Sociology

BRIEF EDITION

Sociology
4th Edition
Exploring the Architecture of Everyday Life

- -

David M. Newman

Los Angeles | London | New Delhi
Singapore | Washington DC

Los Angeles | London | New Delhi
Singapore | Washington DC

FOR INFORMATION:

SAGE Publications, Inc.
2455 Teller Road
Thousand Oaks, California 91320
E-mail: order@sagepub.com

SAGE Publications Ltd.
1 Oliver's Yard
55 City Road
London, EC1Y 1SP
United Kingdom

SAGE Publications India Pvt. Ltd.
B 1/I 1 Mohan Cooperative Industrial Area
Mathura Road, New Delhi 110 044
India

SAGE Publications Asia-Pacific Pte. Ltd.
3 Church Street
#10-04 Samsung Hub
Singapore 049483

Acquisitions Editor: Jeff Lasser
Associate Editor: Nick Pachelli
Production Editor: Libby Larson
Typesetter: C&M Digitals (P) Ltd.
Proofreader: Ellen Brink
Indexer: Sheila Bodell
Cover Designer: Candice Harman
Marketing Manager: Erica DeLuca

Printed in the United States of America

Library of Congress Cataloging-in-Publication Data

Newman, David M., 1958- Sociology : exploring the architecture of everyday life, brief edition / David M. Newman, DePauw University. — Fourth Edition.

pages cm

Includes bibliographical references and index.

ISBN 978-1-4522-7587-1 (pbk. : alk. paper)

1. Sociology. I. Title.

HM585.N48 2014
301—dc23   2014009309

This book is printed on acid-free paper.

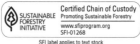

14 15 16 17 18 10 9 8 7 6 5 4 3 2

Brief Contents

Detailed Contents

Preface

It was the first day of the fall semester several years ago. I had just finished making the final adjustments to the first edition of this book, which was due to be published the following January. I felt pretty good about myself, like I'd just accomplished something monumental. Even my two sons were impressed with me (although not as impressed as the time we went to a professional hockey game and I leaped out of my seat to catch an errant, speeding puck barehanded). I walked into the first meeting of my Contemporary Society class eager to start teaching wide-eyed, first-year students a thing or two about sociology.

In my introductory comments to the class that day, I mentioned that I had just written this book. The panicked look in their eyes—a curious combination of awe and fear—calmed when I told them I wouldn't be requiring them to read it that semester. I told them that the process of writing an introductory text helped me immensely in preparing for the course and that I looked forward to passing on to them the knowledge I had accumulated.

The next day after class, one of the students—a bright, freshly scrubbed 18-year-old—approached me. The ensuing conversation would leave a humbling impression even two decades later:

Student: Hi. Umm. Professor Newman . . . I called my parents last night to, like, tell them how my first day in college went. I think they were, like, more nervous than I was. You know how parents can be.

Me: Yes, I sure do. I'm a parent myself, you know.

Student: Yeah, whatever. Anyway, I was telling them about my classes and my professors and stuff. I told them about this class and how I thought it would be pretty cool. I told them you had written a book. I thought that would impress them, you know, make it seem like they were getting their money's worth and everything.

Me: Well, thanks.

Student: So, they go, "What's the book about?" [He laughs sheepishly.] I told them I really didn't know, but I'd find out. So, like, that's what I'm doing . . . finding out.

Me: Well, I'm glad you asked. You see, it's an introductory sociology textbook that uses everyday experiences and phenomena as a way of understanding important sociological theories and ideas. In it I've attempted to . . .

Student: [His eyes, glazed over with boredom, suddenly jump back to life.] Wait, did you say "textbook?"

Me: Why, yes. You see, the purpose of the book is to provide the reader with a thorough and useful introduction to the sociological perspective. I want to convey . . .

Student: [Quite embarrassed now] Oh . . . Professor Newman, I'm really sorry. I misunderstood you. I thought you had written a real book.

Real book. *Real* book. *Real* book. Those words rang in my head like some relentless church bell. At first, I tried to dismiss the comment as the remark of a naïve kid who didn't know any better. But the more I thought about it, the more I realized what his comment reflected. The perception that textbooks aren't real books is widespread.

A few years ago, I heard a radio ad for a local Red Cross book drive. The narrator asked listeners to donate any unused or unwanted books *as long as they weren't textbooks*. Yep, that's what he said. Torn copies of *The Cat in the Hat*? Fine, they'll take 'em. Grease-stained owner's manuals for 1976 Ford Pintos? Sure, glad to have 'em. Textbooks? No way!

Sadly, these sorts of perceptions are not altogether unwarranted. Textbooks hover on the margins of the literary world, somewhere between respectable, intellectual monographs on trailblazing research and Harlequin romance novels. Traditionally, they've been less than titillating: thick, heavy, expensive, and easily discarded for a measly five bucks at the end-of-semester "book buy-back."

My goal—from that very first edition to this one—has always been to write a textbook that reads like a real book. In the first nine editions, I tried to capture simultaneously the essence and insight of my discipline and the reader's interest. From what reviewers, instructors, and students who've read and used the book over the years have said, I think I've been fairly successful. While no Hollywood movie studio has expressed interest in turning this book into a movie (yet!), people do seem to like the relaxed tone and appreciate the consistent theme that ties all the chapters together. Many instructors have commented on how the book enables students to truly understand the unique and useful elements of a sociological perspective. Take that, Red Cross!

FEATURES OF THE 4TH EDITION

To my sons—who believe that I have nothing important to say about anything anyway—continually revising this book has always been clear evidence of my incompetence. Back when he was in middle school, my younger son once asked me, "Why do you keep writing the same book over and over? My English teacher made me rewrite a book report on *To Kill a Mockingbird* because I answered some questions wrong. Is that what's going on here, Dad? Is your publisher making you write the book again because there's too much wrong stuff in it?" I told him

no and that I'd make him read the whole book—cover to cover—if he continued to ask such questions. He stopped . . . although to this day, he's still not convinced I have anything useful to say.

Despite his concerns, sociology textbooks do need to be revised regularly and frequently. No book can be of lasting value if it remains static, locked into a particular style and content. I keep my ears and eyes open, always looking for some new example or current issue to include in the book. My office overflows with stacks of books, newspaper clippings, photocopied journal articles, Post-it notes, and shreds of paper napkins containing scribbled ideas that I write to myself at the breakfast table when I come across something interesting. I've been known to send myself e-mails at 3:00 in the morning so as not to forget the great idea that came to me in the haziness between sleep and wakefulness.

It would be impossible to write an introduction to the discipline of sociology without accounting for the life-altering occurrences—wars, natural disasters, school shootings, political upheavals, court decisions, economic meltdowns, the Kardashians' latest escapades—that we hear about every day. So throughout this book, I've made a special effort to provide some sociological insight into well-known contemporary events and trends, both large and small. In doing so, I intend to show you the pervasiveness and applicability of sociology in our ordinary, everyday experiences in a way that, I hope, rings familiar with you.

As you will see throughout the book, it is impossible to understand what happens to us in our personal lives without taking into consideration broader social and historical phenomena. Several specific recent developments have had—and will continue to have—a dramatic impact on sociological thought and on people's everyday lives: the lingering effects of the recent global economic recession; the second term of Barack Obama's presidency; and the dramatic growth of communication technology, particularly social networking sites. When the economy suffers, everyone—from tycoons to unemployed welfare recipients—experiences some kind of alteration in her or his day-to-day routine. As I was writing this edition, it was quite a challenge to keep up with the most current information on joblessness, hiring trends, home foreclosures, spending patterns, and so on. Likewise, major political events can change what we know and what we take for granted. Although it's still too early to know its full extent, the reelection of the country's first black president will no doubt influence perceptions of race and race relations—locally, nationally, and maybe even globally. And how can we analyze the sociology of everyday life without acknowledging the powerful role online social networking has had in shaping the way we relate to others and define ourselves? Thus, you will see references to these developments throughout the book to illustrate the interconnections between private life and massive historical occurrences.

I also want to call to your attention the fact that many extended examples of sociological theories and concepts throughout the book focus on some aspect of health, illness, and medicine. I have done this for two reasons. First of all, no matter who we are or where we come from, all of us must deal with health matters from time to time. Our own physical and mental well-being is perhaps the most personal and immediate thing in our lives. At the same time, whenever we seek medical attention—whether in a doctor's office, a local pharmacy, or a hospital—or try to figure out how to pay for it, we enter a massive health care system that can sometimes feel immensely bureaucratic and *impersonal*. And as medical costs continue to rise, changes to our health care system—both proposed and enacted—will dominate economic forecasts, newspaper headlines, and legislative action for years to come. Second, beginning in 2015, students taking the Medical College Admissions Test will be required to take a course in sociology. And so these health care–related examples will provide such students with applications and illustrations that are directly relevant to their needs and, hopefully, make them better doctors in the future.

I've also tried to provide the most current statistical information possible. Much of the new statistical information is drawn from the most recent data from sources such as the U.S. Census Bureau, the Population Reference Bureau, the Centers for Disease Control and Prevention, the National Center for Education Statistics, the U.S. Bureau of Labor Statistics, and the U.S. Bureau of Justice Statistics.

TEACHING RESOURCES AND WEBSITE TO ACCOMPANY THE BOOK AND COMPANION READER

For the Instructor

The password-protected Instructor Site at **www .sagepub.com/newmanbrief4e** gives instructors access to a full complement of resources to support

and enhance their courses. The following assets are available on the instructor site:

- A **test bank** with multiple-choice, true/false, short-answer, and essay questions. The test bank is provided on the site in Word format as well as in our Respondus computerized testing software.
- **PowerPoint** slides for each chapter, for use in lecture and review. Slides are integrated with the book's distinctive features and incorporate key tables, figures, and photos.
- **Video resources** that enhance the information in each chapter.
- **SAGE journal articles** for each chapter that provide extra content on important topics from SAGE's sociology journals.
- **Classroom exercises and discussion topics** that suggest group and individual activities to enhance student learning, as well as valuable tools to facilitate discussion.
- **Suggested readings and films** for each chapter that explore recommended literary resources, educational film resources, feature films, and classic/exemplary sociological studies.
- **Web resources** that provide links to websites to encourage additional learning on specific topics.

For the Student

To maximize students' understanding of sociology and promote critical thinking and active learning, we have provided the following chapter-specific student resources on the open-access portion of **www.sage-pub.com/newmabrief4e:**

- **Flashcards** that reiterate key chapter terms and concepts
- **Self-quizzes,** including multiple-choice and true/false questions
- **Video and audio resources** that enhance the information in each chapter
- **SAGE journal articles** for each chapter that provide extra content on important topics from SAGE's sociology journals
- **Web resources** that provide links to websites to encourage additional learning on specific topics

A WORD ABOUT THE "ARCHITECTURE OF SOCIETY"

I have chosen the image of architecture in the subtitle to convey one of the driving themes of this book: Society is a human construction. Society is not "out there" somewhere, waiting to be visited and examined. It exists in the minute details of our day-to-day lives. Whenever we follow its rules or break them, enter its roles or shed them, work to change things or keep them as they are, we are adding another nail, plank, or frame to the structure of our society. In short, society—like the buildings around us—couldn't exist were it not for the actions of people.

At the same time, however, this structure that we have created appears to exist independently of us. We don't usually spend much time thinking about the buildings we live, work, and play in as human constructions. We see them as finished products, not as the processes that created them. Only when something goes wrong—the pipes leak or the walls crack—do we realize that people made these structures and people are the ones who must fix them. When buildings outlive their usefulness or become dangerous to their inhabitants, people must renovate them or, if necessary, tear them down.

Likewise, society is so massive and has been around for so long that it *appears* to stand on its own, at a level above and beyond the toiling hands of individual people. But here, too, when things begin to go wrong—widespread discrimination, environmental degradation, massive poverty, lack of affordable health care, escalating crime rates—people must do something about it.

So the fascinating paradox of human life is that we build society, collectively "forget" that we've built it, and live under its massive and influential structure. But we are not stuck with society as it is. Human beings are the architects of their own social reality. Throughout this book, I examine the active roles individuals play in planning, maintaining, or fixing society.

A FINAL THOUGHT

One of the greatest challenges I have faced in three decades teaching sociology is trying to get my students to see the personal relevance of the course material, to fully appreciate the connection between the individual and society. The true value of sociology lies in its unique ability to show the two-way connection between the most private elements of our lives—our characteristics, experiences, behaviors, and thoughts—and the cultures, groups, organizations, and social institutions to which we belong. The "everyday life" approach in this book uses real-world examples and personal observations as a vehicle for understanding the relationship between individuals and society.

My purpose is to make the familiar unfamiliar—to help you critically examine the commonplace and the ordinary in your own life. Only when you step back and examine the taken-for-granted aspects of your personal experiences can you see that there is an inherent, sometimes unrecognized organization and predictability to them. At the same time, you will see that the structure of society is greater than the sum of the experiences and psychologies of the individuals in it.

It is my conviction that this intellectual excursion should be a thought-provoking and enjoyable one. Reading a textbook doesn't have to be boring or, even worse, the academic equivalent of a painful trip to the dentist (although I personally have nothing against dentists). I believe that one of my responsibilities as a teacher is to provide my students with a challenging but comfortable classroom atmosphere in which to learn. I have tried to do the same in this book. Your instructor has chosen this book not because it makes his or her job teaching your course any easier but because he or she wants you, the student, to see how sociology helps us to understand how the small, private experiences of our everyday lives are connected to this thing we call society. I hope you learn to appreciate this important message, and I hope you enjoy reading this book as much as I enjoyed writing it.

Have fun,

David M. Newman
Department of Sociology and Anthropology
DePauw University
Greencastle, IN 46135
E-mail: dnewman@depauw.edu

Acknowledgments

A book project such as this one takes an enormous amount of time to develop. Over the span of 10 editions, I've spent thousands of hours on this book—typing away at my computer, endlessly searching the web, fretting over what I should and shouldn't include, proofreading for mistakes—either holed up in my isolated and very cluttered third-floor office or tucked away in the quiet corner of a library. Yet as solitary as this project was, I could not have done it alone. Over the years, many people have provided invaluable assistance to make this book a reality. Without their generous help and support, it wouldn't have been written, and you'd be reading some other sociologist's list of people to thank. Because I have revised rather than rewritten this book, I remain indebted to those who have helped me at some point during the writing of all 10 editions.

I would like to extend my sincere gratitude to Eve Oettinger, Diane McDaniel, and Jeff Lasser at SAGE and editors Kim Husband and Libby Larson for their insight and guidance in putting together this newest edition. Having already written nine editions of this book, I was definitely an old dog with absolutely no desire to learn any new tricks when these individuals became involved. To their credit, they let me write as I have always written. For their trust, I am eternally grateful.

I would also like to express my thanks to Gina Cook for creating an excellent instructor's manual and to Professor Harvest Moon from University of Texas at Arlington for creating the student study site materials.

As always, I appreciate the many helpful comments offered by the reviewers of both the full text and this abridged version:

Sharon Abbott, Fairfield University

Deborah Abowitz, Bucknell University

Stephen Adair, Central Connecticut State University

Rebecca Adams, University of North Carolina, Greensboro

Ron Aminzade, University of Minnesota

Afroza Anwary, Carleton College

George Arquitt, Oklahoma State University

Carol Auster, Franklin and Marshall College

Ellen C. Baird, Arizona State University

Ellen Berg, California State University, Sacramento

Mildred Biaku, University of Alabama at Birmingham

Michael G. Bisciglia, Southeastern Louisiana University

David Bogen, Emerson College

Frances A. Boudreau, Connecticut College

David L. Briscoe, University of Arkansas at Little Rock

Todd Campbell, Loyola University, Chicago

Wanda Clark, South Plains College

Thomas Conroy, St. Peter's College

Norman Conti, Duquesne University

Maia Greenwell Cunningham, Citrus College

Doug Currivan, University of Massachusetts, Boston

Karen Dalke, University of Wisconsin, Green Bay

Jeff Davidson, University of Delaware

Kimberly Davies, Augusta State University

Tricia Davis, North Carolina State University

Michelle Deming, University of South Carolina

James J. Dowd, University of Georgia

Laura A. Dowd, University of Georgia, Athens

Charlotte A. Dunham, Texas Tech University

Donald Eckard, Temple University

Charles Edgley, Oklahoma State University

Rachel Einhower, Purdue University

June Ellestad, Washington State University

Shalom Endleman, Quinnipiac College

Rebecca Erickson, University of Akron

Kimberly Faust, Winthrop University

Patrick Fontane, St. Louis College of Pharmacy

Michael J. Fraleigh, Bryant University

Volker Frank, University of North Carolina, Asheville

Sarah N. Gaston, Texas A&M University

Farah Gilanshah, University of Minnesota–Morris

Barry Goetz, University of Dayton

Lorie Schabo Grabowski, University of Minnesota

Valerie Gunter, University of New Orleans

Roger Guy, Texas Lutheran University

John R. Hall, University of California, Davis

Tara Hardinge, California State University, Long Beach

Charles Harper, Creighton University

Douglas Harper, Duquesne University

Lori Heald, East Carolina University

Peter Hennen, University of Minnesota

Max Herman, Rutgers University

Cynthia Hewitt, Morehouse College

Christine L. Himes, Syracuse University

Susan Hoerbelt, Hillsborough Community College

Amy Holzgang, Cerritos College

Kate Hovey, Central New Mexico Community College

W. Jay Hughes, Georgia Southern University

Gary Hytreck, Georgia Southern University

Valerie Jenness, University of California, Irvine

Kimberly Johanek, Boise State

Kathryn Johnson, Barat College

Richard Jones, Marquette University

Tom Kando, California State University, Sacramento

Steve Keto, Kent State University

Peter Kivisto, Augustana College

Lisa Konczal, Barry University

Marc LaFountain, State University of West Georgia

Sharon Melissa Latimer, West Virginia University

Joseph Lengermann, University of Maryland, College Park

Linda A. Litteral, Grossmont Community College

Julie L. Locher, University of Alabama at Birmingham

David G. LoConto, Jacksonville State University

David A. Lopez, California State University, Northridge

Fred Maher, Temple University

Kristen Marcussen, University of Iowa

Benjamin Mariante, Stonehill College

Joseph Marolla, Virginia Commonwealth University

Michallene McDaniel, University of Georgia

James R. McIntosh, Lehigh University

Jerome McKibben, Fitchburg State University

Ted P. McNeilsmith, Adams State College

Dan Miller, University of Dayton

Melinda Milligan, Sonoma State University

John R. Mitrano, Central Connecticut State University

Susannne Monahan, Montana State University

Harvest Moon, The University of Texas at Arlington

Kelly Murphy, University of Pittsburgh

Elizabeth Ehrhardt Mustaine, University of Central Florida

Daniel Myers, University of Notre Dame

Anne Nurse, College of Wooster

Marjukka Ollilainen, Weber State University

Toska Olson, Evergreen State College

Liza A. Pellerin, Ball State University

Larry Perkins, Oklahoma State University, Stillwater

Bernice Pescosolido, Indiana University, Bloomington

Mike Plummer, Boston College

Edward Ponczek, William Rainey Harper College

Tanya Poteet, Capital University

Sharon E. Preves, Grand Valley State University

Kennon J. Rice, North Carolina State University

Judith Richlin-Klonsky, University of California, Los Angeles

Robert Robinson, Indiana University, Bloomington

Mary Rogers, University of West Florida

Sally S. Rogers, Montgomery College

Wanda Rushing, University of Memphis

Michael Ryan, University of Louisiana, Lafayette

Scott Schaffer, Millersville University

Aileen Schulte, State University of New York, New Paltz

Dave Schweingruber, Iowa State University

Mark Shibley, Southern Oregon University

Thomas Shriver, Oklahoma State University

Toni Sims, University of Louisiana, Lafayette

Kathleen Slevin, College of William and Mary

Melissa Sloan, Drew University

Lisa White Smith, Christopher Newport University

Eldon E. Snyder, Bowling Green State University

Nicholas Sofios, Providence College

George Spilker, Clarkson College

Melanie Stander, University of Washington

Beverly Stiles, Midwestern State University

Kandi Stinson, Xavier University

Richard Tardanico, Florida International University

Robert Tellander, Sonoma State University

Kathleen Tiemann, University of North Dakota

Steven Vallas, George Mason University

Tom Vander Ven, Indiana University, South Bend

John Walsh, University of Illinois, Chicago

Gregory Weiss, Roanoke College

Marty Wenglinski, Quinnipiac College

Stephan Werba, Catonsville Community College

Cheryl E. Whitley, Marist College

Norma Williams, University of North Texas

Janelle Wilson, University of Minnesota, Duluth

Mark Winton, University of Central Florida

Judith Wittner, Loyola University, Chicago

Cynthia A. Woolever, Hartford Seminary

Don C. Yost, Mountain State University

Ashraf Zahedi, Stanford University

Stephen Zehr, University of Southern Indiana

I also want to express my appreciation to the many colleagues, students, and friends who, throughout the years, have kept me curious and prevented me from taking myself too seriously.

About the Author

David M. Newman earned his B.A. from San Diego State University in 1981 and his graduate degrees from the University of Washington in Seattle (MA 1984, PhD 1988). After a year at the University of Connecticut, David came to DePauw University in 1989 and has been here ever since. David teaches courses in Contemporary Society, Deviance, Mental Illness, Family, Social Psychology, and Research Methods. He has published numerous articles on teaching and has presented research papers on the intersection of gender and power in intimate relationships. Recently most of his scholarly activity has been devoted to writing and revising several books, including *Sociology: Exploring the Architecture of Everyday Life* (SAGE, 2014); *Identities and Inequalities: Exploring the Intersections of Race, Class, Gender, and Sexuality* (McGraw-Hill, 2012); *and Families: A Sociological Perspective* (McGraw-Hill, 2009). His current work examines the cultural meaning, institutional importance, and social limitations of "second chance" narratives in everyday life.

PART I

The Individual and Society

What is the relationship between your private life and the social world around you? Part I introduces you to the guiding theme of this book: Our personal, everyday experiences affect and are affected by the larger society in which we live. Chapters 1 and 2 discuss the sociological perspective on human life and the ways in which it differs from the more individualistic approaches of psychology and biology. You will read about what society consists of and get a glimpse into sociologists' attempts to understand the two-way relationship between the individual and society.

As you read on, keep in mind a metaphor that will be used throughout the book to help explain the nature of society: architecture. Like buildings, societies have a design discernible to the alert eye. Both are constructed by bringing together a wide variety of materials in a complex process. Both, through their structure, shape the activities within. At the same time, both change. Sometimes they change subtly and gradually as the inhabitants go about their lives; other times they are deliberately redecorated or remodeled. As you make your way through this book, see if you can discover more ways in which buildings and societies are alike.

Taking a New Look at a Familiar World

Sociology and the Individual

The Insights of Sociology

The Sociological Imagination

André graduated from college in 2012. He had been a model student. When not studying, he found time to help kids read at the local elementary school and actively participated in student government at his own school. He got along well with his professors, his grades were excellent, he made the dean's list all four years, and he graduated Phi Beta Kappa. As a computer science major with a minor in economics, André thought his future was set: He would land a job at a top software company or perhaps a stock brokerage firm and work his way up the ladder so that he'd be earning a six-figure income by the time he was 30.

But when André entered the job market and began applying for jobs, things didn't go exactly according to plan. Despite his credentials, nobody seemed willing to hire him full time. He was able to survive only by taking temporary freelance programming jobs here and there and working nights at the Gap. Most of his classmates had similar difficulties finding jobs. Nevertheless, André began to question his own abilities: "Do I lack the skills employers are looking for? Am I not trying hard enough? What the heck is wrong with me?" His friends and family were as encouraging as they could be, but some secretly wondered if André wasn't as smart as they'd thought he was.

Michael and Louise were both juniors at a large university. They had been dating each other exclusively for the past two years. By all accounts, the relationship seemed to be going quite well. In fact, Michael was beginning to imagine them getting married, having children, and living happily ever after. Then one day out of the blue, Louise dropped a bombshell. She told Michael she thought their relationship was going nowhere and perhaps they ought to start seeing other people.

Michael was stunned. "What did I do?" he asked her. "I thought things were going great. Is it something I said? Something I did? I can change."

She said no, he hadn't done anything wrong, they had simply grown apart. She told him she just didn't feel as strongly about him as she used to.

After the breakup, Michael was devastated. He turned to his friends for support. "She wasn't any good for you anyway," they said. "We always thought she was a little flighty. She probably couldn't be in a serious relationship with anybody. It wasn't your fault; it was hers."

In both of these stories, notice that people immediately try to explain an unhappy situation by focusing on the personal characteristics and attributes of the individuals involved. André blames himself for not being able to land a job in his field; others harbor doubts about his intelligence and drive. Michael wonders what he did to sour his relationship with Louise; his friends question her psychological stability. Such reactions are not uncommon. We have a marked tendency to rely on *individualistic explanations*, attributing people's achievements and failures to their personal qualities.

Why can't André, our highly intelligent, well-trained, talented college graduate, land a permanent job? It's certainly possible that he has some personal flaw that makes him unemployable: lack of motivation, laziness, negative attitude, bad hygiene, and so on. Or maybe he doesn't come across as particularly capable during job interviews.

But by focusing exclusively on such individual "deficiencies," we risk overlooking the broader societal factors that may have affected André's job prospects. For instance, the employment situation for college graduates like André was part of a broader economic trend that began with the global financial crisis of 2008 and continues to suppress the job market today. At the time I was writing this chapter, 6.7% of American adults (a little more than 10 million

people) were officially unemployed. Incidentally, the official unemployment rate only counts people who have been actively seeking employment for the past month. Thus it doesn't include the 8.2 million people who were employed part time even though they wanted to work full time, the 2.4 million "marginally attached" unemployed people who had looked for a job sometime in the past year (just not in the past month), and the 917,000 so-called 'discouraged' workers who had lost hope and given up looking for employment (U.S. Bureau of Labor Statistics, 2012b). So you see, a lot of people are in André's boat.

But he's a college graduate. Shouldn't that help? It turns out that college degrees are no longer the guarantee of fruitful employment they once were. Job opportunities for college graduates did improve in the mid 2000s, only to take a steep dive in the late 2000s. Each year between 2004 and 2008, employers increased their hiring of college graduates by an average of 13% over the previous year (cited in Hunsinger, 2009). In fact, the job market became so good in the mid 2000s that newspapers provided advice to college graduates on how to be "picky" when choosing a place to work (Knight, 2006). As late as May 2008, economists were still predicting a favorable job market for new graduates (K. Murphy, 2008).

But all that quickly changed with the economic recession. According to one study, about 53% of recent college graduates are either unemployed or underemployed (that is, working in jobs that don't require a bachelor's degree; cited in Weissmann, 2012). Another study found that 44% of unemployed college graduates have been out of a job for more than 6 months—the so-called long-term unemployed—up from 13% in 2000 (Economic Policy Institute, 2012). The percentage who have given up trying to find a job—roughly 17%—is the highest it's been since 1994, the first year such records were kept (Uchitelle, 2010). Indeed, about 1 out of every 5 unemployed people over the age of 25 is a college graduate, up from less than 1 in 10 in 1979 (Mishel, Bernstein, & Allegretto, 2007; U.S. Bureau of Labor Statistics, 2011).

Although new graduates fare better than other young people without college degrees (Pew Charitable Trusts, 2013), their future outlook is tepid at best. According to the Collegiate Employment Research Institute (2012), about 22% of employers reported definite plans to hire college graduates in the 2012 to 2013 academic year, a 50% decrease compared with the previous year. And 42% of those employers who will be hiring intend to take on fewer people than they did the previous year. Not surprisingly, 82% of young adults in a recent poll said that finding a job is harder for them than it was in their parents' generation (Pew Research Center, 2012b).

What about earnings? College graduates still earn 85% more, on average, than people with only high school diplomas (ProQuest Statistical Abstract, 2013). And having a degree brings higher pay even in fields that don't require a degree, such as dishwasher, hairdresser, and cashier (cited in Leonhardt, 2011). However, the average starting salary for college graduates has stagnated in recent years. For instance, those graduating in 2010 could expect a starting salary of $27,000, down from $30,000 for those who graduated between 2006 and 2008 (Godofsky, Zukin, & Van Horn, 2011). To make matters worse, students who took out loans to pay for their college education have an average debt of about $26,600 after graduation (The Project on Student Debt, 2012).

So you see, André's employability and his chances of earning a good living were as much a result of the economic forces operating at the time he began looking for a job as of any of his personal qualifications. Had he graduated only a few years earlier (when the economy was doing better) or a few years later (when it is projected to improve), his prospects would have been much brighter.

And what about Michael and Louise? It seems perfectly reasonable to conclude that something about either of them or the combination of the two caused their breakup. We tend to view dating relationships—not to mention marriages—as successes or failures based solely on the traits or behaviors of the two people involved.

But how would your assessment of the situation change if you found out that Lee—to whom Louise had always been secretly attracted—had just broken up with his longtime girlfriend, Julie, and was now available? Like it or not, relationships are not exclusively private entities; they're always being influenced by forces beyond our control. They take place within a larger network of friends, acquaintances, ex-partners, coworkers, fellow students, and people as yet unknown who may make desirable or, at the very least, acceptable

dating partners. On social media such as Facebook and Twitter, people routinely post up-to-the-minute changes in the status of their relationships, thereby instantaneously advertising shifts in their availability (Gershon, 2010).

When people believe they have no better alternative, they tend to stay with their present partners, even if they are not particularly satisfied. When people think that better relationships are available to them, they may become less committed to staying in their present ones. Indeed, people's perceptions of what characterizes a good relationship (such as fairness, compatibility, affection) are less likely to determine when and if it ends than the presence or absence of favorable alternatives (Felmlee, Sprecher, & Bassin, 1990). Research shows that the risk of a relationship ending increases as the supply of potential alternative relationships increases (South & Lloyd, 1995).

In addition, Louise's decision to leave could have been indirectly affected by the sheer number of potentially obtainable partners—a result of shifts in the birthrate 20 years or so earlier. Today, there are roughly 120 U.S. men in their 20s who are single, divorced, or widowed for every 100 women in the same categories (Roberts, 2006). For a single, heterosexual woman like Louise, such a surplus of college-age men increases the likelihood that she would eventually find a better alternative to Michael. The number of available alternatives can even vary from state to state. For instance, Michael's attractiveness would rise if he were living in Delaware (where around half of all single young people are men) but sink if he were living in Wyoming (where there are three single men for every two single women; Eligon, 2013). In sum, Michael's interpersonal value, and therefore the stability of his relationship with Louise, may have suffered not because of anything he did but because of population forces over which he had little, if any, control.

Let's take this notion beyond Louise and Michael's immediate dating network. For instance, the very characteristics and features that people consider desirable (or undesirable) in the first place reflect the values of the larger culture in which they live. Fashions and tastes are constantly changing, making particular characteristics (e.g., hairstyle, physique, clothing), behaviors (smoking, drinking, sharing feelings), or life choices (educational attainment, occupation, political affiliation) more or less attractive.

And broad population and economic forces can affect intimate choices even further. In China, where there are about 41 million *more* unmarried young men than women (Tsai, 2012), young single women can be especially choosy when it comes to romantic partners, often requiring that suitors own their own homes before they'll even consider them for a date (Jacobs, 2011).

The moral of these two stories is simple: To understand experiences in our personal lives, we must move past individual traits and examine broader societal characteristics and trends. External features beyond our immediate awareness and control often exert as much influence on the circumstances of our day-to-day lives as our "internal" qualities. We can't begin to explain an individual's employability without examining current and past economic trends that affect the number of jobs available and the number of people who are looking for work. We can't begin to explain why relationships work or don't work without addressing the broader interpersonal network and culture in which they are embedded. By the same token, we can't begin to explain people's ordinary, everyday thoughts and actions without examining the social forces that influence them.

SOCIOLOGY AND THE INDIVIDUAL

Herein lies the fundamental theme of *sociology*—the systematic study of human societies—and the theme that will guide us throughout this book: Everyday social life—our thoughts, actions, feelings, decisions, interactions, and so on—is the product of a complex interplay between societal forces and personal characteristics. To explain why people are the way they are or do the things they do, we must understand the interpersonal, historical, cultural, technological, organizational, and global environments they inhabit. To understand either individuals or society, we must understand both (C. W. Mills, 1959).

Of course, seeing the relationship between individuals and social forces is not always so easy. The United States is a society built on the image of the rugged, self-reliant individual. Not surprisingly, it is also a society dominated by individualistic understandings of human behavior that seek to explain problems and processes by focusing exclusively on the character, the psychology, or even the biochemistry

of each person. Consequently, most of us simply take for granted that what we choose to do, say, feel, and think are private phenomena. Everyday life seems to be a series of free personal choices. After all, we choose what to major in. We choose what to wear when we go out. We choose what and when to eat. We choose our lifestyles, our mates, and so on.

But how free are these decisions? Think about all the times your actions have been dictated or at least influenced by social circumstances over which you had little control. Have you ever felt that because of your age or gender or race, certain opportunities were closed to you? Your ability to legally drive a car, drink alcohol, or vote, for instance, is determined by society's prevailing definition of age. When you're older, you may be forced into retirement despite your skills and desire to continue working. Gender profoundly affects your choices, too. Some occupations, such as bank executive and engineer, are still overwhelmingly male, whereas others, such as registered nurse and preschool teacher, are almost exclusively female. Likewise, the doctrines of your religion may limit your behavioral choices. For a devout Catholic, premarital sex or even divorce is unlikely. Each day during the holy month of Ramadan, a strict Muslim must abstain from food and drink from sunrise to sunset. An Orthodox Jew would never drink milk and eat meat at the same meal.

Then there's the matter of personal style—your choices in hairstyle, dress, music, and the like. Large-scale marketing strategies can actually create a demand for particular products or images. Would One Direction or Nicki Minaj or Justin Bieber have become so popular without a tightly managed and slickly packaged publicity program designed to appeal to adolescents and preadolescents? Your tastes, and therefore your choices as a consumer, are often influenced by decisions made in far-off corporate boardrooms.

National and international economic trends also affect your everyday life. You may lose your job or, like André, face a tight job market as a result of economic fluctuations brought about by increased global competition or a severe recession. Or, because of the rapid development of certain types of technology, the college degree that may be your ticket to a rewarding career today may not qualify you even for a low-paying, entry-level position 10 years from now. In one poll, 75% of young adults who dropped out of college cited the financial need to work full time as the principal reason why it would be hard for them to go back to school (Lewin, 2009b). And if you finish your degree but don't get a good job right out of college, you may have to move back home—like 43% of people between the ages of 20 and 25 these days (Qian, 2012)—and live there for years after you graduate, not because you can't face the idea of living apart from your beloved parents but because you can't earn enough to support yourself.

Government and politics affect our personal lives, too. A political decision made at the local, regional, national, or even international level may result in the closing of a government agency you depend on, make the goods and services to which you have grown accustomed either more expensive or less available, or reduce the size of your paycheck after taxes are taken out. Workplace family-leave policies or medical insurance regulations established by the government may affect your decision whether and when to have a baby or to undergo the elective surgery you've been putting off. If you are homosexual, federal and state governments can determine whether you can be covered by your partner's health care policy, file a joint income tax return, inherit mutually acquired assets, or be involuntarily discharged from the military because of your sexual orientation. In the United States, decisions made by the U.S. Supreme Court can increase or limit your ability to control your fertility, sue an employer for discrimination, use your property however you please, carry a concealed weapon in public, or keep the details of your life a private matter.

People's personal lives can also be touched by events that occur in distant countries:

- In 2005, Hurricane Katrina killed thousands of people, rendered hundreds of thousands homeless and unemployed, contaminated local waterways, and decimated Gulf Coast industries such as tourism and steel, lumber, and oil production. Its economic effects were felt immediately in the rest of the country, where, for instance, gasoline prices skyrocketed. It also had a staggering impact on U.S. exports and on the travel industry—both nationally and internationally.
- In 2008, a stock market plunge in the United States instantly sent markets tumbling in Europe, South America, and Asia. The ensuing recession drove up unemployment rates in just about every

industrialized nation around the world. To this day, some countries, like Greece and Portugal, are on the verge of bankruptcy.

- In 2009, fear over the spread of swine flu dramatically reduced international travel—especially to Mexico, where the flu was purported to originate—thereby affecting global airline companies and cruise operators in the United States and elsewhere. It even reduced exports of pork, despite assurance by health officials that there was no connection between the virus and food consumption.
- In 2011, a massive earthquake and deadly tsunami crippled many Japanese companies that manufacture car parts, resulting in a drop in automobile production in U.S. plants.
- That same year, violent protests in Arab countries like Libya, Egypt, Syria, and Yemen sparked fears of reduced oil imports and drove U.S. gasoline prices up over $4.00 a gallon.

These are only some of the ways in which events in the larger world can affect individual lives.

THE INSIGHTS OF SOCIOLOGY

Sociologists do not deny that individuals make choices or that they must take personal responsibility for those choices. But they are quick to point out that we cannot fully understand the things happening in our lives, private and personal though they may be, without examining the influence of the people, events, and societal features that surround us. By showing how social processes can shape us, and how individual action can in turn affect those processes, sociology provides unique insight into the taken-for-granted personal events and the large-scale cultural and global processes that make up our everyday existence.

Other disciplines study human life, too. Biologists study how the body works. Neurologists examine what goes on inside the brain. Psychologists study what goes on inside the mind to create human behavior. These disciplines focus almost exclusively on structures and processes that reside *within* the individual. In contrast, sociologists study what goes on *among* people as individuals, groups, or societies. How do social forces affect the way people interact with one another? How do individuals make sense of their private lives and the social worlds they occupy? How does everyday social interaction create "society"?

Personal issues like love, sexuality, poverty, aging, and prejudice are better understood within the appropriate societal context. For instance, U.S. adults tend to believe that they marry purely for love, when in fact society pressures people to marry from the same social class, religion, and race (P. L. Berger, 1963). Sociology, unlike other disciplines, forces us to look outside the tight confines of individual anatomy and personality to understand the phenomena that shape us. Consider, for example, the following situations:

- A 14-year-old girl, fearing she is overweight, begins systematically starving herself in the hope of becoming more attractive.
- A 55-year-old stockbroker, unable to find work since his firm laid him off, sinks into a depression after losing his family and his home. He now lives on the streets.
- A 46-year-old professor kills herself after learning that her position at the university will be terminated the following year due to budget cuts.
- The student body president and valedictorian of the local high school cannot begin or end her day without several shots of whiskey.

What do these people have in common? Your first response might be that they are all suffering or have suffered terrible personal problems. If you saw them only for what they've become—an "anorexic," a "homeless person," a "suicide victim," or an "alcoholic"—you might think they have some kind of personality defect, genetic flaw, or mental problem that renders them incapable of coping with the demands of contemporary life. Maybe they simply lack the willpower to pick themselves up and move on. In short, your immediate tendency may be to focus on the unique, perhaps "abnormal," characteristics of these people to explain their problems.

But we cannot downplay the importance of their *social* worlds. There is no denying that we live in a society that exalts a lean body, encourages drinking to excess, and values individual achievement and economic success. Some people suffer under these conditions when they don't measure up. This is not to say that all people exposed to the same social messages inevitably fall victim to the same problems. Some overcome their wretched childhoods, others withstand the tragedy of economic failure and begin anew, and some are immune to narrowly defined cultural images of beauty. But to understand fully the nature of human life or of particular social problems, we must acknowledge the broader social context in which these things occur.

THE SOCIOLOGICAL IMAGINATION

Unfortunately, we often don't see the connections between the personal events in our everyday lives and the larger society in which we live. People in a country such as the United States, which places such a high premium on individual achievement, have difficulty looking beyond their immediate situations. Someone who loses a job, gets divorced, or flunks out of school in such a society has trouble imagining that these experiences are somehow related to massive cultural or historical processes.

The ability to see the impact of these forces on our private lives is what the famous sociologist C. Wright Mills (1959) called the *sociological imagination*. The sociological imagination enables us to understand the larger historical picture and its meaning in our own lives. Mills argued that no matter how personal we think our experiences are, many of them can be seen as products of society-wide forces. The task of sociology is to help us view our lives as the intersection between personal biography and societal history and thereby to provide a means for us to interpret our lives and social circumstances.

Getting fired, for example, is a terrible, even traumatic private experience. Feelings of personal failure are inevitable when one loses a job. But if the unemployment rate in a community hovers at or above 28%—as it does in places hardest hit by the recent economic recession, like El Centro, California, and Yuma, Arizona—then we must see unemployment not as a personal malfunction but as a social problem that has its roots in the economic and political structures of society. Listen to how one columnist described his job loss:

> Five years ago, when the magazine dismissed me, fewer Americans were unemployed than are now, and I felt like a solitary reject in a nation of comfortable successes. . . . If I were to get the same news now, in an era of mass layoffs and major bankruptcies, I wonder if I would suffer as I did then. . . . Maybe I would just shrug instead and head outside for a relaxing bike ride. (Kirn, 2009, p. 13)

Such an easygoing response to being fired is probably uncommon. Nevertheless, his point is important sociologically: Being unemployed is not a character flaw or personal failure if a significant number of people in one's community are also unemployed. We can't explain a spike in the unemployment rate as a sudden increase in the number of incompetent or unprepared individual workers in the labor force. As long as the economy is arranged so that employees are easily replaced or slumps inevitably occur, the social problem of unemployment cannot be solved at the personal level.

The same can be said for divorce, which people usually experience as an intimate tragedy. But in the United States, 4 out of every 10 marriages that begin this year will eventually end in divorce, and divorce rates are increasing in many countries around the world. We must therefore view divorce in the context of broader historical changes occurring throughout societies: in family, law, religion, economics, and the culture as a whole. It is impossible to explain significant changes in divorce rates over time by focusing exclusively on the personal characteristics and behaviors of divorcing individuals. Divorce rates don't rise simply because individual spouses have more difficulty getting along with one another than they used to, and they don't fall because more husbands and wives are suddenly being nicer to each other.

Mills did not mean to imply that the sociological imagination should debilitate us—that is, force us to powerlessly perceive our lives as wholly beyond our control. In fact, the opposite is true. An awareness of the impact of social forces or world history on our personal lives is a prerequisite to any efforts we make to change our social circumstances.

Indeed, the sociological imagination allows us to recognize that the solutions to many of our most serious social problems lie not in changing the personal situations and characteristics of individual people but in changing the social institutions and roles available to them (C. W. Mills, 1959). Drug addiction, homelessness, sexual violence, hate crimes, eating disorders, suicide, and other unfortunate situations will not go away simply by treating or punishing a person who is suffering from or engaging in the behavior.

CONCLUSION

In the 21st century, understanding our place within cultural, historical, and global contexts is more important than ever. The world is shrinking. Communication technology instantly binds us to people on the other side of the planet. Increasing ecological awareness opens our eyes to the far-reaching effects of environmental degradations. The changes associated with colossal events in one country (political revolutions, terrorist attacks, natural disasters, economic crises, school shootings, cultural upheavals) often quickly reverberate around the world. The local and global consequences of such events often continue to be felt for years.

When we look at how people's lives are altered by such phenomena—as they sink into poverty or ascend to prosperity; stand in bread lines or enter a career previously unavailable; or find their sense of ethnic identity, personal safety, or self-worth altered—we can begin to understand the everyday importance of large-scale social change.

However, we must remember that individuals are not just helpless pawns of societal forces. They simultaneously influence and are influenced by society. The next chapter provides a more detailed treatment of this theme. Then, in Part II, I examine how society and our social lives are constructed and ordered. I focus on the interplay between individuals and the people, groups, organizations, institutions, and culture that collectively make up our society. Part III focuses on the structure of society, with particular attention to the various forms of social inequality.

CHAPTER HIGHLIGHTS

◆ The primary theme of sociology is that our everyday thoughts and actions are the product of a complex interplay between massive social forces and personal characteristics. We can't understand the relationship between individuals and societies without understanding both.

◆ The sociological imagination is the ability to see the impact of social forces on our private lives—an awareness that our lives lie at the intersection of personal biography and societal history.

◆ Rather than studying what goes on within people, sociologists study what goes on between people, whether as individuals, groups, organizations, or entire societies. Sociology forces us to look outside the tight confines of our individual personalities to understand the phenomena that shape us.

KEY TERMS

individualistic explanation: Tendency to attribute people's achievements and failures to their personal qualities

sociological imagination: Ability to see the impact of social forces on our private lives

sociology: Systematic study of human societies

Seeing and Thinking Sociologically

How Individuals Structure Society

Social Influence: The Impact of Other People in Our Everyday Lives

Societal Influence: The Effect of Social Structure on Our Everyday Lives

Three Perspectives on Social Order

Twenty years ago, ethnic violence erupted in the small African nation of Rwanda. The Hutu majority had begun a systematic program to exterminate the Tutsi minority. Soon, gruesome pictures of the tortured and dismembered bodies of Tutsi men, women, and children began to appear on television screens around the world. When it was over, close to a million Tutsis had been slaughtered—half of whom died within a three-month period.

Surely such horror must have been perpetrated by bands of vicious, crazed thugs who derived some sort of twisted pleasure from committing acts of unspeakable cruelty. Or maybe these were the extreme acts of angry soldiers, trained killers who were committed to destroying the enemy as completely as possible.

Actually, much of the responsibility for these atrocities lay elsewhere, in a most unlikely place: among the ordinary, previously law-abiding Rwandan citizens. Many of the participants in the genocide were the least likely brutes you could imagine. For instance, here's how one woman described her husband, a man responsible for many Tutsi deaths:

> He came home often. He never carried a weapon, not even his machete. I knew he was a leader. I knew the Hutus were out there cutting Tutsis. With me, he behaved nicely. He made sure we had everything we needed. . . . He was gentle with the children. . . . To me, he was the nice man I married. (quoted in Rwandan Stories, 2011, p. 1)

Pauline Nyiramasuhuko, a former social worker and the country's minister of family and women's affairs, promised the Tutsis in one village that they would be safe in a local stadium. When they arrived there, armed militia were waiting to kill them. She instructed one group of soldiers to burn alive a group of 70 women and girls, adding, "Before you kill the women, you need to rape them" (quoted in Zimbardo, 2007, p. 13). In 2011, a United Nations tribunal found that she had used her political position to help abduct and kill uncounted Tutsi men, women, and children and sentenced her to life in prison (Simons, 2011).

Some of the most gruesome attacks occurred in churches and missions (Lacey, 2006). Two Benedictine nuns and a National University of Rwanda physics professor stood trial for their role in the killings. The nuns were accused of informing the military that Tutsi refugees had sought sanctuary in the church and of standing by as the soldiers massacred them. One nun allegedly provided the death squads with cans of gasoline, which were used to set fire to a building where 500 Tutsis were hiding. The professor was accused of drawing up a list for the killers of Tutsi employees and students at the university and then killing at least seven Tutsis himself (Simons, 2001). A Catholic priest was sentenced to 15 years in prison for ordering his church to be demolished by bulldozers while 2,000 ethnic Tutsis sought refuge there. Indeed, some have argued that Rwandan churches themselves were complicit in the genocide from the beginning (Longman, 2009; Rittner, 2004).

A report by the civil rights organization African Rights provides evidence that members of the medical profession were deeply involved, too (M. C. Harris, 1996). The report details how doctors joined with militiamen to hunt down Tutsis, turning hospitals into slaughterhouses. Some helped soldiers drag sick and wounded refugees out of their beds to be killed. Others took advantage of their positions of authority to organize roadblocks, distribute ammunition, and compile lists of Tutsi colleagues, patients, and neighbors to be sought out and slaughtered. Many doctors who didn't participate in the actual killing refused to treat wounded Tutsis and withheld food and water from refugees who sought sanctuary in hospitals. In fact, the president of Rwanda and the minister of health were both physicians who were eventually tried as war criminals.

Ordinary, well-balanced people—teachers, social workers, priests and nuns devoted to the ideals of charity and mercy, and physicians trained to heal and save lives—had changed, almost overnight, into cold-hearted killers. How could something like this have happened? The answer to this question lies in the sociological claim that individual behavior is largely shaped by social forces and situational contingencies. The circumstances of large-scale ethnic hatred and war have the power to transform well-educated, "nice" people with no previous history of violence into cruel butchers. Tragically, such forces were at work in many of the 20th and 21st centuries' most infamous examples of human brutality, such as the Nazi Holocaust during World War II and, more recently, large-scale ethnic massacres in Cambodia, Iraq, Bosnia, Burma, Kosovo, the Democratic Republic of the Congo, and the Darfur region of Sudan, as well as Rwanda.

But social circumstances don't just create opportunities for brutality; they can also motivate ordinary people to engage in astounding acts of heroism. The 2004 film *Hotel Rwanda* depicts the true story of Paul Rusesabagina, a hotel manager in the Rwandan capital, Kigali, who risked his own life to shelter over a thousand Tutsi refugees from certain death. Rusesabagina was a middle-class Hutu married to a Tutsi and the father of four children. He was a businessman with an eye toward turning a profit and a taste for the finer things in life. But when the genocide began, he used his guile, international contacts, and even water from the swimming pool to keep the refugees alive.

In this chapter, I examine the process by which individuals construct society and the way people's lives are linked to the social environment in which they live. The relationship between the individual and society is a powerful one—each continually affects the other.

HOW INDIVIDUALS STRUCTURE SOCIETY

Up to this point, I have used the word *society* rather loosely. Formally, sociologists define **society** as a population living in the same geographic area who share a culture and a common identity and whose members are subject to the same political authority. Societies may consist of people with the same ethnic heritage or of hundreds of different groups who speak a multitude of languages. Some societies are highly industrialized and complex; others are primarily agricultural and relatively simple in structure. Some are very religious; others are distinctly secular.

According to the 19th-century French philosopher Auguste Comte, all societies, whatever their form, contain both forces for stability, which he called "social statics," and forces for change, which he called "social dynamics." Sometimes, however, people use the term *society* only to mean a "static" entity—a natural, permanent, and historical structure. They frequently talk about society "planning" or "shaping" our lives and describe it as a relatively unchanging set of organizations, institutions, systems, and cultural patterns into which successive generations of people are born and socialized.

As a result, sociology students often start out believing not only that society is powerfully influential (which, of course, it is) but also that it is something that exists "out there," completely separate and distinct from us (which it isn't). It is tempting to view society simply as a "top down" initiator of human activity, a massive entity that methodically shapes the lives of all individuals within it like some gigantic puppeteer manipulating a bunch of marionettes. This characterization is not completely inaccurate. Society does exert influence on its members through certain identifiable structural features and historical circumstances. The concept of the sociological imagination discussed in Chapter 1 implies that structural forces beyond our direct control do shape our personal lives.

But this view is only one side of the sociological coin. The sociological imagination also encourages us to see that each individual has a role in forming a society and influencing the course of its history. As we navigate our social environments, we respond in ways that may modify the effects and even the nature of that environment (House, 1981). To fully understand society, then, we must see it as a human construction made up of people interacting with one another. Communication plays an important role in the construction of society. If we couldn't communicate with one another to reach an understanding about society's expectations, we couldn't live together. Through day-to-day communication, we construct, reaffirm, experience, and alter the reality of our society. By responding to other people's messages, comments, and gestures in the expected manner and by talking about social abstractions as real things, we help shape society (Shibutani, 1961).

Imagine two people sitting on a park bench in 2013 discussing *sequestration*—the series of deep across-the-board spending cuts that were about to automatically take effect because Congress failed to approve a federal debt-reduction plan. Person A is convinced that the fairest way to reduce the enormous national debt would be to raise taxes on the wealthiest Americans and not reduce spending on the federal programs that help the poorest citizens, like Social Security and Medicaid. Person B is convinced that the way to avoid financial ruin would be to impose deep cuts on these expensive programs that add to the debt, thereby avoiding the need to raise anyone's taxes. The debate becomes heated: One thinks that we have a moral obligation to care for our neediest citizens and that it's appropriate that the wealthiest among us pay more; the other feels that increasing taxes to subsidize "bloated" government "handouts" is a sure road to economic disaster. These two people obviously don't agree on the role that the federal government should play in people's lives. But merely by discussing sequestration, they are acknowledging that such a phenomenon exists. In talking about such matters, people give shape and substance to society's ideals and values (Hewitt, 1988).

We live in a world in which our everyday lives are largely a product of structural, or **macrolevel**, societal and historical processes. Society is an objective fact that coerces, even creates us (P. L. Berger, 1963). At the same time, we constantly create, maintain, reaffirm, and transform society. Hence, society is part and parcel of individual-level human interaction (R. Collins, 1981). But although we create society, we then collectively "forget" we've done so, believe it exists independently of us, and live our lives under its influence.

SOCIAL INFLUENCE: THE IMPACT OF OTHER PEOPLE IN OUR EVERYDAY LIVES

We live in a world with other people. I know that's not the most profound statement you've ever read, so you can stop yawning. But it is key to understanding the sociology of human behavior. Our everyday lives are collections of brief encounters, extended conversations, intimate interactions, and chance collisions with other people. In our early years, we may have our parents, siblings, uncles, aunts, and grandparents to contend with. Soon, we begin to form friendships with others outside our families. Over time, our lives also become filled with connections to other people—classmates, teachers, coworkers, bosses, spiritual leaders, therapists—who are neither family nor friends but who have an enormous impact on us. And, of course, we have frequent experiences with total strangers: the barista at the local coffee shop who serves us our daily latte, the chatty traveler who sits next to us on an airplane, the tech support specialist who helps us when our documents won't print or our iPads freeze.

If you think about it, understanding what it means to be alone requires that we know what it's like to be with other people. As I will discuss in Chapters 5 and 6, much of our private identity—what we think of ourselves, the type of people we become, and the images of ourselves we project in public—comes from our contact with others.

Sociologists tell us that these encounters have a great deal of *social influence* over our lives. Whether we're aware of their doing so or not, other people affect our thoughts, likes, and dislikes. Consider why certain songs, books, or films become blockbuster hits. We usually think their popularity is a consequence of a large number of people making their own independent decisions about what appeals to them. But research shows that popularity is a consequence of social influence (Salganik, Dodds, & Watts, 2006). If one object happens to be slightly more popular than others—such as a particular song that gets downloaded a lot from iTunes—it tends to become more popular as more people are drawn to it. As one sociologist put it, "People tend to like what other people like" (Watts, 2007, p. 22).

Imagine for a moment what your life would be like if you had never had contact with other people (assuming you could have survived this long!). You wouldn't know what love is, or hate or jealousy or compassion or gratitude. You wouldn't know whether you were attractive or unattractive, bright or dumb, witty or boring. You'd lack some basic information, too. You wouldn't know what day it was, how much a pound weighs, where Belgium is, or how to read. Furthermore, you'd have no language, and because we use language to think, imagine, predict, plan, wonder, and reminisce, you'd lack these abilities as well. In short, you'd lack the key experiences that make you a functioning human being.

Contact with people is essential to a person's social development. But there is much more to social life than simply bumping into others from time to time. We act and react to things and people in our environment as a result of the meaning we attach to them. At the sight of Mokolodi, my big Labrador retriever, playfully barreling toward it, a squirrel instinctively runs away. A human, however, does not have such an automatic reaction. We've all learned from past experiences that some animals are approachable and others aren't. So we can think, "Do I know this dog? Is it friendly or mean? Does it want to lick my face or tear me limb from limb?" and respond accordingly. In short, we usually interpret events in our environment before we react.

The presence of other people may motivate you to improve your performance—for example, when the high quality of your tennis opponent makes you play the best match of your life. But their presence may at other times inhibit you—as when you forget your lines in the school play because your ex-boyfriend's in the audience glowering at you. Other people's presence is also essential for the expression of certain feelings or bodily functions. We've all experienced the unstoppable urge to yawn after watching someone else yawn. But have you ever noticed the contagion of coughing that often breaks out in class during a lecture or exam? Research has shown that coughing tends to trigger coughing in those who hear it (cited in Provine, 2012). And think about the fact that you can't tickle yourself. Being tickled is the product of a *social* interaction. Indeed, according to one study of laughter, people are about 30 times more likely to laugh when they're around other people than when they're alone (Provine, 2000).

And our personal contentment and generosity can be linked to others as well. One recent study found that just knowing someone who is happy—whether she or he is a relative, friend, or acquaintance—significantly increases your own chances of happiness (Fowler & Christakis, 2008). Such influence can be found in the online world, too. Twitter users prefer to follow other Twitter users who exhibit comparable moods. That is, happy users tend to retweet or reply to other happy users (Bollen, Gonçalves, Ruan, & Mao, 2012). Research also suggests that the presence of female family members (wives, sisters, daughters, mothers) can make men more generous, compassionate, and empathetic. The founder of Microsoft, Bill Gates, has consistently cited the inspiration provided by his wife and mother in setting up his charitable foundation, which has given away more than $28 billion to date (Grant, 2013).

The influence of others goes beyond emotions, behaviors, and performances. Even our physical well-being is affected by those around us. According to researchers in Japan, the risk of heart attack is three times higher among women who live with their husbands and their husbands' parents than among women who live just with their husbands (cited in Rabin, 2008).

And, of course, other people can sometimes purposely influence our actions. I'm sure you've been in situations in which people have tried to persuade you to do things against your will or better judgment. Perhaps someone convinced you to steal a candy bar, skip your sociology class, or disregard the speed limit. On occasion, such social influence can be quite harmful.

SOCIETAL INFLUENCE: THE EFFECT OF SOCIAL STRUCTURE ON OUR EVERYDAY LIVES

Social life is more than individual people affecting one another's lives. Society is not just a sum of its human parts; it's also the way those parts are put together, related to each other, and organized (Coulson & Riddell, 1980). Statuses, roles, groups, organizations, and institutions are the building blocks of society. Culture is the mortar that holds these blocks together. Although society is dynamic and constantly evolving, it has an underlying macro-level structure that persists.

Statuses and Roles

One key element of any society is its collection of *statuses*—the positions that individuals within the society occupy. When most of us hear the word *status*, we tend to associate it with rank or prestige. But here we're talking about a status as any socially defined position a person can occupy: cook, daughter, anthropologist, husband, computer nerd, electrician, Facebook friend, shoplifter, and so on. Some statuses may, in fact, be quite prestigious, such as president. But others carry very little prestige, such as gas station attendant. Some statuses require a tremendous amount of training, such as physician; others, such as ice cream lover, require little effort or none at all.

We all occupy many statuses at the same time. I am a college professor, but I am also a husband, son, uncle, father, brother, friend, sushi lover, dog owner, occasional poker player, aging athlete, homeowner, and author. My behavior at any given moment is dictated to a large degree by the status that's most important at that particular time. When I am training for a half marathon, my status as professor is not particularly relevant. But if I decide to run in a race instead of showing up for the final exam in my sociology course, I may be in big trouble!

Sociologists often distinguish between ascribed and achieved statuses. An *ascribed status* is a social position we acquire at birth or enter involuntarily later in life. Our race, sex, ethnicity, and identity as someone's child or grandchild are all ascribed statuses. As we get older, we enter the ascribed status of teenager and, eventually, old person. These aren't positions we choose to occupy. An *achieved status*, in contrast, is a social position we take on voluntarily or acquire through our own efforts or accomplishments, such as being a student or a spouse or an engineer.

Of course, the distinction between ascribed and achieved status is not always so clear. Some people become college students not because of their own efforts but because of their family's influence. Chances are the religion with which you identify is the one you inherit from your parents. However, many people decide to change their religious membership later in life. Moreover, as we'll see later in this book, certain ascribed statuses (sex, race, ethnicity, and age) influence our access to lucrative achieved statuses.

Whether ascribed or achieved, statuses are important sociologically because they all come with a set of rights, obligations, behaviors, and duties that people occupying a certain position are expected or encouraged to perform. These expectations are referred to as *roles*. For instance, the role expectations associated with the status "professor" include teaching students, answering their questions, grading them impartially, and dressing appropriately. Any out-of-role behavior may be met with shock or suspicion. If I consistently showed up for class in a thong and tank top, that would certainly violate my "scholarly" image and call into question my ability to teach (not to mention my sanity).

Each person, as a result of her or his own skills, interests, and interactional experiences, defines roles differently. Students enter a class with the general expectation that their professor is knowledgeable about the subject and is going to teach them something.

Each professor, however, may have a different method of meeting that expectation. Some professors are very animated; others remain stationary behind a podium. Some do not allow questions until after the lecture; others constantly encourage probing questions from students. Some are meticulous and organized, others spontaneous and absentminded.

People engage in typical patterns of interaction based on the relationship between their roles and the roles of others. Employers are expected to interact with employees in a certain way, as are doctors with patients and salespeople with customers. In each case, actions are constrained by the role responsibilities and obligations associated with those particular statuses. We know, for instance, that lovers and spouses are supposed to interact with each other differently from the way acquaintances or friends are supposed to interact. In a parent–child relationship, both members are linked by certain rights, privileges, and obligations. Parents are responsible for providing their children with the basic necessities of life—food, clothing, shelter, and so forth. These expectations are so powerful that not meeting them may constitute the crime of negligence or abuse. Children, in turn, are expected to abide by their parents' wishes. Thus, interactions within a relationship are functions not only of the individual personalities of the people involved but also of the role requirements associated with the statuses they occupy.

We feel the power of role expectations most clearly when we have difficulty meeting them or when we occupy two conflicting statuses simultaneously. Sociologists use the term *role strain* to refer to situations in which people lack the necessary resources to fulfill the demands of a particular role, such as when parents can't afford to provide their children with adequate food, clothing, or shelter. *Role conflict* describes situations in which people encounter tension in trying to cope with the demands of incompatible roles. People may feel frustrated in their efforts to do what they feel they're supposed to do when the role expectations of one status clash with the role expectations of another. For instance, a mother (who also happens to be a prominent sociologist) may have an important out-of-town conference to attend (status of sociologist) on the same day her 10-year-old son is appearing as a talking pig in the school play (status of parent). Or a teenager who works hard at his job at the local ice cream shop (status of employee) may be frustrated when his buddies arrive and expect him to sit and chat or to give them free ice cream (status of friend).

Role conflict can sometimes raise serious ethical or legal concerns. For instance, in states that use lethal injection as a means of execution, it is necessary to have a licensed anesthesiologist present to ensure that the prisoner is unconscious when paralyzing and heart-stopping drugs are administered. Ordinarily, the role expectations of doctors emphasize ensuring the health and well-being of the people they treat. But when doctors are part of an execution team, they are expected to use their medical skills and judgment to make killing more humane and less painful. Several medical organizations, including the American Medical Association, have condemned physicians' involvement in executions as unethical and unprofessional (P. Elias, 2006).

Groups

Societies are not simply composed of people occupying statuses and living in accordance with roles. Sometimes individuals form well-defined units called groups. A *group* is a set of people who interact more or less regularly with one another and who are conscious of their identity as a group. Your family, your colleagues at work, and any clubs or sports teams to which you belong are all social groups.

Groups are not just collections of people who randomly come together for some purpose. Their structure defines the relationships among members. When groups are large, enduring, and complex, each individual within the group is likely to occupy some named position or status—mother, president, supervisor, linebacker, and so forth.

Group membership can also be a powerful force behind one's future actions and thoughts. Sociologists distinguish between *in-groups*—the groups to which we belong and toward which we feel a sense of loyalty—and *out-groups*—the groups to which we don't belong and toward which we feel a certain amount of antagonism. For instance, a girl who is not a member of the popular clique at school, but wants to be, is likely to structure many of her daily activities around gaining entry into that group.

In addition, like statuses and roles, groups come with a set of general expectations. A person's actions within a group are judged according to a conventional set of ideas about how things ought to be. For example, a coworker who always arrives late for meetings or never takes his or her turn working an undesirable shift is violating the group's expectations and will be pressured to conform.

The smallest group, of course, is one that consists of two people, or a *dyad*. According to the renowned German sociologist Georg Simmel (1902/1950), dyads (marriages, close friendships, etc.) are among the most meaningful and intense connections we have. The problem, though, is that dyads are by nature unstable. If one person decides to leave, the group completely collapses. Hence, it's not surprising that for society's most important dyads (i.e., marriages), a variety of legal, religious, and cultural restrictions are in place that make it difficult for people to dissolve them.

The addition of one person to a dyad—forming what Simmel called a *triad*—fundamentally changes the nature of the group. Although triads might appear more stable than dyads because the withdrawal of one person needn't destroy the group, they develop other problems. If you're one of three children in your family, you already know that triads always contain the potential for *coalitions*—where two individuals pair up and perhaps conspire against the third.

Groups can also be classified by their influence on our everyday lives. A *primary group* consists of a small number of members who have direct contact with each other over a relatively long period of time. Emotional attachment is high in such groups, and members have intimate knowledge of each other's lives. Families and networks of close friends are primary groups. A *secondary group*, in contrast, is much more formal and impersonal. The group is established for a specific task, such as the production or sale of consumer goods, and members are less emotionally committed to one another. Their roles tend to be highly structured. Primary groups may form within secondary groups, as when close friendships form among coworkers, but in general, secondary groups require less emotional investment than primary groups.

Like societies, groups have a reality that is more than just the sum of their members; a change in a group's membership doesn't necessarily alter its basic structure. Secondary groups can endure changing membership relatively easily if some, or even all, individuals leave and new ones enter—as, for example, when the senior class in a high school graduates and is replaced the following year by a new group of students. However, change in primary groups—perhaps through divorce or death—produces dramatic effects on the structure and identity of the group, even though the group itself still exists.

Although people of the same race, gender, ethnicity, or religion are not social groups in the strictest sense of the term, they function like groups in that members share certain characteristics and interests. They become an important source of a person's identity. For instance, members of a particular racial or ethnic group may organize into a well-defined unit to fight for a political cause. The feelings of "we-ness" or "they-ness" generated by such group membership can be constructive or dangerous, encouraging pride and unity in some cases and anger, bitterness, and hatred toward outsiders in others.

Organizations

At an even higher level of complexity are social units called *organizations*, networks of statuses and groups created for a specific purpose. The International Brotherhood of Teamsters, Harvard University, Microsoft, the Federal Emergency Management Agency, the National Organization for Women, and the Methodist Church are all examples of organizations. Organizations contain groups as well as individuals occupying clearly defined statuses and taking on clearly defined roles.

Some of the groups within organizations are transitory; some are more permanent. For instance, a university consists of individual classes that form at the beginning of a semester and disband at its end, as well as more permanent groups such as the faculty, administration, secretarial staff, maintenance staff, and alumni.

Large, formal organizations are often characterized by a *hierarchical division of labor*. Each person in an organization occupies a position that has a specific set of duties and responsibilities, and those positions can be "ranked" according to their relative power and importance. At Honda, for instance, assembly line workers typically don't make hiring decisions or set budgetary policies, and the vice president in charge of marketing doesn't spray paint the underbodies of newly assembled Accords. In general, people occupy certain positions in an organization because they have the skills to do the job required of them. When a person can no longer meet the requirements of the job, she or he can be replaced without seriously affecting the functioning of the organization.

Organizations are a profoundly common and visible feature of everyday social life, as you'll see in Chapter 9. Most of us cannot acquire food, get an education, pray, undergo lifesaving surgery, or earn a salary without coming into contact with or becoming a member of some organization. To be a full-fledged member of modern society is to be deeply involved in some form of organizational life.

Social Institutions

When stable sets of statuses, roles, groups, and organizations form, they provide the foundation for addressing fundamental societal needs. These enduring patterns of social life are called *social institutions*. Sociologists usually think of institutions as the building blocks that organize society. They are the patterned ways of solving the problems and meeting the requirements of a particular society. Although there may be conflict over what society "needs" and how best to fulfill those needs, all societies must have some systematic way of organizing the various aspects of everyday life.

Key social institutions in modern society include the family, education, economics, politics and law, and religion. Some sociologists add health care, the military, and the mass media to the list.

Family. All societies must have a way of replacing their members, and reproduction is essential to the survival of human society as a whole. Within the institution of family, sexual relations among adults are regulated; people are cared for; children are born, protected, and socialized; and newcomers are provided an identity—a "lineage"—that gives them a sense of belonging. Just how these activities are carried out varies from society to society. Indeed, different societies have different ideas about which relationships qualify for designation as family. But the institution of family, whatever its form, remains the hub of social life in virtually all societies (J. H. Turner, 1972).

Education. Young people need to be taught what it means to be a member of the society in which they live and how to survive in it. In small, simple societies, the family is the primary institution responsible for socializing new members into the culture. However, as societies become more complex, it becomes exceedingly difficult for a family to teach its members all they need to know to function and survive. Hence, most modern, complex societies have an elaborate system of schools—preschool, primary, secondary, post-secondary, professional—that not only create

and disseminate knowledge and information but also train individuals for future careers and teach them their "place" in society.

Economy. From the beginning, human societies have faced the problems of securing enough food and protecting people from the environment (J. H. Turner, 1972). Today, modern societies have systematic ways of gathering resources, converting them into goods and commodities, and distributing them to members. In addition, societies provide ways of coordinating and facilitating the operation of this massive process. For instance, banks, accounting firms, insurance companies, stock brokerages, transportation agencies, and computer networks don't produce goods themselves but provide services that make the gathering, producing, and distributing of goods possible. To facilitate the distribution of both goods and services, economic institutions adopt a system of common currency and an identifiable mode of exchange. In some societies, the economy is driven by the value of efficient production and the need to maximize profits; in others, the collective well-being of the population is the primary focus.

Politics and Law. All societies face the problem of how to preserve order, avoid chaos, and make important social decisions. The legal system provides explicit laws or rules of conduct and mechanisms for enforcing those laws, settling disputes, and changing outdated laws or creating new ones (J. H. Turner, 1972). These activities take place within a larger system of governance that allocates and acknowledges power, authority, and leadership. In a democracy, the governance process includes the citizens, who have a say in who leads them; in a monarchy, kings or queens can claim that their birthright entitles them to positions of leadership. In some societies, the transfer of power is efficient and mannerly; in others, it is violent.

Religion. In the process of meeting the familial, educational, economic, and political needs of society, some individuals thrive, whereas others suffer. Hence, all societies also face the problem of providing their less successful members with a sense of purpose and meaning in their lives. Religion gives individuals a belief system for understanding their existence as well as a network of personal support in times of need. Although many members of a given society may actively reject religion, it remains one of the most enduring and powerful social institutions. Although religion provides enormous comfort to some people, it can also be a source of hatred and irreparable divisions.

Health Care. One of the profoundly universal facts of human life is that people get sick and die. In some societies, healing the sick and managing the transition to death involves spiritual or supernatural intervention; other societies rely on science and modern technology. Most modern societies have established a complex system of health care to disseminate medical treatments. Doctors, nurses, hospitals, pharmacies, drug and medical equipment manufacturers, and patients all play an active role in the health care system.

Military. To deal with the possibility of attack from outside and the protection of national interests, many societies maintain an active military defense. However, militaries are used not only to defend societies but also, at times, to attack other countries in order to acquire land, resources, or power. In other cases, the military is used for political change, as when U.S. armed forces were mobilized to overthrow the government of Saddam Hussein in Iraq in 2003.

Mass Media. In very small, relatively close-knit societies, information can be shared through word of mouth. However, as societies become more complex, the dissemination of information requires a massive coordinated system. The modern mass media—radio, newspapers, television, and the Internet—provide coverage of important societal events so individuals can make informed decisions about their own lives. But the media do more than report events of local, national, and international significance. They also actively mold public opinion and project and reinforce a society's values.

From these very brief descriptions, you can see that the social institutions within a society are highly interrelated. Take, for instance, the connections between medical research and economics. A constant stream of recent studies has affirmed the presence of a dangerous "epidemic" in competitive football: severe concussions. It's not uncommon for players—from high school to the pros—to sustain hits to the head equivalent to the impact of a 25-mph car crash. Some studies suggest that as many as 15% of players suffer some type of brain damage each season (cited in Lehrer, 2012). In the past, players who "got their bell rung" were quickly resuscitated after such hits so they could re-enter the game. But it's clear now that the brain damage these hits cause—a condition known as chronic traumatic encephalopathy—can have lasting consequences including long-term memory loss, depression, mood disorders, and suicidal tendencies. According to the Centers for Disease Control and Prevention, 80% of these cases go unrecognized until it is too late (Congeni, 2009). But football is a multibillion-dollar business with far-reaching economic ties. At the college level, football is the number-one revenue-generating activity for most large universities, and the NFL is the most lucrative professional league in the country. Hence it's not surprising that with such deep economic investments, the football industry has been slow to heed medical research and take any sort of significant step to reduce the game's violence, and hence the likelihood of deadly brain injury.

To individual members of society, social institutions appear natural, permanent, and inevitable. Most of us couldn't imagine life without a family. Nor could most of us fathom what society would be like without a stable system of government, a common currency, schools to educate our children, or an effective health care system. It is very easy, then, to think that institutions exist independently of people.

But one of the important themes that will be revisited throughout this book is that we each have a role to play in maintaining or changing social institutions, as when citizens alter the political shape of a country by voting out of office an administration with which they've grown displeased. Although the effects of changes can be felt at the organizational and institutional levels, they are ultimately initiated, implemented, or rejected, and, most important, experienced by individual people.

Culture

The most pervasive element of society is *culture*, which consists of the language, values, beliefs, rules, behaviors, and physical artifacts of a society. Think of it as a society's "personality." Culture gives us codes of conduct—proper, acceptable ways of doing things. We usually don't think twice about it, yet it colors everything we experience.

Culture is particularly apparent when someone questions or violates it. Those who do not believe what the majority believes, see what the majority sees, or obey the same rules the majority obeys are likely to experience punishment, psychiatric attention, or social ostracism. I will discuss the power of culture in more detail in Chapter 4, but here we should look at two key aspects of culture that are thoroughly implicated in the workings of social structure and social influence: values and norms.

Values

Perhaps no word in the English language carries more baggage than *values*. People throw around terms such as *moral values*, *traditional values*, *family values*, and *American values* with little thought as to what they actually mean. Sociologically speaking, a *value* is a standard of judgment by which people decide on desirable goals and outcomes (Hewitt & Hewitt, 1986). Values represent the general criteria on which our lives and the lives of others can be judged. They justify the social rules that determine how we ought to behave. For instance, laws against theft clearly reflect the value we place on personal property.

Different societies emphasize different values. Success, independence, and individual achievement are seen as important values in U.S. society. In other societies, such as Vietnam, people are more likely to value group obligation and loyalty to family.

Values within a society sometimes come into conflict. The value of privacy ("stay out of other people's business") and the value of generosity ("help others in need") may clash when we are trying to decide whether to help a stranger who seems to require assistance. Similarly, although the value of cooperation is held in high esteem in contemporary U.S. society, when someone is taking a final exam in a sociology class, cooperation is likely to be defined as cheating. When the key values that characterize a particular social institution come into conflict, the result may be widespread legal and moral uncertainty among individuals.

Norms

Norms are culturally defined rules of conduct. They specify what people should do and how they should pursue values. They tell us what is proper or necessary behavior within particular roles, groups, organizations, and institutions. Thousands of norms guide the minor and the grand details of our lives,

from the bedroom to the classroom to the boardroom. You can see, then, that norms serve as the fundamental building blocks of social order.

Norms make our interactions with others reasonably predictable. Americans expect that when they extend a hand to another person, that person will grasp it and a brief handshake will follow. They would be shocked if they held out their hand and the other person spit on it or grabbed it and wouldn't let go. In contrast, people in some societies commonly embrace or kiss each other's cheek as a form of greeting, even when involved in a formal business relationship. A hearty handshake in those societies may be interpreted as an insult. In Thailand, people greet each other by placing the palms of their hands together in front of their bodies and slightly bowing their heads. This greeting is governed by strict norms. Slight differences in the placement of one's hands reflect the social position of the other person—the higher the hands, the higher the position of the person being greeted. Norms like these make it easier to "live with others" in a relatively harmonious way (see Chapter 4).

Social Structure in a Global Context

A discussion of social structure would not be complete without acknowledging the fact that statuses, roles, groups, organizations, social institutions, and culture are sometimes influenced by broad societal and historical forces at work in the world. One such force with deep implications for contemporary society is *globalization*, the process through which people's lives all around the world become increasingly interconnected—economically, politically, environmentally, and culturally (see Chapter 9 for more detail).

Cultures have rarely been completely isolated from outside influence, because throughout human history people have been moving from one place to another, spreading goods and ideas. What is different today, though, is the speed and scope of these interactions. Several decades ago, overnight mail service and direct long-distance telephone calls increased the velocity of cross-national communication. Advances in transportation technology have made international trade more cost effective and international travel more accessible to ordinary citizens. And today, the Internet has given people around the world instantaneous access to the cultural artifacts and ideals of other societies, no matter where they're located. Through search engines like Google, Yahoo, and Bing, children in Beirut, Baltimore, or Beijing can easily and immediately mine unlimited amounts of the same information on every conceivable topic.

Clearly, societies are more interdependent than ever, and that interdependence matters for individuals around the world. Sometimes the effects are positive. Pharmaceutical breakthroughs in the United States or Europe, for instance, can save lives around the world. Globalization gives us a chance to learn about other societies and learn from them. Other times, however, global influence can have disastrous consequences. Many of today's most pressing societal problems—widespread environmental devastation, large- and small-scale wars, economic crises, viral epidemics, and so on—are a function of globalization to some degree. Closer to home, the construction of a toy factory in Southeast Asia or a clothing factory in Mexico may mean the loss of hundreds of manufacturing jobs in Kentucky or California.

In short, it is becoming increasingly difficult, if not impossible, to consider ourselves members of a single society unaffected by other societies. All of us are simultaneously members of our own society and citizens of a world community.

THREE PERSPECTIVES ON SOCIAL ORDER

The question of what holds all these elements of society together and how they combine to create social order has concerned sociologists for decades. Sociologists identify three broad intellectual orientations they often use to address this question: the structural-functionalist perspective, the conflict perspective, and symbolic interactionism. Each of these perspectives has its advantages and shortcomings. Each is helpful in answering particular types of questions. For instance, structural functionalism is useful in showing us how and why large, macrolevel structures, such as organizations and institutions, develop and persist. The conflict perspective sheds light on the various sources of social inequality that exist in our own and other societies. And symbolic interactionism is helpful in explaining how individuals construct meaning to make sense of their social surroundings. At times, the perspectives complement one another; at other times, they contradict one another.

Throughout the remaining chapters of this book, I will periodically return to these three

perspectives—as well as several other perspectives—to apply them to specific social phenomena, experiences, and events.

The Structural-Functionalist Perspective

According to sociologists Talcott Parsons and Neil Smelser (1956), two theorists typically associated with the *structural-functionalist perspective*, a society is a complex system composed of various parts, much like a living organism. Just as the heart, lungs, and liver work together to keep an animal alive, so too do all the elements of a society's structure work together to keep society alive.

Social institutions play a key role in keeping a society stable. All societies require certain things to survive. They must ensure that the goods and services people need are produced and distributed; they must provide ways of dealing with conflicts between individuals, groups, and organizations; and they must provide ways to ensure that individuals are made a part of the existing culture.

As we saw earlier in this chapter, institutions allow societies to attain their goals, adapt to a changing environment, reduce tension, and recruit individuals into statuses and roles. Economic institutions, for instance, allow adaptation to dwindling supplies of natural resources or to competition from other societies. Educational institutions train people for the future statuses they will need to fill to keep society going. Religions help maintain the existence of society by reaffirming people's values and preserving social ties among individuals (Durkheim, 1915/1954).

Sociologist Robert Merton (1957) distinguishes between manifest and latent functions of social institutions. *Manifest functions* are the intended, obvious consequences of activities designed to help some part of the social system. For instance, the manifest function of going to college is to get an education and acquire the credentials necessary to establish a career. *Latent functions* are the *unintended*, sometimes unrecognized, consequences of actions that coincidentally help the system. The latent function of going to college is to meet people and establish close, enduring friendships. In addition, college informally teaches students how to live on their own, away from their parents. It also provides important lessons in negotiating the intricacies of large bureaucracies—registering for classes, filling out forms, learning important school policies—so that students figure out how to "get things done" in an organization. These latent lessons will certainly help students who enter the equally large and bureaucratic world of work after they graduate (Galles, 1989).

From the structural-functionalist perspective, if an aspect of social life does not contribute to society's survival—that is, if it is *dys*functional—it will eventually disappear. Things that persist, even if they seem to be disruptive, must persist because they contribute somehow to the survival of society (Durkheim, 1915/1954). Take prostitution, for example. A practice so widely condemned and punished would appear to be dysfunctional for society. But prostitution has existed since human civilization began. Some structural functionalists suggest that prostitution satisfies sexual needs that may not be met through more socially acceptable means, such as marriage. Customers can have their physical desires satisfied without having to establish the sort of emotional attachment to another person that would destroy a preexisting marriage, harm the institution of family, and ultimately threaten the entire society (K. Davis, 1937).

Structural functionalism was the dominant theoretical tradition in sociology for most of the 20th century, and it still shapes sociological thinking to a certain degree today. But it has been criticized for accepting existing social arrangements without examining how they might exploit or otherwise disadvantage certain groups or individuals within the society.

The Conflict Perspective

The *conflict perspective* addresses the deficiencies of structural functionalism by viewing the structure of society as a source of inequality that benefits some groups at the expense of other groups. Conflict sociologists are likely to see society not in terms of stability and acceptance but in terms of conflict and struggle. They focus not on how all the elements of society contribute to its smooth operation and continued existence but on how these elements promote divisions and inequalities. Social order arises not from the societal pursuit of harmony but from dominance and coercion. The family, government, religion, and other institutions foster and legitimate the power and privilege of some individuals or groups at the expense of others.

Karl Marx, perhaps the most famous scholar associated with the conflict perspective, focused exclusively on economic arrangements. He argued that all human societies are structured around the production of goods that people need to survive. The individuals or groups who control the means of production—land in an agricultural society, factories in an industrial society, computer networks and information in a postindustrial society—have the power to create and maintain social institutions that serve their interests. Hence, economic, political, and educational systems in a modern society support the interests of those who control the wealth (see Chapter 10).

Marx believed that when resources are limited or scarce, conflict between the "haves" and the "have-nots" is inevitable and creates a situation in which those in power must enforce social order. He said this conflict is not caused by greedy, exploitative individuals; rather, it is a by-product of a system in which those who benefit from inequality are motivated to act in ways that maintain it.

Contemporary conflict sociologists are interested in various sources of conflict and inequality. One version of the conflict perspective that has become particularly popular among sociologists in the past few decades is the *feminist perspective*. Feminist sociologists focus on gender as the most important source of conflict and inequality in social life. Compared with men, women in nearly every contemporary society have less power, influence, and opportunity. In families, especially in industrialized societies, women have traditionally been encouraged to perform unpaid household labor and childcare duties, whereas men have been free to devote their energy and attention to earning money and power in the economic marketplace. Women's lower wages when they do work outside the home are often justified by the assumption that their paid labor is secondary to that of their husbands. But as women in many societies seek equality in education, politics, career, marriage, and other areas of social life, their activities inevitably affect social institutions (see Chapter 12 for more details). The feminist perspective helps us understand the difficulties men and women face in their everyday lives as they experience the changes taking place in society.

Because this perspective focuses so much on struggle and competing interests, it tends to downplay or overlook the elements of society that different groups and individuals share. In addition, its emphasis on inequality has led some critics to argue that it is a perspective motivated by a particular political agenda and not the objective pursuit of knowledge.

Symbolic Interactionism

The structural-functionalist and the conflict perspectives differ in their assumptions about the nature of society, yet both analyze society mostly at the macro or structural level, focusing on societal patterns and the consequences they produce. In contrast, *symbolic interactionism* attempts to understand society and social structure through an examination of the microlevel interactions of people as individuals, pairs, or groups.

These forms of interaction take place within a world of symbolic communication. A *symbol* is something used to represent or stand for something else (Charon, 1998). It can be a physical object (like an engagement ring, standing for betrothal), a characteristic or property of objects (like the pink color of a triangle, standing for gay rights), a gesture (like a thumb pointed up, standing for "everything's OK"), or a word (like the letters d-o-g, standing for a particular type of household pet, or M-o-k-i, standing for *my* particular pet).

Symbols are created, modified, and used by people through their interactions with others. We concoct them and come to agree on what they should stand for. Our lives depend on such agreement. For instance, imagine how chaotic—not to mention dangerous—automobile travel would be if we didn't all agree that green stands for go and red stands for stop.

Symbols don't bear any necessary connection to nature. Rather, they're arbitrary human creations. There's nothing in the natural properties of "greenness" that automatically determines that green should stand for "go." We could have decided long ago that purple meant go. It wouldn't have mattered as long as we all learned and understood this symbol.

Most human behavior is determined not by the objective facts of a given situation but by the symbolic meanings people attach to the facts (Weber, 1947). When we interact with others, we constantly attempt to interpret what they mean and what they're up to. A gentle pat on the shoulder symbolizes one thing if it comes from someone with whom you are romantically involved but something quite different if it comes from your mother or your boss.

Society, therefore, is not a structure that exists independent of human action. It is "socially constructed," emerging from the countless symbolic interactions that occur each day between individuals. Each time I refer to "U.S. society," "the school system," "the global economy," "the threat of terrorism," or "the Upton family" in my casual conversations with others, I am doing my part to reinforce the notion that these are real things. By examining how and why we interact with others, symbolic interactionism reveals how the everyday experiences of people help to construct and maintain social institutions and, ultimately, society itself.

This perspective reminds us that for all its structural elements, society is, in the end, people interacting with one another. But by highlighting these microlevel experiences, symbolic interactionism runs the risk of ignoring the larger social patterns and structures that create the influential historical, institutional, and cultural settings for people's everyday interactions.

CONCLUSION

Living with others, within a social structure, influences many aspects of our everyday lives. But we must be cautious not to overstate the case. Although the fundamental elements of society are not merely the direct expressions of the personalities of individuals, we must also remember that people are more than "robots programmed by social structure" (G. Swanson, 1992, p. 94).

The lesson I hope you take from this chapter—and, in fact, from the entire book—is that the relationship between the individual and society is reciprocal. One cannot be understood without accounting for the other. Yes, this thing we call "society" touches our lives in intimate, important, and sometimes not altogether obvious ways. And yes, this influence is often beyond our immediate control. But society is not simply a "forbidding prison" that mechanically determines who we are and what we do (P. L. Berger, 1963). We as individuals can affect the very social structure that affects us. We can modify role expectations, change norms, create or destroy organizations, revolutionize institutions, and even alter the path of world history.

CHAPTER HIGHLIGHTS

◆ Although society exists as an objective fact, it is also created, reaffirmed, and altered through the day-to-day interactions of the very people it influences and controls.

◆ Humans are social beings. We look to others to help define and interpret particular situations. Other people can influence what we see, feel, think, and do.

◆ Society consists of socially recognizable combinations of individuals—relationships, groups, and organizations—as well as the products of human action—statuses, roles, culture, institutions, and broad societal forces such as globalization.

◆ There are three major sociological perspectives. The structural-functionalist perspective focuses on the way various parts of society are structured and interrelated to maintain stability and order. The conflict perspective emphasizes how the various elements of society promote inequality and conflict among groups of people. Symbolic interactionism seeks to understand society and social structure through the interactions of people and the ways in which they subjectively define their worlds.

KEY TERMS

achieved status: Social position acquired through our own efforts or accomplishments or taken on voluntarily

ascribed status: Social position acquired at birth or taken on involuntarily later in life

coalition: Subgroup of a triad, formed when two members unite against the third member

conflict perspective: Theoretical perspective that views the structure of society as a source of inequality that always benefits some groups at the expense of other groups

culture: Language, values, beliefs, rules, behaviors, and artifacts that characterize a society

dyad: Group consisting of two people

feminist perspective: Theoretical perspective that focuses on gender as the most important source of conflict and inequality in social life

globalization: Process through which people's lives all around the world become economically, politically, environmentally, and culturally interconnected

group: Set of people who interact more or less regularly and who are conscious of their identity as a unit

in-groups: The groups to which we belong and toward which we feel a sense of loyalty

latent function: Unintended, unrecognized consequences of activities that help some part of the social system

macrolevel: Way of examining human life that focuses on the broad social forces and structural features of society that exist above the level of individual people

manifest function: Intended, obvious consequences of activities designed to help some part of the social system

microlevel: Way of examining human life that focuses on the immediate, everyday experiences of individuals

norm: Culturally defined standard or rule of conduct

organization: Large, complex network of positions created for a specific purpose and characterized by a hierarchical division of labor

out-groups: The groups to which we don't belong and toward which we feel a certain amount of antagonism

primary group: Collection of individuals who are together for a relatively long period, whose members have direct contact with and feel emotional attachment to one another

role: Set of expectations—rights, obligations, behaviors, duties—associated with a particular status

role conflict: Frustration people feel when the demands of one role they are expected to fulfill clash with the demands of another role

role strain: Situations in which people lack the necessary resources to fulfill the demands of a particular role

secondary group: Relatively impersonal collection of individuals that is established to perform a specific task

social institution: Stable set of roles, statuses, groups, and organizations—such as the institutions of education, family, politics, religion, health care, or the economy—that provides a foundation for behavior in some major area of social life

society: A population of people living in the same geographic area who share a culture and a common identity and whose members are subject to the same political authority

status: Any named social position that people can occupy

structural-functionalist perspective: Theoretical perspective that posits that social institutions are structured to maintain stability and order in society

symbol: Something used to represent or stand for something else

symbolic interactionism: Theoretical perspective that explains society and social structure through an examination of the microlevel, personal, day-to-day exchanges of people as individuals, pairs, or groups

triad: Group consisting of three people

value: Standard of judgment by which people decide on desirable goals and outcomes

PART II

The Construction of Self and Society

Part II examines the basic architecture of individual identities and of society: how reality and truth are constructed; how social order is created and maintained; how culture and history influence our personal experiences; how societal values, ideals, and norms are instilled; and how we acquire our sense of self. The tactical and strategic ways in which we present images of ourselves to others are also addressed. You will see how we form relationships and interact within small, intimate groups. The section closes with a look at how we define "acceptable" behavior and how we respond to those who "break the rules."

Building Reality

The Social Construction of Knowledge

Understanding the Social Construction of Reality

Laying the Foundation: The Bases of Reality

Building the Walls: Conflict, Power, and Social Institutions

Appreciating the Contributions of Sociological Research

T he year was 1897. Eight-year-old Virginia O'Hanlon became upset when her friends told her there was no Santa Claus. Her father encouraged her to write a letter to the *New York Sun* to find out the truth. The editor's reply—which included the now famous phrase, "Yes, Virginia, there is a Santa Claus!"—has become a classic piece of American folklore. "Nobody sees Santa Claus," the editor wrote, "but that is no sign that there is no Santa Claus. The most real things in the world are those that neither children nor men [*sic*] can see" ("Is There a Santa Claus?" 1897).

In his book *Encounters With the Archdruid*, John McPhee (1971) examines the life and ideas of David Brower, who was one of the most successful and energetic environmentalists in the United States. McPhee recalls a lecture in which Brower claimed that the United States has 6% of the world's population and uses 60% of the world's resources and that only 1% of Americans use 60% of those resources. Afterward, McPhee asked Brower where he got these interesting statistics:

Brower said the figures had been worked out in the head of a friend of his from data assembled "to the best of his recollection." . . . [He] assured me that figures in themselves are merely indices. *What matters is that they feel right* [italics added]. Brower feels things. (p. 86)

What do these two very different examples have in common? Both reflect the fickle nature of "truth" and "reality." Young Virginia was encouraged to believe in the reality of something she could not and would never perceive with her senses. She no doubt learned a different sort of truth about Santa Claus when she got older, but the editor urged her to take on faith that Santa Claus, or at least the idea of Santa Claus, exists despite the lack of objective proof. That sort of advice persists. A survey of 200 child psychologists around the United States found that 91% of them advised parents not to tell the truth when their young children asked about the existence of Santa Claus (cited in Stryker, 1997).

Likewise, David Brower urges people to believe in something that doesn't need to be seen. What's important is that the information "feels right," that it helps one's cause even if it is not based on hard evidence. More recently, former MTV star Jenny McCarthy published several best-selling books in which she claims that the measles, mumps, and rubella vaccine—something most infants in this country routinely receive—had probably given her son autism. Rather than provide research evidence (principally because there really is none), McCarthy based her conclusion on her own intuition, or what she called "mommy instinct." In fact, the Centers for Disease Control and Prevention, the Institute of Medicine, and the National Academy of Sciences have all concluded there is no link between vaccines and autism. Nevertheless, the contention that vaccines could harm children struck an emotional chord with many fretful parents. Consequently the percentage of children who get this vaccine as well as others has consistently dropped over the past several years. Perhaps not coincidentally, measles outbreaks have recently occurred in several states including New York, California, and Illinois (Mnookin, 2011).

Such precarious uses of truth may appear foolish or even deceitful. Yet much of our everyday knowledge is based on accepting as real the existence of things that can't be seen, touched, or proved—"the world taken-for-granted" (P. L. Berger, 1963,

p. 147). Like Virginia, we learn to accept the existence of things such as electrons, the ozone layer, black holes in the universe, love, and God, even though we cannot see them. And like David Brower and Jenny McCarthy, we learn to believe and use facts and figures as long as they sound right or support our interests.

How do we come to know what we know? How do we learn what is real and what isn't? In this chapter, I examine how sociologists discover truths about human life. But to provide the appropriate context, I must first present a sociological perspective on the nature of reality. How do individuals construct their realities? How do societal forces influence the process?

UNDERSTANDING THE SOCIAL CONSTRUCTION OF REALITY

In Chapter 2, I noted that the elements of society are human creations that provide structure to our everyday lives. They also give us a distinctive lens through which we perceive the world. For example, because of their different statuses and their respective occupational training, an architect, a real estate agent, a police officer, and a firefighter can each look at the same building and see very different things: "a beautiful example of early Victorian architecture," "a moderately priced fixer-upper," "an easy target for a thief," or "a dangerous fire hazard." Mark Twain often wrote about how the Mississippi River—a waterway he saw every day as a child—looked different after he became a riverboat pilot. What he once saw as a place for recreation and relaxation, he later saw for its treacherous currents, eddies, and other potential perils.

What we know to be true or real is always a product of the culture and historical period in which we exist. It takes an exercise of the sociological imagination, however, to see that what we ourselves "know" to be true today—the laws of nature, the causes and treatments of certain diseases, and so forth—may not be true for everyone everywhere or may be replaced by different truths tomorrow (Babbie, 1986). For example, in some cultures, the existence of spirits, witches, and demons is a taken-for-granted part of everyday reality that others might easily dismiss as fanciful. On the other side of the coin, the Western faith in the curative powers of little pills—without the intervention of spiritual forces—might seem far-fetched and naïve to people living in cultures where illness and health are assumed to have supernatural causes.

Ideas about reality also change over time. In 1900, a doctor might have told a patient with asthma to go to the local tobacconist for cigarettes people with colds may have been told to inhale formaldehyde (Zuger, 1999). Many pieces of taken-for-granted 20th-century child development advice—such as infants need to be bathed every day; picking up babies when they're crying spoils them; infants need to be on a strict feeding schedule; and the safest way to put babies to sleep is on their stomachs—have been called into question by contemporary pediatricians (First, 2011). Fifty years ago, obstetricians encouraged pregnant women to have a martini or a glass of wine each night to calm their nerves. Doctors also believed that alcohol prevented premature labor. Hence, women arriving at the hospital in early labor were often handed vodka or even given alcohol intravenously (Hoffman, 2005). In recent years, we've seen the medical field reverse its stand on the rules used to define autism (Carey, 2012), the necessity of vitamin D and calcium supplements (Begley, 2011), routine mammograms for healthy women over 40 (Bleyer & Welch, 2012), and regular blood tests for prostate cancer for healthy men (Harris, 2011b).

According to one researcher, about a third of major medical studies are eventually contradicted by further research (Ioannidis, 2005). The frequency with which medical "truths" emerge only to be reversed or debunked later on led one columnist to write, with a fair amount of exasperation, "Sometimes you really do want to tell the medical profession to just make up its mind" (G. Collins, 2011, p. A23). Quite possibly, people 100 years from now will look back at the early 21st century and regard some of our taken-for-granted truths as mistaken, misguided, or downright laughable.

The process through which facts, knowledge, truth, and so on are discovered, made known, reaffirmed, and altered by the members of a society is called the *social construction of reality* (P. L. Berger & Luckmann, 1966). This concept is based on the simple assumption that knowledge is a human creation. Ironically, most of us live our lives assuming that an objective reality exists, independent of us and accessible through our senses. We are quite sure trees and tables and trucks don't exist simply in our imaginations. We assume this reality is shared by others

and can be taken for granted as reality (Lindesmith, Strauss, & Denzin, 1991).

Hence, reality often turns out to be more a matter of agreement than something inherent in the natural world. On some occasions, taken-for-granted realities change almost instantaneously. Sociologists, particularly those working from the conflict perspective and symbolic interactionism, strive to explain the social construction of reality in terms of both its causes and its consequences. Their insights help explain many of the phenomena that influence our daily lives.

LAYING THE FOUNDATION: THE BASES OF REALITY

Think of society as a building constructed by the people who live and work in it. The building's foundation, its underlying reality, determines its basic shape and dimensions. And the foundation is what makes that building solid and helps it stand up through time and the elements. For students of architecture as well as sociology, the first thing to understand is the way the foundation is prepared.

Symbolic interactionism encourages us to see that people's actions toward one another and interpretations of situations are based on their definitions of reality, which are in turn learned from interactions with those around them. What we know to be real, we share with other members of our culture. Imagine how difficult it would be to believe in something no one else around you thought existed. Psychiatrists use terms such as *hallucination* and *delusion* to describe things experienced by people who see, hear, or believe things that others don't.

The social construction of reality is a process by which human-created ideas become so firmly accepted that to deny them is to deny common sense. Of course, some features of reality are grounded in physical evidence—fire is hot, sharp things hurt. But other features of reality are often based not on sensory experiences but on forces such as culture and language, self-fulfilling prophecies, and faith.

Culture and Language

As I mentioned in Chapter 2, we live in a symbolic world and interact chiefly through symbolic communication—that is, through language.

Language gives meaning to the people, objects, events, and ideas of our lives. In fact, language reflects and often determines our reality (Sapir, 1949; Whorf, 1956). Thus, language is a key tool in the construction of society.

Within a culture, words evolve to reflect the things that have practical significance. Solomon Islanders have nine distinct words for *coconut*, each specifying an important stage of its growth, but they have only one word for all the meals of the day (M. M. Lewis, 1948). The Hanunóo people of the Philippines have different names for 92 varieties of rice, allowing them to make distinctions all but invisible to English-speaking people, who lump all such grains under a single word: *rice* (Thomson, 2000). Yet a traditional Hanunóo coming to this country would be hard pressed to see the distinction between the vehicles we call *sedans*, *SUVs*, *hybrids*, *hatchbacks*, and *station wagons*.

Language reinforces prevailing ideas and suppresses conflicting ideas about the world (Sapir, 1929). In a highly specialized market economy such as the United States, for example, the ability to distinguish linguistically between "real" work, "house" work, and "volunteer" work allows us to telegraph our attitudes about a person's worth to society. In small agricultural societies, where all people typically perform tasks to provide the basic necessities and to ensure the survival of their tight-knit communities, work is work no matter where it takes place or whether or not you're paid to do it.

Language can also pack an enormous emotional wallop. Words can make us happy, sad, disgusted, or angry, or even incite us to violence. Racial, ethnic, sexual, or religious slurs can be particularly volatile. Among heterosexual adolescents, for example, homophobic name-calling (*queer*, *fag*, *dyke*) is one of the most common modes of bullying and coercion in school (Pascoe, 2010). In 2013, the famous cooking show host, Paula Deen, was fired by the Food Network after admitting that she had used the word *nigger*. In 2011, MSNBC radio host Ed Schultz was suspended for calling rival radio personality Laura Ingraham a "right-wing slut." That same year, star basketball player Kobe Bryant was fined $100,000 after television cameras caught him calling referee Bennie Adams a "faggot" during a game. Bryant wasn't disparaging Adams's sexual orientation. I doubt if he even knew whether Adams was gay or straight. Instead, he was enraged by a call Adams

had just made and found this word to be the most effective means of communicating his utter contempt for what he perceived to be terrible officiating.

The emotional effect of words can have health implications, too. Researchers estimate that an antibiotic-resistant intestinal bacterium called *Clostridium difficile* infects about a million people and kills 14,000 in the United States each year (Grady, 2013; Pollan, 2013). Symptoms include profuse diarrhea, uncontrollable vomiting, high fever, and significant weight loss. The most effective treatment for this condition, by far, is a procedure called a "fecal transplant" in which feces taken from healthy donors is infused into patients infected with *Clostridium difficile* (van Nood, 2013). The healthy feces, which contain thousands of types of "good" bacteria, is diluted with salt water, sanitized, and deodorized before being pumped into the patients' intestines. It bears no resemblance, either by sight or smell, to its original form. Yet despite its demonstrable success—as one author put it, "Rarely does medical science come up with a treatment so effective, inexpensive, and free of side effects" (Roach, 2013, pp. 320–321)—many patients who could be helped refuse to consider the treatment. And even though the first fecal transplant was performed over half a century ago, no U.S. insurance company formally recognizes the procedure (Roach, 2013). Why? Because people can't get past the disgust— what some refer to as the "ick factor"—associated with the thought of pumping one person's waste into another person's body.

The broader demands of everyday life also influence the way language is used. For instance, as societies become more developed, the pace of life quickens, and we become impatient. This phenomenon is reflected in the compression (and subsequent speedup) of language over the years. Contractions (like *we're* and *isn't*) shorten words. Portmanteaus combine two existing words into one, like *brunch* for "breakfast and lunch," *docudrama* for "documentary and drama," and *webinar* for "web seminar" (Garner, 2010). Technology contracts language even further. If you do a lot of instant messaging, tweeting, or texting, you have no doubt made use of "shortspeak"—the reduction of words and sentences through the use of abbreviations, acronyms, and emoticons. We don't even have to finish typing our words anymore. The search engine Google offers an enhancement called Google Instant, which begins to reveal search results even before you're done entering the key words. The company claims this feature saves two to five seconds per search. In fact, Google engineers recently discovered that a delay of 400 *milliseconds* between a keyboard click and a computer response—roughly the time it takes to blink an eye—is too long for some people and may actually cause them to use the search engine less. As one engineer put it, "Subconsciously, you don't like to wait. Every millisecond matters" (quoted in Lohr, 2012, p. A1).

Within a culture, certain professions or groups sometimes develop a distinctive language, known as *jargon*, that allows members of the group to communicate with one another clearly and quickly. Surfers, snowboarders, and techies each have a specialized vocabulary (not understandable to most outsiders) through which they can efficiently convey to others information about wave quality, snow conditions, or the latest innovations in microprocessors. Teenagers must keep up with a constantly evolving vocabulary to avoid falling out of favor with their peers. At the same time, jargon can sometimes create boundaries and therefore mystify and conceal meaning from outsiders (Farb, 1983). For instance, first-year medical students spend countless hours memorizing a new vocabulary as if they were learning a foreign language (Hartzband & Groopman, 2011). By using esoteric medical terminology when discussing a case in front of a patient, health care professionals define who is and who isn't a member of their group, reinforce their image as highly trained experts, and keep the patient from interfering too much in their decision making.

This sort of communication roadblock has become a cause for concern in the field of medicine. Many books and websites now help patients overcome their position of powerlessness by instructing them on how and when to ask physicians the right questions so they can make informed decisions about a course of treatment. For their part, some medical schools require their students to be trained in how to avoid jargon (at the same time they're learning it) and how to listen to their patients (D. Franklin, 2006). And there is some evidence that doctor–patient interactions have become a bit more patient centered and collaborative in recent years (Peck & Conner, 2011).

Language is sometimes used to purposely conceal as well. A *euphemism* is an innocuous expression substituted for one that might be offensive. On the surface, people use such terms in the interests of politeness and good taste, such as saying "perspiration" instead of "sweat," "bathroom tissue" instead of "toilet paper," or "no longer with us" instead of "dead." However, euphemisms also shape perceptions and emotions. Does it matter, for instance, whether an economic crisis is called a *downturn, slump, recession, crash, depression,* or *meltdown*?

In sum, words help frame or structure social reality and give it meaning. Language also provides people with a cultural and group identity. If you've ever spent a significant amount of time in a foreign country or even moved to a new school, you know you cannot be a fully participating member of a group or a culture until you share its language.

Self-Fulfilling Prophecies

As you will recall from Chapter 2, we do not respond directly and automatically to objects and situations; instead, as the symbolic interactionist perspective points out, we use language to define and interpret them, and then we act according to those interpretations. By acting on the basis of our definitions of reality, we often create the very conditions we believe exist. A *self-fulfilling prophecy* is an assumption or prediction that, purely as a result of having been made, causes the expected event to occur and thus confirms the prophecy's own "accuracy" (Merton, 1948; Watzlawick, 1984).

Every holiday season, we witness the stunning effects of self-fulfilling prophecies on a national scale. Each September the toy industry releases the results of its annual survey of retailers, predicting which toys will be the top sellers at Christmas. Usually, one toy in particular emerges as the most popular, hard-to-get gift of the year. In the 1980s, it was Cabbage Patch Kids. In the early 1990s, it was Mighty Morphin Power Rangers and Ninja Turtles. More recently, items such as Beanie Babies, SpongeBob SquarePants toys, Razor scooters, ripsticks, Bratz dolls, toy digital cameras, Harry Potter paraphernalia, and Xbox Kinect and Wii video games have taken their turn as the "must have" toy of the year. By around November, we begin to hear the hype about unprecedented demand for the toy and the likelihood of a shortage. Powerful retail store chains, such as Toys "R" Us and Wal-Mart, may announce the possibility of rationing: one toy per family. Fueled by the dreaded image of a disappointed child's face at Christmas, thousands of panicked parents and grandparents rush to stores to make sure they're not left without. Some hoard extras for other parents they know. As a result, supplies of the toy—which may not have been perilously low in the first place—become severely depleted, thereby bringing about the predicted shortage. The mere belief in some version of the reality creates expectations that can actually make it happen.

Self-fulfilling prophecies are particularly powerful when they become an element of social institutions. In schools, teachers can subtly and unconsciously encourage the performance they expect to see in their students. For instance, if they believe their students are especially intelligent, they may spend more time with them or unintentionally show more enthusiasm when working with them. As a result, these students may come to feel more capable and intelligent and actually perform better (R. Rosenthal & Jacobson, 1968).

Faith and Incorrigible Propositions

David Blaine is a famous street performer and illusionist who combines sophisticated magic tricks with a hint of comedy. In one of his more astounding stunts, he appears to rise up and float several inches off the ground for a few seconds. Suppose you saw him perform such a feat in person. He looks as if he is levitating, but you "know better." Even though your eyes tell you he is floating in midair, you have learned that it's just not possible. Rather than use this experience to entirely abandon your belief that people can't float in midair, you'll probably come up with a series of "reasonable" explanations: "Maybe it's an optical illusion, and it just appears like he's floating." "Perhaps there are wires holding him up." To acknowledge the possibility that he is literally floating is to challenge the fundamental reality on which your everyday life is based. It is an article of faith that people aren't capable of levitating.

Such an unquestionable assumption, called an ***incorrigible proposition***, is a belief that cannot be proved wrong and has become so much a part of common sense that one continues to believe it even in the face of vast contrary evidence. By explaining away contradictions with "reasonable" explanations, we strengthen the correctness of the initial premise (Watzlawick, 1976). In the process, we participate in constructing a particular version of

reality. For instance, if an incorrigible proposition for you is that women are inherently less aggressive than men, seeing an especially violent woman might lead you toward explanations that focus on the peculiar characteristics of *this particular* woman. Maybe *she's* responding to terrible circumstances in her life; maybe *she* has some kind of chemical imbalance or neurological disorder. By concluding that she is an exception to the rule, the rule is maintained.

In 2011, some evangelical Christians claimed that on May 21 of that year, God would send devastating earthquakes and begin a process that in five months would destroy the world. Believers would be spared and raised to heaven in "the rapture." When doomsday didn't materialize and the world still existed on May 22, those who believed in the prophecy provided a variety of rationalizations that allowed them to maintain the original belief. For instance, some pointed to human fallibility: "I don't know where we went wrong other than that we obviously don't understand Scriptures in the way that we should" (quoted in Hagerty, 2011, p. 1). Others argued that May 21 only marked the beginning of a five-month countdown to the end of the world and that the *real* day to worry about was *October* 21. When that didn't happen either, some claimed that the prayers of the believers actually worked and that God delayed judgment so that more people could be saved.

BUILDING THE WALLS: CONFLICT, POWER, AND SOCIAL INSTITUTIONS

We, as individuals, play an important role in coordinating, reproducing, and giving meaning to society in our daily interactions. But we are certainly not completely free to create whatever version of social reality we want to create. We are, after all, born into a preexisting society with its norms, values, roles, relationships, groups, organizations, and institutions. Just as the walls of a building constrain the ability of the inhabitants to move about, directing them through certain predetermined doorways and corridors, these features of society influence our thoughts and deeds and consequently constrain our ability to freely construct our social world (Giddens, 1984). As Karl Marx (1869/1963) wrote, "[People] make their own history, but they do not make it just as they please; they do not make it under circumstances chosen by themselves, but under circumstances directly encountered, given and transmitted from the past" (p. 15).

As the conflict perspective points out, certain people or groups of people are more influential in defining reality than others. In any modern society, where socioeconomic classes, ethnic and religious groups, age groups, and political interests struggle for control over resources, there is also a struggle for the power to determine or influence that society's conception of reality (Gans, 1971). Those who emerge successful gain control over information, define values, create myths, manipulate events, and influence what the rest of us take for granted. Conflict theorists therefore argue that people with more power, prestige, status, wealth, and access to high-level policymakers can turn their perceptions of the world into the entire culture's perception. In other words, "He who has the bigger stick has the better chance of imposing his definitions of reality" (P. L. Berger & Luckmann, 1966, p. 109). That "bigger stick" can be wielded in several ways. Powerful social institutions and the people who control them play a significant role in shaping and sustaining perceptions of reality for everybody else. But if you wish to develop the sociological imagination, you need to understand the role of not only these larger forces in shaping private lives but also private individuals who struggle to shape public reality.

The Economics of Reality

Definitions of reality frequently reflect underlying economic interests. The key concerns from the conflict perspective are who benefits economically and who loses from dominant versions of reality. Take mental illness, for example. The number of problems officially defined by the American Psychiatric Association (APA) as mental disorders and defects has now reached nearly 400 (Horwitz, 2002). In defining what constitutes a mental disorder, the APA unwittingly reflects the economic organization of U.S. society. In the United States, individuals seldom pay the total costs of health care services out of their own pockets. Most of the money for medical treatment comes from the federal and state governments or from private insurance companies. Only if problems such as gambling, depression, anorexia, and cocaine addiction are formally defined as illnesses is their treatment eligible for medical insurance coverage.

In 2010, the U.S. Department of Veterans Affairs changed its definition of posttraumatic stress disorder, making it substantially easier for hundreds of thousands of veterans to receive compensatory benefits. Posttraumatic stress disorder is a condition characterized by emotional numbness, irritability, and flashbacks following the experience or observation of some traumatic event. In the past, only soldiers who had been in combat and who could document specific firefights, bomb blasts, or mortar attacks qualified for benefits. Under the new rule, veterans only have to prove they served in a war zone and in a job consistent with the events they say caused their condition. The rule also allows compensation for service members who have a good reason to fear traumatic events even if they didn't experience them firsthand. It's estimated that this new rule will cost the government $5 billion in treatment costs over the next several years (Dao, 2010b).

The Politics of Reality

The institution of politics is also linked to societal definitions of reality. To a great extent, politics is about controlling public perceptions so people will do things or think about issues in ways that political leaders want them to. During important political campaigns, we can see such attempts to influence public perception. Mudslinging, euphemistically called "negative campaigning," has become as common an element of the U.S. electoral process as speeches, debates, baby kissing, and patriotic songs.

Most politicians know that if you say something untrue or unproven about an opponent often enough, people will believe it. In fact, while companies that sell consumer products must meet some standard of accuracy in their advertising, we have no federal truth-in-advertising laws for political campaign ads. Candidates have the legal right to lie ("Bunk Busters," 2007). Ironically, constant public denials of bogus charges often reinforce their reality and keep them in the news. In 2011, President Obama was forced to hold a news conference and present his birth certificate because the false claims that he isn't a U.S. citizen—which first arose during the 2008 election campaign—wouldn't go away. In some states, over half of Republican registered voters believed he was born outside the United States (D. Jackson, 2011). The validity of claims becomes irrelevant as accusations are transformed into "fact" and become solidified in the minds of the voting public. The problem has become so acute that a website, FactCheck.org, exists solely to monitor the factual accuracy of what major U.S. politicians say in TV ads, debates, speeches, interviews, and news releases.

When the lives of thousands of citizens are at stake and public opinion is crucial, information control becomes particularly tight. Between September 2001 and the invasion of Iraq in March 2003, the Bush administration worked diligently to foster a belief that Iraq and its then dictator, Saddam Hussein, played a direct role in the September 11 attacks and had stockpiles of weapons of mass destruction. They were quite successful. At the time of the attacks, national opinion polls showed that only 3% of Americans mentioned Iraq or Saddam Hussein when asked who was responsible. But by January 2003, 44% of Americans reported that either "most" or "some" of the hijackers were Iraqi citizens. In fact, none were (Feldmann, Marlantes, & Bowers, 2003). Two years later, 69% of Americans said in a *Washington Post* poll that they thought it at least likely that Hussein was involved in the attacks, even though the link between Iraq and al-Qaeda was never established (Milbank & Deane, 2003). Nevertheless, these beliefs provided the kind of public support necessary to justify the military invasion and occupation of Iraq. In 2008, the Center for Public Integrity (2008) concluded that the administration had made close to 1,000 false public statements on either the existence of weapons of mass destruction or the link between al-Qaeda and Iraq. Such a molding of public perception is accomplished most notably through the media.

The Medium Is the Message

Communication media are the primary means by which we are entertained and informed about the world around us (see Chapter 5). But the messages we receive from the media also reflect dominant cultural values (Gitlin, 1979). In television shows and other works of fiction, the way characters are portrayed, the topics addressed, and the solutions imposed on problems all link entertainment to the economic system and prevailing societal tastes in consumption.

The media are also our primary source of information about local, national, and international events and people. News broadcasts and newspapers

tell us about things we cannot experience directly, making the most remote events meaningful (Molotch & Lester, 1974). The way we look at the world and define our lives within it is therefore shaped and influenced by what we see on Internet news sites, watch on TV news shows, hear on the radio, or read in our daily papers.

Because the news is the means by which political realities are disseminated to the public, it is an essential tool in maintaining social order (Hallin, 1986; Parenti, 1986). In many societies, news sources don't even try to hide the fact that they are mouthpieces of one faction or another. In repressive societies, the only news sources allowed to operate are those representing the government. In North Korea, for instance, the flow of news information is clearly controlled by the government. People who live in societies with a cultural tradition of press independence, in contrast, assume that news stories are purely factual—an accurate, objective reflection of the "world out there" (Molotch & Lester, 1975). Like everything else, however, news is a constructed reality.

Hundreds, perhaps thousands, of potentially newsworthy events occur every day. Yet we'll see maybe 10 of them on our favorite evening broadcast or the home page of our favorite online news service. These events exist as news not because of their inherent importance but because of the practical, political, or economic purposes they serve. The old newsroom adage "If it bleeds, it leads" attests to the fact that events with shocking details—which appeal to the public's fondness for the sensational—are those most likely to be chosen. At its most independent, the news is still the product of decisions made by reporters, editors, network executives, and corporation owners, all of whom have their own interests, biases, and values (Molotch & Lester, 1974).

Although "freedom of expression" and "freedom of the press" are core American values, media manipulation of information has been not only tolerated but encouraged in some situations. Take the coverage of the military actions in Iraq and Afghanistan following the attacks of September 11, 2001. During the initial stages of the war, press coverage seemed to be relatively open. The Pentagon allowed hundreds of "embedded" reporters to accompany fighting forces and transmit their stories from the front battle lines. According to one study, 61% of their reports during the first three days of the war were live and unedited (Project for Excellence in Journalism, 2005). By granting such unprecedented access, Pentagon officials hoped that these reporters would convey the "heroism and hard work" of American soldiers to a worldwide audience and in the process discredit Iraqi propaganda (Getlin & Wilkinson, 2003).

But even then, some media critics were concerned that the reporters were tools of the military, especially given their often close attachment to the soldiers with whom they were traveling. The Pentagon required embedded journalists to sign a contract giving the military control over the content of their stories (Jamail, 2007). According to one study, 80% of early embedded reports included no commentary at all from soldiers (Project for Excellence in Journalism, 2005).

For everyday news stories, even in societies that restrict the press, official censorship is usually unnecessary. Because of the economic pressures to attract audiences and keep their attention, TV networks and newspapers usually censor themselves (Bagdikian, 1991). Reporters pursue stories that are relatively easy to research and that have immediate interest for audiences. Less exciting, more complicated stories don't get enough journalistic resources or are cut in the editing process. We usually have no way of knowing which events have *not* been selected for inclusion in the day's news or which plausible alternatives are kept out of the public eye.

The economic and political motivation for such selectivity becomes apparent when we consider who owns the media. For instance, one company, Clear Channel, owns about 850 local radio stations in all 50 states, reaching more than 110 million listeners every week; Clear Channel also owns over 1 million outdoor advertising displays in 45 countries on 5 continents (Clear Channel Communications, 2012). Cumulus Media owns 525 local radio stations and reaches 65 million listeners a week. In addition, its websites yield 70 million page views a month (Cumulus Media, 2012). Another, the Sinclair Broadcast Group (2012), owns and operates 74 television stations in 45 markets and reaches an estimated 26.3% of U.S. television-watching households.

We can see such consolidation of ownership at the national level as well. In 1983, 50 companies controlled 90% of all U.S. media outlets. By 2011, just six companies—Comcast, Disney, News Corp, Time Warner, Viacom, and CBS—owned 90% of all media outlets, concentrating control over what we see, hear, and read (Free Press, 2012; Sanders & Copps, 2012).

Many media observers fear that the concentration of corporate-owned news outlets twists certain stories to promote particular economic or political interests. In recent years, media owners have refused to run advertisements, stories, or commentaries that supported single-payer health insurance, criticized U.S. military intervention, or opposed certain international trade agreements. Television and print journalists have been fired, forced to resign, or reassigned for presenting stories critical of subsidiaries owned by the parent company (Parenti, 2006).

As the viewing and listening public, our recourse is difficult. To criticize faulty government policies and consider solutions to difficult social problems, we need solid information, which is frequently unavailable or difficult to obtain. The recent growth in popularity of podcasting, blogs, Internet Protocol television, micro radio stations, and subscription satellite networks may be a sign that some citizens are growing weary of the filtered and sometimes partisan information they receive from traditional news sources. Indeed, distrust of the news media has become so acute that some people turn to deliberately fake news/comedy shows like *The Daily Show* and *The Colbert Report* to keep abreast of national and world events.

So the challenge we face in our own private lives is to recognize the processes at work in the social construction of reality and to take them into account as we "consume" the news. A critical dimension of the sociological imagination is the ability to "read silences"—to be attentive to what the mass media *don't* say. Fortunately, one of the purposes of sociology is to scientifically amass a body of knowledge that we can use to assess how our society really works.

APPRECIATING THE CONTRIBUTIONS OF SOCIOLOGICAL RESEARCH

Up to this point, I've been describing how individuals, groups, organizations, and various social institutions go about constructing reality. We've seen that these realities sometimes shift with time, place, and individual perception. Faced with this type of fluctuation, sociologists, as well as scholars in other disciplines, seek to identify a more "real" reality through systematic, controlled research. The rules sociologists abide by when conducting research give them confidence that they are identifying more than just a personal version of reality. They hope to determine a reality as it exists for a community of people at a particular point in time.

Moving beyond the level of individual conclusions about the nature of social reality is crucial if we are to escape the distortions of personal interests and biases. A danger of relying solely on individual perceptions is that we are likely to conclude that what we experience is what everyone experiences. For example, the famous psychiatrist Sigmund Freud used his own childhood as the ultimate "proof" of the controversial concept called the Oedipus complex (the belief that sons are secretly in love with their mothers and jealous of their fathers). He wrote to a friend in 1897, "I have found, in my own case too, being in love with the mother and jealous of the father, and I now consider it a universal event of early childhood" (quoted in Astbury, 1996, p. 73).

To avoid the risk of such overgeneralizations, sociologists try to determine what most people believe or how most people behave. But in doing so, they sometimes run the risk of simply restating what people already know. Indeed, a criticism of sociology you hear from time to time is that it is just a fancy version of common sense. A lot of the things that we think are obvious based on our personal observations, however, turn out not to be so straightforward under the closer scrutiny of social research. Consider the following "commonsense facts":

- Rape, assault, and murder occur most often between total strangers.
- Because of the high divorce rate in the United States, people are reluctant to get married.
- American children today are more likely to live in a single-parent household than they were 100 years ago.

Most of us probably assume these statements are true. Given what you've read or seen on television, they probably make a lot of sense. But how accurate are they?

According to the U.S. Bureau of Justice Statistics (2011), over the past three decades, only 14% of all homicides in the U.S. were perpetrated by strangers. In addition, only 44% of assaults involve strangers. The rest occur between acquaintances, friends, colleagues, romantic partners, and family members. In 79% of rapes and sexual assaults that involve a female victim, the attacker is a nonstranger, either an intimate partner, friend, acquaintance, or relative of the victim (U.S. Department of Justice, 2013).

According to the U.S. Bureau of the Census (ProQuest Statistical Abstract, 2013), 9.4% of men and 8.7% of women between the ages of 55 and 64 have never been married. In fact, about two thirds of divorced women and three fourths of divorced men eventually remarry (Cherlin, 1992). Although we have become increasingly willing to end a bad marriage, we still tend to place a high value on the institution of marriage itself.

The percentage of children who don't live with both their parents—about 32% of all children (ProQuest Statistical Abstract, 2013)—is roughly the same as it was a century ago. At that time, life expectancy was much lower than it is today, so it was highly likely that before reaching adulthood a child would lose at least one parent to death (Kain, 1990).

As you can see, sometimes commonsense "facts" don't hold up under the weight of evidence provided by social research.

The Empirical Nature of Sociological Research

Research is all around us. Throughout our lives, we are flooded with statistics that are supposedly the result of scientific studies—which detergents make clothes brighter, which conditioners repair hair better, which dog food tastes best, which wireless providers have the widest 4G coverage, which chewing gum dentists recommend for their gum-chewing patients. Many of the important decisions we make, from purchasing a car to opting for a particular surgical procedure, are supported by some sort of research.

In addition, a significant proportion of our own lives is spent *doing* research. Every time we seek out the opinions of others, gauge the attitude of a group, or draw conclusions about an event, we engage in a form of research. Say, for example, you thought your exam scores would improve if you studied with others, so you formed a study group. After the exam, you compared your grade with the grade you received on the previous exam (when you just studied on your own) to see if there was any significant improvement. If there was, you would likely attribute your better performance to the study group. This is the essence of research: You had an idea about some social process, and you went out and tested it to see if you were correct.

Although useful and common, such casual research is fraught with problems. We may make inaccurate or selective observations, overgeneralize on the basis of a limited number of observations, or draw conclusions that protect our own interests (Babbie, 1992). Maybe your exam score would have improved even without the study group because you had a better understanding of the material this time and had a better sense of what the instructor expected.

Sociological research, which is a much more sophisticated and structured form of the sort of individual inquiry we use every day, can avoid some of these pitfalls. Of course, sociological researchers are human beings, and they too make errors in observation, generalization, and analysis. But they have a greater chance of avoiding these errors because, first and foremost, sociological research is an empirical endeavor. *Empirical research* operates on the assumption that answers to questions about human behavior can be ascertained through controlled, systematic observations in the real world. Individuals can reach naïve conclusions based on their personal impressions of what happens in society. Great scholars can spend years thinking about human life and developing logical explanations about particular social phenomena. But for most sociologists, the strength of an explanation depends on how much empirical support it has.

Another characteristic of sociological research that makes it a better reflection of social reality than individual inquiry is that it is *probabilistic.* Instead of making absolute predictions, most sociologists prefer to state that under certain conditions, particular phenomena are likely to occur. In other words, human behavior operates within the laws of probability. Whenever sociologists set out to find the reasons, say, for why people hold prejudiced beliefs or why some countries have a higher birthrate than others, they are searching for the factors that would explain these phenomena most but not all of the time. For instance, adults with less than a high school education are more likely than adults with college degrees to be prejudiced against members of other ethnoracial groups. But that doesn't mean that every single high school dropout is a bigot or that every person

with a PhD embraces those who are ethnically or racially different. By focusing on the probability of some phenomenon occurring while at the same time allowing for exceptions and variations, sociologists provide a view of reality that simultaneously reflects the way things are and the way they can be.

Qualitative and Quantitative Research

In contrast to the casual way we carry out our personal research, sociologists seek to define reality through a careful process of collecting information and answering questions. Some sociologists collect nonnumeric information (text, written words, phrases, symbols, observations) that describes people, actions, or events in social life (called *qualitative research*; Neuman, 1994). Others collect numeric data and rely on precise statistical analysis (called *quantitative research*). And some use a combination of both.

Qualitative researchers often go out and observe people and events as they happen in society. For instance, qualitative researchers interested in how additional children affect parents' ability to balance the demands of work and home may spend an entire day with a family, listening, observing, and asking questions. Once they've collected enough information, they go about interpreting their observations, looking for identifiable patterns in people's everyday lives.

Quantitative sociological researchers methodically record observations across a variety of situations; they design and choose questions in advance and ask them in a consistent way of a large number of people; they use sophisticated techniques to ensure that the characteristics of the people in a study are similar to those of the population at large; and they use computers to generate statistics from which confident conclusions can be drawn.

Both kinds of sociological research are subjected to the scrutiny of peers, who will point out any mistakes and shortcomings. Researchers are obligated to report not only their results but also the methods they used to record observations or collect data and the conditions surrounding the study. Such detailed explanations allow other researchers to replicate a study—that is, to perform it themselves to see if the same results are obtained. The more a particular research result is replicated, the greater its acceptance as fact in the sociological community.

Theories, Variables, and Hypotheses

Whether qualitative or quantitative, social research is purposeful. Unlike personal research, which may be motivated by a hunch, whim, or immediate need, most social research is guided by a particular theory. A *theory* is a set of statements or propositions that seeks to explain or predict a particular aspect of social life (Chafetz, 1978). Theory does not, as is popularly thought, mean conjecture or speculation. Ideally, theories explain the way things are, not the way they ought to be.

Research and theory closely depend on each other. Research without any underlying theoretical reasoning is simply a string of meaningless bits of information (C. W. Mills, 1959); theory without research is abstract and speculative.

Some theories—such as structural functionalism, the conflict perspective, and symbolic interactionism—are quite broad, seeking to explain why social order exists or how societies work overall. Other theories are more modest, seeking to explain more narrowly certain behaviors among specific groups of people. For example, Travis Hirschi (1969) developed a theory of juvenile delinquency called "social control theory," in which he argued that delinquent acts occur when an individual's bond to society is weak or broken. These bonds are derived from a person's attachments to others who obey the law, the rewards a person gains by acting nondelinquently (commitments), the amount of time a person engages in nondelinquent activity (involvements), and the degree to which a person is tied to society's conventional belief system.

To test theories, sociologists must translate abstract propositions into testable hypotheses. A *hypothesis* is a researchable prediction that specifies the relationship between two or more *variables*. A variable is any characteristic, attitude, behavior, or event that can take on two or more values or attributes. For example, the variable "marital status" has several categories: never married, cohabiting, married, separated, divorced, widowed. The variable "attitudes toward capital punishment" has categories ranging from "strongly in favor" to "strongly oppose."

Hirschi was interested in why juveniles engage in delinquent behavior. Such a question is far too general to study empirically, so he developed a clear, specific, empirically testable prediction, or hypothesis, specifying a relationship between two variables:

Strong "social bonds" will be associated with low levels of "delinquency."

In developing their hypotheses, sociologists distinguish between independent and dependent variables. The *independent variable* is the factor presumed to influence or create changes in another variable. The *dependent variable* is the one assumed to depend on, be influenced by, or change as a result of the independent variable. If we believe that gender affects people's attitudes toward capital punishment, then "gender" would be the independent variable influencing "attitudes toward capital punishment," the dependent variable. For Hirschi's theory of juvenile delinquency, the strength of the social bond was the independent variable, and level of delinquency was the dependent variable.

The assumption behind most research that tests a hypothesis is that the independent variable *causes* changes to occur in the dependent variable—for instance, that a weak social bond *causes* a young person to become delinquent. But just because two variables seem to be related doesn't necessarily mean a causal relationship exists.

In fact, the two variables may not be related at all but merely seem to be associated with each other due to the effect of some third variable. Sociologists call such misleading relationships spurious. A classic example of a *spurious relationship* is the apparent association between children's shoe size and reading ability. It seems that as shoe size increases, reading ability improves (Babbie, 2007). Does this mean that the size of one's feet (independent variable) *causes* an improvement in reading skills (dependent variable)? Certainly not. This illusory relationship is caused by a third factor, age, that is related to shoe size (older kids have bigger feet) as well as reading ability (older kids can read better than younger kids). Hence, when researchers attempt to make causal claims about the relationship between an independent and a dependent variable, they must control for—or rule out—other variables that may be creating a spurious relationship. Can you think of a third variable that might strengthen or weaken a person's social bond *and* influence his or her tendency toward delinquent behavior?

Aside from concern with spuriousness, quantitative social researchers, like Hirschi, face the problem that many of the concepts that form the basis of theories are abstract and not easy to observe or measure empirically. We can't directly see concepts such as "attachments" or "commitments." So they must be translated into **indicators**: events, characteristics, or behaviors that can be observed or quantified.

In his survey of 1,200 boys in Grades 6 through 12, Hirschi derived a set of indicators for his independent variable, the strength of the social bond. To determine young people's attachments to law-abiding others, Hirschi measured their attraction to parents, peers, and school officials. To determine the degree to which they derived rewards from acting nondelinquently (commitment), he asked them to assess the importance of things such as getting good grades. To determine the proportion of their lives spent in conventional activities (involvement), he asked them how much time they spent in school-oriented activities. Finally, to determine their ties to a conventional belief system, he asked them questions about their respect for the law and the police.

Hirschi measured the dependent variable, delinquent activity, by asking the boys if they'd ever stolen things, taken cars for rides without the owner's permission, banged up something on purpose that belonged to somebody else, or beaten up or hurt someone on purpose. In addition, he used school records and police records to measure delinquent acts that had come to the attention of authorities.

The empirical data he collected supported his hypothesis. The boys who indicated close attachments to their parents and peers, who got good grades, who were involved in lots of school-related activities, and who had high levels of respect for the law were the boys who didn't get into trouble. Hirschi was therefore able to use these results to strengthen the power of his original theory.

Modes of Research

Although the answers to important sociological questions are not always simple or clear, the techniques sociologists use to collect and examine data allow them to draw informed and reliable conclusions about human behavior and social life. The most common techniques are experiments, field research, surveys, and unobtrusive research.

Experiments

An **experiment** is typically a research technique designed to elicit some sort of behavior under closely controlled laboratory circumstances. In its ideal form, the experimenter randomly places participants into two groups, then deliberately manipulates or introduces changes into the environment of one group of participants (called the experimental group) and not the other (called the control group). Care is taken to ensure that the groups are relatively alike except for the variable that the experimenter manipulates. Any observed or measured differences between the groups can then be attributed to the effects of the experimental manipulation.

Experiments have a significant advantage over other types of research because the researcher can directly control all the relevant variables. Thus, conclusions about the independent variable causing changes in the dependent variable can be made more convincingly. The artificial nature of most laboratory experiments, however, may make subjects behave differently than the way they would in their natural settings, leading some people to argue that laboratory experimentation in sociology is practically impossible (Silverman, 1982).

To overcome this difficulty, some researchers have created experimental situations outside the laboratory. In 2010, the City of New York embarked on a multi-year experimental test of the effectiveness of its six-year-old homelessness prevention program, a $23 million endeavor called Homebase. Half of the test subjects—people who are unable to pay their rent and therefore risk eviction—are being denied assistance from the program as researchers observe them to see if they become homeless. The other half receive the program's regular assistance services, including tenant–landlord mediation, emergency rental assistance, and job training (Buckley, 2010). The city hopes to determine if the program's intervention actually makes a difference in reducing the number of homeless. Some public officials have denounced the experiment as unnecessarily cruel.

Field Research

In **field research**, qualitative sociologists observe events as they actually occur, without selecting experimental and control groups or purposely introducing any changes into the subjects' environment. Field research can take several forms. In **nonparticipant observation**, the researcher observes people without directly interacting with them and without their knowing that they are being observed. Sociologist Lyn Lofland (1973), for example, studied how strangers relate to one another in public places by going to bus depots, airports, stores, restaurants, and parks and secretly recording everything she saw.

Participant observation requires that the researcher interact with subjects. In some cases, the researcher openly identifies herself or himself. For instance, to gain insight into how people balance work and family, sociologist Arlie Russell Hochschild (1997) observed employees over a period of three years at a large public relations company she called Amerco. She was particularly interested in why employees tend not to take advantage of available family leave policies. At Amerco, only 53 of 21,000 employees—all of them women—chose to switch to part-time work in response to the arrival of a new baby. Less than 1% of the employees shared a job or worked at home, even though the company permits it. Most of the workers worked a lot of overtime, coming in early and staying late. So why were these workers so unwilling to change their work lives to spend more time with their families even when the company would have supported them in doing so? Through her long-term observations of Amerco, Hochschild came to the conclusion that work has become a form of "home" and home has become "work." For many people at Amerco, home had become a place of frenzied activity and busy schedules, whereas work had become a sort of nurturing refuge where they could relax and share stories with friends. So they actually preferred spending more time at work.

This type of qualitative field research can be quite time consuming. Researchers can conduct only a limited number of interviews and can observe only a limited number of people and events. Hochschild collected rich information about people's work–family trade-offs, but she could study only one corporation. It's risky to generalize from the experiences of a small group of workers in one company in one society to all workers in all sorts of work environments.

In more delicate situations where the people being studied don't want their actions made public, the researcher may have to conceal his or her identity in order to gather accurate information. For instance, researchers have gone "undercover" to study everything from doomsday cults (Festinger, Riecken, & Schacter, 1956) to college sororities (Robbins, 2004). Sociologist Julia O'Connell Davidson (2002) wanted to examine the issue of power and control in the relationships between prostitutes and their clients.

To study this topic, she posed as a "receptionist" for a prostitute she called "Desiree," fielding phone calls and supervising the "waiting room" for the clients who had arrived to see Desiree. While Desiree knew O'Connell Davidson was a sociologist, the clients did not. If these men knew they were being studied, they might have altered their conversations and behaviors to cover up potentially damaging information.

Surveys

When it is impossible or impractical to carry out field observations or to set up a controlled experimental situation, social researchers use the survey method. *Surveys* require that the researcher pose a series of questions to respondents either orally, electronically, or on paper. The questions should be sufficiently clear so they are understood by the respondent the way the researcher wants them to be understood and measure what the researcher wants them to measure. In addition, the respondent is expected to answer the questions honestly and thoughtfully. The answers are often recorded in numerical form so they can be statistically analyzed.

Surveys typically use standardized formats. All subjects are asked the same questions in the same way, and large samples of people are used as subjects. One survey that has provided the basis for much sociological research on families is the National Survey of Families and Households. First conducted in the late 1980s, it includes information derived from interviews with over 13,000 respondents. A second wave of the survey, conducted between 1992 and 1994, and a third wave between 2001 and 2003 included interviews with surviving members of the original sample. The sample covers a diverse array of households, including single-parent families, families with stepchildren, cohabiting couples, and recently married persons. A great deal of family information was collected from each respondent, including family arrangements in childhood, dating experiences, experiences of leaving home, marital and cohabitation experiences, details of contact with kin, and data on economic well-being, as well as education, childbearing, and employment histories. Some of the research discussed in this book is based on analyses of data collected from this survey.

When sociologists Philip Blumstein and Pepper Schwartz (1983) undertook a massive study of intimate couples in the United States, they sent questionnaires to people from every income level, age group, religion, political ideology, and educational background. Some of their respondents were cohabiting; others were married. Some had children; others were childless. Some were heterosexual, others homosexual. All couples filled out a 38-page questionnaire that asked questions about their leisure activities, emotional support, housework, finances, sexual relations, satisfaction, relations with children, and so forth. More than 6,000 couples participated. From these surveys, Blumstein and Schwartz were able to draw conclusions about the importance of money, work, sexuality, power, and gender in couples' lives.

Unobtrusive Research

All the methods I've discussed so far—whether quantitative or qualitative—require the researcher to have some contact with the people being studied: giving them tasks to do in an experiment, watching them (with or without their knowing that they are participating in social research), or asking them questions. But the very act of intruding into people's lives may influence the phenomena being studied. This problem, known as *reactivity*, calls into question the accuracy of the data that are collected, thereby threatening the credibility of the research.

In the late 1920s, an engineer and a time study analyst (Roethlisberger & Dickson, 1939) were hired to study working conditions and worker productivity at an electric company in Hawthorne, Illinois. They were interested in finding out whether changing certain physical conditions in the plant could improve workers' productivity and satisfaction. They quickly discovered that increasing the lighting in the workroom was linked with workers' producing more. Increasing the brightness of the lights again the next day increased productivity even further. To bolster their conclusion, they decided to dim the lights to see if productivity dropped. Much to their dismay, productivity increased again when they darkened the room. They soon realized that the workers were responding more to the attention they were receiving from the researchers than to changes in their working conditions. This phenomenon is known as the "Hawthorne effect."

To avoid such influence, sociologists sometimes use another research technique, unobtrusive research, which requires no contact with people at all. *Unobtrusive research* is an examination of the evidence of social behavior that people create or leave behind. There are several types of unobtrusive research.

Analysis of existing data (also known as secondary data) relies on data gathered earlier by someone else for some other purpose. Analysis of existing data is still used extensively by sociologists today. One of the most popular and convenient sources of data is the U.S. Census. Studies that examine broad, nationwide trends (e.g., marriage, divorce, or premarital childbearing rates) typically use existing census data.

Content analysis is the study of documented communications—books, speeches, poems, song lyrics, television commercials, websites, and so forth. This method is particularly useful for documenting cultural shifts over time. Psychologists Jean Twenge, Keith Campbell, and Brittany Gentile (2012) analyzed the content of American books published between 1960 and 2008 using the Google Books Ngram database. This search engine allows you to assess how often a particular word or phrase appears in the millions of digitized books found in the database. The researchers found that over the span of 48 years, individualistic words and phrases like "personalized," "self," "unique," "I come first," and "I can do it myself" became more common, while words that reflected a more communal orientation, such as "community," "collective," "share," "united," and "common good" became less common. From these data they were able to argue that we are experiencing a shift in language usage reflective of a larger cultural ethos that has been increasingly characterized by a focus on the self and a reduced sense of group identity and responsibility.

Historical analysis relies on existing historical documents as a source of research information. Sociologist Kai Erikson (1966) was interested in how communities construct definitions of acceptable and unacceptable behavior. For his book *Wayward Puritans*, he studied several "crime waves" among the Puritans of the Massachusetts Bay Colony in the late 17th century. Erikson examined court cases, diaries, birth and death records, letters, and other written documents of the period. Piecing together fragments of information 300 years old was not easy, but Erikson was able to draw some conclusions. He found that each time the colony was threatened in some way—by opposing religious groups, betrayals by community leaders, or the king of England's revocation of its charter—the number of convicted criminals and the severity of punishments significantly increased. Erikson believed that these fluctuations occurred because the community needed to restate its moral boundaries and reaffirm its authority.

All these methods allow sociological researchers to collect information without intruding on and possibly changing the behavior of the people and groups they're studying.

The Trustworthiness of Social Research

Most sociologists see research as not only personally valuable but central to improving human knowledge and understanding. However, as consumers of this research, we must always ask "How accurate is this information?" Moreover, because we have a tendency to believe what we read in print or see reported on television or posted on websites, much of what we see may be either inaccurate or misleading. To evaluate the results of social research, we must examine the researcher's samples, the indicators used to measure important variables, and the researcher's personal qualities—namely, values, interests, and ethics.

Samples

Frequently, sociological researchers are interested in the attitudes, behaviors, or characteristics of large groups—college students, women, Twitter subscribers, single parents, and so on. It would be impossible to interview, survey, observe, or experiment on all of these people directly. Hence, researchers must select a smaller *sample* of respondents from the larger population. The characteristics of this subgroup are supposed to approximate the characteristics of the entire population of interest. A sample is said to be *representative* if the small group being studied is in fact typical of the population as a whole. For instance, a sample of 100 students from your university should include roughly the same proportion of first-year students, sophomores, juniors, and seniors that characterizes the entire school population. Sampling techniques have become highly sophisticated, as illustrated by the relative accuracy of polls conducted to predict election results.

In the physical sciences, sampling is not such an issue. Certain physical or chemical elements are assumed to be identical. One need only study a small number of vials of liquid nitrogen, because one vial of nitrogen should be the same as any other. Human beings, however, vary widely on every imaginable characteristic. You couldn't make a general statement about all Americans on the basis of an interview with one person. For that matter, you couldn't draw conclusions about all people from observing a sample consisting only of Americans, men, or teenagers. Samples that are not representative can lead to inaccurate and misleading conclusions.

Note the sampling problems revealed in the following letter to the editor of a small-town newspaper in the rural Midwest:

> I went to a restaurant yesterday for lunch. I began to feel guilty, when I reached into my pocket for a cigarette.... I was thinking of the government figures which estimated cigarette smokers at 26% of the population of the United States. But everywhere I looked inside that room, people were smoking. I decided to count them. There were 22 people in the room.... I was surprised to discover that the government's figures were an outright fabrication.... Seventeen people out of the 22 were cigarette smokers ... that accounts for over 77% of the people in that restaurant.... The government's figures are understated by 51% and just plain wrong! (*Greencastle Banner Graphic*, 1992)

This letter writer assumed that the 22 people who frequented a small restaurant in a small, relatively poor rural town on a single day were an accurate representation of the entire U.S. population. Such a conclusion overlooks some important factors. Government studies show that the lower a person's income, the greater the likelihood that person will be a smoker. Furthermore, people in blue-collar or service jobs are more likely to smoke than people in white-collar jobs. Finally, the prevalence of smoking tends to be higher in rural areas of the Midwest and South than in other parts of the country (U.S. Department of Health and Human Services, 2006).

Indicators

As you recall, one problem sociologists face when doing research is that the variables they are interested in studying are often difficult to see. What does powerlessness look like? How can you identify marital satisfaction? How would you recognize alienation or social class? Sociologists thus resign themselves to measuring indicators of things that cannot be measured directly. Researchers measure events and behaviors commonly thought to accompany a particular variable, hoping that what they are measuring is a valid indicator of the concept they are interested in.

Suppose you believe that people's attitudes toward abortion are influenced by the strength of their religious beliefs, or "religiosity." You might hypothesize that the stronger a person's religious beliefs, the less accepting he or she will be of abortion rights. To test this hypothesis, you must first figure out what you mean by "religious." What might be an indicator of the strength of someone's religious beliefs? You could determine whether the subjects of your study identify themselves as members of some organized religion. But this indicator might not tell you how religious your subjects are because many people identify themselves as, say, Catholic or Jewish but are not religious at all. Likewise, some people who consider themselves quite religious don't identify with any organized religion. So this measure would focus on group differences but would fail to capture the intensity of a person's beliefs or the degree of religious interest.

Perhaps a better indicator would be some quantifiable behavior, such as the frequency of attendance at formal religious services (Babbie, 1986). Arguably, the more someone attends church, synagogue, or mosque, the more religious that person is. But here, too, we run into problems. Church attendance, for instance, may reflect family pressure, habit, or the desire to visit with others rather than religious commitment. Furthermore, many very religious people are unable to attend services because they are sick or disabled. As you can see, indicators seldom perfectly reflect the concepts they are intended to measure.

Surveys are particularly susceptible to inaccurate indicators. A loaded phrase or an unfamiliar word in a survey question can dramatically affect people's responses in ways unintended by the researcher. For instance, opinion polls show a majority of people oppose programs that give "preferences to minorities." However, polls also show a majority of people *in favor of* programs that "make special efforts to help minorities get ahead in order to make up for past discrimination" (Sussman, 2010, p. 5). In 2009, during the heated debate over health care reform, several news agencies conducted polls to determine

people's feelings about altering the health care system. A *New York Times*/CBS News poll found overwhelming support (66%) for the so-called public option. Fox News, however, reported the support at a much lower 44%. Such an inconsistency had more to do with the way each agency worded its survey question than with the fluid, fluctuating nature of people attitudes. The *New York Times*/CBS poll asked people how they felt about "a government administered health insurance plan—something like the Medicare coverage that people 65 and older get." Fox News asked about "a government-run health insurance plan" (Sussman, 2010, p. 5).

Values, Interests, and Ethics in Sociological Research

Along with samples and indicators, the researcher's own qualities can influence social research. Ideally, research is objective and nonbiased and measures what is and not what should be. However, the questions researchers ask and the way they interpret observations always take place in a particular cultural, political, and ideological context (Ballard, 1987; Denzin, 1989).

Consider the impact of values and interests. If prevailing social values identify an intact nuclear family as the best environment for children, then most researchers will be prone to notice the disadvantages and perhaps ignore the advantages of other family arrangements. Furthermore, research is sometimes carried out to support a narrowly defined political interest (as when environmental groups fund research showing the damaging effects of global warming) or economic interest (as when tobacco companies fund research that downplays the relationship between cigarette smoking and cancer). Following the 2011 killing of 6 people and the wounding of Arizona representative Gabrielle Giffords outside a Tucson supermarket, the National Rifle Association used its political sway to choke off government funding for scientific research on the impact of firearms in society (M. Luo, 2011). In 2009, a legal investigation found that between 1998 and 2005, 26 scientific journal articles on the use of the hormone replacement drugs Premarin and Prempro for menopausal women were written by ghostwriters who were on the payroll of Wyeth, the pharmaceutical company that manufactured Premarin (Singer, 2009). That same year, an investigation by the Department of

Health and Human Services found that the Food and Drug Administration does almost nothing to monitor financial conflicts of interest of doctors who conduct clinical trials of drugs and medical devices (cited in G. Harris, 2009).

But it's not just a problem of unscrupulous researchers or financial benefactors. Academic journals are notoriously reluctant to publish studies that show no support for the hypothesized relationship between one variable and another. A reexamination of clinical trial studies of antidepressants conducted between 1987 and 2004 found that medical journals had a significant bias toward publishing studies with positive results (E. H. Turner, Matthews, Linardatos, Tell, & Rosenthal, 2008). This problem has become so bad that an organization of 12 major medical journals proposed that pharmaceutical companies be required to register clinical trials at *the beginning* of drug studies so that negative and not just positive results would be publicly available (Meier, 2004).

We must remember that sociologists are people just like the rest of us, with their own biases, preconceptions, and expectations. Sociologists' values determine the kinds of information they gather about a particular social phenomenon. If you were conducting research on whether the criminal justice system is fair, would you study criminals, politicians, law enforcement personnel, judges, or victims? Each group would likely provide a different perception of the system. The most accurate picture of reality is likely to be based on the views of all subgroups involved.

In fact, values can influence the questions that researchers find important enough to address in the first place (Reinharz, 1992). For instance, research on families has historically reflected the interests of men. The term *labor force* has traditionally referred to those working for pay and has excluded those doing unpaid work, such as housework and volunteer jobs—areas that have always been predominantly female. Thus, findings on labor force participation are more likely to reflect the significant elements of men's lives than of women's lives. You can see that a lack of data does not necessarily indicate that a phenomenon or a problem doesn't exist. Perhaps all it indicates is that no researcher has yet undertaken a systematic study of it.

Ethics is another personal quality that affects the trustworthiness of social research. Research, as I mentioned earlier, often represents an intrusion into people's lives; it may disrupt their ordinary activities, and it often requires them to reveal personal information about themselves. Ethical researchers agree, therefore, that they should protect the rights of subjects and minimize the amount of harm or disruption subjects might experience as a result of being part of a study. Ethical researchers agree that no one should be forced to participate in research, that those who do participate ought to be fully informed of the possible risks involved, and that every precaution ought to be taken to protect the confidentiality and anonymity of participants. Sociologists almost always conduct their research under the scrutiny of university review committees for the protection of human participants.

At the same time, however, researchers must attempt to secure the most accurate—and perhaps most useful—information possible. Sometimes, this requirement conflicts with ethical considerations. In 2007, the federal government began a 5-year, $50 million project designed to improve the way hospital patients are treated after car accidents, shootings, heart attacks, and other emergencies. Because such patients are often unconscious when they arrive at the hospital, researchers were allowed to conduct medical experiments on them without their consent, something that goes against usual ethical research protocol (R. Stein, 2007).

And what about research that requires information about people who may be involved in dangerous or criminal behavior or who do not want or cannot have their identities revealed? Sociologist Patricia Adler (1985) was interested in studying the worlds of drug dealers and smugglers. The illegal nature of their work makes them, by necessity, secretive, deceitful, and mistrustful—not the sort of individuals who make ideal surveyor interview respondents. So Adler had to establish a significant level of rapport and trust. Although she never became actively involved in drug trafficking, she did become a part of the dealers' and smugglers' social world and participated in their daily activities. Only by studying these criminals in their natural setting was she able to see the full complexity of the world of drug smuggling. Her research, however, raises important questions related to trustworthiness and ethics: Did her closeness to her subjects make it impossible to study them objectively? Did she have an obligation to report illegal activity to law enforcement officials?

CONCLUSION

In this chapter, I have described some of the processes by which reality is constructed, communicated, manipulated, and accepted. Reality, whether in the form of casual observations or formal research, is ultimately a human creation. Different people can create different conceptions of reality.

This issue can be raised from a personal level to a global one. People in every culture believe that their reality is the paramount one. Who is right? Can we truly believe that a reality in direct conflict with ours is equally valid? If we profess that everyone should have the right to believe what she or he wants, are we acknowledging the socially constructed nature of reality or merely being tolerant of those who are not "smart enough" to think as we do? Do we have the right to tell other people or other cultures that what they do or believe is wrong only because it conflicts with our definition of reality? Exasperating and complex, these questions lie at the core of international relations, global commerce, and everyday life.

CHAPTER HIGHLIGHTS

◆ The social construction of reality (truth, knowledge, etc.) is the process by which reality is discovered, made known, reinforced, and changed by members of society.

◆ Language is the medium through which reality construction takes place. It enables us to think, interpret, and define. Linguistic categories reflect aspects of a culture that are relevant and meaningful to people's lives.

◆ Not all of us possess the same ability to define reality. Individuals and groups in positions of power have the ability to control information, define values, create myths, manipulate events, and ultimately influence what others take for granted.

◆ The purpose of a discipline such as sociology is to amass a body of knowledge that provides the public with useful information about how society works. This is done, quantitatively and qualitatively, through systematic social research—field research, surveys, and unobtrusive research. It is important to keep in mind, however, that this form of reality is also a social construction, shaped by the people who fund, conduct, and report on social research.

KEY TERMS

analysis of existing data: Type of unobtrusive research that relies on data gathered earlier by someone else for some other purpose

content analysis: Form of unobtrusive research that studies the content of recorded messages, such as books, speeches, poems, songs, television shows, websites, and advertisements

dependent variable: Variable that is assumed to be caused by, or to change as a result of, the independent variable

empirical research: Research that operates from the ideological position that questions about human behavior can be answered only through controlled, systematic observations in the real world

experiment: Research method designed to elicit some sort of behavior, typically conducted under closely controlled laboratory circumstances

field research: Type of social research in which the researcher observes events as they actually occur

historical analysis: Form of social research that relies on existing historical documents as a source of data

hypothesis: Researchable prediction that specifies the relationship between two or more variables

incorrigible proposition: Unquestioned cultural belief that cannot be proved wrong no matter what happens to dispute it

independent variable: Variable presumed to cause or influence the dependent variable

indicator: Measurable event, characteristic, or behavior commonly thought to reflect a particular concept

moral entrepreneurs: Groups that work to have their moral concerns translated into law

nonparticipant observation: Form of field research in which the researcher observes people without directly interacting with them and without letting them know that they are being observed

participant observation: Form of field research in which the researcher interacts with subjects, sometimes hiding his or her identity

probabilistic: Capable only of identifying those forces that have a high likelihood, but not a certainty, of influencing human action

qualitative research: Sociological research based on nonnumeric information (text, written words, phrases, symbols, observations) that describes people, actions, or events in social life

quantitative research: Sociological research based on the collection of numeric data that uses precise statistical analysis

reactivity: A problem associated with certain forms of research in which the very act of intruding into people's lives may influence the phenomenon being studied

representative: Typical of the whole population being studied

sample: Subgroup chosen for a study because its characteristics approximate those of the entire population

self-fulfilling prophecy: Assumption or prediction that in itself causes the expected event to occur, thus seeming to confirm the prophecy's accuracy

social construction of reality: Process through which the members of a society discover, make known, reaffirm, and alter a collective version of facts, knowledge, and "truth"

spurious relationship: A false association between two variables that is actually due to the effect of some third variable

survey: Form of social research in which the researcher asks subjects a series of questions verbally, online, or on paper

theory: Set of statements or propositions that seeks to explain or predict a particular aspect of social life

unobtrusive research: Research technique in which the researcher, without direct contact with the subjects, examines the evidence of social behavior that people create or leave behind

variable: Any characteristic, attitude, behavior, or event that can take on two or more values or attributes

CHAPTER

4

Building Order

Culture and History

Dimensions of Culture

Cultural Expectations and Social Order

Cultural Variation and Everyday Experience

In Madagascar, the harvest months of August and September mark the *famadihana*—the "turning of the bones." Families receive messages from *razana*—their dead loved ones—who may say they are uncomfortable or need new clothes. In an elaborate ceremony that can last for days, families feast, sing, and dig up the graves of the deceased. The bodies are wrapped in shrouds and seated at the dinner table. Loved ones run their fingers over the skeletons through the shroud. Family news is whispered to them, and toasts are drunk. Widows and widowers can often be seen dancing with the bones of their dead spouses. The exhumed bones are then oiled and perfumed and laid back onto their "beds" inside the family tomb (Bearak, 2010; Perlez, 1991).

In the late 19th and early 20th centuries, dating and courtship in North America were based on a ritualized system known as "calling." Although the process varied by region and social class, the following general guidelines were involved:

When a girl reached the proper age or had her first "season" (depending on her family's social level), she became eligible to receive male callers. At first her mother or guardian invited young men to call; in subsequent seasons the young lady . . . could bestow an invitation

47

to call upon any unmarried man to whom she had been properly introduced at a private dance, dinner, or other "entertainment" . . . young men . . . could be brought to call by friends or relatives of the girl's family, subject to her prior permission. . . . The call itself was a complicated event. A myriad of rules governed everything: the proper amount of time between invitation and visit (two weeks or less); whether or not refreshments should be served . . . ; chaperonage (the first call must be made on mother and daughter . . .); appropriate topics of conversation (the man's interests, but never too personal); how leave should be taken (on no account should the woman accompany [her caller] to the door nor stand talking while he struggles with his coat). (B. L. Bailey, 1988, pp. 15–16)

How could anybody dig up a relative's corpse? Why would young men and young women follow such elaborate rules just so they could go on a date? These practices may seem peculiar, silly, or backward to most of us, but to the people involved, they are or were simply the taken-for-granted, "right" ways of doing things.

Some of the things you do may seem equally incomprehensible to an outside observer:

- You may think a Spaniard's fondness for bullfighting is "absurd," yet millions of people in the United States shell out a lot of money each year to watch large men in brightly colored shirts and helmets knock each other down while they chase, throw, carry, and kick an inflated object made out of the hide of a dead animal.

- You may pity the turn-of-the-century woman who squeezed her body into an ultratight corset to achieve the wasp-waisted figure men considered attractive, yet many women today (and some men) routinely use harsh chemicals to change the color of their hair, pay to have someone cut into their faces to decrease the size of their noses or tighten the skin around their chins, or reduce their food intake to the point of starvation in order to become slender.

- Most Americans would likely be horrified by a particular practice of the Parsi in Mumbai, India: leaving the bodies of their dead relatives on the rooftops of some buildings so they can be eaten by vultures (Harris, 2012). Yet some of those same Americans might pay hundreds of dollars to have the cremated remains of their loved ones stuffed into shotgun shells and ceremoniously fired into the air (Ingold, 2012).

Clearly, the legitimacy of certain practices and ideas can be understood only within the unique context of the group or society in which they occur. What is considered abnormal in one case may be perfectly normal, even necessary, in another. It takes a sociological imagination to see that time and place have a great influence on what people consider normal.

Ancestor worship in Madagascar is a custom that has been around for centuries, impervious to the arrival of Christian churches and Western ideals. To the people who practice it, the ritual of burial, disinterment, and reburial is more important than marriage. The physical body may die, but the *fanahy*, or soul, lives on. The Malagasy believe that spirits stay with the bones and have needs for earthly goods like food and clothing. It's up to the living to provide these things. In exchange, the dead take care of living relatives by determining their health, wealth, and fertility and by helping them communicate with God. As one man said after tending to the remains of his dead grandfather, "It is good to thank the ancestors in person because we owe them everything.... I am asking them for good health, and of course if they would help me to accumulate wealth, this is also a good idea" (quoted in Bearak, 2010, p. A7). In short, the custom is quite rational and beneficial: The individual's own earthly well-being and spiritual salvation depend on it.

Likewise, the practice of calling was an integral part of late-19th-century U.S. culture. It maintained the social class structure by serving as a test of suitability, breeding, and background (B. L. Bailey, 1988). Calling enabled the middle and upper classes to protect themselves from what many at the time considered the "intrusions" of urban life and to screen out the disruptive effects of social and geographic mobility, which reached unprecedented levels at the turn of the century. It also allowed parents to control the relationships of their children, thereby increasing the likelihood that their pedigree would remain intact.

These phenomena illustrate the important role played by culture and history in creating social order. Whether we're talking about our own ordinary rituals or those practiced by some distant society, the normative patterns that mark the millions of seemingly trivial actions and social encounters of our everyday lives are what make society possible. They tell us what to expect from others and what others should expect from us. In this chapter, by looking at the various taken-for-granted aspects of culture that lend structure to our daily lives, I examine how order is created and maintained in society. In the process, I compare specific aspects of our culture with others, past and present.

DIMENSIONS OF CULTURE

In Chapter 2, you saw that culture is one of the key elements that shape the structure of a society. It consists of the shared, taken-for-granted values, beliefs, objects, and rules that guide people's lives. In everyday conversation, however, the term *culture* is often used only when discussing something "foreign." We rarely feel the need to question why we do certain things in the course of our daily lives—we just do them. It's other people in other lands whose rituals and beliefs need explaining. What we often fail to realize is that culture is "doing its job" most effectively when it is unnoticed. Only in times of dramatic social change and moral uncertainty or when circumstances force us to compare our society with another—like when you travel abroad—do we become aware that a distinct set of cultural rules and values influences us, too.

To a large degree, we are products of the culture and historical epoch in which we live. From a very young age we learn, with a startling amount of accuracy, that certain types of shelter, food, tools, clothing, modes of transportation, music, sports, and art characterize our culture and make it different from others. Without much conscious effort, we also learn what to believe, what to value, and which actions are proper or improper both in public and in private.

Material and Nonmaterial Culture

Culture consists of all the products of a society that are created over time and shared by members of that society. These products may be tangible or intangible. The term *nonmaterial culture* refers to all the nonphysical products of society that are created over time and shared: knowledge, beliefs, customs, values, morals, and so on. Nonmaterial culture also includes common patterns of behavior and the forms of interaction appropriate in a particular society. It is a "design for living" that distinguishes one society from another. Like an owner's manual for social life, nonmaterial culture tells us how our society works, what is possible, what to value, how to conduct our everyday lives, and what to do if something breaks down. Without an understanding of a society's nonmaterial culture, people's behaviors—not to mention the symbolic significance of their material world—would be thoroughly incomprehensible.

Material culture includes the physical artifacts and objects that shape or reflect the lives of members of a particular society: distinctive clothing and architecture, inventions, food, artwork, music, and so on. Some of the most important elements of material culture are technological achievements, which are the ways in which members of a society apply knowledge to adapt to changing social, economic, or environmental conditions. For instance, plastic products have provided people with cheaper and more convenient packaging of needed goods—and in the process have forever altered shopping and consumption patterns.

Similarly, the advent of the automobile in the early 20th century gave people greater mobility to take advantage of economic or residential opportunities elsewhere and thereby dramatically changed how and where they lived. It's impossible to imagine society without cars. Today, the average number of cars per household (2.1) almost matches the average number of people per household (2.55; Bureau of Transportation Statistics, 2012; ProQuest Statistical Abstract, 2013). Since the interstate highway system was developed in 1956, the distance Americans drive annually has increased from 628 million miles to over 3 billion (cited in R. Sullivan, 2006), although in the past few years factors like higher gas prices, new licensing laws, and improvements in technology that support alternative transportation have actually reduced the number of miles young people drive (U.S. PIRG Education Fund, 2012). The highway system made suburban living and cross-country travel possible. Moreover, our national economy would crumble without the ubiquitous long-haul trucks that transport needed goods to every corner of the country. The influence of the automobile is especially noticeable today in places such as Nepal and rural China, where it is beginning to have a similar dramatic impact on people's lives.

Changes in material culture often transform the physical environment, creating the need for additional alterations in material and nonmaterial culture. The enormous amount of nonbiodegradable plastic piling up in overflowing landfills, for example, has spawned a vast array of advances in recycling and other ecofriendly technologies. Likewise, a heavy reliance on automobiles has created several serious problems throughout the world: air pollution, depletion of fossil fuel reserves, suburban sprawl, and constant traffic. These problems in turn have created the need for changes in travel patterns and arrangements as well as further material developments, such as an entire "green" industry that includes pollution-reducing devices, hybrid automobiles, and alternative-fuel sources (for more, see Chapter 14).

Global Culture

Although culture gives each society its distinctive character, cultural "purity" is all but obsolete (Griswold, 1994). Transnational media, global communication and transportation systems, and centuries of international migration have contributed to a worldwide swapping of cultural elements. For instance, even in bad economic times, U.S. retailers are a common fixture around the globe. More than 200 million people worldwide shop at one of Wal-Mart's 10,000 stores in 27 countries each year (Wal-Mart, 2012). Starbucks has nearly 18,000 coffeehouses in 60 countries (Starbucks, 2012). American pizza, too, which originally came to us from Naples, Italy, has migrated to every corner of the globe. Domino's Pizza now has 10,040 restaurants in 70 countries (Domino's, 2012). And Yum! Brands—which owns American fast food chains such as Taco Bell, Kentucky Fried Chicken, Pizza Hut, and Long John Silver's—has over 38,000 restaurants in 120 countries and territories (Yum! Brands, 2012).

But in many societies, people see the imported elements of culture as dangerous encroachments on long-held traditions and national unity. In 2012, the president of South Africa, Jacob Zuma, proclaimed that keeping a pet, like a dog or a cat, was a dangerous encroachment of "white culture" that black South Africans were spending too much time trying to emulate ("South Africa," 2012).

Of special concern is the increasing influence of U.S. culture on other countries. A decade ago or so, culture ministers from 20 different countries on four continents met to discuss how best to maintain their own cultures in a global environment dominated by U.S. media (Croteau & Hoynes, 2000). They were responding to examples like these:

- Approximately two thirds of French respondents to a survey feel that the United States exerts too much cultural influence on Europe (Daley, 2000). France is now the most successful market for McDonald's in Europe (Sexton, 2009); hence the fast food restaurant has become a symbol of what many French consider to be the despicable intrusion of U.S. food culture. Several years ago, a French sheep farmer named José Bové became something of a national hero for vandalizing McDonald's restaurants. Bové is now a spokesperson for *Via Campesina*, an organization that promotes "food sovereignty," the right of countries to define their own food systems.

- In Austria, an organization called the Pro-Christkind Association launched a campaign against Santa Claus several years ago, claiming that he is nothing more than an advertising symbol of American culture and consumption habits (Landler, 2002). The group now has an anti–Santa Facebook page.

- Okinawa, Japan, has historically had the highest proportion of people over the age of 100 in the world and the greatest life expectancy of any region in Japan. But, increasingly, Okinawans are living and eating like Americans. They walk less, eat fewer vegetables, and eat more hamburgers than they used to. Okinawa now has the most American-style fast food restaurants of any city in Japan. As a result, average weight and rates of heart disease, cerebral hemorrhage, and lung cancer have all increased. Okinawans now rank 26th in life expectancy among the Japanese administrative regions (Onishi, 2004; Takayama, 2003).

Emotions can run especially high when the integrity of a culture's language is at stake. About 60% of all existing languages have fewer than 10,000 speakers (R. G. Gordon, 2005). These languages are highly vulnerable to disappearance in a global culture. Indeed, linguists predict that half of the 7,000 or so languages spoken worldwide today will disappear sometime this century (cited in Wilford, 2007). Taking their place will be a handful of dominant languages that, in a technologically connected world, are seen as "linguistic passports" to education and a successful economic future (P. H. Lewis, 1998). This phenomenon is known as "linguistic imperialism."

Foremost among these major languages, of course, is English, which today shapes communication all over the world. People in Japan will order bottles of *bi-ru* (pronounced beer-oo) in pubs and spread *bata* on their bread. In many Spanish-speaking countries, people type e-mails on a *computadora* and text on a *telefono móvil*. The French commonly use terms like *cool, le weekend,* and *le buzzword.* People are recognizing that in a world of collapsing borders, a common language is useful. And because of pervasive U.S. cultural influences and technologies, English is an understandable choice. For instance, even though the number of non–English Internet users grows each year, about 80% of the world's electronically stored information is in English (Crystal, 2003). It is estimated that 500 million to 1 billion people now speak English as either a first or a second language (N. Cohen, 2006). In fact, there are more people who speak English as their second language than there are people who speak it as their first (Mydans, 2007).

The growth of English as a sort of world language—what one author refers to as "Globish" (Chotiner, 2010)—has had a profound effect on the way people in other countries go about their business. For example, a while back the Swiss government decreed that all Swiss children above the age of six must learn English. In Chile, the government wants to make all of its 15 million citizens fluent in English within a generation (Rohter, 2004).

But not everyone is happy about such developments. In French-speaking Quebec, Canada, large American retailers like Costco, Wal-Mart, Toys "R" Us, and Best Buy are required by law to serve their customers in French and post signs in French along the aisles (Austen, 2012). In 2013, French legislators proposed a law that would require universities to teach more of their courses in English. Supporters argued that the lack of English was a major factor in France's declining economic competitiveness around the world. Opponents, however, took to the streets in loud and fierce protest. One scholar called the proposal a "suicidal project" and a "sacrifice to Americanization"; another called it a "drive toward self destruction" (quoted in de la Baume, 2013, p. A10).

In the United States, many people are concerned with the encroaching influence not of English but of Spanish. Today, nearly 37 million U.S. residents speak Spanish as their first language; in Los Angeles, 43.4% of residents over the age of five speak Spanish at home (ProQuest Statistical Abstract, 2013). Immigrants are actually making the transition to speaking English more quickly than in the past, and over 90% of residents with a foreign-born parent prefer to speak only English at home (Kent & Lalasz, 2006). Indeed, over three quarters of the children who speak Spanish as their first language speak English "very well" (ProQuest Statistical Abstract, 2013). Nevertheless, many U.S. citizens fret about the primacy of English

when they see street signs, billboards, election ballots, and automated teller machines in Spanish. Up until a few years ago, the state of Arizona sent government monitors into classrooms to make sure that teachers didn't have heavy Spanish accents. Those who did were cited for violations and required, with the help of their school districts, to improve their English (Lacey, 2011). Indeed, 31 states and at least 19 cities have declared English as their official language (Robbie Brown, 2009; U.S. English, 2011).

Subcultures

Sociologists and anthropologists usually speak of culture as a characteristic of an entire society. But culture can also exist in smaller, more narrowly defined units. A *subculture* consists of the values, behaviors, and physical artifacts of a group that distinguish it from the larger culture. Think of it as a culture within a culture. Certain racial and ethnic groups, religions, age groups, and even geographic areas can all constitute subcultures.

We don't usually think of people with sensory deficits as constituting a subculture, but many people who are deaf identify themselves as members of a subculture and take pride in its unique values and norms. This issue received national attention in 2006, when the board of trustees at Gallaudet University, a liberal arts university for the deaf, proposed hiring a new president. But students immediately protested because they felt the candidate—who was deaf herself—wasn't committed enough to deaf identity and culture. They mocked her for not learning sign language until she was 23 and criticized her for focusing too much attention on technologies to "fix" deafness, like cochlear implants and more powerful hearing aids, and not enough on advocating for deaf rights (Schemo, 2006). The university eventually relented and abandoned its candidate.

To see a more common subculture, you don't have to look any further than your own school. You're probably well aware of the material and nonmaterial subculture that is unique to your campus. Perhaps some landmark—a bell tower or ornate archway—is the defining symbol of the university, or maybe a boulder or tree or fountain occupies a hallowed place in campus lore. I'm sure you know your school mascot and the school colors. In addition, when you first arrived at school, you probably had to learn a tremendous amount of new information about the nonmaterial subculture just to survive—how to register for courses;

how to address a professor; where to eat and study; what administrators, faculty, and fellow students expect of you; and so on. At my university, the student newspaper publishes a glossary of common words, phrases, acronyms, and nicknames at the beginning of each academic year to aid first-year students in their adjustment to life on campus. Just as you have to learn how to be a member of your society, you have to learn how to be a member of your university subculture.

CULTURAL EXPECTATIONS AND SOCIAL ORDER

Despite periodic shifts in the acceptability of certain acts, culture and history provide people with a common bond—a sense of shared personal experiences. That we can live together at all depends on the fact that we share a tremendous amount of cultural and historical knowledge. This knowledge allows us to predict, with a fair amount of certainty, what most people will do in a given situation. For instance, I can assume that when I say "Hi, how are you?" you will reply "Fine." You probably won't launch into some long-winded explanation of your mental, physical, and emotional condition at that precise moment, because doing so would violate the cultural rules governing such casual greetings.

The actions of individuals are not simply functions of personality types or psychological predispositions; rather, they are also a reflection of shared cultural expectations. Culture provides us with information about which of these actions are preferred, accepted, or disapproved of at a given time (McCall & Simmons, 1978). Take, for example, sexuality. American culture is often characterized as a *heteronormative culture*—that is, a culture where heterosexuality is accepted as the normal, taken-for-granted mode of sexual expression. Social institutions and social policies reinforce the belief that sexual relationships ought to exist between males and females. Cultural representations of just about every aspect of intimate and family life—dating, sex, marriage, childbearing, retirement, and so on—presume a world in which men are sexually and affectionately attracted to women and women to men (Macgillivray, 2000). Think of the flurry of magazine and TV advertisements we're subjected to in the weeks prior to Valentine's Day that depict men and women embracing, gazing longingly into each other's eyes, and buying each other expensive jewelry. Adolescent girls

seeing a gynecologist for the first time can expect to be given information on birth control, highlighting the assumption that they will have sex with men—it's just a matter of when. In 2008, the online dating service eHarmony was sued for discrimination because the site offered only two options to its customers: "man seeking woman" or "woman seeking man" (L. Miller, 2008). Even some sports reflect a heteronormative culture. In competitive figure skating, the "pairs" competition always consists of women partnered with men (Wildman & Davis, 2002). The 2007 film *Blades of Glory* humorously satirized this basic assumption by depicting two men skating with one another in the pairs event.

Recall from Chapter 2 that norms are the rules that govern the routine social encounters in which we all participate. Although many everyday norms are sometimes difficult to identify and describe, they reflect commonly held assumptions about conventional behavior. For instance, people who live in large cities like New York or Chicago quickly learn a large array of rules for walking along busy sidewalks: avoid bumping into others (while staying comfortably close), follow whoever is in front of you, and keep up with those next to you. These rules are so well learned that most residents automatically adjust their walking behavior to those around them:

> While striding forward, we turn ever so slightly to the side, pulling in our bellies and leading with the shoulder instead of the nose. This lets us barely brush against passing pedestrians, our hands to our torsos and faces turned away politely (Horowitz, 2012, p. 5)

Norms can be generalized to similar situations within a culture. That is, we can be reasonably certain that grocery store or doctor's office or restaurant behavior that is appropriate in Baton Rouge will be appropriate in Bakersfield or Butte as well. Our experiences in these places would be chaotic if there weren't a certain degree of agreement over how we should act. Without such unspoken rules and expectations, every situation would have to be interpreted, analyzed, and responded to as if it were an entirely new occasion. Social life would be utterly unmanageable.

Social Institutions and Cultural Norms

Large social institutions are closely tied to culture. For one thing, some institutions reflect deeply held cultural values. A free-market economy, for instance, reflects the cultural values of achievement, competition, material acquisition, and so on. A democratic government reflects the values of individual freedom and citizen participation. As we'll see in the following chapter, other institutions—such as education, religion, and family—provide the mechanisms through which culture and subculture are transmitted across generations.

Institutions are also strongly supported by cultural norms. When a pattern of behavior becomes widely accepted within a particular social institution and is taken for granted in society, sociologists say it has become an ***institutionalized norm*** (DiMaggio & Powell, 1991). For instance, the institutionalized (i.e., culturally acceptable) way of becoming financially successful in many developed societies is to earn a college degree, get a job in an entry-level position somewhere, and eventually work your way to the top. Even things that most of us would condemn have, at times, been institutionalized and encouraged by society. Slavery, for example, was for several hundred years a culturally, politically, and economically acceptable practice in the United States. The buying and selling of slaves was strongly approved by the nation's most powerful forces as well as by many ordinary people (Birenbaum & Sagarin, 1976).

Institutionalized norms constrain people's behavior by making some lines of action unthinkable. But they don't just limit options; they also establish the setting in which people discover their preferences and begin to see the world in a particular way (DiMaggio & Powell, 1991). The military ritualizes the process of becoming a full-fledged member through training, oaths of allegiance, and public recognition of the passage from one rank to another. In doing so, it ensures conformity to military norms and an understanding of the "rules of engagement," the specific norms that govern fighting on the battlefield. Religious congregations reinforce "appropriate" lifestyles and downplay inappropriate ones through collective worship services.

Shifts in one institution are often linked to shifts in another. The abolition of slavery in the United States, for instance, meant that the entire economic system of the South had to be restructured, from an agrarian plantation economy to one characterized by smaller landholdings and increased industrial production. In Russia, the collapse of communism two decades ago strengthened the role of religious organizations in providing people with normative guidelines. In the United States today, the fact that women are no longer expected to be the sole caretakers of children has meant an increase in the number of mothers who enter the paid labor force, which in turn has created a higher demand for organized day care as well as increased pressure on legislatures to enact laws protecting the interests of working parents.

Institutionalized Emotions

To illustrate the power of institutionalized norms in our private experiences, I turn to a common element of everyday life: emotions. We all experience emotions as physical, sometimes instantaneous responses to life events. Thus, we're inclined to see emotions as natural and universal. Yet emotional display comes under the strict control of cultural norms. In rural areas of Greece, widows traditionally are expected to mourn over the loss of their husbands—most notably by wearing black—for the rest of their lives. That would be seen as excessive in the United States, where more than two months of grieving might be considered an indicator of a major depressive episode (Horwitz, 2002).

Every society has unwritten rules about which emotions are appropriate to feel, which are appropriate to display, and how intense the emotional display should be under specific circumstances. For instance, in our culture, we're supposed to be sad at funerals, happy at weddings, and angry when we are insulted. We're supposed to feel joy when we receive good news but not show too much of it if our good fortune is at someone else's expense. In extreme cases, the violation of emotional display norms can lead to grave sanctions, such as a diagnosis of mental illness (Pugliesi, 1987; Thoits, 1985).

When people hide or alter their emotions to fit the situation, they are playing a significant role in maintaining social order within broader social institutions. Take the popular TV show *American Idol*, for example. In the season finale, when the field is finally reduced to the last two contestants, the camera zooms in on both of them. They stand on stage holding hands in shaky anticipation of the final verdict. The lights are dimmed. When the winner is announced, the runner-up is the picture of grace and charm, all smiles and congratulations. But we know better. This person has just lost the contest of her or his life on national television and has got to be sad, angry, or at the very least disappointed. To add insult to injury, she or he is then gently escorted offstage so the winner can have the spotlight. Why does the runner-up suppress the urge to show true emotions? Part of the reason is that he or she understands that there's more at stake than personal feelings. Imagine what would happen to the *American Idol* phenomenon if the runners-up started displaying their bitterness onstage—screaming at the host, threatening the judges, shunning the winners, or demanding a recount.

Norms about expressing emotions are often linked to institutional concerns and needs. In her book *The Managed Heart*, Arlie Russell Hochschild (1983) describes the feeling rules required by occupations in which employees have a great deal of contact with the public. Flight attendants, for example, must constantly be good natured and calm under dangerous conditions. They must make their work appear effortless and handle other people's feelings as deftly as their own. This ability is not just a matter of living up to social expectations—it is part of their job description. A "smile" becomes an economic asset and a public relations tool.

Likewise, doctors and nurses are trained to show compassionate concern for their patients, not disgust or alarm. Furthermore, they cannot become too emotionally involved with patients, because they see pain, suffering, and death every day. It is difficult not to become attached to patients, but such emotional outlay would inevitably lead to burnout, making effective job performance impossible. We want our health care providers to show that they like us, but doctors and nurses are most successful in their jobs when they can keep their emotions under control.

Although it is not surprising that organizations would have an interest in emotional displays by members, it is perhaps less obvious that particular emotions are linked to larger societal concerns such as politics and economics, often as a method of social control (Kearl & Gordon, 1992). For instance, the conflict perspective points out that some regimes may use fear to quell dissent and enforce obedience. In the early 20th century, in response to the increasing political and economic strength of African Americans, many white Southerners used fear to control Blacks through the threat of lynching and other forms of violence. Similarly, religious leaders often use the fear of eternal damnation to make sure their followers cooperate.

The effectiveness of invoking emotions such as guilt, anxiety, and shame waxes and wanes as social climates change. In the past, when communities were smaller and life was more interdependent, social behavior could be easily regulated by the threat of shame. If people broke a law or violated some norm of morality, they would bring humiliation on themselves, their families, and the community at large. But as societies became more complex, such close ties began to disappear. Today, the political control of behavior through emotion is more likely to be directed inward, in the form of guilt and anxiety. For instance, if working mothers are implicated by politicians as contributing to the "breakdown" of the traditional family by leaving the raising of their children to others, more and more mothers will experience guilt when they seek employment outside the home (Berg, 1992).

Norms governing the expression of emotions give us a way to communicate and maintain social order. They perpetuate institutions by creating powerful cultural expectations that are difficult to violate.

Norms and Sanctions

Most norms provide only a general framework of expectations; rarely do they tell us exactly how to act, and rarely are they obeyed by all people at all times. Furthermore, norms may be ambiguous or contradictory. It is no surprise, then, that actual behavior sometimes departs markedly from normative expectations. When it does, negative **sanctions** may be applied. A sanction is a direct social response to some behavior; a negative sanction is one that punishes or otherwise discourages violations of social norms and symbolically reinforces the culture's values and morals.

Different norms evoke different sanctions when violated. **Mores** (pronounced MORE-ayz) are norms, sometimes codified into laws, that are taken very seriously by society. Violation of some mores can elicit severe, state-sponsored sanctions, such as serving time in prison for armed robbery. Other mores may be equally serious but much less formally stated. Sanctions for violating these norms may take the form of public ostracism or exclusion from the group, as when one is excommunicated for going against the moral doctrine of one's church.

The vast majority of everyday norms are relatively minor, however; violations of these norms, called **folkways**, carry much less serious punishment. For instance, if I chew with my mouth open and food dribbles down my chin, others may show outward signs of disapproval and consider me a "disgusting pig." I may receive fewer dinner invitations as a result, but I won't be arrested or banished from my community.

The difference between mores and folkways is not always clear. Recently the Spanish village of La Toba passed an ordinance outlawing dozens of "rude" public behaviors including burping, slurping soup, picking one's nose, coughing without covering one's mouth, and adjusting underwear (Wilson, 2012). Some economists advocate taxing behaviors that, although not illegal, might be damaging or annoying to others, such as playing music too loudly or driving in congested city areas at peak traffic times. In London, drivers have to pay what amounts to about $16 to enter the central part of the city during rush hours (Davidson, 2013).

According to the structural-functionalist perspective, each time a community moves to sanction an act, it strengthens the boundaries between normative and nonnormative behavior (Erikson, 1966). In the process, the rest of us are warned of what is in store if we, too, violate the norms. In the 17th century, for example, criminals and religious heretics were executed at high noon in the public square for all to see. The spectacle was meant to be a vivid and symbolic reaffirmation of the community's norms. Today, such harsh sanctions are likely to be hidden from the public eye. However, the publicity surrounding executions, as well as the visibility of less severe sanctions, serves the same purpose—to declare to the community where the line between acceptable and unacceptable behavior lies. By sanctioning the person who violates a norm, society informs its members what type of person cannot live "normally" within its boundaries (Pfohl, 1994).

Cultural Relativism and Ethnocentrism

When it comes to examining the cultures of different societies, sociologists are inclined to adopt a position of *cultural relativism*, the principle that people's beliefs and activities should be interpreted in terms of their own culture. In other words, practices that might conflict with our cultural values are still considered valid because they reflect the values of that culture. Maintaining a culturally relativist position becomes especially difficult when the practice in question is considered brutal or oppressive. Take, for instance, the practice of female genital mutilation/cutting (FGM/C), a procedure that entails the removal of a young girl's clitoris and/or the destruction of the labia and vulva. In the countries where FGM/C is practiced, women are expected to be virgins when they marry. The ritual therefore serves to control young women's sexuality and ensure their "marriageability." But to people in societies that acknowledge or even celebrate female sexuality, such a practice is abhorrent and a violation of human rights. A decades-long worldwide campaign to end FGM/C has led many countries to ban the practice. However, it persists as a local custom in 29 countries in Africa and the Middle East. Overall, about 125 million girls and women worldwide are living with the consequences of this procedure, which is usually carried out sometime between infancy and age 15 (UNICEF, 2013). In Africa alone, an estimated 101 million girls over the age of 10 have undergone FGM/C (World Health Organization, 2013).

Cultural relativism is not part of the way most of us are raised. People tend to evaluate other cultures in comparison to their own. This tendency is called *ethnocentrism*. As children, most people are taught that they live in the greatest country on earth. Many also learn to take pride in their religious, racial, or ethnic group. But the belief that one group or country is the "best" means that others are "not the best." Sixty percent of Americans believe that their culture is superior to others. The figure rises to 90% in South Korea and Indonesia (cited in Rieff, 2006).

Ethnocentrism results from the nature of human interaction itself. Much of our everyday lives is spent in groups and organizations. By their very character, these collectivities consist of individuals with some, though not necessarily all, shared interests. The same is true for larger cultures. To the extent that we spend a majority of our time with others "like us," our interactions with others "not like us" will be limited, and they will remain "foreign" or "mysterious." Similarity breeds comfort; difference breeds discomfort. For example, despite laws against the practice, many Japanese shopkeepers are so uncomfortable dealing with foreigners that they refuse to serve them (French, 1999a). In fact, when Japanese citizens who have lived abroad for a long time return to Japan, they find that they are no longer regarded as fully Japanese and are treated with the sort of cold disdain foreigners there often experience (French, 2000).

Another reason for the existence of ethnocentrism is the loyalty we develop to our particular culture or subculture (Charon, 1992). Different values, beliefs, and behaviors come to be seen not merely as different ways of thinking and acting but as threats to our own beliefs and values. Such perceptions, for instance, underlie much of the resentment of and hostility toward recently arrived immigrants. Even groups whose position in society is strong and secure can find the encroachment of other ways of life threatening:

- A Honolulu restaurant made headlines recently for its policy of adding a 15% gratuity to the checks of all non–English-speaking patrons. The owner claimed he put the policy into place because Asian guests routinely fail to tip. "It's not a part of their culture," he said. "They spend a lot of money, but they don't tip" (quoted in McKinley, 2011, p. A16).
- A school superintendent in Mustang, Oklahoma, got into trouble a few years ago for including references to Kwanzaa and Chanukah as well as Christmas in an annual school play and for removing a live nativity scene from the conclusion of the play so as not to highlight one faith too much over others. Christian parents became outraged, suing the school for discrimination and voting down an $11 million school bond (Zernike, 2004).
- In 2011, a bill introduced in the California legislature sought to ban the sale and possession of shark fins because of the brutal way the fins are hacked off live sharks. Similar bills have been presented in Oregon and Washington. But shark fins are a centuries-old delicacy among Chinese residents, who perceive the proposed law as an assault on their cultural traditions (P. L. Brown, 2011).

Cultural loyalty is also encouraged by institutional ritual and symbolism. In this country, saying the Pledge of Allegiance at the beginning of the school day, playing the "Star-Spangled Banner" and "God Bless America" at sports events, and observing holidays such as Memorial Day, the Fourth of July, Veterans Day, and Flag Day all reinforce loyalty to U.S. culture. The American flag is considered such an important national symbol that an entire code of etiquette with specific instructions on how to display it exists to ensure that it is treated with reverence. These are the "sacred objects" of U.S. culture (Durkheim, 1915/1954). The importance of these objects is especially pronounced when people in society feel threatened. You will recall the enormous number of American flags, patriotic songs, pins, T-shirts, and magnetic ribbons on cars

that exploded onto the cultural landscape after the September 11, 2001, attacks and during the wars in Iraq and Afghanistan. Religious artifacts and symbols, uniforms and team colors, and distinctive ethnic clothing all foster a sense of pride and identity and hold a community of similar people together, often to the exclusion of others.

CULTURAL VARIATION AND EVERYDAY EXPERIENCE

As populations grow more ethnically and racially diverse and as the people of the world become linked more closely by commerce, transportation, and communication, the likelihood of individuals from different cultures and subcultures living together increases. An awareness of cultural differences helps ease everyday interactions in a multicultural society and can be crucial in international relations:

- In Iran, people are expected to give false praise and make insincere promises. They are expected to tell others what they want to hear in order to avoid conflict or offer hope when, clearly, there is none. This practice, known as *taarof*, is considered polite, not offensive. Children learn from an early age to pick up on nuances in others' comments. The practice has its historical roots in centuries of occupation by foreign powers, which taught Iranians the value of hiding their true feelings. As one Iranian psychologist put it, "When you tell lies, it can save your life" (quoted in Slackman, 2006, p. 5).
- In Afghanistan, the thumbs-up gesture—a sign of approval in the United States—is the equivalent of giving someone "the finger." To reduce potentially dangerous cultural clashes, the U.S. Marine Corps distributes "Culture Smart Cards" to U.S. military personnel on their arrival in these countries. The cards contain instructions on matters such as how to shake hands, what gestures are appropriate, and how to act when in Afghan homes (Edidin, 2005).
- In India, waiting lines do not carry the same set of cultural expectations they do in the U.S. When a line appears to be too long to some, they will create their own lines by standing next to someone toward the front of the original line and hoping that others will line up behind them. Pretty soon the original line has sprouted multiple branches. People will push their entire bodies against the person in front of them in hopes of deterring cutters. But that rarely works:

[Cutters] hover near the line's middle, holding papers looking lost in a practiced way, then slip in somewhere close to the front. When confronted, their refrain is predictable: "Oh, I didn't see the line." (Giridharadas, 2010a, p. 5)

In all these cases, you can see how important it is for soldiers, diplomats, negotiators, and tourists to know of such tendencies. Without such knowledge, the risk of misunderstandings and perhaps even conflict increases.

Cultural variation reflects more than just differences in people's habits and customs. It indicates that even the most taken-for-granted truths in our lives, the things we assume are universal and unambiguous, are subject to different interpretations and definitions worldwide. Two important examples of such variation are beliefs about health and illness and definitions of sex.

Health and Illness

A prominent doctor once said, "A disease does not exist until we name it" (quoted in Kolata, 2011, p. 3). In other words, we can't claim to have a disease that is not recognized as real in our culture. In Malaysia, a man may be diagnosed with *koro*, a sudden, intense anxiety that his sexual organs will recede into his body, causing death. In some Latin American countries, a person can suffer from *susto*, an illness tied to a frightening event that makes the soul leave the body, causing unhappiness and sickness (American Psychiatric Association, 2013). One psychiatrist estimates that as many as one million Japanese youth (or about 1% of the population) suffer from *hikikomori*, a phenomenon whereby alienated adolescents withdraw from social life and sequester themselves in their rooms for six months or longer (some have lived in isolation for over a decade; M. Jones, 2006). None of these conditions exists as a medical diagnosis in other parts of the world. But they are not simply anthropological curiosities. They show that culture shapes everyday notions of health and illness.

Even more compelling, though, are the dramatic cultural differences in medical treatment among societies that share many other values, beliefs, norms, and structural elements. In the United States, medical treatment tends to originate from an aggressive "can do" cultural spirit. Diseases are enemies that need to be conquered. Words like "fight" and

"battle" are frequently invoked to describe the struggles of people receiving cancer treatment. Their stoicism in facing the disease, undergoing surgery, or enduring the powerful side effects of chemotherapy are often considered signs of "bravery." If they recover, they've "beaten" or "defeated" the cancer; if they succumb, they've "lost the good fight" (Jennings, 2010).

In contrast, British medicine is much more subdued. British physicians don't recommend routine examinations, seldom prescribe drugs, and order about half as many X-ray studies as U.S. doctors do. British patients are also much less likely to have surgery. These attitudes also influence perceptions of patients. People who are quiet and withdrawn—something U.S. doctors might consider symptoms of clinical depression—tend to be seen by British psychiatrists as perfectly normal.

Ironically, despite their more aggressive approach, Americans are actually much sicker than their British counterparts, even though the U.S. spends more than twice as much on health care per person than Great Britain (Emanuel, 2011). They suffer higher rates of conditions like diabetes, heart disease, and obesity and have a lower life expectancy. These differences exist even when controlling for social class. According to one study, the richest one third of U.S. citizens are in worse health than the poorest one third of Britons (Banks, Marmot, Oldfield, & Smith, 2006). In fact, when compared to other wealthy, industrialized countries—not just Great Britain—Americans fare worse in such major health indicators as infant mortality, HIV/AIDS, drug-related deaths, obesity and diabetes, heart disease, and chronic lung disease (Institute of Medicine, 2013). Americans younger than 50 also rank below 16 other high-income nations in life expectancy (National Academies, 2013).

In addition to determining the nature of illness, cultural attitudes determine what it means to be sick and how individuals experience sickness. Each society has a **sick role**, a widely understood set of rules about how people are supposed to behave when sick (Parsons, 1951). The sick role entails certain obligations (things sick people are expected to do) as well as certain privileges (things sick people are entitled to). Here are some common elements of the sick role in U.S. society:

- Because we tend to think of most illnesses as things that happen to people, individuals may be exempted from responsibility for the condition itself. At the same time, though, they're expected to recognize the condition as undesirable and something that should be overcome as soon as possible.

- Individuals who are allowed to occupy the sick role are excused from ordinary daily duties and expectations. This privilege varies with the severity of the illness. Compare someone with cancer to someone with a cold, for instance. National legislation—in the form of the Family and Medical Leave Act—and private workplace sick leave policies are the institutional manifestations of these expectations.

- Depending on the magnitude of the malady, sick people may be given relief from the ordinary norms of etiquette and propriety. Think of the nasty moods, actions, or insults you're able to "get away with" when you're sick that people wouldn't tolerate from you if you were well.

- Sick people are entitled to ask for and receive care and sympathy from others. But sympathy requests operate under their own set of cultural regulations. For instance, one should not claim too much sympathy, for too long, or for too many problems. In other words, sick people are expected to downplay their problems to avoid the appearance of self-pity. At the same time, though, they are expected to graciously accept some expressions of sympathy so as not to appear ungrateful (C. Clark, 1997).

- People occupying the sick role are required to take the culturally prescribed actions that will aid in their recovery, including, if the condition is serious enough, seeking help from a culturally appropriate health care professional (Parsons, 1951). Sometimes, to obtain the privilege of exemption from normal social obligations, people must be documented as officially ill from a culturally acceptable source. In the United States, that means a "doctor's note" (Lorber, 2000). Without such validation, your boss might not give you the day off, or your instructor might not allow you to miss an exam and reschedule it for a later date.

- Sick people are obligated to think of others as well as themselves. Hence, they are required to take precautions to avoid infecting those around them. In some cultures, sick people are expected to wear surgical masks in public to prevent contamination.

Failure on the part of sick people either to exercise their rights or to fulfill the obligations of the sick role—as when a person shows up at work with a persistent cough and a 102-degree fever—may elicit sanctions from the group (Crary, 2007). Moreover, those who do not appear to want to recover or who seem to enjoy being sick quickly lose sympathy. Parents who, because of their religious beliefs, prevent culturally approved medical intervention for their sick children have been arrested and charged with child endangerment or worse. A person may also give up legal rights by not seeking or following expert advice. If you are hospitalized and your attending physician doesn't think you ought to be discharged, but you leave anyway, your records will indicate that you have left "AMA"—against medical advice. This designation protects the doctor and the hospital from any liability should your condition worsen.

Like illness itself, sick role expectations are culturally influenced. For instance, when recent Latin American immigrants to the United States fall ill, they are likely to make a visit to the local *botanica* rather than a doctor. *Botanicas* are stores that sell all manner of folk remedies, religious objects, amulets, oils, perfumes, and other products purported to have curative powers. These practices, which combine alternative medicine with Roman Catholicism and other spiritual practices, are used to treat everything from arthritis to financial problems (Trotter & Chavira, 1997).

While different cultures define the sick role differently, it can also vary considerably along social class lines within the same culture (Freund & McGuire, 1991). Someone might have a debilitating disease, but without health insurance she or he may not have the wherewithal to seek the care of health professionals (and receive an official diagnosis) or may not be able to take time off from work for fear of losing her or his job. In short, socioeconomic factors may preclude such people from claiming sick role status.

The Sexes

The culture we grow up in shapes our most fundamental beliefs, even about what most people would consider the basic, universal facts of life. For instance, we take for granted that humans can be divided into two clearly identifiable sexes that are genetically determined at the moment of conception. If you asked someone how to distinguish between males and females, the response would probably focus on observable physical characteristics—body shape, hair, voice, facial features, and so on. When biologists distinguish between the sexes, they too refer to biological traits—for example, chromosomes (XX for female, XY for male), sex glands (ovaries or testes), hormones (estrogen or testosterone), genitalia (vagina or penis), reproductive capacities (pregnancy or impregnation), germ cells produced (ova or sperm), and secondary sex characteristics (hips and breasts or facial hair and deep voice).

These characteristics, and hence the two sex categories, male and female, are usually assumed to be biologically determined, permanent, universal (males are males and females are females no matter what country or what era you live in), exhaustive (everyone can be placed into one or the other category), and mutually exclusive (you can only be one or the other sex; you can't be both). This set of beliefs is called the *sexual dichotomy.*

If you think about it, our entire culture is built around the sexual dichotomy. We have separate clothing sections for men and women, separate hygienic products, separate sections in shoe stores, separate public restrooms, and so on. The sexual dichotomy is so obvious that we simply assume it to be in the nature of things. Our casual references to the "opposite" sex reinforce how much we take the sexual dichotomy for granted; when two things are opposite, it implies there's nothing in between.

But on closer inspection, the natural reality of the sexual dichotomy begins to break down. Throughout human history and across all societies, certain people have transcended the categories of male and female. They may be born with anatomical and/or genital configurations that are ambiguous. Or they may simply choose to live their lives in ways that don't conform to existing gender expectations associated with their sex (see Chapter 5 for more information about the distinction between sex and gender). *Transsexuals*—people who identify with a different sex and sometimes undergo hormone treatment and surgery to change their sex—challenge the idea that male and female are permanent biological characteristics. It's estimated that 1 in 30,000 men and 1 in 100,000 women in the United States undergo sex reassignment surgery each year, although many advocates consider this figure an underestimate (cited in Jost, 2006a). In 2008, a female-to-male transsexual named Thomas Beatie made international headlines when he gave birth to a baby girl. Although Thomas had his breasts removed, was taking testosterone (which deepened his voice and gave him facial hair), and was legally a man, he had kept his female reproductive organs.

The impermanence of sex received official recognition of sorts when the International Olympic Committee's executive board approved a proposal to allow transsexuals to compete in the 2004 Athens Olympic Games. Athletes who had undergone sex reassignment surgery were eligible to compete as long as they had been legally recognized as a member of the "new" sex and it had been at least two years since their surgery. Shortly afterward, the Ladies European Golf Tour enacted a similar policy, allowing a 37-year-old Danish male-to-female transsexual to play in one of its professional tournaments. Today, over half a dozen states have policies that allow transgender high school students to compete on teams that correspond to their current stated sex rather than the sex listed on their school records (Lovett, 2013a).

Although transsexuals challenge the assumption of sexual permanence, they don't challenge the belief that there are only two sex categories. But that assumption is contested in some cultures. In Navajo culture, for instance, one could be identified as male, female, or *nadle*—a third sex assigned to those whose sex-typed anatomical characteristics were ambiguous at birth (Lang, 1998). Physically normal individuals also had the opportunity to choose to become *nadle* if they so desired. The gender status of *nadle* is simultaneously masculine and feminine. They are allowed to perform the tasks and take up the occupations of both men and women. In Samoa, *fa'afafines* are biological men who embody female traits and live their lives as women. The *hijras* of India are born as men, but by choice they have their genitals surgically removed (Reddy, 2005). This operation transforms them not into women but into *hijras*, who appear feminine—dressing, standing, walking, and sitting as women. Many figures in Hindu mythology are neither male nor female. Hence, Indian culture not only accommodates the *hijras* but views them as meaningful, even powerful beings.

Such cross-cultural examples illustrate that our taken-for-granted beliefs about sex and gender are not held worldwide. In other cultures, sex is not dichotomous, exhaustive, or permanent.

The sexual dichotomy is not challenge-free in the United States either. Consider the standard of mutual exclusivity, for example. *Intersexuals* are individuals in whom sexual differentiation is either incomplete or indistinct. They may have the chromosomal pattern of a female but the external genitals of a male, or they may have both ovaries and testicles. Experts estimate that about 1% of all babies born have some form of intersexuality, meaning that they are born with sexual organs that don't completely fit into the standard sex categories (Fausto-Sterling, 2000; Jost, 2006a).

It is interesting to note that the medical response to intersexuals supports the cultural and historical belief that there are two and only two sexes. Intersexuality is usually defined by doctors and medical researchers as a defective combination of the two existing categories and not as a third, fourth, or fifth category unto itself. Furthermore, on diagnosis of intersexuality, a decision is always made to define the individual as either male or female. In societies with advanced medical technology, surgical and chemical means may be used to establish consistency between visible anatomy and the social label. Every month, dozens of sexually ambiguous newborns are "assigned" a sex and undergo surgery to confirm the designation (Cowley, 1997). About 90% are designated female because creating a vagina is considered surgically easier than creating a penis (Angier, 1997b).

However, an increasingly vocal group of intersexuals protest that many of the surgical techniques used to "correct" the problem of visually ambiguous genitals are mutilating and potentially harmful. They cite cases of intersexuals being robbed of any sexual sensation in the attempt to surgically "normalize" them—that is, give them the physical appearance of either a male or a female. The founder of the Intersex Society of North America eloquently summed up her organization's frustration: "They can't conceive of leaving someone alone" (quoted in Angier, 1997a, p. A10).

The medical profession can't leave these individuals alone because to do so would undermine our cultural understanding of sex. Drastic surgical intervention is undertaken in these cases not because the infant's life is threatened but because our entire social structure is organized around having two and only two sexes (Lorber, 1989). The male-female dichotomy in our culture is so essential to our way of life that those who challenge it are often considered disloyal to the most fundamental of biological "facts." To suggest that the labels "male" and "female" are not sufficient to categorize everyone is to threaten a basic organizing principle of social life. So pervasive is the sexual dichotomy that one doctor estimated her chances of persuading the parents of an intersexual child *not* to choose surgery at zero (Weil, 2006).

CONCLUSION

Over the span of a year or two, most cultures seem to have a stable set of norms about the acceptability of certain behaviors. This stability is illusory, however. From the perspective of a generation or even a decade later, that sense of order would give way to a sense of change (McCall & Simmons, 1978). Behaviors, values, beliefs, and morals fluctuate with startling frequency. Thus, comparisons across eras, in addition to comparisons across cultures, can provide rich insight into shifting definitions of acceptability, the nature of everyday life, and ultimately large-scale social change and stability.

The cultural and historical underpinnings of our private lives help us see the relationships among the individual, society, and social order. Cultural practices add continuity and order to social life.

To an individual, culture appears massive and unrelenting; but at the same time, it cannot exist without people. Norms govern our lives, whether we live by them or rebel against them. But to fully understand the relationship between the individual and society, we must look beyond the fact that culture and history shape our lives; we must see them as human constructions as well.

CHAPTER HIGHLIGHTS

◆ Culture provides members of a society with a common bond, a sense that we see certain facets of society in similar ways. That we can live together at all depends on the fact that members of a society share a certain amount of cultural knowledge.

◆ Norms—the rules and standards that govern all social encounters—provide order in our lives. They reflect commonly held assumptions about conventional behavior. Norm violations mark the boundaries of acceptable behavior and symbolically reaffirm what society defines as right and wrong.

◆ The more ethnically and culturally diverse a society, the greater the likelihood of normative clashes between groups.

◆ Over the span of a few years, most cultures present an image of stability and agreement regarding normative boundaries. This agreement is illusory, however. Over a generation or even a decade, that sense of order is replaced by a sense of change.

KEY TERMS

cultural relativism: Principle that people's beliefs and activities should be interpreted in terms of their own culture

ethnocentrism: Tendency to judge other cultures using one's own as a standard

folkway: Informal norm that is mildly punished when violated

heteronormative culture: Culture in which heterosexuality is accepted as the normal, taken-for-granted mode of sexual expression

institutionalized norm: Pattern of behavior within existing social institutions that is widely accepted in a society

intersexuals: Individuals in whom sexual differentiation is either incomplete or ambiguous

material culture: Artifacts of a society that represent adaptations to the social and physical environment

mores: Highly codified, formal, systematized norms that bring severe punishment when violated

nonmaterial culture: Knowledge, beliefs, customs, values, morals, and symbols that are shared by members of a society and that distinguish the society from others

sanction: Social response that punishes or otherwise discourages violations of a social norm

sexual dichotomy: Belief that two biological sex categories, male and female, are permanent, universal, exhaustive, and mutually exclusive

sick role: Set of norms governing how one is supposed to behave and what one is entitled to when sick

subculture: Values, behaviors, and artifacts of a group that distinguish its members from the larger culture

transsexuals: People who identify with a different sex and sometimes undergo hormone treatment and surgery to change their sex

5

Building Identity
Socialization

Genes, Social Structure, and the Construction of Human Beings

Socialization: Becoming Who We Are

Socialization and Stratification: Growing Up With Inequality

Institutions and Socialization

When I was little, my family lived in a suburb just outside New York City. One day, shortly after my ninth birthday, my parents sat me down and told me that we were going to be moving. They had narrowed down our ultimate destination to two possibilities: Laredo, Texas, or a suburb of Los Angeles called Burbank. After some rather intense debate, they chose Burbank. And so we headed "out West," where from age 9 to age 18, I lived in the shadow of the entertainment industry and all its glamour, glitz, and movie stars.

It wasn't long before I became a typical sun-worshipping Southern California kid. I often wonder how differently I would have turned out if my parents had chosen Laredo and I had spent my formative years along the Texas-Mexico border instead of in the middle of Tinseltown. Would I have a fondness for cowboy hats and snakeskin boots instead of flip-flops and shorts? Would I have grown up loving country music instead of the Beach Boys? Would my goals, beliefs, or sense of morality be different? In short, would I be a different person?

Try to imagine what your life would be like if you had grown up under different circumstances. What if your father had been a harpsichord enthusiast instead of a diehard Cubs fan? What if your family had been Muslim instead of Episcopalian? What if you had an older brother instead of a younger sister? What if you had lived on a farm instead of in a big city? What if you had been born in the 1960s instead of the 1990s? Your tastes, preferences, and hobbies, as well as your values, ambitions, and aspirations, would no doubt be different. But more profoundly, your self-concept, self-esteem, personality—the very essence of who you are—would be altered, too.

Consider the broader social and historical circumstances of your life. What kind of impact might they have had on the type of person you are? Talk to elderly people who were children back in the 1930s, and they will speak of the permanent impact that the Great Depression had on them (Elder & Liker, 1982). Imagine spending your childhood as a Jew in Nazi Germany. That couldn't help but shape your outlook on life. The same can be said for growing up poor and black in the American South in the segregated 1950s or wealthy and white in Salt Lake City during the George W. Bush presidency.

Becoming the person you are cannot be separated from the people, historical events, and social circumstances that surround you. In this chapter, I examine the process of socialization—how we learn what's expected of us in our families, our communities, and our culture and how we learn to behave according to those expectations. The primary focus will be on the development of identity. *Identity* is our most essential and personal characteristic. It consists of our membership in various social groups (race, ethnicity, religion, gender, etc.), the traits we show to others, and the traits they ascribe to us. Our identity locates us in the social world, thoroughly affecting everything we do, feel, say, and think in our lives. Most people tend to believe that our self-concept, our sense of "maleness" or "femaleness," and our racial and ethnic identities are biologically or psychologically determined and therefore permanent and unchangeable. But as you will discover, these characteristics are social constructions: as much a product of our social setting and the significant people in our lives as a product of our physical traits and innate predispositions.

GENES, SOCIAL STRUCTURE, AND THE CONSTRUCTION OF HUMAN BEINGS

The question of how we become who we are has for centuries occupied the attention of biologists, psychologists, anthropologists, sociologists, philosophers, poets, and novelists. The issue is typically framed as a debate between *nature* (we are who we are because we were born that way) and *nurture* (we are who we are because of the way we were treated while growing up). Are we simply the predetermined product of our genes and biochemistry, or are we "created" from scratch by the individuals and social institutions that surround us?

The answer to this question swings back and forth depending on the dominant cultural mood. In the late 19th and early 20th centuries, genetic inheritance became a popular explanation for human behavior, including a host of social problems ranging from poverty and crime to alcoholism and mental deficiency. Scientists, borrowing from the selective breeding practices used with thoroughbred racehorses and livestock, advocated programs of *eugenics*, or controlled mating, to ensure that the "defective" genes of troublesome individuals would not be passed on to future generations. Similar theories of genetic inferiority became the cornerstone of Adolf Hitler's horrors in Nazi Germany during World War II. After the war, most people wanted to get as far away from such "nature" arguments as possible. So in the 1950s and 1960s, scholars heavily emphasized environmental influences on behavior, especially the role of early family experiences in shaping children's future personalities (Gould, 1997).

Today, because of the growing cultural emphasis on scientific technology, genetic explanations of human behavior have again become fashionable. In recent years, researchers have claimed that such diverse social phenomena as shyness, impulsiveness, intelligence, aggression, obesity, alcoholism, and addiction to gambling are at least partly due to heredity. An economist raised eyebrows recently when he argued in his book that because of the power of genetic inheritance, parenting hardly matters. Children's destiny is pretty much genetically predetermined. Healthy, smart, happy, virtuous parents tend to have matching offspring no matter what they do to and for their children. So, he wrote, they should just relax and let their children do, essentially, what they want (B. Caplan, 2011). Similarly, the authors of the best-selling book *Freakonomics* wrote, "It isn't so much a matter of what you *do* as a parent; it's who you are (Levitt & Dubner, 2009, p. 175). Advances in genetic testing technology, like the Human Genome Project—an undertaking, completed in 2003, that mapped all the 20,000 to 25,000 genes in human DNA—and a recently developed technique that uses only a blood sample from a pregnant mother and saliva from the father to map the entire genetic configuration of a fetus (and thereby detect thousands of diseases prenatally; Pollack, 2012) will no doubt add fuel to "nature" arguments in the years to come.

Yet apparently we're not quite ready to say that nurture plays no role. In 2011, a prominent Yale law professor struck a blow for the environmental influence on kids when she argued in her popular book that the educational success of Asian children is due largely to the heavy-handed role of mothers, whom she refers to as "Tiger Mothers." She recommends—to all parents, no matter what their ethnic backgrounds—that the prescription for a successful child consists of stressing academic performance, never accepting a mediocre grade, insisting on drilling and practice, and instilling unwavering respect for authority (Chua, 2011). Some affluent parents have even gone so far as to move to another country for a year so their children can be immersed in another culture and become cultivated, global citizens (L. Miller, 2011).

Indeed, when it comes to certain traits, heredity is meaningful only in the context of social experiences. Take intelligence. Many geneticists argue that heredity determines the limits of intelligence (Kirp, 2006). They base this claim on studies that have found that differences in IQ scores between identical twins (who share all their genes) are smaller than differences between fraternal twins (who share only half their genes). But it's impossible to understand intelligence without examining how our genetic makeup interacts with our social experiences. As one author put it,

> You've got genes that are going to give you a certain range of height, or a certain range in the color of your eyes, and a certain range of your intelligence. But we can't say that there's this separate nature that just does its thing separately from nurture. The genes literally do come first, but the way the genes act, their influence, actually doesn't take place before

they interact with their environment. Everything is dependent on this interaction. (Shenk, 2010, p. 44)

Other researchers have found that children's socioeconomic environment can make an enormous difference in their intelligence. One study of seven-year-old children found that while genetics accounts for most of the variation in IQ scores among twins with wealthy parents, the opposite is the case for twins from impoverished families. In these families, the IQs of identical twins vary just as much as the IQs of fraternal twins (Turkheimer, Haley, Waldron, D'Onofrio, & Gottesman, 2003). The researchers conclude that home life is critical. In a poor and unstable home environment, children's genetic potential cannot be reached. Conversely, affluent families are better equipped to provide the cognitive stimulation needed for neurological development.

As you might suspect, most sociologists would argue that human beings are much more than a collection of genetic predispositions and biological characteristics. But that doesn't mean that nature is irrelevant. Certainly, our outward appearance, our physical strength, and our inherited predisposition to sickness have some effect on our personal development. Furthermore, our every thought and action is the result of a complex series of neurological and electrochemical events in our brains and bodies. When we feel the need to eat we are reacting to a physiological sensation—stomach contractions—brought about by a lowering of blood sugar. Satisfying hunger is clearly a biological process. But the way we react to this sensation cannot be predicted by physiology alone. What, when, how, and how often we eat are all matters of cultural forces that we learn over time. When you say something like "I'm starving, but it's too early to eat dinner," you're signaling the power of cultural training in overriding physiological demands.

Likewise, society can magnify genetic and physical differences or cover them up. We've collectively decided that some differences are socially irrelevant (e.g., eye color) and that some are important enough to be embedded in our most important social institutions (e.g., sex and skin color), giving rise to different rights, duties, expectations, and access to educational, economic, and political opportunities.

The relatively new field of *epigenetics* focuses on how gene expression or suppression is dictated by environmental influences. The life we lead and the world we live in can therefore be just as powerful as our genetic code in the development of temperament, body shape, and predisposition to disease (Shulevitz, 2012). So while our genes may have a role to play in who we become, the behaviors and attitudes of significant people in our lives and the cultural and institutional forces that structure our lives are just as, if not more, important (Eliot, 2010). As these things change, so do we. This proposition is not altogether comforting. It implies that who we are may in some ways be "accidental," the result of a series of social coincidences; chance encounters; decisions made by others; and political, economic, and historical events that are in large measure beyond our control—like growing up in California rather than Texas.

SOCIALIZATION: BECOMING WHO WE ARE

The structural-functionalist perspective reminds us that the fundamental task of any society is to reproduce itself—to create members whose behaviors, desires, and goals correspond to those that particular society deems appropriate and desirable. Through the powerful and ubiquitous process of *socialization*, the needs of the society become the needs of the individual.

Socialization is a process of learning. To be socialized is to be trained to think and behave appropriately. It is the means by which people acquire a vast array of important social skills, such as driving a car, converting fractions into decimals, speaking the language correctly, or using a fork instead of a knife to eat peas. But socialization is also the way we learn how to perceive our world; how to interact with others; what it means to be male or female; how, when, why, and with whom to be sexual; what we should and shouldn't do to and for others under certain circumstances; what our society defines as moral and immoral; and so on. In short, it is the process by which we internalize all the cultural information I discussed in Chapter 4.

This learning process is carried out by the various individuals, groups, organizations, and institutions a person comes into contact with during the course of his or her life. These entities—whom sociologists refer to as *agents of socialization*—can be family, friends, peers, teammates, teachers, schools, religious institutions, and the media. They can influence our self-concepts, attitudes, tastes, values, emotions, and behavior.

Although socialization occurs throughout our lives, the basic, formative instruction of life begins early on. Young children must be taught the fundamental values, knowledge, and beliefs of their culture. Some of the socialization that occurs during childhood—often called *anticipatory socialization*—is the primary means by which young individuals acquire the values and orientations found in the statuses they will likely enter in the future (Merton, 1957). Household chores, a childhood job, organized sports, dance lessons, dating, and many other types of experiences give youngsters an opportunity to rehearse for the kinds of roles that await them in adulthood.

The Acquisition of Self

The most important outcome of the socialization process is the development of a sense of self. The term *self* refers to the unique traits, behaviors, and attitudes that distinguish one person from the next. The self is both the active source of behavior and its passive object (Mead, 1934).

As an active source, the self can initiate action, which is frequently directed toward others. Imagine, for example, that Donna and Robert are having dinner in a restaurant. Donna has a self that can perceive Robert, talk to him, evaluate him, tell him what to order, and maybe even try to persuade him to act in a way that is consistent with her interests. At the same time, Donna has a self that is a potential object of others' behavior: She can be perceived, talked to, evaluated, directed, or persuaded by Robert.

Donna can also direct these activities toward herself. She can perceive, evaluate, motivate, and even talk to herself. This is called *reflexive behavior*. To have a self is to have the ability to plan, observe, guide, and respond to one's own actions (Mead, 1934). Think of all the times you have tried to motivate yourself to act by saying something such as "All right, if I read 20 more pages of my boring sociology book, I'll make myself a hot fudge sundae" or "I won't go on Facebook until I write five more pages of this chemistry paper." To engage in such activities, you must simultaneously be the motivator and the one being motivated—the seer and the seen.

At this very moment, you are initiating an action: reading this nonboring sociology book. But you also have the ability (now that I've mentioned it!) to be aware of your reading behavior, to reflexively observe yourself reading, and even to evaluate how well you are doing. This may sound like some sort of mystical out-of-body experience, but it isn't. Nothing is more fundamental to human thought and action than this capacity for reflexive self-awareness. It allows us to control our own behavior and interact smoothly with other self-aware individuals.

At birth, human babies have no sense of self. This is not to say that infants don't act on their own. Anyone who has been around babies knows that they have a tremendous ability to initiate action, ranging all the way from snapshot-worthy cute to downright disgusting. They cry, eat, sleep, play with squeaky rubber toys, and eliminate waste, all with exquisite flair and regularity. From the very first days of life, they respond to the sounds, sights, smells, and touches of others.

But this behavior is not characterized by the sort of reflexive self-awareness that characterizes later behavior. Babies don't say to themselves "I wonder if Mom will feed me if I scream" or "I can't *believe* how funny my babbling sounds right now." As children grow older, though, they begin to exert greater control over their actions. Part of this transformation is biological. As they mature, they become more adept at muscle control. But physical development is only part of the picture. Humans must acquire certain cognitive capacities through interactions with others, including the abilities to differentiate between self and others, to understand and use symbolic language, and to take the roles of others.

Language Acquisition and the Looking-Glass Self

The next important step in the acquisition of self is the development of speech (Hewitt, 1988). Symbolic interactionism points out that mastery of language is crucial in children's efforts to differentiate themselves as distinct social as well as physical objects (Denzin, 1977). Certainly, language acquisition relies on neurological development. But the ability to grasp the nuances of one's own language requires input from others. Most parents talk to their children from the start. Gradually, children learn to make sounds, imitate sounds, and use sounds as symbols for particular physical sensations or objects. Children learn that the sounds "Mama" and "Dada" are associated with two important objects in their life. Soon children learn that other objects—toys, animals, foods, Aunt

Anita, Uncle Marc—have unique sounds associated with them as well.

This learning process gives the child access to the preexisting linguistic world in which his or her parents and others live (Hewitt, 1988). The objects named are not only those recognized within the larger culture but also those recognized within the child's family and social groups. The child learns the names of concrete objects (balls, buildings, furniture) as well as abstractions that cannot be directly perceived (God, happiness, peace, idea).

By learning that people and other objects have names, the child also begins to learn that these objects can be related to one another in a variety of ways. Depending on who is talking to whom, the same person can be called several different names. The object "Dad" is called "David," "Dave," "Dov," "Dr. Newman," "Professor Newman," "Mr. Newman," and "New Man" by various other people. Furthermore, the child learns that different people can be referred to by the same name. All those other toddlers playing in the park have someone they also call "Mama."

Amid these monumental discoveries, young children learn that they too are objects that have names. A child who learns that others are referring to her when they make the sound "Emma," and that she too can use "Emma" to refer to herself, has taken a significant leap forward in the acquisition of self. The child now can visualize herself as a part of the named world and the named relationships to which she belongs.

Children learn the meaning of named objects in their environment by observing the way other people act toward those objects. By witnessing people sitting on a chair, they learn what *chair* means. Parental warnings allow them to learn that a "hot stove" is something to be avoided. Similarly, by observing how people act toward them, they learn the meaning of themselves. People treat children in a variety of ways: care for them, punish them, love them, neglect them, teach them. If parents, relatives, and other agents of socialization perceive a child as smart, they will act toward her or him that way. Thus, the child eventually comes to define herself or himself as a smart person. One of the earliest symbolic interactionists, Charles Horton Cooley (1902), referred to this process as the acquisition of the *looking-glass self*. He argued that we use the reaction of others toward us as looking glasses (that is, mirrors) in which we see ourselves and determine our self-worth. Through this process, we imagine how we might look to other people, we interpret their responses to us, and we form a self-concept. If we think people perceive us favorably, we're likely to develop a positive self-concept. Conversely, if we detect unfavorable reactions, our self-concept will likely be negative. Hence, self-evaluative feelings like pride or shame are always the product of the reflected appraisals of others.

The Development of Role Taking

The socialization process would be pretty simple if everyone in our lives saw us in exactly the same way. But different people expect or desire different things from us. Children eventually learn to modify their behavior to suit a variety of others. Four-year-old Ahmed learns, for instance, that his three-year-old sister loves it when he sticks his thumb up his nose, but he also knows that his father doesn't find this behavior at all amusing. So Ahmed will avoid such conduct when his father is around but proceed to amuse his sister with this trick when Papa is gone. The ability to use other people's perspectives and expectations in formulating one's own behavior is called *role taking* (Mead, 1934).

Role taking ability develops gradually, paralleling the increasing maturation of linguistic abilities. Operating from the symbolic interactionist perspective, George Herbert Mead (1934) identified two major stages in the development of role taking ability and, ultimately, in the socialization of the self: the play stage and the game stage. The *play stage* occurs when children are just beginning to hone their language skills. Role taking at the play stage is quite simple in form, limited to taking the perspective of one other person at a time. Very young children cannot yet see themselves from different perspectives simultaneously. They have no idea that certain behaviors may be unacceptable to a variety of people across a range of situations. They know only that this particular person who is in their immediate presence will approve or disapprove of this particular act. Children cannot see that their father's displeasure with public nose picking reflects the attitudes of a larger group and is always unacceptable no matter where or when it takes place. This more sophisticated form of self-control develops at the next stage of the socialization process: the game stage.

The *game stage* occurs about the time when children first begin to participate in organized activities such as school events and team sports. The difference between role taking at the play and game stages parallels the difference between childhood play and game behavior. "Play" is not guided by a specific set of rules. It has no ultimate object, no clearly organized competition, and no winners and losers. Children playing baseball at the play stage have no sense of strategy and may not even be aware of the rules and object of the game. They may be able to hit, catch, and throw the ball but have no idea how their behavior is linked to that of their teammates. If a little girl is playing shortstop and a ground ball is hit to her, she may turn around and throw the ball to the left fielder, not because it will help her team win the game but because that's where her best friend happens to be.

Game behavior, in contrast, requires that children understand the object of the game. They realize that each player on the team is part of an organized network of roles determined by the rules of the game. Children know they must continually adapt their behavior to the team's needs in order to achieve a goal. To do so, they must imagine the group's perspective and anticipate how both their teammates and their opponents will act under certain circumstances. Now our little shortstop will throw the ball to first base to get the batter out, but only after assessing how many outs there are and checking to make sure the opposing runner on second base is not trying to advance to third. It doesn't matter whether she likes or hates the first baseman; her team's success depends on her making this play.

With regard to role taking at the game stage, not only does the child learn to respond to the demands of several people, but she or he can also respond to the demands of the community or even society as a whole. Sociologists call the perspective of society and its constituent values and attitudes the *generalized other*. The generalized other becomes larger as a child matures, growing to include family, peer group, school, and finally the larger social community. "Dad doesn't like it when I take off my pants in a restaurant" (play stage) eventually becomes "It's never acceptable to take off one's pants in public" (game stage). Notice how such an understanding requires an ability to generalize behavior across a variety of situations and audiences. The child realizes that "public" consists of restaurants, shopping malls, school classrooms, parks, neighbors' living rooms, and so forth.

This ability is crucial because it enables the individual to resist the influence of specific people who happen to be in his or her immediate presence. The boy who defies his peers by not joining them in an act of petty shoplifting is showing the power of the generalized other ("Stealing, no matter where or with whom, is bad"). During the game stage, the attitudes and expectations of the generalized other are incorporated into one's values and self-concept.

Real life is not always that simple, though. Sometimes people succumb to the pressures of particular others and engage in behaviors they know are socially unacceptable. Furthermore, individuals from markedly different backgrounds are likely to internalize different sets of group attitudes and values. A devout Catholic contemplating divorce, for instance, is taking the role of a different generalized other than an atheist contemplating divorce. Likewise, the social worlds and social standards of men and women are different, as are those of children and adults, parents and nonparents, middle-class and working-class people, and people who grew up in different cultures.

Nor is role taking ability static. It changes in response to interactions with others. When people feel that they can understand another person's perspective—say, that of an intimate partner—they are likely to become concerned about or at least aware of how their behavior will affect that other person (Cast, 2004). Furthermore, as we move from one institutional setting to another, we adopt the perspective of the appropriate group and can become, for all intents and purposes, a different person. At school we behave one way, at church another, and at Grandma's house still another. We are as many different people as there are groups and organizations to which we belong.

In sum, the ability to imagine another person's attitudes and intentions and thereby to anticipate that person's behavior is essential for everyday social interaction. Through role taking, we can envision how others perceive us and imagine what their response may be to some action we're contemplating. Hence, we can select behaviors that are likely to meet with the approval of the person or persons with whom we are interacting and can avoid behaviors that might meet with their disapproval. Role taking is thus a crucial component of self-control and

social order. It transforms a biological being into a social being who is capable of conforming her or his behavior to societal expectations. It is the means by which culture is incorporated into the self and makes group life possible (Cast, 2004).

Resocialization

Socialization does not end when childhood ends; it continues throughout our lives. Adults must be *resocialized* into a new set of norms, values, and expectations each time they leave behind old social contexts or roles and enter new ones (Ebaugh, 1988; Pescosolido, 1986; Simpson, 1979). For instance, we have to learn how to think and act like a spouse when we marry (P. L. Berger & Kellner, 1964), like a parent when we have kids (A. Rossi, 1968), and like a divorced person when a marriage ends (Vaughan, 1986). Every new group or organization we enter, every new friendship we form, every new life-changing experience we have requires the formation of new identities and socialization into new sets of norms and beliefs.

Certain occupations require the formal resocialization of new entrants. Often, the purpose is simply to make sure people who work in the organization share the same professional values, methods, and vocabulary. Many large companies, for example, have orientation programs for new employees to teach them what will be expected of them as they begin their new jobs. Sometimes the purpose is to make new entrants abandon their original expectations and adopt a more realistic view of the occupation. Police recruits who believe their job is to protect people must learn that deadly force is appropriate and sometimes necessary in the line of duty (Hunt, 1985). Medical students may become less idealistic and more realistic as they learn about the exhausting demands of their profession (Becker & Geer, 1958; Hafferty, 1991).

Sometimes resocialization is forceful and intense. According to sociologist Erving Goffman, this type of resocialization often occurs in *total institutions* (E. Goffman, 1961). Total institutions are physical settings in which groups of individuals are separated from the broader society and forced to lead an enclosed, formally administered life. Prisons, mental hospitals, monasteries, and military training camps are examples of total institutions. In these locations, previous socialization experiences are systematically destroyed and new ones developed to serve the interests of the larger group. Take military boot camp, for example. The Army alone spends several billion dollars a year and employs thousands of people to turn civilians into battle-ready warriors who look, act, and think like soldiers and learn to see the world from the soldier's perspective (Tietz, 2006). The process is called "total control." To aid in this transformation, recruits are stripped of old civilian identity markers (clothes, personal possessions, hairstyle) and forced to take on new ones that nullify individuality and also identify the newcomers' subordinate status (uniforms, identification numbers, similar haircuts). The newcomer is also subjected to constant scrutiny. Conformity is mandatory. Any misstep is met with punishment or humiliation. Eventually, the individual learns to identify with the ideology of the total institution.

In the boot camp, the uniformity of values and appearance is intended to create a sense of solidarity among the soldiers and thereby make the military more effective in carrying out its tasks. Part of the reason for all the controversy over diversity in the military—first with the inclusion of African Americans, then with women, and now with gay men and lesbians—is that it introduces dissimilar beliefs, values, appearances, and lifestyles into a context where, from an institutional perspective, similarity is essential.

The Self in a Cultural Context

When we imagine how others will respond to our actions, we choose from a limited set of lines of conduct that are part of the wider culture. In the United States, the self is likely to incorporate key cultural virtues such as self-reliance and individualism. Hence, personal goals tend to be favored over group goals (Bellah, Madsen, Sullivan, Swidler, & Tipton, 1985). In the United States, people will readily change their group membership as it suits them—leaving one career for another, moving from neighborhood to neighborhood, switching political allegiances or even religions.

The United States is said to be an *individualist culture*, where personal traits and accomplishments are a key part of one's self-concept. We've always admired independent people whose success—usually measured in financial terms—is based on their own achievements and self-reliance (Bellah et al., 1985).

Hence, the amount of respect people deserve is determined in large part by their level of individual expertise. For example, before a public speech, a guest lecturer in the United States will likely be introduced to her audience as "a distinguished scholar, a leader in her field" along with a list of academic credentials and scholarly achievements.

In many non–Western cultures, however, people are more likely to subordinate their individual goals to the goals of the larger group and to value obligations to others over personal achievements. In such a setting, known as a *collectivist culture*, personal identity is less important than group identity (Gergen, 1991). In India, for instance, feelings of self-esteem and prestige originate more from the reputation and honor of one's family than from any individual attainments (Roland, 1988). In a collectivist setting, high value is placed on preserving one's public image so as not to bring shame on one's family, tribe, or community (Triandis, McCusker, & Hui, 1990). Overcoming personal interests and temptations to show loyalty to one's group and other authorities is celebrated. Guest lecturers in a collectivist culture would be considered self-centered and egotistical if they mentioned their personal accomplishments and credentials. Japanese public speakers, for instance, commonly begin their lectures by telling the audience how *little* they know about the topic at hand (Goleman, 1990).

But even in an individualist society such as the United States, our personal identities are inseparable from the various groups and organizations to which we belong. Thus, to fully understand how we become who we are, we must know the norms and values of our culture, family, peers, coworkers, and all the other agents of socialization who are a part of our lives.

SOCIALIZATION AND STRATIFICATION: GROWING UP WITH INEQUALITY

Socialization does not take place in a vacuum. Your social class, your race and ethnicity, and your sex and gender all become significant features of your social identity. Were you born into a poor or a well-to-do family? Are you a member of a racial minority or a member of the dominant group? Are you male or female? These elements of identity shape your experiences with other people and the larger society and will direct you along a certain life path. In most societies, social class, race and ethnicity, and gender are the key determinants of people's opportunities throughout their lives.

Social Class

Social classes consist of people who occupy similar positions of power, privilege, and prestige. People's positions in the class system affect virtually every aspect of their lives, including political preferences, sexual behavior, religious affiliation, diet, and life expectancy. The conflict perspective points out that even in a relatively open society such as the United States, parents' social class determines children's access to certain educational, occupational, and residential opportunities. Affluent children grow up in more abundant surroundings than less affluent children and therefore have access to more material comforts and enriching opportunities such as good schools, chances to travel to far-off places, private music lessons, and so on. Furthermore, the lower the income of a child's family, the greater that child's risk of living in a single-parent household, having unemployed parents, having more than one disability, and dropping out of school (Mather & Adams, 2006).

But the relationship between class and socialization is not simply about parents' providing (or not providing) their children with the trappings of a comfortable childhood. Parents' class standing also influences the values and orientations children learn and the identities they develop.

In Chapter 10, you will learn much more about how social class affects attitudes, behaviors, and opportunities. The important point here is that social class and socialization are closely linked. Sociologist Melvin L. Kohn (1979) interviewed 200 working-class and 200 middle-class American couples who had at least one child of fifth-grade age. He found that the middle-class parents were more likely to promote values such as self-direction, independence, and curiosity than were the working-class parents. A more recent study found that middle-class parents are more likely than working-class parents to foster their children's talents through organized leisure activities and experiences that require logical reasoning (Lareau, 2003). Other researchers have found this tendency especially strong among middle-class mothers (Xiao, 2000).

Conversely, working-class parents are more likely than middle-class parents to emphasize conformity to external authority, a common characteristic of the blue-collar jobs they're likely to have later on (M. L. Kohn, 1979). Principally, they want their children to be neat and clean and to follow the rules.

Of course, not all middle-class parents, or working-class parents, raise their children in these ways, and many factors other than social class influence parental values (J. D. Wright & Wright, 1976). Nevertheless, Kohn found that these general tendencies were consistent regardless of the sex of the child or the size and composition of the family. In a study of African American women, those from middle-class backgrounds reported that their parents had higher expectations of them and were more involved in their education than African American women from working-class backgrounds reported (N. E. Hill, 1997). Moreover, others have found that despite cultural differences, social class standing influences child socialization in societies in Europe (Poland, Germany) and Asia (Japan, Taiwan; Schooler, 1996; Williamson, 1984; Yi, Chang, & Chang, 2004).

Sudden shifts in social class standing—due, for instance, to an unexpected job loss—can also affect the way parents socialize their children. Parents who lose their jobs can become irritable, tense, and moody and their disciplinary style more arbitrary. They may come to rely less on reasoning and more on hostile comments and physical punishment. As a result, children's sense of self, their aspirations, and their school performance suffer (cited in Rothstein, 2001).

Class differences in socialization are also directly related to future goals. Working-class parents tend to believe that eventual occupational success and survival depend on their children's ability to conform to and obey authority (M. L. Kohn, 1979). Middle-class parents are likely to believe that their children's future success will result from assertiveness and initiative. Hence, middle-class children's feelings of control over their own destinies are likely to be much stronger than those of working-class children.

Race and Ethnicity

Similarly, race and ethnicity can have a powerful impact on socialization. For white children, learning about their racial identity is less about defining their race than it is about learning how to handle the privileges and behaviors associated with being white in a predominantly white society (Van Ausdale

& Feagin, 2001). Chances are good that schools and religious organizations will reinforce the socialization messages expressed to white children in their families—for example, that "you can be anything you want as long as you work hard."

For children who are members of ethnoracial minorities, however, learning about their race takes place in a different and much more complex social environment (Hughes & Chen, 1997). These children must live simultaneously in two different worlds: their ethnoracial community and the "mainstream" (i.e., white) society. Hence, they're likely to be exposed to several different types of socialization experiences while growing up: those that include information about the mainstream culture, those that focus on their minority status in society, and those that focus on the history and cultural heritage of their ethnoracial group (L. D. Scott, 2003; Thornton, 1997). Parents often emphasize one type of orientation over others. In ethnoracial groups that have been able to overcome discrimination and achieve at high levels—such as some Asian American groups—ethnic socialization can focus simply on the values of their culture of origin. But among groups that by and large remain disadvantaged, such as African Americans, Native Americans, and Latino/as, parents' discussion of race is more likely to focus on preparing their children for prejudice, ethnic hatred, and mistreatment in a society set up to ignore or actively exclude them (McLoyd, Cauce, Takeuchi, & Wilson, 2000; Staples, 1992). For instance, these children may be taught that "hard work" alone may not be enough to get ahead in this society. Even African American children from affluent homes in racially integrated neighborhoods need reassurances about the racial conflicts they will inevitably encounter. These are lessons that children in the dominant racial group seldom require, for reasons explored in greater depth in Chapter 11.

Gender

As you recall from Chapter 4, the sexual dichotomy—the belief that there are two and only two sexes—is not universal. Cultures are even more likely to differ in what is expected of people based on their sex and in how male and female children are to be socialized.

Before discussing this aspect of socialization, it's necessary to distinguish between two concepts: sex and gender. *Sex* is typically used to refer to a person's biological maleness or femaleness. *Gender* designates masculinity and femininity: the psychological, social, and cultural aspects of maleness and femaleness (Kessler & McKenna, 1978). This distinction is important because it reminds us that male-female differences in behaviors or experiences do not spring naturally from biological differences between the sexes (Lips, 1993).

The gender socialization process begins the moment a child is born. A physician, nurse, or midwife immediately starts that infant on a career as a male or female by authoritatively declaring whether it is a boy or a girl. In most U.S. hospitals, the infant boy is wrapped in a blue blanket, the infant girl in a pink one. From that point on, the developmental paths of U.S. males and females diverge. The subsequent messages that individuals receive from families, books, television, and schools not only teach and reinforce gender-typed expectations but also influence the formation of their self-concepts.

New parents can be very sensitive about the correct identification of their child's sex. Even parents who claim to consider sex and gender irrelevant may spend a great deal of time ensuring that their child has the culturally appropriate gender appearance. Parents of a girl baby who has yet to grow hair (a visible sign of gender in many cultures) will sometimes tape pink ribbons to their bald daughter's head to avoid potential misidentification. In many Latin American countries, families have infant girls' ears pierced and earrings placed in them to provide an unmistakable marker of the child's sex and gender.

In a culture where sex and gender are centrally important and any ambiguity is distasteful, the correct gender identification of babies maintains social order. When my elder son was an infant, I dressed him on several occasions in a pink, frilly snowsuit in order to observe the reactions of others. (Having a sociologist for a father can be rather difficult from time to time!) Inevitably, someone would approach us and start playing with the baby and some variation of the following interchange would ensue:

"Oh, she's so cute! What's your little girl's name?"

"Zachary."

"Isn't Zachary a boy's name?"

"He's a boy."

At this point, the responses would range from stunned confusion and awkward laughter to nasty looks and outright anger. Clearly, people felt that I had emotionally abused my son somehow. I had purposely breached a fundamental gender norm and thereby created, in their minds, unnecessary trauma (for him) and interactional confusion (for them).

Both boys and girls learn at a very young age to adopt gender as an organizing principle (Hollander, Renfrow, & Howard, 2011). By the age of three or so, most children can accurately answer the question, "Are you a boy or a girl?" (e.g., Kohlberg, 1966). To a young child, being a boy or a girl is simply another characteristic, like having brown hair or 10 fingers. The child at this age has no conception that gender is a category into which every human can be placed (Kessler & McKenna, 1978). But by the age of five or so, most children have developed a fair number of gender stereotypes (often incorrect) that they then use to guide their own perceptions and activities (C. L. Martin & Ruble, 2004). They also use these stereotypes to form impressions of others. A boy, for instance, may avoid approaching a new girl who's moved into the neighborhood because he assumes that she will only be interested in "girl" things. Acting on this assumption reinforces the original belief that boys and girls are different. Indeed, to children at this age, gender is typically seen as a characteristic that is fixed and permanent. Statements such as "Doctors are men" and "Nurses are women" are uttered as inflexible, objective "truths." Children's views of gender differences reach their "peak rigidity" between five and seven years of age (Trautner et al., 2005). A few years later, though, their attitudes toward gender become considerably more flexible, although such flexibility isn't always reflected in their actual behaviors (C. L. Martin & Ruble, 2004).

It's important to note that gender socialization is not a passive process in which children simply absorb the information that bombards them. As part of the process of finding meaning in their social worlds, children actively construct gender as a social category (Liben & Bigler, 2002). From an early age, they are like "gender detectives," searching for cues about gender, such as who should and shouldn't engage in certain activities, who can play with whom, and why girls and boys differ (C. L. Martin & Ruble, 2004, p. 67).

Parents and other family members sometimes provide children with explicit instructions on proper gender behavior, such as "Big boys don't cry" or "Act like a young lady." More commonly, though, such instruction is more subtle. Decades' worth of research shows that parents speak differently to and play differently with their sons and daughters, often without realizing it. For instance, one study of mothers' reactions to their children's misbehaviors found that they tend to be more concerned about injuries and safety issues with their daughters and tend to focus more on disciplinary issues with their sons (Morrongiello & Hogg, 2004). In another study, parents were instructed to tell their children stories about their own childhoods. In doing so, they were more likely to highlight themes of autonomy and independence when they had sons than when they had daughters (Fiese & Skillman, 2000). Fathers spend more time with their sons and engage in more physical play with them than with their daughters, whereas mothers are more emotionally responsive to girls and encourage more independence with boys (Lanvers, 2004; Raley & Bianchi, 2006). Interestingly, parents—especially parents who claim to be gender neutral in the raising of their children—often fail to acknowledge their socializing role and resort to biological explanations about "hard wiring" when their kids behave in gender stereotypical ways (Kane, 2006).

As children grow older, parents tend to encourage increasingly gender-typed activities (Liben & Bigler, 2002). Research consistently shows that children's household tasks differ along gender lines (Antill, Goodnow, Russell, & Cotton, 1996). For instance, boys are more likely to mow the lawn, shovel snow, take out the garbage, and do the yard work, whereas girls tend to clean the house, wash dishes, cook, and babysit their younger siblings (L. White & Brinkerhoff, 1981). These discrepancies are clearly linked to the different social roles ascribed to men and women, which are discussed in more detail in Chapter 12.

Gender instructions seem to be particularly rigid and restrictive for U.S. boys. Indeed, the social costs for "gender-inappropriate" behavior are disproportionately severe for boys. One study found that girls' play patterns become less stereotypical as they age; boys, however, must remain ardently masculine (Cherney & London, 2006). As one author put it, girls can still be girls, but boys *must* be boys (Orenstein, 2008).

It's worth noting, however, that not all parents subscribe so tightly to traditional gender expectations when it comes to raising their sons. A small but growing number of parents have begun to advocate a gender-fluid approach to childrearing by, for instance, allowing their sons to wear dresses and high heels, if that's what they want to do. They refer to their children as "pink boys"—males with a strong interest in traditionally female presentation who still identify as boys (Padawer, 2012). They want their children to occupy the "middle space" between traditional boyhood and traditional girlhood. Although they are fully aware of the problems these boys will face when they display their appearance preferences in public (both from other children as well as adults), they argue that nobody fits the dichotomous gender categories perfectly anyway, so why should they crush their child's individuality by forcing them uncomfortably into a traditional gender group? But their battle is an uphill one as they fight against a community of others whose responses range from confused to hostile.

For the most part, parents participate in gender socialization through the things they routinely provide for their children: clothes, adornments, books, toys, videos, and so forth. Clothes not only provide visible markers of gender; they also send messages about how that person ought to be treated and direct behavior along traditional gender lines (Shakin, Shakin, & Sternglanz, 1985). Frilly outfits do not lend themselves easily to rough-and-tumble play. Likewise, it is difficult to walk quickly or assertively in high heels and tight miniskirts. Clothes for boys and men rarely restrict physical movement in this way. Toys and games are an especially influential source of gender information parents provide their children.

INSTITUTIONS AND SOCIALIZATION

It should be clear by now that becoming who we are is a complex process embedded in the larger social structure. We are much more than the sum of our anatomical and neurological parts. Cultural attitudes toward class, race, and gender can dramatically affect our personal identities. But various social institutions—in particular, the educational system, religious organizations, and the mass media—exert considerable influence on our self-concept, our values, and our perspectives as well.

Education

In contemporary industrial societies, the most powerful institutional agent of socialization, after the family, is education. In fact, according to the structural-functionalist perspective, the primary reason schools exist is to socialize young people. Children formally enter the school system around age five, when they begin kindergarten, although many enter earlier in preschool or nursery school. At this point, the "personalized" instruction of the family is replaced by the "impersonalized" instruction of the school, where children in most developed countries will remain for the next 13 years or longer. No other nonfamily institution has such extended and consistent control over a person's social growth.

Although schools are officially charged with equipping students with the knowledge and skills they need to fulfill various roles in society (e.g., reading, writing, mathematics, science), they also teach students important social, political, and economic values. When students set up simulated grocery stores or banks, they are learning about the importance of free enterprise and finance in a capitalist society; when they hold mock elections, they are being introduced to a democratic political system; when they spend time tending a school garden or setting up recycling bins, they are learning to nurture the earth.

More subtly, schools teach students what they can expect for themselves in the world. In many school districts, children are grouped into different programs, or tracks, based on an assessment of their academic abilities. In a typical high school, for example, some students will take courses designed to prepare them for college, whereas others will take more general or vocational courses designed to prepare them for work after they graduate. *Tracking* clearly determines future outcomes: Students in the higher tracks often go on to prestigious universities; those in the lower tracks may not go to college at all. Tracking can, therefore, ultimately affect employment opportunities, income levels, and overall quality of life.

Some sociologists argue that schooling in most cultures is designed not so much to provide children with factual information and encourage creativity as to produce passive, nonproblematic conformists who will fit into the existing social order (Gracey, 1991). Although American schools still, for the most part, emphasize order and discipline, educators are beginning to pay more attention to the importance of creativity, developing curricula that incorporate innovation and problem solving into all subject areas, not just the arts. Some schools even work to instill values that seem at odds with existing social arrangements. One school system in Minnesota, for example, is experimenting with a novel approach to teaching and learning in its elementary schools. Instead of forcing students to sit still during class time, teachers allow them to stand up and move around as much as they want. Even the desks are adjustable so students can stand at them to work if they like. Teachers claim that students sustain their attention longer and learn better than those in more traditional classrooms (Saulny, 2009b).

Because formal education is so important in the everyday lives of most children, the agenda of a particular school system, regardless of its philosophy or method, cannot help but influence the types of people they will eventually become.

Religion

As the structural-functionalist perspective tells us, religion is the social institution that tends to the spiritual needs of individuals and serves as a major source of cultural knowledge. It plays a key role in developing people's ideas about right and wrong. It also helps form people's identities by providing coherence and continuity to the episodes that make up each individual's life (Kearl, 1980). Religious rites of passage, such as baptisms, bar and bat mitzvahs, confirmations, and weddings, reaffirm an individual's religious identity while impressing on him or her the rights and obligations attached to each new status (J. H. Turner, 1972).

Religion occupies a complex place in U.S. life. Structural changes in society have made religious affiliation somewhat unstable in recent years. For instance, as people move from one location to another, many of the ties that bind them to the same religion—most notably, networks of family and friends—are broken. Less than 40% of U.S. residents attend religious services once a week or more (Pew Forum on Religion and Public Life, 2012a). The percentage of Americans who identify with *no* religion grew from 15% in 2008 to 20% in 2012. This group includes over 13 million self-described atheists and agnostics as well as 33 million people who say they have no religious affiliation (Pew Forum on Religion & Public Life, 2012a). The trend is especially pronounced among those younger than 30.

Nevertheless, religion still remains a fundamental socializing agent in most Americans' lives. Compared with most other Western democracies—such as

Canada, Germany, France, Great Britain, and Australia—people in the United States stand out for the depth of their religious beliefs (Zoll, 2005). Consider these facts:

- Eighty-four percent of U.S. adults say that religion plays a big role in their lives (cited in Zoll, 2005). In contrast, 52% of Norwegians and 55% of Swedes say that God doesn't matter to them at all (cited in Ferguson, 2004).
- Ninety-three percent of Americans—including those who report no religious affiliation—believe in God or a "higher power" (cited in Weiner, 2011).
- Eighty-three percent of Americans pray in a given week (The Barna Group, 2007).
- Two thirds of Americans feel that it is important that an American president have strong religious beliefs (Pew Forum on Religion and Public Life, 2004) and that they'd be less likely to vote for a political candidate who didn't believe in God (cited in M. Luo, 2007).
- Two thirds of married Americans had religious weddings and two thirds of Americans, in general, expect to have a religious funeral (Kosmin & Keysar, 2009).
- Among 18- to 29-year-olds who are *not* affiliated with any existing religion, 46% believe in heaven, 54% believe in life after death, and 58% believe in miracles (Pew Forum on Religion and Public Life, 2010).

Furthermore, we still consider ourselves "one nation under God," and our money still proclaims our trust in God. It's virtually impossible these days to watch a music awards show without seeing a winner acknowledging God's role in her or his success or a sporting event without seeing a baseball player cross himself before batting, a football player point skyward after scoring a touchdown, or a basketball player in a postgame interview thank God for guiding the shot that led to his team's victory. Some public schools around the country continue to hold prayer services or bible studies, in spite of the threat of lawsuits by organizations like the American Civil Liberties Union (Eckholm, 2011). Sales of Christian books, computer games, videos, and toys remain robust. Enrollment in evangelical colleges has grown steadily in recent years (MacDonald, 2006), as has the number of families choosing to homeschool their children for religious reasons (Talbot, 2000a).

Mass Media

Another powerful institutional agent of socialization is the media. Newspapers, magazines, television, radio, film, and the Internet transmit persuasive messages on the nature of reality. They are the gatekeepers of political, economic, and social information, defining what is and isn't important (Marger, 2005). They also tell us the type of person we "should" be, from how we should perform our jobs to how different social classes live to what our sexual relationships and families are supposed to look like. The media teach us about prevailing values, beliefs, myths, stereotypes, and trends (Gitlin, 1979) and provide an avenue through which we learn new attitudes and behavior (Bandura & Walters, 1963).

Media exposure is pervasive in the United States. Young people between the ages of 8 and 18 spend an average of six and a half hours a day—or about 45 hours a week—with some type of media, such as television, radio, magazines, and computers (Rideout, Roberts, & Foehr, 2005). And children under the age of eight are spending more time with electronic media than ever—on the order of three and a half hours a day (Common Sense Media, 2011).

With each mass killing—in places like Aurora, Colorado, or Newtown, Connecticut—attention refocuses on the role of violent media in such tragedies. So it's not surprising that sociologists, psychologists, and, of course, politicians continue to debate the degree to which sex and violence in film, television, and video games influence behavior, particularly among young people.

The socializing role of the media is especially apparent when it comes to gender. Children's books, for instance, teach youngsters what other little boys or girls in their culture do and what is expected of them. In the early 1970s, Lenore Weitzman and her colleagues studied the portrayal of gender in popular U.S. preschool books (Weitzman, Eifler, Hodada, & Ross, 1972). They found that boys played a more significant role in the stories than girls by a ratio of 11 to 1. Boys were more likely to be portrayed in adventurous pursuits or activities that required independence and strength; girls were likely to be confined to indoor activities and portrayed as passive and dependent. These gender stereotypes in children's books decreased only slightly over the next several decades (S. B. Peterson & Lach, 1990). Recent attempts to publish more nonsexist children's books have had little impact on the overall market. For instance, elementary school reading textbooks still primarily portray males as aggressive, argumentative, and competitive (L. Evans & Davies, 2000). "Gender equality" in children's books usually involves female characters taking on characteristics and roles typically associated with males. These books rarely, if ever, portray male characters exhibiting feminine traits (Diekman & Murnen, 2004).

Similarly, film and television continue to portray males and females in stereotypical ways. Consider these facts (Geena Davis Institute on Gender in Media, 2012):

- Males outnumber females 3 to 1 in family films, despite the fact that over half the U.S. population is female.
- In feature films, females are almost four times as likely as males to be shown in sexy attire. Further, females are nearly twice as likely as males to be shown with a diminutive waistline that leaves little room for internal organs. In general, unrealistic figures are more likely to be seen on females than males.
- From 2006 to 2009, not one female character in a G-rated family film was depicted in the field of medical science, as a business leader, in law, or in politics. In these films, 8 out of 10 working characters were male, which is a contrast to real world statistics, where women comprise over 50% of the workforce.

Similar gender portrayals exist on television. About 40% of characters on prime-time television drama series are female. The figure drops to 30% on children's shows. Only on reality TV does the proportion of female characters approach that of males (48%). When it comes to occupational depiction on television, traditional gender stereotypes remain. On prime-time shows, women comprise 14% of corporate executives, 28% of high-level politicians, 29% of doctors, and 21% of scientists/engineers (Smith, Choueiti, Prescott, & Pieper, 2012). Even the media coverage of female sports events tends to focus on the physical appearance and sexual attractiveness of the athletes and not just their competitive accomplishments (Billings, Angelini, & Eastman, 2005; Shugart, 2003). In order to revive flagging interest in its sport during the 2012 Summer Olympics, the Badminton World Federation issued an edict requiring all female players to wear short skirts to create a more "attractive presentation" (Longman, 2011).

All of these gender images have a strong influence on children's perceptions and behaviors (Witt, 2005). Children who watch a lot of television are more likely to hold stereotypical attitudes toward gender, exhibit gender-related characteristics, and engage in gender-related activities than children who watch little television (M. Morgan, 1987; Signorielli, 1990). In one study, girls who did not have stereotypical conceptions of gender to begin with showed a significant increase in such attitudes after two years of heavy television watching (M. Morgan, 1982). The more high school students watch talk shows and prime-time programs that depict a lot of sexual activity, the more likely they are to hold traditional sexual stereotypes (Ward & Friedman, 2006).

CONCLUSION

Becoming the people we are is a complex social process. Those intimate characteristics we hold so dear—our self-concept, our gender, and our racial and ethnic identity—reflect larger cultural attitudes, values, and expectations. Yet we are not perfect reflections of society's values. Despite all the powerful socializing institutions that pull our developmental strings, we continue to be and will always be individuals.

Sometimes we ignore our generalized others and strike out on our own with complete disregard for community standards and attitudes. Sometimes we form self-concepts that contradict the information we receive from others about ourselves. Sometimes we willingly violate the expectations associated with our social class, gender, or race. Societal influence can go only so far in explaining how we become who we are. The rest—that which makes us truly unique—remains a fascinating mystery.

CHAPTER HIGHLIGHTS

◆ Socialization is the process by which individuals learn their culture and learn to live according to the norms of a particular society. It is how we learn to perceive our world, gain a sense of our own identity, and interact appropriately with others. It also tells us what we should and should not do across a range of situations.

◆ One of the most important outcomes of socialization for an individual is the development of a sense of self. To acquire a self, children must learn to recognize themselves as unique physical objects, master language, learn to take the roles of others, and, in effect, see themselves from another's perspective.

◆ Socialization is not just a process that occurs during childhood. Adults must be resocialized into a new galaxy of norms, values, and expectations each time they leave or abandon old roles and enter new ones.

◆ Through socialization, we learn the social expectations that go with our social class, racial or ethnic group, and gender.

◆ Socialization occurs within the context of several social institutions—family first, and then schools, religious institutions, and the mass media.

KEY TERMS

agents of socialization: Various individuals, groups, and organizations that influence the socialization process

anticipatory socialization: Process through which people acquire the values and orientations found in statuses they will likely enter in the future

collectivist culture: Culture in which personal accomplishments are less important in the formation of identity than group membership

eugenics: Control of mating to ensure that "defective" genes of troublesome individuals will not be passed on to future generations

game stage: Stage in the development of self during which a child acquires the ability to take the role of a group or community (the generalized other) and conform his or her behavior to broad societal expectations

gender: Psychological, social, and cultural aspects of maleness and femaleness

generalized other: Perspective of the larger society and its constituent values and attitudes

identity: Essential aspect of who we are, consisting of our sense of self, gender, race, ethnicity, and religion

individualist culture: Culture in which personal accomplishments are a more important component of one's self-concept than group membership

looking-glass self: Sense of who we are that is defined by incorporating the reflected appraisals of others

play stage: Stage in the development of self during which a child develops the ability to take a role, but only from the perspective of one person at a time

reflexive behavior: Behavior in which the person initiating an action is the same as the person toward whom the action is directed

resocialization: Process of learning new values, norms, and expectations when an adult leaves an old role and enters a new one

role taking: Ability to see oneself from the perspective of others and to use that perspective in formulating one's own behavior

self: Unique set of traits, behaviors, and attitudes that distinguishes one person from the next; the active source and passive object of behavior

sex: Biological maleness or femaleness

socialization: Process through which one learns how to act according to the rules and expectations of a particular culture

total institution: Place where individuals are cut off from the wider society for an appreciable period and where together they lead an enclosed, formally administered life

tracking: Grouping of students into different curricular programs, or tracks, based on an assessment of their academic abilities

Supporting Identity

The Presentation of Self

Forming Impressions of Others

Managing Impressions

Mismanaging Impressions: Spoiled Identities

O n Christmas Day, 1981, I met my (former) wife's family for the first time. We had just started dating, so I knew for this group of important strangers, I had to be on my best behavior and say and do all the right things. I wanted to make sure the impression they formed of me was that of a likable fellow whom they'd be proud to call a member of the family someday.

As people busily opened their presents, I noticed the wide and gleeful eyes of my wife's 14-year-old sister as she unwrapped what was to her a special gift—her very own basketball. Being the youngest in a family of eight kids, she didn't have much she could call her own, so this was a significant moment for her. She had finally broken away from a life filled with hand-me-downs and communal equipment. She hugged that ball as if it were a puppy.

I saw my chance to make the perfect first impression. "I'm not a bad basketball player," I thought to myself. "I'll take her outside to the basketball hoop in the driveway, dazzle her with my shooting skills, become her idol, and win family approval."

"Hey, Mary," I said, "let's go out and shoot some hoops." After we stepped outside, I grabbed the new ball from her. "Watch this," I said as I flung it toward the basket from about 40 feet away. We both watched as the ball arced gracefully toward its destination, and for a brief moment, I actually thought it was going to go in. But that was not to be.

As if guided by the taunting hand of fate, the ball struck an exposed bolt that protruded from the supporting pole of the hoop. There was a sickeningly loud pop, followed by a hissing sound as the ball fluttered to the ground like a deflated balloon. It sat there lifeless, never having experienced the joy of "swishing" through a net. For that matter, it had never even been bounced on the ground in its short-lived inflated state.

For a few seconds, we both stood numb and motionless. Then I turned to apologize to the 14-year-old girl, whose once cheerful eyes now harbored the kind of hate and resentment usually reserved for ax murderers and IRS auditors. In a flash, she burst into tears and ran into the house shrieking, "*That guy* popped my ball!" It was hardly the heroic identity I was striving for. As the angry mob poured into the backyard to stare at the villainous and still somewhat unknown perpetrator, I became painfully aware of the fragile nature of the self-images we try to project to others.

We all have been in situations—a first date, a job interview, a first meeting with a girlfriend or boyfriend's family—in which we feel compelled to "make a good impression." We try to present a favorable image of ourselves so that others will form positive judgments of us. This phenomenon is not only an important and universal aspect of our personal lives but a key element of social structure as well.

In this chapter, I examine the social creation of images. How do we form impressions of others? What do we do to control the impressions others form of us? I also discuss the broader sociological applications of these actions. What are the institutional motivations behind individuals' attempts to control others' impressions of them? How do groups and organizations present and manage collective impressions? Finally, what happens when these attempts fail and images are spoiled, as mine was when my errant jump shot murdered a girl's brand-new basketball?

FORMING IMPRESSIONS OF OTHERS

When we first meet someone, we form an immediate impression based on observable cues such as age, ascribed status characteristics such as race and sex, individual attributes such as physical appearance, and verbal and nonverbal expressions. This process of *impression formation* helps us form a quick picture of the other person's identity.

Keep in mind that the importance of this information—the value attached to a certain age, race, or sex; the particular physical or personality traits a society defines as desirable; the meaning of certain words and gestures—varies across time and place. Hence, the impressions that people form of others must always be understood within the appropriate cultural and historical contexts. For instance, an emotionally expressive person in the United States may give the impression of being energetic and outgoing; in the United Kingdom such a person may seem boorish and rude; and in Thailand or Japan that person may be considered dangerous or crazy.

Social Group Membership

We can often determine people's age, sex, race, and to a certain degree ethnicity merely by looking at them; social class is less obvious but sometimes becomes known early in an encounter with another person through her or his language, mannerisms, or dress. Our socialization experiences have taught us to expect that people displaying these signs of social group membership have certain characteristics in common. For instance, if all you know about a person you've not yet met is that she's 85 years old, you might predict that she has low energy, a poor memory, and a conservative approach to life. Think about your expectations when you learn that your new roommate is from a different region of this country—or, for that matter, from a different country. Of course, such expectations are rarely completely accurate. Nevertheless, we typically begin social interactions with these culturally defined conceptions of how people from certain social groups are likely to act, what their tastes and preferences might be, and what values and attitudes they are likely to hold.

This information is so pervasive and so quickly processed that we usually notice it only when it is ambiguous or unavailable. If you spend a lot of time texting or tweeting with strangers, you may have noticed how difficult it can be to form a friendship or carry on a discussion when you don't know whether you are conversing with someone of the same sex or with someone of a different sex or whether the person is much older or much younger than you are. Social group membership provides the necessary backdrop to all encounters between people who have little if any prior knowledge of one another.

Physical Appearance

We confirm or modify early impressions based on social group membership by assessing other characteristics that are also readily perceivable, such as a person's physical appearance (Berndt & Heller, 1986). The way people dress and decorate their bodies communicates their feelings, beliefs, and group identity to others. People's clothes, jewelry, hairstyles, and so on can also indicate their ethnicity, social class, age, cultural tastes, morality, and political attitudes.

But again, these impressions can be influenced by our cultural background. Physical appearance is enormously important in U.S. culture. Everywhere we turn, it seems, we are encouraged to believe that if our skin isn't perfect, if we are too short or too tall, if we are over- or underweight, if our hair isn't stylish, if our clothes don't reflect the latest fashion trend, we have fallen short of some attractiveness threshold. Although we readily acknowledge that using a person's physical appearance to form an impression is shallow and unfair, most of us do it anyway.

The famous Greek philosopher Aristotle once said, "personal beauty is a greater recommendation than any letter of introduction." Contemporary research confirms that physical appearance affects our perceptions of others. Attractive men are perceived as more masculine, and attractive women more feminine than their less attractive counterparts (Gillen, 1981). We often assume that good-looking people possess other desirable traits, such as sensitivity, kindness, strength, and sexual responsiveness (Dion, Berscheid, & Walster, 1972). Such judgments can sometimes be converted to financial gain. Economists have coined the term "beauty premium" to refer to the economic advantages attractive people enjoy:

> Handsome men earn, on average, 5% more than their less-attractive counterparts (good-looking women earn 4% more); pretty people get more attention from teachers, bosses, and mentors. . . . Fifty seven percent of hiring managers [in a recent survey indicated that] qualified but unattractive candidates are likely to have a harder time landing a job, while more than half advised spending as much time and money on "making sure they look attractive" as on perfecting a résumé. (J. Bennett, 2010, p. 47)

But beauty is not always associated with positive impressions. For instance, people might assume that those who are extremely attractive are spoiled or aren't particularly intelligent. In Malawi, a southeast African country with a high rate of HIV infection, women who are *too* beautiful are often subject to suspicious gossip. People who are HIV positive tend to be extremely thin as AIDS takes its toll on the body. Some of the most effective treatments for HIV are antiretroviral drugs (ARVs; see Chapter 14). One of the side effects of the drug is weight gain and smooth skin. Hence others might presume that women who look *too* healthy must be taking ARVs, meaning that they are HIV positive and not desirable sexual partners (Koenig, 2011).

On the flip side, ugliness has always occupied a lowly place on the social landscape. In literature and film, ugliness is usually associated with evil and fear, characterizing all manner of monsters, witches, and villains (Kershaw, 2008). Beyond fictional portrayals, unattractiveness can have serious everyday consequences. For instance, one study found that even in occupations where looks have no bearing on a person's ability to do his or her job—like computer programming—unattractive workers suffer discrimination (Mobius & Rosenblat, 2006). Many parents these days are becoming less tolerant of any flaw in their children's appearance. Numerous websites now offer retouching services so that parents can airbrush photos of their children to remove blemishes, crooked teeth, and other facial imperfections (J. Bennett, 2008).

Physical attractiveness is still a more salient interpersonal and economic issue for women than for men, even though women have more money, political clout, and legal recognition today than ever. For instance, 61% of hiring managers indicate that it's advantageous for a woman to "show off her figure" in the workplace (cited in J. Bennett, 2010). An article about a talented, all-female chamber music trio called Eroica stated, "The Eroica Trio not only plays beautiful music, it has also created a marketing sensation for being 'easy on the eye'" (W. Smith, 2002, p. 4). Here's how one columnist described the way Australians treated that country's first female prime minister:

> For the three years and three days that Julia Gillard was prime minister of Australia, we debated the fit of her jackets, the size of her bottom, the exposure of her cleavage, the cut of her hair, the tone of her

voice, the legitimacy of her rule and whether she had chosen, as one member of Parliament . . . put it, to be "deliberately barren" (Baird, 2013, p. A17).

It's hard to imagine physical appearance being the hub of this kind of attention for male political leaders, not to mention male employees or classical musicians.

Women around the world routinely inflict serious pain and injury on themselves as they alter their bodies to conform to cultural definitions of beauty. In China, for example, hundreds of women each year, convinced that being taller would improve their job and marriage prospects, subject themselves to a procedure in which their leg bones are broken, separated, and stretched. Metal pins and screws pull the bones apart a fraction of a millimeter a day, sometimes for close to two years. Many Chinese women have lost the ability to walk from this treatment; others have suffered permanent, disfiguring bone damage (C. S. Smith, 2002). In the United States, affluent women sometimes undergo potentially dangerous cosmetic foot surgery to reduce the size of their toes so that they can fit into fashionable, narrow high-heeled shoes (G. Harris, 2003). In 2010, girls and women began wearing decorative "circle lenses," brightly colored contact lenses that make eyes appear larger because they cover not just the iris, as ordinary lenses do, but part of the Whites as well (Saint Louis, 2010). These lenses, which give wearers a childlike, doe-eyed appearance, are available online without a prescription, much to the chagrin of eye doctors who fear the damage they may cause. A spokesperson for the Food and Drug Administration wrote that consumers risk significant eye injury, even blindness, when they buy contact lenses without a valid prescription.

At the individual level, the emphasis on physical appearance devalues a person's other attributes and accomplishments; at the institutional level, it plays an important role in the nation's economy by sustaining several multibillion-dollar enterprises, including the advertising, fashion, cosmetics, and weight-loss industries.

Verbal and Nonverbal Expression

Another important piece of information we use in forming impressions of others is what people express to us verbally or nonverbally. Obviously, we form impressions of others based on what they tell us about themselves. But beyond speech, people's movements, postures, and gestures provide cues about their values, attitudes, sentiments, personality, and history (Stone, 1981). Sometimes people use these forms of communication purposely to convey meaning, as when they put on a smile so that others will find them approachable. However, some physical expressions, such as a shaky voice, a flushed face, and trembling hands, are difficult to control. They transmit an impression whether we want to or not.

Most of us are quite proficient at "reading" even the subtlest nonverbal messages. We learn early on that a raised eyebrow, a nod of the head, or a slight hand gesture can mean something important in a social encounter. So crucial is this ability in maintaining orderly interactions that some psychologists consider a deficiency in it to be a learning disability akin to severe reading problems (Goleman, 1989).

MANAGING IMPRESSIONS

People form impressions of others and present impressions of themselves at the same time. This ability to influence the impressions others make of us is the defining feature of human interaction. Naturally, we try to create impressions of ourselves that give us advantages—by making us seem attractive or powerful or otherwise worthy of people's attention and esteem. Of course, that's what I was trying to do when I attempted the ill-fated jump shot with my future sister-in-law's new basketball.

The process by which people attempt to present a favorable public image of themselves is called *impression management*. Erving Goffman (1959), the sociologist most responsible for the scholarly examination of impression management, portrays everyday life as a series of social interactions in which a person is motivated to "sell" a particular image to others. The primary goal of impression management is to project a particular identity that will increase the likelihood of obtaining favorable outcomes from others in particular social situations (E. E. Jones & Pittman, 1982; Stryker, 1980). To do so, we can strategically furnish or conceal information. At times, we may need to advertise, exaggerate, or even fabricate our positive qualities; at other times, we conceal or camouflage behaviors or attributes that we believe others will find unappealing.

The prominent role that social media now plays in our lives has created new challenges for impression management. Recall our discussion of role taking in Chapter 5. In our "offline" lives, we interact with various people each day: family, acquaintances, coworkers, friends from different corners of our lives. Consequently, we have the opportunity to express multiple selves and manage different impressions that suit our different immediate needs. You need not be the same person with your friends as you are with your grandparents. As long as you keep these disparate groups apart, you're OK. But online—when, say, we're selecting a picture or posting photos on our Facebook page—we have one shot at managing the impression we want others to form of us. And it's an impression various people who have come to know us under very different circumstances could have access to. Similarly, on Twitter, once we tweet, it's out there forever, remaining in the feed of whoever is following us. That's a lot of pressure. Facebook seems to acknowledge the necessity for managing multiple selves by allowing users to customize impressions to particular selected audiences through privacy settings and friend lists.

Whether it occurs online or in offline, face-to-face interaction, obtaining favorable outcomes through impression management is usually associated with social approval—that is, with being respected and liked by others. However, different circumstances may require projecting different identities (E. E. Jones & Pittman, 1982). Perhaps you've been in situations where you've tried to appear helpless in order to get someone else to do a task you really didn't want to do, or maybe you've tried to appear mean and fearsome to intimidate someone. Perhaps you've "played dumb" to avoid challenging a superior (Gove, Hughes, & Geerkin, 1980). As social beings, we have the ability to tailor our images to fit the requirements of a particular situation.

Goffman argues that impression management is not used just to present false or inflated images of ourselves. Many authentic attributes we possess are not immediately apparent to others; sometimes our actions may be misinterpreted. Imagine yourself taking the final exam in your sociology course. You look up from your paper and make brief eye contact with the instructor. You're not cheating, but you think the instructor may interpret your wandering eyes as an indication of cheating. What do you do? Chances are you will consciously overemphasize your noncheating behavior by acting as though you're deep in thought or by glancing up at the clock to highlight your "law-abiding" image.

Frequently people try to present a favorable image of themselves by altering their physical appearance.

Clothing and body adornment can be used to manipulate and manage the impressions others form of us. People can dress to convey the impression that they are worthy of respect or, at the very least, attention (Lauer & Handel, 1977). Some research has shown that women who dress in a traditionally masculine way during a job interview are more likely to be hired. Likewise, students perceive teachers who dress formally as more intelligent than teachers who dress casually (cited in Blakeslee, 2012).

Children often signal their entry into the world of adolescence by wearing the clothing of their peers and refusing to wear the clothing chosen by their parents (Stone, 1981). The purveyors of various music subcultures like pop, hip-hop, heavy metal, rave, hipster, dance/house/techno, and goth use clothing and hairstyle as an expression of identity and social rebellion. And as you are well aware, fashion is a significant element of the student subculture on most college campuses (Moffatt, 1989). In short, by what they wear, people tell one another who they are, where they come from, and what they stand for.

Interestingly, a growing scientific field called "embodied cognition" takes the importance of clothing one step further, arguing that what we wear can actually change how we perform. In one psychological experiment, subjects who were given white lab coats to wear made about half as many errors in a test of sustained attention and memory as subjects who wore regular clothes. Even when they were given a painter's coat but *told* it was a doctor's coat, they outperformed others (cited in Blakeslee, 2012).

Dramaturgy: Actors on a Social Stage

"All the world's a stage, / And all the men and women merely players: / They have their exits and their entrances; / And one man in his time plays many parts," wrote William Shakespeare in *As You Like It*. Analyzing social interaction as a series of theatrical performances—what sociologists call **dramaturgy**—has been a staple of symbolic interactionism for decades. Like Shakespeare, Goffman (1959) argues that people in everyday life are similar to actors on a stage. The "audience" consists of people who observe the behavior of others, "roles" are the images people are trying to project, and the "script" is the content of their communication with others. The goal is to enact a performance that is believable to a particular audience and that allows us to achieve the goals we desire. Just about every aspect of social life can be examined dramaturgically, from the ritualized greetings of strangers to the everyday dynamics of our family, school, and work lives.

Front Stage and Back Stage

A key structural element of dramaturgy is the distinction between front stage and back stage. In the theater, front stage is where the performance takes place for the audience. In contrast, back stage is where makeup is removed, lines are rehearsed, and performances are rehashed, and where people can fall "out of character."

In social life, *front stage* is where people maintain the appropriate appearance as they interact with others. For workers in a restaurant, front stage is the dining room where the customers (the audience) are present. Here, the servers (the actors) are expected to present themselves as upbeat, happy, competent, and courteous. *Back stage*, however, is the region where people can knowingly violate their impression management performances. In the restaurant, back stage is the kitchen area where the once courteous servers now shout, shove dishes, and even complain about or mock the customers.

As in the theater, the barrier between front and back stage is crucial to successful impression management because it blocks the audience from seeing behavior that would ruin the performance. During a therapy session (front stage), psychiatrists usually appear extremely interested in everything their patients say and show considerable sympathy for their problems. At a dinner party with colleagues or at home with family (back stage), however, they may express total boredom with and disdain for their patients' disclosures. If patients were to see such back stage behavior, not only would it disrupt the performance, but it would damage the psychiatrist's professional credibility and reputation as well. One study found that beneath their masks of neutrality, many psychiatrists harbor strong and professionally inappropriate feelings—including hatred, fear, anger, and sexual arousal—toward their patients (cited in Goleman, 1993).

Props

Successful impression management also depends on the control of objects, called props, that convey identity. In the theater, props must be handled deftly for an effective performance. A gun that doesn't go off when it's supposed to or a chair that unexpectedly collapses can destroy an entire play. The same is true in social interaction. For instance, college students may make sure their schoolbooks are in clear view and beer bottles disposed of as they prepare for an upcoming visit from their parents. Similarly, someone may spend a great deal of time setting a romantic mood for a dinner date at home—the right music, the right lighting, pictures of former lovers hidden from view, and so on.

Sometimes people use props to create an environment that reinforces some individuals' authority over others. Note the way props were used to intimidate this professor as he testified before Congress:

> And then I was called to the witness stand. Now, the chair is something nobody talks about. It is low and extremely puffy. When you sit in it your butt just keeps sinking, and suddenly the tabletop is up to your chest. The senators peer down at you from above, and the power dynamic is terrifying. (H. Jenkins, 1999, p. 21)

Props needn't be inanimate objects. To convey to potential clients and investors what they believe will be an air of prestige, money, and crucial global connections, some Chinese companies now "rent" white foreigners to pose as fake employees. The companies hope that the presence of these individuals will help to secure a contract or simply support the company's claim of being internationally successful. An ad in a Chinese newspaper for a company called Rent-a-*Laowai* (Chinese for "foreigner") read: "Occasionally companies want a foreign face to go to meetings and conferences or to go to dinners and lunches and smile at the clients and shake people's hands" (quoted in Farrar, 2010, p. 1).

Viewing impression management from a dramaturgical perspective reminds us that our everyday actions rarely occur in a social vacuum. Indeed, our behaviors are often structured with an eye toward how they might be perceived by particular "audiences."

Image Making

In our individualistic, competitive society, appearances can sometimes provide a critically important edge. A person's desire to maximize prestige, wealth, and power can be the driving force behind a thorough makeover. These efforts are not things a person undertakes on his or her own. Whole industries have evolved that are devoted to making and remaking images for the public eye.

The desire to manage impressions by changing physical appearance motivates some people to do far more than try a new hairstyle, get a tattoo, or buy a new outfit or two. Even in economic hard times, people in the United States are willing to spend huge sums of money to medically alter their looks. According to the American Society of Plastic Surgeons (2011), there were 1.6 million cosmetic surgery procedures and close to 12 million minimally invasive, nonsurgical procedures (such as Botox injections, cellulite treatments, and chemical peels) in the United States in 2010. Ninety-one percent of the patients were women. These figures represent a 77% increase over 2000. The overall cost for these procedures was about $10.2 billion. The desire to surgically alter one's appearance is not unique to the United States:

- Doctors perform more plastic surgeries per capita in South Korea than anywhere else in the world; the U.S. ranks sixth. It's estimated that one in five women in Seoul have had some kind of cosmetic surgery (International Society of Aesthetic Plastic Surgery, 2011). One of the most common procedures is blepharoplasty, an eyelid surgery that gives a rounder, more "Western" look to the eye (*Daily Mail*, 2012).
- Brazil leads the world in the number of liposuction procedures and nose jobs performed each year (International Society of Aesthetic Plastic Surgery, 2011). In 2001, the Brazilian contestant in the Miss Universe contest scandalized many non-Brazilians by speaking freely and publicly about her breast implants, cheekbone reconstruction, silicone remolding of her chin, pinned-back ears, and liposuction. She told reporters, "I have to work on my figure to get it where I want it. It's something I need for my profession. . . . I have a doctorate in body measurement" (Kulick & Machado-Borges, 2005, p. 128).
- In China, the growing cosmetic surgery industry takes in over $2.4 billion a year as people with new-found affluence rush to go under the knife. As one Chinese student put it, "In China we say there are no ugly women, only lazy women" (quoted in Savacool, 2009, p. 62). The number of Chinese receiving cosmetic plastic surgery doubles each year. As in South Korea, the most commonly requested procedure is one designed to make the eyes appear larger and

more "Western" (LaFraniere, 2011). In fact, China now hosts an annual *Renzao Meinu* or "artificial beauty" contest, where people from all over the globe compete to become the world's most beautiful product of plastic surgery (Savacool, 2009).

The growing popularity of cosmetic surgery reflects an alarming level of discontent among people about the way they look. Researchers estimate that 30% to 40% of U.S. adults have concerns about some aspect of their physical appearance (Gorbis & Kholodenko, 2005). And over 2% of the population is so self-conscious about their looks that their lives are constricted in some significant way, from feeling inhibited during lovemaking to becoming homebound or even suicidal (American Psychiatric Association, 2013). This condition, called "body dysmorphic disorder," has become more common over the past decade or so (Wartik, 2003). About half of these individuals seek some sort of professional medical intervention, like surgery or dermatological treatment (Gorbis & Kholodenko, 2005). Indeed, the number of Americans undergoing weight reduction surgery, such as stomach banding, has increased seven-fold over the past decade, at a cost of over $6 billion annually (cited in Hartocollis, 2012b).

Social Influences on Impression Management

Up to this point, I've described impression management and dramaturgy from the viewpoint of individual actors driven by a personal desire to present themselves in the most advantageous light possible. But social group membership may also influence the sorts of images a person tries to present in social interaction. The elements of one's identity—age, gender, race and ethnicity, religion, social class, occupational status—influence others' immediate expectations, which can be self-fulfilling. In other words, members of certain social groups may manage impressions somewhat differently than nonmembers because of society's preconceived notions about them. Race or ethnicity and social status are among the most notable influences on impression management.

Race and Ethnicity

In a society where race is a primary source of inequality, people of color often learn that they will be rewarded if they assimilate to "white norms" and hide the elements of their ethnoracial culture.

According to Kenji Yoshino (2006), a law professor, the pressure to "act white" means that people of color must suppress the nonwhite aspects of their hairstyles, clothing, and speech. They must also monitor their social activities, participation in ethnic or race-based organizations or political causes, and friendship networks. The comedian Dave Chappelle once said that African Americans must be "bilingual" if they want to make it in this society. In other words, they become adept at identifying situations, like job interviews, where they must eliminate "black" patterns of speech and "speak white" (Chaudhry, 2006).

Such impression management strategies may increase the likelihood of economic benefit, but they are not without social costs. As then-Senator Barack Obama said in a 2004 speech at the Democratic National Convention, "Children [of color] can't achieve unless we raise their expectations and . . . eradicate the slander that says a black youth with a book is acting white" (quoted in Fryer, 2006, p. 53). People of color who "act white" in some situations but perform a different version of their identity when with others like themselves run the risk of being considered sellouts or tagged as "Oreo cookies," "bananas," or "coconuts"—that is, black or yellow or brown on the outside and white on the inside—by members of their ethnoracial communities (Chaudhry, 2006).

Moreover, it's only the relatively affluent who have the opportunity to learn how to act white. Others—Pakistani cab drivers, Latina housekeepers, Korean grocery store clerks, to name a few—have no such option. Indeed, living up (or down) to certain ethnoracial stereotypes may be one of the few ways people can participate actively in public life while retaining their own cultural identity. In the past, for example, Native Americans often complained that in interactions with members of other ethnoracial groups, they were expected to "act Indian" by wearing traditional garb or speaking in the stilted manner of media stereotypes. Contemporary rap and hip-hop stars are often criticized for conforming to unflattering black stereotypes in order to appeal to white, middle-class audiences. But while individuals from disadvantaged groups may appear to fit common racial or ethnic stereotypes in public (front stage), an analysis of private (back stage) behavior often indicates that they are keenly aware of the identities they've been forced to present.

Social Status

A person's relative position in society can also influence impression management. Some working-class youths, frustrated by their lack of access to the middle-class world and their inability to meet the requirements of "respectability" as defined by the dominant culture, may present themselves as malicious or dangerous. A tough image helps them gain attention or achieve status and respect within their group (A. Campbell, 1987; A. K. Cohen, 1955).

Conversely, those who occupy the dominant classes of society can get the attention and respect we all want with very little effort (Derber, 1979). They get special consideration in restaurants, shops, and other public settings. They monopolize the starring roles in politics and economics and also claim more than their share of attention in ordinary interactions. By displaying the symbolic props of material success—large homes, tasteful furnishings, luxury cars, expensive clothes and jewelry—people know that they can impress others and thereby reinforce their own sense of worth and status.

Prior to the recent economic recession, the visual trappings of social class had become harder to spot. When credit was easily available, more U.S. adults had access to the traditional high-end props of the well to do. A middle-class family could own a flat-screen television or a fancy sports car. Just a few years ago, 81% of respondents in one study indicated that they had felt some pressure to buy high-priced goods (cited in Steinhauer, 2005). So the extremely wealthy ratcheted up the visual display of social status, buying even more expensive products, such as $130,000 cars, $7,000 smartphones, and $400 bottles of wine, and using posh services like personal chefs and private jets. Tougher times, however, have led even the super rich to become a bit more discreet in their public displays of wealth:

> Fabulous home theaters are tucked into the basements of plain suburban houses. Bespoke jeans that start at $1,200 can be detected only by a tiny red logo on the button. The hand-painted Italian bicycles that flash across Silicon Valley on Saturday mornings have become the new Ferrari. (Sengupta, 2012, p. A1)

Indeed, ostentatious displays of wealth have become the object of public anger and ridicule. You may recall the firestorm that erupted in the media in 2009, when the chief executives of the major U.S. automakers flew to Washington, DC, in their private jets to appeal for federal bailout money. In fact, some public figures—like Facebook CEO Mark Zuckerberg and his trademark hoodie—take great pains to distance themselves from their upper-class or "elite" backgrounds. Every election cycle, we watch all manner of exceedingly wealthy candidates go through the charade of altering their clothing, mannerisms, tastes, and vocabulary to show voters that "they're less loftily removed from the so-called common man than they really are" (Bruni, 2012, p. 3).

Status differences in impression management permeate the workplace as well. Those at the very top of an organization need not advertise their high status because it is already known to the people with whom they interact regularly. Their occupational status is a permanently recognized "badge of ability" (Derber, 1979, p. 83). Others, however, must consciously solicit the attention to which they feel they are entitled. For example, physicians in hospitals may wear stethoscopes and white lab coats to communicate their high-status identity to patients; female doctors are especially inclined to wear the white coats so they will not be mistaken for nurses. These status markers become especially powerful when compared with patients, who are often required to shed their own clothes and don revealing hospital-issue garments. It's hard to appear powerful and be taken seriously in a conversation with a doctor when you're barefoot and naked under a paper gown (D. Franklin, 2006).

Some indicators of occupational status have become the source of conflict, however. In recent years, thousands of nurses have returned to school to earn their PhDs in nursing. As a result, they are entitled to—and often do—refer to themselves as "Doctor So-and-So" while at work in hospitals. Needless to say, many physicians oppose the use of such titles, seeing it as a threat to their professional authority and stature (Harris, 2011a). And they're fighting back. A bill proposed in the Florida state senate would bar nurses from calling themselves doctors, no matter what their degree. In Arizona and Delaware, nurses, pharmacists, and other health care providers who aren't physicians are forbidden from referring to themselves as "Doctor" unless they immediately identify their profession (Waldrop, 2013).

Impression management plays a prominent role in the socialization process within many professions (Hochschild, 1983). Managers and CEOs in large companies, for instance, become acutely aware through their rise up the corporate ladder of the image they must exude through dress and demeanor. Salespeople are trained to present themselves as knowledgeable, trustworthy, and, above all, honest. Medical students learn how to manage their emotions in front of patients and to present the image of "competent physicians." New teachers learn what images are most effective in getting students to comply. This teacher's assessment of the importance of impression management more than 50 years ago still rings true today:

> You can't ever let them get the upper hand on you or you're through. So I start out tough. The first day I get a new class in, I let them know who's boss. . . . You've got to start off tough, then you can ease up as you go along. If you start out easygoing, when you try to be tough, they'll just look at you and laugh. (E. Goffman, 1959, p. 12)

In any given interaction, one person is likely to have more power than others (Wrong, 1988). When we first hear the word *power*, we think of it in terms of orders, threats, and coercion. But noncoercive forms of power—the signs and symbols of dominance, the subtle messages of threat, the gestures of submission—are much more common to impression management in social encounters (Henley, 1977). The humiliation of being powerless is felt by people who are ignored or interrupted, are intimidated by another's presence, are afraid to approach or touch a superior, or have their privacy freely invaded by another.

The norms that govern the way people address each other also reflect underlying power differences. For instance, the conversations that take place between friends or siblings are commonly marked by the mutual use of informal terms such as first names or nicknames. When status is unequal, though, the lower-status person is often required to use terms of respect such as *Sir* or *Ma'am* or *Doctor*. In the South in years past, every white person had the privilege of addressing any black person by first name and receiving the respectful form of address in return. A president's fondness for making up funny nicknames for people on his staff or members of Congress may appear amiable and friendly, but it also reinforces power differences. These people are still required to address him as "Mr. President."

MISMANAGING IMPRESSIONS: SPOILED IDENTITIES

While impression management is universal, it's not always successful. We may mishandle props, blow our lines, mistakenly allow the audience to peek back stage, or otherwise destroy the credibility of our performances. Some of us manage to recover from ineffective impression management quite quickly; others suffer an extended devaluation of their identities. What happens when impression management is unsuccessful? What do we do to regain identities and restore social order?

Embarrassment

A common emotional reaction to impression mismanagement is *embarrassment*, the spontaneous feeling we experience when the identity we are presenting is suddenly and unexpectedly discredited in front of others (E. Gross & Stone, 1964). An adolescent boy trying to look "cool" in front of his friends may have his tough image shattered by the unexpected arrival of his mother in the family minivan. We can see his embarrassment in the fixed smile, the nervous hollow laugh, the busy hands, and the downward glance that hides his eyes from the gaze of others (E. Goffman, 1967). Embarrassment can come from a multitude of sources: lack of poise (e.g., stumbling, saying something stupid, spilling a drink, inappropriately exposing body parts), intrusion into the private settings of others (a man walking into a women's restroom), improper dress for a particular social occasion, and so on.

Embarrassment is sociologically important because it has the potential to destroy the orderliness of a social situation. Imagine being at your high school graduation. As the class valedictorian is giving the commencement address, a gust of wind blows her note cards off the podium. As she reaches down to collect them, she hits her head on the microphone and tears her gown. In front of hundreds of people she stands there, flustered, not knowing what to say or do. The situation would be uncomfortable and embarrassing not only for her but for you and the rest of the audience as well.

Because embarrassment is disruptive for all concerned, it is in everyone's best interest to cooperate in reducing or eliminating it. To call attention to such an act may be as embarrassing as the original episode itself, so we may pretend not to notice the faux pas (Lindesmith, Strauss, & Denzin, 1991). By suppressing signs of recognition, we make it easier for the person to regain composure (E. Goffman, 1967). A mutual commitment to supporting others' social identities, even when those identities are in danger, is a fundamental norm of social interaction.

At times, however, embarrassment is used strategically to disrupt another person's impression management. Practical jokes, for instance, are intentional attempts to rein in conceit or overconfidence and cause someone to lose identity. More seriously, groups and organizations may use embarrassment or the threat of embarrassment (e.g., hazing) to encourage a preferred activity or discourage behavior that may be damaging to the group. In that sense, embarrassment reasserts the power structure of the group, because only certain people can legitimately embarrass others. A low-status employee, for instance, has much less freedom to embarrass a superior or make him or her the target of a joke than vice versa (Coser, 1960).

Organizations themselves may also experience embarrassment from time to time:

- In 2010, British Petroleum (BP) faced a massive public image crisis when a deepwater oil rig in the Gulf of Mexico exploded, creating a catastrophic oil spill that devastated the local economy and ecosystem. As if the accident weren't bad enough, Tony Hayward, chief executive officer of BP, and Carl-Henric Svanberg, its chairman, embarrassed the company further when they made insensitive public comments belittling the disaster, shirking responsibility for it, and trivializing the suffering of the Gulf Coast residents affected by it.

- In 2012, McDonald's launched two Twitter hashtags, #McDStories and #MeettheFarmers, which were intended to solicit adoring tweets from loyal McDonald's customers. Instead, it had the opposite embarrassing effect as thousands of people chimed in to complain about the restaurant and its food with tweets like, "I once got food poisoning from eating a Big Mac" and "McDonalds is where dreams of being healthy and fit go to die" (Kuperinsky, 2012).

- In a collectivist culture like Japan, organizational misdeeds or mistakes can create considerable public humiliation, shame, and embarrassment for top officials. In 2010, Toyota faced worldwide condemnation and was forced to recall some 8 million vehicles when it could no longer deny published reports of fatal accidents in which accelerator pedals had gotten stuck at high speeds. A year later, some officials in Japanese government agencies were forced to resign for trying to downplay the public health crisis that occurred after a nuclear reactor sustained major damage from the earthquake and tsunami.

When events challenge an organization's public image, leaders are often compelled to engage in activities that protect, repair, and enhance that image (Ginzel et al., 2004). Most government agencies and large corporations like BP, McDonald's, and Toyota have massive public relations departments or crisis management teams that carefully oversee the organization's image by controlling negative publicity. For instance, Southwest Airlines has a full-time employee, called Senior Manager of Proactive Customer Communications, whose sole responsibility is to write apology letters to customers who are annoyed about flight delays, cancellations, or shoddy plane conditions. He writes about 20,000 such letters a year (J. Bailey, 2007).

Remedies for Spoiled Identities

Organizations and governments can enlist the aid of experts to overcome the debilitating effects of negative images, but individuals are usually left to their own devices. Fixing a spoiled identity is not easy. The mere knowledge that we are being evaluated negatively can impede our thoughts, speech, and action. Nevertheless, the major responsibility for restoring order lies with the person whose actions disrupted things in the first place.

To restore social order and overcome a spoiled identity, the transgressor will use an *aligning action* (Stokes & Hewitt, 1976). Sometimes aligning can be done easily and quickly. If you step on a person's foot while standing in line at a cafeteria, a simple apology may be all that's needed to avoid the impression that you're a clumsy oaf.

By apologizing, you acknowledge that such an act is wrong and send the message that you are not ordinarily a breaker of such social norms. Other situations, however, call for more detailed repair:

- An *account* is a verbal statement designed to explain unanticipated, embarrassing, or unacceptable behavior (C. W. Mills, 1940; M. Scott & Lyman, 1968). For example, an individual may cite events beyond her or his control ("I was late for the wedding because there was a lot of traffic on the highway") or blame others ("I spilled my beer because somebody pushed me"). An alternative is to define the offending behavior as appropriate under the circumstances, perhaps by denying that anyone was hurt by the act ("Yeah, I stole the car, but no one got hurt"), by claiming that the victim deserved to be victimized ("I beat him up, but he had it coming"), or by claiming higher, unselfish motives ("I stole food, but I did it to feed my family").

- A *disclaimer* is a verbal assertion given before the fact to forestall any complaints or negative implications (Hewitt & Stokes, 1975). If we think something we're about to do or say will threaten our identity or be used by others to judge us negatively, we may use a disclaimer. Phrases such as "I probably don't know what I'm talking about, but . . ." or "I'm not a racist, but . . ." introduce acts or expressions that ordinarily might be considered undesirable. As long as a disclaimer is provided, a self-proclaimed nonexpert can pretend to be an expert and a person claiming to be nonracist feels he or she can go ahead and make a racist statement.

Accounts and disclaimers are important links between the individual and society. We use them to explicitly define the relationship between our questionable conduct and prevailing cultural norms. That is, by using aligning actions, we publicly reaffirm our commitment to the social order that our conduct has violated and thereby defend the sanctity of our social identities and the "goodness" of society.

Other people may also try to deal with a transgressor's spoiled identity through a process called *cooling out* (E. Goffman, 1952): gently persuading someone who has lost face to accept a less desirable but still reasonable alternative identity. People engaged in cooling out seek to persuade rather than force offenders to change. It's an attempt to minimize distress. The challenge is to keep the offender from realizing that he or she is being persuaded.

Cooling out is a common element of social life; it is one of the major functions of consumer complaint departments, coaches, doctors, and priests. Cooling out also plays a major part in informal relationships. A partner who terminates a dating or courting relationship might persuade the other person to remain a "good friend," gently pushing the person into a lesser role without completely destroying her or his self-worth.

Stigma

The permanent spoiling of someone's identity is called *stigma*. A stigma is a deeply discrediting characteristic, widely viewed as an insurmountable obstacle preventing competent or morally trustworthy behavior (E. Goffman, 1963). Stigmas spoil the identities of individuals regardless of other attributes those individuals might have. According to Goffman, the three types of stigma are (1) defects of the body (e.g., severe scars, blindness, paralyzed or missing limbs), (2) defects of character (e.g., dishonesty, a weak will, a history of imprisonment or substance abuse), and (3) membership in devalued social groups, such as certain races, religions, or ethnicities. The impression management task when faced with stigma is not so much to recapture a tarnished identity as to minimize the social damage.

Some stigmas are worse than others. For instance, the use of eyeglasses to compensate for one sensory deficiency (poor vision) is usually considered far less stigmatizing than the use of hearing aids to compensate for a different sensory deficiency (poor hearing). Contemporary hearing aids are designed to be as small and unnoticeable as possible. Eyeglasses, on the other hand, have become a common fashion accessory, often sold in their own trendy boutiques.

Stigma varies across time and culture as well. For instance, being a Christian in the 21st century is very different from being one in AD 100, and being a Christian in the United States is different from being one in the Arab Middle East (Ainlay, Becker, & Coleman, 1986). Ancient Mayans considered being cross-eyed desirable, so parents encouraged babies to focus on objects that forced their eyes to cross (Link & Phelan, 2001). In contemporary Sierra Leone, the stigma of epilepsy is so severe that those who suffer from the condition are considered uneducable, unemployable, and unmarriageable (Baruchin, 2011). Obesity is stigmatized in contemporary Western societies but was seen as desirable, attractive, and symbolic of status and wealth in the past and is still seen that way in some other cultures today.

Even different situations within the same culture can yield different perceptions of stigma. For example, in the business world, *non*drinking can stigmatize people and limit their career trajectory. Those who abstain often find it harder to get ahead than those willing to drink with coworkers or clients. On Wall Street, nondrinkers complain that they have difficulty closing deals or negotiating with clients simply because they don't drink. In fact, some research suggests that nondrinkers have a harder time climbing the corporate ladder than moderate drinkers. As one director of an alcohol treatment program put it, "If you say you don't drink, you have to deal with the suspicion that you can't play the game" (quoted in Quenqua, 2012b, p. 1).

Interactions between the stigmatized and the nonstigmatized—called "mixed contacts"—can sometimes be uneasy. We have all felt uncomfortable with people who are "different" in appearance or behavior. Stigma initiates a judgment process that colors impressions and sets up barriers to interaction (E. E. Jones et al., 1984).

Whether intentionally or not, nonstigmatized individuals often pressure stigmatized people to conform to "inferior" identities. A person in a wheelchair who is discouraged from going camping or a blind person who is discouraged from living on her or his own is not given the chance to develop important skills and is thus kept dependent.

Nonstigmatized people often avoid mixed contacts because they anticipate discomfort and are unsure how to act (E. Goffman, 1963). Research shows that when interacting with a person who is physically disabled, an able-bodied person is likely to be more inhibited and more rigid and to end the interaction sooner than if the other person were also able bodied (Kleck, 1968; Kleck, Ono, & Hastorf, 1966). On the one hand, the able-bodied person may fear that showing direct sympathy or interest in a disabled person's condition could be regarded as rude or intrusive. On the other hand, ignoring it may make the interaction artificial and awkward or create impossible demands (Michener, DeLamater, & Schwartz, 1986).

As for people with stigmatizing conditions, they often sense that others are evaluating them negatively. One study of people diagnosed with a mental disorder found that they had all at one time or another been shunned, avoided, patronized, or discriminated against when others found out about their condition (Wahl, 1999). Consider also the case of Mark Breimhorst, a Stanford University graduate. Mr. Breimhorst has no hands. When he was applying to business schools in 1998, he was given 25% more time to complete the Graduate Management Admission Test. His results were mailed to prospective graduate schools with the notation "Scores obtained under special circumstances." Mr. Breimhorst was not admitted to any of the business schools to which he applied. He filed a federal lawsuit against the testing service, challenging the way they flagged the scores of students who needed accommodations. Such notations, he argued, were stigmatizing because they created suspicion that the scores were less valid than others (Lewin, 2000). In 2003, the testing service stopped flagging the results of students who receive special accommodations.

Faced with the strong possibility of discrimination, people with stigmatizing conditions often use coping strategies to establish the most favorable identity possible. One strategy is to try to hide the stigma. People who are hard of hearing, for instance, may learn to read lips or otherwise interact with people as if they could hear perfectly; those with bodily stigmas may opt for surgery to permanently conceal their condition.

Some stigmatized individuals, particularly those whose conditions are not immediately observable, use a strategy of selective disclosure. Sociologist Charlene E. Miall (1989) interviewed and surveyed 70 infertile women, nearly all of whom characterized infertility as something negative, an indication of failure, or an inability to function "normally." Most of the women were concerned that others' knowledge of their infertility would be stigmatizing. So they engaged in some form of information control. Many simply concealed the information from everyone except medical personnel and infertility counselors. Others used medical accounts, saying, "It's beyond my control." Some disclosed the information only to people they felt would not think ill of them. Some even used the disclosure of their infertility to gain control of a situation by deliberately shocking their "normal" audience (Miall, 1989).

Of course, not all stigmas can be hidden. Some individuals can only minimize the degree to which their stigmas intrude on and disrupt the interaction. One tactic is to use self-deprecating humor—telling little jokes about their shortcomings—to relieve the tension felt by the nonstigmatized. Others may try to focus on attributes unrelated to the stigma. For instance, a person in a wheelchair may carry around esoteric books in a conspicuous manner to show others that he or she still has a brain that works well. Still others with stigmas boldly call attention to their condition by mastering areas thought to be closed to them (such as mountain climbing for an amputee).

And some organize a movement to counter social oppression. For instance, organizations like the National Association to Advance Fat Acceptance and the Council on Size and Weight Discrimination help fat people (*fat* is their preferred adjective, by the way) cope with a society that hates their size by lobbying Congress and state legislatures to combat "size discrimination" and promote "weight diversity" (Saulny, 2009a). They have organized civil rights protests in Washington, DC, lobbied health care professionals for tolerance and acceptance, publicly condemned weight-loss TV shows like *The Biggest Loser* for bullying overweight contestants, and organized campaigns against insurance discrimination and the dubious "science" of weight-loss programs (LeBesco, 2004; National Association to Advance Fat Acceptance, 2013).

But overcoming the problems created by stigma cannot be accomplished solely through individual impression management or collective demonstrations. Long-lasting improvements can be accomplished only by changing cultural beliefs about the nature of stigma (Link, Mirotznik, & Cullen, 1991). As long as we hold stigmatized individuals solely responsible for dealing with the stigma, only some of them will be able to overcome the social limitations of their condition.

CONCLUSION

After reading this chapter, you may have an image of human beings as cunning, manipulative, and cynical play actors whose lives are merely a string of phony performances carefully designed to fit the selfish needs of the moment. The impression manager comes across as someone who consciously and fraudulently presents an inaccurate image in order to take advantage of a particular situation. Even the person who seems not to care about her or his appearance may be consciously cultivating the image of "not caring."

There's no denying that people consciously manufacture images of themselves that allow them to achieve some desired goal. Most of us go through life trying to create the impression that we're attractive, honest, competent, and sincere. To that end, we carefully manage our appearance, present qualities we think others will admire, and hide qualities we think they won't. When caught in an act that may threaten the impression we're trying to foster, we strategically use statements that disclaim, excuse, or justify it.

So who is the real you? If people freely change their images to suit the expectations of a given audience, is there something more stable that characterizes them across all situations?

If you are aware that the impression you are managing is not the real you, then you must have some knowledge of what *is* the real you. And what you are may, in fact, transcend the demands of particular situations. Some basic, pervasive part of your being may allow you to choose from a repertoire of identities the one that best suits the immediate needs of the situation. As you ponder this possibility, realize that your feelings about impression management reflect your beliefs about the nature of individuals and the role society and others play in our everyday lives.

CHAPTER HIGHLIGHTS

◆   A significant portion of social life is influenced by the images we form of others and the images others form of us.

◆   Impression formation is based initially on our assessment of ascribed social group membership (race, age, gender, etc.), individual physical appearance, and verbal and nonverbal messages.

◆   While we are gathering information about others to form impressions of them, we are fully aware that they are doing the same thing. Impression management is the process by which we attempt to control and manipulate information about ourselves to influence the impressions others form of us. Impression management can be both individual and collective.

◆   Impression mismanagement can lead to the creation of damaged identities, which must be repaired in order to sustain social interaction.

KEY TERMS

account: Statement designed to explain unanticipated, embarrassing, or unacceptable behavior after the behavior has occurred

aligning action: Action taken to restore an identity that has been damaged

back stage: Area of social interaction away from the view of an audience, where people can rehearse and rehash their behavior

cooling out: Gently persuading someone who has lost face to accept a less desirable but still reasonable alternative identity

disclaimer: Assertion designed to forestall any complaints or negative reactions to a behavior or statement that is about to occur

dramaturgy: Study of social interaction as theater, in which people ("actors") project images ("play roles") in front of others ("the audience")

embarrassment: Spontaneous feeling experienced when the identity someone is presenting is suddenly and unexpectedly discredited in front of others

front stage: Area of social interaction where people perform and work to maintain appropriate impressions

impression formation: The process by which we define others based on observable cues such as age, ascribed status characteristics such as race and gender, individual attributes such as physical appearance, and verbal and nonverbal expressions

impression management: Act of presenting a favorable public image of oneself so that others will form positive judgments

performance team: Set of individuals who cooperate in staging a performance that leads an audience to form an impression of one or all team members

stigma: Deeply discrediting characteristic that is viewed as an obstacle to competent or morally trustworthy behavior

Building Social Relationships

Intimacy and Families

Life With Others

Social Diversity and Intimate Choices

Family Life

Family and Social Structure

Family Challenges

So far, the 21st century has been a challenging time for the types of close relationships we commonly think of as the foundation of social life:

- Among college students, traditional dating has been replaced by *hooking up*—in which two people hang out in a dorm room or meet at a party, go somewhere private, and engage in some form of sexual contact, which can range from kissing to intercourse (England & Thomas, 2007). Alcohol is usually involved. Intimacy and romance? Not so much.

- There are about 33 million single-person households in the United States, up from 23 million in 1990 (ProQuest Statistical Abstract, 2013). Indeed, in 2010, the number of adults between the ages of 25 and 34 who had never been married surpassed the number who were married for the first time in over a century (Eckholm, 2010).

- Forty million adults have tried online dating. Twenty percent of current committed relationships began online and 17% of marriages that began in 2011 were between people who had met online (Online Dating Statistics, 2012). Internet dating is now the quickest and cheapest way to find a lover since people can choose from a huge pool of potential mates. Consequently, however, it has made people more picky and dating partners more disposable (Brooks, 2011). As one psychologist put it, "You could . . . easily see a world in which online dating leads to people leaving relationships the moment they're not working—an over all weakening of commitment" (quoted in Slater, 2013, p. 4).

- Forty percent of men and 32% of women between the ages of 18 and 24 live with their parents (Fry, 2013). These figures include people who have never left home and those who have left and returned, perhaps more than once. According to one survey, 13% of parents with grown children said that one of their sons or daughters had moved back home within the past year (Wang & Morin, 2009).

- Nearly four in 10 respondents to a national survey said they felt marriage is becoming obsolete (Pew Research Center, 2010a).

- The number of Americans with children who live together but are not married has increased 12-fold since 1970; children are now more likely to have unmarried parents than divorced parents (cited in Tavernise, 2011a).

- In 1970, 11% of all births in the United States were to unmarried mothers; today that figure is 36% (Shattuck & Kreider, 2013). About 58% of these births occur within cohabiting relationships (Haub, 2013).

- At the time of this writing, two people of the same sex can legally marry in seventeen states—California, Connecticut, Delaware, Hawaii, Illinois, Iowa, Maine, Maryland, Massachusetts, Minnesota, New Hampshire, New Jersey, New Mexico, New York, Rhode Island, Vermont, and Washington—plus the District of Columbia.

Some people might see these events as "proof" that society is going downhill fast; others may see them as signs that relationships are keeping up with a changing culture.

Like every other aspect of our individual lives, intimacy and family must be understood within the broader contours of our society. This chapter takes a sociological peek into their private and public aspects and explores the role that close relationships, especially family bonds, play in our everyday experience. Why are these relationships so important to us? How do societal factors such as social institutions, gender, race, and social class affect our perceptions of intimacy and belonging? How do they affect family life? And why are the desirable aspects of these relationships so often outweighed by the negative aspects, such as family violence?

LIFE WITH OTHERS

The quality and quantity of our relationships with others are the standards against which many of us judge the well-being of our lives (A. Campbell, Converse, & Rodgers, 1976). We spend a tremendous amount of time worrying about these relationships, contemplating new ones, obsessing over past ones, trying to make current ones more satisfying, or fretting over how to get into or out of one.

Although we hunger for closeness in our lives, it can often be a challenge to maintain. For more than a century, sociologists have been writing that people who live in complex, urban, industrial, or postindustrial societies gradually become less integrated and connected to others (Durkheim, 1893/1947; Riesman, 1950; Tönnies, 1887/1957). In the late 20th and early 21st centuries, membership in church-related groups, civic organizations (e.g., Red Cross, Boy Scouts, PTA), and fraternal organizations (e.g., Lions, Elks, Shriners) decreased (Putnam, 1995). According to one study, only 43% of Americans know all or most of their neighbors by name (cited in Blow, 2010). Today, single people who have never married make up 27% of the adult population in this country—up from 24% in 2000 (ProQuest Statistical Abstract, 2013).

Some sociologists attribute these trends to U.S. culture's emphasis on individualism, which takes away a sense of community, diminishes our ability to establish ties with others, and makes it easier for people to walk away from groups they see as unfulfilling (Bellah, Madsen, Sullivan, Swidler, & Tipton, 1985; Sidel, 1986). The high value that contemporary society places on self-reliance and individual achievement can sometimes make social relationships, even family relationships, seem expendable.

In contrast, in collectivist societies such as China and Japan, group ties play a more substantial role in people's everyday lives. There, people consider duty, sacrifice, and compromise more desirable traits than personal success and individual achievement. They assume that group connections are the best guarantee for an individual's well-being. Hence, feelings of group loyalty and responsibility for other members tend to be strong.

Despite the inevitable conflicts in close relationships and the difficulties of maintaining these ties in an individualistic, mobile, high-tech society, people still place a high value on belonging and intimacy and take great pains to achieve them. For instance, a growing number of older women who are single, widowed, or divorced look for support not through marriage but through long-term friendships with other women who are at a similar stage in their lives (J. Gross, 2004). Similarly, we spend more time than ever at work (Galinsky et al., 2006), perhaps to the detriment of relationships with our families. But for many people, forming ties with coworkers can be just as emotionally fulfilling (Wuthnow, 1994). And many of us spend a great deal of time in local hangouts (such as bars and coffee shops), where we can find comfort and good company (Oldenburg & Brissett, 1982). Many people find the sense of belonging they crave in these small groups of friends and like-minded neighbors and coworkers.

SOCIAL DIVERSITY AND INTIMATE CHOICES

Our bonds with coworkers, neighbors, relatives, and friends (real or virtual) are certainly an important part of our social lives, but the sense of belonging and closeness that comes from intimate, romantic relationships has become one of the prime obsessions of the 21st century. Magazines, self-help books, supermarket tabloids, websites, blogs, and talk shows overflow with advice, warnings, and pseudoscientific analyses of every conceivable aspect of these relationships.

Most people in the United States assume that love is all they need to establish a fulfilling, long-lasting relationship. But their intimate choices are far from free and private. The choices they make regarding whom to date, live with, or marry are governed by two important social rules that limit the field of eligible partners: exogamy and endogamy.

Exogamy

At any given time, each of us is a member of many groups simultaneously. We belong to a particular family, a friendship group, a set of coworkers, a religion, a race, an ethnicity, an age group, a social class, and so on. Entering into intimate relationships with fellow members of some of these groups is considered inappropriate. So society follows a set of customs referred to as *exogamy* rules, which require that an individual form a long-term romantic or sexual relationship with someone *outside* certain social groups to which she or he belongs. For instance, in almost all societies, exogamy rules define marrying or having sex with people in one's own immediate family—siblings, parents, and children—as incest. Presumably, these rules exist in order to prohibit procreation between people who are genetically related, thereby reducing the chance that offspring will inherit two copies of a defective gene.

Exogamy prohibitions typically extend to certain relatives outside the immediate family too, such as cousins, grandparents, aunts, uncles, and, in some societies, stepsiblings. In the United States, 25 states completely prohibit marriage between first cousins; 6 others allow it under certain circumstances, such as when both partners are over 65 or when one is unable to reproduce (National Conference of State Legislatures, 2009).

Informally, opposition to romantic relationships between coworkers or, on college campuses, between people who live on the same dorm floor (called "dormcest") illustrates a common belief that relationships work best when they occur between people who aren't in constant close proximity. One college advice blog identifies some the pitfalls of dormcest—mismatched expectations, seeing sex partners at their worst, nonexclusivity in a shared living space, keeping things fresh—and provides some strategies to overcome them (A. Jones, 2010).

Different cultures apply the rules of exogamy differently. For example, in South Korea, it was once illegal to marry someone with the same surname—not a trivial law, considering that 55% of the population is named Kim, Park, Lee, Choi, or Chong (WuDunn, 1996b). This rule originated centuries ago as a way of preventing marriages between members of the same clan and was written into Korean law in 1957. The ban was deemed unconstitutional in 1997. However, most single people still try to avoid lovers with the same name. As one college student put it, "When I'm introduced to someone, I very casually ask what her name is, and if I find out that it's the same as mine, it puts a mark against her right there" (WuDunn, 1996b, p. A4).

In other places, the violation of exogamy rules can lead to severe sanctions. In 2003, a young Indian couple was beaten to death by members of their own families for being lovers. In their community, it was considered incest for two people from the same village to fall in love. A resident of the village said, "In our society all the families living in a village are all sons and daughters of the whole village. We are like brothers and sisters. The marriage of brothers and sisters is not accepted" (quoted in Waldman, 2003, p. A4).

Endogamy

Simultaneously, less formal, but just as powerful, are the rules of *endogamy*, which limit people's intimate choices to those *within* certain groups to which they belong. The vast majority of marriages in the United States, for example, occur between people from the same religion, ethnoracial group, and social class. These rules of endogamy increase the likelihood that the couple will have similar backgrounds and therefore share common beliefs, values, and experiences. But more important, from a sociological point of view, rules of endogamy reflect our society's traditional distaste for relationships that cross social-group boundaries.

Religious Endogamy

Throughout history, many societies have had endogamy rules relating to religion: Only people with the same religious background were allowed to marry. Marrying outside one's religion is more common than it once was in industrialized countries, however, because greater mobility and freer communication bring people from diverse religious backgrounds into contact. In the United States, it's estimated that between one quarter and one half of all marriages occur between people of different religions ("Breaking the Rules," 2002; B. A. Robinson, 1999).

Nevertheless, most religious leaders still actively discourage interfaith marriages. They worry about maintaining their religion's influence over how people identify themselves within a diverse and complex society (M. M. Gordon, 1964). In 2004, the Vatican issued an official church document discouraging marriage between Catholics and non-Christians, especially Muslims (Feuer, 2004). The concern was that such marriages would further weaken people's religious beliefs and values, lead to the raising of children in a different faith, or encourage family members to abandon religion entirely.

The situation facing U.S. Jews provides a good example of the consequences of marriages that break rules of religious endogamy. Although only 1 Jew in 10 married a non-Jew in 1945, more than one in two does so today (Goodstein, 2013). A lower birthrate among Jews compared with other groups, coupled with the likelihood that interfaith couples will not raise children as Jews, explains, in part, why the Jewish population has been dropping steadily (Goodstein, 2003). Between 1990 and 2008, the number of Jews in the U.S. population declined from 3.1 million to 2.6 million (Kosmin & Keysar, 2009). Many Jewish leaders fear that the outcome of this trend will be not only the shrinking of the Jewish population but also the erosion and perhaps extinction of an entire way of life.

Racial and Ethnic Endogamy

Racial and ethnic endogamy is a global phenomenon, forming the basis of social structure in most societies worldwide (Murdock, 1949). The issue is an especially volatile one in U.S. society, however, given how racially and ethnically diverse we are. The first law against interracial marriage was enacted in Maryland in 1661, prohibiting Whites from marrying Native Americans or African slaves. Over the next 300 years or so, 38 more states put such laws on the books, expanding their coverage to include Chinese, Japanese, and Filipino Americans. It was believed that a mixing of the races (then referred to as "mongrelization") would destroy the racial purity (and superiority) of Whites. The irony, of course, is that racial mixing had been taking place since the 17th century, much of it through white slave owners raping and impregnating their black slaves.

Legal sanctions against interracial marriage persisted well into the 20th century. In 1958, for example, when Richard Loving (who was white) and his new wife, Mildred Jeter Loving (who was black), moved to their new home in Virginia, a sheriff arrived to arrest them for violating a state law that prohibited interracial marriages. The Lovings were sentenced to one year in jail but then learned that the judge would suspend the sentence if they left the state and promised not to return for 25 years. At the time, the majority of states, including California, Oregon, Indiana, all the mountain states, and every state in the South, legally prohibited interracial marriage (Liptak, 2004). The Lovings found a home in Washington, DC, where interracial marriage was not prohibited, and had three children. While there, they embarked on an appeal of their conviction. In 1967, the U.S. Supreme Court ruled in favor of the Lovings, concluding that using racial classifications to restrict freedom to marry was unconstitutional.

A half-century later, attitudes are becoming more tolerant, and people are no longer banished for violating racial endogamy rules. Although the vast majority of U.S. marriages remain racially endogamous, relationships that cross racial or ethnic lines are becoming more common. The number of interracial and interethnic marriages in the U.S. has grown dramatically, from 3.2% of all existing marriages in 1980 to 8.4% today (Pew Research Center, 2012a). These figures grow each year. Of all the marriages that began in 2010, a little over 15% consisted of two people of different racial or ethnic groups, up from 6.7% of marriages that began in 1980 (Pew Research Center, 2012a). Over 40% of people say that an increase in interracial marriages has been a change for the better in U.S. society, compared to 11% who think it has hurt society (Pew Research Center, 2012a).

Nevertheless, people involved in interracial relationships still face problems. About half of the black–white couples in one study felt that biracial marriage makes things harder for them, and about two thirds reported that their parents had a problem with the relationship, at least initially (Fears & Deane, 2001). Many interracial couples—especially black–white couples—still experience a lack of family support when choosing to marry each other (R. Lewis & Yancey, 1997). Everyday activities may require more time and effort for interracial couples than for couples of the same race. For instance, when planning vacations, interracial couples often have to do extensive advance research of potential leisure destinations to see how accepting they are of relationships like theirs (Hibbler & Shinew, 2005). Even today, judges can sometimes make it difficult for interracial couples to marry. In 2009, newspapers reported that a Louisiana justice of the peace regularly refused to issue marriage licenses to interracial couples, claiming that he was doing it to protect children because of

the instability of such marriages. As one woman in an interracial marriage put it, "In a perfect world, race wouldn't matter, but that day's a while off" (quoted in Saulny, 2011, p. 4).

Social Class Endogamy

If we based our ideas about the formation of romantic relationships on what we see in movies, we might be tempted to conclude that divisions based on social class don't matter in U.S. society or perhaps don't exist at all. Popular films such as *Titanic*, *The Wedding Planner*, *Maid in Manhattan*, *Good Will Hunting*, *Sweet Home Alabama*, *The Prince and Me*, *Pretty Woman*, *Good Deeds*, and of course *Cinderella* send the message that the power of love is strong enough to blow away differences in education, pedigree, resources, and taste. When it comes to love, Hollywood's United States is a classless society.

In reality, however, social class is a powerful determinant of whom we choose to marry. Around the world, people face strong pressures to choose marital partners of similar social standing (H. Carter & Glick, 1976; Kalmijn, 1994). Even if two individuals from different races, ethnic groups, or religions marry, chances are they will have similar socioeconomic backgrounds (Rosenfeld, 2005). Certainly some people do marry a person from a different social class, but the class tends to be an adjacent one—for instance, an upper-middle-class woman may marry a middle-class man. Cinderella-like marriages, between extremely wealthy and extremely poor people, are quite rare.

One reason this occurs is because individuals of similar social classes are more likely to participate in activities together, where they come into contact with people who share their values, tastes, goals, expectations, and backgrounds (Kalmijn & Flap, 2001). Our education system plays a particularly important role in bringing people from similar class backgrounds together. The proportion of married couples who share the same level of schooling is the highest it's been in 40 years. The odds of someone with only a high school education marrying a college graduate have been decreasing since the 1970s (C. R. Schwartz & Mare, 2005).

Moreover, neighborhoods—and thus neighborhood schools—tend to be made up of people from similar social classes. College often continues this class segregation. People from upper-class backgrounds are considerably more likely to attend costly private schools, whereas those from the middle class are most likely to enroll in state universities and those from the working class are most likely to enroll in community colleges. These structural conditions increase the odds that the people with whom college students form intimate relationships will come from the same class background.

FAMILY LIFE

To most people's way of thinking, committed intimate romantic relationships form the cornerstone of families. Of all the groups we belong to, family is usually the most significant. Our ancestors provide us with a personal history, and they, along with the families we build later in life, provide much of our identity. Because of its importance in everyday life, sociologists consider family one of the main social institutions, a social structure that addresses not only our personal needs but also the fundamental needs of society (see Chapter 2).

Defining Family

Ironically, as important as family is, it is an elusive term to define. When most people hear the word *family*, they usually think of the **nuclear family**: a unit consisting of parents and siblings. Others may think of the **extended family**: other kin, such as grandparents, aunts, uncles, and cousins. In everyday usage, people may use the word *family* more loosely to describe those with whom they've achieved a significant degree of emotional closeness and sharing, even if they're not related. If I choose to think of my father's best friend, my barber, and even my dog as members of my family, I can.

But we don't live our lives completely by ourselves, and so we don't have complete freedom to define our own families. Not only do we come into fairly regular contact with people who want to know what our family looks like, but we also must navigate a vast array of organizations and agencies that have their own definitions of family and may, at times, impose them on us. Local, state, and federal governments manage many programs that provide certain benefits only to groups they officially define as "families."

The federal government regularly compiles up-to-date statistics on the number of individuals, married couples, and families that live in this country.

Obviously it must have some idea of what a family (or what a marriage) is before it can start counting. In its official statistics, the U.S. Bureau of the Census distinguishes between households and families. A **household** is composed of one or more people who occupy the same housing unit. A **family** consists of "two or more persons, including the householder, who are related by birth, marriage, or adoption, and who live together as one household" (U.S. Bureau of the Census, 2005). Not all households contain families. If we accept this narrow definition of family, then other arrangements—people living alone, roommates, cohabitors, and various forms of group living—cannot be considered families in the strict sense of the word. Such a definition is reflected in many people's beliefs. In a recent national study, respondents were twice as likely to identify unmarried couples (both heterosexual and homosexual) *with* children as families as they were to identify unmarried couples *without* children as families (B. Powell, Bolzendahl, Geist, & Steelman, 2010). According to the government's definition, over 40% of U.S. households are not families.

Having one's household legally recognized as a family has many practical implications. Benefits such as inheritance rights, insurance coverage, spousal immigration benefits, savings from joint tax returns, the ability to make medical decisions for another person, and visitation rights in prisons and hospital intensive care units are determined by marital or family status. Members of relationships not defined as family relationships, no matter how committed, economically interdependent, or emotionally fulfilling, are not eligible. For instance, homosexual partners of victims of the September 11 attack on the Pentagon were not eligible for the same survivor benefits in the state of Virginia that surviving heterosexual spouses were entitled to (Farmer, 2002).

Historical Trends in Family Life

Many functionalist sociologists have voiced concern over the current state of family as a social institution. Over time, they argue, the family has lost many, if not all, of its traditional purposes (Lasch, 1977). Historically, the family was where children received most of their education and religious training. It was where both children and adults could expect to receive emotional nurturing and support. It was the institution that regulated sexual activity and reproduction. And it was also the economic center of society, where family members worked together to earn a living and support one another financially.

But as the economy shifted from a system based on small, privately owned agricultural enterprises to one based on massive industrial manufacturing, the role of family changed. Economic production moved from the home to the factory, and families became more dependent on the money that members earned outside the home. Schools began to take over the teaching of skills and values that were once a part of everyday home life. Even the family's role as a source of emotional security and nurturing began to diminish as it became less able to shield its members from the harsh realities of modern life (Lasch, 1977).

For all of these reasons, many people are concerned about the survival of the contemporary family. Anxiety over the future of families has generated some strident calls for a return to the "good ol' days" of family life. The belief in a lost "golden age" of family has led some to depict the present as a period of rapid decline and inevitable family breakdown (Coontz, 2005; Hareven, 1992; Skolnick, 1991). Critics often pessimistically cite high divorce rates, large numbers of out-of-wedlock births, changing gender roles (most notably, the increase in working mothers), and a de-emphasis on heterosexual marriage as troublesome characteristics of contemporary families (The National Marriage Project, 2010). However, although marriage is no longer the only relationship where people can make lifelong commitments, most Americans still marry eventually (Coontz, 2013). Moreover, families have always been diverse in structure and have always faced difficulties in protecting members from economic hardship, internal violence, political upheaval, and social change. Calls for a return to the "good ol' days" are calls for a return to something that has never truly existed. By glorifying a mythical and idealized past, we artificially limit ourselves to an inaccurate image of what we think a "normal" family ought to look like.

Trends in Family Structure

The reality of U.S. family life has never quite fit its nostalgic image. In the 19th century, U.S. adults had a shorter life expectancy than adults today, so due to the death of a parent, children were actually more likely then than they are now to live in a single-parent home (Kain, 1990). Even children fortunate enough to come from intact families usually left home to work as servants or apprentices in other people's homes. Furthermore, although nearly 22% of U.S. children live in poverty today (DeNavas-Walt, Proctor, & Smith, 2012), a comparable proportion lived in orphanages at the beginning of the 20th century—but not just because their parents had died. Many were there because their parents simply couldn't afford to raise them. Rates of alcohol and drug abuse, domestic violence, and school dropouts were also higher a century ago than they are today (Coontz, 1992).

Also contrary to popular belief, father-breadwinner/mother-homemaker households were not the universal family form in the 19th and early 20th centuries. For instance, by 1900, one fifth of U.S. women worked outside the home (Staggenborg, 1998). But the experiences of employed women varied along class and race lines. For middle- and upper-class white women, few professions other than teaching and nursing were available. Because their income was probably not essential for the survival of the household, most could enter and exit the labor force in response to family demands. In contrast, poor women were likely to work long hours, mostly in unskilled jobs in clothing factories, canning plants, or other industries.

Family life for women of color was even more affected by economic necessity. Black domestic servants, for instance, were often forced to leave their own families and live in their employers' homes, where they were expected to work around the clock. And most of them had little choice. Throughout U.S. history, black women have rarely had the luxury of being stay-at-home spouses and parents. In 1880, 73% of black single women and 35% of black married women reported holding paid jobs. Only 23% of white single women and 7% of white married women reported being in the paid labor force at that time (cited in Kessler-Harris, 1982).

Trends in Household Size

Perhaps the most pervasive myth regarding U.S. families of the past is that of the primacy of the extended family with several generations living under the same roof. Today's more isolated nuclear family is often compared unfavorably with the image of these large, close-knit support networks. But research shows that U.S. families have always been fairly small and primarily nuclear (Blumstein & Schwartz, 1983;

W. J. Goode, 1971; Hareven, 1992). The United States has no strong tradition of large, extended multigenerational families living together. In fact, the highest proportion of extended-family households ever recorded existed between 1850 and 1885 and was only around 20% of all households (Hareven, 1978). Because people didn't live as long then as they do today, most died before ever seeing their grandchildren. Even in the 1700s, the typical family consisted of a husband, a wife, and approximately three children.

When households of the past were large, it was probably due to the presence of nonfamily members: servants, apprentices, boarders, and visitors. The reduction in average household size we've seen over the past several centuries was caused not by a decline in the number of extended relatives but by a decrease in the number of nonfamily members living in a household, a reduction in the number of children in a family, and an increase in the number of young adults living alone (Kobrin, 1976).

As people migrated to the United States from countries that did have a tradition of extended families, such as China, Greece, and Italy, often their first order of business was to leave their extended family members so they could create their own households. Reducing the size of their families was seen as a clear sign that they had become American. Large, multigenerational families simply didn't make economic sense. Being able to move to a different state to pursue a job would be next to impossible with a bunch of grandparents, aunts, uncles, and cousins in tow.

In addition, it's not at all clear that families today are as isolated as some people make them out to be. More U.S. residents than ever have grandparents alive, and most adults see or talk to a parent on the phone at least once a week (Coontz, 1992). Extended family members may not live under the same roof, but they do stay in contact and provide advice, emotional support, and financial help when needed (K. Newman, 2005).

Trends in Divorce

Another oft-cited indicator of the demise of the U.S. family based on faulty conceptions of the past is the current high divorce rate. Many observers fear that the intact middle-class family depicted in 1950s television shows such as *Ozzie and Harriet*, *Father Knows Best*, and *Leave It to Beaver* has crumbled away forever. The rise in the divorce rate in the late 20th century has been attributed to the cultural movement toward "swinging singles, open marriages, alternative lifestyles, and women's liberation" in the 1960s and 1970s (Skolnick, 1991). True, this was a revolutionary period in U.S. history, and norms governing all aspects of social life were certainly changing.

What these conclusions overlook, however, is the longer historical trend in divorce in this country. Until World War II, it had been increasing steadily for more than 100 years. It rose sharply right after the war, most likely because of short courtships before the young men shipped out and the subsequent stress of separation. In the 1950s, the rate dropped just as sharply. The high divorce rates of the 1970s, then, represented a return to a national trend that had been developing since the beginning of the 20th century. Indeed, since the mid 1980s, the rate has actually been declining (ProQuest Statistical Abstract, 2013).

Furthermore, the rate of "hidden" marital separation 100 years ago was probably not that much less than the rate of "visible" separation today (Sennett, 1984). For financial or religious reasons, divorce was not an option for many people in the past. For instance, divorce rates actually fell during the Great Depression of the 1930s. With jobs and housing scarce, many couples simply couldn't afford to divorce. Rates of marital unhappiness and domestic violence increased. A significant number of people turned to the functional equivalents of divorce—desertion and abandonment—which have been going on for centuries. So you can see that the divorce rate may have been lower in the past, but families found other ways to break up. The image of a warm, secure, stable family life in past times is at odds with the actual history of U.S. families (Skolnick, 1991).

Cultural Variation in Intimacy and Family

Families can be found in every human society, and from a structural-functionalist perspective, they all address similar societal needs. However, the way families go about meeting these needs—their structure, customs, patterns of authority, and so on—differ widely across cultures. Thus, ideas about what a family is and how people should behave within it are culturally determined.

Most of us take for granted that *monogamy*, the practice of being married to only one person at a time, is the fundamental building block of the family. Some families do exist without a married couple, and some people may have several spouses over their lifetimes. But monogamous marriage is the core component of our image of family (Sudarkasa, 2001).

In the United States, monogamous marriage between one man and one woman continues to be the only adult intimate relationship that is legally recognized, culturally approved, and endorsed by the Internal Revenue Service. It's still the only relationship in which sexual activity between the partners is not only acceptable but expected. No other relationship has achieved such a status. Despite the growing number of couples choosing cohabitation over marriage and overall public concern regarding the disintegration of marriage, monogamous heterosexual marriage remains the cultural standard against which all other types of intimate relationships are judged.

It may be hard to imagine a society that is not structured around the practice and primacy of monogamy, but many societies allow an individual to have several husbands or wives at the same time. This type of marriage is called *polygamy*. Some anthropologists estimate that about 75% of the world's societies prefer some type of polygamy, although few members within those societies actually have the resources to afford more than one spouse (Murdock, 1957; Nanda, 1994). Often polygamy is an adaptation to population or economic conditions. In Russia, for instance, some people, mostly women, have lobbied the government to legalize polygamy because of population pressures: The Russian population is falling by 3% each year and there are 9 million fewer men than women. Polygamy would give more women, particularly in rural areas, an opportunity to have a husband and therefore legal rights to his financial and physical support as well as legitimacy for their children. According to one anthropologist, the scarcity of potential husbands has led many Russian women to conclude that "half a good man is better than none at all" (quoted in Katbamna, 2009, p. 3).

Even in the United States, certain groups practice polygamy. Thousands of members of a dissident Mormon sect in Utah live in households that contain one husband and two or more wives (T. McCarthy, 2001). Although these marriages are technically illegal, few polygamists are ever prosecuted. For most of the past century, practitioners were tolerated as long as they kept to themselves. However, every once in a while a case garners widespread publicity.

For instance, in 2006, Warren Jeffs, leader of the Fundamentalist Church of Jesus Christ of Latter Day Saints, drew national attention when he was placed on the FBI's Ten Most Wanted list for unlawful flight to avoid prosecution on charges that he arranged illegal marriages between his adult male followers and underage girls. In 2007, he was convicted of this crime as well as rape and incest and sentenced to 10 years to life in a Utah prison. In 2008, law enforcement officials removed 400 children from his polygamous compound in Eldorado, Texas, and placed them in state custody. The popularity of recent television shows such as *Big Love* and *Sister Wives* has sparked even more public interest in the private everyday lives of American polygamists.

Societies differ in other taken-for-granted facets of family life as well. Take living arrangements, for example. In U.S. society, families tend to follow the rules of **neolocal residence**; that is, young married couples are expected to establish their own households and separate from their respective families when financially possible. However, only about 5% of the world's societies are neolocal (Murdock, 1957; Nanda, 1994). In most places, married couples are expected to live with or near either the husband's relatives (called "patrilocal" residence) or the wife's relatives (called "matrilocal" residence).

Child-rearing philosophies vary cross-culturally, too. Most people in the United States believe that young children are inherently helpless and dependent: They feel that if parents attend to the child's drives and desires with consistency, warmth, and affection, that child will learn to trust the parents, adopt their values, develop a sturdy self-concept, and turn out to be a well-rounded, normal individual. Most U.S. child development experts believe that neglect and physical punishment can deaden the child's spirit and lead to violence later in life (Dugger, 1996). In contrast, in the highlands of Guatemala, parents believe that their child's personality is determined by the date of birth. The parents are almost entirely uninvolved in the child's life, standing aside so he or she can grow as nature intended. In many societies— Nigeria, Russia, Haiti, the Dominican Republic, and Mexico, to name a few—most parents think that the best way to teach children to be respectful and studious is to beat them when they misbehave. Despite these dramatic differences in child-rearing practices, most children in all of these cultures grow up equally well adapted to their societies.

FAMILY AND SOCIAL STRUCTURE

All of us have experience with families of one form or another, so it's very tempting to look at this topic in individualistic, personal terms. However, the sociological imagination encourages us to think about how social forces affect this aspect of our private lives. As you will see, a focus on the influence of social structure—social institutions as well as sources of social inequality, such as gender, race, and class—can help us understand some of the dilemmas facing contemporary families.

How Other Institutions Influence Family

As a social institution, family is connected to other institutions in important ways. Consider, for instance, the effect that the recent wars in Iraq and Afghanistan have had on family life. For as long as there have been wars, military families have been disrupted when one parent—almost always the father—either shipped out to sea or was deployed in another part of the world. But the structure of U.S. families had changed in many ways by the time the current wars began. According to the United States Department of Defense (2010), there were 148,000 single parents serving in the military in 2008. However, the military as an institution has no special programs in place to assist single parents when they are deployed. Raising a child in the military has always been hard, but being a single parent raises special challenges and difficult choices, not the least of which is what to do with the children while the parent is gone. According to the Servicemembers' Civil Relief Act, military personnel cannot be evicted or have their property seized during deployment. But this law does not protect them from losing custody of their children, if that's what a judge decides. In 2010, a single mother was days away from her yearlong deployment in Afghanistan when her mother backed out of an agreement to take care of her 10-month-old son while she was away. With no other choice, she stayed home and missed her flight to Afghanistan. She was immediately arrested by military police and faced court martial charges and jail time until she agreed to a "less-than-honorable discharge" (Dao, 2010a).

The legal, political, religious, and economic forces that shape society are perhaps the institutions that most influence the identities and actions of individuals within family relationships. Keep in mind that individuals within families can act to influence society as well.

The Influence of Law and Politics

The relationship between the family and the law is obvious. Marriage, for instance, is a legal contract that determines lawful rights and responsibilities. In the United States, each state legislature determines the age at which two people can marry, the health requirements, the length of the waiting period required before marriage, rules determining inheritance, and the division of property in case of divorce (Baca Zinn & Eitzen, 1996). Sometimes the legislature sets limits on specific types of marriage. For instance, to protect noncitizens from potential abuse, the U.S. Congress enacted the International Marriage Broker Regulation Act, which requires that men who seek foreign brides over the Internet disclose information about their criminal record and marital history before any contracts are signed (Porter, 2006).

In the case of same-sex unions, the law's power to either forbid or grant family rights and privileges is especially obvious and controversial. In some countries, gay men and lesbians can have their relationships legally ratified. Belgium, Spain, Portugal, Canada, Iceland, South Africa, Argentina, the Netherlands, Norway, and Sweden allow gay couples to legally marry. France, Denmark, Germany, and several other European countries allow same-sex couples to enter "civil unions" (sometimes called "domestic partnerships" or "registered partnerships"), which grant them many of the legal and economic benefits and responsibilities of heterosexual marriage.

The matter is far from resolved in the United States, however. In 2004, Massachusetts became the first state to allow same-sex couples who are state residents to legally marry. Since then, California, Connecticut, Delaware, Hawaii, Illinois, Iowa, Maine, Maryland, Minnesota, New Hampshire, New Jersey, New Mexico, New York, Rhode Island, Vermont, and Washington and the District of Columbia have followed suit. Wisconsin, Colorado, and Oregon provide at least some spousal rights to same-sex couples. In addition, 285 of the Fortune 500 companies provide domestic partner health benefits for their gay and lesbian workers (Human Rights Campaign, 2011b). Almost a third of all private-sector gay and lesbian workers now have access to employer-provided health care benefits for their partners (Human Rights Campaign, 2011a).

But most states have moved in the opposite direction. Thirty-three states explicitly ban same-sex marriage either by constitutional amendment or by state law.

At the federal level, the status of same-sex marriage is just as murky. The 1996 Defense of Marriage Act—written at a time when there was no legal same-sex marriage in any state—formally reaffirms the definition of marriage as the union of one man and one woman; authorizes all states to refuse to accept same-sex marriages from other states where it is legal; and denies federal benefits such as Social Security survival payments and spousal burials in national military cemeteries to same-sex couples. However, in 2010, a federal judge in Massachusetts ruled that this restrictive definition of marriage is discriminatory in that it violates the equal-protection provisions of the Constitution. In 2010, President Obama approved policies allowing gay workers to take family and medical leave to care for sick or newborn children of a same-sex partner and authorizing them to make medical decisions on behalf of their partners (Pear, 2010; Stolberg, 2010). That same year, he mandated that hospitals extend visitation rights to the partners of gay and lesbian patients and respect patients' choices about who may make critical health care decisions on their behalf (Shear, 2010). And in 2012, he publicly stated that same-sex couples should have the right to legally marry.

In 2013, when the U.S. Supreme Court began hearing arguments in a case testing the constitutionality of the Defense of Marriage Act, over 200 companies—including Citigroup, Apple, Mars, and Alcoa—signed a "friend of the court brief" in support of recognizing same-sex marriage. They argued that the Defense of Marriage Act imposed serious administrative and financial costs on their operations (Eckholm, 2013). In the summer of 2013, the Supreme Court ruled that the Defense of Marriage Act is unconstitutional, meaning that gay and lesbian couples who live in states where same-sex marriage is legal are entitled to all the federal marriage benefits that heterosexual couples are entitled to. The ruling, however, does not require other states to legalize same-sex marriage.

State and federal laws usually reflect public opinion, which, as you might suspect, is mixed on the matter of legalizing same-sex marriage. While acceptance of gays and lesbians in the workplace, in elementary schools, in the military, and in elected office has grown over the past several decades, support of laws allowing gay couples to marry has been slower to grow. In 2001, roughly one-third of American adults supported gay marriage (35%), while 57%

opposed it. But by 2012, for the first time, more people approved of same-sex marriage (48%) than opposed it (43%; Pew Forum on Religion and Public Life, 2012b). And younger people seem especially inclined to support it. Sixty-four percent of 18- to 34-year-olds in a recent survey support same-sex marriage rights, compared with 41% of people between 48 and 66 (cited in Winerip, 2012). As an institutional indicator of this shift in attitudes, the National Cathedral in Washington, DC, began performing same-sex wedding ceremonies in 2013.

Politics and family are interconnected in other ways, too. Many of today's most pressing political issues, such as affordable health insurance, quality education, guaranteed parental leave in the workplace, Social Security, and poverty are fundamentally family problems. For example, abortion didn't become a significant political issue until the late 1960s, when it became part of the larger movement for women's rights and reproductive freedom. Later, the right-to-life movement framed the abortion debate not only as a moral and political issue but also as a symbolic crusade to define (or redefine) the role of motherhood and family within the larger society (Luker, 1984).

The Influence of Religion

You saw in Chapter 5 that religion is an important feature of everyday life and a powerful agent of socialization. Religion can also play a role in virtually every stage of family life. One of the key aspects of religion is that it constrains people's behavior, or at the very least encourages them to act in certain ways. This normative aspect of religion has important consequences for people's family experiences. For instance, all the major religions in the United States are strong supporters of marriage and childbearing.

In recent years, more churches have begun requiring engaged couples to participate in premarital counseling and education programs before the wedding. In addition, religions almost universally prohibit sexual relations outside marriage. Some religions prohibit divorce or don't permit remarriage after divorce. In 2003, the Roman Catholic pope publicly urged women worldwide to pay heed to what he called their "lofty vocation" as wives and mothers ("Pope Exalts Women," 2003). In highly religious families, a sacred text such as the Bible, the Qur'an, or the Talmud may serve not only as a source of faith but as a literal guidebook for every aspect of family life, from dating, marriage, and sexuality to child discipline, responses to illness and death, and household division of labor.

Religion's influence on family life needn't be so direct, however. For example, among Muslims and members of certain Christian denominations, families are expected to tithe, or donate, a certain amount of their income (10% in most cases) to support their religious establishment. Although it is a charitable thing to do, tithing obligations can create problems for families that are already financially strapped.

Most evidence suggests that religious involvement has positive effects, especially for families raising children, such as higher levels of marital commitment (Larson & Goltz, 1989) and more positive parent–child relationships (L. D. Pearce & Axinn, 1998; Wilcox, 2000). "Spiritual wellness" is often cited as one of the most important qualities of family well-being (Stinnett & DeFrain, 1985).

However, in some situations the link between religious beliefs and actual family behavior may not be as strong as we might think. Even in highly religious families, the practical demands of modern life can make it difficult for people to always subscribe to religious teachings. For instance, although fundamentalist Christians believe wives should stay at home and submit to the authority of their husbands, many fundamentalist women do work outside the home and exert powerful influence over family decisions (Ammerman, 1987). Moreover, although many religions stress the value of keeping families intact, increased religious involvement does not do much to strengthen troubled marriages (Booth, Johnson, Branaman, & Sica, 1995). It may slightly decrease thoughts about divorce, but it doesn't necessarily enhance marital happiness or keep spouses from fighting.

The Influence of Economics

The economy affects virtually every aspect of family life, from the amount of money coming into the household to the day-to-day management of finances and major purchasing decisions. Money matters are closely tied to feelings of satisfaction within family relationships. When couples are disappointed with how much money they have or how it is spent, they find all aspects of their relationships less satisfying (Blumstein & Schwartz, 1983). Sustaining a supportive, nurturing family environment is nearly impossible without adequate income or health care. When economic foundations are weak, the emotional bonds that tie a family together can be stretched to the breaking point.

Financial problems are not just private troubles. Rather, they are directly linked to larger economic patterns. A deep recession and a high national unemployment rate have obvious effects on family life. At the global level, the competitive pressures of the international marketplace have forced many businesses and industries to make greater use of so-called disposable workers—those who work part time or on a temporary contract. These jobs offer no benefits and no security and therefore make family life less stable. Other companies have reduced their costs by cutting salaries, laying off workers, or encouraging early retirement. Some businesses end up relocating either to other countries or to other parts of the United States where they can pay lower wages (see Chapter 10 for a more detailed discussion). Relaxed rules on foreign investment and export duties have made it easy for U.S. companies to open low-wage assembly plants abroad. The companies obviously benefit from higher profits, and the impoverished workers in these countries benefit from the added income. But displaced U.S. workers and their families may suffer.

The financial strains of living in the 21st century have made it difficult for most young couples to survive on only one income. For instance, it's estimated that it will cost two-parent, middle-income families more than $220,710 to raise a child from birth to the age of 17, up from $25,230 in 1970 (Lino, 2012; U.S. Department of Agriculture, 2001). Since the mid 1970s, the amount of an average family budget earmarked for mortgage payments increased 69%. And the cost of a college degree has increased 1,120% over the past three decades (Jamrisko & Kolet, 2012).

But incomes have not risen proportionately. In fact, in constant dollars, median household incomes have remained stagnant since 1999 (ProQuest Statistical Abstract, 2013). Consequently, among families with children, nearly half (45%) are headed by two working parents; and fewer than one in three children now have a stay-at-home parent, compared to half in 1975 (Glynn, 2012).

How Social Diversity Influences Family

We cannot talk about structural influences on family life without discussing the role of gender, class, and race. Gender is especially influential, explaining a variety of phenomena in family relationships, such as the way people communicate, how they express themselves sexually, how they deal with conflict, and what they feel their responsibilities are. Culturally defined gender expectations in families are certainly changing. But men and women are still likely to enter relationships with vastly different prospects, desires, and goals.

As you learned in Chapter 5, traditional gender role socialization encourages women to be sensitive, express affection, and reveal weakness, whereas men are taught to be competitive, strong, and emotionally inexpressive. These stereotypes have some basis in fact. Research has consistently shown that women have more close friends than men and are more romantic in their intimate relationships (Perlman & Fehr, 1987). Furthermore, women have been shown to be more concerned about, attentive to, and aware of the dynamics of their relationships than men are (see, e.g., Fincham & Bradbury, 1987; Rusbult, Zembrodt, & Iwaniszek, 1986). Women even think more and talk more about their relationships than men do (Acitelli, 1988; Holtzworth-Munroe & Jacobson, 1985).

Ironically, such attentiveness and concern do not necessarily mean that women get more satisfaction out of family relationships than men do. In fact, the opposite may be true. According to one sociologist, every marriage actually contains two marriages—"his" and "hers"—and "his" seems to be the better deal (J. Bernard, 1972). Both married men and married women live longer and healthier lives than their single counterparts, but husbands typically are sick less often and have fewer emotional problems (Gove, Style, & Hughes, 1990; Ross, Mirowsky, & Goldstein, 1990; Waite & Gallagher, 2000). They are more likely to receive regular checkups, maintain healthy diets, and exercise regularly than unmarried men (Fustos, 2010b). One study found that compared with married women, married men have lower rates of back pain, headaches, serious psychological distress, and physical inactivity (Schoenborn, 2004).

The reason for these differences may lie in the relationship between cultural gender expectations and family demands. Because of the continued pressures of gender-specific family responsibilities, married women are more likely than married men to experience the stresses associated with parenthood and homemaking. Men have historically been able to feel they are fulfilling their family obligations by simply being financial providers. While some evidence suggests that fathers are struggling just as much as mothers in balancing work and family obligations (Harrington, Van Deusen, & Ladge, 2010), most people still interpret a father's long hours on the job as an understandable sacrifice for his family's sake. Fathers rarely spend as much time worrying about the effect their work will have on their children as mothers do.

In contrast, even in the relatively "liberated" United States, women's employment outside the home is often perceived as optional or, more seriously, as potentially damaging to the family. Even though women work for the same reasons men work—because they need the money—and are now either the primary breadwinners or co-breadwinners in two-thirds of families with children (Glynn, 2012), women have traditionally had to justify why working outside the home is not an abandonment of their family duties. You'd be hard pressed to find many journalists and scholars fearfully describing the perilous effects of *men's* outside employment on the family. But a mountain of articles, editorials, and research reports over the years—not to mention a steady stream of Hollywood films—have focused on the difficulties women have in juggling the demands of work and family and on the negative effects of mothers' employment on their children's well-being. Newspaper accounts of studies showing that children who spend time in day care have more behavioral problems than children who don't—even if the effect is slight—perpetuate the idea that mothers' labor force choices can have dire consequences (Carey, 2007).

Social class has a substantial effect on family life, too. You saw in Chapter 5 that social class can determine the lessons that parents instill in their children. Social class affects families in other ways, too. All families, no matter what their class standing, face the same issues: work, leisure, child rearing, and interpersonal relations (L. Rubin, 1994). But beneath the similarities, we see dramatic differences in how these issues are handled. For example, because of heightened concern over class boundaries, ancestry, and maintenance of prestige, upper-class parents exert much more control over the dating behaviors of their children than lower-class parents do (Domhoff, 1983; M. K. Whyte, 1990). Upper-class families are also better able to use their wealth and resources in coping with some of the demands of family life. Finding adequate childcare arrangements will probably not pose much of a dilemma to parents who can afford a full-time, live-in nanny.

FAMILY CHALLENGES

Given all the pressures on families from the society around them, it should be no surprise that some families experience serious problems. Those problems include divorce and its aftereffects and family violence.

Divorce

Although divorce is more common and more acceptable in some places than in others, virtually all societies have provisions—legal, communal, or religious—for dissolving marriages (McKenry & Price, 1995). As a general rule, divorce rates worldwide tend to be associated with socioeconomic development. The developing countries of Latin America (e.g., Ecuador, Nicaragua, and Panama) and Asia (e.g., Malaysia, Mongolia, and Sri Lanka) have substantially lower divorce rates than the developed countries of Western Europe and North America (Nugman, 2002).

Iran provides a vivid example of how development and modernization can influence divorce rates, even in a restrictive environment. Recent economic development there has created more job opportunities for women than ever before. And female college undergraduates now outnumber males two to one. Hence, more women now see divorce as an available way out of an unsatisfying marriage. As one Iranian sociologist put it,

> This economic freedom has had an effect on the behavior of women in the home. In the past, if a housewife left her home, she would go hungry; now there is a degree of possibility of finding a job and earning an income. (quoted in Yong, 2010, p. A4)

Consequently, between 2000 and 2010, the number of Iranian divorces per year tripled.

Even in societies that we would consider modern and developed, powerful religious forces can sometimes suppress divorce. For instance, in 1995, the Irish government began a campaign against the Catholic Church over the country's constitutional ban on divorce. The government estimated at that time that at least 80,000 people were trapped in broken marriages and that they deserved the right to end them and remarry. The Catholic bishops launched a massive advertising counterattack, arguing that even unhappily married people have an obligation to keep their marriages intact to provide a good example for society. The referendum passed by a minuscule margin, and in 1997, for the first time, people in Ireland had the right to legally divorce.

Although the dissolution of marriage is virtually universal, no society values divorce highly. In fact, in most societies, people who divorce are somehow penalized, either through formal controls such as fines, prohibitions against remarriage, excommunication, and forced alimony and child support or through informal means such as censure, gossip, and stigmatization.

The Normalization of Divorce

Fifty years ago, divorce was a topic people talked about in whispers if they talked about it at all. Today, of course, things are quite different. You'd be hard pressed to find an eight-year-old who doesn't know what the word *divorce* means or who hasn't witnessed the end of a marriage, either that of her or his parents or of someone close. Divorce has become a part of everyday life. It's in our movies, television shows, and novels. The children's sections of bookstores stock picture books showing little dinosaurs or bears worrying about the possibility of their parents divorcing. Hallmark has an entire line of greeting cards for parents whose children live elsewhere.

Although the U.S. divorce rate has declined a bit since reaching a peak in 1981 (Stevenson & Wolfers, 2007), it still remains high. Consider these statistics:

- Roughly 2.4 million U.S. adults divorce each year (ProQuest Statistical Abstract, 2013). That works out to just under 20 divorces per 1,000 existing marriages.
- About 40% of men and women in their 50s have been divorced at least once (U.S. Bureau of the Census, 2007).
- About 23% of marriages—not to mention 55% of cohabitations—end in divorce or separation within the first five years (Fustos, 2010a). The figure jumps to 33% after 10 years and 43% after 15 years (Bramlett & Mosher, 2002).

- Eighty-three percent of women who married between 1960 and 1964 reached their fifth anniversary, but only 74% of women who married between 1990 and 1994 did so (Kreider & Ellis, 2011).

Such figures frighten people who are about to enter a "lifetime" relationship and distress those already married who want some sense of permanence.

Despite the traditional "family values" rhetoric we hear so much about these days, divorce in the United States tends to be unaffected by religious restrictions or political conservatism. For instance, several studies have found that born-again Christians are just as likely as anyone else to divorce (cited in Belluck, 2004). In addition, divorce rates are lowest in the so-called liberal states of the Northeast and upper Midwest and are highest in the conservative, heavily religious states of the South, such as Alabama, Arkansas, Oklahoma, and Kentucky (D. Elliott & Simmons, 2011). Some sociologists argue that other factors more commonly found in these states—namely younger age at marriage, less education, and lower socioeconomic status—render religiosity irrelevant. No matter how religious they are, young people who drop out of school and marry quickly not only lack emotional maturity but are highly susceptible to the economic strains that can create insurmountable problems in a marriage.

At a cultural level, the causes of the high divorce rates in Western societies include things such as the weakening of the family's traditional economic bonds and the stress of shifting gender roles (D. Popenoe, 1993). One particularly important factor has been a cultural change in the perception of marriage. Marriage has become a voluntary contract system that can be ended at the discretion of either spouse. In the past, when economic needs—not to mention constraints such as parental expectations or religious norms—held couples together, people "made do" with loveless, unsatisfying marriages because they had to. But when these constraints do not exist, people are less willing to make do (Coontz, 2005). Women's increasing earning power and decreasing economic dependence on men have made it easier to end an unsatisfying marriage.

In addition, people's overall attitudes toward divorce have become more accepting. In the 1960s, a divorced politician didn't stand a chance of being elected in the United States. Today, many of our most influential lawmakers are divorced. In the 1980s,

Ronald Reagan's divorce and remarriage didn't prevent him from being elected—twice. In the 2008 presidential election, people barely mentioned candidate John McCain's divorce and remarriage. Most people now recognize that a divorce may be preferable to an unhappy marriage. In short, divorce is as much a part of U.S. family life as, well, marriage.

Changing perceptions of marriage and changing cultural attitudes toward divorce are typically accompanied by other institutional changes. In the United States, modifications of existing divorce laws in the past four decades have made it easier for people to end an unsatisfying marriage. Historically, evidence of wrongdoing—adultery, desertion, abuse, and so forth—was required for courts to grant a divorce. But since the early 1970s, every state has adopted a form of no-fault divorce. No-fault laws have eliminated the requirement that one partner be found guilty of some transgression. Instead, marriages are simply declared unworkable and terminated. Furthermore, no-fault divorce can reduce various forms of personal distress. For instance, whenever a state adopted a no-fault divorce law, rates of female suicide and domestic violence dropped significantly in that state (Stevenson & Wolfers, 2003). Today, couples can download the appropriate forms and get online help filling them out. As one divorcing man put it, "I filled out the forms in the course of a night—it took three hours—and saved $2,000" (quoted in Crary, 2003, p. A6).

Many critics argue that these laws and innovations have made divorce *too* easy and *too* quick. Indeed, there seems to be a desire in some areas of the country to return to more restrictive divorce laws. Some states, like Vermont, New Jersey, North Carolina, and South Carolina, have mandatory "cooling off" periods that require couples to be separated for six months to a year before filing for divorce. Arkansas requires an 18-month period of separation. Some states, like Rhode Island and Nebraska, have mandatory waiting periods of several months between when a couple files for divorce and when it can be finalized (Stonington & McIntyre, 2011). Other states have toyed with the idea of providing discounted marriage licenses to couples who participate in premarital counseling. In 1997, the Louisiana State Legislature passed a measure forcing engaged couples to choose between a standard marriage contract that permits no-fault divorce and a "covenant marriage," which can be dissolved only by a mutually agreed-on two-year separation (2½ years if children are present) or proof of fault—chiefly adultery, abandonment, or abuse (Fee, 2013). Arizona followed suit in 1998, as did Arkansas in 2001. Critics of such measures note that instead of having a positive impact on family life, the result might be an increase in contentious, expensive, potentially child-harming divorces and unhappy, perhaps even dangerous marriages.

Children, Divorce, and Single Parenting

More than 1 million U.S. children see their parents divorce each year (D. Elliott & Simmons, 2011). When we combine divorce, separation, widowhood, and out-of-wedlock births, a significant number of children grow up living with one parent. In 1960, 91% of children under 18 lived with both of their parents; by 2011, the figure had fallen below 69% (ProQuest Statistical Abstract, 2013; U.S. Bureau of the Census, 2011b). In fact, 8% of children who live with their mothers will witness three or more maternal partnerships (either marriage or cohabitation) by the time they reach 15 (Fustos, 2010a).

Although divorce can be traumatic for adults, most recover after a period of years. Children, however, have a more difficult time adjusting. For them, divorce may set a series of potentially disruptive changes in motion. They may have to move to a new home in a new neighborhood, make new friends, and go to a new school. Because the overwhelming majority of children of divorced parents live with their mothers (D. Newman, 2009), they often experience a decline in their standard of living. The earning capacity of women is generally lower than that of men to begin with. Furthermore, noncustodial fathers do not always pay child support. In 55% of divorces in which mothers have sole physical custody, fathers are required to pay child support (ProQuest Statistical Abstract, 2013). Of these, only 42% receive the full amount they are awarded, 28.5% receive partial payments, and 29.5% receive nothing (Grall, 2011). Hence, more than half of divorced mothers with custody of children don't receive all the financial assistance they have been granted.

The relationship that children have with their noncustodial parent also tends to deteriorate over time. Some research indicates that noncustodial fathers rarely see their children regularly or maintain close relationships with them (Furstenberg & Harris, 1992). What contact they do have with their children often diminishes over time (W. D. Manning & Smock,

1999). One study found that 75% of noncustodial fathers never attend their child's school events, 85% never help them with their homework, and 65% never take them on vacations (Teachman, 1991). Another found that fewer than one in five noncustodial fathers have a significant influence over their children's health care, education, religion, or other matters important to their welfare (Arendell, 1995).

What are the long-term effects of divorce on children? A substantial body of research shows that regardless of race or education of parents, children raised in single-parent homes have more problems at every stage of life than children from two-parent families. An extensive review of studies published during the 1990s found that children from divorced families fare worse in terms of academic success, psychological adjustment, self-concept, social competence, and long-term health than children from intact, two-parent families (Amato, 2000). When they reach adulthood, they are at greater risk of low socioeconomic attainment, increased marital difficulties, and divorce (Diekmann & Engelhardt, 1999).

These differences are typically attributed to factors such as the absence of a father, increased strain on the custodial parent to keep the household running, and emotional stress and anger associated with the separation. However, the causes of these problems are just as likely to be factors found in two-parent families: low income, poor living conditions, lack of parental supervision, and marital discord (Amato & Sobolewski, 2001; Cherlin, 1992).

Some critics argue that the standard research design in studies on the impact of divorce on children—comparing children whose parents have divorced with children in happy, intact families—is flawed. Indeed, if we compare kids from divorced families with kids from intact families whose parents are unhappily married or whose families experience a great deal of conflict, we find that the type and frequency of emotional and interpersonal problems are similar for both sets of children (Cherlin et al., 1991). In fact, children who grow up in intact families marked by frequent conflict may actually suffer more. This research suggests that behavioral problems are caused not by the divorce itself but by exposure to conflict between the parents both before and after the divorce (Stewart, Copeland, Chester, Malley, & Barenbaum, 1997). In short, the simple fact of growing up in a single-parent family may not be as important in the development of a child as the way parents relate to each other and to the child.

Family Violence

Ironically, relationships in families—with the people who are supposed to nourish us when the outside world has sucked away our life energy—can also be some of the most violent relationships in a society.

Intimate-Partner Violence

Wife beating occurs in about 85% of the world's societies. According to the World Health Organization, women everywhere face the greatest threat of violence in their own homes (Garcia-Moreno, Jansen, Ellsberg, Heise, & Watts, 2006). A study of intimate violence in developing countries found that about one third of women in Egypt and Nicaragua and close to one half of women in Peru, Colombia, and Zambia have been beaten by their spouses or partners (Kishor & Johnson, 2004). In some countries—Indonesia, Ghana, India, and Uganda, for instance—it's not unusual for women to condone intimate violence against them. They are actually more likely than men to believe that it's acceptable for a husband to beat his wife if she argues with him or refuses to have sex with him (Population Reference Bureau, 2011).

Husband beating occurs less frequently—in about 27% of societies—and occurs less often than wife beating in societies where both are present (Levinson, 1989). In the United States, for instance, women are five times more likely than men to be beaten by an intimate partner (Catalano, 2012).

Exact statistics about the prevalence of violence among intimates are notoriously difficult to collect. In the United States, domestic violence typically occurs in private, beyond the watchful eyes of relatives, neighbors, and strangers. Even with the more stringent rules for police reporting that have been instituted in the past decade or two, most incidents of domestic violence are never reported; others are dismissed as accidents. It's been estimated that only about half of the cases of nonlethal violence against women are reported to the police (Rennison & Welchans, 2000).

The statistics on intimate-partner abuse that do exist indicate that it is a widespread problem, although it has declined somewhat over the past two decades. According to the U.S. Bureau of Justice Statistics, in 2010 (the last year for which figures were available at the time of this writing), there were about 906,000 incidents of rape or assault committed by current or former spouses, boyfriends, or girlfriends in the United States. About 85% of victims were women; and 76% of these women were previously victimized by the same offender (Catalano, 2012).

Other studies place the prevalence rate for intimate-partner violence significantly higher. For instance, the National Intimate Partner and Sexual Violence Survey of 16,500 women and men across the country found that nearly 36% of surveyed women and 28% of men said they'd been raped, physically assaulted, and/or stalked by a spouse, partner, or date at some point in their lifetimes. In addition, 6% of women and 5% of men report being victimized in the past 12 months (Black et al., 2011). If we extrapolate from these estimates to the general population, several million men and women are assaulted by an intimate partner annually in the United States, well above the Bureau of Justice Statistics official figure of 906,000.

Tragically, intimate partner violence can sometimes be lethal. According to the FBI, about 2,000 people were killed by an intimate partner in 2010; two thirds of these victims were women (cited in Fox, 2012). Often these murders are not isolated incidents but are the culmination of a pattern of violence. For instance, one study found that almost half the women murdered by their intimate partners had visited the emergency room within the two years before they were killed (Crandall, Nathens, Kernic, Holt, & Rivara, 2004).

But women don't just suffer disproportionate physical consequences. Female victims of intimate violence are also more likely than male victims to suffer psychologically (e.g., from depression, anxiety, or low self-esteem) and socially (e.g., isolation from friends). The economic costs can be steep, too. It's estimated that intimate violence costs about $8.3 billion a year in direct costs (medical and mental health care) and indirect costs (lost productivity due to time away from work; Centers for Disease Control and Prevention, 2009). Women who experience severe forms of abuse are also more likely than women who experience less serious forms of abuse to lose their jobs or to go on public assistance.

Although domestic violence between heterosexual partners gets most of the attention, same-sex couples are not immune to the problem. Indeed, same-sex intimate violence is widespread. It's estimated that between 42% and 79% of gay men and 25% and 50% of lesbians have experienced some type of intimate violence (cited in Burke & Owen, 2006).

In fact, some researchers claim that more violence occurs in long-term homosexual relationships than in heterosexual relationships (P. Cameron, 2003).

Child Abuse

Children are even more likely to be victims of intimate violence than adult family members. In some poverty-stricken countries, children may be consigned to unpleasant and dangerous labor, sold to buy food for the rest of the family, or even murdered in infancy if their parents don't want them or can't afford them. In the United States, there were about 754,000 victims of child abuse and/or neglect in 2010 (ProQuest Statistical Abstract, 2013). Because the vast majority of child abuse incidents involve victims who can't protect themselves or report the abuse and remain hidden from the police and social service agencies, many researchers think the actual figure is much higher. And if we take violence against children to mean any act of physical aggression directed by an adult toward a child—including spanking and slapping—perhaps as many as 9 of every 10 U.S. children under the age of three have been the object of violence at the hands of their parents or caretakers (Straus & Gelles, 1990).

Because of the relative size of victims and abusers, child abuse can sometimes be fatal. It's estimated that 1,740 children nationally died from abuse or neglect in 2008, and 71% were killed by one or both parents. About 80% of these victims were younger than four years old at the time of their death (Child Welfare Information Gateway, 2010).

Intimate Violence in a Cultural Context

Individual-level factors such as frustration over money, stress, and alcohol and drug use are frequently cited as major causes of domestic violence. To some analysts, batterers are either psychopaths or people who are just plain prone to violence. Although it would be comforting to believe that intimate violence is rare and occurs only in families that harbor a "sick" partner, parent, or spouse, it actually happens with alarming frequency and is likely to be committed by people we would otherwise consider "normal." Intimate-partner abuse and child abuse—not to mention elder abuse and violence between siblings—occur in every culture, class, race, and religion. It is not an aberration; it is a fundamental characteristic of the way we relate to one another in private, intimate settings. So to fully understand intimate violence, we

must take a look at some important characteristics of the society in which it occurs.

The United States is fundamentally committed to the use of violence to achieve desirable ends (Straus, 1977). For many people, violence is considered the appropriate means by which to resolve certain problems. Furthermore, violence pervades the culture. It is in our schools, our movies, our toy stores, our video games, our spectator sports, our government, and even our clothes. The Woolrich clothing company, for example, markets a line of pants, vests, and jackets designed to "fashionably" conceal a weapon (Richtel, 2012). It's in our everyday language, too. How many times have you heard a parent "playfully" warn a misbehaving child that she or he is "cruisin' for a bruisin'"?

In addition to the pervasiveness of violence in the culture, families have several characteristics that increase the probability of conflict. For instance, we spend a lot of time with family members and interact with them across a wide range of situations. The intimacy of these interactions is intense. Emotions run deep. The anger we may feel toward a stranger or an acquaintance never approaches the intensity of the anger we feel toward a spouse—or for that matter, toward a sibling or a child.

Moreover, we also know more about family members than we know about other people in our lives. We know their likes and dislikes, their fears, and their desires. And they know these things about us, too. If someone in your family insults you, you know immediately what you can say to get even. Spouses usually know the "buttons" they can push to hurt or infuriate each other. Arguments can escalate into violence when one partner focuses on the other's vulnerabilities and insecurities.

Finally, family life contains endless sources of stress and tension. For one thing, we expect a lot from our families: emotional and financial support, warmth, comfort, and intimacy. When these expectations aren't fulfilled, stress levels escalate. Life circumstances also contribute to family tension (Gelles & Straus, 1988). The birth and raising of a child, financial problems, employment transitions, illness, old age, death, and so on are all events that potentially increase stress. Indeed, a pregnant or recently pregnant woman is more likely to be the victim of a homicide than to die of any other cause (Horon & Cheng, 2001).

We must also look at the broader conceptions of gender that exist within a society. Male dominance in human societies has a long and rather infamous history. Roman law, for instance, justified a husband's killing his wife for reasons such as adultery, wine drinking, and other so-called inappropriate behaviors (Steinmetz, Clavan, & Stein, 1990). Most societies in the world remain dominated by and built around the interests of men. Men typically occupy the high-status positions, make important decisions and exercise political power, tend to dominate interpersonal relationships, and occupy the roles society defines as most valuable (see Chapter 12).

Men who beat their partners are not necessarily psychotic, deranged, "sick" individuals. Rather, they are often men who believe that male dominance is their birthright. Such men are actually living up to cultural prescriptions that are cherished in many societies—aggressiveness, male dominance, and female subordination (Dobash & Dobash, 1979). We have a deeply entrenched tendency to perceive intimate violence as "normal"—as something that, although not necessarily desirable, is not surprising or unexpected, either. Consequently, much of the research in this area has focused on the victims rather than on the perpetrators.

Personal and Institutional Responses to Intimate Violence

One question that has captured the attention of many marriage and family researchers is why people, especially women, stay in abusive relationships in societies where divorce is readily available. During the 1960s, the *masochism thesis*—that is, that women like being humiliated and hurt—was the predominant reason offered by psychiatrists (see, e.g., Saul, 1972). Even today, many psychiatrists believe that masochism—or *dependent personality disorder*, as it is now called—is a "legitimate" medical explanation for women who stay in abusive relationships. Other contemporary explanations focus on the woman's character flaws, such as a weak will or a pathological emotional attachment.

All of these explanations focus on the individual victim while paying little attention to her social situation. From a conflict perspective, we can see that in a society reluctant to punish male abusers, many women may perceive that they have no alternatives and may feel physically, economically, and emotionally trapped in their relationships. Many of them leave, sometimes on several occasions, but find that the opportunities outside the relationship are not sufficient and end up returning (D. J. Anderson, 2003). Indeed, the broader economic structure conspires to keep vulnerable women in abusive relationships.

Women who are unemployed and cannot support themselves financially are significantly less likely to leave an abusive marriage than women who are employed and who therefore have their own source of income (Strube & Barbour, 1983).

In some cases, the social organizations and institutions that are designed to help battered women contribute to their inability to escape abuse. As recently as 20 years ago, for instance, emergency room workers routinely interviewed battered women about their injuries with their husbands present. The courts, too, historically treated spousal violence less seriously than other crimes, making it even more difficult for women to seek help. Even today, about 80% of domestic violence victims don't have lawyers to guide them through the legal process (Prah, 2006). Most states require that volunteers who work on domestic violence hotlines complete 40 to 50 hours of training, but no such training is required for police personnel, lawyers, and judges (Prah, 2006).

Sometimes the resources in place to assist battered women are simply inadequate. Several states have waiting lists of intimate violence victims in need of counseling. If shelters are filled—as is often the case—victims may have to be bused hundreds of miles away to a place where shelter is available. This remedy may get them out of harm's way, but it may also wreck their work lives, endanger welfare checks, take them away from the support of extended family and friends, and disrupt their children's schooling.

In rural areas, there may be no services available at all. And if there's no public transportation, the shelters that do exist may be inaccessible to women who live miles away and don't own a car. In small towns, confidentiality is virtually impossible. The fact that people tend to know one another can dissuade a woman from calling a local sheriff's office for help, because the person answering might be a friend or relative of her abusive partner.

Broader societal circumstances may also play a role. In the months following the September 11, 2001, attacks, for instance, many battered women made the decision not to leave their relationships, clinging to familiar surroundings and coming to believe that a bad home was better than none in such unstable times. As a consequence, shelters reported dwindling demand for beds in their facilities in the immediate aftermath of the attacks (Lewin, 2001). In their need to acknowledge such realities, battered women are no different from any other individuals seeking to negotiate the complexities of social life.

CONCLUSION

Close relationships form the center of our personal universes. Life with intimates provides us with the sense of belonging that most of us need. However, although these relationships are the principal source of identity, community, happiness, and satisfaction for many, they can be the source of tremendous anguish and suffering for others.

Family, the most structured and culturally valued intimate relationship, is simultaneously a public and a private institution. True, most intimate and family behavior occurs away from the watchful eyes of others; we alone have access to our thoughts, desires, and feelings regarding those with whom we are intimately involved. But people around us,

the government, and even society as a whole have a vested interest in what happens in our intimate lives.

The social institutions and culture that make up our society also shape the very nature and definition of "family." Today, the boundaries of that definition are being pushed by rapidly increasing numbers of "nontraditional" families—dual-earner couples, single-parent households, cohabitors, same-sex married couples, and so on.

Every family relationship, whether it violates or conforms to current social norms, reflects the dominant ideals and beliefs regarding what a marriage or a family ought to look like. Although each relationship is unique, this uniqueness will always be bounded by the broader constraints of our cultural, group, and institutional values.

CHAPTER HIGHLIGHTS

◆ In this culture, close relationships are the standard against which we judge the quality and happiness of our everyday lives. Yet in complex, individualistic societies, they are becoming more difficult to establish and sustain.

◆ Many people in the United States long for a return to the "golden age" of the family. But the image of the U.S. family of the past is largely a myth.

◆ Although monogamous marriage is the only sexual relationship that has achieved widespread cultural legitimacy in the United States, other forms of intimacy (e.g., extra- and premarital sex, polygamy) are considered legitimate in other societies.

◆ Although we like to think that the things we do in our family relationships are completely private experiences, they are

continually influenced by large-scale political interests and economic pressures. Furthermore, our choices of romantic partners are governed to some degree by cultural rules that encourage us to form relationships within certain social groups and outside others.

◆ Divorce is not a solely private experience, either. It occurs within a cultural, historical, and community context. The high rate of remarriage after divorce indicates that people still view the institution of marriage as desirable.

◆ Instead of viewing domestic violence (spouse abuse and child abuse) as a product of "sick" individuals, sociologists are likely to view it as the product of a culture that tolerates violence in a variety of situations, traditionally grants men authority over women in family roles, and values family privacy and autonomy over the well-being of individual members.

KEY TERMS

endogamy: Marriage within one's social group

exogamy: Marriage outside one's social group

extended family: Family unit consisting of the parent–child nuclear family and other relatives, such as grandparents, aunts, uncles, and cousins

family: Two or more persons, including the householder, who are related by birth, marriage, or adoption and who live together as one household

household: Living arrangement composed of one or more people who occupy a housing unit

monogamy: The practice of being married to only one person at a time

neolocal residence: Living arrangement in which a married couple sets up residence separate from either spouse's family

nuclear family: Family unit consisting of at least one parent and one child

polygamy: Marriage of one person to more than one spouse at the same time

Constructing Difference

Social Deviance

Defining Deviance

Explaining Deviant Behavior

Linking Power, Deviance, and Social Control

I n 1984, 22-year-old Kelly Michaels moved to New York to pursue her dream of becoming an actress. She was a mild-mannered, devout Catholic who loved children. To support herself, she began working at the Wee Care Preschool in a New Jersey suburb. By all accounts, the kids there loved her (Hass, 1995).

Two weeks after Michaels left Wee Care for a better-paying job at another preschool, a four-year-old boy who was enrolled at Wee Care was taken to a doctor. A nurse rubbed his back and explained that she was going to take his temperature rectally. He said something like "That's what teacher [Michaels] does to me at nap time." Although it was unclear exactly what he meant by this—Michaels sometimes rubbed children's backs to get them to sleep and did take their temperature with a plastic forehead strip—the boy's alarmed mother, who happened to be the daughter of a local judge, called the school and the police (Michaels, 1993). The police questioned the child, as well as other children at Wee Care, searching for evidence that Michaels had sexually abused them. As word spread of the investigation, worried parents phoned other parents to share stories about the latest allegations. The police encouraged parents to seek state-funded psychological help for themselves as well as their children. In turn, the therapists encouraged the parents to cooperate with authorities in investigating Michaels.

That casual comment made by one little boy in a doctor's office touched off a 16-month investigation by the Division of Youth and Family Services, which eventually ended in a 235-count indictment against Michaels. During the investigation, scores of parents became convinced that Michaels had raped their children with silverware, wooden spoons, Legos, and light bulbs; that she had played "Jingle Bells" on the piano while naked; and that she had licked peanut butter off children's genitals, made them drink her urine, and forced them to eat excrement off the floor (Hass, 1995). By the time the trial began, Kelly was already being called the "most hated woman in all of New Jersey."

From the start, the case was filled with a host of inconsistencies and questionable legal tactics. For instance, an analysis of interview transcripts found that investigators led the children by introducing suggestive information, providing them with praise when they said things that implicated Kelly Michaels, expressing disbelief when they said good things about her, and inviting them to pretend or speculate about alleged events (Schreiber et al., 2006). Prosecutors never provided any substantiated evidence of abuse, yet they portrayed Michaels as "actressy" and "deviously charming." Everything she did was interpreted from the assumption that she was a "monster." For instance, if she was kind and patient with the children, that meant she was trying to seduce them.

None of the other teachers at the day care center had heard or seen anything, even though most of the alleged abuse took place during the children's nap time in a room set off only by a plastic curtain. The judge in the trial allowed the children to testify on closed-circuit TV while seated on his lap and denied the defense attorneys the opportunity to cross-examine them. One of the prosecution's witnesses—a child therapist—testified that the children who denied being molested by Ms. Michaels suffered from something called "child sexual abuse accommodation syndrome," a psychological condition that made them deny the abuse. In fact, the more the children denied it, the more certain the child therapist was that the abuse had actually happened.

Michaels was found guilty on 115 counts of assault, sexual abuse, and terrorist threats and sentenced to 47 years in prison. As if to add insult to injury, while in prison she received a bill from the Essex County public defenders office charging her $800,000 in legal fees (L. Manning, 2007). In 1993, after she had spent five years in prison—including an 18-month stint in solitary confinement—a state appellate court overturned the conviction. Later, the New Jersey Supreme Court upheld the appellate court's decision, decrying the original conviction with outrage. The court wrote that all 20 children who testified against Michaels had been led, bribed, or threatened (Hass, 1995).

You might think that a formal declaration of innocence from such a powerful body as a state supreme court would change people's feelings about Kelly Michaels. Yet she remained a target of hate. Several civil suits were filed against Michaels by parents who still believed their children had been sexually abused. One mother said she would try to kill Michaels with her bare hands if she had the chance. To date, no Wee Care parents have ever publicly retracted their accusations against their child's former teacher (L. Manning, 2007).

Why was it so hard for people to admit that Michaels was innocent? For one thing, at a time when child molestation was becoming a national obsession, the case reflected our darkest collective fears. The terrifying message was that our children could be hurt not only by creepy, middle-aged men but also by seemingly safe, 22-year-old college women. In the frenzy over children's safety, no one seemed willing to protect the principle that a defendant is innocent until proven guilty.

Even more striking about this case is what it says about the way people think. Once members of the community concluded that Kelly Michaels had committed these horrible acts, no amount of conflicting evidence was going to sway them to believe otherwise. Deviant labels and what they imply in people's minds can overshadow everything else about that person. When Michaels was convicted and formally tagged a criminal, the public degradation acquired legal legitimacy. From that point on, she would never again be able to reclaim a normal life and in many people's minds would forever be a "child molester." Long after Michaels's conviction on sexual abuse charges had been overturned, the media continued to identify her as a criminal. An Associated Press news release about her thwarted attempt to sue the county and the state was titled "Sex Offender's Case Denied in Court" (2001).

Few of us have spent five years in prison as a wrongly convicted child molester. But people are unjustifiably tagged as deviant all the time. Perhaps there have been times in your life when you acquired some sort of unflattering but inaccurate reputation that you couldn't shed. In this chapter, I examine several questions related to this phenomenon: What is deviance? How does society attempt to control deviant behavior? Who gets to define what is and is not deviant? And what are the consequences of being identified by others as deviant?

DEFINING DEVIANCE

In its broadest sense, *deviance* is socially disapproved behavior—the violation of some agreed-on norm that prevails in a community or in society at large. Staring at a stranger in an elevator, talking to oneself in public, wearing outlandish clothes, robbing a bank, and methodically shooting dozens of children in an elementary school can all be considered deviant acts. If we define deviance simply as any norm violation, then most deviance is rather trivial—even "normal"—like driving over the speed limit or walking across an intersection when the light is red. Most of us, at some point in our lives, occupy statuses or engage in behaviors that others could regard as deviant. But most sociologists focus on deviant acts that are assaults on mores, the most serious of a society's norms. It's this type of deviance to which I will devote most of my attention in this chapter.

The determination of which behaviors or characteristics are deviant and which are normal is complex. We usually assume there's a fair amount of agreement in a society about what and who is deviant. For instance, no one would challenge the notion that child abuse is bad and that child abusers ought to be punished. But the level of agreement within a given society over what specific acts constitute child abuse can vary tremendously. Spanking may be a perfectly acceptable method of discipline to one person but be considered a cruel form of abuse by another.

To further complicate the issue, some sociologists who are identified with structural functionalism (e.g., Durkheim, 1895/1958; Erikson, 1966) argue that deviance, as a class of behaviors, is not always bad for society and may actually serve a useful purpose. As you recall from Chapter 4, norm violations help define the cultural and moral boundaries that distinguish right from wrong and increase feelings of in-group togetherness among those who unite in opposition to deviance from group norms. At the

surface level, individual acts of deviance disrupt everyday life and generate varying degrees of social condemnation, but at a deeper level, they can contribute to the maintenance and continuity of society. Deviance can also create needed change (Durkheim, 1895/1958). During the 1950s and 1960s, civil rights protestors purposely broke laws they considered discriminatory, such as those that prevented Blacks from entering certain establishments or attending certain schools. These acts of deviance eventually helped convince many voters and politicians to support legislation ending legal segregation.

As you may have guessed, sociologists usually don't judge whether a given behavior should or shouldn't be considered deviant. Instead, they examine how deviance comes about and what it means to society. One of their primary concerns is whether people respond to deviance from the perspective that all human behavior can be classified as essentially good or bad (absolutism) or from the perspective that definitions of deviance are socially constructed (relativism).

Absolutist Definitions of Deviance

According to *absolutism*, there are two fundamental types of human behavior: (1) that which is inherently proper and good and (2) that which is intrinsically improper, immoral, evil, and bad. To those who subscribe to such a position, the distinction is clear and identifiable. The rightness or wrongness of an act exists prior to socially created rules, norms, and customs and independently of people's subjective judgments (Erich Goode, 1994).

Absolutist definitions of deviance imply something about society's relationship with the person who is considered deviant. Many people consider "deviants" to be psychologically, and perhaps even anatomically, different from ordinary, rule-abiding people. The attribute or behavior that serves as the basic reason for defining a person as deviant in the first place is considered pervasive and essential to his or her entire character (Hills, 1980). Respectable, conventional qualities become insignificant. It doesn't matter, for instance, that the "sexual deviant" has an otherwise ordinary life, that the "drug addict" no longer uses drugs, or that the violent act of the "wife batterer" was completely atypical of the rest of his life. In short, the deviant act or trait determines the overall worth of the individual (J. Katz, 1975). Being defined as deviant means being identified as someone who cannot and should not be treated as an ordinary member of society.

There's another element of unfairness involved in the absolutist approach to deviance. People routinely make judgments about deviants based on strongly held stereotypes. If you ask someone to imagine what a typical drug addict looks like, for instance, chances are she or he will describe a dirty, poor, strung-out young man living on the streets and resorting to theft to support his illegal habit. The image probably wouldn't be one of a middle-class, stay-at-home mother or clean-shaven, hardworking physician hooked on prescription drugs, even though these groups constitute a higher percentage of drug addicts than any other in U.S. society (Pfohl, 1994).

In U.S. society, the consequences of absolute deviant stereotypes fall heavily on members of ethnoracial minorities. Latino/as and African Americans make up over 70% of the U.S. inmate population even though they compose only about 27% of the general population (U.S. Sentencing Commission, 2011). Black males are incarcerated at a rate 2.4 times higher than Latino males and almost 7 times higher than white males (Tsai & Scommegna, 2012). On any given day, young black men without a high school diploma are more likely to be behind bars (37%) than to be employed (26%; Pettit, 2012).

Although some people may see such figures as clear evidence of higher rates of minority involvement in crime, other statistics seem to suggest something different. For instance, African Americans make up about 13% of the population, but they account for 38% of all arrests for violent crime, 29% of arrests for property crimes, and 32% of arrests for drug violations. Blacks are nearly four times more likely than Whites to be arrested on charges of marijuana possession, even though the two groups use the drug at comparable rates (cited in Urbina, 2013). In addition, African Americans account for 39% of convictions for violent crimes, 34% of convictions for property crimes, and 46% of convictions for drug crimes (U.S. Bureau of Justice Statistics, 2012). Since the death penalty was reinstated in 1977, 42% of defendants who have been executed have been Latino/a or African American, and 56% of the current death row population is Latino/a or African American (Snell, 2011).

Absolutist images of deviants are often oversimplified and fall short of accounting for every individual. The vast majority of African Americans do not commit crimes, just as the vast majority of gay men are not sexual predators; the vast majority of Italians are not involved in the Mafia; and the vast majority of Muslims are not terrorists. Nevertheless, the degree to which an entire group is characterized by an absolutist stereotype is important, because it determines individual and societal responses. If affluent housewives and businesspeople who abuse drugs are not considered typical drug addicts, they will never be the focus of law enforcement attention, collective moral outrage, political rhetoric, or public policy.

Relativist Definitions of Deviance

Reliance on a strict absolutist definition of deviance can lead to narrow and often inaccurate perceptions of many important social problems. This shortcoming can be avoided by employing a second approach to defining deviance, *relativism*, which draws from symbolic interactionism and the conflict perspective. This approach—which parallels the more general "cultural relativism" discussed in Chapter 4—states that deviance is not inherent in any particular act, belief, or condition; instead, it is socially constructed, a creation of collective human judgments and ideas. Like beauty, it is in the eye of the beholder. Consequently, no act is universally or "naturally" deviant. The relativist approach is useful when the focus of study is the process by which some group of people or some type of behavior is defined as deviant.

For the relativist, complex societies consist of different groups with different values and interests. Sometimes these groups agree and cooperate to achieve a common goal, as when different segments of society join together to fight a foreign enemy. But more often than not there is conflict and struggle among groups to realize their own interests and goals.

Different people or groups can thus have dramatically different interpretations of the same event. In 1995, a 35-year-old white ex-Marine named William Masters was taking his usual armed, late-night walk through a barren neighborhood in Los Angeles. He came upon two young Latino men spray painting graffiti beneath a freeway overpass. Masters wrote down the license number of their car on a small piece of paper. When the men saw him and demanded the paper, Masters pulled out his 9-millimeter pistol and shot them, wounding one and killing the other. He told the police that the men had threatened him with a screwdriver and he had acted in self-defense, even though both were shot in the back. He was not charged with murder. Eventually, he was found guilty on one count of carrying a concealed gun in public and one count of carrying a loaded gun in public—charges that carried a maximum of 18 months in jail and a $2,000 fine.

Shortly after his arrest, Masters made a case for why his actions shouldn't be defined as deviant. He told one interviewer he was sure people were glad that he, the intended victim, had gotten away and that no jury would ever convict him (Mydans, 1995). Many people agreed. Callers to radio talk shows and letters to newspapers applauded him for his vigilant antigraffiti efforts and for his foresight in carrying a weapon for self-protection. A few suggested that society would be better off with more people like William around (Mydans, 1995). But others expressed dismay at the verdict and argued that Masters was simply a racist out looking for trouble. They felt he was a deviant who literally got away with murder.

All those who expressed opinions on this case would likely agree on one thing: "Murder" is a deviant act at the far end of the spectrum of social acceptability. However, their perceptions of whether William Masters was a "murderer" were quite different. Was he a "hero" or a "killer"? The answer lies not in the objective act of taking another's life but in the way others define and respond to such an act.

To fully understand the societal and personal implications of deviance designations, we must look at how these definitions are created and perpetuated. One key factor is who is doing the defining. One person's crime is another person's act of moral conscience; one group's evil is another group's virtue; one culture's terrorist is another culture's freedom fighter.

Definitions of deviance are also relative to particular cultural standards:

- In Singapore, a young vandal is a serious deviant (punishable by caning), as is a person who leaves chewed gum where it can be stepped on. The fine for bringing one stick of gum into Singapore is $10,000.
- In Thailand, it is illegal to step on a *baht*, the nation's currency, or insult the king in any way.
- In Malaysia, a Muslim woman can be whipped for drinking alcohol in public or arrested for snacking during the daylight fasting hours of Ramadan.
- In some Indonesian cities, it is illegal for women to straddle motorbikes or hold on to a male driver while riding on the back of one.

- In Japan, a drunk driving conviction carries the possibility of a three- to five-year prison sentence, depending on the level of intoxication, and passengers who either provide the alcohol or provide the vehicle face criminal charges as well.

Deviance definitions undergo changes over time as well. For instance, several states at one time had laws designed specifically to protect women's virtue. Florida had a law that prohibited women from parachuting on Sundays. Michigan law made it a crime for men to use profanity in front of women. In Texas, it was a crime for women to adjust their stockings in public. The state of Washington still has a law on the books that makes it illegal to call a woman a "hussy" or "strumpet" in public (Kershaw, 2005). Sometimes new laws outlawing previously acceptable behavior seem just as ludicrous.

Conflict over deviance definitions often reflects differing cultural expectations. In 2005, for instance, an appeals court in Florida upheld a judge's earlier ruling that a Muslim woman could not wear a burka—a traditional veil that covers all but a woman's eyes—in her driver's license photo. In 2005, the U.S. Supreme Court ruled that the federal government could prohibit the medicinal use of marijuana even in those states that explicitly permit it (L. Greenhouse, 2005). Even though people in the United States who wear burkas or smoke marijuana for medical purposes don't consider themselves deviant, these court rulings meant they could be defined and treated as such by the dominant culture.

The absolutist approach assumes that certain individual characteristics are typical of all deviants, but the relativist approach acknowledges that there is no typical deviant. In fact, the same act committed by two different people may yield very different community responses. In 1980, a Bayonne, New Jersey, teacher named Diane Cherchio was caught kissing and groping a 13-year-old male student at an eighth-grade dance. A few years later, after being promoted to guidance counselor, she had sex with an 11th grader, became pregnant, and eventually married him upon his graduation in 1985. Yet instead of being fired or even reprimanded, she was allowed to continue working in the public school district for two decades. When the son she gave birth to grew to be a teenager, Ms. Cherchio began having sex with one of his friends. She used her school authority to rearrange the boy's schedule so they had time for their sexual trysts. When that boy's parents found out and complained to the police, she was arrested. Again, she was not fired. School officials instead allowed her to take an early retirement package that increased her pension. They even gave her a gala farewell party. When she finally pleaded guilty to sexual assault charges in 2005, glowing references from coworkers convinced the judge to sentence her to probation and to spare her from registering as a sex offender (Kocieniewski, 2006).

Cherchio was eventually punished, as have been other older women who've had sexual relationships with teenage boys. Nevertheless, it's hard to imagine a school accommodating or defending a male teacher who seduced teenage girls in such a way. Because she was a young, attractive, intelligent woman whose victims were willing teenage boys, people in her community looked the other way. When *she* did it, somehow it wasn't so bad. One author summed up the public response to such incidents: "A teenage boy who gets to live his fantasy? What can be the harm?" (Levy, 2006, p. 2).

From a relativist approach, immediate situational circumstances, such as the time and location of an act, can also influence definitions of deviance. For example, drinking alcohol on the weekend is more acceptable than drinking during the week, and drinking in the evening is more acceptable than drinking in the morning. Twenty-four states have "stand your ground" laws, which justify deadly force if a person feels threatened not just in their home but in any other place they have "a right to be" (Currier, 2012). Had William Masters lived in any of these places instead of Los Angeles, he wouldn't have faced even minor criminal charges; he would have simply been a citizen exercising his legal right. These laws came under national scrutiny recently when an unarmed Florida teenager named Trayvon Martin was gunned down on a Sanford, Florida, sidewalk by a neighborhood watch captain who claimed he felt threatened by the boy and was acting in self-defense. A jury agreed, finding the man not guilty of the second-degree murder charge he faced.

If deviance is relative, then even acts of extreme violence may be defined as acceptable under certain circumstances. Killings committed under the auspices of the government—shooting looters during a riot, killing enemy soldiers during wartime, or executing convicted murderers—fall outside the category of behaviors deemed deviant and problematic in society. However, a relativist approach to defining deviance doesn't mean that we can't be upset by activities that some people consider acceptable:

> Relativity does not require moral indifference, and it does not mean that one can never be . . . horrified by what one experiences in another group or culture. . . . [It] just reminds us that our personal beliefs or our cultural understandings are not necessarily found everywhere. (Curra, 2000, p. 13)

Relativists, like absolutists, acknowledge that every society identifies certain individuals and certain behaviors as bothersome and disruptive and therefore as justifiable targets of social control, whether through treatment, punishment, spiritual healing, or correction. However, to a relativist the main concerns in defining deviance are not so much what is committed but rather who commits the act, who labels it, and where and when it occurs. Some people have the wherewithal to avoid having their acts defined as deviant; others may fit a certain profile and be defined as deviant even if they've done nothing wrong. Definitions of deviant behavior change over time, and certain acts are acceptable to some groups and not others. The definitions most likely to persevere and become part of the dominant culture are those that have the support of influential segments of the population or have widespread agreement among the members of that society.

The Elements of Deviance

The two perspectives on defining deviance raise some complex and controversial issues. The definition of *deviance* most applicable to both perspectives is this: behavior (how people act), ideas (how people think), or attributes (how people appear) that some people in society—though not necessarily all people—find offensive, wrong, immoral, sinful, evil, strange, or disgusting.

This definition has three important elements (Aday, 1990):

- *An expectation*: Some sort of behavioral expectation must exist, a norm that defines appropriate, acceptable behavior, ideas, or characteristics. The expectations may be implicit or explicit, formal or informal, and more or less widely shared.
- *A violation*: Deviance implies some violation of normative expectations. The violation may be real or alleged; that is, an accusation of wrongdoing may

be enough to give someone the reputation of being a deviant.

- *A reaction*: An individual, group, or society must react to the deviance. The reaction can take several forms: avoidance, criticism, warnings, punishment, or treatment. It may accurately reflect the facts, or it may bear little relation to what really happened, as when people are punished or ostracized for acts they did not commit.

Deviance, then, cannot exist if people don't have some idea of what's appropriate, if someone hasn't been seen or accused of violating some social norm, and if others haven't reacted to the alleged transgression.

EXPLAINING DEVIANT BEHAVIOR

The question of how certain acts and certain people come to be defined as deviant is different from the question of why people do or don't commit acts that are considered deviant. Psychological or biological theories addressing this question might focus on the personality or physical characteristics that give rise to deviant behavior, such as psychological proneness to violence or addiction, genetic predispositions, chemical imbalances, or neurological defects. Most sociological theories, however, focus on the environmental forces that act upon people and the effectiveness of various methods to control them.

The structural-functionalist perspective, for instance, tells us that it is in society's interest to socialize everyone to strive for success so that the most able and talented people will come to occupy the most important positions. Sociologist Robert Merton's "strain theory" (1957) argues that the probability of committing deviant acts increases when people experience a strain or contradiction between these culturally defined success goals and access to legitimate means by which to achieve them. The despair and hopelessness that accompany sudden economic hardship can sometimes evoke anger and blame, leading to violence. Some criminologists noted an unprecedented spike in mass murders in 2009 during the height of the economic recession. For instance, in the span of one month, there were eight mass murders that took the lives of 57 people (cited in Rucker, 2009).

More commonly, though, those who believe that being wealthy and achieving the "American dream" are important goals but have no money,

employment opportunities, or access to higher education will be inclined to achieve the goal of financial success through illegitimate means (Merton, 1957). One of the most consistent findings in criminal research is the correlation between unemployment (a factor closely associated with economic disadvantage) and property crime (Hagan, 2000). In this sense, people who sell, say, illegal drugs or stolen cell phones to get rich are motivated by the same desire as people who sell real estate or automobiles to make money. But people who lack access to legitimate means to achieve success may also reject the culturally defined goal of success and retreat from society altogether. According to Merton, deviants such as vagrants, chronic drunks, drug addicts, and the mentally ill fall into this category.

Another sociologist, Edwin Sutherland, bases his theory of deviance (Sutherland & Cressey, 1955) on the symbolic interactionist principle that we all interpret life through the symbols and meanings we learn in our interactions with others. Sutherland argues that individuals learn deviant patterns of behavior from the people with whom they associate on a regular basis: friends, family members, peers. Through our associations with these influential individuals, we learn not only the techniques for committing deviant acts (e.g., how to pick a lock or how to snort cocaine) but also a set of beliefs and attitudes that justify or rationalize such behavior (Sykes & Matza, 1957). To commit deviant acts on a regular basis, we must learn how to perceive those acts as normal.

Deterring Deviance

Some sociologists have turned away from the issue of why some people violate norms to the issue of why most people don't (see, e.g., Hirschi, 1969). Their concern is with the mechanisms society has in place to control or constrain people's behavior. *Deterrence theory* assumes that people are rational decision makers who calculate the potential costs and benefits of a behavior before they act. If the benefits of a deviant act (e.g., money or psychological satisfaction) outweigh the costs (e.g., getting caught and punished), we will be inclined to do it. Conversely, if the costs exceed the benefits, the theory predicts that we'll decide it's not worth the risk (van den Haag, 1975).

The controversy surrounding capital punishment is, essentially, a debate over its true capacity to deter potentially violent criminals. According to deterrence theory, a punishment, to be effective, must be swift as well as certain and severe. However, capital punishment is anything but swift. Currently, about 3,200 inmates are on death row in the United States, but only 1,234 prisoners have been executed since 1977, when the death penalty was reinstated. On average, death row inmates spend close to 15 years awaiting execution, a figure that has been growing steadily for three decades (Snell, 2011).

In addition, opponents of the death penalty argue that violent offenders are often under the influence of drugs or alcohol or are consumed by passion when they commit acts of violence; their violence is more or less spontaneous. Hence, they may not be thinking rationally (weighing the potential benefits of the act against the costs of punishment) at the time of the crime. The threat of being condemned to death may not deter such people when they are committing the act. Researchers have, indeed, found little empirical support for the argument that the threat of capital punishment reduces murders (W. C. Bailey, 1990; Galliher & Galliher, 2002). Nor have they found that well-publicized executions deter homicides (R. D. Peterson & Bailey, 1991). In fact, over the past two decades, the homicide rate in states with the death penalty has consistently been about 50% higher than the rate in non–death penalty states (Death Penalty Information Center, 2013b). According to one study, 9 out of 10 leading criminologists don't think the death penalty deters homicides (Amnesty International, 2013),

Most societies around the world have abandoned the use of capital punishment for both moral and practical reasons: It's inhumane, and it doesn't reduce crime. Even in China, a country responsible for most of the world's court-ordered executions, legislators voted in 2006 to bar all but the nation's highest court from approving death sentences ("China Changes," 2006). Nevertheless, the majority of U.S. citizens—about 62% according to one study—continue to favor the death penalty (Pew Research Center for People and the Press, 2012). Legislative efforts to increase the number of offenses punishable by death and to reduce the number of "death row" appeals an offender can file reflect this popular attitude. However, such a position can sometimes conflict with economic realities. During the recent recession, lawmakers in several states pushed bills to abolish the death penalty, not on moral grounds but to cut costs. Some argued that capital punishment cases cost states nearly three times as much as homicide cases where the death penalty was not sought (Urbina, 2009).

Labeling Deviants

These theories help us explain why some people engage in deviant acts and others don't, but they bypass the question of why certain acts committed by certain people are considered deviant in the first place. *Labeling theory* attempts to answer this question by characterizing a deviant person as someone—such as the preschool teacher Kelly Michaels—to whom the label "deviant" has been successfully applied (Becker, 1963; Lemert, 1972). According to this theory, the process of being singled out, defined, and reacted to as deviant changes a person in the eyes of others and has important life consequences for the individual. Once the label sticks, others may react to the labeled deviant with rejection, suspicion, withdrawal, fear, mistrust, and hatred (A. K. Cohen, 1966). A deviant label suggests that the person holding it is habitually given to the types of undesirable motives and behavior thought to be typical of others so labeled. The "ex-convict" is seen as a cold-blooded and ruthless character incapable of reforming, the "mental patient" as dangerous and unpredictable, the "alcoholic" as weak willed, the "prostitute" as dirty and immoral.

The problem, of course, is that such labels overgeneralize and can be misleading. For instance, psychologists recently found that upper-class individuals behave more unethically than lower-class people. They are more likely to break the law while driving, take things from others, lie in negotiations, and cheat to increase the chances of winning a prize (Piff, Stancato, Côté, Mendoza-Denton, & Keltner, 2012).

The type of deviant who receives the harshest expressions of public outrage changes with some regularity. At various times, child molesters, crack addicts, and drug dealers have claimed the title of society's most despised deviant. Currently, foreign terrorists, greedy Wall Street executives, steroid-fueled athletes, and cyberstalkers fit the bill. Often, collective hostility is directed toward people who don't seem to pose a grave societal threat, like those who talk loudly on cell phones in public places. Cigarette smoking used to be seen as a sign of sophistication; nowadays many people consider smoking filthy and disgusting, and smokers are often banished from buildings and forced to keep their distance from entryways. Across the country, landlords of privately owned multiple housing units have begun to forbid smoking *inside* people's apartments.

Cities around the country sometimes use humiliating labels as an alternative to incarceration. For example, a Cleveland woman who had driven her SUV on a sidewalk to avoid stopping for a school bus was ordered by a judge to stand on a street corner holding a sign that read "Only an idiot would drive on the sidewalk to avoid a school bus" (Palmer, 2012). Some cities post the pictures of drug offenders, deadbeat dads, men who solicit prostitutes, even public urinators on billboards. In some states, convicted drunk drivers have to put special license plates on their cars, and convicted shoplifters must take out ads in local newspapers that use their photographs and announce their crimes. The Chicago police department posts on its website photographs and partial addresses of men arrested for soliciting prostitution, even though they've not yet been convicted. Kansas City posts this information on a government-owned local television station. Such penalties are designed to shame the labeled individuals into behaving properly and to deter others from committing such crimes. In the process, they satisfy the public's need for dramatic moral condemnation of deviants (Hoffman, 1997).

Deviant labels can impair an individual's eligibility to enter a broad range of socially acceptable roles. Many state penal systems use an instrument called the "Psychopathy Checklist–Revised" to decide an inmate should be awarded parole. The battery of questions yields a score that allegedly determines if the individual is a "psychopath" or not. If an inmate is found to be a "psychopath" and therefore not eligible for parole, the label stays on his or her permanent record, rendering future positive parole decisions unlikely or even impossible ("This American Life," 2011b). Indeed, some psychologists believe that fledgling psychopaths can be identified as early as kindergarten. Others, however, feel that branding a child at such an early age can be devastating:

> This isn't like autism, where the child and parents will find support. Even if accurate it's a ruinous diagnosis. No one is sympathetic to the mother of a psychopath (quoted in Kahn, 2012, p. 35).

Consider also the impact of the 1994 Federal Crime Bill on convicted sex offenders. This law requires states to register and track convicted sex offenders for 10 years after their release from prison and to privately notify police departments when the sex offenders move into their community. A website, Family Watchdog, provides information on released sexual offenders in all 50 states, including their names, addresses, convictions, and photographs. Many states have "sexually violent predator" statutes that give officials the power to commit violent sex offenders to mental hospitals involuntarily or to retain them in prison indefinitely *after* their prison terms are up. Because of laws that allow registered sex offenders to live in towns as long as their residence is more than 2,000 feet from a school or park, some communities around the country have found a new way of excluding these individuals from their midst: they've begun creating "pocket parks" out of tiny parcels of land in the community, thereby forcing sex offenders who live nearby to move. These parcels, which can be as small as 1,000 square feet, are often parks in name only, containing no playground equipment or even children. Their sole purpose is to keep sex offenders out of the neighborhood (Lovett, 2013b). These convicts have "paid their debt" to society by serving their mandated punishment. But convicted sex offenders can never fully shed their deviant identities. Finding a decent place to live or a decent job may be a problem for the rest of their lives.

And it's not just sex offenders who must navigate the stigmatizing effects of their deviant labels. Several states are seeking to establish online registries for offenders who engage in a wide range of crimes including arson, drunk driving, methamphetamine production, and animal cruelty (Erica Goode, 2011). The appeal of these laws is hard to understate. According to one law professor, "You'd be hard pressed to find a more politically popular movement in recent years. Whether it's actually good public policy is a distinct and independent question from whether it's politically popular and makes us feel good" (quoted in Erica Goode, 2011, p. A12).

All ex-offenders experience the "stickiness" of labels to some degree, despite legislative efforts to help them. In 2007, Congress passed the Second Chance Act, which funds a variety of services and resources for ex-offenders in hopes of aiding their reentry into society. Nevertheless, potential employers still commonly refuse to hire ex-convicts, even when the crime has nothing to do with the job requirements. Like the public at large, many employers believe that prisons do not rehabilitate but actually make convicts more deviant by teaching them better ways to commit crimes and by providing social networks for criminal activity outside the prison (R. Johnson, 1987). In recent years—particularly in the wake of the attacks of September 11, 2001—the criminal background check industry has grown dramatically. The public now has greater access to criminal history records of ex-offenders than ever before through such websites as CriminalSearches .com and ScreenStaff.com. Nine out of 10 companies—both large and small—now use criminal background checks as part of their hiring process. An examination of jobs posted on Craigslist found several hundred ads that contained statements that the company wouldn't consider applicants with criminal records: for example, "Do not apply with any misdemeanors/felonies;" "You must not have any felony or misdemeanor convictions on your record. Period;" and "We are looking for people with . . . spotless background/criminal history" (M. N. Rodriguez & Emsellem, 2011).

In addition, being labeled as deviant may actually increase the probability that the behavior itself will stay the same or become worse (Archer, 1985). A great many ex-convicts in the United States do return to prison. According to the U.S. Department of Justice, a little over two thirds of all ex-convicts released in 1994 were arrested for a new offense within three years, and 47% were convicted again (Langan & Levin, 2002).

Deviant labels are so powerful that a mere accusation of dangerous activity can taint a person's character. In 2009, two Muslim immigrants from Morocco enlisted in the Army National Guard. They both successfully completed basic training, but just prior to leaving the base in South Carolina, they were questioned by military investigators who suspected them and three other Moroccan immigrants of plotting to poison fellow soldiers. They were placed under military arrest. For the next month and a half, the Army prevented them from calling their families without military personnel present, barred them from speaking to each other in Arabic, and required them to go to the mess hall and bathroom with an escort. It wasn't until 2010 that the Army concluded that the allegations against them were completely unfounded. However, despite their innocence, the FBI has kept its investigation open. As a result, the two men have been unable to receive security clearances, become citizens, obtain concealed weapons permits, or get government jobs (Dao, 2011).

LINKING POWER, DEVIANCE, AND SOCIAL CONTROL

Because deviance is socially defined, the behaviors and conditions that come to be called "deviant" can at times appear somewhat arbitrary. Sociologists working from the conflict perspective would say that definitions of and responses to deviance are often a form of social control exerted by more powerful people and groups over less powerful people and groups. In U.S. society, the predominant means of controlling those whose behavior does not conform to the norms established by the powerful are criminalization and medicalization. Labeling people either as criminals or as sick people gives socially powerful individuals, groups, and organizations a way to marginalize and discount certain people who challenge the status quo. Criminalization and medicalization also have economic and other benefits for certain powerful groups.

The Criminalization of Deviance

Presumably, certain acts are defined as crimes because they offend the majority of people in a given society. Most of us trust our legal institutions—legislators, courts, the police, and prisons—to regulate social behavior in the interest of the common good. But according to the conflict perspective, most societies ensure that offenders who are processed through the criminal justice system are members of the lowest socioeconomic class (Reiman & Leighton, 2010). Poor people are more likely to get arrested, be formally charged with a crime, have their cases go to trial, get convicted, and receive harsher sentences than more affluent citizens (Parenti, 1995; Reiman & Leighton, 2010). In some places, people who can't afford to pay fines—say, for speeding tickets—often end up in jail (Bronner, 2012). Furthermore, although the accused have a constitutional right to an attorney even if they can't afford one, many poor people still face legal proceedings alone. It turns out that this constitutional provision only applies to criminal cases, not civil ones. Hence in civil matters like home foreclosures, job loss, and child support, poor people often end up representing themselves, which usually means they lose because they don't present necessary evidence, commit procedural mistakes, and fail to examine witnesses thoroughly. It's estimated that 80% of the legal needs of the poor in the United States go unmet (Bronner, 2013).

The quality of legal representation for defendants in criminal cases is also skewed along socioeconomic lines. When wealthy or powerful individuals are tried for capital crimes (an occurrence that, in and of itself, is rare), they can usually afford effective legal representation. In contrast, poor defendants in such cases are often represented by public defenders, who have fewer resources available for investigative work and who may have little, if any, experience in such matters. Supreme Court Justice Ruth Bader Ginsburg summed up the situation this way:

> People who are well represented at trial do not get the death penalty. . . . I have yet to see a death case among the dozens coming to the Supreme Court on eve-of-execution stay applications in which the defendant was well represented at trial. (quoted in Death Penalty Information Center, 2013a, p. 1)

Consider the case of Leroy White, a poor black Alabama man who was facing the death penalty. After being convicted, Mr. White's appeals attorney withdrew from the case without telling White. He admitted that he let his client miss a critical appeal deadline, shortening the appeals process. This attorney, who took over White's case after another member of his firm was suspended, practiced transactional tax and corporate law and had never been in a courtroom. Mr. White was executed in 2011 (Death Penalty Information Center, 2013a).

Cases like these have intensified the national debate over class—not to mention racial—disparities in the quality of legal representation. Ninety-eight percent of chief district attorneys in death penalty states are white; 1% are black. Since 1977, 19 white defendants have been executed for murdering black victims; during the same period, 264 black defendants have been executed for killing white victims (The Criminal Justice Project, 2012).

Persistent imbalances in the justice system go beyond the way disadvantaged people are treated by the police, judges, attorneys, and juries. If they were simply a matter of discrimination, the situations would be relatively easy to address. Instead, they occur because the actions of poor individuals are more likely to be *criminalized*—that is, officially defined as crimes in the first place. When poor people do commit certain crimes—car theft, burglary, assault, illegal drug use, and so on—they become "typical criminals" in the public eye (Reiman & Leighton, 2010).

The Social Reality of Crime

Followers of the conflict perspective point out that powerful groups often try to foster a belief that society's rules are under attack by deviants and that official action against them is needed. The strategy has worked well. In polls taken in the United States in the 1980s and 1990s, an average of 83% of respondents felt that the justice system was not harsh enough in dealing with criminals (Gaubatz, 1995). Ever since, governments at the state and federal level have responded to popular sentiment by "getting tough on crime"—cracking down on drug users and dealers, reviving the death penalty, scaling back parole eligibility, lengthening prison sentences, and building more prisons.

Not surprisingly, the inmate population in this country has grown. In 1970, there were fewer than 200,000 people in state and federal prisons; today that figure is 1.6 million (Carson & Sabol, 2012). Another 735,000 are in local jails (Minton, 2012). Add in the 1.5 million or so ex-offenders who exit supervision each year because they've completed their probation (Glaze & Bonczar, 2010) and you get what one author called "a nation of ex-cons" (Gonnerman, 2004). This situation is less a function of some staggeringly high number of serious criminals in this country than it is of the "tough on crime" policies that have taken hold in the last few decades. In 2011, the U.S. incarceration rate was 716 prisoners per 100,000 people (International Centre for Prison Studies, 2012). No other industrialized country comes close to this figure.

High rates of incarceration have been accompanied by heightened police surveillance and supervision in poor communities. The number of police per capita has increased dramatically in the past several decades (A. Goffman, 2009). Hovering police helicopters and video cameras mounted on streetlights have become the ubiquitous markers of poor urban neighborhoods. As a consequence, a climate of fear and suspicion has gripped these communities. In such an environment, life for everyone is anxious and unsettled: "Family members and friends are pressured to inform on one another and young men live as suspects and fugitives, with the daily fear of confinement" (A. Goffman, 2009, p. 353).

Newly released inmates—who are likely to be poor and members of ethnoracial minorities—are also significantly less likely than their counterparts of two decades ago to find jobs and stay out of the kind of trouble that leads to further imprisonment (Butterfield, 2000). Many states have sharply curtailed education, job training, and other rehabilitation programs inside prison. In addition, parole officers are quicker to rescind a newly released inmate's parole for relatively minor infractions, such as failing a drug test.

The question you might ask is "Who benefits when it becomes so hard for ex-convicts to stay out of prison?" According to advocates of the conflict perspective, the law is not merely a mechanism that protects good people from bad people; it is a political instrument used by specific groups to further their own interests, often at the expense of others' (W. Chambliss, 1964; Quinney, 1970). Law is, of course, determined by legislative action. But legislatures are greatly influenced by powerful segments of society, such as lobbying groups, political action committees, individual campaign contributors, and so on.

Tellingly, the acts that threaten the economic or political interests of the groups that have the power to influence public policy are more likely to be criminalized (and more likely to be punished) than are the deviant acts members of these groups are likely to commit. For instance, it's against the law to fail to report income on one's annual tax return. But poor working people are far more likely to be audited by the Internal Revenue Service (IRS) than wealthy people (Johnston, 2002). That's not surprising, given that the IRS looks for tax cheating by wage earners much more closely than it does for cheating by corporations or by people whose money comes from their own businesses, investments, partnerships, and trusts.

Through the mass media, dominant groups influence the public to look at crime in ways that are favorable to them. The selective portrayal of crime plays an important role in shaping public perceptions of the "crime problem" and therefore its "official" definition. For instance, decades of research show that the crimes depicted on television are significantly more likely to be violent than actual crimes committed in the real world (cited in Reiman & Leighton, 2010). When politicians talk about fighting the U.S. crime problem or when news shows report fluctuations in crime rates, they are almost always referring to street crimes (illegal drug use, robbery, burglary, murder, assault, etc.) rather than corporate crimes, governmental crimes, or crimes committed by people in influential positions.

Such coverage creates a way of perceiving crime that becomes social reality. We accept the "fact" that certain people or actions are a threat to the well-being of the entire society and therefore a threat to our own personal interests.

Corporate and White-Collar Crime

Consequently, people in the United States take for granted that street crime is our worst social problem and that corporate crime is not as dangerous or as costly (Reiman & Leighton, 2010). Unsafe work conditions; dangerous chemicals in the air, water, and food; faulty consumer products; and unnecessary surgery actually put people who live in the United States in more constant and imminent physical danger than do ordinary street crimes (Mokhiber, 1999). Approximately 13,000 Americans were murdered in 2010 (ProQuest Statistical Abstract, 2013). At the same time,

- About 4,700 Americans die on the job annually (U.S. Bureau of Labor Statistics, 2012a).
- Approximately 20,000 U.S. cancer deaths each year are attributable to occupational exposure (Centers for Disease Control and Prevention, 2011b).
- Almost 100,000 people die annually from infections they contract in hospitals or clinics (Klevens et al., 2007).

Add in the nearly 3 million Americans who suffer from nonfatal workplace injuries and illnesses each year (U.S. Bureau of Labor Statistics, 2012d) and you can see that street crime is not the biggest threat to our health and safety.

Organizational misbehaviors and white-collar crimes also pose greater economic threats to U.S. citizens than does street crime. The FBI estimates that burglary and robbery cost the United States $3.8 billion a year. Unnecessary medical treatments alone, such as unwarranted scans, blood tests, and surgical procedures, cost at least $210 billion annually (cited in Parker-Pope, 2012b). And the total cost of white-collar crimes like corporate fraud, bribery, embezzlement, insurance fraud, and securities fraud amounts to close to $500 billion a year (Reiman & Leighton, 2010).

To be fair, some people actually do view certain types of corporate malfeasance as a more serious form of deviance than street crimes (Huff, Desilets, & Kane, 2010). Indeed, the financial crisis that first gripped the nation in 2008 created a firestorm of public anger that cast unprecedented scrutiny on white-collar misconduct. President Obama vowed to crack down on Wall Street bankers for their "reckless practices" (P. Baker & Herszenhorn, 2010). Across the country, attorneys began to indict loan processors, mortgage brokers, and bank officials on various types of financial fraud. Congress and the Department of Justice plotted strategies for an all-out federal attack (Segal, 2009).

In a few high-profile cases, executives convicted of corporate crimes have, indeed, received harsh prison sentences:

- In 2006, Jeffrey Skilling, former CEO of Enron, received a 24-year sentence for securities fraud and other crimes.
- In 2009, a wealthy stockbroker and financial adviser named Bernard Madoff pleaded guilty to charges of securities fraud, investment fraud, mail fraud, wire fraud, money laundering, and theft from an employee benefit plan, to name a few. Prosecutors estimated that these schemes cost his clients about $65 billion. The judge called Madoff's actions "extraordinarily evil" and sentenced him to 150 years in prison, an act that was largely symbolic since Madoff was 71 years old at the time (Henriques, 2009).
- In 2011, billionaire hedge fund manager Raj Rajaratnam was found guilty of securities fraud and conspiracy. He was sentenced to 11 years in prison (though the government recommended a sentence twice that long).

But responses like these have been directed largely at individual white-collar criminals. Corporations themselves rarely receive heavy criminal punishment when their dangerous actions violate the law (Reiman & Leighton, 2010). For example, even after it was revealed that Bayer AG—a German pharmaceutical company—had failed to disclose the results of a study showing that a widely used heart surgery medicine increases the risk of death and stroke, the Food and Drug Administration (FDA) did not take the drug off the market (G. Harris, 2006). In 2004, the pharmaceutical company GlaxoSmithKline agreed to settle a $2.5 million lawsuit brought by New York State alleging that the company had hidden the results of drug trials showing that its antidepressant Paxil might have deadly side effects, such as increasing suicidal thoughts in children.

At congressional hearings, lawmakers berated executives from GlaxoSmithKline and other drug companies for hiding study results that challenged the effectiveness of their drugs. In response, the companies promised to do better. But according to studies financed by the National Institutes of Health, crucial facts about many clinical trials continue to be withheld from the FDA (cited in Berenson, 2005).

To ease the inconvenience of prosecution for corporate wrongdoers, the U.S. Department of Justice has instituted a form of corporate probation. Several major companies that have been charged with billions of dollars' worth of accounting fraud, bid rigging, and other illegal financial schemes—including American International Group, PNC Financial Services Group, Merrill Lynch, AOL–Time Warner, and American Express—have agreed to *deferred prosecutions*, in which they accept responsibility for wrongdoing, agree not to fight the charges, agree to cooperate with investigations, pay a fine, and implement changes in their corporate structure to prevent future criminal wrongdoing. If a company abides by the agreement for a specified time—usually 12 months—prosecutors will drop all charges (Mokhiber & Weissman, 2004). Since 2007, the Department of Justice has made over 150 deferred prosecution agreements with companies accused of criminal activity (Henning, 2012). In 2009, UBS AG, Switzerland's largest bank, entered a deferred prosecution agreement on charges that it had helped U.S. taxpayers hide accounts from the IRS. In exchange for a dismissal of the charges, the bank agreed to pay $780 million in fines, penalties, interest, and restitution; acknowledge responsibility for its actions and omissions; and continue cooperating with Justice Department officials (U.S. Department of Justice, 2009).

Such arrangements are meant to avoid more drastic punishment, which could destroy these companies and cost thousands of innocent employees their jobs. For instance, when the government aggressively prosecuted the Arthur Andersen accounting firm in 2002 for its criminal role in the famous Enron scandal, 28,000 employees lost their jobs (Lichtblau, 2008). But the penalties companies do receive are usually relatively minor and don't do much to deter their future law violations. Fines of hundreds of millions of dollars or even several billion dollars may sound like a hefty sum to you and me, but for companies that earn *hundreds of billions* of dollars annually, they barely make a dent. For instance, in the five years leading up to the 2010 Gulf of Mexico drilling rig explosion that killed 11 people and dumped nearly 5 million barrels of oil into the water, British Petroleum had received more than $550 million in fines for violations of safety codes, environmental laws, and antitrust statutes. Those fines added up to one tenth of a percent of its revenue over that period. In 2010, the Securities and Exchange Commission imposed a $550 million fine on Goldman Sachs for securities fraud. It was the largest penalty ever paid by a Wall Street firm. However, the company earned $51.7 billion that year, so the fine worked out to about four *days* of earnings ("Do Fines Ever," 2010). In 2012, GlaxoSmithKline (yes, the same drug company that had gotten into trouble 8 years earlier) pleaded guilty to charges that it had promoted unapproved uses of its best-selling antidepressants and had failed to report safety data about its top diabetes drug. The company agreed to pay $3 billion in fines, the largest settlement involving a drug company to date. However, some industry observers argue that even fines of this magnitude will do little to prevent drug companies from such unlawful behavior in the future (Thomas & Schmidt, 2012). It's no wonder that many large corporations consider the punishments they receive for wrongdoing simply a cost of doing business.

The imbalance in the legal response to these crimes versus street crimes is glaring. If you were an individual thief who had robbed a bank at gunpoint, a shop owner who had defrauded your customers of millions of dollars, or a small-businessperson who had knowingly manufactured a potentially lethal product, it's highly unlikely that you would be allowed to avoid any criminal prosecution simply by "cooperating with the investigation." Our massive law enforcement and criminal justice machinery would no doubt mobilize its vast resources to see that you were prosecuted to the fullest extent of the law. Yet large corporations engage in such activities every day, largely without much public outcry or moral panic. In fact, most aren't even prosecuted under criminal statutes. Between 1982 and 2002, about 170,000 American workers died on the job. During that same period, federal and state workplace safety agencies investigated 1,798 fatality cases in which companies had *willfully* violated workplace safety laws—for instance, by removing safety devices to speed up production, denying workers proper safety gear, or simply ignoring explicit safety warnings. But only 104 of these cases were ever prosecuted. And of those, only 16 resulted in criminal convictions (Barstow, 2003).

Why aren't these dangerous and costly corporate acts considered deviant the way face-to-face street crimes are? According to sociologists Jeffrey Reiman and Paul Leighton (2010), the answer resides in the perceived circumstances surrounding these acts. People typically see the injuries caused by corporate crime as unintentional, indirect, and a consequence of an endeavor culturally defined as legitimate or socially productive: making a profit. In most people's minds, someone who tries to harm someone else is usually considered more evil than someone who harms without intending to. Moreover, harming someone directly seems more deviant than harming someone indirectly. Finally, harm that results from illegitimate activities is usually considered more serious than harm that is a by-product of standard business activities.

The Menace of "Illegal" Drugs

Different cultures show varying levels of tolerance when it comes to drug use. For instance, throughout the South Pacific, people commonly chew betel nuts for their stimulant effects. In the Bolivian and Peruvian Andes, people chew coca leaves during their ordinary workday. The Huichol of central Mexico ingest peyote—a small cactus that produces hallucinations—as part of their religious rituals.

In the United States, we wink at the use of many substances that alter people's state of mind, such as coffee, chocolate, and alcohol. In 2011, companies began marketing baked goods with names like "Lazy Cakes," "Kush Cakes," and "Lulla Pies" that contain the sleep-inducing substance melatonin. The pastries bear labels warning against operating heavy machinery or driving after eating them. One consumer said, "It knocks you out—in a good way, not a bad way. For me, it's not to chill. For me, it's to get a good night's sleep" (quoted in Saint Louis, 2011, p. 4). Nevertheless, because they look and taste like sweet desserts, these products are considered food, not drugs.

But when it comes to illegal drugs, U.S. attitudes change dramatically. Like the term *terrorist*, the term *drugs* is an easy and popular scapegoat on which to heap our collective hatred. The United States has been characterized as a *temperance culture* (Levine, 1992)—one in which self-control and industriousness are perceived as desirable traits of productive citizens. In such an environment, drug-induced states of altered consciousness are likely to be perceived as a loss of control and thus feared as a threat to the economic and physical well-being of the population.

The United States has been in an ill-defined, undeclared, but highly publicized "war" against illegal drugs for more than 40 years at a cost of about $1 trillion and hundreds of thousands of lives (Mendoza, 2010). The Drug Enforcement Administration, the FBI, and the U.S. Customs Service seized about 5 million pounds of illegal drugs in 2010, about three and a half times as much as was seized in 2000 (ProQuest Statistical Abstract, 2013). Federal spending on antidrug campaigns increased from $420 million in 1973 to $25.2 billion in 2012 (Katel, 2006; Office of National Drug Control Policy, 2012).

With so much attention and resources now focused on homeland security, it would seem that the fight against drug dealers and users is no longer a national priority. Indeed, cuts in the federal budget have reduced the availability of resources devoted to drug enforcement, and some antidrug programs and agencies have been folded into antiterrorism efforts. Nevertheless, there remains a widespread belief that although terrorists pose an external danger, drug users and drug dealers are slowly destroying the country from within and therefore need to be stopped.

Many conflict sociologists, however, argue that antidrug campaigns and legislative activities are driven chiefly by political interests (see, e.g., Erich Goode, 1989). The war on drugs in the United States has permitted greater social control over groups perceived to be threatening, such as young minority men, and has mobilized voter support for candidates who profess to be "tough" on drugs. Capitalizing on the "drug menace" as a personal and societal threat is a common and effective political tactic (Ben-Yehuda, 1990).

As with deviance in general, the very definition of which substances are "illegal" is influenced by powerful interests. Behind the phrase "war on drugs" is the assumption that illegal drugs (marijuana, ecstasy, cocaine, methamphetamines, heroin, etc.) are the most dangerous substances and the ones that must be eradicated. However, the difference between legal and illegal drugs is not necessarily a function of their relative danger.

For instance, each year about 1,700 U.S. college students die from alcohol-related injuries, nearly 100,000 are victims of alcohol-related sexual assault and rape, 700,000 are assaulted by another student who has been drinking, and close to 3 million are cited for drunken driving (National Institute on Alcohol Abuse and Alcoholism, 2007). But alcohol is big business: Sales of alcoholic beverages reached $156 billion in 2010 (ProQuest Statistical Abstract, 2013). Hence, efforts to completely criminalize it are few and far between. While most colleges now offer "alcohol-free" housing, encourage students to "drink responsibly," or sponsor alcohol-free social events, few have become "dry" campuses, banning alcohol outright.

Tobacco is an even clearer health risk than alcohol—or marijuana and heroin for that matter (Reiman & Leighton, 2010). But aside from some age restrictions, it is legally available to anyone. According to the World Health Organization (2011), 6 million people around the world die each year from tobacco-related causes. In the United States, cigarette smoking is responsible for one in five deaths annually, or about 443,000 deaths a year (Centers for Disease Control and Prevention, 2011c). If those figures are accurate, more people die from smoking-related causes than from AIDS, illegal drug use, alcohol use, motor vehicle injuries, suicides, and murders combined. The costs of smoking are financial as well as physical. It's estimated that smoking costs the U.S. economy nearly $193 billion annually in both health care costs and lost productivity due to illness (American Lung Association, 2008).

And tobacco doesn't affect just those who choose to consume it directly. According to the Centers for Disease Control and Prevention (2010), about 88 million nonsmoking U.S. residents over the age of three are exposed to secondhand smoke at home, in vehicles, at work, and in public places each year. Such exposure, even for brief periods, can cause health problems. Nonsmokers who inhale secondhand smoke at work or at home increase their risk of heart disease by 30% and risk of cancer by 25% (Centers for Disease Control and Prevention, 2006). Almost 50,000 of the above-cited 443,000 cigarette-related deaths are the result of exposure to secondhand smoke (Centers for Disease Control and Prevention, 2011c). Thirty of the country's 50 largest cities now have comprehensive smoke-free laws that restrict smoking in public places, up from one city in 2000 (Centers for Disease Control, 2012). Health experts are now paying attention to the harmful effects of "thirdhand" smoke, the residue of tobacco smoke left on walls, furniture, clothes, and house dust.

In 2003, the U.S. Department of Justice took the unprecedented step of demanding that the nation's biggest cigarette makers forfeit $289 billion in profits derived from more than 50 years of dangerous and "fraudulent" marketing practices, such as manipulating nicotine levels, lying to customers about the health effects of smoking, and directing advertising campaigns at children (Lichtblau, 2003). Yet knowing the hazards of selling and smoking cigarettes has not prompted our society to outlaw them entirely, as we have methamphetamine and cocaine use. It's true that some states have enacted smoking bans in bars, restaurants, and other enclosed public places and some cities have banned outdoor smoking as well (Springen, 2006). And in 2009, President Obama signed into law the Family Smoking Prevention and Tobacco Control Act, which gives the FDA more power to impose stricter controls on the production and sale of cigarettes (D. Wilson, 2009b). But this bill stopped short of completely criminalizing tobacco, which would have had a disastrous impact on many large corporations and on several states whose economies depend on this crop.

The tobacco industry has one of the most powerful lobbies in Washington. In fact, in 2005, the Justice Department decided to reduce the amount it sought in its case from $289 billion to a mere $10 billion, out of concern over the financial impact that the original amount would have on the tobacco companies (Leonnig, 2005). But as efforts to limit or prohibit smoking in this country become more successful (the proportion of 18- to 24-year-olds who currently smoke dropped from 24% in 2005 to 20% in 2010; ProQuest Statistical Abstract, 2013), tobacco companies are stepping up efforts to combat regulations in other parts of the world. They are fighting advertising limits in Great Britain, larger health warnings in South America, and higher taxes in the Philippines and Mexico. In addition, tobacco companies are spending billions of dollars each year on promotional advertising in Africa (D. Wilson, 2010).

The response to illegal drug users also shows how conceptions of deviance are socially constructed. Take, for instance, discrepancies in prison sentences for the possession and use of cocaine. Although the two types of cocaine—powdered and crack—cause similar physical reactions, the sentences for those convicted of selling them are vastly different. The average length of a sentence for selling less than 25 grams of crack cocaine is 65 months; for powdered cocaine, it is 14 months (Coyle, 2003). According to federal law, possession of 28 grams of crack cocaine yields

a five-year mandatory minimum sentence for a first offense; it takes 500 grams of powder cocaine to prompt the same sentence (Drug Policy Alliance, 2013).

Many law enforcement officials argue that the different levels of punishment are justified because crack cocaine is more closely associated with violence than powdered cocaine; it is more dangerous to the user; and it is more likely to cause birth defects in babies whose mothers use it while pregnant. However, a study of the physiological and psychoactive effects of different forms of cocaine found that they are so similar as to make the existing discrepancy in punishment "excessive." In addition, other research has found that the effects of crack use by pregnant women on fetuses are no different from those of tobacco or alcohol use (cited in Coyle, 2003).

Some sociologists point out that the problems associated with crack use have as much to do with class and race as with the drug itself. Harsh sentences for crack offenses have had a disproportionate effect on black men in poor urban areas, where crack is much more common than the powdered cocaine favored by white users. In 2009, nearly 80% of those convicted of crack possession were black; only 10% were white. In contrast, 28% of those convicted of powdered cocaine possession were black and 17% were white (cited in Kurtzleben, 2010). In 2009, the Judiciary Committee of the U.S. House of Representatives began hearings on the mandatory sentence disparity between crack and powdered cocaine, and in 2010, President Obama signed into law the Fair Sentencing Act, which aims to reduce these sentencing disparities. In 2011, the U.S. Sentencing Commission voted unanimously to reduce the unfairly long sentences for crack offenders already in prison so that they are more in line with shorter terms given powder cocaine offenders (Serrano, 2011).

Meanwhile, little has been accomplished in the way of stopping the illegal activities of the rich and powerful interests that participate in the drug industry. Established financial institutions often launder drug money, despite laws against it (Parenti, 1995). Massive international crime organizations that ensure the flow of illicit drugs into the country have grown bigger and richer, despite a decades-long attempt to stop them (Bullington, 1993). Unlike low-status users and small-time dealers of illegal drugs, these organizations wield tremendous economic power and political influence (Godson & Olson, 1995).

The Medicalization of Deviance

One of the most powerful forces in defining deviance in the United States today is the medical profession. Throughout the 20th century, the medical profession gained in prestige, influence, and authority. This professional dominance gave medicine jurisdiction over anything that could be designated "healthy" or "sick" (Conrad & Leiter, 2004). This trend, what sociologists call *medicalization*, is the process through which deviant behavior is defined as a medical problem or illness, and the medical profession is mandated or licensed to provide some type of treatment for it (Conrad, 2005). Each time we automatically refer to troublesome behavior or people as "sick," we help to perpetuate the perception that deviance is like an illness. Many physicians, psychologists, psychiatrists, therapists, and insurance agents, not to mention the entire pharmaceutical industry, benefit from a medicalized view of certain deviant acts.

According to some, we're currently in the midst of an "epidemic of diagnoses" (Welch, Schwartz, & Woloshin, 2007), meaning that more and more actions that were once categorized simply as misbehaviors are being redefined as psychiatric diseases, disorders, or syndromes. Between 1952 and 2000, the number of mental disorders officially recognized by the American Psychiatric Association increased from 110 to close to 400 (P. J. Caplan, 1995; Horwitz, 2002). Many of these designations seem to have nothing to do with illness. Take, for instance a malady called "conduct disorder," a diagnosis restricted to children and adolescents. According to the American Psychiatric Association (2013), the "symptoms" of this disorder include bullying or threatening behavior toward others, physical cruelty, destruction of property, theft, and violations of other rules like staying out late despite parental prohibition. In another era, this sort of misbehavior was called juvenile delinquency.

To accommodate the growing number of "illnesses," the number of psychiatric professionals has almost tripled over the past two decades, as has the number of people seeking psychiatric help. The combined indirect and direct costs of serious mental "illness" in this society, including lost productivity, lost earnings due to illness, disability benefits, and health care expenditures, are estimated to exceed $317 billion annually (National Institute of Mental Health, 2010). According to the National Institute of Mental

Health (2009), 26.2% of U.S. adults had suffered from a diagnosable mental disorder during the previous 12-month period and 46.4% had at some point in their lives. Along with alcoholism, drug addiction, and serious mental illness, these disorders now include overeating; undereating; shyness; school stress; distress over a failed romance; poor performance in school; hoarding; addiction to using the Internet; public tantrums; and excessive gambling, shopping, and sex.

For their part, drug companies sometimes create medicalized conceptions of deviance by influencing the way conditions are defined and then by marketing disorders and selling drugs to treat them. According to one study, 56% of psychiatrists involved in defining disorders for the latest revision of the American Psychiatric Association's *Diagnostic and Statistical Manual* had financial ties to drug companies (Cosgrove, Bursztajn, & Krimsky, 2009).

In 1997, Congress passed the Food and Drug Administration Modernization Act, allowing drug companies to advertise directly to the public and create heightened demand for their products. Between 1996 and 2000, drug company spending on television advertising increased by 600%, to $2.5 billion, and it's been rising ever since. They now spend as much money on this direct-to-consumer advertising as they spend on advertising to physicians in medical journals (Conrad, 2005).

Why has the medical view of deviance become so dominant? One reason is that medical explanations of troublesome social problems and deviant behaviors appeal to a society that wants simple explanations for complex social problems. If violent behavior is the result of a dysfunction in a person's brain, it then becomes a problem of defective, violent individuals, not of the larger societal context within which violent acts occur. Likewise, when our doctor or therapist tells us our anxiety, depression, crabbiness, and insecurity will vanish if we simply take a drug, we are spared the difficult task of looking at the social complexities of our lives or the structure of our society.

The medicalization of deviance also appeals to our humanitarian values. The designation of a problem as an illness replaces legal punishment and moral scrutiny with therapeutic treatment (Zola, 1986). The alcoholic is no longer a sinner or a criminal but a victim, someone whose behavior is an "illness" beyond her or his control. Children who have trouble learning in school aren't disobedient and disruptive, they are "sick." If people are violating norms because of a disease that has invaded their bodies, they should not be held morally responsible. Medicalization creates less social stigma and condemnation of people labeled deviant.

Despite its enormous public appeal, the tendency to medicalize deviance has serious social consequences (Conrad & Schneider, 1992). These include the individualization of complex social issues and the depoliticization of deviance.

Individualizing Complex Social Issues

Individualistic medical explanations of deviance are not necessarily wrong. Some violent people do have neurological diseases, and some people diagnosed with clinical depression do have imbalances of chemicals in their brains. But when we pursue these explanations for everyone whose behavior diverges from social expectations, the solutions we seek focus on the perpetrator to the exclusion of everything else.

Consider the problem of attention-deficit/hyperactivity disorder (ADHD), one of the most commonly diagnosed maladies among U.S. children today. A child diagnosed with ADHD is difficult to deal with at home and in the classroom. He or she fidgets and squirms, has difficulty remaining seated, can't sustain attention in tasks or play activities, can't follow rules, talks excessively, and is easily distracted (American Psychiatric Association, 2013).

Fifty years ago, such children were considered bad or troublesome and would have received punishment or even expulsion from school. Today, however, most hyperactive behavior is diagnosed as a symptom of a mental disorder, and drugs are prescribed to treat it. Somewhere between 4% and 12% of all school-aged children in the U.S. will be diagnosed with ADHD at some point in their youth, and three quarters of these children are boys (Getahun et al., 2013). From 2000 and 2010, diagnoses of ADHD increased 66%, from 6.2 million to 10.4 million (IMS Health, 2012). The number of prescriptions for these drugs written for U.S. children is growing at a faster rate than for any other drug; more prescriptions are written for them than for antibiotics or asthma medication (Conrad, 2005). Between 2006 and 2010, total sales of ADHD drugs increased 83%, from $4.05 billion to $7.42 billion (cited in Harris, 2011b). The overall annual cost of treating ADHD is between $36 billion and $52.4 billion (Getahun, et. al., 2013).

This growth is part of an alarming trend toward the increased use of drugs for children in general (Safer, Zito, & dosReis, 2003). For instance, between one quarter and one half of all kids who attend summer camps take daily prescription medications (J. Gross, 2006). A doctor in Georgia prescribes the ADHD drug, Adderall, for his low-income patients who are struggling in elementary school, not because they actually *have* ADHD but because he sees this remedy as the only means he has available to prevent these kids from falling even further behind (Schwarz, 2012). Critics worry not only about the safety of these drugs but also about the mixed messages children receive when they are handed a daily pill to medicate away their troublesome behavior while at the same time they are told to "say no" to other drugs (Koch, 1999).

Despite occasional adverse side effects, the drugs used to treat ADHD are generally successful in quieting unruly and annoying behavior (Whalen & Henker, 1977). And certainly a medical response to ADHD is preferable to harsh punishment. But are we ignoring the possibility that hyperactive behavior may be a child's adaptation to his or her social environment (Sroufe, 2012)? Some pediatricians, for instance, argue that the symptoms of ADHD may just be children's natural reaction to living in a fast-paced, stressful world (Diller, 1998). According to one neuroscientist, the inability to sustain attention, regulate rage, or tolerate normal types of sensory input may be as much a function of living in a "culture of excess and self-indulgence" as faulty brain wiring (cited in Warner, 2010). Others have argued that ADHD may, in part, be a response to an educational system that discourages individual expression (Conrad, 1975) or that expects more self-control from young children than they're capable of exercising (Duncan, 2007). Narrowly defined norms of acceptable behavior make it difficult if not impossible for children to pursue their own desires and needs.

I'm not suggesting that all children who are diagnosed with ADHD are disruptive simply because they live in a multitasking society, are bored in school, or have had their individual creativity and vitality squashed by unsympathetic teachers. Some children do have neurological disorders that create debilitating behavioral problems in need of treatment. The point is that from an institutional perspective, the tendency to label disruptiveness simply as an individual disorder protects the school system's legitimacy and authority. The institution simply cannot function if disruptiveness is tolerated (Tobin, Wu, & Davidson, 1989). But imagine if our educational system promoted and encouraged free individual expression rather than obedience and discipline. In such an environment, overactivity wouldn't be considered disruptive and wouldn't be a problem in need of a medical solution.

When inconvenient or annoying behavior is translated into an individual sickness, medical remedies (usually drugs) become a convenient tool for enforcing conformity and upholding the values of society. When parents say they want "better children," they typically mean they want children who are in line with our culture's values: "well adjusted, well-behaved, sociable, attentive, high-performing, and academically adept" (President's Council on Bioethics, 2003, p. 73). Parents who *don't* want their children to have these characteristics become objects of suspicion.

Depoliticizing Deviance

The process of individualizing social problems robs deviant behavior of its power to send a message about malfunctioning elements in society. Disruptive behaviors or statements automatically lose their power to prompt social change when they are seen simply as symptoms of individual defects or illnesses. We need not pay attention to the critical remarks of an opponent if that opponent is labeled as mentally ill. Totalitarian regimes often declare political dissidents insane and confine them to hospitals in an attempt to quiet dangerous political criticism. In 2007, a Russian activist was held in a psychiatric clinic for months after publishing an article detailing the harsh treatment of patients in the same hospital. In China, people who file complaints against local government officials often find themselves involuntarily committed to mental institutions. Although there are no reliable statistics on how often these confinements occur, human rights activists say they're increasing because local authorities are under intense pressure to quell social unrest these days. One Chinese woman, who was confined for seven months after complaining that she had been unfairly denied a government job, said, "What they are trying to do is completely destroy your mind and weaken your body to the point where you go crazy. That's when you will stop petitioning, they hope" (quoted in LaFraniere & Levin, 2010, p. A14).

Such practices are found not only in foreign countries. In the early 1990s, a *Dallas Morning News* investigation discovered that high-ranking U.S. military commanders were trying to discredit and intimidate subordinates who reported security and safety violations or military overpricing by ordering them to undergo psychiatric evaluations or sending them to a mental ward (Timms & McGonigle, 1992). When a low-ranking naval officer reported that fellow sailors had raped three women while stationed in Bermuda, he was committed to a psychiatric hospital for a week (Zwerdling, 2004). An officer in the Air Force contended that his forced hospitalization was part of retaliation for reporting payroll abuses at the Dallas Naval Air Station. He insightfully describes the power of medical labels to discredit his political criticism:

> What happened was nobody would speak to me. Let's face it. After someone has gone to a mental ward, you kind of question what's going on. It was a nice ploy, and it worked. What they did was totally neutralize me. (quoted in Timms & McGonigle, 1992, p. F1)

Creating the image of deviants as sick people who must be dealt with through medical therapies is a powerful way for dominant groups in society to maintain conformity and protect themselves from those whom they fear or who challenge the way "normal" social life is organized (Pfohl, 1994). The seemingly merciful medical labels not only reduce individual responsibility but also reduce the likelihood that such potentially contagious political criticism will be taken seriously (Hills, 1980).

CONCLUSION

When we talk about deviance, we usually speak of extreme forms: crime, mental illness, substance abuse, and so on. These activities are indeed troublesome, but for most people they remain comfortably distant phenomena. I think most of us would like to cling to the belief that deviants are "them" and normal people are "us."

The lesson I hope you take away from this chapter, however, is that the issue of deviance is, essentially, an issue of social definition. As a group, community, or society, we decide which differences are benign and which are dangerous. Standards and expectations change. Norms come and go. The consequence is that each of us could be considered deviant to some degree by some audience. We have all broken unspoken interactional norms; many of us have even broken the law. To a lesser degree, we are all potentially like Kelly Michaels, subject to being erroneously labeled deviant and unfairly treated as a result. Given the right—or wrong—circumstances, all of us risk being negatively labeled or acquiring a bad reputation.

This chapter has examined deviance as both a microlevel and a macrolevel sociological phenomenon, as something that plays a profound role in individual lives and in society as a whole. Although sociologists are interested in the broad social and political processes that create cultural definitions of deviance, they are also interested in the ways these definitions are applied in everyday life. Societal definitions have their most potent effect when expressed face to face. We can talk about powerful institutions such as medicine creating definitions of deviance that are consistent with broader political or economic interests, but if these definitions aren't accepted as appropriate to some degree by the majority, they will be ineffectual. Again, we see the value of developing the sociological imagination, which helps us understand the complex interplay between individuals and the culture and community within which they live.

CHAPTER HIGHLIGHTS

◆ According to an absolutist definition of deviance, there are two fundamental types of behavior: that which is inherently acceptable and that which is inherently unacceptable. In contrast, a relativist definition of deviance suggests that it is not a property inherent in any particular act, belief, or condition. Instead, deviance is a definition of behavior that is socially created by collective human judgments. Hence, like beauty, deviance is in the eye of the beholder.

◆ The labeling theory of deviance argues that deviance is a consequence of the application of rules and sanctions to an offender. Deviant labels can impede individuals' everyday social life by forming expectations of them in the minds of others.

◆ According to conflict theory, the definition of deviance is a form of social control exerted by more powerful people and groups over less powerful ones.

◆ The criminal justice system and the medical profession have had a great deal of influence in defining, explaining, and controlling deviant behavior. Criminalization is the process by which certain behaviors come to be defined as crimes. Medicalization is the depiction of deviance as a medical problem or illness.

KEY TERMS

absolutism: Approach to defining deviance that rests on the assumption that all human behavior can be considered either inherently good or inherently bad

criminalization: Official definition of an act of deviance as a crime

deterrence theory: Theory of deviance positing that people will be prevented from engaging in a deviant act if they judge the costs of such an act to outweigh its benefits

deviance: Behavior, ideas, or attributes of an individual or group that some people in society find offensive

labeling theory: Theory stating that deviance is the consequence of the application of rules and sanctions to an offender; a deviant is an individual to whom the identity "deviant" has been successfully applied

medicalization: Definition of behavior as a medical problem, mandating the medical profession to provide some kind of treatment for it

relativism: Approach to defining deviance that rests on the assumption that deviance is socially created by collective human judgments and ideas

PART III

Social Structure, Institutions, and Everyday Life

U p to this point, I have been discussing how our everyday lives are constructed and ordered. But that is only part of the picture. What does social life look like from the top down? Once the architecture is constructed and in place, what influence does it exert on our everyday lives? To answer these questions, the remaining chapters investigate the organizational and institutional pressures on everyday life and the various sources of structural inequality in society: social class and wealth, race and ethnicity, and gender. Global institutions and population trends are other structural influences on everyday life. These facets of society may seem ominous and impenetrable. However, you will see that our lives don't completely fall under the control of the social structure. As the concept of the sociological imagination suggests, the collective actions of individuals often bring about fundamental changes in society.

The Structure of Society

Organizations, Social Institutions, and Globalization

Social Structure and Everyday Life

Social Dilemmas: Individual Interests and Structural Needs

The Structure of Formal Organizations

Organizations and Institutions

Globalization and Social Institutions

History will no doubt mark the 2000 presidential election as one of the most bizarre political events of all time. The chaos began on election night. Early in the evening, Al Gore, the Democratic candidate, was projected as the winner of Florida's 25 electoral votes, giving him the inside track to the presidency; a few hours later, that projection was rescinded, and Florida was labeled "too close to call." In the early morning hours of the following day, George W. Bush, the Republican candidate, was projected as the winner of Florida and therefore of the election, only to have that projection withdrawn when Florida, again, was declared "too close to call." The ensuing month brought a daily dose of street protests, charges of voter fraud, recounts, debates over absentee votes, lawsuits, countersuits, and legal rulings. On November 26, the Florida State canvassing board certified that

George Bush was the winner. The Florida Supreme Court overruled and ordered another recount. But on December 13, the U.S. Supreme Court issued its definitive ruling, on a 5–4 vote, that the Florida recount was unconstitutional. George W. Bush was thus declared the next president of the United States, even though he had received over half a million fewer votes nationwide than Gore.

To listen to the domestic and foreign news media describe it at the time, the most powerful country in the world was in a state of utter political confusion. The situation was described in either mocking or apocalyptic terms. U.S. citizens were losing their moral authority to lecture other countries about the virtues of democracy. We were about to face a "constitutional crisis" that could paralyze the government. We were going to be a country without a leader. We were on the brink of anarchy.

Of course, none of that happened. As one journalist put it, "The apparatus of government is still in place, skilled politicians and career civil servants still keep things running, and ultimately nothing apocalyptic is likely to happen. . . . The system will work and life will go on" (Belluck, 2001, p. A9). Indeed, for the average U.S. citizen, nothing really changed during the electoral confusion. Buses, trains, and planes still ran on time. Food was still delivered to grocery store shelves. Municipal services were still provided. Even the stock market remained solid. We all simply went about our business, pausing now and then to witness the political spectacle or to debate with friends, family, and coworkers.

Why didn't the country collapse during this electoral epic? To answer that question, we must turn to one of the key concepts of this book: social structure. Despite strong emotions, dire predictions, and confrontational behavior, the political system remained intact. Whether we agreed with the ultimate outcome of that election or not, our legal and political institutions worked as they were designed to. From local precincts and campaign organizations to state legislatures to the highest court in the land, the system continued to function. To be sure, the motives of some of the individual players were highly partisan. But the structure itself rose above the actions of these individuals and prevented the sort of large-scale catastrophe media pundits predicted. One of the great sociological paradoxes of human existence is that we are capable of producing a social structure that we then experience as something other than a

human product. It is ironic that we spend most of our lives either within or responding to the influence of larger structural entities—particularly in a society such as the United States, which so fiercely extols the virtues of rugged individualism and personal accomplishment.

This chapter focuses on our relationship with the social structure we construct and maintain, both locally and globally. This focus requires us to examine the structure not only from the individual's perspective but also from the macrosociological perspective of the organizations and institutions themselves. Many important social issues look quite different depending on the perspective we use to understand them.

SOCIAL STRUCTURE AND EVERYDAY LIFE

As you recall from Chapter 2, *social structure* is the framework of society that exists above the level of individuals and provides the social setting in which individuals interact with one another to form relationships. It includes the organizations, groups, statuses and roles, culture, and institutions that add order and predictability to our lives. The concept of social structure is important because it implies a patterned regularity in the way we live and in the way societies work. We could not draw any meaningful conclusions about human behavior if we started with the notion that society is haphazard and that things occur by chance alone.

If you know what to look for, you can see social structure everywhere. Consider, for instance, the components of social structure that affect the experience of going to high school. Within this broad U.S. educational institution, there are examples of every component of social structure:

- *Organizations*: National Education Association, state teachers' associations, accrediting agencies, local school boards, school districts, and so on
- *Groups*: faculty, administrators, classes, clubs, teams, cafeteria staff, and so on
- *Statuses*: teacher, student, principal, vice principal, counselor, nurse, secretary, custodian, coach, librarian, and so on
- *Role expectations*: teaching, learning, disciplining, making and taking tests, advising, coaching, feeding, and so on

- *Cultural beliefs*: for example, the belief that education is the principal means of achieving financial success, that it makes possible a complex division of labor, and that it makes a technologically advanced society possible
- *Institutionalized norms*: for example, the expectation that everyone attend school until at least the age of 16, school rules that determine acceptable behavior (not running in the halls, not screaming in class, staying on the school grounds until classes are over; Saunders, 1991)

The massive structure of the educational system is a reality that determines life chances and choices. You can choose which science class to take in high school, whether to go on to college, and what to major in once you get there, but the admissions policies of potential colleges and the availability of jobs to people with and without a college degree are factors beyond your control. You're reading this book right now not because of your fondness for fine literature but because of the structural requirements of being a college student. You know you must graduate to increase your chances of getting a good job, and to graduate you must get good grades in your classes. To get good grades in your classes, you must keep up with the material so you're prepared for exams. You probably would rather be doing a number of other things right now—reading a better book, watching TV, texting, tweeting, blogging, sleeping, staring into space—but personal preferences must take a backseat for the time being to the more immediate structural demands of college life.

The structural requirements of the educational system have a broader impact as well. Course grades, standardized test scores, and class rankings are emphasized so much and create such personal anxiety for students that they may actually overshadow learning and intellectual growth.

This competitive educational atmosphere can sometimes create incompatibility between the needs of the individual student and the needs of the system. Suppose your sociology instructor told you that she was going to give everyone in the class an A as long as they showed up each day. Your immediate reaction might be joy, because such a grade would no doubt improve your grade point average (GPA). But what if all instructors in all courses at your school decided to do the same thing? Every student who simply showed up for all of her or his classes would

graduate with a perfect GPA. How would you feel then? Your joy might be tempered by the knowledge that the reputation of your school would suffer. As long as our educational system is structured on the principle of "survival of the fittest"—the assumption that only the smartest or hardest-working students earn the top grades—outsiders would perceive such changes as a sign that your school is academically inferior. Hence, your long-term personal interests may actually be best served by a highly competitive system that ensures that some of your fellow students will get lower grades than you do.

Even when it's operating as it's designed to, social structure can cause problems. Mistakes are sometimes the result of a chain of events set in motion by a system that either induces errors or makes them difficult to detect and correct. For instance, it's estimated that as many as 25% of hospitalized patients a year will experience a preventable medical error of some sort, and some 100,000 will die as a result (Landrigan et al., 2010). Some patients are particularly vulnerable. An annual study of the experiences of Medicare patients in U.S. hospitals estimates that between 2007 and 2009, there were more than 700,000 safety incidents and close to 80,000 preventable deaths attributable to medical errors such as anesthesia complications, drug mix-ups, infections due to medical care, accidental lacerations, and various other postoperative complications (Health Grades, 2011). To make matters worse, only about one out of every seven errors, accidents, or other events that harm these patients is actually reported (Pear, 2012).

The tendency to hold individual doctors or nurses responsible in such cases demonstrates an overwhelming cultural perception that these errors are caused by personal incompetence. But what appear to be obvious errors in human judgment or ineptitude are often, on closer inspection, linked to broader structural failures. An analysis of 334 drug errors in hospitals found that structural failure was responsible for most of them—for example, poor dissemination of drug knowledge to doctors, inadequate availability of patient information, faulty systems for checking correct dosage, and inefficient hospital procedure (Leape & Bates, 1995). Even the institutional method of training doctors may bear some responsibility. One study found that the overall adequacy and quality of medical care in hospitals decreases significantly in the summer months, not because doctors are distracted by thoughts of beach vacations but because of the timing of new physician residency programs. Summer is when brand new residents fresh out of medical school begin to learn how to care for patients; and they inevitably make mistakes (Young et al., 2011). This problem is so well known in the health care system that it even has a nickname: the July Effect.

To date, the United States, unlike some European countries, has no federal agency charged specifically with hospital oversight. Instead, responsibility for protecting the health and safety of hospital patients lies with a patchwork of state health departments and a nonprofit group called the Joint Commission, which sets quality standards. As a result, bad hospitals are rarely closed and are seldom hit with significant financial penalties for patient suffering (Berenson, 2008). Furthermore, hospitals may actually profit from their own mistakes because insurance companies usually pay for the longer stays and extra care that result from preventable errors (Eappen, 2013).

Some structural improvement is taking place, though. To curb the incidence of medical errors, many hospitals around the country have switched to electronic medical record systems and have invested heavily in tablets, smartphones, and other devices to give medical staff instant access to patients' data, drug information, and case studies. Although, the novelty of these systems can create some distractions and glitches (Richtel, 2011), there is some evidence that hospital performance is improving nationwide (Sack, 2011). At the federal level, hospitals will soon face financial punishments if they don't reduce the number of medical mistakes (Kalb, 2010b).

SOCIAL DILEMMAS: INDIVIDUAL INTERESTS AND STRUCTURAL NEEDS

Although social structure can clearly affect the lives of individuals, individual actions can also have an enormous effect on social structure and stability. Sometimes those actions are coordinated to benefit a collection of individuals, and sometimes they're undertaken independently and for personal gain. Let's say a group of residents want to make sure that their neighborhood is free of crime. Each individual could go on a personal crusade to stop crime, but it seems more logical and efficient for everyone to volunteer at some point to "patrol" at night or to chip in money to improve street lighting.

In actuality, though, people seldom voluntarily act to achieve a common objective. Instead, they usually act to ensure their own personal interests (J. Cross & Guyer, 1980; Dawes & Messick, 2000; Olsen, 1965). Say that your neighbors decide to fight crime by improving street lighting. They ask people in the community for voluntary donations. Some residents may decide that the rational thing to do is not to donate money for a new streetlight because they figure others will do so. That way, they could enjoy the benefits of safer, well-lit streets without spending their own money. But if every person individually decides not to donate, they may save some cash in the short run, but the new streetlights will never be purchased, and everyone will suffer in the long run. The experience of each person in a group pursuing his or her self-interest regardless of the potential ruin for everyone is known as a *social dilemma* (Messick & Brewer, 1983).

Major social problems, such as environmental pollution, can be understood as stemming, at least in part, from social dilemmas. If I fling one bag of trash out of my car window and onto the highway, it won't seem significant or destructive. Large numbers of people doing the same thing, though, would be very destructive.

If we think of nations as individual actors and the planet as the community to which they belong, many problems that have global significance—including energy shortages, massive climate change, and species extinction—can be understood from this perspective. Two important types of social dilemmas, at both the local level and broader levels, are the tragedy of the commons and the free-rider problem.

The Tragedy of the Commons

The term *commons* was originally used to describe the public pasture ground, often located in the center of medieval towns, where all the local herders could bring their animals to graze. When villagers used the commons in moderation, the grass could regenerate, resulting in a perpetual supply of food for the herds (Hardin & Baden, 1977). However, each herder soon realized that she or he could benefit individually by letting the animals eat as much as they wanted, thereby increasing their size and the price they could fetch at market. Unfortunately, when many of the herders came to this same conclusion and allowed their herds to eat without limit, the grass in the commons could not regenerate fast enough to feed them all. The tragic result was that the commons collapsed and the herds that grazed on it died or were sold off. The short-term needs of the individual overshadowed the long-term collective needs of the group.

In this illustration, the common resource was grazing land, and the group was relatively small. However, the *tragedy of the commons* model can be applied to any situation in which indispensable but finite resources are available to everyone. Consider the aggravating slowdowns we sometimes experience when accessing wireless cell and data networks. These networks, like any other common resource, are not unlimited. Once they reach their bandwidth capacity—at, say, peak usage times—there's not enough to go around and everybody suffers. Cell phone companies and network operators usually respond by expanding carrying capacity and building more cell towers. But these remedies cost money (which means higher rates for consumers) and will inevitably bump up against further electromagnetic limits, known as the "spectrum crunch." So as long as we continue to use our gadgets whenever we want for texting a friend who's standing 10 feet away, seeking GPS assistance when we already have directions, or searching for the nearest microbrewery when we should be studying for a sociology exam, we will have to deal with the inevitable and inconvenient "tragedy" of wireless congestion.

The impulse to seek individual gain over the collective good becomes particularly tempting when personal well-being is at stake. In the flood-prone summer of 1993, a river overflowed its banks in Des Moines, Iowa, wiping out a filtration system and making the municipal water supply unsafe. To restore full water service, the system had to be refilled with clean water. The situation was urgent. Without full water pressure in the city's water pipes, not only were the residents without regular water service but fire engines also couldn't use the hydrants. Local officials asked everyone to voluntarily refrain from using tap water in their homes and businesses for a few days. If all the city's residents had complied, everyone in the community would have had water within a couple of days. For some individuals, however, the temptation to use water secretly in the privacy of their own homes was too hard to resist. So many residents violated the city's request that the resumption of full water service had to be delayed for many more days (Bradsher, 1993). The entire community suffered as a result of individuals seeking their own short-term benefits.

Why do such dilemmas occur? Part of the problem is lack of communication and lack of trust among individual members of a community. I may want to be a good citizen and conserve water by using it sparingly, but if I think my neighbors are hoarding it, I too will hoard it to make sure I don't go without. Hence, I may follow a line of action that results in a positive outcome for me in the short run but that may eventually have a negative outcome for the community in the long run.

The problem is made worse when individuals think that meeting their individual needs won't have a noticeable effect on the community. "Is my using an extra gallon of water during a drought *really* going to harm the community?" The tragedy of the commons arises when everyone, or at least a substantial number of people, conclude that it will not. As we collectively ignore or downplay the consequences of our actions, we collectively overuse the resource and pave the way for disasters that none of us has caused individually (Edney, 1979).

The Free-Rider Problem

Social dilemmas can also occur when people refrain from contributing something to a common resource because the resource will be available regardless of their contribution. Why pay for something that you can get for free? For example, it is irrational, from an individual's point of view, to donate money to public television and radio. I can enjoy *Sesame Street*, *Frontline*, and *This American Life* without paying a penny. My small personal donation wouldn't be more than a tiny drop in public broadcasting's budgetary bucket anyway. I have no incentive to incur any costs when I don't have to. If everyone acted this way, however, we would all eventually lose the resource. If public television and radio depended solely on voluntary donations made during those annoying fund drives, it would have disappeared a long time ago. Member station fees, grants from universities and the federally funded Corporation for Public Broadcasting, and corporate sponsorships actually keep it going.

Sociologists sometimes refer to this situation as the *free-rider problem* (Olsen, 1965). As the term implies, a free rider is an individual who acquires goods or services without risking any personal costs or contributing anything in return. Free-rider behavior can be seen in a variety of everyday activities, from reading a magazine at a newsstand without buying it to downloading music files for free from other people's online collections. We all enjoy the benefits our tax dollars provide—police, firefighters, smooth roads, and many other municipal services. But if taxes were voluntary, would anyone willingly pay for these services?

We can see evidence of the free-rider problem at the institutional level. People often talk about children as a vital resource on whom the future of the country and the planet depend. The care and education of all children can be seen as a public resource. The whole society benefits when children are well educated and in good physical and psychological health. Yet taxpayers—especially those without children—often protest against tax increases to improve schools, raise teachers' salaries, or hire more youth social workers because they fail to see how such increases will benefit them personally in the long run.

THE STRUCTURE OF FORMAL ORGANIZATIONS

Social life has far more complex functions than simply trying to balance individual and collective interests. Those of us who live in a complex society are all, to varying degrees, organizational creatures. We are born in formal organizations, are educated in them, spend most of our adult lives working for them, and will most likely die in them (E. Gross & Etzioni, 1985). Organizations help meet our most basic needs.

Think about the food on your dinner plate. The farm where the food is produced is probably a huge organization, as are the unions that protect the workers who produce the food and the trucking companies that bring it to your local stores. And all this is controlled by a vast network of financial organizations that set prices and by governmental agencies that ensure the food's safety.

To prepare the food that is produced, delivered, and sold, you have to use products made by other organizations—a sink, a refrigerator, a microwave, a stove. To use those appliances, you have to make arrangements with organizations such as the water and power departments, the gas company, and the electric company. And to pay those bills, you must use still other organizations—the postal service, your Internet provider, your bank, credit companies, and so on.

Most likely, the money to pay the bills comes from a job you or someone in your household has. If you are employed, you probably work for yet another organization. And when you receive a paycheck, the Internal Revenue Service steps in to take its share.

What about the car you use to get to that job? No doubt a huge, multinational corporation manufactured it. Such corporations also produced and delivered the fuel on which the car runs. The roads you travel on to get to your destinations are built and maintained by massive organizations within the state and federal governments. You aren't even allowed to drive unless you are covered by insurance, which is available only through an authorized organization.

And what if things aren't going well? If you become sick, have an accident, or have a dispute with someone, you have to use organizations such as hospitals, police departments, and courts to rectify the situation.

You get the picture? Life in a complex society is a life touched by public and private organizations at every turn. In such a society, things must be done in a formal, planned, and unified way. For instance, the people responsible for producing our food can't informally and spontaneously make decisions about what to grow and when to grow it, and the people responsible for selling it to us can't make its availability random and unpredictable. Imagine what a mess your life would be if you didn't know when your local supermarket would be open or what sorts of food would be available for purchase. What if one day it sold nothing but elbow macaroni, the next day only mangoes, and the day after that just salad dressing?

In a small-scale community where people grow their own food and the local mom-and-pop store provides everything else, the lack of structure might not be a problem. But this type of informal arrangement can't work in a massive society. There must be a relatively efficient and predictable system of providing goods and services to large numbers of people. The tasks that need to be carried out just to keep that system going are too complex for a single person to manage. This complexity makes bureaucracy necessary.

Bureaucracies: Playing by the Rules

The famous 19th-century sociologist Max Weber (VAY-ber) was vitally interested in understanding the complexities of modern society. He noted that human beings could not accomplish feats such as building cities, running huge enterprises, and governing large and diverse populations without bureaucracies. Bureaucracies were certainly an efficient and rational means of managing large groups of people, although Weber acknowledged that these qualities could easily dehumanize those who work in and are served by those organizations.

Today we tend to see bureaucracies primarily as impersonal, rigid machines that trespass into our personal lives. Bureaucracies conjure up images of rows of desks occupied by faceless workers, endless lines and forms to fill out, and frustration over "red tape" and senseless policies. Indeed, the word *bureaucrat* has taken on such a negative connotation that to be called one is an insult. Keep in mind, however, that in a sociological sense, **bureaucracy** is simply a large hierarchical organization that is governed by formal rules and regulations and that has a clear specification of work tasks.

The bureaucratic organization has three important characteristics:

- *Division of labor*: The bureaucracy has a clear-cut **division of labor**, which is carefully specified by written job descriptions for each position. Theoretically, a clear division of labor is efficient because it employs only specialized experts, every one of whom is responsible only for the effective performance of his or her narrowly defined duties (Blau & Meyer, 1987). Division of labor enables large organizations to accomplish more ambitious goals than would be possible if everyone acted independently. Tasks become highly specific, sometimes to the point that it is illegal to perform someone else's task. In hospitals, for instance, orderlies don't prescribe drugs, nurses don't perform surgery, and doctors don't help patients fill out their insurance forms.
- *Hierarchy of authority*: Not only are tasks divided in a bureaucracy, but they are also ranked in a **hierarchy of authority** (Weber, 1946). Most U.S. bureaucracies are organized in a pyramid shape with a small number of people at the top who have a lot of power and many at the bottom who have virtually none. In such a chain of command, people at one level are responsible to those above them and can exert authority over those below. Authority tends to be attached to the position and not to the person occupying the position, so that the bureaucracy will not stop functioning in the event of a retirement or a death. The hierarchy of authority

in bureaucracies not only allows some people to control others but also justifies paying some people higher salaries than others. When applied to political organizations, the hierarchy of authority can create an **oligarchy**, a system in which many people are ruled by a privileged few (Michels, 1911/1949). In such a setting, leaders can often distance themselves from the public, becoming less accountable for their actions in the process.

- *Impersonality*: Bureaucracies are governed by an elaborate system of rules and regulations that ensure a particular task will be done the same way by each person occupying a position. Rules help ensure that bureaucrats perform their tasks impartially and impersonally. Ironically, the very factors that make the typical bureaucrat unpopular with the public— an aloof attitude, lack of genuine concern—actually allow the organization to run more efficiently. We may want the person administering our driver's license examination to be friendly and to care about us, but think of how you'd feel if the examiner had decided to stop for a bite to eat with the person who was taking the driver's test before you.

Your school is a clear example of a bureaucratic organization. It has a definite division of labor that involves janitors, secretaries, librarians, coaches, professors, administrators, trustees, and students. The tasks that people are responsible for are highly specialized. Professors in the Spanish department don't teach courses in biology. In large universities, the specialization of tasks is even more narrowly defined. Sociology professors who teach criminology probably don't teach courses on family.

Although the power afforded different positions varies from school to school, all universities have some sort of hierarchy of authority. Usually, this hierarchy consists of janitors, groundskeepers, and food service workers at the bottom, followed by students, staff employees, teaching assistants, part-time instructors, professors, and department chairs. At the administrative level are associate deans, deans, vice presidents, and ultimately the president of the university and the board of trustees.

In addition, universities are governed by strict and sometimes exasperating bureaucratic rules. There are rules regarding when and how students register for classes, graduation requirements, behavioral policies, and when grades must be turned in by professors. Strict adherence by university employees to these rules and policies is likely to give universities their final characteristic: impersonality.

As people are fitted into roles within bureaucracies that completely determine their duties, responsibilities, and rights, they often become rigid and inflexible and are less concerned about the quality of their work than about whether they and others are playing by the rules. Hence, people become oriented more toward conformity than toward problem solving and critical thinking. They are the source of frustrating procedures and practices that often seem designed not to permit but to prevent things from happening (G. Morgan, 1986). Relief efforts after Hurricane Katrina decimated the Gulf Coast in 2005 were blocked by many bureaucratic obstacles (Goodman, 2005):

- Out-of-state doctors were told they needed a Louisiana license to practice before they could help Katrina victims in New Orleans.
- In cities as far away as Dallas and Houston, attempts to provide shelter were thwarted by building codes and zoning restrictions.
- Both before and after the storm, car owners who offered to haul people out of New Orleans for $5 or $10 were told they were breaking local laws.
- When it came to housing, medical care, and transportation, poor people—as is always the case—did not have the resources to purchase these services on their own and so had to rely on large bureaucratic organizations to provide them, which meant long delays.

Although Weber (1947) stressed the functional necessity of bureaucracies in complex Western societies, he warned that they could take on a life of their own, becoming impersonal "iron cages" for those within them. He feared that bureaucracies might one day dominate every part of society, locking people into a system that allows movement only from one dehumanizing bureaucracy to another. Weber's fears have been largely realized. The bureaucratic model pervades every corner of modern society. The most successful bureaucracies not only dominate the business landscape but have come to influence our entire way of life.

The Construction of Organizational Reality

According to the symbolic interactionist perspective, organizations are created, maintained, and changed through the everyday actions of their members (G. Morgan, 1986). The language of an organization is one of the ways it creates its own reality.

At one level, new members must learn the jargon of the organization to survive within it. To function within the military system, for example, a recruit must learn the meaning of a dizzying array of words, phrases, slang, sounds, and symbols that are unintelligible to outsiders (Evered, 1983). More important, language helps generate and maintain the organization by marking boundaries between insiders and outsiders.

For an organization to work well, everyone must also internalize the same rules, values, and beliefs. But people still have their own ideas and may develop their own informal structure within the larger formal structure of the organization (Meyer & Rowan, 1977). For example, many college instructors tell their students that class discussion is an important component of the course. Yet rarely does every student in a class, or even a majority of students, participate. Most college students know that a few classmates can usually be counted on to respond to questions asked by the professor or to comment on any issue raised in class. These students relieve the remainder of the class from the burden of having to talk at all (Karp & Yoels, 1976). But although these talkative students are carrying the discussion for the entire class, they tend to be disliked by others. A strong norm among many students is that people shouldn't talk too much in class (Karp & Yoels, 1976). Students who speak up all the time upset the normative arrangement of the classroom and, in the students' eyes, may increase the instructor's expectations, hurting everyone in the long run. Other students indicate their annoyance by audibly sighing, rolling their eyes, or openly snickering when a classmate talks too much.

One of the ironies of large complex organizations is that if everyone followed every rule exactly and literally, the organization would eventually self-destruct. For example, the goal of the highly bureaucratized criminal court system is to ensure justice by punishing those who have violated society's laws. The U.S. Constitution's 6th amendment guarantees each person accused of committing a serious crime a timely court trial by a jury of peers. However, public defenders, district attorneys, private attorneys, and judges actually work closely together to bypass the courtroom and move offenders through the system in an orderly fashion (Sudnow, 1965). In the 1970s, 1 in 12 felony cases went to trial; today it's estimated that fewer than 1 in 40 do (cited in Oppel, 2011).

If judges and attorneys followed the procedural rules to the letter and provided all of their clients with the jury trial that is their constitutional right, the system would break down. The courts, already overtaxed, would be incapable of handling the volume of cases. As one author put it, "If everyone charged with crimes suddenly exercised his [or her] constitutional rights, there would not be enough judges, lawyers, or prison cells to deal with the ensuing tsunami of litigation" (Alexander, 2012, p. 5). Thus, the informal system of plea bargaining has taken root, allowing the courts to continue functioning. Those who play exclusively by the rules, such as a young, idealistic public defender who wants to take all her or his cases to trial, are subjected to informal sanctions by judges and superiors, such as inconvenient trial dates or heavier caseloads.

In sum, organizational life is a combination of formal structural rules and informal patterns of behavior. Codified rules are sometimes violated and new, unspoken ones created instead. Stated organizational goals often conflict with the real ones. Despite what may appear to be a clear chain of command, the informal structure often has more of an impact on how things are done.

ORGANIZATIONS AND INSTITUTIONS

Understanding the influence of organizations on our everyday lives tells only part of the story. Organizations themselves exist within a larger structural context, acting as a sort of liaison between people and major social institutions such as the economic system, government, religion, health care, and education. As we saw in Chapter 2, institutions are stable sets of statuses, roles, groups, and organizations that provide the foundation for behavior in certain major areas of social life. They are patterned ways of solving the problems and meeting the needs of a particular society.

Organizational Networks Within Institutions

Like individual people, organizations are born, grow, become overweight, slim down, migrate, form relationships with others, break up, and die. They interact with one another, too, cooperating on some occasions and competing on others, depending on the prevailing economic and political winds. They even lie, cheat, and steal from time to time. As with people, some organizations are extremely powerful and can dictate the manner in which other organizations go about their business.

The state of Texas accounts for about 15% of the entire national textbook market (Stille, 2002). A provision in the Texas Education Code states that textbooks should promote decency, democracy, patriotism, and the free enterprise system. A coalition of various watchdog organizations in Texas scours textbooks each year in search of material they consider inappropriate or offensive. For instance, over the past few years, the Texas Board of Education has asked publishers to delete favorable references to Islam, discussions of global warming, references to the fossil record and evolution, and illustrations of breast and testicular self-examinations (Simon, 2009; E. Smith, 2010). In 2010, the Board approved a social studies curriculum that requires history and economics textbooks to stress the superiority of American capitalism, highlights Christian influences of the Founding Fathers, and presents conservative political philosophy in a positive light (McKinley, 2010; Shorto, 2010). The economic importance of Texas forces many publishers to write their books with that state's rules in mind.

Similarly, when giant corporations, such as General Electric, Apple, Exxon-Mobil, and Coca-Cola, decide to downsize or expand their operations, the effects are felt throughout the entire financial community. But even powerful organizations like these cannot stand alone. Massive networks of organizations are linked by common goals and needs. The networks are often so complex that organizations from very different fields find themselves dependent on one another for survival.

Consider the U.S. health care system, one of our most important social institutions. Think about the vast networks of organizations that are necessary for a single patient in a single hospital to receive treatment. First of all, the hospital is tightly linked to all the other hospitals in the area. A change in one hospital, such as a reduction in the number of patients treated in the emergency room or the opening of a new state-of-the-art trauma center, would quickly have consequences for all the others. The linkage among hospitals enables the transfer of equipment, staff, and patients from one to another when necessary.

To be accredited and staffed, the hospital must also connect to formal training organizations, such as medical schools, nursing schools, and teaching hospitals. These organizations usually affiliate with larger universities, thus expanding the links in the network. And, of course, the American Medical Association and various licensing agencies oversee the establishment of training policies and credentials.

To survive financially, the hospital must also make connections to funding organizations. Hospitals have traditionally been owned and operated by a variety of governmental, religious, nonprofit, and for-profit organizations. They must operate under a set of strict regulations, which means they must also link to the city, state, and federal governmental agencies responsible for certification, such as the Joint Commission. Add to these relationships their links to the medical equipment industry, the pharmaceutical industry, food service providers, the legal profession, charities, political action committees working on health care legislation, patients' rights groups, and most notably health insurance companies, and the system becomes even more complex. Indeed, the recent highly contentious debate over and subsequent passage of health care reform legislation was essentially a fight to protect competing economic, political, and personal interests.

But despite the health care system's complexity, size, and importance, when patients go to a hospital they don't see it as a node in a vast network. Patients are obviously much less interested in the hospital's organizational links than they are in whether their nurse is friendly, the food is good, or their doctor treats them honestly and compassionately. Yet in a 2003 study, one out of three doctors reported purposely withholding information from patients about potentially helpful treatments because those treatments weren't covered by the patient's health insurance (Wynia, VanGeest, Cummins, & Wilson, 2003). The needs of the larger system can sometimes clash with an individual's health care needs, making even face-to-face interactions problematic and, possibly, even detrimental to the patient's health.

Institutional Pressures Toward Similarity

If you think about how many varieties of organizations exist in the world, you might be tempted to focus on their obvious differences. Some are large, others small. Some are formal and complex, others informal and simple. Some have a pyramid-shaped chain of command; others are more egalitarian (Gross & Etzioni, 1985). Sociologists have long been interested in the unique ways in which different organizations adapt to changing political, economic, cultural, or environmental circumstances. However, organizations seem to be more similar than different and even tend to imitate one another's actions as they become established in a particular institution (DiMaggio & Powell, 1983).

Organizational similarity is not really that surprising. Because of the nature of the problems that organizations in the same industry have to address, they come to adopt similar methods of dealing with them. When Apple sought to corner the electronic gadget market with the popular iPad, it was inevitable that other companies would follow suit with their own tablet devices. The same thing could be said for hybrid cars, Greek yogurt, energy drinks, minimalist running shoes, and 3D televisions.

Often the similarities become overwhelming. There's an old adage among Hollywood filmmakers that goes, "There's no success like a previous box office hit" (Dargis, 2011). Likewise, the major U.S. commercial television networks—NBC, ABC, CBS, and Fox—see the profits one network makes with a particular kind of program and try to attract viewers in much the same way. As you well know, the perceived popularity of a certain type of television show creates an irritating avalanche of similar shows on other networks—like shows where people compete with one another to see who will perform the grossest or the most fearsome feats (*Survivor* and *Fear Factor*), wedding shows (*Bridezillas* and *Say Yes to the Dress*), glorified talent contests (*American Idol*, *America's Got Talent*, *The Voice*, *Dancing With the Stars*, and *The X Factor*), model/fashion shows (*Project Runway* and *America's Next Top Model*), and shows about people who save all their junk (*Hoarders* and *Hoarding: Buried Alive*). In short, instead of adjusting directly to changes in the social environment, such as the shifting tastes of the television-viewing public, organizations end up adjusting to what other organizations are doing (DiMaggio & Powell, 1983).

The surprising fact is that the imitated practices are not necessarily more effective or successful. After once-novel strategies have spread throughout an industry, they may no longer improve the organization's performance. Viewers eventually get sick of seeing the same types of shows. The net effect of the imitations is to reduce innovation within the industry.

The tendency for organizations to emulate one another is especially strong in times of institutional uncertainty (DiMaggio & Powell, 1983). When new technologies are poorly understood, when the physical environment is undergoing dramatic changes, or when local, state, and federal governments are creating new regulations or setting new agendas, organizations are likely to be somewhat confused about how things ought to be done. Just as individuals look to one another to help define ambiguous situations and determine an appropriate course of action, so do organizations.

Take changes in the field of higher education. Many colleges and universities across the country face the problem of how to attract more students. Such was the case several years ago at the university where I teach. An outside consultant was called in to design a new marketing program for the school. He had some clear strategies for "packaging" the school's image to make it more attractive to prospective students: redesigned brochures, a new recruitment video, a flashy website, Twitter feed, and Facebook page, and so on. But he was also consulting for several other schools competing for the same shrinking pool of students and admitted that many of the "novel" strategies he advised us to use were things other universities were already using. We were addressing a new and uncertain dilemma by replicating the practices of other organizations in the network.

In sum, certain organizational forms dominate not necessarily because they are the most effective means of achieving goals but because social forces such as institutional uncertainty and the power of professions to provide individuals with a single normative standard create pressures toward similarity. Such similarity makes it easier for organizations to interact with one another and to be acknowledged as legitimate and reputable within the field (DiMaggio & Powell, 1983). But this homogeneity is not without its costs. When organizations replicate one another, institutional change becomes difficult, and the iron cage of bureaucracy becomes harder to escape.

GLOBALIZATION AND SOCIAL INSTITUTIONS

You've seen in this book so far the enormous effect that globalization is having on everyday life. Many

of our important social institutions have become international in scope—notably economics, education, and religion. How do such global institutions meet the needs of human beings around the world?

Economics

Looking around my office at this moment, I notice that my cell phone was made in Japan; my desk and chair in the United States; my watch in Switzerland; my stapler in Great Britain; my calculator in Taiwan; my shoes in Korea; my pants in Hong Kong; my bottled water in Croatia; my briefcase in Indonesia; the frame holding my kids' picture in Thailand; and my paper clips, scissors, computer, travel mug, and iPhone in China. Because of the rapid increase in economic links among producing nations in recent years, your life is probably similarly filled with products made in other countries. Japan is experiencing a troubling shortage of bluefin tuna—the most desirable fish used in sushi—because of growing demand in the United States, Europe, and other countries in Asia (Issenberg, 2007).

Economic globalization is more than just a matter of more goods being shipped from one place to another. For instance, there's a pretty good chance that if you contact someone online or by phone to prepare your taxes, provide legal advice, track your lost luggage, solve your software problem, or review your long-distance phone bill, you'll be dealing with someone working at a call center in India (Friedman, 2005). The large pool of English-speaking, technologically savvy Indian workers willing to work for low wages has attracted the phone service operations of companies such as American Express, Sprint, Citibank, General Electric, Ford, Hewlett-Packard, and IBM (Lakshmi, 2005).

If a product wasn't entirely manufactured in another country, it's a good bet that some of its components were. Even domestic products can have a complex international pedigree. Take, for instance, a loaf of good old American white bread. Its ingredients include honey (Vietnam, Brazil, Uruguay, Canada, Mexico, and Argentina), calcium propionate (Netherlands), guar gum (India), flour enrichments (China), beta-carotene (Switzerland), vitamin D3 (China), and wheat gluten (France, Poland, Russia, and Australia; Barrionuevo, 2007).

The economic processes involved in globalization have made national boundaries less relevant.

Multinational corporations, businesses that have extended their markets and production facilities globally, have become increasingly powerful over the past several decades. U.S.-based multinational corporations alone employ more than 36 million workers worldwide (ProQuest Statistical Abstract, 2013). These companies control a significant portion of the world's wealth, heavily influence the tastes of people everywhere, and don't owe their allegiance to any one country's political authority or culture. At the same time, international financial organizations, such as the World Bank, the World Trade Organization, and the International Monetary Fund, loan money to countries all over the world to finance development and reconstruction projects. (For more on the global economic impact of international financial organizations and multinational corporations, see Chapter 10.) With the costs of communication and computing falling rapidly, barriers of time and space that traditionally separated national markets have also been falling. Even the most remote rural villagers are linked to the global economy as they carry out transactions over the Internet and send and receive goods around the world.

A global economy has its everyday advantages. Goods manufactured and services provided in a country where wages are lower are less expensive for consumers in other countries. Universally accepted credit cards make international travel more convenient. Snack bars in overseas airports accept American money, as do foreign establishments around the world that are near U.S. borders or military bases. Global economic influence has also enabled a significant portion of the world's population to be healthier, eat better, and live longer than the royalty of past civilizations (Kurtz, 1995).

We may barely be aware of how the taken-for-granted elements of our daily lives connect to the economic well-being of people in faraway places. For instance, most of today's popular electronic devices couldn't work without a little-known gritty, super-heavy mud called columbite-tantalite (coltan, for short). Once coltan is refined in U.S., Japanese, and European factories, it becomes tantalum, a remarkably heat-resistant conductor of electricity. Capacitors made of tantalum can be found inside practically every laptop, tablet, video game system, and smartphone in the world. But there isn't nearly enough coltan in the United States, Europe, or Japan to meet these needs. Its largest quantities lie in the rain forests of eastern Congo, where it is mined in much the same way gold was mined in California in the 1800s. Miners spend days in the muck, digging up mud and sloshing it around in plastic tubs until the coltan settles to the bottom. On a good day, a miner can produce about a kilogram of the stuff. Miners earn up to $50 a week, quite a high figure considering that most people in this region live on the equivalent of $10 a month ("What Is Coltan?" 2002).

But global trade has also created some interesting everyday dilemmas. For instance, for centuries, workers in Spain and some Latin American countries have enjoyed the workday *siesta*, a long afternoon nap or an extended lunch, sometimes lasting until 5 P.M. But the owners of factories and retail stores have realized that shutting down operations every afternoon so workers can take their siestas is incompatible with growing integration into the global economy. As the president of a Spanish research group that advocates doing away with the siesta put it, "In a globalized world, we have to have schedules that are more similar to those in the rest of the world so we can be better connected" (quoted in R. McLean, 2005, p. 4). Spain officially cut lunch breaks from three hours to one hour for government workers in 2006 (R. McLean, 2006). Mexico did so in 1999.

Global financial institutions must also keep close track of holidays around the world to avoid trying to do business on nonbusiness days. In some countries, holidays are determined by the lunar calendar, which not only varies from year to year but may vary from area to area within a country based on local customs. In other countries, such as France, the dates of some bank holidays are a matter of negotiation between the banks and the unions that represent their employees. Even weekends are defined differently in different countries. In Taiwan, the weekend consists of every Sunday and the second and fourth Saturdays of each month. In Malaysia, it is every Sunday and only the first Saturday of every month. And in Lithuania, one-day weekends are occasionally followed by four-day weekends (Henriques, 1999).

Economic globalization has fostered more serious social problems as well, including higher levels of unemployment in countries that maintain labor and environmental protections and exploitation of workers in poor, developing countries. The result is a worldwide system of inequality whose problems are often invisible to consumers (see Chapter 10). For instance, many of the best and most beautiful roses Americans buy for their loved ones each year come from the rich volcanic soil of Ecuador. These flowers help generate about $240 million a year and tens of thousands of jobs for this once impoverished region. But the Ecuadorian workers who harvest roses are exposed each day to a toxic mix of pesticides and fungicides (G. Thompson, 2003). They work with severe headaches and rashes for the benefit of wealthier customers around the world, who are largely unaware of the conditions under which these fragrant symbols of romance are produced. We may wish to do our part to make life better for the rose harvesters of Ecuador as well as other poor workers around the world, but it's hard to take any effective action. For instance, boycotts of exploitative manufacturers are a double-edged sword. The origin of products is seldom clear-cut, and local workers are typically glad to have jobs they wouldn't have had otherwise. Pressure to compete in the global marketplace also erodes the ability of governments to set their own economic policies, protect national interests, or adequately protect workers and the environment.

Education

The prospect of international competition in a global economy can foster changes in a country's educational system. For instance, U.S. primary school students attend school an average of 180 days a year, compared with 204 days in Korea, and 210 days in Japan (Bush, 2009). Moreover, during the four years of high school, the average American student devotes approximately 1,462 hours to math, science, language, and social studies. The average Japanese student will spend 3,190 hours studying these subjects (cited in Bainbridge, 2005). Not surprisingly, students in these and other industrialized countries consistently outperform U.S. students in fields such as math and science (National Center for Education Statistics, 2012b). For instance, only 7% of American eighth graders reach the advanced level in math, compared to 48% of eighth graders in Singapore and 47% in South Korea (cited in Rich, 2012). Indeed, according to some education experts, American high schoolers are about one full school year behind high schoolers in other industrialized countries (cited in Dillon, 2010).

Concern over our ability to compete in the global marketplace has led to nationwide calls for educational reforms such as heavier emphasis on math and science; more time spent on foundational skills, such as reading and writing; increased computer literacy; and training in political geography and international relations. To address this concern, the National Math and Science Initiative provides cash incentives and other forms of support to faculty and students in over 400 schools around the country. Students in participating schools earn $100 for every Advanced Placement (AP) exam they pass while teachers earn salary bonuses for each of their students who passes an AP exam (Matthews, 2012).

Pressures to achieve academically are present from the beginning. Even though research shows that play is essential for healthy development, children as early as kindergarten spend significantly more time on lessons and testing than on play, exercise, and imagination. According to a study of New York and Los Angeles kindergartens (E. Miller & Almon, 2009), children spend four to six times as long being instructed and tested in math skills and literacy (two to three hours a day) as in free play (20 to 30 minutes a day). Standardized testing and preparation for testing are now daily activities in most kindergartens. Play materials like blocks, sand, water tables, and props for dramatic play have largely disappeared from the classroom. Some school districts in Atlanta, New York, Chicago, New Jersey, and Connecticut have opted to eliminate recess, even to the point of building new schools in their districts without playgrounds (Sindelar, 2004).

Education reformers have consistently called for longer school days and shorter vacations so U.S. students can catch up to their peers elsewhere in the world. Some point out that the school calendar—with its six-and-a-half-hour day and 180-day year—was created for the farm-based economy of the past, not today's high-tech one (Ubiñas & Gabrieli, 2011). At his confirmation hearing in 2009, Secretary of Education Arne Duncan stated, "Our school day is too short, our school week is too short, our school year is too short" (quoted in Dillon, 2011, p. A14). In response, according to the National Center on Time and Learning (2013), over 1,000 schools have expanded their school days in recent years by an average of 1.1 hours a day over conventional schools. And other schools have extended their calendars to 190 or even 200 days a year. But even at a time when concern over global competitiveness is more acute than ever, economic hard times are forcing many schools to cut back rather than expand their educational services. School districts in major cities across the country have laid off thousands of teachers, school psychologists, and custodians. Some districts have trimmed bus service, discontinued field trips, shortened the school day, eliminated summer school, and reduced the school week to four days (Dillon, 2008, 2011; Ubiñas & Gabrieli, 2011).

Moreover, some critics still feel that we already place far too much emphasis on performance and achievement in this society and that children end up suffering as a result (Mannon, 1997). They often point to Japan, not as a model but as a cautionary tale, the dangerous effects of performance pressure seen elsewhere. Many Japanese children attend classes all day, then go to one of the many private "cram" schools, where they study for college entrance exams until 10 or 11 P.M. Even three-year-olds may spend hours a day memorizing stories, learning vocabulary, and taking achievement tests (WuDunn, 1996a). But Japanese educational accomplishments often come at a steep price. Some Japanese sociologists blame the intense competitive pressures children face for the dramatic rise in youth crime over the past few years. Historically, passing grueling exams and getting into the top high schools and elite colleges was a virtual guarantee of a prestigious job. But Japan's economic stagnation and record unemployment in the 2000s shattered the implicit social contract that once justified all the hard work and sacrifice (French, 1999b). About one in three Japanese elementary school teachers has experienced at least one disruptive classroom incident, such as students mocking their authority, walking out of class, or even physically attacking them (cited in French, 2002).

Few people in the United States would argue that we should emulate the pressurized Japanese educational model. At the same time, though, the demands of the global economy and concerns over Americans' ability to compete internationally will continue to exert influence on legislators and education reformers.

Religion

Another institution influenced by globalization is religion. Despite the enormous variety of cultures and ethnicities that exist today, nearly two thirds of the world's population belongs to just three major religions—Christianity, Hinduism, and Islam—which have successfully crossed national boundaries for centuries.

Some denominations are globalizing to deal with shrinking memberships in the countries where they originated. For example, outside the United States and Canada, the Mormon Church has grown by over 500% since 1980 (cited in Kress, 2005). The Methodist Church lost 1 million U.S. members between 1980 and 1995 but gained about 500,000 elsewhere, mostly in Africa (Niebuhr, 1998). Indeed, during the 20th century, the population of Christians in Africa grew from 10 million to 360 million. The Anglican Church, in particular, is growing faster in Africa than in its traditional bases, Great Britain and North America; Nigeria alone has 25% of the world's Anglicans (Rice, 2009).

Ironically, this globalization of religion is creating crises for religious communities. Exposure to competing worldviews challenges traditional beliefs. In some cases, religions have reacted with a forceful revitalization of ancient, fundamentalist traditions (Kurtz, 1995). Witness the growing trend toward governments defining themselves in narrowly religious terms. The ascension of fundamentalist Islamic government in Iran, the growing influence of Orthodox Jews in Israeli politics, and the continuing conflict between Hindus and Muslims in Kashmir and between Sunni and Shiite Muslims in Iraq attest to the fact that many people today believe religion cannot be separated from a nation's social and political destiny.

The rise of religious nationalism around the world has created an obvious threat to global security. The attacks of September 11, 2001, are the most glaring illustration. Radical elements sometimes use religious texts—in this case the Qur'an—as justification for violence against societies that they blame for moral decline and economic exploitation. Elsewhere, the possibility of violence by supporters of religious nationalist movements has brought down political regimes, changed the outcomes of elections, strained international relations, and made some parts of the world dangerous places for travelers (Juergensmeyer, 1996).

But religion has also played a positive role in world affairs and has created dramatic social changes. According to Max Weber (1904/1977), the spread of Protestant beliefs throughout Europe made the growth of modern capitalism possible. Protestantism maintained that worldly achievements, such as the accumulation of wealth through hard work, are a sign of God's favor. But the early Protestants also believed that God frowns on vulgar displays of wealth, such as big houses, fancy clothes, and so forth.

So people were motivated to save and reinvest their wealth rather than spend it frivolously. You can see how such beliefs made large-scale and long-term economic growth possible (Weber, 1904/1977). A study of 59 Christian, Buddhist, Muslim, and Hindu countries found that strong religious beliefs tend to stimulate economic growth because of their association with individual traits like honesty, work ethic, thrift, and openness to strangers (Barro & McCleary, 2003).

The influence of religious movements on social life continues. In the 1960s, television pictures of Buddhist monks setting themselves on fire in Vietnam to protest the war fed the growing antiwar movement in the United States. In the 1970s and 1980s, images of Catholic priests and nuns challenging government policies in Central and South America provoked a heightened awareness worldwide of the plight of indigenous people there. In the early 2000s, followers of the Dalai Lama raised global awareness of the plight of Tibetans who seek independence from China, leading to the establishment of the worldwide International Campaign for Tibet. In 2007, tens of thousands of Buddhist monks in Myanmar marched in the streets to protest against that country's oppressive military regime. Their actions sparked organized protests in more than two dozen Asian, European, and North American cities.

CONCLUSION

More than three centuries ago, John Donne wrote, "No man is an island, entire of itself; every man is a piece of the continent, a part of the main." The same can be said of contemporary social life. We are not isolated individuals whose lives are simply functions of personal characteristics and predispositions. We are social beings. We are part of aggregations of other social beings. We have a powerful need to belong to something larger than ourselves. As a result, we constantly affect and are affected by our associations with others, whether face to face or in well-structured groups, massive bureaucratic organizations, or all-encompassing social institutions.

Throughout Part II of this book, I discussed how society and culture affect everyday experiences and how those experiences help to construct and maintain social order. The development of self and self-controlled behavior, the influence of cultural norms, responses to deviance, and so on are all topics that provide insight into how we are able to live together in a relatively orderly and predictable way. In this chapter, however, you can see that the social structure, though created and maintained by the actions of individuals, is more than just the sum of those actions. Organizations interact at a level well above the individual; institutions are organized in a massive, global system.

Social structure is bigger than any of us, exerts enormous control over our lives, and is an objectified reality that appears to exist independently of us. But it cannot exist without us. I'm reminded of a skit from the old British comedy show *Monty Python's Flying Circus,* in which a high-rise apartment building stood erect only because its inhabitants believed in it. When they doubted its existence, it began to crumble. Like that building, social structure requires constant human support. Once we as a society are no longer able to sustain our organizations or believe in our institutions, they fall apart.

CHAPTER HIGHLIGHTS

◆ Social structure is both a source of predictability and a source of problems in our everyday life. Sometimes individual interests coincide with structural needs; other times they conflict.

◆ By virtue of living in society, we are all organizational creatures. We are born in organizations, are educated in them, spend most of our adult lives working in them, and will probably die in them.

◆ A common form of organization in a complex society is the bureaucracy. A bureaucracy is a large hierarchical organization that is governed by a system of rules and regulations, has a clear specification of work tasks, and has a well-defined division of labor.

◆ The everyday experience of bureaucratic organizations is determined by where one fits into the hierarchical structure.

Bureaucracies look very different depending on whether one is situated at the top, middle, or bottom.

◆ Organizations are more than structures, rules, policies, goals, job descriptions, and standard operating procedures. Each organization, and each division within an organization, develops its own norms, values, and language.

◆ Organizations exist within highly interconnected networks. In times of institutional or environmental uncertainty, organizations tend to imitate one another, adopting similar activities, policies, and goals.

◆ As national borders become increasingly permeable, cultures and social institutions become more global in nature.

KEY TERMS

bureaucracy: Large hierarchical organization governed by formal rules and regulations and having clearly specified work tasks

division of labor: Specialization of different people or groups in different tasks, characteristic of most bureaucracies

free-rider problem: Tendency for people to refrain from contributing to the common good when a resource is available without any personal cost or contribution

hierarchy of authority: Ranking of people or tasks in a bureaucracy from those at the top, where there is a great deal of power and authority, to those at the bottom, where there is very little power and authority

McDonaldization: Process by which the characteristics and principles of the fast food restaurant come to dominate other areas of social life

multinational corporation: Company that has manufacturing, production, and marketing divisions in multiple countries

oligarchy: System of authority in which many people are ruled by a privileged few

social dilemma: Potential for a society's long-term ruin because of individuals' tendency to pursue their own short-term interests

social structure: Framework of society—social institutions, organizations, groups, statuses and roles, cultural beliefs, and institutionalized norms—that adds order and predictability to our private lives

tragedy of the commons: Situation in which people acting individually and in their own self-interest use up commonly available (but limited) resources, creating disaster for the entire community

The Architecture of Stratification

Social Class and Inequality

Stratification Systems

Sociological Perspectives on Stratification

Class Inequality in the United States

Global Development and Inequality

I f you've seen the 1997 Hollywood film *Titanic*, you know that the famous ship had every amenity and comfort: Turkish baths, the finest orchestras, intricately tiled walls, the best cuisine. What it didn't have when it hit an iceberg and began to sink was enough lifeboats. There was room for only 1,178 of the 2,207 passengers and crew members on board. Over the span of two hours on that cold April night in 1912, as the "unsinkable" ocean liner was engulfed by the frigid waters of the North Atlantic, more than 1,500 people lost their lives.

This part of the story is well known. What is less known is that some of the passengers actually had a much better chance of survival than others. More than 60% of the people from the wealthy first-class deck survived, compared with 36% of the people from the second-class deck and 24% of the people from the lowest, or "steerage," class. The figures were even more striking for women and children, who, by virtue of mannerly tradition, were entitled to be spared first. In first class, 97% of the women and children survived; in second class, 89% survived. However, only

42% of the women and children in steerage were saved (W. Hall, 1986).

One reason so many wealthier passengers survived was that the lifeboats were accessed from the higher first- and second-class decks. The locked doors and other barriers erected to keep third-class passengers from venturing to the upper decks during the cruise remained in place when disaster struck. In addition, little effort was made to save the people in steerage. Some were forcibly kept down by crew members standing guard.

For passengers on the *Titanic*, social inequality meant more than just differences in the comfort of accommodations or the quality of the food. It literally meant life or death. This situation serves as a metaphor for what many people face in today's society. Those at the top have easy access to various "lifeboats" in times of social or economic disaster; others face locked gates, segregated decks, and policies that make even survival exceedingly difficult (Sidel, 1986).

Let's turn the clock ahead to the summer of 2005, when Hurricane Katrina killed more than 1,000 people in the Gulf Coast region of the U.S. South. Most of these people died not because of the hurricane's torrential rains and high winds but because of the flooding that occurred when the levees that ordinarily protect the low-lying areas of New Orleans (which were in need of repair to begin with) were breached. In addition to the fatalities, hundreds of thousands of people lost everything they owned and were forced to relocate.

The storm and its aftermath did not affect all residents equally. The neighborhoods with significant flooding had a lower median income, a higher poverty rate, and a higher percentage of households without a vehicle than the areas that experienced little or no flooding (J. Schwartz, Revkin, & Wald, 2005). Those of us watching the tragedy unfold on television could not help but notice that the vast majority of the evacuees who suffered for days in the sweltering darkness of the Louisiana Superdome and convention center in New Orleans were poor people of color who came from the most vulnerable parts of the city. These were individuals who either didn't have the necessary transportation to evacuate prior to the hurricane or who stayed behind to tend to sick and elderly relatives who couldn't be moved. Poor, displaced children who were forced to live in ramshackle government trailer parks after the hurricane continue to suffer from various ailments, including

anemia, respiratory infections, and depression (Carmichael, 2008). Again we see how lack of economic resources can have direct, physical consequences in people's lives.

In this chapter, I look at class inequality and stratification. In subsequent chapters, I explore two other facets of inequality: race and/or ethnicity and gender. It's important to note, however, that although class, race and ethnicity, and gender are covered in separate chapters, these components of our identities are not experienced separately. They are all interrelated, and they combine to determine individuals' positions in society. For instance, a person doesn't live his life just as a working-class person, just as a man, or just as an Asian American. He is all these things—and more—simultaneously (D. Newman, 2012).

STRATIFICATION SYSTEMS

Inequality is woven into the fabric of all societies through a structured system of *stratification*, the ranking of entire groups of people that perpetuates unequal rewards and life chances in a society. Just as geologists talk about strata of rock, which are layered one on top of another, the "social strata" of people are arranged from low to high. All societies, past and present, have had some form of stratification, although they vary in the degree of inequality between strata. The four main forms of stratification that sociologists have identified—all of which continue to exist in contemporary societies—are slavery, caste, estate, and social class systems.

Slavery

One of the most persistent forms of stratification in the world is slavery. *Slavery* is an economic form of inequality in which some people are the property of others. Their lives are owned, controlled, coerced, and restricted. One can become a slave in a variety of ways: through birth, military defeat, debt, or, as in the United States until the mid 19th century, capture and commercial trade (Kerbo, 1991). Because slaves are considered possessions, they are denied the rights and life chances other people take for granted. Slavery has occurred in various forms almost everywhere in the world at some time. Mexico, Great Britain, France, Russia, and Holland all abolished slavery before the United States; Spain, Korea, Cuba, and Brazil did so afterward (D. B. Davis, 2006). Several

Middle Eastern countries—Saudi Arabia, Yemen, Oman, United Arab Emirates—didn't abolish slavery until the latter part of the 20th century. Though theoretically against the law, tens of thousands of people in the West African nations of Niger, Burkina Faso, Mali, and Mauritania are born into slavery today ("A Continuing Abomination," 2008). In South Asia, there are millions of "bonded laborers" whose employers force them to work for no wages in order to pay off a debt (Appiah, 2007). The International Labor Organization estimates that 20.9 million adults and children are bought, sold, transported, or kept against their will in the world today (U.S. Department of State, 2012).

Caste Systems

Some societies today retain a second form of stratification: a *caste system*. Traditionally, one's caste, which determines lifestyle, prestige, and occupational choices, was fixed at birth and couldn't be changed. Ancient Hindu scriptures, for instance, identified the strict hierarchy of elite, warrior, merchant, servant, and untouchable castes. The rights and duties associated with membership in each caste were clear. In India, "untouchables"—members of the lowest caste—were once required by law to hide from or, if that wasn't possible, to bow in the presence of anyone from a higher caste. They were routinely denied the right to enter Hindu temples or to draw water from wells reserved for members of the higher castes, who feared they would be contaminated if they touched or otherwise came in contact with an untouchable.

According to Human Rights Watch (2009), more than 260 million people—mostly in India, Nepal, Bangladesh, Pakistan, and Sri Lanka but also in Japan, Yemen, and several African countries—continue to suffer severe caste discrimination. They are victims of exploitation and violence and face massive obstacles to their full attainment of civil, political, economic, and cultural rights.

Things are beginning to change, however. In India, for instance, where 16% of the population belongs to so-called Scheduled Castes (or Dalits, as they prefer to be called; Human Rights Watch, 2012), laws have been passed that prohibit caste-based discrimination. More Dalits now vote than members of the higher castes (Dugger, 1999). In fact, the benefits Dalits now receive—such as reserved spaces in universities and governmental jobs—have prompted members of the next highest caste of farmers and shepherds to lobby the government to have its caste status *downgraded* so as to be eligible for these benefits (Gentleman, 2007).

But the caste system still serves as a powerful source of stratification, especially with regard to marriage and political power (Sankaran, 2013). Even Indians living in the United States find that caste sometimes colors their experiences with friends and business associates (J. Berger, 2004).

Estate Systems

A third form of stratification is the *estate system*, or *feudal system*, which develops when high-status groups own land and have power based on their noble birth (Kerbo, 1991). Estate systems were most commonly found in preindustrial societies. In medieval Europe, the highest "estate" in society was occupied by the aristocracy, who derived their wealth and power from extensive landholdings. The clergy formed the next estate. Although they had lower status than the aristocracy, they still claimed considerable status because the Catholic Church itself owned a great deal of land and exerted influence over people's lives. The last, or "third," estate was reserved for commoners: serfs, peasants, artisans, and merchants. Movement between estates was possible, though infrequent. Occasionally, a commoner might be knighted, or a wealthy merchant might become an aristocrat.

Some reminders of the estate system can still be seen today. In Great Britain, for instance, Parliament's House of Lords is still occupied primarily by people of "noble birth," and a small group of aristocratic families still sit at the top of the social ladder, where they enjoy tremendous inherited wealth and exercise significant political power. For a moment, this system seemed to be changing. In 2007, the British House of Commons (the so-called lower house) voted overwhelmingly to introduce elections to the House of Lords. It also voted to remove the last remaining "hereditary peers," whose presence in the House of Lords is based solely on their noble lineage (Cowell, 2007). A week later, the House of Lords soundly rejected the measure.

Social Class Systems

Stratification systems in contemporary industrialized societies are most likely to be based on social class. A *social class* is a group of people who share a similar economic position in society based on their wealth and income. Class is essentially, therefore, an economic stratification system. It is a means of ranking people or groups that determines access to important resources and life chances. Less obviously, perhaps, social class provides people with a particular understanding of the world and where they fit into it compared with others.

Class systems differ from other systems of stratification in that they raise no legal barriers to *social mobility*—the movement of people or groups from one level to another. Theoretically, all members of a class system, no matter how destitute they are, can rise to the top. In practice, however, mobility between classes may be difficult for some people. For instance, where you live can influence your chances of upward mobility. Climbing the income ladder is less common in the Southeast and industrial Midwest and more likely in the Northeast and West where poor people have a greater chance of living in mixed-income neighborhoods with better elementary schools and high schools and more civic engagement (Leonhardt, 2013).

In addition, some economists say that it often takes five or six generations to erase the advantages or disadvantages of a person's economic origins (Krueger, 2002). Within the span of a single generation, there isn't much social mobility—wealthy parents tend to have wealthy children; poor parents tend to have poor children. In fact, the United States has significantly less social mobility than comparable nations. For instance, 42% of Americans who grew up in the bottom fifth of incomes remain there as adults. In Denmark, the figure is 25% and in Britain it's 30% (Jäntti, 2006). Likewise, race and gender have historically determined a person's access to educational, social, and employment opportunities. Women of color are especially likely to face barriers to upward mobility, in terms of both economic disadvantage and lack of emotional support from their families (Higginbotham & Weber, 1992).

SOCIOLOGICAL PERSPECTIVES ON STRATIFICATION

Sociologists have long been interested in explaining why societies are stratified. Two perspectives—the structural-functionalist perspective and the conflict perspective—offer insights into the sources and purposes of social inequality. They are often presumed to be competing views, but we can actually use them together to deepen our understanding of why social inequality exists, how it develops, and why it is so persistent.

The Structural-Functionalist View of Stratification

From a structural-functionalist perspective, the cause of stratification lies in a society's inevitable need for order. Because social inequality is found in some form in all societies and thus is apparently unavoidable, inequality must somehow be necessary for societies to run smoothly.

As with bureaucracies, the efficient functioning of society requires that various tasks be allocated through a strictly defined division of labor. If the tasks associated with all social positions in a society were equally pleasant and equally important and required the same talents, it wouldn't make a difference who occupied which position. But structural functionalists argue that it does make a difference. Some occupations, such as teaching and medicine, are more important for the well-being of society than others and require greater talent and training. Society's dilemma is to make sure that the most talented people perform the most important tasks. One way to ensure this distribution of tasks is to assign higher rewards—better pay, greater prestige, more social privileges—to some positions in society so that they will be attractive to people with the necessary talents and abilities (Davis & Moore, 1945). Presumably, if these talented people were not offered sufficiently high rewards, they would have no reason to take on the difficult and demanding tasks associated with important positions. Why would someone go through the agony and costs of many years of medical school, for instance, without some promise of compensation and high prestige?

Just because a position is important, however, does not mean it is generously rewarded (Davis & Moore, 1945). Imagine what our society would be like without people who remove our trash. Not only would our streets be unsightly, but our collective health would suffer. Therefore, garbage collectors serve a vital social function. But they don't get paid very much—on average, about $481 a week, according to the U.S. Bureau of Labor Statistics (2010)—and trash removal is certainly not a highly respected occupation. Why aren't garbage collectors higher up in the hierarchy of occupations? According to the structural-functionalist perspective, it is because we have no shortage of people with the skills needed to collect garbage. Physicians also serve the collective health needs of a society. But because of the skills and training needed to be a doctor, society must offer rewards high enough to ensure that qualified people will want to enter the medical profession. Doctors—even those just starting out—can expect to make, on average, four to five times more than garbage collectors (U.S. Bureau of Labor Statistics, 2010).

This explanation may make some sense. But when we examine the pay scales of actual occupations more closely, it comes up short. For instance, despite the fact that they're in the same profession and have gone through similar training, a registered nurse in a doctor's office can make close to four times as much as a registered nurse working in a high school or junior college. A plumber at a city hospital makes more than twice what a plumber at a decent-sized hotel makes (Davidson, 2011).

But let's not stop there. One look at the salary structure in today's society reveals obvious instances of highly paid positions that don't seem as functionally important as positions that receive lower wages. For instance, Oprah Winfrey makes about $165 million a year. Filmmakers Michael Bay and Steven Spielberg earn $160 million and $130 million a year respectively. Tiger Woods makes $58 million. Justin Bieber, $55 million a year. Seth MacFarlane pulls in $36 million (*Forbes* Magazine, 2013). You might say that TV personalities, filmmakers, golfers, singers, and comedians serve vital social functions by providing the rest of us with a recreational release from the demands of ordinary life; and the best entertainers and athletes do have rare skills, indeed. However, society probably can do without another TV show, megahit movie, or concert more easily than it can do without competent physicians, scientists, computer programmers, teachers, or even trash collectors, who earn substantially less in a year than what many celebrities earn in a day.

Furthermore, the structural-functionalist argument that only a limited number of talented people are around to occupy important social positions is probably overstated. Many people have the talent to become doctors. What they lack is access to training. And why are some people—women and members of racial and ethnic minorities—paid less for or excluded entirely from certain jobs? The debates over equal employment opportunity and equal pay for equal work are essentially debates over how the functional importance of certain positions is determined.

Finally, when functionalists claim that stratification serves the needs of society, we must ask, whose needs? A system of slavery obviously meets the economic needs of one group at the expense of another, but that doesn't make it acceptable. In a class-stratified society, individuals who receive the greatest rewards have the resources to make sure they continue receiving such rewards. Over time, the competition for the most desirable positions will become less open and less competitive. The offspring of "talented"—that is, high-status—parents will inevitably have an advantage over equally talented people who are born into less successful families. Hence, social background and not personal aptitude may become the primary criterion for filling important social positions (Tumin, 1953).

The structural-functionalist perspective gives us important insight into how societies ensure that all positions in the division of labor are filled. Every society, no matter how simple or complex, differentiates people in terms of prestige and esteem and possesses a certain amount of institutional inequality. But this perspective doesn't address the fact that stratification can be unjust and divisive, a source of social *disorder* (Tumin, 1953).

The Conflict View of Stratification

Conflict theorists are among those who argue that social inequality is neither a societal necessity nor a source of social order. They see it as a primary source of conflict, coercion, and unhappiness. Stratification ultimately rests on the unequal distribution of resources—some people have them, others don't. Important resources include money, land, information, education, health care, safety, and adequate housing. Those high in the stratification system can control these resources because they are the ones who set the rules. The conflict perspective takes it as a fundamental truth that stratification systems serve the interests of those at the top and not the survival needs of the entire society.

Resources are an especially important source of inequality when they are scarce. Sometimes, their scarcity is natural. For instance, there's only a finite amount of land on earth that can be used, inhabited, and owned. At other times, however, the scarcity of a resource is artificially created. For instance, in 1890, the founder of De Beers, the South African company that currently controls two thirds of the international diamond market, realized that the sheer abundance of diamonds in southern Africa would make them virtually worthless on the international market. So he decided to carefully limit the number of diamonds released for sale each year. This artificially created rarity, coupled with a carefully cultivated image of romance, is what made diamonds so expensive and what continues to make companies such as De Beers so powerful today (Harden, 2000).

Rich and politically powerful individuals frequently work together to create or maintain privilege, often at the expense of the middle and lower classes (Phillips, 2002). The U.S. Congress is dominated by both Republicans and Democrats who are far richer than the citizens they represent. The median net worth of a member of Congress is about $966,000, 14 times more than that of a typical American household. It's even higher for freshmen members elected in 2012 ($1,066,155). Indeed, the average per capita net worth of the 10 wealthiest members of Congress is about $210 million (Center for Responsive Politics, 2013).

Thus, from the conflict perspective, it's not at all surprising that politicians would make decisions that benefit the wealthy over others. For instance, while Congress continues to search for ways to cut spending on programs designed to help low-income Americans, such as Medicaid (the health insurance system that covers poor adults and their dependents), low-income housing programs, legal services for the poor, and supplemental nutrition for poor families (Greywolfe359, 2011), the wealthiest 20% of the population gets over half of the overall savings from breaks in the U.S. tax code (for things like mortgage interest and rental expenses; Congressional Budget Office, 2013). In fact, Americans earning over $1 million a year receive about $30 billion a year in federal grants and subsidies (Stone & Colarusso, 2011). Furthermore, although the federal tax rate on corporate profits is 35%, wealthy corporations actually enjoy a tax rate of only around 12.6% due to legal deductions and loopholes (Schwartz, 2013). Indeed, when called upon to provide financial relief to the victims of natural disasters like hurricanes and tornadoes, many members of Congress favor paying for the aid by cutting the budgets of existing social programs that help other needy citizens rather than by repealing tax cuts for upper-class Americans (Pappas, 2013).

There's some evidence that a growing number of Americans perceive tensions between those at the top and the rest of the population, as the conflict perspective would predict. The Occupy Wall Street movement that began in 2011 drew public attention to the inequality between the wealthiest 1% and the rest of the population. A 2011 poll by the Pew Research Center found that about two-thirds of Americans believe that there are "very strong" or "strong" conflicts between the rich and poor; less than half held similar beliefs just two years earlier (cited in Kohut, 2012). In addition, nearly 6 in 10 people believe that the rich pay too little in taxes and 55% believe that rich people are more likely than the average person to be greedy.

What the conflict perspective gives us that the structural-functionalist perspective doesn't is an acknowledgment of the interconnected roles that economic and political institutions play in creating and maintaining a stratified society.

The Marxian Class Model

Karl Marx and Friedrich Engels (1848/1982) were the original proponents of the view that societies are divided into conflicting classes. They felt that in modern societies, two major classes emerge: *capitalists* (or the bourgeoisie), who own the **means of production**—land, commercial enterprises, factories, and wealth—and are able to purchase the labor of others, and *workers* (or the proletariat), who neither own the means of production nor have the ability to purchase the labor of others. Workers, instead, must sell their own labor to others in order to survive. Some workers, including store managers and factory supervisors, may control other workers, but their power is minimal compared with the power exerted over them by those in the capitalist class. Marx and Engels supplemented this two-tiered conception of class by adding a third tier, the *petite bourgeoisie*, which is a transitional class of people who own the means of production but don't purchase the labor power of others. This class consists of self-employed skilled laborers and businesspeople who are economically self-sufficient but don't have a staff of subordinate workers (R. V. Robinson & Kelley, 1979).

Capitalists have considerable sway over what and how much will be produced, who will get it, how much money people will be paid to produce it, and so forth. Such influence allows them to control other people's livelihoods, the communities in which people live, and the economic decisions that affect the entire society. In such a structure, the rich inevitably tend to get richer, to use their wealth to create more wealth for themselves, and to act in ways that will protect their interests and positions in society.

Ultimately, the wealthy segments of society gain the ability to influence important social institutions such as the government, the media, the schools, and the courts. They have access to the means necessary to create and promote a reality that justifies their exploitative actions. Their version of reality is so influential that even those who are harmed by it come to accept it. Marx and Engels called this phenomenon *false consciousness*. False consciousness is crucial because it is the primary means by which the powerful classes in society prevent protest and revolution. As long as large numbers of poor people continue to believe that wealth and success are solely the products of individual hard work and effort rather than structured inequalities in society—that is, they believe what in the United States has been called the American Dream—resentment and animosity toward the rich will be minimized and people will perceive the inequalities as fair and deserved (R. V. Robinson & Bell, 1978).

Neo-Marxist Models of Stratification

In Marx's time—the heyday of industrial development in the mid 19th century—ownership of property and control of labor were synonymous. Most jobs were either on farms or in factories. Lumping all those who owned productive resources into one class and all those who didn't into another made sense. However, the nature of capitalism has changed a lot since then. Today, a person with a novel idea for a product or service, a computer with high-speed Internet access, and a smartphone can go into business and make a lot of money. Corporations have become much larger and more bureaucratic, with a long, multilevel chain of command. Ownership of corporations lies in the hands of stockholders (foreign as well as domestic), who often have no connection at all to the everyday workings of the business. Thus, ownership and management are separated. The powerful people who run large businesses and control workers on a day-to-day basis are frequently not the same people who own the businesses.

In light of changing realities, more contemporary conflict sociologists, such as Ralf Dahrendorf (1959), have offered models that focus primarily on differing levels of authority among the members of society. What's important is not just who owns the means

of production but who can exercise influence over others. *Authority* is the possession of some status or quality that compels others to obey (Starr, 1982). A person with authority has the power to order or forbid behavior in others (Wrong, 1988). Such commands don't require the use of force or persuasion, nor do they need to be explained or justified. Rulers simply have authority over the ruled, as do teachers over students, employers over employees, and parents over children. These authority relationships are not fixed, of course: Children fight with their parents, students challenge their teachers, and workers protest against their bosses. But although the legitimacy of the authority may sometimes be called into question, the ongoing dependence of the subordinates maintains it. The worker may disagree with the boss, and the student may disagree with the teacher; but the boss still signs the paycheck, and the teacher still assigns final grades.

Like Marx and Engels, Dahrendorf believed that relations between classes inherently involve conflicts of interest. Rulers often maintain their position in society by ordering or forcing people with less authority to do things that benefit the rulers. But by emphasizing authority, Dahrendorf argued that stratification is not exclusively an economic phenomenon. Instead, it comes from the social relations between people who possess different degrees of power.

Dahrendorf's ideas about the motivating force behind social stratification have since been expanded. Sociologist Erik Olin Wright and his colleagues (Wright, 1976; Wright, Costello, Hachen, & Sprague, 1982; Wright & Perrone, 1977) have developed a model that incorporates both the ownership of means of production and the exercise of authority over others. The capitalist and petite bourgeoisie classes in this scheme are identical to those of Marx and Engels. What is different is that the classes of people who do not own society's productive resources (Marx and Engels's worker class) are divided into two classes: managers and workers.

Wright's approach gives us a sense that social class is not simply a reflection of income or the extent to which one group exercises authority over another. Lawyers, plumbers, and cooks, for instance, could each conceivably fall into any of the four class categories. They may own their own businesses and hire assistants (placing them in the capitalist class), work for a large company and have subordinates (placing them in the manager class), work for a large company without any subordinates (placing them in the worker class), or be self-employed (placing them in the petite bourgeoisie; R. V. Robinson & Kelley, 1979).

Wright's approach also emphasizes that class conflict is more than just a clash between the rich and the poor. Societies have, in fact, multiple lines of conflict— economic, political, administrative, and social. Some positions, or what Wright calls *contradictory class locations*, fall between two major classes. Individuals in these positions have trouble identifying with one side or the other. Middle managers and supervisors, for instance, can align with workers because both are subordinates of capitalist owners. Yet because middle managers and supervisors can exercise authority over some people, they may also share the interests and concerns of owners.

Weber's Model of Stratification

Other conflict sociologists have likewise questioned Marx's heavy emphasis on wealth and income as the sole factors that stratify society. Max Weber (1921/1978) agreed with Marx that social class is an important determinant of stratification. However, he observed that the way people are ranked is not just a matter of economic inequality. Weber added two other dimensions—status (or what he called prestige) and power—to his model of stratification, preferring the term *socioeconomic status*—the prestige, honor, respect, and power associated with different class positions in society—rather than class to describe social inequality (Weber, 1970).

The existence of these other dimensions makes the conflict model of class stratification more complex than simply a battle between the rich and the poor. *Prestige* is the reverence and admiration given to some people in society. It is obviously influenced by wealth and income, but it can also be derived from *achieved* characteristics, such as educational attainment and occupational status, and from *ascribed* characteristics, such as race, ethnicity, gender, and family pedigree. While wealth and prestige often go hand in hand, they don't necessarily have to. Drug dealers, for example, may be multimillionaires, but they aren't well respected and therefore aren't ranked high in the stratification system. On the flip side, professors may earn a modest salary, but they can command a fair amount of respect. *Power*, for Weber, is a person's ability to affect decisions in ways that benefit him or her. Again, power is usually related to

wealth and prestige, but it need not be. Sometimes low-income individuals can band together and influence decisions at the societal level, as happened in 2012 when several thousand janitors effectively shut down the city of San Francisco by going on strike and marching through the streets to demand higher wages and better working conditions.

CLASS INEQUALITY IN THE UNITED STATES

One of the ideological cornerstones of U.S. society is the belief that all people are created equal and that only individual shortcomings can impede a person's progress up the social ladder. After all, the United States is billed as the "land of opportunity." Our folklore is filled with stories of disadvantaged individuals who use their courage and resolve to overcome all adversity. We don't like to acknowledge that class inequality exists or that some people face immovable obstacles on the path to success that others will never have to face. But sociologists tell us that our place in the stratification system determines the course of our lives, in obvious and subtle ways.

Class and Everyday Life

Class standing in the United States has always determined a whole host of life chances, including access to higher education; better-paying jobs; and healthier, safer, and more comfortable lives:

- A study of street repair work in Indianapolis found that the average time it took between the filing of a complaint and the fixing of a pothole was 11 days in neighborhoods with an average annual income of more than $55,000; in neighborhoods with an average income of less than $25,000, it took an average of nearly 25 days (T. Evans & Nichols, 2009).
- For an annual fee, ranging from a few thousand to as much as twenty thousand dollars, wealthy individuals can buy "boutique" or "concierge" medical care, which includes special access to their physician via 24/7 cell phone and e-mail; same-day appointments with a guaranteed waiting time of no more than 15 minutes; nutrition and exercise physiology exams at the patients' homes; nurses to accompany them when they go to see specialists; and routine physicals that are so thorough they can last up to

three days (Belluck, 2002; Garfinkel, 2003; Zuger, 2005). For those wealthy individuals who end up in the hospital, the pampering continues. New York-Presbyterian/Weill Cornell Hospital offers a luxury penthouse wing whose deluxe accommodations rival the world's best hotels: chef-prepared gourmet menus, the finest Italian bed linens, a marble bathroom, and a butler (Bernstein, 2012).

- On airplanes, more affluent passengers can luxuriate in the spacious first-class section that often includes flatbed seats. First-class cabins usually contain more flight attendants per person than coach, and first-class attendants respond more quickly to call buttons. In addition, most airlines now have special express security lines for first-class passengers so as to avoid inconvenient delays. And it's not just about shorter waits, better service, and roomier seats. Emirates Airlines offers first-class passengers their own enclosed suites—complete with minibar, 19-inch television, bed, and "dine on demand" room service—as well as access to one of two shower spas on board (Rosato, 2004). In Paris's Charles De Gaulle Airport, Air France offers its high-end customers a dedicated first-class lounge with a spa and a restaurant catered by one of the city's finest chefs. In addition, immigration officers come directly into the lounge to check passports and passengers are driven from the lounge to the airplane in a limousine (Monawad, 2011).

This sort of exclusive personal attention reinforces feelings of power and privilege. On the other side of the coin, people who are less well off routinely face frustrating barriers in their daily lives. They must often make use of public facilities (health clinics, Laundromats, public transportation, and so on) to carry out the day-to-day tasks that wealthier people can carry out privately.

Social class also determines access to everyday resources that can contribute to long-term advantages. Consider, for instance, something we all now take for granted: Internet access. It would seem as if the Internet has become a truly universal resource. Over the last decade, inexpensive web access over wireless phone lines has brought the Internet to millions of working-class people who may not have been able to afford it in the past. However, the emergence of services like video on demand, videoconferencing, online medicine, and web classrooms has restratified digital access. These functions require the

kind of high-speed wired connections that tend to be available only through expensive contracts. Half of middle and high school students from higher-income families have high-speed Internet access at home, compared to 20% of middle-income children and only 3% of poor children (cited in Kang, 2013). High-speed access can provide many educational, technological, occupational, and quality-of-life opportunities that lower-speed connections can't. As a result, those with slower connection speeds may experience lower-quality health services, entertainment outlets, career opportunities, and education options (Crawford, 2011).

We can see similar imbalances when it comes to college admissions. We would like to think that admissions decisions are based solely on a student's merit: high academic achievement (reflected in high school grades) and strong intellectual potential (reflected in scores on standardized aptitude tests like the SAT). What could be fairer than the use of these sorts of objective measures as the primary criteria for determining who gets an elite education that will open doors for a lifetime?

Would it disturb you to know that your SAT score may depend as much on your parents' financial status as on your own intellect? Obviously, simply coming from a well-to-do family doesn't guarantee a high score on the SAT, but it can help. If you were fortunate enough to attend high school in an affluent, upper-class neighborhood, chances are your school offered SAT preparation courses. In some of these schools, students take practice SAT exams every year until they take the real one in their senior year. Even if a school doesn't provide such opportunities, private lessons from test preparation coaches are available to those who can afford them. Wealthy high schools are also significantly more likely than mid-level or poor high schools to offer Advanced Placement courses, another important tool that college admissions officers use to measure applicants (Berthelsen, 1999). In 2012, Congress voted to cut federal financing for programs that provided students in poor schools money to cover the registration costs for Advanced Placement exams. It's estimated that 30,000 fewer low-income students took these exams that year because they couldn't afford the $87 fee (Lewin, 2012b).

Access to these opportunities pays off. In 2010, the average combined SAT score for students whose families earned less than $20,000 a year was 1329.

The average score for students whose families earned more than $200,000 a year was 1721 (National Center for Fair and Open Testing, 2011).

But social class is not just about differences in access to technological, educational, or economic opportunities. People create and maintain class boundaries through their perceptions of moral, cultural, and lifestyle distinctions (Lamont, 1992). For example, some communities forbid residents to dry their clothes outdoors on clotheslines because it gives the neighborhood a shabby appearance. A few years ago, the town of Wilson, North Carolina, voted to prohibit people from keeping old sofas on their front porches (Bragg, 1998). For generations, poor people in the area—unable to purchase expensive outdoor furniture—had kept their worn-out sofas and chairs on the porch, where they could still be used. But more affluent residents saw the practice as "low class" and approved the ban to make neighborhoods more presentable.

Class Distinctions

Although the boundaries between classes tend to be fuzzy and subjective, distinct class designations remain a part of everyday thinking, political initiatives, and social research. The *upper class* (which some sociologists define as the highest-earning 5% of the U.S. population) is usually believed to include owners of vast amounts of property and other forms of wealth, major shareholders and owners of large corporations, top financiers, rich celebrities and politicians, and members of prestigious families. The *middle class* (roughly 45% of the population) is likely to include college-educated managers, supervisors, executives, owners of small businesses, and professionals. The *working class* (about 35% of the population) typically includes industrial and factory workers, office workers, clerks, and farm and manual laborers. Most working-class people don't own their own homes and don't attend college. Finally, about 15% of the population consists of people who work for minimum wage or who are chronically unemployed. They are the *poor* (sometimes referred to as the underclass or the lower class; Walton, 1990; E. O. Wright et al., 1982).

The Upper Class

The upper class in the United States is a small, exclusive group that occupies the highest levels of status and prestige. For some, membership in the upper class is relatively recent, acquired through personal financial achievement. These families are usually headed by high-level executives in large corporations and highly compensated lawyers, doctors, scientists, entertainers, and professional athletes. Such individuals may have been born into poor, working-class, or middle-class families, but they have been able to climb the social ladder and create a comfortable life. They are sometimes called "the new rich."

Others, however, are born into wealth gained by earlier generations in their families (Langman, 1988). The formidable pedigree of "old wealth," not to mention the wealth itself, provides them with insulation from the rest of society. Their position in society is perpetuated through a set of exclusive clubs, resorts, charitable and cultural organizations, and social activities that provides members with a distinctive lifestyle and a perspective on the world that distinguishes them from the rest of society.

Sociologists G. William Domhoff (1983, 1998) and C. Wright Mills (1956) have made the case that members of the upper class can structure other social institutions to ensure that their personal interests are met and that the class itself endures. They control the government, large corporations, the majority of privately held corporate stock, the media outlets, universities, councils for national and international affairs, and so on (Domhoff, 1998). Hence, members of this class enjoy political and economic power to a degree not available to members of other classes.

For example, the educational system plays not only a key socializing role (see Chapter 5) but also an important role in perpetuating or reproducing the U.S. class structure. Children of the upper class often attend private schools, boarding schools, and well-endowed private universities (Domhoff, 1998). In addition to the standard curriculum, these schools teach vocabulary, inflection, styles of dress, aesthetic tastes, values, and manners (R. Collins, 1971). Required attendance at school functions; participation in esoteric sports such as lacrosse, squash, and crew; the wearing of school blazers or ties; and other "character-building" activities are designed to teach young people the unique lifestyle of the ruling class. In many ways, boarding schools function like "total institutions" such as prisons and convents (E. Goffman, 1961), isolating members from the outside world and providing them with routines and traditions that are highly effective agents of socialization.

In a study of more than 60 elite boarding schools in the United States and Great Britain, Peter Cookson and Caroline Persell (1985) showed how the philosophies and programs of boarding schools help transmit power and privilege. This school experience forms an everlasting social, political, and economic bond among all graduates, and the schools act as gatekeepers into prestigious universities. After graduates leave these universities, they connect with one another at the highest levels in the world of business, finance, and government.

The privileged social status that is produced and maintained through the elite educational system practically guarantees that the people who occupy key political and economic positions will form a like-minded, cohesive group with little resemblance to the majority whose lives depend on their decisions.

The Middle Class

In discussing the U.S. class system, it is tempting to focus on the very top or the very bottom, overlooking the chunk of the population that falls somewhere in the ill-defined center: the middle class. Ironically, the middle class has always been important in defining U.S. culture. Every other class is measured and judged against the values and norms of the middle class. It is a universal class, a class that supposedly represents everyone (Ehrenreich, 1990). Not surprisingly, the middle class is a coveted political constituency. Liberal and conservative politicians alike court it. Policies are proclaimed on its behalf.

But the lofty cultural status of the middle class in U.S. society belies the difficulties it experiences. Economists, pundits, and sociologists have long been fond of talking about the middle class being "under assault," "endangered," or "fragile" (T. A. Sullivan, Warren, & Westbrook, 2000). While corporate profits rose sharply during the 2000s, the take-home pay of middle-income U.S. workers has failed to keep up. Median household incomes rose steadily throughout the 1980s and 1990s but have leveled off and even fallen a bit ever since. In 1980, the median household income (in current dollars) across all ethnoracial groups in the United States was $44,059. By 2011, it had only increased to $50,054 (DeNavas-Walt, Proctor, & Smith, 2012). Between 1980 and 1990, median household income grew by about 8%. But between 2000 and 2007, median income actually shrank by about 1%; it fell an additional 1.5% between 2010 and 2011 (DeNavas-Walt, Proctor, &

Smith, 2012). Moreover, between 2007 and 2010, the average value of a middle-class household's assets (or net worth) fell 40%, from $126,400 to $77,300 (Bricker, Kennickell, Moore, & Sabelhaus, 2012).

The recent economic recession took its toll on every sector of the population, including the middle class. Hourly earnings, weekly earnings, and employer-provided benefits like pensions and retirement accounts have either stagnated or fallen since 2007 (Mishel, Bivens, Gould, & Shierholz, 2013). The number of workers who earn at least $20 an hour (a wage that once symbolized "middle class") has dropped nearly 60% over the past three decades (cited in Uchitelle, 2008). Indeed, after adjusting for inflation, the median hourly wage today is only $16.71 (U.S. Bureau of Labor Statistics, 2013e). In addition to lower wages, many workers across the country are seeing their hours cut—for instance, by being moved from full time to part time or by losing opportunities for overtime. According to data from the U.S. Bureau of Labor Statistics (2013b), in 2013, about 8 million workers had to cut their hours to fewer than 35 a week due to slack work conditions or the inability to find full-time work.

Today, even families with good incomes live close to the financial edge, one layoff or medical emergency away from financial crisis. Consequently, Americans now see a middle class with fewer opportunities to get ahead, less disposable income, and lower job security than the middle class of previous generations. According to one recent poll, 85% said it was more difficult now than a decade ago to maintain their standard of living (cited in Blow, 2013).

Not only do middle-class jobs pay less than they used to, but there are fewer of them to go around. Many people who have followed the institutionalized path to success—getting college degrees, developing marketable skills, building impressive résumés—are finding themselves out of work as companies cut costs to stay afloat. Hundreds of thousands of once-solid jobs in high tech, communication, and finance have disappeared. And with a national unemployment rate that hovers around 7%, many people who were once middle class are either marginally attached to the labor force or completely discouraged over their job prospects.

To add insult to injury, economists predict that even as the economy continues to recover, the job market will be weak. Many companies that are currently laying off people don't plan to rehire at prerecession levels once things get better (Lowenstein, 2009).

In 2011, the economy was actually producing as much as it was prior to the recession, but with 7 million fewer workers than there were prior to the recession. In other words, companies have learned to produce more cost efficiently with a smaller workforce. Furthermore, since 2010, equipment and software prices have dropped 2.4% while labor costs have risen 6.7%. So when companies grow, they quickly realize that it's much cheaper to buy new machines than to hire more people. In 1999, the typical new business started with 7.7 employees; today that figure is 4.7 (cited in Rampell, 2012). Said one executive, "I want to have as few people touching our products as possible. Everything should be as automated as it can be" (quoted in Rampell, 2011, p. A1).

Moreover, the types of jobs that will be available in the future may not be the sort that will strengthen people's economic status. For instance, employers are increasingly turning to temporary and part-time workers rather than full-time, permanent workers (who would be eligible for benefits). In 2010, one quarter of the 1.17 million private-sector jobs that were added were temporary jobs (cited in Rich, 2010).

And even the permanent jobs that are created may not pay enough to ensure people's middle-class standing. Twenty-one percent of the jobs lost during the recent recession were low-wage occupations—those with a median hourly wage of $7.69 to $13.83. However, as employment began pick up in the last few years, these occupations accounted for 58% of all job growth (National Employment Law Project, 2012). By most accounts, middle-class jobs will continue to be in short supply, meaning that many college-educated people will be thwarted in their attempts to earn a comfortable living. Economists project that incomes for middle-class households won't reach their 2000 levels again until 2018 (Mishel, Bivens, Gould, & Shierholz, 2013). It's no wonder that many middle-class adults feel like they're on a treadmill that constantly threatens to throw them into a less desirable social class (Blow, 2013).

The Working Class

Members of the working class—people who work in factory, clerical, or low-paying sales jobs—are even more susceptible to economic fluctuations than those in the middle class. Most working-class people have only a high school education and earn an hourly wage rather than a weekly or monthly salary. Although they may earn enough money to survive, they typically don't earn enough to accumulate significant savings or other assets. Under the best circumstances, they usually have difficulty buying a home or paying for a child's education. When times are bad, they live their lives under the constant threat of layoffs, factory closings, and unemployment.

The middle class may be under siege, but the working class always suffers disproportionately from downturns in the U.S. economy. Consequently, they are far more pessimistic about their futures than wealthier Americans. For instance, one survey found that people who make less than $30,000 a year are more likely to expect to be laid off or take a pay cut and to say they have had trouble paying for medical care or paying the rent (Pew Research Center, 2011).

Their fears are real. To save money, many large companies first reduce their low-wage workforce. In 2011, American employers initiated 6,597 "extended mass layoff events" (where at least 50 employees from a single employer file for unemployment insurance benefits and are out of work for 30 days or more), resulting in the loss of more than 1.1 million jobs, mostly in manufacturing and retail (U.S. Bureau of Labor Statistics, 2012c).

Many working-class people who remain employed haven't had raises in years but have seen the cost of living (in particular, food, energy, and health care) rise steadily. Nearly 22% of people living in households with an income between $25,000 and $49,000 had no health insurance during 2011 (DeNavas-Walt et al., 2012). And about 80% of low-wage earners get no paid sick days off from work (Herbert, 2007).

The Poor

In an affluent society like the United States, the people at the very bottom of the social class structure face constant humiliation in their everyday lives. You've heard the old saying "Money can't buy happiness." The implication is that true satisfaction in life is more than just a matter of being wealthy. Indeed, research shows that compared with others, people with high incomes aren't happier, don't spend more time in enjoyable activities, and tend to be more tense (Kahneman, Krueger, Schkade, Schwarz, & Stone, 2006). Yet such information provides little comfort to people who can't pay their bills, don't know where their next meal is coming from or whether their job will exist tomorrow, suffer from ill health, or have no home. The legendary vaudeville singer Sophie Tucker once said, "I've been rich and I've been poor—and believe me, rich is better."

What Poverty Means in the United States

We hear the word *poverty* all the time. In common usage, poverty is usually conceived, in economic terms, as the lack of sufficient money to ensure an adequate lifestyle. Sociologists, though, often distinguish between absolute and relative poverty. The term **absolute poverty** refers to the minimal requirements a human being needs to survive. The term **relative poverty** refers to one's economic position compared with the living standards of the majority in a given society. Absolute poverty means not having enough money for minimal food, clothing, and shelter. But relative poverty is more difficult to gauge. It reflects culturally defined aspirations and expectations. Poor people "generally feel better if they know that their position in life does not compare too badly with others in society" (quoted in D. Altman, 2003, p. 21). An annual family income of $5,000, which would constitute abject poverty in the United States, is perhaps five times higher than the *average* income in many developing countries. As Kentucky senator Rand Paul once said, "The poor in our country are enormously better off than the rest of the world" (Paul, 2010, p. 16). Although such a statement reflects a common perception that life in a U.S. slum is luxurious when compared with life in destitute regions in other parts of the world, it overlooks the very real suffering associated with American poverty.

The Poverty Line

The U.S. government uses an absolute definition of poverty to identify people who can't afford what they need to survive. The U.S. *poverty line* identifies the amount of yearly income a family requires to meet its basic needs. Those who fall below the line are officially poor. The official poverty line is based on pretax money income only, which doesn't include food stamps, Medicaid, public housing, and other noncash benefits. The figure does vary according to family size, and it is adjusted each year to account for inflation. But it doesn't take into account regional differences in cost of living. In 2012, the official poverty line for a family of four—two parents and two children—was an annual income of $23,283.

That dollar amount is established by the U.S. Department of Agriculture and for decades has been based on something called the Thrifty Food Plan. This plan, developed in the early 1960s, is used to calculate the cost of a subsistence diet, which is the bare minimum a family needs to survive. This cost is then multiplied by three because research at the time showed that the average family spent one third of its income on food each year. The resulting amount was adopted in 1969 as the government's official poverty line. Even though the plan is modified periodically to account for changes in dietary recommendations, the formula itself and the basic definition of poverty have remained the same for nearly five decades.

Many policymakers, economists, sociologists, and concerned citizens question whether the current poverty line provides an accurate picture of basic needs in the United States. Several things have changed since the early 1960s. For instance, today food costs account for less than 14% of the average family's budget because the price of other things, such as housing and medical care, has increased at much higher rates (U.S. Bureau of Labor Statistics, 2013d). In addition, there were fewer dual-earner and single-parent families in the past, meaning that fewer families had to pay for childcare. In short, today's family has many more expenses and therefore probably spends a greater proportion of its total income on nonfood items. The consequence is that the official poverty line is probably set too low and therefore underestimates the hardships that struggling Americans experience (Swarns, 2008a).

In 2011, the U.S. Census Bureau proposed a new way of determining the poverty line called the supplemental poverty measure. This new formula is based on an estimate of expenditures on food, clothing, shelter, and utilities. It also takes into consideration medical spending, taxes, commuting costs, and childcare (Short, 2012). Using this model, the poverty line for a family of four would rise to an annual income of around $25,000.

Deciding who is and isn't officially poor is not just a matter of words and labels. When the poverty line is too low, we fail to recognize the problems of the many families who have difficulty making ends meet but who are not officially defined as poor. A needy family earning an amount slightly above the poverty line may not qualify for a variety of public assistance programs, such as housing benefits, Head Start, Medicaid, or Temporary Assistance for Needy

Families. As a result, its standard of living may not be as good as that of a family that earns slightly less but qualifies for these programs.

Some economists suggest that the exclusive focus on income in setting the poverty line underestimates the harmful long-term effects of poverty. Obviously, when families don't have enough income, they can't buy what they need—adequate food, clothing, and shelter. But when families don't have any assets, such as savings and home equity, they lose economic security and their ability to plan, dream, and pass on opportunities to their children (Block, Korteweg, & Woodward, 2013).

The Near-Poor

Interestingly, the government seems to agree implicitly that the poverty line is set too low. The U.S. Bureau of the Census defines individuals or families who earn up to 25% more than the official poverty line amount as the **near-poor** or **working poor**. Individuals and families that fall into this category can be eligible for certain government assistance programs. For instance, the Affordable Health Care Act (also known as "Obamacare") extends Medicaid coverage to people earning 38% more than the official poverty line.

The existence of the near-poor is fraught with irony. For one thing, they tend to defy stereotypes of how poor people live. Half live in married-couple households, 49% live in the suburbs, 42% have private health insurance, and 28% work full time (DeParle, Gebeloff, & Tavernise, 2011). Because they fall above the poverty line, they tend to escape academic, policy, and public attention. Yet they are everywhere, doing the tasks with which others come into contact and on which they depend on a daily basis:

> They serve you Big Macs and help you find merchandise at Wal-Mart. They harvest your food, clean your offices, and sew your clothes. In a California factory, they package lights for your kids' bikes. In a New Hampshire plant, they assemble books of wallpaper samples to help you redecorate. (Shipler, 2004, p. 3)

When nothing out of the ordinary happens, the near-poor can manage. But an unexpected event—a sickness, an injury, the breakdown of a major appliance or automobile—can destroy a family financially and sink it into poverty. As one near-poor mother of two put it, "We're O.K. unless something—anything at all—goes wrong" (quoted in Davey, 2011, p. A22).

It has been estimated that about one quarter of the near-poor will fall below the poverty line at some point in their lives, and then they have some difficult decisions to make. One study of 34,000 people nationwide found that during the cold winter months, families spend less on food and reduce their caloric intake by an average of 10% in order to pay their fuel bills (Bhattacharya, DeLeire, Haider, & Currie, 2003). Imagine being a poor single mother with a sick child. One trip to the doctor might cost an entire week's food budget or a month of rent. Dental work or an eye examination is easily sacrificed when other pressing bills need to be paid. If she depends on a car to get to work and it breaks down, a few hundred dollars to fix it might mean not paying the electric bill that month. When gasoline prices approach $5 a gallon—as they did for a while in 2011—many near-poor families find that they have to cut down on food purchases so they can afford to drive to work. These are choices that wealthier families never face.

The Poverty Rate

The **poverty rate**—the percentage of residents whose income falls below the official poverty line—is the measure that the U.S. government uses to track the success of its efforts to reduce poverty. In 2011 (the most recent year for which data are available), 15% of the population—or more than 46 million Americans—fell below the official poverty line, up from 11.3% in 2000. Of this group, twenty million live in "deep poverty" (earning less than half the poverty line (Abramsky, 2012). If we add in the near-poor, the number of people who suffer financially in this country increases to about 61 million, or about 20% of the population (DeNavas-Walt et al., 2012). By the way, if we used the supplemental poverty measure I described earlier, the poverty rate would go up to 16%, adding about 3 million people to the officially poor (Short, 2012).

When used to describe national trends in poverty, the overall poverty rate can obscure important differences among subgroups of the population. For example, in 2011, 9.8% of people who identified themselves as non–Hispanic whites and 12.3% of Asian Americans fell below the poverty line. That same year, 27.6% of Blacks and 25.3% of Latino/as (who could be of any race) were considered poor. The poverty rate in the South (16.0%) and West (15.8%) is higher than the rate in the Midwest (14.0%) and Northeast (13.1%). Finally, poverty is higher in rural areas (17.0%) than in metropolitan areas (14.6%), although it's highest in inner cities (20.0%; DeNavas-Walt et al., 2012).

Although racial and ethnic minorities have consistently been rated among the poorest Americans, other groups have seen their status change over time. Before Social Security was instituted in 1935, many of the most destitute were those over age 65. As recently as 1970, 25% of U.S. residents over age 65 fell below the poverty line. Today, only 8.7% of the people in this age group are officially poor (DeNavas-Walt et al., 2012).

Taking their place among the poor, however, are children. Although the rate of child poverty has declined a bit since the mid 1990s, 21.9% of U.S. residents under the age of 18 (over 16 million kids) are poor. As you might suspect, poverty figures for American children vary dramatically along ethnoracial lines. About 38.8% of African American and 34.1% of Latino/a children under 18 live in poverty—compared with 18.6% of white children and 13.5% of Asian children (ProQuest Statistical Abstract, 2013).

The United States has the highest child poverty rate of any industrialized nation (DeNavas-Walt et al., 2012). To put that 21.9% figure into perspective, the average child poverty rate in the 33 other member nations of the Organisation for Economic Cooperation and Development (2012) is 12.4%. Rates in Scandinavian countries are especially low, ranging from 3.7% to 7.0% (Bertelsmann Stiftung, 2011).

The recent recession affected poverty rates in general but hit children particularly hard (DeParle & Tavernise, 2011). Between 2007 and 2009, the number of children who lived in homes affected by foreclosure and who had at least one unemployed parent more than doubled (cited in Davey, 2011).

To make matters worse, about 8 million poor American children now live in "high-poverty" neighborhoods (defined as areas with poverty rates of 30% or more). That marks a 25% increase since 2000. Growing up in these neighborhoods increases the risk of health problems, teen pregnancy, dropping out of school, and a host of other social and economic problems that limit a child's ability to successfully transition into adulthood (Mather & Dupuis, 2012).

Several factors explain why the poverty rate among U.S. children is high compared with that of older U.S. residents. For one thing, family structure is closely related to child poverty. The poverty rate for families headed by single mothers is 31.2%, compared with 16.1% for families headed by single fathers and 6.2% for married-couple families (DeNavas-Walt et al., 2012). In addition, government spending on programs for the elderly (Medicare, Social Security) has increased dramatically over the past four decades (Mishel et al., 2013), while spending on families and children (cash assistance, health care, food and nutritional aid, etc.) has dropped and will continue to drop into the foreseeable future (Davey, 2011; Steuerle, 2007). Not surprisingly, young families with children are six times as likely to be poor as elderly families (cited in Tavernise, 2011b).

The Consequences of Poverty

Poverty isn't just about rates, trends, and official definitions. It is a never-ending burden borne on the shoulders of those who are least equipped to endure it. Being poor clearly influences people's physical and intellectual well-being.

Poverty and Health

With each step down the income ladder comes increased risk of headaches, varicose veins, respiratory infection, hypertension, stress-related illness, low-birth-weight babies, stroke, diabetes, and heart disease (Krugman, 2008; Pérez-Peña, 2003; Shweder, 1997). Recent studies have found a troubling increase in tropical parasitic diseases like Dengue fever and typhus in poverty-stricken areas of the South and Southwest that were heretofore confined to poor countries in Latin America. These parasites thrive where there is poor street drainage, plumbing, sanitation, and garbage disposal (Hotez, 2012).

Among children, decades of research show that rates of chronic illness, injury, ear disease, asthma, and physical inactivity all increase as socioeconomic status decreases (E. Chen, Matthews, & Boyce, 2002). And poor children covered by Medicaid/CHIP (Children's Health Insurance Program) are more likely than children with private health insurance to be denied appointments with medical specialists. In addition, they wait an average of 22 days longer for an appointment, even for serious medical problems (Bisgaier & Rhodes, 2011).

Even after controlling for age, sex, race, family size, and education, the risk of death steadily increases as income goes down (Marmot, 2004). And the gap is growing. According to data from the U.S. Department of Health and Human Services, in 1980, the most affluent U.S. citizens could expect to live 2.8 years longer than the poorest citizens; today the difference in life expectancy is about 6.5 years (cited in Sanders, 2011). The health status of poor people in the United States is so bad that volunteer medical groups that were created to provide free medical services in destitute third-world countries like Ghana, Tanzania, and Haiti now set up mobile medical facilities in poor rural areas of the United States (Towell, 2007).

One of the obvious reasons for these health gaps is lack of access to adequate health care. Over the last 20 years, for instance, one quarter of urban and suburban hospitals, particularly those serving poor residents, have closed their emergency rooms (Rabin, 2011). Furthermore, even if they do have access to medical facilities, many poor people aren't able to pay for care. According to the U.S. Bureau of the Census (ProQuest Statistical Abstract, 2013), 29.6% of poor people have no health insurance, even though they may be eligible for government health insurance (Medicaid). In fact, only 47% of poor people actually receive Medicaid benefits (ProQuest Statistical Abstract, 2013). The dangers of having no health insurance are undeniable:

- Uninsured people are less likely than people who have health insurance to see a doctor when needed and are more likely to report being in poor health (Robert Wood Johnson Foundation, 2005).
- Uninsured people (and those covered by Medicaid) are more likely than those with private health insurance to receive diagnoses of cancer in its late stages, diminishing their chances of survival (Virning, 2008).
- A study of trauma units and emergency departments around the country found that even after controlling for age, gender, and type and severity of injury, uninsured patients were 50% more likely than insured patients to die from their injuries; the gap was worst for ethnoracial minorities (cited in Noonan, 2008).

In addition to inadequate or nonexistent health care, approximately 14.5% of American households are "food insecure"—meaning that some members don't have enough to eat or the family uses strategies like eating less varied diets, participating in food assistance programs, or getting emergency food from community food pantries (ProQuest Statistical Abstract, 2013). That means that about 49 million poor Americans—including more than 16 million children—now live in households that experience hunger or the risk of hunger, an increase of 13 million since 2007.

Lower-income families actually pay higher-than-average prices for food (Brookings Institution, 2006). Large supermarket chains, for example, hesitate to open stores in very poor neighborhoods because of security fears. Hence, residents who are without transportation must rely on small neighborhood grocery stores, which usually charge more for food than large supermarkets do.

Poverty and Education

The educational deck is likewise stacked against poor people. A report by the Education Trust (2002) showed that in most states, school districts with the neediest students receive far less state and local tax money—on average, around $1,000 less per student—than districts with the fewest poor students. Teachers in poor districts tend to be less experienced and are paid less than teachers in more affluent districts (LaCoste-Caputo, 2007). Without adequate resources, teachers become frustrated and do not teach; children become cynical and do not learn. The consequences are striking. While differences in standardized test scores between black and white students have narrowed over the past 50 years, differences between rich and poor students have grown dramatically. The achievement gap between children from high- and low-income families is roughly 30% to 40% greater among children born in 2001 than among those born 25 years earlier (Reardon, 2011).

Even if they graduate from high school, most poor children can't afford to attend college. Those who do are more likely to attend community colleges or state universities, which are less expensive but lack the prestige, and often the quality, of their more expensive counterparts. In one study, 15% of high-income students who graduated from high school in 2004 enrolled in a highly selective university;

however, fewer than 5% of middle-income and 2% of low-income students did (Reardon, 2013).

Despite nationwide efforts to increase access to higher education, universities have not been particularly successful in recruiting and retaining poor students (Pérez-Peña, 2013). In 2012, 74% of the entering class at selective top-tier universities came from the quarter of households with the highest income; only 3% came from the bottom quarter (Krugman, 2012). Indeed, a greater proportion of college students today come from wealthy families than was the case two decades ago. Of course, students without family wealth do sometimes attend top universities with the help of need-based scholarships. But these schools, by and large, have no systematic plans for identifying, recruiting, or admitting low-income students.

Furthermore, once they get into college, poor students don't fare as well as their more affluent counterparts. According to the Department of Education, a little over 25% of college students from families with annual incomes of under $25,000 earn a bachelor's degree within six years. For students from families with incomes more than $70,000, the figure is 56% (Hebel, 2007). Such a gap is especially significant because a bachelor's degree is essential in today's global economy. According to the U.S. Bureau of the Census (ProQuest Statistical Abstract, 2013), people with some college experience but no degree earn, on average, just under $32,000 a year. College graduates on average earn more than $57,000 a year. Such numbers demonstrate that the educational system often seals the fate of poor people instead of helping them succeed within the U.S. class structure.

Out on the Streets

The most publicly visible consequence of poverty is homelessness. No one knows for sure exactly how many homeless people live in the United States. The National Alliance to End Homelessness (2013) estimates that there are more than 633,000 homeless people, 38% of whom are completely unsheltered. But because people move in and out of homelessness or are homeless for a short period of time, it's estimated that somewhere between 2.3 and 3.5 million people experience some type of homelessness over the course of a year. According to a 2012 survey of 25 major American cities, on an average night, 64% of homeless people are single adults, 35% are

persons in families, and 1% are children on their own. Of the homeless, 17% are employed, and 13% are military veterans (U.S. Conference of Mayors, 2012).

The causes of homelessness in the United States are typically institutional ones: stagnating wages, changes in welfare programs, and, perhaps most important, lack of affordable housing. Nearly three quarters of homeless families cite lack of affordable housing as the principal cause of their homelessness (U.S. Conference of Mayors, 2012). When rising wealth at the top of society drives up housing prices, the poor are left unable to afford decent housing and without federal and state programs to help (Shipler, 2004).

According to the federal government, housing is considered "affordable" if it costs 30% of a family's income. The poorest fifth of the population spend about 78% of their wages on housing. By comparison, the wealthiest fifth of the population spend only 19% of their income on housing (cited in Swartz, 2007). In 2012, the nationwide median housing wage—the minimum amount of money a person would have to make to afford two-bedroom rental housing—was $18.25 an hour (or an annual income of $37,960, assuming full-time, year-round employment). That's more than double the federal minimum wage. Nowhere in the United States does a full-time, minimum-wage job provide enough income to afford adequate housing, and in some states—New York, California, Connecticut, Maryland, and Massachusetts to name a few—a household would need the income of at least three minimum-wage jobs. In Hawaii, *four* minimum-wage jobs wouldn't be enough (National Low Income Housing Coalition, 2012). With foreclosure rates rising steadily (National Alliance to End Homelessness, 2013), the housing future for the neediest Americans looks even bleaker.

Why Poverty Persists

Even in the best of times, a prosperous country such as the United States has a sizable population of poor people. Why, in such an affluent society, is poverty a permanent fixture? To explain the persistence of poverty, we must look at enduring imbalances in income and wealth, the structural role poverty plays in larger social institutions, and the dominant cultural beliefs and attitudes that help support it.

Enduring Disparities in Income and Wealth

One reason poverty is so persistent in the United States is the way income and wealth are distributed. According to the U.S. Bureau of the Census (ProQuest Statistical Abstract, 2013), the average annual income of the top 5% of U.S. households is $186,000 while the average annual income of the bottom 20% of households is under $21,000.

This wide income gap between the richest and poorest segments of the population has been growing steadily over the past few decades. The most affluent 1% of American households now accounts for 17% of all the income earned in a given year, up from under 8% in 1979 (cited in Pear, 2011). Since 1979, incomes of the top 1% have grown 275%; during the same time, incomes for the bottom 20% have grown only 18% (Congressional Budget Office, 2011). As the country recovers from the recent recession, the wealthy do better than anyone else. In 2010, 93% of income growth went to the wealthiest 1% of American households. By comparison, the wealthiest 1% accounted for only 45% of the nation's income growth following the economic downturn of the early 1990s (Saez, 2012).

Meanwhile, compensation for those at the very top continues to soar. In 1964, the average compensation for a top executive in an American company was about $822,000; by the mid 2000s it approached $5 million (Whoriskey, 2011). In the early 1980s, chief executives earned $42 for every $1 earned by the average production worker; by 2012, that figure had increased to $354 (AFL-CIO, 2013). We may want to believe that personal effort and hard work solely determine our success, but it's hard to imagine that a CEO of, say, an electronics company works 354 times harder than a person who actually assembles the TVs and cell phones.

Tax laws also work to the advantage of those at the top. The rich do pay a lot of taxes as a total percentage of all taxes collected; however, they don't pay a lot of taxes as a percentage of what they earn and can afford. In the 1940s, the tax rate for the wealthiest tax bracket was about 90%; in 1980 it was 49%. Today it's 42%. Incidentally, the threshold for that top bracket is $379,150 (Sorkin, 2011). Any income above that is taxed at the same rate. In other words, someone earning $40 million a year pays the same tax percentage as someone earning $380,000 a year.

Although most U.S. residents paid more taxes as a percentage of income during the late 1990s and early 2000s than they had in previous decades, many of the wealthiest citizens paid less. Families earning more than $1 million a year have seen their federal tax rates drop more sharply than those of any other group in the country (Andrews, 2007). In fact, federally mandated tax cuts in 2008 had virtually no effect on low-income families. However, families in the top 1% of income earners saw annual tax savings of more than $50,000 (Mishel et al., 2009).

As a result, the United States has the greatest income disparity between poor and wealthy citizens of any industrialized nation. As we've seen, the wealthiest fifth of U.S. families earns almost nine times more than the poorest fifth (ProQuest Statistical Abstract, 2013). In France, the richest fifth earns seven times more than the poorest fifth, and in Japan they earn four times more (Phillips, 2002). But to be fair, the income gap between rich and poor is worse in some developing countries. For example, the richest 20% of Brazilians earns 64% of the country's income, whereas the poorest 20% earns 2.5% (Romero, 1999). Similar disparities exist in other Latin American countries and in most of sub–Saharan Africa.

Inequalities in income lead to even more striking inequalities in wealth. A lifetime of high earnings and inheritance from privileged parents creates a lasting advantage in ownership of property; of durable consumer goods such as cars, houses, and furniture; and of financial assets such as stocks, bonds, savings, and life insurance. The wealthiest 1% of U.S. households controls 35% of all the country's wealth. By comparison, the bottom 90% controls only 23% of all the wealth. Moreover, the top 1% has a median net worth 288 times as large as the average American household (Mishel, et al., 2013). We will never live in a society with a perfectly equal distribution of income and wealth. Some people will always earn more, have more, and maybe even deserve more than others. But the magnitude of the gap between rich and poor in the United States challenges the notion that we live in a society where everyone is valued equally. As disparities in income and wealth grow, so does the gap in quality of life and access to opportunity between those at the top of society and those at the bottom.

The Social "Benefits" of Poverty

Recall the structural-functionalist assertion that stratification is necessary because it ensures that the most qualified and valuable people in society will occupy the most important positions. Social conditions exist and persist only if they are functional to society in some way. But functional for whom? If you were to survey people on the street and ask them if poverty is a good or bad thing, most, I'm sure, would say, "Bad." Yet according to sociologist Herbert Gans (1971, 1996), within a free-market economy and competitive society such as the United States, poverty plays a necessary institutional role. Although structural functionalism has often been criticized for its propensity to justify the status quo, Gans combines it with conflict thinking to identify several economic and social "functions" served by poverty that benefit all other classes in society:

- Poverty provides a ready pool of low-wage laborers who are available to do society's "dirty work." Poor people work at low wages primarily because they have little choice. When large numbers of poor people compete for scarce jobs, business owners can pay lower wages.
- Poverty ensures that there will be enough individuals, especially during times of high unemployment, to populate an all-volunteer military. To people with limited educational and occupational opportunities, military service holds the promise of an escape from poverty through stable employment, comprehensive insurance coverage, a living wage, free schooling, and the development of marketable skills. Those with lower family income are significantly more likely to join the military than those with higher family income (Lutz, 2008). As you might guess, American casualties in Iraq and Afghanistan have been overwhelmingly from families of modest means who live in sparsely populated rural counties (Cushing & Bishop, 2005; Golway, 2004). By 2006, 34% of U.S. military personnel killed in Iraq came from the poorest quarter of families, while only 17% came from the richest quarter (cited in "Price Paid," 2006).
- Poverty supports occupations that either serve the poor or protect the rest of society from them: police officers, welfare workers, social workers, lawyers, pawnshop owners, and so on. Even drug dealers and loan sharks depend on the presence of a large population of poor people willing to pay for their illegal services.
- Poverty is the reason some people purchase goods and services that would otherwise go unused: secondhand appliances; day-old bread, fruits, and vegetables; deteriorated housing; dilapidated cars; care from incompetent physicians; and so forth. In 2002,

dozens of Coca-Cola employees in Texas revealed that, for years, they had been required to sell expired Coke to stores in poor neighborhoods. They were instructed to strip cans from their boxes, stuff them into fresh boxes with new dates stamped on the side, and stock them on store shelves in poor neighborhoods as if they were new (Winter, 2002). Clearly, this merchandise had little or no monetary value outside the poverty market; it was believed that the beverages couldn't be sold to wealthier Coke drinkers because they'd have noticed the difference.

- Poverty is a visible reminder to the rest of society of the "legitimacy" of the conventional values of hard work, thrift, and honesty. By violating, or seeming to violate, these mainstream values, the poor reaffirm these virtues. If poor people are thought to be lazy, their presence reinforces the ethic of hard work; if the poor single mother is condemned, the two-parent family is idealized.
- Poverty provides scapegoats for society's institutional problems. The alleged laziness of the jobless poor and the anger aimed at street people and beggars distract us from the failure of the economic system to adequately deal with the needs of all citizens. Likewise, the alleged personal shortcomings of slum dwellers and the homeless deflect attention from shoddy practices within the housing industry.

This explanation of poverty's persistence can easily be dismissed as cold and heartless. We certainly don't want to admit that poor people allow the rest of us to avoid unpleasant or even dangerous tasks and enjoy comfortable lifestyles. Yet this explanation is quite compelling. Just as society needs talented people to fill its important occupational positions, it also needs a stable population of poor people to fill its "less important" positions. If society fostered full equality, who would do the dirty work?

If we are truly serious about reducing poverty, we must find alternative ways of performing the societal functions it currently fulfills. But such a change will assuredly come at a cost to those who can now take advantage of poverty's presence. In short, poverty will be eliminated only when it becomes dysfunctional for people who *aren't* poor.

The Ideology of Competitive Individualism

Poverty also persists because of cultural beliefs and values that support the economic status quo. An important component of this value system in U.S.

society is the belief in *competitive individualism* (Feagin, 1975; M. Lewis, 1978; Neubeck, 1986). As children, most of us are taught that nobody deserves a free ride. The way to be successful is to work hard, strive toward goals, and compete well against others. We are taught that we are fully responsible for our own economic fates. Rags-to-riches stories of people who rose above terrible conditions to make it to the top reinforce the notion that anybody can be successful if she or he simply has the desire and puts in the necessary effort.

The dark side of the U.S. belief in competitive individualism is that it all too easily justifies the unequal distribution of rewards and the existence of poverty. If people who are financially successful are thought to deserve their advantages, allegedly because of individual hard work and desire, then the people who are struggling financially must likewise deserve their plight—because of their *lack* of hard work and desire. People in the United States have an intense need to believe that good things happen to good people and bad things happen to bad people (Huber & Form, 1973; Lerner, 1970). In short, most of us want to believe that if a poor person is suffering, he or she "must have" done something to deserve it. The people who succeed, in contrast, "must have" been born smarter, stayed in school longer, or worked harder. The belief in competitive individualism gives people the sense that they can control their own fate.

But the depth of such beliefs depends on where people are in the stratification system. When asked why people succeed, lower-income people are more likely than wealthy people to downplay competitive individualism and cite things like "coming from a wealthy family" or "knowing the right people." Upper-class individuals, on the other hand, are more likely than their lower-income counterparts to contend that opportunities for success and advancement are available to everyone, meaning that success is a result of individual merit. They are likely to cite "natural ability," "a good education," and "hard work" as factors that are essential to getting ahead in life. Hence, they can justify inequality by emphasizing equal chances (cited in J. Scott & Leonhardt, 2005).

Such attitudes don't take into consideration the possibility that the competition itself may not be fair. Competitive individualism assumes that opportunities to learn a high-level trade or skill or enter a profession are available to everyone. Every person is supposed to have the chance to "be all that she or he can be." But the system may be rigged to favor those who already have power and privilege.

The contemporary U.S. welfare system does little to alter these conditions. Instead, it reflects the belief that the best way to reduce poverty is to change poor people's lifestyles. In 1994, more than 5 million U.S. families were on government assistance. By 2012, that figure had dropped to 1.7 million (ProQuest Statistical Abstract, 2013). You might think that such a drop reflects the fact that fewer citizens need government aid, but much of the reduction was actually due to the eligibility limitations of a new welfare system that began in 1996. This system includes a mandatory work requirement (or enrollment in vocational training or community service) after two years of receiving assistance and a five-year lifetime limit to benefits for any family. Despite soaring unemployment rates and the worst economic recession in decades, 16 states have cut their welfare caseloads since 2008, sometimes by as much as 50% (cited in DeParle, 2012).

Contrary to popular belief, the financial help that people receive on public assistance is rarely enough to sustain a life that is remotely comfortable. For example, in Indiana—where benefits are among the lowest and eligibility rules among the tightest in the nation—the cash assistance limit for a family of three is a mere $288 per month. To qualify for this assistance, such a family cannot earn more than $378 a month (Groppe, 2010). That works out to an annual "income" below $8,000.

Some of the people who leave welfare do, in fact, find sustained employment (Duncan & Chase-Lansdale, 2001). However, more than half of the decrease in welfare rolls in the first decade after welfare reform went into effect reflected a decline in government assistance to families that were poor enough to qualify for aid rather than an increase in the number of families who no longer needed the assistance. Indeed, even in the rather affluent 1990s, the poverty rate decreased by only 14% (U.S. Bureau of the Census, 2009), and it has increased significantly ever since. Moreover, the 20 million Americans who earn less than half the poverty line represent the highest rate of "deep" poverty we've seen in 15 years (DeNavas-Walt et al., 2012; National Center for Law and Economic Justice, 2010).

You'd think that with all the political rhetoric over "ending welfare as we know it," the welfare system would be the largest drain on the federal budget. However, programs to assist the poor constitute only about 11% of the entire federal budget. In 2013, the federal government spent approximately $170 billion on welfare assistance, including Temporary Assistance for Needy Families (TANF), food and nutrition programs, and housing assistance. That same year, it spent more than $1.5 *trillion* on Social Security, unemployment insurance, and Medicare—the government-subsidized health care program for the elderly (usgovernmentspending.com, 2013).

Nonetheless, the assumptions behind welfare reform are clear: Making work mandatory will teach welfare recipients important work values and habits, make poor single mothers models of these values for their children, and cut the nation's welfare rolls. The underlying idea is that hard work will lead to the moral and financial rewards of family self-reliance. It will cure poverty and welfare dependence and ensure that new generations of children from single-parent families will be able to enter the American mainstream. Like competitive individualism, however, this ideology protects the nonpoor, the larger social structure, and the economic system while blaming poor people for their own plight.

GLOBAL DEVELOPMENT AND INEQUALITY

As you've seen elsewhere in this book, it is becoming increasingly difficult to understand life in any one society without understanding that society's place in the larger global context. The trend toward globalization (see Chapter 9) may have brought the world's inhabitants closer together, but they are not all benefiting equally. Nations have differing amounts of power to ensure that their interests are met. The more developed and less developed countries of the world experience serious inequalities in wealth that have immediate consequences for their citizens. Just as an economic gap exists between rich and poor citizens within a single country, economic gaps exist between rich and poor countries. Consider these facts:

- The average per-capita yearly income in Western Europe, the United States, Canada, Japan, and other developed countries is $33,460; in the less developed countries of the world, it's $5,900 (Population Reference Bureau, 2012).
- About 0.13% of the world's population controls 25% of the world's financial assets. On the other end of the economic spectrum, more than 1.3 billion people in less developed countries live on the equivalent of less than $1.25 a day (World Hunger Education Service, 2012), and close to half of all people living in sub–Saharan Africa survive on $1 a day (World Bank, 2006).
- The wealthiest 20% of the world accounts for about 77% of all private consumption (Shah, 2009). Twelve percent of the world's population (who happen to reside in developed countries) uses 85% of its water. The United States alone consumes one quarter of the world's oil ("Burning Through Oil," 2008).

Explanations for Global Stratification

How has global stratification come about? The conflict perspective explains not only stratification within a society but also stratification between societies. One way a country can use its power to control another is through *colonization*—invading and establishing control over a weaker country and its people in order to expand the colonizer's markets. Typically, the native people of the colony are forced to give up their culture. The colony serves as a source of labor and raw materials for the colonizer's industries and a market for their high-priced goods. Much of North and South America, Africa, and Asia were at one time or another under the colonial control of wealthier nations.

Although the direct conquest of weak countries is rare today, wealthy countries are still able to exploit them for commercial gain. Powerful countries can use weaker countries as a source of cheap raw materials and cheap labor. They can also exert financial pressure on poorer nations by setting world prices on certain goods (Chase-Dunn & Rubinson, 1977). Because their economic base is weak, poor countries often have to borrow money or buy manufactured goods on credit from wealthy countries. The huge debt they build up locks them into a downward spiral of exploitation and poverty. They cannot develop an independent economy of their own and thus remain dependent on wealthy countries for their very survival (Frank, 1969).

Global Financial Organizations

It's not just powerful nations that have the ability to hold poor nations in their grip. International financial organizations play a significant role in determining the economic and social policies of developing countries. For instance, the World Bank funds reconstruction and development projects in poor countries through investments and loans. It spends about

$35 billion annually to better the lives of destitute people worldwide (World Bank, 2012). Similarly, the International Monetary Fund (IMF) tries to foster economic growth and international monetary cooperation through financial and technical assistance. The World Trade Organization (WTO) oversees the rules of trade between nations.

These organizations spend a lot of money to improve the standard of living in many poor countries by funding projects such as new roads or water treatment plants. And they've been somewhat successful. Funding from the World Bank helped cut the proportion of the world's population living in extreme poverty from 43% in 1990 to 21% in 2010 (Lowrey, 2013).

But global financial organizations may, from time to time, do more harm than good. The WTO, for example, can impose fines and sanctions on debtor countries that don't act as it dictates. It has, in the past, forced Japan to accept greater levels of pesticide residue on imported food, prevented Guatemala from outlawing deceptive advertising on baby food, and eliminated asbestos bans and car emission standards in various countries (Parenti, 2006).

In fact, countries that receive the aid of these organizations sometimes end up even more impoverished than before. When the World Bank and the IMF provide development credit, they do so with certain conditions attached. The conditions, referred to as "structural adjustments," typically reflect a Western-style, free-market approach: reducing government spending, lifting import and export restrictions, privatizing public services, removing price controls, increasing interest rates, eliminating food subsidies, and devaluing the country's currency (Shah, 2013). For instance, countries might be required to lift trade restrictions, enhance the rights of foreign investors, cut social spending, increase exports, or balance their budgets in exchange for aid.

You can see that global financial relationships between international lending institutions and poor countries are a double-edged sword. The countries certainly receive much-needed financial assistance. But in the process, they sometimes become even more dependent and less able to improve conditions for their citizens.

Multinational Corporations

Global stratification has been made even more complex by the growth of massive multinational corporations, which can go outside their countries' borders to pursue their financial interests if domestic opportunities aren't promising. They can invest their money in more lucrative foreign corporations or establish their businesses or factories abroad. U.S.-based multinational corporations employ more than 23 million people worldwide and have total assets of $27.7 trillion (ProQuest Statistical Abstract, 2013).

But such success often comes at a price. The largest U.S.-based multinational corporations continue to achieve record earnings while hiring fewer American workers than ever. Between 2009 and 2011, 35 of the largest U.S.-based multinational corporations—including Wal-Mart, International Paper Company, and United Parcel Service—added 446,000 jobs, a growth rate substantially higher than other U.S. companies. However, three quarters of these new jobs went to workers overseas (Thurn, 2012).

With their ability to quickly shift operations to friendly countries, multinational corporations find it easy to evade the governance of any one country. Their decisions reflect corporate goals and not necessarily the well-being or interests of any particular country.

From a structural-functionalist perspective, a U.S. company locating a production facility in a developing country would seem to benefit everyone involved. The host country benefits from the creation of new jobs and a higher standard of living. The corporation, of course, benefits from increased profits. And consumers in the country in which the corporation is based benefit from paying lower prices for products that would cost more if manufactured at home. Furthermore, the entire planet benefits because these firms form alliances with many different countries and therefore might help pressure them into settling their political disputes peacefully.

Multinational corporations are indeed a valuable part of the international economy, as we saw in Chapter 9. However, the conflict perspective argues that in the long run, multinationals can actually perpetuate or even worsen global stratification. One common criticism of multinationals is that they exploit local workers and communities. Employees in foreign plants or factories often work under conditions that wouldn't be tolerated in wealthier countries. The most obvious inequity is the wage people earn. For example, according to the National Labor Committee for Worker and Human Rights (2001), senior seamstresses with six years' experience at a Bangladesh factory that makes Disney clothing earn

17 cents an hour. Most work more than 15 hours a day, seven days a week.

In addition, environmental regulations and occupational safety requirements that tend to drive up the cost of finished products, such as protection against dangerous conditions or substances, sometimes don't exist in other countries. Hence, local workers may become sicker and the environment more polluted when foreign manufacturers set up facilities. Conditions in foreign factories were so bad and criticism from human rights organizations so strong that a 1997 presidential task force created a code of conduct on wages, working conditions, and child labor for apparel factories that U.S. companies own and operate around the world.

The host countries themselves are equally likely to be exploited. The money multinational corporations earn is rarely reinvested in the host country. In fact, 85% of the profit from exported products ends up in the hands of the multinational corporations, bankers, traders, and distributors (Braun, 1997). For example, in Brazil, one of the world's largest agricultural exporters, shipments abroad of fruits, vegetables, and soybeans have grown considerably over the past several decades. During the same period, however, the number of Brazilians who were undernourished grew from one third to two thirds of the population (Braun, 1997).

Local economies can suffer too. For instance, supermarket chains owned by large multinational corporations have revolutionized food distribution worldwide. They are popular with consumers all over the world because of their lower prices and greater variety and convenience (Dugger, 2004). But these stores tend to get their produce from large conglomerates that have more money and marketing know-how than small, local suppliers and can therefore provide cheaper fruits and vegetables. Hence, the livelihoods of millions of struggling small farmers have been destroyed, widening the gap between the haves and the have-nots in developing countries.

Not all multinationals are hardhearted organizations that ignore the well-being of their workers abroad, the well-being of the workforce at home whose jobs are being exported to other countries, or the health and welfare of poor people in developing nations. For many multinationals, relocating manufacturing facilities to another country where labor is less expensive is a necessary response to global economic pressures as well as the demands of domestic consumers for inexpensive products.

But the processes that drive corporate decisions do sometimes drive individuals out of work, contribute to environmental and health problems, and reinforce global inequality.

CONCLUSION

In Chapter 1, I pondered the question of how free we really are to act as we wish. I described some of the personal, interpersonal, and structural considerations that limit or constrain our choices. In this chapter, you have seen how this fundamental issue is affected by social stratification and inequality. Certain groups of people have a greater capacity to control their own lives than others. Your position in the stratification system can determine not only your ability to influence people and exert authority but a whole host of life chances as well, from financial stability to housing, education, and health care. The unequal distribution of economic resources, whether between wealthy and poor individuals in the same society or between wealthy and poor countries worldwide, has created a seemingly indestructible system of haves and have-nots.

The profound imbalances in wealth, power, and prestige that exist in the United States are especially ironic given how loudly and frequently U.S. citizens boast of their cultural commitment to the values of equality and justice. Nevertheless, the U.S. system is set up, like most others in the world, to promote, enhance, and protect the interests of those who reside at or near the top of the stratification system. Authority, wealth, and influence grant rights that are unknown to the vast majority of people.

It's rather shocking that in a country as wealthy as the United States, a comfortable, healthy, and stable life is well beyond the reach of tens of millions of people. Constant media images of wealth remind poor and working-class people that they are outsiders who can only watch and long to be part of that affluent world. And when disaster strikes, like Hurricane Katrina, poor people receive the message once again that their marginal status in society can have deadly consequences.

We speak of the poor as if they were an unchanging and faceless group to be pitied, despised, or feared. To talk of the "poverty problem" is to talk about some depersonalized, permanent fixture on the U.S. landscape. But poverty is people. It's people standing in soup kitchen lines and welfare lines. It's people living in rat-infested projects. It's people sleeping on sidewalks. It's people struggling to acquire things the rest of society takes for granted. It's people coming up short in their quest for the American Dream.

When we look at the institutional causes of poverty, we see that the personality or "cultural" traits often associated with poverty—low ambition, rejection of the work ethic, inability to plan for the future—might be better understood as the consequences of poverty rather than its causes. As long as the structural obstacles to stable employment, adequate wages, and a decent education continue to exist, so will the characteristic hopelessness associated with poverty.

CHAPTER HIGHLIGHTS

◆ Stratification is a ranking of entire groups of people, based on race, gender, or social class, which perpetuates unequal rewards and life chances in society.

◆ Social class is the primary means of stratification in many societies, including the United States. Contemporary sociologists are likely to define one's class standing as a combination of income, wealth, occupational prestige, and educational attainment. Social class is more than an economic position; it is a way of life that affects how we experience every facet of our lives.

◆ The structural-functionalist explanation of stratification is that higher rewards, such as prestige and large salaries, are afforded to the most important positions in society, thereby ensuring that the most qualified individuals will occupy the highest positions. Conflict theory argues that stratification reflects an unequal distribution of power in society and is a primary source of conflict and tension.

◆ The official U.S. poverty line, the dollar cutoff point that defines the amount of income necessary for subsistence living, may actually be set too low, thereby underestimating the proportion of the population that is suffering financially.

◆ Poverty persists because it serves economic and social functions. The ideology of competitive individualism—that to succeed in life all one has to do is work hard and win in competition with others—creates a belief that poor people are to blame for their own suffering. In addition, poverty receives institutional "support" from a distribution of wealth and income that is growing increasingly unequal.

◆ Stratification exists not only among different groups within the same society but also among different societies within a global community. Wealthy nations are better able to control the world's financial resources than poor nations are.

KEY TERMS

absolute poverty: Inability to afford the minimal requirements for sustaining a reasonably healthy existence

authority: Possession of some status or quality that compels others to obey one's directives or commands

caste system: Stratification system based on heredity, with little movement allowed across strata

colonization: Process of expanding economic markets by invading and establishing control over a weaker country and its people

competitive individualism: Cultural belief that those who succeed in society are those who work hardest and have the best abilities and that those who suffer don't work hard enough or lack the necessary traits or abilities

culture-of-poverty thesis: Belief that poor people, resigned to their position in society, develop a unique value structure to deal with their lack of success

estate system (feudal system): Stratification system in which high-status groups own land and have power based on noble birth

false consciousness: Situation in which people in the lower classes come to accept a belief system that harms them; the primary means by which powerful classes in society prevent protest and revolution

means of production: Land, commercial enterprises, factories, and wealth that form the economic basis of class societies

middle class: In a society stratified by social class, a group of people who have an intermediate level of wealth, income, and prestige, such as managers, supervisors, executives, small business owners, and professionals

near-poor: Individuals or families whose earnings are between 100% and 125% of the poverty line (see also **working poor**)

poor: In a society stratified by social class, a group of people who work for minimum wage or are chronically unemployed

poverty line: Amount of yearly income a family requires to meet its basic needs, according to the federal government

poverty rate: Percentage of people whose income falls below the poverty line

power: Ability to affect decisions in ways that benefit a person or protect his or her interests

prestige: Respect and honor given to some people in society

relative poverty: Individuals' economic position compared with the living standards of the majority in the society

slavery: Economic form of inequality in which some people are legally the property of others

social class: Group of people who share a similar economic position in a society, based on their wealth and income

social mobility: Movement of people or groups from one class to another

socioeconomic status: Prestige, honor, respect, and lifestyle associated with different positions or groups in society

stratification: Ranking system for groups of people that perpetuates unequal rewards and life chances in society

upper class: In a society stratified by social class, a group of people who have high income and prestige and who own vast amounts of property and other forms of wealth, such as owners of large corporations, top financiers, rich celebrities and politicians, and members of prestigious families

working class: In a society stratified by social class, a group of people who have a low level of wealth, income, and prestige, such as industrial and factory workers, office workers, clerks, and farm and manual laborers

working poor: Employed people who consistently earn wages but do not make enough to survive (see also **near-poor**)

The Architecture of Inequality

Race and Ethnicity

Race and Ethnicity: More Than Just Biology

Histories of Oppression and Inequality

Racial and Ethnic Relations

Global Perspectives on Racism

Just like millions of other Americans, I sat transfixed in front of my television on the night of November 4, 2008, watching the presidential election results trickle in. At about 11:00 P.M. Eastern time, the networks made the astounding projection: Barack Obama—a man with a black Kenyan father and a white American mother—would be the 44th president of the United States. I sat in semi-disbelief. Had this country, one with such a difficult, painful, and deadly racial history, really just elected a black man to the highest office in the land? A development that would have been unthinkable 50, 25, or even 10 years earlier had just happened. People of all colors and classes here and abroad danced in the streets. Jesse Jackson, Oprah Winfrey, Colin Powell, and countless other less famous people wept with joy. Parents named their newborns "Barack."

Sociologists, columnists, and political analysts tried to find the most memorable and most articulate way to capture the historical significance of the moment. Some speculated that it might mark the end of racial inequality and exclusion in this country; others wondered if we'd become a "postracial" society, where traditional racial categories no longer matter. In a national poll the day before Obama's inauguration, more than two thirds of African Americans said they believed that Martin Luther King's famous 1963 dream (of a country where race and ethnicity are losing their status as major criteria for judging the content of a person's character) had been fulfilled (CNN.com, 2009). And surveys since the election consistently show that college-age Blacks are as optimistic and upbeat about their economic futures as Whites (Cose, 2011).

As I tried to absorb the magnitude of what took place that night, I began to think about the other important but less dramatic educational, economic, political, and cultural gains that people of color have made over the past few years:

- Close to half of all Latino/as and Blacks between 18 and 24 are now enrolled in college (Pérez-Peña, 2012). The percentage of African American and Latino/a college graduates has also risen steadily over the past 15 years, as has the proportion of ethnoracial minority families that could be considered middle or upper class.
- In the 2012 election, Blacks voted at a higher rate than Whites (Wheaton, 2013); 1 out of every 10 voters was Latino/a (Gonzalez, 2012). More Latino/as, Asian Americans, and Native Americans are in elected offices at the national, state, and local levels than ever before. In fact, 2012 marked the first time in our history that no white Protestant, either Democrat or Republican, occupied a top political position—president, vice president, Supreme Court justices, Speaker of the House, or Senate Majority Leader (Leonhardt, Parlapiano, & Waananen, 2012.
- African American artists like Jay-Z, Beyoncé, and Drake have achieved remarkable crossover success. In recent years, some of the most successful athletes in what were once exclusively white sports—tennis and golf—are black: Serena Williams and Tiger Woods. Three out of every 10 major league baseball players today is Latino, and, for the first time in history, there are more head coaches of color than white coaches in the NBA (Lapchick, 2013).

Yet as I think of the significant strides ethnoracial minorities have made, I can't get past a very different

reality. Despite the progress they've attained, African Americans, Latino/as, and Native Americans still remain, on average, the poorest and most disadvantaged of all groups in the United States. Their average annual income is still substantially lower than that of Whites and Asian Americans. The unemployment rate of Blacks who don't attend college is nearly twice as high as that of Whites and Asians who don't attend college. And the rate of home ownership among Blacks and Latino/as is below 50%, compared to 70% among Whites (ProQuest Statistical Abstract, 2013). Of all ethnoracial groups in this society, African Americans have the lowest life expectancy; highest rate of infant mortality; highest rates of most cancers, diabetes, heart disease, high blood pressure, and HIV/AIDS; and highest rates of death from treatable illnesses, gunshot wounds, and drug- or alcohol-induced causes (American Sociological Association, 2005; Centers for Disease Control and Prevention, 2011a; ProQuest Statistical Abstract, 2013). Whites even get more and better quality sleep than people of other races (Quenqua, 2012a).

I also think of specific violent events in the recent past that further belie the image of racial progress and harmony:

- In 2012, four East Haven, Connecticut, police officers were accused of systematically mistreating Latino/as in the community by conducting unreasonable searches of residents; slapping, hitting, and kicking suspects when in custody; and regularly harassing customers as they emerged from Latino/a-owned businesses (Barron, 2012).
- Also in 2012, a Wisconsin man murdered six congregants and wounded a police officer at a Sikh temple, probably because he thought the Sikhs were Muslim. A day later, a mosque in Joplin, Missouri, was burned to the ground (Beinart, 2012).
- Between 2000 and 2012, the number of known hate groups whose ideology is organized against specific racial or religious groups grew from 602 to 1,007 (Southern Poverty Law Center, 2013).
- One week after President Obama's 2012 reelection, posts on a neo-Nazi website included comments like "Gentlemen, prepare to defend yourselves!" and "White folks need to stick together. We should secede!" (quoted in Feldman & Weinberg, 2012).

So how far have we really come? Which is the real United States? Is it the one that overcame centuries of racial conflict and elected a black president? Or is it the one perpetually plagued by economic inequality, prejudice, and hatred?

In the previous chapter, I examined the class stratification system. But social class doesn't create unequal life chances on its own. This chapter focuses on another important determinant of social inequality: race and ethnicity.

RACE AND ETHNICITY: MORE THAN JUST BIOLOGY

To most people, *race* is a category of individuals labeled and treated as similar because of common inborn biological traits, such as skin color; color and texture of hair; and shape of eyes, nose, or head. It is widely assumed that people who are placed in the same racial category share behavioral, psychological, and personality traits that are linked to their physical similarities. But sociologists typically use the term *ethnicity* to refer to the nonbiological traits—such as shared culture, history, language, patterns of behavior, and beliefs—that provide members of a group with a sense of common identity. Whereas ethnicity is thought to be something that we learn from other people, race is commonly portrayed as an inherited and permanent biological characteristic that can easily be used to divide people into mutually exclusive groups.

But the concept of race isn't nearly so straightforward. For instance, people who consider themselves "white" may actually have darker skin and curlier hair than some people who consider themselves "black." In addition, some groups have features that do not neatly place them in one race or another. Australian Aborigines have black skin and "Negroid" facial features but also have blond, wavy hair. The black-skinned !Kung, who live in the Kalahari Desert of southern Africa, have epicanthic eye folds, a characteristic typical of East Asian peoples.

Not surprisingly, there are no universal racial categories. South Africa has four legally defined races—black, white, colored, and Indian—but in England and Ireland the term *black* is used to refer to all people who are not white. In one small Irish town that experienced an unprecedented influx of refugees in the late 1990s, anyone who wasn't Irish was considered black. As one resident put it, "Either Romanians or Nigerians, we don't know the difference. They're all the same. They're all black" (quoted in Lyall, 2000, p. A6). Conversely, some African Americans visiting Ghana are shocked when people there refer to them as *obruni*, or "white foreigner" (Polgreen, 2005).

In some places, racial identification can shift throughout the course of an individual's life, reflecting changes in economic standing, not skin color. For instance, Brazilians who climb the class ladder through educational and economic achievement may find themselves in a different racial category, as illustrated by popular Brazilian expressions such as "Money whitens" or "A rich Negro is a white man, and a poor white man is a Negro" (Marger, 1994, p. 441). Educated nonwhite parents in Brazil are significantly more likely to classify their children as white than are less-educated nonwhite parents (Schwartzman, 2007). In Puerto Rico, a U.S. territory, conceptions of race are markedly more fluid than they are in the United States. Race is seen as a continuum of categories with different shades of color as the norm and classifications that can change as one's socioeconomic circumstances change (C. E. Rodriguez & Cordero-Guzman, 2004). But even in this country, racial definitions can fluctuate. One nationwide survey showed that over a third of African Americans believe that because of a widening gap between middle-class and poor Blacks, "black" can no longer be thought of as a single race (cited in Gates, 2007).

The complex issue of defining race points to a complicated biological reality. Since the earliest humans appeared, they have consistently tended to migrate and interbreed. Some surveys estimate that at least 75% of U.S. Blacks have some white ancestry (cited in Mathews, 1996). Indeed, there is no gene that is 100% of one form in one race and 100% of a different form in another race (P. Brown, 1998).

That is not to say that race has absolutely *no* connection to biology. Geneticists and public health officials have known for quite a while that some diseases are not evenly distributed across racial groups. The overwhelming majority of cases of sickle cell anemia, for instance, are among people of African descent; it is rare among non-Hispanic whites (Blackhealthcare.com, 2003). In 2005, the Food and Drug Administration approved the cardiac drug BiDil, which is intended to be used exclusively by African Americans, who have been shown to be genetically predisposed to heart disease. Hemochromatosis, a digestive disorder that causes the body to absorb too much iron, affects Whites of Northern European descent much more frequently than it does people of color. Among African Americans, Asian Americans, Latino/as, and American Indians, the disease is virtually nonexistent. Among Whites, about five people out of 1,000—0.5%—carry two copies of the hemochromatosis gene and are susceptible to developing the disease. One out of every 8 to 12 Whites is a carrier of one abnormal gene (National Digestive Diseases Information Clearinghouse, 2011). However, no disease is found *exclusively* in one racial group. Furthermore, it's unclear whether these differences are solely due to some inherited biological trait or to the life experiences and historical, geographical, and/or environmental location of certain groups.

For most sociologists, then, race is more meaningful as a social category than as a biological one (Gans, 2005). That is, the characteristics a society selects to distinguish one ethnoracial group from another shape social rankings and determine access to important resources. But they have less to do with innate physical differences or genetic predispositions than with what the prevailing culture defines as socially significant (American Sociological Association, 2002). For instance, Jews, the Irish, Italians, and even some Germans were once defined as members of inferior races. They came to be seen as "white" only when they entered the mainstream culture and gained economic and political power (Bronner, 1998a).

Historical changes in the categories used by the U.S. government in its decennial population censuses further illustrate shifting conceptions of race (S. M. Lee, 1993):

- In 1790, the first U.S. census used the following classifications: Free White Males, Free White Females, All Other Free Persons, and Slaves.
- In 1870, there were five races: White, Colored (Black), Mulatto (people with some black blood), Chinese, and Indian.
- Race categories in the 1890 census reflected white people's concern about race mixing and racial purity. Eight races were listed, half of them applying to black or partly black populations: White, Colored (Black), Mulatto (people with three-eighths to five-eighths black blood), Quadroon (people with one-fourth black blood), Octoroon (people with one-eighth black blood), Chinese, Japanese, and Indian.
- In 1900, Mulatto, Quadroon, and Octoroon were dropped, so that any amount of "black blood" meant a person had to be classified as "black."

- In 1910 and 1920, Mulatto returned to the census form, only to disappear for good in 1930.
- Between 1930 and 2000, some racial classifications (such as Hindu, Eskimo, part Hawaiian, and Mexican) appeared and disappeared. Others (Filipino, Korean, Hawaiian) made an appearance and have remained since.
- Individuals filling out the 2010 census form had a wide array of racial categories from which to choose: White, Black, American Indian or Alaska Native, Asian Indian, Chinese, Filipino, Japanese, Korean, Vietnamese, Native Hawaiian, Guamanian or Chamorro, or Samoan.

You may have noticed that Latino/a or Hispanic is not included in the list of races on the latest census form. With the exception of the inclusion of "Mexican" in 1930, Spanish-speaking people have routinely been classified as "white." But because Latino/as can be members of any race, "Hispanic origin" appears on the census form, not as a race but as an ethnicity. In fact, the 2010 form explicitly states that "Hispanic origins are not races."

This way of thinking has not been received well by all Latino/as. Recent census data show that 87% of Americans born in Cuba and 53% born in Mexico identify themselves as white; but a majority of those born in the Dominican Republic and El Salvador refused to identify themselves by any of the racial categories on the census form (cited in Roberts, 2010). In the 2010 census, many Latino/as chose to use "American Indian" to identify their race. Consequently, the number of American Indians who also identified themselves as Hispanic tripled between 2000 and 2010 (cited in Decker, 2011). The U.S. Census Bureau is currently considering a combined "race or origin" question for the 2020 census that would include "Hispanic, Latino, or Spanish Origin" as a category along with "White," "Black, African American, or Negro," "American Indian or Alaskan Native," "Asian," and "Native Hawaiian or Other Pacific Islander" (Haub, 2012a).

In short, racial categories are not natural, biological groupings. They are created, inhabited, transformed, applied, and destroyed by people (Omi & Winant, 1992). What ties individuals together in a particular racial group is not a set of shared physical characteristics—because there aren't any physical characteristics shared by all members of a particular racial group—but the shared experience of identifying, and being identified by others, as members of that group (Piper, 1992). The power of this experience is reflected by the fact that people who identify as one race but are perceived by others as a member of another race suffer higher levels of depression and psychological distress than people who are "correctly" classified (M. E. Campbell & Troyer, 2007).

HISTORIES OF OPPRESSION AND INEQUALITY

A quick glance at the history of the United States reveals a record of not just freedom, justice, and equality but also of conquest, discrimination, and exclusion. Racial and ethnic inequalities have manifested themselves in phenomena such as slavery and fraud; widespread economic, educational, and political deprivation; the violent and nonviolent protests of the civil rights movement; and racially motivated hate crimes. Along the way, such injustices have constricted people's access to basic necessities, including housing, health care, a stable family life, and a means of making a decent living.

Every ethnoracial minority has its own story of persecution. European immigrants—Germans, Irish people, Italians, Poles, Jews, Greeks—were objects of hatred, suspicion, and discrimination when they first arrived in significant numbers in the United States. For instance, Benjamin Franklin once expressed fear that white Pennsylvanians would be "overwhelmed by swarms of swarthy Germans, who 'will soon so out number us, that all the advantages we have will not . . . be able to preserve our language, and even our government will become precarious'" (quoted in Roberts, 2008, p. 6). Nineteenth-century newspaper job ads routinely noted, "No Irish need apply." Jews were refused admission to many U.S. universities until the mid 20th century. The National Origins Act of 1924 restricted immigration from southern Europe (mainly Greece and Italy) until the 1960s. But because these groups had the same skin color as the dominant white Protestants, they eventually overcame most of these obstacles and gained entry into mainstream society. Most recently, immigrants from Asia, Latin America, and the Middle East have become popular targets of hostility. For people of color in this country, racial equality has always been elusive.

Native Americans

The story of Native Americans includes racially inspired massacres, takeover of ancestral lands, confinement on reservations, and unending governmental exploitation. Successive waves of white settlers seeking westward expansion in the 18th and 19th centuries pushed Native Americans off any land the settlers considered desirable (U.S. Commission on Human Rights, 1992). A common European belief that Native Americans were "savages" who should be displaced to make way for civilized Whites provided the ideological justification for conquering them.

According to the Fourteenth Amendment to the U.S. Constitution, "All persons born or naturalized in the United States, and subject to the jurisdiction thereof, are citizens of the United States and of the state wherein they reside." But despite the broad wording of this amendment, Native Americans were excluded from citizenship. In 1884, the U.S. Supreme Court ruled that Native Americans owed their primary allegiance to their tribe and so did not automatically acquire citizenship at birth. Not until 1940 were all Native Americans born in the United States considered U.S. citizens (Haney López, 1996).

Despite their history of severe oppression and continuing disadvantaged economic status compared with other groups, some Native Americans have shown a remarkable ability to endure and in a few cases to shrewdly promote their own financial interests. In the Pacific Northwest, for instance, some Indian tribes have successfully protected their rights to lucrative fishing waters (F. G. Cohen, 1986). Casinos and resorts have made some tribes wealthy. The Connecticut Sun, a professional women's basketball franchise, plays its home games on the grounds of a casino owned by the Mohegan tribe. Elsewhere, organizations have been formed to advance the financial concerns of Native Americans in industries such as gas, oil, and coal, where substantial reserves exist on Indian land (Snipp, 1986). However, intense struggles between large multinational corporations and Native American tribes continue today over control of these reserves.

Latino/as

The history of Latino/as in this country has been diverse. Some groups have had a relatively positive experience. For instance, Cuban immigrants who streamed into this country in the late 1950s, fleeing Fidel Castro's communist political regime, received an enthusiastic welcome (Suarez, 1998). Many early Cuban immigrants were wealthy business owners who set up lucrative companies, particularly in South Florida. Today, Cuban American families are the most economically and educationally successful of any Latino/a group.

But other groups have experienced extreme resentment and oppression. For instance, when the United States expanded into the Southwest, white Americans moved into areas already inhabited by Mexicans. After a war that lasted from 1846 to 1848, Mexico relinquished half its national territory to the United States, including what are now the states of Arizona, California, Colorado, New Mexico, Texas, Nevada, and Utah, as well as parts of Kansas, Oklahoma, and Wyoming.

In theory, Mexicans living on the U.S. side of the new border were to be given all the rights of U.S. citizens. In practice, however, their property rights were frequently violated, and they lost control of their mining, ranching, and farming industries. The exploitation of Mexican workers coincided with a developing economic system built around mining and large-scale agriculture, activities that demanded a large pool of cheap labor (J. Farley, 1982). Workers often had to house their families in primitive shacks with no electricity or plumbing for months on end while they performed seasonal labor.

Today, the status of Latino/as is mixed. They account for more than 40% of the 81 million people added to the U.S. population over the last 30 years and now represent a bigger proportion of the U.S. population than Blacks (ProQuest Statistical Abstract, 2013). By 2050, 3 out of every 10 persons in the United States will be Latino/as (Saenz, 2010). Larger numbers mean not only greater influence on the culture but more political clout. In 2012, Latino/as voted for Barack Obama over his Republican opponent, Mitt Romney, by a margin of nearly 3 to 1. In states with heavy Latino/a populations, like California, Florida, and Colorado, their vote was key to Obama's victory.

Economically and educationally, however, the situation is less rosy. The average annual income for Latino/a individuals and families is still substantially lower than that of other groups (ProQuest Statistical Abstract, 2013), and they were hit hardest by the recent recession. Between 2005 and 2009, median net worth among Latino/as decreased by 66%, compared with 53% for Blacks, 54% for Asians, and 16% for Whites (Kochhar, Fry, & Taylor, 2011). In addition, Latino/as are significantly more likely to drop out of school and less likely to go to college than are white, Asian American, or African American children. Their low levels of education, coupled with geographic concentration in economically distressed areas of the country, has made Latino/as, particularly men, especially vulnerable to downsizing and unemployment (Mather & Jacobsen, 2010).

African Americans

The experience of African Americans has been unique among ethnoracial groups in this country because of the direct and indirect influences of slavery. From 1619, when the first black slaves were sold in Jamestown, Virginia, to 1865, when the Thirteenth Amendment was passed, outlawing slavery, several million Blacks in this country endured the brutal reality of forced servitude. Slave owners controlled every aspect of a slave's life. They determined which slaves could marry and which marriages could be dissolved. Wedding vows among slave couples often substituted the phrase "until distance do us part" for "until death"—or "the white man"—"do us part" (Hunter, 2011). The economic value of children (i.e., future slaves) meant that slave owners had an interest in keeping slave marriages intact. But even the possibility of stable family life was an illusion. When economic troubles forced the sale of slaves to raise money, slave owners didn't hesitate to separate the very slave families they had once advocated. The daily threat of separation hung over every slave family.

Even after slavery was abolished, the conditions of life for U.S. Blacks showed little improvement. Following emancipation, freed Blacks in the South found themselves arrested on trumped-up charges like selling produce after dark or talking loudly to white women in public. Vagrancy was criminalized so that Blacks who couldn't show proof of employment were fined and thrown in jail. When they couldn't pay their fines, thousands were "leased" to county officials or private companies and forced to work—sometimes in shackles—under conditions that were actually worse than what they had experienced during slavery (Blackmon, 2009).

Later on, "Jim Crow" laws established rigid lines between the races. In 1896, the U.S. Supreme Court ruled that racial segregation in public facilities was constitutional. Unequal access to public transportation, schools, hotels, theaters, restaurants, campgrounds, drinking fountains, the military, and practically every other aspect of social life continued until the middle of the 20th century. Conditions were so bad that Blacks often had to take extra precautions simply to engage in everyday activities. For instance, from the 1930s to the 1960s, many Blacks wouldn't embark on a long-distance automobile trip without a guidebook called *The Negro Motorist Green Book*. This book provided Blacks with city-by-city information about where they could drive, sleep, eat, buy gas, or shop without being harassed, humiliated, or attacked (McGee, 2010).

Despite advances, the quality of life for most African Americans remains below that of Whites. The median annual income for black households is $32,229, compared with $52,214 for white households (ProQuest Statistical Abstract, 2013). Black unemployment is twice as high as that of Whites. As one author put it, "The era that ushered in the first black president has also introduced the highest levels of unemployment and poverty for African Americans in 20 years" (Samuels, 2011, p. 46). Nevertheless, blatant discrimination has declined in the past four decades, and some economic, educational, and political advances have been made. For instance, black-owned businesses generate more than $137 billion in annual sales (ProQuest Statistical Abstract, 2013). The average annual household income of $32,229 represents a significant increase over the average income of black households in 1980 ($27,973).

Asian Americans

When large numbers of Chinese men came to this country in the second half of the 19th century to work in the mines and on the expanding railroad system, they were treated with hostility. The image of the "yellow peril" was fostered by rampant fears that hordes of Chinese workers would take away scarce jobs and eventually overrun native-born Whites. In the late 19th and early 20th centuries, several laws, such as the Chinese Exclusion Act, the Scott Act, and the Geary Act, barred Chinese immigrants from entering the country and stripped those already here of many of their legal rights. For instance, Chinese laborers were legally prevented from becoming permanent citizens, from bringing their wives with them, and from marrying Whites when they got here.

Early Japanese Americans faced similar circumstances. Like the Chinese, Japanese families created tight-knit, insulated communities where they were able to pool money and resources and achieve relative success. But their perceived success motivated lawmakers to enact legislation that barred all further Japanese immigration. Hostility toward the Japanese reached a peak in 1941, following Japan's attack on Pearl Harbor. President Franklin Roosevelt signed an executive order authorizing the relocation and internment of Japanese immigrants and U.S. citizens of Japanese descent in camps surrounded by barbed wire, watchtowers, and armed guards.

The irony of race for Chinese, Japanese, Koreans, Vietnamese, Cambodians, Laotians, Indians, and other Asian groups is that they are often perceived as "model minorities" or "America's greatest success story." For instance, the average total SAT scores for Asian high school seniors is 1641, compared with 1578 for Whites and 1498 for the general population (Jaschik, 2012). Nine of the 11 finalists at the 2013 Scripps National Spelling Bee were of Asian descent. Almost twice the percentage of Asian Americans as Whites complete college, their median household income is actually higher than that of the population as a whole, and they are more likely than other groups to be married and to raise their children in a two-parent household (ProQuest Statistical Abstract, 2013).

But the expectations and resentment associated with being the "model minority" can be as confining and oppressive as those created by more negative labels. By overemphasizing Asian American success, the label downplays the problems Asian Americans continue to face from racial discrimination in all areas of public and private life. Furthermore, it portrays Asian American success as proof that the United States provides equal opportunities for those who conform and work hard, even though many ethnoracial groups continue to suffer.

The "model minority" image can also turn ugly when equated with perceptions that Asians are overstudious loners who can't be trusted. These stereotypes bubbled to the surface in the immediate aftermath of the 2007 massacre at Virginia Tech University, in which a Korean American student went on a rampage and killed 32 people. Although it turned out that the gunman suffered from serious mental problems and the feared anti-Korean backlash never materialized, media portrayals continued to highlight both his ethnicity and his lack of social skills, perpetuating the idea that shy, bookish Asian American college students might be ticking time bombs.

Muslim Americans

Although their numbers are small compared with those of other ethnoracial minority groups and their arrival has been more recent, few groups have evoked stronger negative feelings or are as misunderstood as Muslim Americans. While the tendency is to see them as a monolithic, homogeneous group, they are actually quite culturally and racially diverse. Sixty-five percent of Muslim Americans are first-generation immigrants. About a third come from the Arabic-speaking countries of the Middle East and North Africa and another 27% from South Asia. Despite the heavy presence of immigrants, more than three quarters of Muslims in this country are U.S. citizens (Pew Research Center, 2007).

In terms of educational attainment and income level, Muslim Americans mirror the rest of U.S. society. The proportion of Muslims who have earned college degrees is the same as it is for the general population. In addition, 41% of Muslim American adults report annual household incomes of more than $50,000, compared with 44% of all U.S. adults. In fact, Muslims in the United States are in far better shape economically than those in France, Spain, Germany, or Great Britain (Pew Research Center, 2007) and are more likely to have non-Muslim friends than their counterparts in other countries (Thomson-DeVeaux, 2013).

Overall, Muslim Americans are quite assimilated into mainstream U.S. society. The vast majority believe that their communities are good places to live in and that hard work will pay off. Most are happy to be in the United States and condemn Islamic extremism. Fewer than 1 in 10 U.S. Muslims feel that violence against civilians is ever justified to defend Islam (Pew Forum on Religion and Public Life, 2013). A recent poll found that most Muslim Americans say they are loyal to the United States and optimistic about the future, despite reporting high levels of discrimination (Younis, 2011).

Nevertheless, the equation of Muslims with violent terrorism has been a common prejudice for decades, dating back to the murder of 11 Israeli athletes during the 1972 Summer Olympics in Munich. The September 11, 2001, attacks bolstered anti-Muslim prejudice and continue to make their lives significantly more difficult. Most Muslims believe that the government and law enforcement agencies single them out for increased surveillance and monitoring (Pew Research Center, 2007). This belief is not unwarranted. For instance, the New York Police Department recently used a film, titled *The Third Jihad*, as part of its training program of new police recruits. The film depicts Muslim terrorists shooting Christians in the head and exploding car bombs; images of "executed" American children covered by sheets; and a doctored photograph showing an Islamic flag flying over the White House (Powell, 2012).

Despite knowing more about Muslims than ever before, almost half of U.S. adults have an unfavorable view of them, believing that Islam encourages violence more than other religions (Jost, 2006b). People are equally divided over whether Islamic values are consistent with the American way of life (Thomson-DeVeaux, 2013). During the primary campaign leading up to the 2012 presidential campaign, one Republican candidate said that if elected, he'd never appoint a Muslim to his cabinet. Another insinuated that a Muslim woman who served as the Chief of Staff for then Secretary of State Hillary Clinton was a secret agent of Egypt's Muslim Brotherhood (Beinart, 2012).

The expression of anti-Muslim sentiment is more open than such sentiments applied to other ethnoracial groups. In 2010, voters in Oklahoma overwhelmingly approved a ballot measure that would prohibit the use of Sharia law—the body of law based on the Qur'an—in state courts. Although the measure was blocked by a federal judge, several other states have considered similar legislation. Given such fear and distrust, it's not surprising that Muslim Americans are one of the most openly despised ethnoracial groups in the country today.

RACIAL AND ETHNIC RELATIONS

U.S. society's long history of racial tension is unlikely to fade away anytime soon. Increasing numbers of ethnoracial minorities and an influx of non–English-speaking immigrants are heightening competition and conflict over society's resources, including various forms of wealth, prestige, and power. The unequal distribution of resources is often motivated by *racism*, the belief that humans are subdivided into distinct groups so different in their social behavior and mental and physical capacities that they can be ranked as superior or inferior (Marger, 1994). Racism can be expressed at the personal level through individual attitudes and behavior, at the cultural level in language and collective ideologies, and at the macrostructural level in the everyday workings of social institutions.

Personal Racism

Personal racism is the expression of racist attitudes or behaviors by individual people. This type of racism takes many obvious forms, such as individuals who use derogatory names when they refer to other ethnoracial groups or those who show clear disdain for and hostility toward members of other groups during face-to-face contact. However, subtle forms of personal racism, such as the high school guidance counselor who steers minority students away from "hard" subjects and toward those that do not prepare them for higher-paying jobs, are much more common. Whether blatant or subtle, personal racism rests on two important psychological constructs—stereotypes and prejudice.

Stereotypes

The word *stereotype* was first used by the political commentator Walter Lippmann in 1922. He defined it as an oversimplified picture of the world, one that satisfies our need to see our social environment as a more understandable and manageable place than it really is (Lippmann, 1922). When applied to race, it is the overgeneralized belief that a certain trait, behavior, or attitude characterizes all members of some identifiable group.

Casual observations easily refute the accuracy of common racial or ethnic stereotypes. Most African Americans aren't on welfare, most Jews aren't greedy, few Italians belong to the Mafia, not all Asian Americans excel in math, and so on. Overgeneralizations are never true for every member of a group. Yet despite their obvious inaccuracy, stereotypes remain a common part of our everyday thinking. We all know what the stereotypes are, even if most of us choose not to express them or act on them.

The contemporary view is that stereotyping is a universal aspect of human thought (D. L. Hamilton, 1981). Our brains tend to divide the world into distinct categories: good and bad, strong and weak, them and us (Rothenberg, 1992). By allowing us to

group information into easily identifiable categories, stereotypes make the processing of information and the formation of impressions more efficient. As you saw in Chapter 6, our lives would be utterly chaotic if we weren't able to quickly categorize and form expectations about people in terms of gender, race, age, ethnicity, and so on. What's important to remember, though, is that the actual content of stereotypes is by no means natural; it must be learned.

The media provide large audiences with both real and fantasized images of racial, religious, and ethnic groups: the savage American Indian; the sassy, confrontational, overweight black woman; the spoiled, pampered, shopping-obsessed Jewish woman; the fanatical Arab terrorist; and so on. Asians are frequently depicted as camera-wielding tourists, scholastic overachievers, or sinister warlords. Latino/as have historically been cast as "Latin lovers," "banditos," "greasers," or "lazy good-for-nothings" (Reyes & Rubie, 1994). Popular contemporary characters like Mike and Tina Chang on *Glee,* Rajesh Koothrappali on *The Big Bang Theory,* and Gloria Delgado-Pritchett on *Modern Family* continue to present Chinese, Indian, and Latina characters in a stereotypical manner.

An analysis of a random sample of television news shows aired in Los Angeles and Orange counties in California revealed that Whites were more likely than African Americans and Latino/as to be portrayed on television news as victims of crime. Conversely, African Americans and Latino/as were more likely to be portrayed on news shows as lawbreakers than as crime victims (Dixon & Linz, 2000). Another study found that although people of color appear regularly in prime-time TV commercials, they usually appear as secondary characters. Furthermore, Whites are more likely to appear in ads for upscale products, beauty products, and home products. People of color, in contrast, are more likely to appear in ads for low-cost, low-nutrition products (like fast foods and soft drinks) and in athletic or sports equipment ads (Henderson & Baldasty, 2003).

Prejudice and Discrimination

When stereotypes form the basis of a set of rigidly held, unfavorable attitudes, beliefs, and feelings about members of a racial or ethnic group, they constitute *prejudice* (Allport, 1954). A good example of how prejudice affects social interaction is a study in which a group of whites was shown a photograph of a white person holding a razor blade while arguing with a black person on a New York subway. Subjects were shown the picture for a split second and then asked to write down what they saw. More than half said they saw the black man holding the razor against the white man's throat (cited in Helmreich, 1992). The belief that all Blacks are violent was so powerful that it distorted people's perceptions. Such perceptions can influence policy. New York City's "stop and frisk" law, for example, gives police the power to stop and detain someone based on "reasonable suspicion" of involvement in criminal activity. Although not defined in racial terms, the policy has been applied overwhelmingly to young black men since its inception (Harris-Perry, 2012).

These sorts of perceptions can be life threatening as well. To many observers, the 2012 murder of Trayvon Martin, the unarmed African American teenager who was gunned down by the neighborhood-watch coordinator in the gated community where Trayvon was staying, reflected the depth of the presumptions people make about "dangerous" young black men. Even those who work in law enforcement are not immune to such attitudes. In New York City, for example, undercover black police officers have, on occasion, been shot and wounded or killed by white officers who mistook them for dangerous criminals. As one black officer put it, "If you speak with nine out of 10 [undercover] officers of color they would tell you that when they hear sirens, in their head they are thinking: 'I hope these cops know that I'm one of the good guys'" (quoted in M. Powell, 2009, p. 18). Over the years, there have been calls for the department to appoint panels to examine the underlying racial assumptions of white officers and to provide cadets with extra training.

Prejudices can change as social conditions change. When people feel their cultural integrity or their economic livelihood is being threatened—by either the real or the perceived infiltration of other ethnoracial groups—prejudicial attitudes can become more open and hostile. For instance, widespread anti-Catholic sentiment became especially virulent in the late 19th and early 20th centuries as waves of Catholic immigrants entered the country looking for a better life (Gusfield, 1963).

Prejudiced beliefs would be of little significance if they didn't lead sometimes to discrimination. *Discrimination* is the unfair treatment of people based on some social characteristic. The 1964 Civil Rights Act prohibits discrimination or segregation on the grounds of race, color, religion, or national origin. This act has produced tremendous progress in U.S. race relations. Nevertheless, discrimination still exists.

When we think of discrimination, we usually think of its most blatant forms—racial epithets, racially inspired hate crimes, barriers to employment, and so on. Most of the time, though, discrimination is much more subtle, expressed as suspicion or avoidance; in fact, the person engaging in it may not even realize she or he is doing so. We are generally so unaware of our own nonverbal behavior that if we unwittingly give off signs of our dislike, we don't interpret others' subsequent behavior as a reaction to our nonverbal cues. Rather, we attribute it to some inherent trait in them. We may unknowingly prompt the very actions that we then use as evidence of some flaw or deficiency in that group.

These understated forms of discrimination are often harder to fight than overt bigotry. If you are excluded from a job because you're Asian or denied membership in a club because you're Jewish, you can fight to open those doors. Today, quite a few people have made it in (Blauner, 1992). But once inside, they still have many interpersonal barriers to overcome.

When such subtle behavior becomes common among large numbers of people, prejudice and discrimination become mutually reinforcing. Defining one group as inferior and thus denying its members access to a decent education and jobs becomes a self-fulfilling prophecy, producing the very inferiority that the group was believed to possess in the first place.

Prejudice and discrimination based on skin color may also occur *within* a particular ethnoracial group. Some see this phenomenon, known as *colorism*, as just as bad a problem as racial hatred expressed toward the group by outsiders. For instance, skin tone has been associated with social advantage among Blacks since the days of slavery, when light-skinned slaves were often allowed to work in the main house but dark-skinned slaves were relegated to the fields (Graham, 1999). During the early to mid 20th century, many African American churches, social clubs, fraternities, and other organizations still used skin color to determine the suitability of candidates for membership. The so-called brown bag test restricted membership to those whose skin was lighter than the color of a brown paper bag (Graham, 1999). More recent studies have found that lighter-skinned Blacks have higher educational attainment, more prestigious occupations, and higher annual incomes than darker-skinned Blacks, regardless of their sex, region of residence, age, marital status, or parents' socioeconomic status (M. E. Hill, 2000; Keith & Herring, 1991). As a result, darker-skinned Blacks sometimes resent light-skinned Blacks, accusing them of "selling out" in an attempt to conform to white standards of beauty as well as behavior (F. J. Davis, 1991).

Colorism is not limited to African Americans. Among Latino/as, the degree of "Indianness," or the darkness of one's skin, has long determined a person's status. After controlling for all other relevant factors, researchers have found that dark-skinned Mexican Americans who have a Native American physical appearance have fewer years of education than light-skinned Mexican Americans (Murguia & Telles, 1996) and they consistently earn lower wages (Telles & Murguia, 1990).

The Privilege of Having No Color

People who are members of a racial majority sometimes have trouble appreciating the humiliating effects of everyday encounters with prejudice and discrimination. They don't have to experience the petty indignities of racism, such as repeatedly being watched with suspicion in stores and on streets. Consequently, many Whites in the United States pay little attention to their own race, think people of color are obsessed with race and ethnicity, and find it difficult to understand the emotional and intellectual energy people of color devote to the subject (Haney López, 1996).

In a society in which they dominate statistically and culturally, U.S. Whites rarely define their identity in terms of race. Whiteness is so obvious and normative that white people's racial identity is, for all intents and purposes, invisible. Whites enjoy the luxury of *racial transparency*, or "having no color" (Haney López, 1996). People in the United States are far more likely to hear "black" or "Asian" or "Latino" used as an adjective (e.g., the black lawyer, the Latino teacher) than "white" (the white lawyer, the white teacher). Whites have the luxury of choosing whether to include their specific ethnic ancestry in descriptions of their identity (Waters, 2008). In this sense, ethnicity is optional, voluntary, and perhaps even recreational—as when white people

embrace their Irishness on St. Patrick's Day. In short, Whites for the most part enjoy the privilege of not having to constantly think about race or identify their ethnicity.

Such a luxury provides benefits to Whites whether or not they approve of the way social advantage has been conferred on them. One white author (McIntosh, 2001) catalogued all the everyday privileges she enjoyed (and often didn't notice) simply because she was white. These included the ability to shop alone in a department store without being followed by suspicious salespeople, to buy greeting cards or children's picture books featuring people of her race, and to find bandages that match her skin color. In other words, Whites need not be bigots or feel racially superior or more deserving than others to enjoy the privileges that their skin color brings.

Class, Race, and Discrimination

Some sociologists have argued that discriminatory treatment, as well as the unequal social and political status of some racial groups, is more a function of social class than of race. If this belief were completely accurate, the lives of middle- and upper-class people of color would be relatively free of discrimination. The election and reelection of Barack Obama clearly show that well-educated, highly qualified members of ethnoracial minorities are no longer barred from the highest positions in society. However, some civil rights advocates believe Obama's victories are isolated successes and fear many people will mistakenly conclude that racial discrimination is over (Swarns, 2008b). After all, African Americans still remain twice as likely as Whites to be unemployed, three times as likely to live in poverty, and six times as likely to be incarcerated (National Urban League, 2009). As the former chair of the U.S. Commission on Civil Rights put it, "It's like saying that because some poor white person made it, there's no poverty" (quoted in Cose, 2009, p. 43).

Indeed, even for many financially successful people of color, lack of respect, faint praise, low expectations, and outright harassment and exclusion continue to be common features of their lives (Feagin & McKinney, 2003). Minority professionals often bemoan the tendency of others to assume they bring to every interaction the perspective of their entire group. A successful law professor, who happens to be Chinese American, once said, "I suspect . . . that at every appearance . . . my audience continues to see and hear me as a spokesperson on behalf of Asian Americans" (Wu, 2002, p. 37).

Everyday life can be trying as well. Wealthy black residents of affluent neighborhoods all over the country sometimes complain that they are watched closely when shopping in upscale stores or that the police view them with suspicion simply because their skin color doesn't match the neighborhood. Situations like these are disturbing and frustrating not only because of the racist attitudes that lie behind them but also because the people who experience them had come to believe that their upward social mobility protected them from such treatment. Racial discrimination is still very prevalent in the lives of members of ethnoracial minorities, including those who are affluent. In fact, such discrimination is more apparent than that experienced by low-income people because the affluent individuals have entered previously inaccessible social spaces (Bonilla-Silva, 2008). One study even found that Blacks with college degrees experience more discrimination than those without degrees (Forman, Williams, & Jackson, 1997).

The days of NO NEGROES and NO INDIANS signs on public facilities may be gone, but less blatant contemporary expressions of personal racism serve as a constant reminder that in the 21st century, members of ethnoracial minorities—no matter what their class standing—are still stereotyped, prejudged, and discriminated against every day.

Quiet Racism

Clearly, the nature of public attitudes in the United States toward racial and ethnic groups has changed over the past few decades, prompting many sociologists to rethink their ideas of what constitutes personal racism. One nationwide poll found that the proportion of U.S. residents who feel that race relations are improving and that progress has been made in reducing racial discrimination is the highest it's been since the early 1990s (cited in J. Cohen & Agiesta, 2008). However, other surveys indicate that different groups have very different perceptions of the state of race relations:

- Sixty percent of Blacks think racism is a big problem compared to 19% of Whites; 70% of Whites believe that Blacks and Whites have an equal chance of getting a job they're qualified for compared to only 25% of Blacks (Romano & Samuels, 2012).
- Seventy-two percent of Whites believe that Blacks overestimate the amount of discrimination against them; conversely, 82% of Blacks believe that Whites underestimate the amount of discrimination Blacks suffer (cited in Blow, 2008).
- Almost half of white respondents oppose programs that make special efforts to help minorities get ahead; 27% feel that too much has been made of the problems facing black people (cited in Blow, 2009).
- In a study of residents in Durham, North Carolina, 50% of black respondents said they had the most in common with Latino/as; however only 17% of Latino/as said they had the most in common with Blacks. Similarly, 78% of Latino/as said they had the most in common with Whites, but only 22% of Whites felt that way about Latino/as (McClain et al., 2006).

These paradoxes have led some to argue that a subtle form of racism has emerged (Ansell, 2000; Bonilla-Silva, 2008; Sniderman & Tetlock, 1986). **Quiet racism** is linked to the traditional forms of personal racism by negative feelings toward certain groups. However, the feelings common to quiet racism are not necessarily hate or hostility but discomfort, uneasiness, and sometimes fear, which tend to motivate avoidance and passivity rather than outright confrontation (Trepagnier, 2013). Quiet racists are people who maintain that discrimination against a person because of his or her race or ethnicity is unfair but who nonetheless cannot entirely escape the cultural forces that give rise to racist beliefs in the first place. What complicates the situation is that this type of racism is often expressed by people who consider themselves unbiased and nonprejudiced.

The changing face of racism has serious institutional consequences as well. When racism remains quiet, people are tempted to assume that it has disappeared and thus to forget about helping groups that have traditionally been the objects of discrimination (Bonilla-Silva, 2003). Recent efforts to eliminate programs designed to help ethnoracial minorities exemplify this trend. Many Whites now believe that the only reason so many Blacks are unsuccessful is that they lack motivation and aren't committed to the "white" values of hard work, individualism, delayed gratification, and so on (Schuman & Krysan, 1999). Although these beliefs are more subtle than overt acts of bigotry, they have the same effect: On the basis of stereotypes, they promote prejudice toward individuals.

The Cultural Ideology of Racism

If I stopped here in my discussion of racism, you might be inclined to consider it an individual-level phenomenon that could best be stopped by changing the way people think or by personal acts of kindness and respect. But the sociologically important thing about racism is that it exists not just in the minds and actions of individuals but in a cultural belief system that both justifies the domination of some groups over others and provides a set of social norms that encourages differential treatment for these groups (O'Sullivan-See & Wilson, 1988). From a conflict perspective, the ideology of racism that exists in our language and in our prevailing cultural beliefs contributes to racial and ethnic inequality.

Racism in Language

Certainly, racial slurs and derogatory words reflect underlying racism. But racism in language is often less obvious. Consider the use of *panethnic labels*—general terms applied to diverse subgroups that are assumed to have something in common (D. Newman, 2012). Today, we use the general terms *Native American* or *American Indian* to refer to all 560 or so native nations living in the United States, despite their different languages and cultures. *Asian American* refers to a variety of peoples from dozens of countries whose ethnic heritages and lifestyles are quite different from one another. Similarly, *Hispanic* or *Latino* refers to people whose backgrounds include culturally diverse areas such as Mexico, the Caribbean, Central America, and South America. To some, even the term *African American*, which is widely considered to be a positive racial label, glosses over the thousands of ethnic groups, class interests, and indigenous religions that exist on the continent of Africa. Reliance on panethnic labels allows users to overlook and ignore variations within a particular labeled group, thereby reinforcing stereotypes. In response to these concerns, the University of California expanded the number of Asian American categories on its application forms from 8 to 23, allowing prospective students to claim a more specific ethnic identity.

Racial identifiers often become equated with negative meanings. Consider, for instance, connotations

of the words *black* and *white*. Among the definitions of *black* in *Webster's New Universal Unabridged Dictionary* are "soiled and dirty," "thoroughly evil," "wicked," "gloomy," "marked by disaster," "hostile," and "disgraceful." The definition of *white,* in contrast, includes "fairness of complexion," "innocent," "favorable," "fortunate," "pure," and "spotless." The pervasive "goodness" of white and "badness" of black affects children at a very young age and provides white children with a false sense of superiority (R. B. Moore, 1992). Young children know the difference between a black lie, which is harmful and inexcusable, and a white lie, which is small, insignificant, and harmless. Also important are the political implications of racially tinged terminology. Terms such as *economically disadvantaged*, *underclass*, *inner city*, and *underdeveloped* sound unprejudiced, but they are often used as code for racial terms.

Language is just a small part of the overall problem of racist ideology in U.S. society. It seemingly pales in comparison with more visible issues such as racial violence and economic discrimination. We must remember, however, that language filters our perceptions. It affects the way people think from the time they first learn to speak. Fortunately, efforts are being made today to address the issue of language and its crucial role in maintaining racism and oppression. People are becoming more aware of the capacity of words to both glorify and degrade (R. B. Moore, 1992).

The Myth of Innate Racial Inferiority

Scientific-sounding theories of the innate inferiority of certain ethnoracial groups have long been used to explain why some groups lag behind others in areas such as educational achievement and financial success. These theories combine with the belief in competitive individualism (see Chapter 10) to justify all forms of prejudice and discrimination.

Appeals to biology and nature have been used throughout history to define the existing stratification system as proper and inevitable (Gould, 1981). What would you think of a person who harbored the following beliefs about Blacks?

[Blacks] have less hair on the face and body. They secrete less by the kidneys [sic], and more by the glands of the skin, which gives them a very strong and disagreeable odour [sic]. . . . They are at least as brave, and more adventuresome. But this may perhaps proceed from a want of forethought, which prevents their seeing a danger till it be present. . . . In imagination, they are dull, tasteless, and anomalous. . . . The improvement of the blacks in body and mind, in the first instance of their mixture with the whites, has been observed by everyone, and proves that their inferiority is not the effect merely of their condition of life. . . . I advance it therefore . . . that the blacks . . . are inferior to the whites in the endowments both of body and mind.

A white supremacist? A raving bigot? An ignorant fanatic? How would your assessment of this person change if you found out that this passage was written by none other than Thomas Jefferson (1781/1955, pp. 138–143)? In the 18th and 19th centuries, no white person—not even one apparently committed to protecting people's right to "life, liberty and the pursuit of happiness"—doubted the validity of natural racial rankings: Indians below Whites, and Blacks below everyone else. Other idols of Western culture—George Washington, Abraham Lincoln, Charles Darwin—held similar beliefs about the "natural inferiority" of some races, beliefs that were commonly accepted knowledge at the time but would at the very least be considered racially insensitive today.

From a conflict perspective, beliefs about racial inferiority provide advantages for the dominant group. These beliefs discourage subordinate groups from questioning their disadvantaged status. In addition, they provide moral justification for maintaining a society in which some groups are routinely deprived of their rights and privileges. Nineteenth-century Whites could justify the enslavement of Blacks, and 20th-century Nazis could justify the extermination of Jews and other "undesirables," by promoting the belief that those groups are biologically subhuman.

Despite energetic searches over the centuries, a link between "inferior" race-based genes and certain traits and abilities has not been found (Hacker, 1992). For one thing, comparing racial groups on, say, intelligence overlooks the range of differences within and between groups. Many African Americans are more intelligent than the average white person; many Whites are less intelligent than the average Native American.

Variations such as these are difficult to explain in terms of the genetic superiority of one race. Moreover,

treating the more than 240 million "white" people in the United States as a single (and intellectually superior) group is problematic at best and misleading at worst. It can't account for the wide variation in academic achievement among Whites of different national backgrounds. For instance, at the time *The Bell Curve* was written, 21% of white Americans of Irish descent completed college, whereas 22% of Italian Americans, 33% of Scottish Americans, and 51% of Russian Americans did so (Hacker, 1994). Finally, such comparisons also ignore a problem I described earlier in this chapter: that race itself is a meaningless biological category. How can we attribute racial differences in intelligence to genes when race itself is not traceable to a single gene?

Nevertheless, the idea that racial inferiority is innate remains appealing. If observable, physical differences among races are inherited, the argument goes, then why not differences in social behavior, intelligence, and leadership ability? Like the belief in competitive individualism we examined in the previous chapter, the belief in innate racial inferiority places the blame for suffering and economic failure on the individual rather than on the society in which that individual exists.

Institutional Racism: Injustice Built Into the System

Anyone can be personally racist, whether overtly or quietly. Members of any ethnoracial group can develop a set of beliefs or a vocabulary that denigrates outsiders. But one form of racism, less obvious and perhaps more dangerous, can work only to the advantage of those who wield power in society: institutional racism. **Institutional racism** consists of established laws, customs, and practices that systematically reflect and produce racial inequalities in society, whether or not the individuals maintaining these practices have racist intentions (J. M. Jones, 1986). Thus, a society can be racist even if only a small proportion of its members harbor personally racist beliefs. Because African Americans, Latino/as, Asian Americans, Native Americans, and other groups have historically been excluded from key positions of authority in social institutions, they often find themselves victimized by the routine workings of such structures.

Sometimes institutional discrimination is obvious and codified into the law. Until the early 1990s, for example, South Africa operated under an official system of *apartheid*: Nonwhite groups were legally segregated and subjected to sanctioned forms of political and economic discrimination. In the United States, the forceful relocation of Native Americans in the 19th century, the repressive Jim Crow laws in the 20th-century South, and the internment of Japanese Americans during World War II are all examples of legislated policies that purposely worked to the disadvantage of already disadvantaged groups.

Understanding less obvious forms of institutional racism is a great test of the sociological imagination. Because it is a built-in feature of social arrangements, institutional racism is often much more difficult to detect than acts of personal racism. Consider one well-established practice for granting home mortgage or home improvement loans. Many banks use zip codes to mark off the neighborhoods they consider high risk—that is, where property values are low and liable to drop even further. These practices make it difficult for individuals in such areas to borrow money to buy or improve a home. Unfortunately, these are precisely the areas where minorities, with lower-than-average incomes, are most likely to find an affordable home to purchase. Thus, although individual bank officers are not denying loans to people because of their race— they are merely following their employers' policy—the resulting discrimination is the same.

Sometimes institutional racism is camouflaged behind claims that may on the surface seem quite reasonable. For instance, taxi companies protect the safety of their drivers by refusing service to what they consider dangerous neighborhoods. Similarly, home delivery businesses, such as pizza parlors, sometimes refuse to deliver to certain neighborhoods. Several years ago, Domino's Pizza was criticized in the media when it was revealed that the company was distributing software to its outlets to let them mark addresses on computers as green (deliver), yellow (curbside only), or red (no delivery). Businesses defend such policies as a rational response to the threat of sending easy-to-spot, cash-carrying delivery personnel into unsafe areas ("Pizza Must Go," 1996). Although such practices may be considered "good" business policy and are not intentionally racist, their consequences are discriminatory because high-risk neighborhoods tend to be inhabited predominantly by people of color. Institutional racism is difficult to address in these cases because no individual "bad guy," no identifiable bigot, is the source of the discrimination.

The National Fair Housing Alliance (2012) conservatively estimates that there are approximately 4 million fair-housing violations every year. Apart from incidents of landlords discriminating against families with small children or against people with disabilities, most of these cases involve ethnoracial minorities. On occasion, such housing discrimination is personal, the result of individuals' blatant "we don't want you people here" attitudes. More commonly, though, it's institutional, politely and subtly driven by company policies (D. Pearce, 1979). Discriminatory policies include making fewer houses or rental units available to minorities, limiting minorities' access to financial assistance, and steering them toward particular neighborhoods. Because these policies restrict opportunities for people of color, they are much more likely than white families to live in neighborhoods that have a shortage of important commercial, educational, and financial resources (National Fair Housing Alliance, 2012).

One study found that African Americans were twice as likely as Whites, and Latino/as one and a half times as likely as Whites, to be denied a conventional 30-year home loan (cited in Kilborn, 1999). When they do receive home loans, African Americans and Latino/as are significantly more likely than Whites to have to pay substantially higher "subprime" interest rates (cited in Bajaj & Fessenden, 2007; Mui, 2012). Some argue that the discrepancy in rates is justified because borrowers who have poor credit histories are higher risks or because Blacks and Latino/as have fewer assets and therefore have less money for down payments than white borrowers (Blanton, 2007). But the discrepancy is even found between minority and white borrowers with similar credit scores (Bocian, Ernst, & Li, 2006). In 2012, the U.S. Justice Department reached a multimillion-dollar settlement with SunTrust and Bank of America over charges that these institutions imposed loan fees—what some called a "racial surtax"—on black borrowers; white borrowers with similar credit histories and qualifications were not charged these fees (Mui, 2012).

Racial Inequality in the Economic System

Institutional racism is readily apparent throughout the U.S. economy. Consider participation in the labor force. With the exception of Asian Americans, workers of color have always been concentrated in lower-paying jobs. African Americans make up

10.8% of the entire civilian U.S. workforce but only 5.3% of lawyers, 5.3% of physicians, and 5.2% of architects and engineers. Similarly, Latino/as make up 14.5% of the labor force but are underrepresented in the fields of law (3.2%), medicine (6.6%), and architecture/engineering (6.4%; ProQuest Statistical Abstract, 2013). This underrepresentation becomes more acute in the higher echelons of certain professions. For instance, while 17% of attorneys in U.S. law firms are members of ethnoracial minorities, only 5% ever become partners in those firms (cited in Glater, 2006).

Because ethnoracial minorities are occupationally concentrated in low-paying jobs, they are particularly vulnerable to economic downturns. The recent economic recession, for instance, has not hit all races equally. The rate of unemployment for Blacks and Latino/as is consistently higher than that of other groups. In the summer of 2013, the unemployment rate for Blacks was 13.5%, compared with 9.1% for Latino/as, 6.7% for Whites, and 4.3% for Asians (U.S. Bureau of Labor Statistics, 2013c).

Members of ethnoracial minorities can sometimes find their employment opportunities limited or blocked by the institutional practices and beliefs common in certain industries. Take, for instance, the restaurant business. Researchers in one study (Restaurant Opportunities Center of New York, 2009) hired white, black, Asian, and Latino/a people to act as job applicants for advertised server positions in 181 upscale New York City restaurants. The applicants were paired up—one white and one nonwhite—and matched for age, appearance, gender, and work experience. They were also trained to have similar mannerisms and answer questions in similar ways. So theoretically, the only thing distinctive about the two people in a pair was their race. Their arrival at restaurants was staggered so that they showed up about 30 minutes apart. This way the restaurant managers had no way of knowing the "applicants" were part of a study. Overall, white applicants were significantly more likely than applicants of color to have their work experience accepted without probing, to be granted an interview, and to be offered a position. The researchers concluded that this differential treatment was not a result of "a few bad apples" with racist intent. Instead, they identified industry-wide trends and practices as the culprit. For instance, a pervasive "culture of informality" exists in the restaurant business. Although such informality creates a casual, "familylike" work environment, it also creates subjective recruitment and hiring practices that rely on word-of-mouth and friendship networks rather than the formal procedures and explicit hiring criteria that could protect against conscious and unconscious biases and stereotypes.

People of color also remain marginal participants in the economy as owners of their own small businesses. Loan companies usually demand a credit history, some form of collateral, and evidence of potential success before they will lend money to prospective businesses. These are standard practices—and not in and of themselves racist—but they perpetuate racial inequalities because members of groups that have been exploited in the past tend to be poorer and thus have poor credit ratings and no collateral. Admittedly, poor people are greater credit risks than those with economic resources, and businesses in poorer communities must pay more for insurance because of the greater likelihood of theft or property damage. But the higher costs of doing business in a poor community usually make small business loans to minority members even more necessary.

Racial Inequality in the Health Care System

As I pointed out at the beginning of this chapter, the economic and educational advances of ethnoracial minority groups over the past decade or so have been tempered by continuing disparities—and in some cases, worsening disparities—in health and health care (U.S. Department of Health and Human Services, 2012). For example, members of ethnoracial minorities are routinely underrepresented as subjects in research on medical and psychiatric drug treatments (Vedantam, 2005). Members of ethnoracial minorities are also less likely than Whites to have access to health insurance. About 30.1% of Latino/as (especially those from Mexico and Central America) and 19.5% of African Americans lack any kind of health insurance, compared with 11.1% of non-Hispanic whites (DeNavas-Walt, Proctor, & Smith, 2012). As the president of the American Medical Association put it, "When people don't have health insurance, they live sicker and they die younger" (quoted in D. Wilson, 2009a, p. 16).

Ethnoracial health imbalances are most glaring when it comes to the most serious diseases. For instance, a study of heart failure among 5,000 black and white men and women over a 20-year period found that Blacks had a rate 20 times higher than Whites (Bibbins-Domingo, 2009). Although rates of new HIV/AIDS cases have dropped among all groups over the past decade, they remain stubbornly high among some groups. African Americans constitute 42% of all people living with HIV/AIDS in the United States (ProQuest Statistical Abstract, 2013), and young gay black men now account for 45% of all new diagnoses among people under 25 (Doucleff, 2012). HIV/AIDS is the leading cause of death among African Americans between the ages of 25 and 44—ahead of heart disease, cancer, accidents, and homicides (Andriote, 2005).

Sometimes personal stereotyping and bias are to blame for health outcomes. For instance, in one study, doctors described African American patients— no matter what their education and income levels—as less intelligent, less likely to follow medical advice, less likely to participate in rehabilitation, and more likely to abuse alcohol and drugs than white patients (Van Ryn & Burke, 2000). Another study found that doctors often stereotype Asian patients as compliant and "problem free" (cited in American Sociological Association, 2005). When time and medical resources are limited, such beliefs can drive the treatment decisions doctors make.

But we can't simply blame ruthless and bigoted individuals for all racial imbalances in the health care system. Instead, the financial considerations that drive the health care system create a context ripe for institutional racism. Consider racial differences in organ transplants. According to the Organ Procurement and Transplant Network (2013), the 2013 national kidney transplant waiting list consisted of 37.7% Whites and 34% African Americans. (This figure in and of itself is telling: African Americans make up only about 13% of the population yet account for over one third of people in need of kidney transplants.) However, that same year, Whites received 59.7% of all kidney transplants, while African Americans received only 20%. Such a discrepancy is likely linked to hospitals' determination of a candidate's ability to pay before approving an expensive procedure. These policies are sometimes referred to as "green screens" or "wallet biopsies." For example, the total cost of a liver transplant—including preoperative and postoperative care—can run over $570,000 (Transplant Living, 2013). So it's not surprising that most hospitals would screen potential recipients for some kind of evidence up front that their insurance will cover the procedure. Because ethnoracial minorities are less likely than Whites to have medical insurance, they are less likely to receive a referral for transplant surgery (Stolberg, 1998). Financial concerns, not outright racial prejudice, lie at the heart of these policies.

Sometimes the institutional racism underlying threats to people's health is less obvious than shoddy medical care or unethical research. For instance, people in neighborhoods where hazardous waste treatment plants, toxic vacant lots, landfills, and petrochemical plants or other sources of industrial pollution exist are disproportionately exposed to the unhealthful effects of air pollution, water pollution, and pesticides. The decisions on where to place such facilities are usually based not on the ethnoracial makeup of an area but on factors such as the cost of land, population density, and geological conditions. However, because the less desirable residential areas (and hence more desirable industrial areas) are disproportionately inhabited by poor people of color, these decisions have the effect of discriminating against them (Velázquez, 2002). For instance, Native American reservations, which have less stringent environmental regulations than other areas, have been targeted by the U.S. military for stockpiles of nuclear, chemical, and biological weapons and by private companies for solid waste landfills, hazardous waste incinerators, and nuclear waste storage facilities (Hooks & Smith, 2004). When it comes to the federal government cleaning up polluted areas, predominantly white communities see faster action, better results, and stiffer penalties for polluters than do communities where ethnoracial minorities predominate (Bullard, 2001).

People of color make up the majority of residents who live in neighborhoods within two miles of the nation's hazardous waste treatment facilities (Dosomething.org, 2007). The predominantly Latino/a neighborhoods south of Tucson are exposed to twenty times the acceptable levels of the carcinogenic solvent trichloroethylene, and rates of cancer, birth defects, and genetic mutations in those neighborhoods far outpace national averages (Velázquez, 2002). Poor African American communities often have the worst conditions. Several oil refineries and several hundred heavy industrial plants are situated along a stretch of the Mississippi River between Baton Rouge and New Orleans known as "cancer alley" (Koeppel, 1999). At one time, a study of toxic emissions in this area by the Environmental Protection Agency showed that 9 of the 10 major sources of industrial pollution were in predominantly black neighborhoods (Cushman, 1993). Overall, the greater the proportion of black residents in a community, the more likely it is that there will be industrial sources of air pollution within a two-mile radius of people's homes (Perlin, Sexton, & Wong, 1999). Indeed, Blacks are 79% more likely than Whites to live in areas where air pollution levels constitute serious health risks (cited in Little, 2007).

Racial Inequality in the Educational System

In 1954, the U.S. Supreme Court ruled in *Brown v. Board of Education of Topeka* that racially segregated schools were unconstitutional because they were inherently unequal. School districts around the country were placed under court order to desegregate. But within the past 10 years, courts have lifted desegregation orders in at least three dozen school districts around the country. In 2007, the Supreme Court reversed itself and ruled that public school systems could not try to achieve or maintain integration through actions that take explicit account of students' race. At the time of the ruling, such programs were in place in hundreds of school districts around the country (L. Greenhouse, 2007). Some districts have resorted to using integration plans based on children's socioeconomic disadvantage, rather than race, to skirt these restrictions (Bazelon, 2008).

You might assume that the court took this action because desegregation plans based on students' race were no longer needed. However, African American and Latino/a students are actually more isolated from white students today than they were 30 years ago (Orfield & Lee, 2007). The average black and Latino/a student attends a school in which at least 70% of the students are not white. In Southern California, two fifths of Latino/a students and one third of black students attend schools where 90% to 100% of the students are not white (Orfield, Siegel-Hawley, & Kucsera, 2011). In contrast, the average white student attends a school in which almost 80% of the students are white (Orfield & Lee, 2007). In New York City, half of the public schools are over 90% black and Latino/a (Kleinfield, 2012).

And it's not just students who are segregated. In general, white teachers have very little experience with racial diversity. They are likely to teach in schools where almost 90% of their faculty

colleagues and over 70% of the students are white (Frankenberg, 2006).

Schools where the majority of students are not white are likely to be schools where poverty is concentrated. Almost 86% of schools in which black and Latino/a students represent more than 90% of the enrollment are also schools in which more than half the students came from poor families. This is not the case with majority-white schools, which almost always enroll high proportions of middle-class students. Just 12% of schools with less than 10% black and Latino/a students are schools where a majority of students are poor (Frankenberg, 2006).

The racial mix of the classroom has important implications for the quality of the education students receive. Segregation has long been associated with lower academic performance and lack of preparation for the interracial world that awaits students of color after graduation (Kleinfield, 2012). Schools in poor communities lack the financial and therefore educational resources that schools in more affluent communities have (see Chapter 10). For instance, poor school districts are less likely than wealthier districts to offer Advanced Placement (AP) programs. And because poor schools tend to be in minority communities, fewer students of color have access to AP courses. So while African Americans make up 14% of high school graduates, they constitute only 8% of those taking AP exams and 4% of those with passing scores (cited in Lewin, 2009a). Furthermore, poor schools hire fewer teachers with credentials in the subjects they're teaching and have more unstable enrollments, higher dropout rates, and more students with untreated health problems. Despite attempts to rectify the problem, black and Latino/a students still lag behind white and Asian students at all levels of the educational system (ProQuest Statistical Abstract, 2013).

Lack of money isn't the only problem, however. Common institutional assumptions and practices within the educational system can also lead to unequal outcomes. For instance, nationwide, black students are significantly more likely than other students to be subjected to disciplinary practices in school. According to 2012 data from the U.S. Department of Education, black students made up 18% of those enrolled in the schools that were studied, yet they accounted for 35% of one-time suspensions, 46% of multiple suspensions, and 39% of expulsions. Black and Latino/a students, particularly those with disabilities, are also more likely to be subjected to seclusion and physical restraints than Whites who exhibit similar behavioral problems (cited in Lewin, 2012a).

Consider also the widespread use of standardized tests, which are often used as the basis for "tracking" students—that is, as Chapter 5 explains, assigning them to different educational programs based on their intellectual abilities. Standardized tests supposedly measure innate intelligence. Many educational experts agree, however, that these tests are culture bound, tapping an individual's familiarity with a specific range of white, middle-class experiences rather than indicating innate intelligence (Hout & Lucas, 2001). Hence, members of ethnoracial minorities consistently score lower on these tests than Whites (C. Jencks & Phillips, 1998).

Despite the potential for bias, more and more states across the country require high school students to pass a standardized test to graduate. And, as you recall from Chapter 9, the government uses standardized test scores to determine school funding under No Child Left Behind laws. At the same time, though, many universities and other educational organizations have begun seeking alternative ways to determine eligibility for admission. For instance, some universities use a "strivers" approach, whereby college applicants whose SAT scores fall in the borderline range for many selective colleges but who manage to exceed the historical average for students from similar backgrounds are deemed "strivers" and given special consideration (Kahlenberg, 2013). The Texas legislature went a step further, ordering the University of Texas system to accept all students who graduate in the top 10% of their class, regardless of their SAT scores. In 1999, a U.S. district court judge ruled that the NCAA (National Collegiate Athletic Association) could no longer use SAT scores to determine athletic eligibility. The court concluded that the test is culturally biased and therefore discriminates against underprivileged students.

These changes indicate a significant effort to undermine institutional racism in the educational system, which is, according to some sociologists, the largest barrier to racial equality that exists in this country today (Jencks & Phillips, 1998).

Remedies for Institutional Racism

If tomorrow all people in the United States were to wake up harboring absolutely no hatred, prejudice, or animosity toward other groups, institutional racism would still exist. It is part of the structure of society. Thus, it requires a structural solution.

You have already seen how the educational system and the legal system are undertaking limited measures to overcome certain types of institutional racism. However, the most far-reaching structural solution to the problem of institutional racism has been *affirmative action*. Affirmative action is a governmental policy, developed in the early 1960s, that requires organizations to draft a written plan on how they will seek out members of minority groups and women for educational or occupational positions from which they had previously been excluded. One assumption is that past discrimination has left certain people ill equipped to compete with others as equals today. Another assumption is that organizations will not change discriminatory policies unless they are forced to do so.

Contrary to popular belief, employers and university admissions officers are not compelled to institute hiring or admissions quotas or to compromise standards to meet affirmative action goals. They are simply required to gather all relevant information on all applicants, to interview qualified minority candidates, and to make sure underrepresented groups have access to needed information. For instance, companies doing business with the government can set numerical hiring goals based on the availability of qualified candidates in the particular field. However, affirmative action guidelines specify that such goals cannot be quotas:

> Numerical goals do not create set-asides for specific groups, nor are they designed to achieve proportional representation or equal results. Rather, the goal-setting process in affirmative action planning is used to target and measure the effectiveness of affirmative action efforts to eradicate and prevent discrimination . . . . The regulations . . . specifically prohibit quota and preferential hiring and promotions under the guise of affirmative action numerical goals. In other words, discrimination in the selection decision is prohibited. (United States Department of Labor, 2011, p. 1)

For close to half a century, affirmative action policies have been successful in helping members of ethnoracial minorities get ahead (Katel, 2008). Businesses, unions, universities, and local governments accused of discrimination in hiring or admissions have been sued under the 1964 Civil Rights Act. In part because of such actions, more than 40%

of U.S. colleges and universities reported enrollment gains among African Americans and Latino/as during the mid 1990s (cited in Worsnop, 1996). People of color now hold a greater percentage of management, white-collar, and upper-level blue-collar jobs than ever before. Even young black men—historically the most economically disadvantaged and alienated group in the United States—have made some employment gains (Nasar & Mitchell, 1999). Wages and salaries, relative to those of Whites, have also improved somewhat (although, as we've seen, they still lag behind).

Despite its successes, affirmative action remains highly controversial. In one national survey, for example, 93% of respondents agreed that society has an obligation to help hardworking people overcome disadvantages so they can succeed in life. However, when asked whether a fictitious low-income college applicant who happens to be black should be given preference over a high-income student who happens to be white, only 36% agreed (Carnevale & Rose, 2003).

Opposition to affirmative action comes from all directions. Some politically liberal critics, for example, argue that the lives of people for whom affirmative action policies were originally designed—the poorest and most disadvantaged—remain largely unchanged. Although the percentages of Blacks and Whites earning midrange incomes are roughly the same now, there continues to be a large discrepancy at the top and bottom income levels (ProQuest Statistical Abstract, 2013). Top U.S. colleges admit more students of color today than ever before. But these students tend to come from middle- or upper-class backgrounds. For example, of the 8% of Harvard's undergraduates who are black, only a handful are from poor families in which all four grandparents were born in this country and are descendents of slaves (Rimer & Arenson, 2004). In addition, many schools don't provide enough support to ensure that students from historically disadvantaged groups actually graduate. The six-year graduation rate for Native American, Latino/a, and African American students is well below 50%, compared with 60% for white students and 67% for Asian students (National Center for Education Statistics, 2011). Because a college degree is associated with success later in life (bachelor's degree holders earn about twice as much a year as those with high school diplomas), such educational disappointment can have far-reaching social and personal effects.

Conservative critics argue that preferential treatment of any group, even one whose rights have been historically unrecognized, is demeaning to the people it's supposed to help and unfair to everyone else, amounting to a form of "reverse" discrimination. After the Supreme Court's 2007 ruling that barred the use of race in school desegregation plans, the Chief Justice said, "The way to stop discrimination on the basis of race is to stop discriminating on the basis of race" (quoted in L. Greenhouse, 2007, p. 1). Some go further, arguing that affirmative action isn't needed because discrimination is already illegal and nothing more is required. And others maintain that it's not working because the problems that disadvantaged people face have more to do with economics or with inherent character flaws than with race (Fish, 2000). After four decades of such criticisms, many people have come to believe that affirmative action in all its forms should be abolished.

Ironically, however, other modes of preferential treatment continue to operate with virtually no criticism. For instance, applicants who are most likely to receive favored treatment when it comes to college admissions are white, affluent "legacies," or children of alumni. Playing favorites with alumni children is a common practice at almost every private college and many public institutions as well. At some highly selective universities, legacies are twice as likely to be accepted as unconnected applicants with similar or better credentials (Larew, 2003). Some schools reserve a certain number of spaces for legacies. In one recent year at Harvard, marginally qualified white legacies outnumbered all African American, Mexican American, Puerto Rican, and Native American students combined.

Yet all around the country, voters have been approving bans on race-based affirmative action. Five states—California, Florida, Michigan, Nebraska, and Washington—forbid racial preferences for historically underrepresented groups in college admissions as well as employment. The California case has served as a model for other states considering bans on racial preferences. In 1996, voters there approved Proposition 209, a landmark referendum that bans the consideration of race, ethnicity, and sex in the public sector, including college admissions. Prior to the ban, African Americans, Latino/as, and Native Americans made up 23.1% of first-year students in the University of California system. The first year after the ban went into effect, that figure fell to

10.4% (Bronner, 1998b). In California, Blacks and Latino/as make up 42% of the state's population. However, they accounted for only about 15% of first-year admissions in the University of California system in 2006. At the same time, Asians, who make up about 12% of the state's population, accounted for about half of first-year admissions (Egan, 2007). That year, UCLA had its lowest first-year black enrollment in 30 years (Lewin, 2007). In 2013, the U.S. Supreme Court ruled that universities can still consider applicants' race and ethnicity in admissions decisions but only if they can prove their methods are narrowly tailored to reflect a compelling interest in achieving diversity.

Clearly, affirmative action remains a divisive issue. In a society with a tradition of racial stratification, what is the best way to overcome institutional inequality? Does it take discriminating in the opposite direction to "make things equal," or is it enough simply to treat people equally from this point on?

In sum, just because opportunities have been equalized in the present doesn't mean that the accumulated disadvantages of the past have been entirely overcome (Shapiro, 2008). Such is the problem we face today. We can legislate hiring and admission policies that do away with unfair advantages to any group, but is that action enough to address a long history of exclusion? For a long time to come, members of certain groups will continue to be underrepresented in traditionally white positions. Can U.S. citizens achieve complete equality without forcing those who have benefited historically to give up some of their advantages? The answer to this question is complex, controversial, and emotionally charged and will have a great impact on the nature of ethnoracial relations in the United States in the foreseeable future.

GLOBAL PERSPECTIVES ON RACISM

Given the focus of this chapter so far, you might be tempted to conclude that racism and racial inequality are purely U.S. phenomena. Certainly, these problems are very obvious in a society such as the United States, which is so ethnically and racially diverse and which has had such a long history of bitter conflict. But ethnoracial tension is the worldwide rule, not the exception.

Like disadvantaged ethnoracial groups in the United States, minority groups in other countries suffer discrimination that limits their opportunities for success:

- During soccer matches all across Europe, black players are routinely subjected to racist taunts, derisive chanting, monkey noises, and hurled bananas from white fans (Longman, 2006).
- Police in Paris, France, stop young Arab and black men for identity checks in train stations about seven times more often than young Whites (Erlanger, 2009). In 2011, France became the first country in Europe to ban Muslim women from wearing facial veils in public (de La Baume, 2011).
- In Israel, Ashkenazic Jews (who are of European descent) are more likely to be hired and earn more money for the same job than Sephardic Jews (who are of West Asian or North African descent; Rosner, 2013).
- In Eastern European countries such as Slovakia, Romania, Hungary, and the Czech Republic, discrimination against the Roma—or Gypsies—is the norm. They have been despised for centuries as thieving subhumans with no respect for the law and are stereotyped as loud, dirty, indecent, and sloppy (Erlanger, 2000). As a result of such attitudes, Roma suffer disproportionately from poverty, interethnic violence, discrimination, illiteracy, and disease (Wood, 2005). Such treatment is not confined to countries where Romas have long resided. In 2010, France embarked on a major push to reduce crime and illegal immigration by forcibly expelling some Romas and demolishing the camps they live in, even though such mass expulsion based on ethnicity violates European Union law (Erlanger, 2010; Sayre, 2012).
- In Mexico, all citizens are considered legally equal under the country's constitution. Yet it is a society deeply divided along racial lines, particularly between dark-skinned people of Indian descent and light-skinned people of Spanish descent. Ironically, most Mexicans are of mixed lineage, so that nearly all of them could be considered at least part Indian. But Mexicans who are considered Indians are the object of severe discrimination. They have significantly lower educational attainment and occupational status than lighter-skinned Mexicans. In addition, they are more likely to live in poverty (Villarreal, 2010).

Sociologists once believed that the global forces of industrialization and modernization would create ethnoracially diverse societies where people's loyalty would be directed to the national society rather than their racial or ethnic community (Deutsch, 1966). But the opposite has happened. At a time when people from every corner of the globe are linked technologically, economically, and ecologically and when mass migrations mix people from different races, religions, and cultures in unprecedented numbers, racial and ethnic hostilities are at an all-time high (Barber, 1992).

So much ethnic conflict is going on in the world today that we might conclude that hostility between groups is among the most universal of human feelings (Schlesinger, 1992). Look at any online news service and you will see stories of ethnic, religious, or racial conflict: Jews and Palestinians in Israel and Gaza, Buddhists and Muslims in Myanmar, Chechens and Russians in the former Soviet Union, Janjaweed and Darfurians or Sudanese and Nubans in Sudan, Hindus and Muslims or Bengalis and Gurkhas in India, the Han and Uighurs in western China, Lendus and Hemas in the Democratic Republic of the Congo, Georgians and Ossetians in Georgia, Sunis and Shiites in Iraq, Orma and Pokomo in Kenya, Tajiks and Pashtuns in Afghanistan, the Kyrgyz and Uzbeks in Kyrgyzstan, and the Ijaw and Itsekiri in Nigeria. In Great Britain, France, and Germany, loud and sometimes violent resentment occurs between the native born and immigrants from Africa, Eastern Europe, and the Middle East. In the United States, such animosity is likely to be directed toward immigrants from Latin America and Asia (see Chapter 13 for more details). When people feel that their survival is threatened, they often blame others for their problems, particularly newly arrived others who look and act differently. Racial and ethnic hatreds claim the lives of millions of people each year.

But global forces don't just increase ethnoracial tension and inequality; sometimes they help to resolve it. In South Africa, for example, the end of apartheid in the early 1990s was the result of an international boycott. In the 1980s, the global media brought the world pictures and stories of the brutal treatment of South African blacks. When consumers in the United States and other industrial nations stopped buying products from companies that held investments in South Africa, the companies began to withdraw their money. The minority white government felt the sting as domestic economic problems mounted. As a result of these pressures, the white population of South Africa voted to abolish apartheid. Shortly thereafter, the first black president, Nelson Mandela, was elected. In 1996, a new constitution was adopted that officially and peacefully completed South Africa's transition from white supremacy to nonracial democracy. The document renounces the racism of the past and guarantees all South Africans broad freedoms of speech, movement, and political activity (Daley, 1996). Although serious inequalities and animosities remain, the country is moving toward unity and stability.

More recently, we've seen how political developments in one country can reverberate around the globe. Shortly after the 2008 U.S. presidential election, social observers in Europe began to speculate on how Barack Obama's ascendency to the highest office in the land would influence race relations in their own countries. As an editor of a French blog put it, "They always said, 'You think race relations are bad here in France, check out the U.S.' But that argument can no longer stand" (quoted in Erlanger, 2008, p. 1). France's defense minister pondered how Obama's victory might serve as a lesson to the French on dealing with issues of immigration and integration. However, others in Italy, Great Britain, and Germany were more skeptical about the ultimate impact it would have on race relations there. I guess we'll just have to wait and see.

CONCLUSION

On April 16, 1963, the Reverend Martin Luther King Jr., was arrested and jailed for leading a civil rights demonstration in Birmingham, Alabama. At that time, not only were Blacks being subjected to daily doses of fear, violence, and humiliation, but they also had to constantly fight what Dr. King called "a degenerating sense of nobodiness." Torn between the brutal reality of a racist society and a fierce optimism for the future, he wrote from his jail cell,

> Let us all hope that the dark clouds of racial prejudice will soon pass away and the deep fog of misunderstanding will be lifted from our fear-drenched communities and in some not too distant tomorrow the radiant stars of love and brotherhood will shine over our great nation with all of their scintillating beauty. (King, 1991, p. 158)

A half century later, our society—like most societies around the globe—still struggles with the debilitating effects of personal and institutional discrimination based on race, religion, and ethnicity. In the United States, lynchings and state-supported segregation have given way to a form of racism that resides not in bloodshed and flagrant exclusion but in the day-to-day workings of our major social institutions. Despite recent gains, people of color still suffer noticeable disadvantages in economics, education, politics, employment, health care, vulnerability to crime, and many other areas. When opportunities to learn, legislate, and make a living are unequally distributed according to race, all facets of life remain unequal.

Fifty years after racial segregation was ruled unconstitutional in the United States, the complete integration of fundamental social institutions such as public schools, government, and business has only partially been achieved. And some are questioning the very value of integration. One reason race relations are so problematic today is that public debate over the issue confuses personal racism and institutional racism. Different types of racism require different solutions. We cannot put an end to economic deprivation or massive residential segregation by trying to convince people not to stereotype other groups.

I realize that this chapter has been rather depressing. After reading it, you may have a hard time imagining a society without racial or ethnic stratification, one where skin color is about as relevant in determining people's life chances as eye color.

We must remember, however, that differences do not have to imply inequality. The transformation from difference to disadvantage is a social construction. The people of every society decide which differences should be irrelevant and which should be the primary criteria for making social and legal distinctions between groups of people. The good news is that because we construct these differences, we can tear them down.

CHAPTER HIGHLIGHTS

◆ The history of race and ethnicity in U.S. society is an ambivalent one. Famous sayings about equality conflict with the experiences of most ethnoracial minorities—experiences of oppression, violence, and exploitation. Opportunities for life, liberty, and the pursuit of happiness have always been distributed along racial and ethnic lines.

◆ Personal racism is manifested in the form of bigotry, prejudice, and individual acts of discrimination. Quiet racism is expressed not directly but rather indirectly through anxiety about or avoidance of minorities.

◆ Racism can also be found in language and norms prescribing differential treatment of certain groups.

◆ Institutional racism exists in established institutional practices and customs that reflect, produce, and maintain ethnoracial inequality. Institutional racism is more difficult to detect than personal racism and hence is more difficult to stop. Because such racism exists at a level above personal attitudes, it will not disappear simply by reducing people's prejudices.

◆ Ethnoracial conflict is not just an American phenomenon. It is a global reality.

KEY TERMS

affirmative action: Program designed to seek out members of minority groups for positions from which they had previously been excluded, thereby seeking to overcome institutional racism

colorism: Skin color prejudice within an ethnoracial group, most notably between light-skinned and dark-skinned blacks

discrimination: Unfair treatment of people based on some social characteristic, such as race, ethnicity, or sex

ethnicity: Sense of community derived from the cultural heritage shared by a category of people with common ancestry

institutional racism: Laws, customs, and practices that systematically reflect and produce racial and ethnic inequalities in a society, whether or not the individuals maintaining these laws, customs, and practices have racist intentions

panethnic labels: General terms applied to diverse subgroups that are assumed to have something in common

personal racism: Individual expression of racist attitudes or behaviors

prejudice: Rigidly held, unfavorable attitudes, beliefs, and feelings about members of a different group based on a social characteristic such as race, ethnicity, or gender

quiet racism: Form of racism expressed subtly and indirectly through feelings of discomfort, uneasiness, and fear, which motivate avoidance rather than blatant discrimination

race: Category of people labeled and treated as similar because of allegedly common biological traits, such as skin color, texture of hair, and shape of eyes

racial transparency: Tendency for the race of a society's majority to be so obvious, normative, and unremarkable that it becomes, for all intents and purposes, invisible

racism: Belief that humans are subdivided into distinct groups that are different in their social behavior and innate capacities and that can be ranked as superior or inferior

stereotype: Overgeneralized belief that a certain trait, behavior, or attitude characterizes all members of some identifiable group

The Architecture of Inequality

Sex and Gender

Sexism at the Personal Level

The Ideology of Sexism: Biology as Destiny

Institutions and Gender Inequality

The Global Devaluation of Women

A t a women's rights convention held in Seneca Falls, New York, participants created a modified version of the Declaration of Independence. They called it the Declaration of Sentiments and Resolutions. Here are some excerpts from that document:

We hold these truths to be self-evident: that all men and women are created equal. . . . The history of mankind is a history of repeated injuries . . . on the part of man toward woman, having in direct object the establishment of an absolute tyranny over her:

He has compelled her to submit to laws, in the formation of which she had no voice.

He has monopolized nearly all profitable [occupations], and from those she is permitted to follow, she receives but a scanty remuneration. He closes against her all the avenues to wealth and distinction which he considers most honorable to himself.

He has endeavored, in every way that he could, to destroy her confidence in her own powers, to lessen her self-respect, and to make her willing to lead a dependent and abject life.

In view of their social degradation and in view of the unjust laws above mentioned, and because women do feel themselves aggrieved, oppressed, and fraudulently deprived of the most sacred rights, we insist that they have immediate admission to all the rights and privileges which belong to them as citizens of the United States.

The women who wrote this declaration were not the women's liberationists of the 1960s and 1970s or the radical feminists of the 1990s and 2000s. They were participants in the first convention in support of women's rights ever held in the United States—in 1848 (Declaration of Sentiments and Resolutions, 2001, pp. 449–450). We tend to think that women of the past were either content with their second-class status or unaware that it could be otherwise. As you can see from the preceding declaration, though, 166 years ago U.S. women were anything but passive, ignorant victims of discrimination.

Many people are also inclined to believe that the battle against gender inequality has been won. Beginning with the civil rights movement of the 1960s and the so-called sexual revolution of the 1970s, a process of liberation has given contemporary U.S. women opportunities that equal men's. After all, as many U.S. women as men work in the paid labor force; the majority of college students these days are women; and women play a prominent role in business, politics, and entertainment. In 2013, there were 101 women serving in Congress, the most ever, and five states had female governors. Perhaps you will be surprised to learn in this chapter, then, that women's struggle to overcome economic, legal, and social inequality is as relevant in the 21st century as it was in 1848.

In Chapter 5, I discussed the difference between sex and gender and how we learn to become boys and girls and men and women within the appropriate social and cultural contexts. Being placed in a gender category affects everything we do in life. But gender is more than just a source of personal identity that sets societal expectations; it is a location in the stratification system and a major criterion for the distribution of important resources in most societies.

In this chapter, I will address several important questions: What are sexism and gender discrimination? How are they expressed and felt at the personal level? How is inequality based on sex and gender supported by cultural beliefs and symbols? At the institutional level, how is inequality related to family and work roles? What are its legal and economic consequences? And finally, how pervasive is gender inequality around the world?

SEXISM AT THE PERSONAL LEVEL

What do you think of when you hear the word *sexism*? The husband who won't let his wife work outside the home? The construction worker who whistles and shouts vulgar comments at female passersby? Perhaps you think of the woman who mocks men's interpersonal skills or their clumsy attempts at romance? Sexism is all those things, to be sure. But sociologically speaking, **sexism** refers to a system of beliefs that asserts the inferiority of one sex and that justifies discrimination based on gender—that is, on feminine or masculine roles and behaviors. At the personal level, sexism refers to attitudes and behaviors communicated in everyday interaction.

In male-dominated societies, or **patriarchies**, which exist in every quadrant of the globe, cultural beliefs and values typically give higher prestige and importance to men than to women. Throughout such societies, inequality affects girls and women in everything from the perceptions, ambitions, and social interactions of individuals to the organization of social institutions. Above all, gender inequality in a patriarchy provides men with privileged access to socially valued resources and furnishes them with the ability to influence the political, economic, and personal decisions of others. **Matriarchies**, which are societies that give preference to women, are rare in the contemporary world.

Even the most democratic societies tend to be male dominated to some degree. Research on U.S. gender stereotypes, for instance, has shown that they haven't changed all that much over the years (D. L. Berger & Williams, 1991; Eagly & Karau, 2002; Fine, 2010; Rudman & Glick, 1999). Some researchers have shown that women are consistently perceived as more passive, emotional, easily influenced, and dependent than men (Broverman, Vogel, Broverman, Clarkson, & Rosenkrantz, 1972; Deaux & Kite, 1987; Tavris & Offir, 1984). Others have noted the myriad ways personal sexism is expressed in U.S. society, both overtly and subtly, through physical domination, condescending comments, sabotage, and exploitation (Benokraitis & Feagin,

1993). One study found that although some forms of personal sexism are motivated by hostility, others are motivated by benevolence, as when men assume women are helpless and thus feel compelled to offer assistance (Glick & Fiske, 1996). Such attitudes and behaviors not only place women in a lower-status position compared with men but also channel them into less advantageous social opportunities.

Men, of course, aren't the only ones who can be personally sexist. Certainly, some women dislike men, judge them on the basis of stereotypes, hold prejudiced attitudes toward them, objectify them sexually, consider them inferior, and even discriminate against them socially or professionally. We must keep in mind, though, that male sexism occupies a very different place in society from female sexism. The historical balance of power in patriarchal societies has allowed men as a group to subordinate women socially and sometimes legally to protect male interests and privileges. Because men still tend to hold most positions of power, their sexism has more cultural legitimacy, is more likely to be reflected in social institutions, and has more serious consequences than women's sexism.

Sexism and Social Interaction

Everyday social life is fraught with reminders of gender imbalances. Men and women interact with each other a lot, but rarely do these interactions occur between two people who are of equal status (Ridgeway & Smith-Lovin, 1999). The average woman is reminded frequently of her subordinate position, through subtle—and sometimes not so subtle—ways. Men often have a hard time understanding women's reactions to personal encounters between the sexes. Just as white people enjoy racial transparency (see Chapter 11), members of the dominant sex take for granted the social arrangements that serve their interests.

For example, consider the following tongue-in-cheek quote from a female newspaper columnist:

By whistling and yelling at attractive but insecure young men, we women may actually help them feel better about themselves, and give them new appreciation of their bodies. Some might say women were descending to the level of male street-corner oafs, but I'm willing to take that risk. If, with so little effort, I can bring joy to my fellow man, then I am willing

to whistle at cute guys going down the street. (Viets, 1992, p. 5)

If you're a man, you may wonder why the columnist is bothering to make fun of "wolf whistles." The answer simply is that this behavior means different things when directed at men versus women. Unsolicited sexual attention may be an enjoyable, esteem-enhancing experience for men because it doesn't have the weight of a long tradition of subordination attached to it; nor is it linked in any way to the threat of violence. Men aren't subjected to **objectification**—that is, to being treated like objects rather than people—in the same way that women are. Sure, women gawk at and swoon over good-looking men from time to time (just watch reruns of *Sex and the City* sometime). But men's entire worth is rarely condensed into a quick and crude assessment of their physical appearance. For women, who must often fight to be taken seriously in their social, private, and professional lives, whistles and lewd comments serve as a reminder that their social value continues to be based primarily on their looks.

The implicit, nonverbal messages of social interaction—body movements, facial expressions, posture—also have more serious implications and consequences for women than for men. For example, femininity is typically gauged by how little space women take up; masculinity is judged by men's expansiveness and the strength of their gestures. Women's bodily demeanor tends to be restrained and restricted (Henley, 1977). What is typically considered "ladylike"—crossed legs, folded arms—is also an expression of submission. Men's freedom of movement—feet on the desk, legs spread, straddling a chair—conveys power and dominance. Such interactional norms place women who are in authoritative positions in a no-win situation. If, on the one hand, they meet cultural definitions of femininity by being passive, polite, submissive, and vulnerable, they fail to meet the requirements of authority. If, on the other hand, they exercise their authority by being assertive, confident, dominant, and tough, their femininity may be called into question (J. L. Mills, 1985).

Women are also routinely exposed to assorted forms of sexual harassment—unwelcome leers, comments, requests for sexual favors, and unwanted physical contact—in a variety of institutional settings, from schools to workplaces. According to the American Association of University Women (2013),

56% of all girls in Grades 7 to 12 experience verbal, physical, or electronic sexual harassment in a given year and 87% say it had a negative effect on them. In addition, about 30% of teenage girls are bullied at school and another 7.2% report being cyber-bullied (ProQuest Statistical Abstract, 2013). And nearly two thirds of female college students experience sexual harassment at some point during their college careers, though fewer than 10% tell a university official and an even smaller number file an official complaint (C. Hill & Silva, 2006).

The U.S. Equal Employment Opportunity Commission (2012) resolved more than 12,500 cases of workplace sexual harassment in 2011 to the tune of over $52 million in compensation to victims. But these figures obviously don't include incidents that are never reported. According to one national poll, perhaps as many as one third of female workers are sexually harassed on the job (cited in Sexual Harassment Support, 2009).

Some occupations are particularly vulnerable to sexual harassment and assault. For instance, sexual affronts from male guests are an everyday safety hazard for female hotel workers (S. Greenhouse, 2011). It is so common, in fact, that hotel managers routinely provide their housekeeping staff with a list of safety precautions, for example, to always carry a panic button (or mace) in your pocket, always clean rooms in tandem with another housekeeper, and always prop the door open when cleaning a room (J. Bernstein & Ellison, 2011; McGeehan, 2012).

From a conflict perspective, cases of sexual harassment are expressions of and attempts to reinforce positions of dominance and power (Uggen & Blackstone, 2004). Indeed, the vast majority of harassment cases involve male assertions of power over women. But women aren't the only victims. Sometimes an overbearing, sexually aggressive female boss may harass a male subordinate; but more commonly, men are victimized when other men create a hostile environment through bullying, hazing, sexual insults, and other boorish behaviors. According to the Equal Employment Opportunity Commission (2012), sexual harassment charges filed by men increased from 11.6% of all cases in 1997 to 16.3% of all cases in 2011. Sometimes men are victimized in settings where you'd least expect it. The Pentagon estimates that close to 14,000 male service members experienced unwanted sexual contact in 2012, mostly by other men (Dao, 2013).

As troubling as this figure is, however, women face a far less welcoming and more dangerous environment in the military. A survey conducted by the U.S. Department of Defense (2013) found that 6.1% of active female service members said they had experienced sexual assault at least once in the past year. Perhaps as many as one in three female soldiers has been sexually assaulted at some point during their military careers (cited in Risen, 2012). And such figures don't even include the countless number of female soldiers who regularly face degradation, hostility, and loneliness instead of the camaraderie every soldier depends on for comfort and survival. Many female military personnel end up waging what amounts to two wars—one against the enemy and one against their fellow soldiers (Benedict, 2009).

Sexual Orientation

Prejudices expressed at the personal level often combine gender and sexual orientation. For many decades, gays and lesbians have been rejected, ridiculed, and condemned on moral, religious, criminal, or even psychiatric grounds. Today, homosexuals and bisexuals—as well as people assumed to be or accused of being gay or bisexual—routinely experience discrimination, interpersonal rejection, or even violence (Herek, 2000a). Such sexual prejudice varies along gender lines. According to one study (Herek, 2000b), women tend to express fewer antigay attitudes, beliefs, and behaviors than men. But the object of attitudes is also gender specific. Heterosexual men tend to have more negative attitudes toward and feel more discomfort around gay men than they feel toward lesbians. Heterosexual women, in contrast, hold similar attitudes toward gay men and lesbians. Demonstrating one's heterosexuality and one's conformity to traditional gender roles seems to be of greater concern to men than to women, which may explain the heightened male hostility toward gay men.

Often the attitudes are unabashedly virulent. According to the Federal Bureau of Investigation (2012), there were close to 1,230 documented cases of antihomosexual hate crimes in 2011. Several years ago, a gay college student in Wyoming, Matthew Shepard, was pistol-whipped, tied to a fence, and left to die. At his funeral, protestors from a church in Topeka, Kansas, held up signs reading "God Hates Fags!" The church's website had a picture of Matthew depicted burning in hell. The same website had a similar photo of a lesbian who was mauled to death by two dogs a few years earlier. Above her picture, it read "God used literal dogs to kill a figurative dog." More recently, nine attackers lured a 30-year-old gay man into a house, where they stripped him, tied him to a chair, burned his nipples and penis with a cigarette, whipped him with a chain, and sodomized him with a baseball bat while shouting antigay slurs at him (M. Wilson & Baker, 2010). According to one researcher, gay, lesbian, and bisexual youth are about five times as likely as heterosexuals to attempt suicide (Hatzenbuehler, 2011). In 2010, a rash of suicides among harassed and bullied gay teenagers in New Jersey, California, Texas, and Indiana focused national attention on the problem. In one Minnesota school district alone, four gay and lesbian teenagers committed suicide in 2011 (Erdely, 2012).

Harassment can also occur in settings purported to be more tolerant, such as universities. In a nationwide study of gay, lesbian, and bisexual college students, 89% had been the recipient of derogatory remarks, 49% had received verbal threats and 2% had been physically assaulted. Close to 20% feared for their physical safety because of their sexual orientation (Rankin, 2003). These students are not only more likely than heterosexuals to be harassed by fellow students but also are at greater risk of being harassed by teachers and school employees (C. Hill & Silva, 2006).

Violence Against Women

The epitome of sexual domination expressed at the personal level is sexual violence. Forcible rape and other forms of sexual assault exist throughout the world, in the most democratic societies as well as in the most repressive.

In the United States, rape is the most frequently committed but least reported violent crime. Less than 40% of these crimes ever come to the attention of the police—compared with 68% of robberies and 58% of aggravated assaults (Planty, Langton, Krebs, Berzofsky, & Smiley-McDonald, 2013; Truman & Rand, 2010). According to the National Crime Victimization Survey—an annual assessment of crime victimization carried out by the U.S. Bureau of Justice Statistics (Planty et al., 2013)—more than 270,000 women over the age of 12 said they'd been raped or sexually assaulted in 2008, more than double the roughly 126,000 incidents of rape and sexual

assault officially reported to the police in a given year (ProQuest Statistical Abstract, 2013).

Rape is also the most personal of violent crimes. In 78% of rapes and sexual assaults, the victim knows the attacker (Planty et al., 2013). On college campuses, where about 3% of college women experience a completed or attempted rape during a typical college year, 90% of the victims know their attackers (U.S. Bureau of Justice Statistics, 2001).

Rape as a Means of Social Control

According to the conflict perspective, stratification along sex and gender lines has long distorted our understanding of rape. Throughout history, women have been viewed socially and legally as the property of men, as either daughters or wives. Thus, in the past, rape was defined as a crime against men or, more accurately, against men's property (Siegel, 2004). Any interest a husband took in another man sexually assaulting his wife probably reflected a concern with his own status, the loss of his male honor, and the devaluation of his sexual possession. Even when women are not seen as men's property, their lives are controlled by rape and sexual assault. Lesbians in South Africa are sometimes raped by men who believe it will "cure" them of their sexual orientation. These violent acts are known as "corrective rapes." Lesbians are sexually assaulted twice as often as heterosexual women (Hunter-Gault, 2012). As one woman put it,

> We get insults every day, beatings if we walk alone, you are constantly reminded that . . . you deserve to be raped, they yell, "if I rape you then you will go straight . . . you will buy skirts and start to cook because you will have learned how to be a real woman." (quoted in ActionAid, 2009, p. 15)

Around the world, rape is a time-tested wartime tactic of terror, revenge, and intimidation, not only against female victims but also against husbands, sons, and fathers whose idea of honor is connected to their ability to protect "their" women (Amnesty International, 2004; Enloe, 1993; Sengupta, 2004). In Somalia, for example, the militant group Al-Shabab routinely seizes and gang rapes women and girls as a way of supporting its reign of terror in the southern part of the country (Gettleman, 2011). In the Democratic Republic of the Congo, bands of soldiers have been "waging a war of rape and destruction against women" since the 1980s (Herbert, 2009, p. A17). Congolese girls and women of all ages have been publicly gang raped, had their reproductive organs deliberately destroyed, and been violated with loaded guns. In one four-day stretch during 2010, gangs of marauding Congolese soldiers raped at least 200 women in one village, despite the fact that United Nations peacekeepers were based just up the road (Gettleman, 2010). The devastation of these atrocities extends beyond the psychological humiliation, physical wounds, and deaths of individual victims. Entire families and neighborhoods are traumatized when husbands are forced to watch their wives being raped; parents, their daughters; or children, their mothers.

According to some feminist sociologists, men have used rape and the threat of rape throughout history to exert control over women (Brownmiller, 1975). The mere existence of rape limits women's freedom of social interaction, denies them the right of self-determination, and makes them dependent on and ultimately subordinate to men (Griffin, 1986).

The fear of rape goes beyond simply making life terrifying and uncomfortable for women. It also can restrict their economic opportunities. Women may avoid some neighborhoods with affordable housing because of potential danger. If a woman has a job that requires night work, she may be forced to buy a car to avoid walking at night or using public transportation. The threat of sexual assault restricts where and when she is able to work, thereby limiting her money-earning choices and perhaps keeping her financially dependent on others.

Women are also harmed by the larger cultural ideology surrounding rape. I think most of us are inclined to believe that men who rape must be insane or abnormally violent. All one has to do to avoid being raped, then, is to avoid strange/dangerous guys. However, rapists as a group have not been shown to be any more disturbed than nonrapists (Griffin, 1986; Warshaw, 1988). In fact, most rapists are quite "normal" by usual societal standards. As I mentioned earlier, the vast majority of rapes involve people the victim knows—friends, acquaintances, classmates, coworkers, or relatives. But when rape is generally perceived to be perpetrated by psychologically defective strangers, it doesn't implicate the dominant culture or established social arrangements. In other words, rape isn't considered the fault of society; it's the fault of flawed men who can't abide by society's

rules. This assumption may explain why date or acquaintance rape, marital rape, and other forms of sexual violence that don't fit the typical image have, until quite recently, been ignored or trivialized.

We must therefore examine the crime of rape within a broader cultural context that encourages certain types of behavior between men and women (S. Jackson, 1995). When we do so, rape becomes less an act of deviance and more an act of overconformity to cultural expectations; less an act committed by abnormal individuals and more an act of "normal" men taking cultural messages about power and assertiveness to their violent extreme. As one author wrote over two decades ago, rape is the "all-American crime," involving precisely those characteristics traditionally regarded as desirable in American men: strength, power, domination, and control (Griffin, 1989).

Victim Blaming

Globally, cultural beliefs about gender, sexuality, and intimacy influence societal and legal responses to rape and rape victims (Faleiro, 2013; Morgan, 1996; Rubin, 2011):

- In Afghanistan, a married woman who is raped can be charged with adultery and imprisoned; a condition of release is that she marry the man who raped her. In Colombia, a man who rapes a woman—whether he knows her or not—can be absolved of all charges if he simply offers to marry her.
- In Senegal, single women who are rape victims may be killed by their families because as nonvirgins they can no longer command a high dowry; a married woman who's been raped may be killed by her "dishonored" husband.
- In Iran, because Islamic tradition forbids the execution of virgins, any woman condemned to die must first lose her virginity through rape.
- Many political leaders in India attribute that country's increasing incidence of rape to women's use of cell phones and their inclination to go out at night. Said one, "Just because India achieved freedom at midnight does not mean that women can venture out after dark" (quoted in Faleiro, 2013, p. A19).

Arguably, the United States has a more sympathetic reaction to rape victims. But the legal response here still tends to be consistent with men's interests, focusing on women's complicity or blameworthiness.

In rape cases, unlike any other crime, victims typically must prove their innocence rather than the state having to prove the guilt of the defendant. Many women who have been victimized come to the conclusion that reporting their experiences would, at best, be embarrassing and useless (Sanday, 1996). As one psychologist put it, "there is no other crime I can think of where the victim is more victimized" (quoted in Brody, 2011, p. D7).

The conflict perspective provides one explanation for the widespread tendency to hold women responsible for their own victimization: The common definition of rape is based on a traditional model of sexual intercourse—penile-vaginal penetration—rather than on the violent context within which the act takes place. The primary focus on the sexual component of the crime has long required that information about the intimate circumstances of the act and about the relationship between the people involved be taken into consideration—all of which tends to put female rape victims at a disadvantage during criminal proceedings. Research consistently shows that observers attribute more blame to the victims and minimize the seriousness of the assault when the perpetrator is an acquaintance, date, or steady partner (S. T. Bell, Kuriloff, & Lottes, 1994). One study of convicted rapists found that those who assaulted strangers received longer prison sentences than those who were acquaintances or partners of their victims, regardless of the amount of force used or physical injury to the victim (McCormick, Maric, Seto, & Barbaree, 1998).

Rape victims are often expected to provide clear evidence that they were "unwilling" and tried to resist. Anything short of vigorous and repeated resistance can still call the victim's motives into question. Indeed, research suggests that police, prosecutors, and juries are less likely to believe allegations of rape if there is no evidence of violence (McEwan, 2005).

No other serious crime requires that the victim prove lack of consent. People aren't asked if they wanted their house broken into or if they enticed someone to beat them up and steal their wallet. Yet if women cannot prove that they resisted or cannot find someone to corroborate their story, consent (or even latent desire) may be presumed (Siegel, 2004). A few years ago, while in a hospital waiting room after being brutally raped, a woman from Madison, Wisconsin, was required to submit a "statement of nonconsent" swearing that she hadn't given her

knife-wielding assailant permission to rape, cut, and rob her (Lueders, 2006).

Certain states have reconsidered the issue of what constitutes consent. In most states a woman may withdraw her consent to have sex at any time, and if the man continues, he is committing rape. However, in North Carolina, once a woman gives consent, she cannot rescind it. Such an understanding of consent rests on the belief that at a certain point during arousal, a man loses the ability to stop (Lee-St. John, 2007).

Public perceptions are slow to change. Many people regard female rape victims as at least partly to blame if they put themselves in risky situations, for instance, by behaving seductively, wearing "provocative" clothing, drinking too much, or telling dirty jokes. In one study, male and female high school students were given a list of statements and asked to indicate the extent to which they agreed with them (Kershner, 1996). Of the male and female subjects, 52% agreed that most women fantasize about being raped by a man; 46% felt that women encourage rape by the way they dress; and 53% said they felt that some women provoke men into raping them. Moreover, 31% agreed that many women falsely report rapes, and 35% felt that the victim should be required to prove her innocence during a rape trial. Research has linked such attitudes to a heightened risk of rape and sexual assault occurring (Ching & Burke, 1999) as well as increased likelihood of holding rape victims responsible (Frese, Moya, & Megías, 2004).

The important sociological point of these findings is that many men and even some women don't always define violent sexual assault as a form of victimization. They think it is either something women bring on themselves or something men understandably do under certain circumstances.

Some progress is being made regarding cultural perceptions of rape. Myths are being debunked, the violent sexual exploitation of women in the media is being protested, and the rules governing admissible evidence in rape trials are being changed. Rates of rape and sexual assault have dropped steadily since the mid 1990s (Planty et al., 2013). Moreover, the federal government has recently sought to expand the definition of rape to include forcible anal and oral penetration and penetration with an object or body part other than the penis. And in 2013, the U.S. Department of Justice (2013) issued new victim-centered protocols to improve the way rape victims are treated by first responders and hospital personnel. However, as long as we live in a culture that objectifies women and glorifies male assertiveness, we will continue to face the problem of sexual violence.

THE IDEOLOGY OF SEXISM: BIOLOGY AS DESTINY

The domination of one group over another is always endorsed by a set of beliefs that explains and justifies that domination. You saw in the previous chapter that racism is often justified by the belief in innate racial inferiority. With sexism, it is the belief that men and women are biologically and naturally different that has been used historically to rationalize unequal treatment (Fine, 2010).

For 19th- and early-20th-century physicians, few "truths" were more incontestable than the fact that women were the products and prisoners of their anatomy. One French scientist noted a century ago that women have smaller brains than men, which explained their "fickleness, inconstancy, absence of thought and logic, and incapacity to reason" (quoted in Angier & Chang, 2005, p. A1). Even today, there's no shortage of books purporting to show that female tendencies in self-control, risk taking, intuition, empathy, anxiety, aggression, emotions, and even decision making can all be traced to the structure and function of their brains (Baron-Cohen, 2003; Brizendine, 2006; Mansfield, 2006).

Likewise, women's reproductive systems have been the object of scientific attention and concern for centuries (Scull & Favreau, 1986). Everything supposedly known about women that made them different from men—their subordinate place in society, their capacity for affection, their love of children and aptitude for child rearing, their "preference" for domestic work, and so on—could be explained by their uterus and ovaries (Ehrenreich & English, 1979; Scull & Favreau, 1986). Scholars in the past warned that young women who studied too much were struggling against nature, would badly damage their reproductive organs, and would perhaps even go insane in the process (Fausto-Sterling, 1985). So the exclusion of women from higher education was not only justifiable but necessary for health reasons and for the long-term good of society.

Some structural-functionalist sociologists have also used the bodily differences between men and women to explain gender inequality. The fact that men tend to be physically stronger and that women bear and nurse children has created many culturally recognized sex-segregated social roles, especially at work and in the family (Parsons & Bales, 1955). This specialization of roles is the most effective way to maintain societal stability, structural functionalists believe. By giving birth to new members, by socializing very young children, and by providing affection and nurturing, women make invaluable contributions to society. The common occupations women have traditionally had outside the home—teacher, nurse, day care provider, maid, social worker, and so on—tend therefore simply to be extensions of their "natural" tendencies.

Similarly, men's physical characteristics have been presumed to better suit them for the roles of economic provider and protector of the family. And if it's true that men are "naturally endowed" with traits such as strength, assertiveness, competitiveness, and rationality, then they are best qualified to enter the serious and competitive world of work and politics (Kokopeli & Lakey, 1992). Sociologist Steven Goldberg (1999) argues that because male rule and male dominance seem to characterize the vast majority of human societies, this gender difference must be rooted in evolutionary biology.

The problem with depicting masculinity and femininity as natural, biological phenomena is that it confuses sex with gender. The underlying assumption of sexist ideology—that gender is as "unchangeable" as sex—overlooks extensive similarities between the sexes and extensive variations within each sex. The distributions of men and women on most personality and behavioral characteristics generally overlap (Carothers, 2013). For instance, men as a group do tend to be more aggressive than women as a group. But these differences are a matter of degree, not kind. Hence some women are much more aggressive than the average man, and some men are much less aggressive than the average woman. Indeed, social circumstances may have a greater impact on aggressive behavior than any innate, biological traits. Some studies show that when women are rewarded for behaving aggressively, they can be just as violent as men (Hyde, 1984).

Furthermore, the reliance on biology ignores the wide cultural and historical variation in conceptions of masculinity and femininity. For instance, although every known society has a division of labor based on sex, what's considered "men's work" and "women's work" differs. In most societies, men fish, hunt, clear land, and build boats and houses, but in some societies, women regularly perform these tasks. In most societies, women do the cooking; but in some societies, cooking is typically a male responsibility (Eitzen & Baca Zinn, 1991).

Although women have become prominent in the U.S. workforce, many people still believe that they are less capable than men of performing certain tasks outside the home. Some still may find female doctors or lawyers unusual. Legislators and military officials continue to debate the role of female soldiers in direct ground combat. The controversy in several churches over whether women should be ordained as ministers and priests illustrates the depth and intensity of people's feelings about gender-appropriate career pursuits.

Moreover, the qualities we consider naturally feminine are usually seen as less socially valuable than those considered masculine. Girls do suffer sometimes when their behavior is considered "boylike." But accusing a boy of acting like a girl is the ultimate schoolyard insult. Even when they get older, many men can be easily whipped into aggressive responses by accusations of femininity, such as when coaches call their male players "girls" or "ladies."

The biological rationale for gender inequality—what one psychologist calls "neurosexism" (Fine, 2010)—is difficult to justify these days. Technological advances—including bottled baby formula, contraceptives that give women more choices over childbearing, and innovations that lessen the need for sheer physical strength—have made it possible for women and men to fulfill many of the same responsibilities. Nevertheless, as long as people believe that gender-linked roles and societal contributions are determined by nature, they will continue to accept inequality in women's and men's opportunities, expectations, and outcomes. If people consider it "natural" for women to play nurturing, weak, and dependent roles, then limiting women to such positions seems neither unfair nor oppressive.

INSTITUTIONS AND GENDER INEQUALITY

The subordination of women that is part of the everyday workings of social institutions (or

institutional sexism) has far greater consequences for women as a group than personal expressions of sexism. When sexism in social institutions becomes part of the ongoing operation of large-scale organizations, it perpetuates and magnifies women's disadvantages, making social equality all the more difficult to attain. But not only can social institutions be sexist, they can also be gendered. In other words, institutions and organizations segregate, exploit, and exclude women solely on the basis of their physical characteristics and then compound the impact of their sexism by incorporating values and practices based on traditional expectations for women and men (Kimmel, 2004).

Masculinized Institutions

More often than not, institutions incorporate masculine values—which is not surprising because, historically, men have developed, dominated, and interpreted most institutions. Take competitive sports, for example. Most of us would agree that to be successful, an athlete must be aggressive, strong, and powerful—attributes typically associated with masculinity. By celebrating these traits, a sport such as football symbolically declares itself an arena that women cannot or should not enter (except, of course, as spectators, cheerleaders, or sideline reporters).

But even sports such as gymnastics and figure skating, which have traditionally valued more "feminine" traits like grace, beauty, and balance, have made their judging criteria more masculine. For a woman to be a world-class gymnast or skater these days, she must also be physically strong and exhibit explosive acrobatic power. Indeed, the popularity of women's team sports in this country coincides with the increasing presence of traditionally male traits such as physical strength and competitive vigor in female athletes.

Similarly, most bureaucracies in institutional areas such as business, politics, and the military operate according to taken-for-granted masculine principles. Successful leaders and organizations are usually portrayed as aggressive, goal oriented, competitive, and efficient—all characteristics associated with masculinity in this society. Rarely are strong governments, prosperous businesses, or efficient military units described as supportive, nurturing, cooperative, kind, and caring (Acker, 1992). When institutions are gendered in these ways, everyday inequalities become apparent.

Gender Inequality in Health and Health Care

Gender inequality has created some curious discrepancies in the way the medical establishment treats men and women. For instance, prior to the health care reform bill signed into law in 2010, it was legal in most states for insurance companies selling individual policies—those for people who don't have group insurance coverage through their employers—to charge women higher premiums than men for the same medical coverage . . . a practice known as "gender rating." The difference in price ranged from 4% to 48% and collectively cost women about $1 billion annually. Only 14 states currently ban this practice; in those that don't, 92% of best-selling plans charge women higher premiums than men (National Women's Law Center, 2013). The obvious justification for this practice is the belief that women use the health care system more than men do because of all the medical procedures associated with childbirth. But discrepancies exist even for policies that don't cover maternity costs (Pear, 2008). The Department of Health and Human Services has vowed to end the practice of "gender rating" when health care reforms go into effect in 2014, raising hopes that the health care–related cost of being a woman will be reduced.

Ironically, in every developed country, men tend to have more health problems and a shorter life expectancy than women (Read & Gorman, 2010). They occupy more physically demanding jobs and engage in more dangerous physical activity. Hence, they've historically been at greater risk for various bodily injuries and stress-related ailments. According to figures from the U.S. Bureau of the Census (ProQuest Statistical Abstract, 2013), men also have higher rates of cancer (excluding breast, cervical, and ovarian types) than women do.

Yet women have historically been the focus of intrusive medical attention more than men (B. K. Rothman, 1984). Women are more likely than men to undergo surgical and diagnostic procedures. Indeed, the three most common short-stay surgical procedures for women—repair of lacerations during childbirth, cesarean sections, and hysterectomy—all deal with female anatomy and physiology. The three most common short-stay procedures for men—cardiac catheterization, reduction of fractures, and coronary artery bypass grafting—are not sex specific (ProQuest Statistical Abstract, 2013). Women are also more likely than men to receive diagnoses for conditions that have unclear causes, like fibromyalgia and chronic fatigue syndrome (Edwards, 2013). Not surprisingly, physicians often specialize in *women's* health care, but rarely do they specialize in *men's*. Obstetricians and gynecologists deal exclusively with the reproductive and sexual matters of female patients. There are no comparable specialties of medicine devoted solely to men's reproductive health (urologists address men's reproductive issues, but they also see female patients).

Normal biological events in women's lives—menstruation, pregnancy, childbirth, and menopause—have long been considered problematic conditions in need of medical intervention. For instance, the American Psychiatric Association (2013) now officially recognizes a psychiatric diagnosis called "premenstrual dysphoric disorder" in its official manual of mental disorders. Indisputably, many women around the world experience irritability, moodiness, and other symptoms related to hormonal cycles. The issue, however, is whether these symptoms ought to be labeled as a medical and/or mental problem (Lander, 1988). To do so not only promotes the selling of drugs to healthy women (C. A. Bailey, 1993; Figert, 1996) but fosters the belief that women, biologically frail and emotionally erratic because of their hormones, cannot be allowed to work too hard or be trusted in positions of authority (Fausto-Sterling, 1985).

Given the special attention women's health problems receive, it's ironic that, outside obstetrics and gynecology, research on women's general health needs has been rather limited. More than 20 years ago, the U.S. Public Health Service reported that a lack of medical research on women limited our understanding of their health concerns (B. K. Rothman & Caschetta, 1999). The reason often given for their exclusion from medical studies was that their menstrual cycles complicated the interpretation of research findings. In addition, medical researchers have historically been reluctant to perform research on women of childbearing age for fear that exposing them to experimental manipulations might harm their reproductive capabilities. In fact, in the 1970s and 1980s, federal policies and guidelines actually called for the blanket exclusion of women of childbearing potential from certain types of drug research. That meant that any woman who was physically capable of becoming pregnant, regardless of her own desire to do so, could be excluded. Concerns were less about threats to women's health than they were about the possibility of liability if reproductive damage due to exposure to the experimental drug occurred (J. A. Hamilton, 1996).

The exclusion of women from medical research became so problematic that Congress passed a law in 1993 stipulating that women must be included in clinical trials in numbers sufficient to provide evidence of the different ways men and women respond to drugs, surgical treatments, and changes in diet or behavior. Nevertheless, a study in 2000 found that many researchers were not complying with the law (cited in Pear, 2000). In 2003, the Agency for Healthcare Research and Quality reported that research on coronary heart disease (CHD) still either excludes women entirely or includes them only in limited numbers. Consequently, the therapies used to treat women with CHD—a disease that kills 250,000 women a year—are still based on studies conducted primarily on middle-aged men (cited in "Research Findings Affirm," 2003).

Gender Inequality in Families

Much of the inequality women face revolves around the traditional view of their family role: keepers of the household and producers, nurturers, and socializers of children. Although in other times and places, women have had different levels of responsibility for homemaking, they have always been responsible for reproduction.

One of the major consequences of the industrial revolution of the 18th and 19th centuries was the separation of the workplace and the home. Prior to industrialization, most countries were primarily agricultural. People's lives centered on the farm, where husbands and wives were partners not only in making a home but also in making a living (Vanek, 1980). Farm couples were interdependent; each person needed the other for survival. It was taken for granted that women provided for the family along with men (J. Bernard, 1981). Although the relationship between husbands and wives on the farm was never entirely equal—wives still did most if not all of the housekeeping and family care—complete male dominance was offset by women's indispensable contributions to the household economy (Vanek, 1980).

With the advent of industrialization, things began to change. New forms of technology and the promise of new financial opportunities and a good living drew people (mostly men) away from the farms and into cities and factories. For the first time in history, the family economy in some societies was based outside the household. Women no longer found themselves involved in the day-to-day supervision of the family's business as they had once been. Instead, they were consigned to the only domestic responsibilities that remained necessary in an industrial economy: the care and nurturing of children and the maintenance of the household. Because this work was unpaid and because visible goods were no longer being produced at home, women quickly found their labor devalued in the larger society (Hareven, 1992).

However, as we saw in Chapter 7, men weren't the only ones who left home each day to work in factories. At the turn of the century, hundreds of thousands of children worked in mines, mills, and factories (Coontz, 1992). And contrary to popular belief, one fifth of U.S. women worked outside the home in 1900, especially women of color (Staggenborg, 1998).

Today, the devaluation of "women's work" is the result of a separation of the public and private spheres (Sidel, 1990). As long as men dominate the public sphere—the marketplace and the government—they will wield greater economic and political power within society and also be able to translate that power into authority at home. "Women's work" within the relatively powerless private sphere of the home will continue to be hidden and undervalued.

According to the conflict perspective, the problem is not that housewives don't work; it's that they work for free outside the mainstream economy, in which work is strictly defined as something one is paid to do (Ciancanelli & Berch, 1987; Voyandoff, 1990).

Ironically, however, domestic work is actually invaluable to the entire economic system. If a woman were to be paid the minimum going rate for all her labor as mother and housekeeper, including childcare, transportation, housecleaning, laundry, cooking, bill paying, and grocery shopping, her yearly salary would be comparable to that of women who are employed full time, year round. One recent study found that if we apply average hourly wage rates to the typical daily amounts of childcare mothers of children under 12 provide, a low-end estimate of the monetary value of this work is about $33,000 a year (Folbre & Yoon, 2006). But because societal and family power is a function of who brings home the income, such unpaid work does not afford women the prestige it might if it were paid labor.

Despite significant shifts in U.S. attitudes toward gender roles and the accelerated entry of women into the paid labor force in the past few decades, housework continues to be predominantly female (U.S. Bureau of Labor Statistics, 2013a). Husbands do play a more prominent role in the raising of children than they did two decades ago, and they've increased their contribution to housework somewhat (Bianchi, Robinson, & Milkie, 2006), especially when compared with men in other industrialized countries (Fuwa, 2004). But the household work that husbands do is typically quite different from the work that wives do. Women's tasks tend to be essential to the daily functioning of the household (Fuwa, 2004); men's chores are typically infrequent, irregular, or optional:

> They take out the garbage, they mow the lawns, they play with children, they occasionally go to the supermarket or shop for household durables, they paint the attic or fix the faucet; but by and large, they do not launder, clean, or cook, nor do they feed, clothe, bathe, or transport children. These . . . most time-consuming activities . . . are exclusively the domain of women. (Cowan, 1991, p. 207)

From a structural-functionalist perspective, one could argue that traditional gendered household responsibilities actually reflect an equitable, functional, interdependent division of labor. That is, the husband works in the paid labor force and supports the family financially; the wife takes care of the household work and childcare. Each person provides essential services in exchange for those provided by the other. But research in this area indicates that the gender discrepancy in housework responsibilities does not diminish when women work full time outside the home. On average, working women spend about 19 hours per week on housework, while men spend only about 10 hours (Bianchi et al., 2006). The hours that women spend on housework are down from 35 hours in the mid 1960s, and men have increased their contribution from 4 hours per week, but still men contribute only half as much time as women do to the maintenance of the household. According to a survey conducted by the U.S. Bureau of Labor Statistics (2013a), women devote three times as much of their day to housework and food preparation and twice as much to childcare as men do.

Because working women continue to be primarily responsible for housework, they often end up working what amounts to two full-time jobs. Even when a husband is unemployed, he does less housework than a wife who puts in a 40-hour week. Indeed, recently laid-off men tend to take on fewer household tasks—rather than more—when they lose their jobs. In contrast, laid-off women double the time they spend on childcare and household chores (Dokoupil, 2009).

Interestingly, couples who profess egalitarian, nonsexist values also experience discrepancies in the division of household labor (P. Blumstein & Schwartz, 1983). Husbands who say that all the housework should be shared still spend significantly less time doing it than their wives (Institute for Policy Research, 2002). The fact that housework is still predominantly women's work gives us some sense of how pervasive and powerful our sexist ideology continues to be.

Gender Inequality in Education

Another institutional setting in which gender inequality persists is education. In elementary school and beyond, teachers are likely to treat their male and female students differently (Sadker, Sadker, Fox, & Salata, 2004):

- Girls receive less teacher attention and less useful feedback than boys.
- Girls talk significantly less in class than boys, and when they do speak up, they are more likely than boys to be reminded to raise their hands.
- Girls are more likely than boys to be the focus of unwanted sexual attention in school.

Over the course of their school careers, such differential treatment takes its toll on girls. Since it is sometimes quite subtle, most people are unaware of the hidden sexist lessons and quiet losses it creates (Sadker & Sadker, 1999).

In elementary school and middle school, girls outperform boys on almost every standard measure of academic achievement (Legewie & DiPrete, 2012; Tyre, 2006). Boys are more likely than girls to repeat a grade, drop out, be put in special education, or be diagnosed as having an emotional problem, a learning disability, or attention-deficit disorder (Lewin, 1998). Yet boys have higher expectations for themselves and higher self-esteem than girls, a gap that widens with each passing year in the school system. According to one study, around the ages of eight and nine, about two thirds of both boys and girls report feeling confident and positive about themselves. By high school, however, the percentage drops to 29% for young women (Freiberg, 1991). As girls make the transition from childhood to adolescence, they are faced with a conflict between the way they see themselves and the way others, particularly teachers, see them (Gilligan, 1990).

These gender-typed patterns pervade high school. Teenage boys' sense of their own masculinity tends to be derived primarily from their achievements, such as participation in organized sports (Messner, 2002). Boys are also likely to be encouraged by counselors and teachers to formulate ambitious career goals. In contrast, prestige and popularity for teenage girls are still likely to come largely from their physical appearance and from having a boyfriend (Lott, 1987). Not surprisingly, by the end of high school, boys perform better than girls. For instance, although 54% of all SAT takers are girls, boys' average total score is higher (1511 for boys vs. 1486 for girls; National Center for Fair and Open Testing, 2012).

Gender differences in academic performance are usually a cultural by-product as opposed to some innate intellectual difference. Take, for instance, the common belief that boys are naturally better at science and mathematics than girls. Cross-cultural evidence shows that many Asian and Eastern European countries consistently produce girls with strong mathematical abilities, while other countries (chiefly the United States) do not (Andreescu, Gallian, Kane, & Mertz, 2008). In fact, girls in developing countries are far more likely than girls in industrialized countries to indicate that they like math and science and would like to work in those fields (M. Charles, 2011). In the United States, girls who excel in national and international mathematical competitions are likely to be the daughters of immigrants. Researchers locate the reason for this discrepancy in a culture that doesn't value, actively discourages, or even socially penalizes mathematical excellence in girls. For instance, in the early 1980s, boys identified as "highly gifted" in mathematics—that is, those who scored in the 90th percentile of the math section of the SAT even though they were still too young to take the test—outnumbered girls 13 to 1. By 2005, that ratio had dropped to less than three to one (Andreescu et al., 2008).

Gender inequality is evident in postsecondary education, too. Over 2 million more U.S. women than men are enrolled in college (ProQuest Statistical Abstract, 2013). And women earn nearly 59% of all associate's, bachelor's, and advanced college degrees. Moreover, college women study more and have higher grade point averages than men. They're also more likely to complete their bachelor's degrees in four or five years (cited in Lewin, 2006). However, men are more likely to take rigorous courses geared for math and science majors and achieve higher grades in those courses than women (The College Board, 1998). Many of the majors that lead to high-paying or high-prestige careers remain dominated by men (engineering, economics, mathematics, earth sciences, etc.), whereas women are concentrated in fields such as nursing, education, and social services (Dey & Hill, 2007). Here, too, however, we see cross-cultural differences. In countries that we typically view as repressive when it comes to women's rights—such as Iran, Saudi Arabia, and Malaysia—women earn the majority of science degrees (M. Charles, 2011).

Gender Inequality in the Economy

Because of their difficulty converting educational achievements into high pay, women have historically been prevented from taking advantage of the occupational opportunities and rewards to which most men have had relatively free access. Today, women continue to have much less earning power in the labor market than men.

The unequal economic status of women not only results from the personal sexism of potential employers but is tied to larger economic structures and institutional forces. The standard assumptions that drive the typical workplace often work against women, both at work and at home. For instance, during the current economic recession, many mortgage lenders have become skittish about approving home loans for expectant parents. They fear that these couples will inevitably experience a temporary drop in income if the mother goes on temporary maternity leave—or perhaps a permanent loss of income if she decides to leave the workforce entirely—and therefore will be unable to make their mortgage payments (T. S. Bernard, 2010).

More generally, think of the things one generally has to do to be considered a good worker by a boss: put in extra hours, travel to faraway business meetings, go to professional conferences, attend training programs, be willing to work unpopular shifts, or entertain out-of-town clients. These activities assume that employees have the time and the freedom from familial obligations to do them. Because women, especially mothers, still tend to have the lion's share of responsibility at home, they are less able than their male colleagues to "prove" to their bosses that they are good, committed employees. Even if women are able to commit extra time to work, employers frequently assume that, because they are women, they won't. A famous hedge fund billionaire recently stated that in the world of global trading, babies are a "killer" for women's careers: "As soon as that baby's lips touch that girl's bosom, forget it" (quoted in J. Johnson, 2013, p. 1). Indeed, working mothers continue to earn significantly less than other employed women (Porter, 2012).

Furthermore, even when companies provide "family-friendly" workplace policies—such as flexible work schedules or the opportunity to temporarily reduce hours—women may be penalized for using them. Women who opt for these provisions risk being seen as less competent and less committed to their work. Interestingly, men who seek work flexibility may be stigmatized even more than women because employers tend to view them as deviating from traditional male breadwinner expectations. In fact, men who take leave for the birth of a child are less likely than men who don't to get promoted or receive raises (Williams, Blair-Joy, & Berdahl, 2013).

But for the most part, women continue to face obstacles men never do. For instance, although it is against federal law for a company with 15 or more employees to discriminate against pregnant job seekers, it can be difficult for a woman to get hired if she lets prospective bosses know she's pregnant. Hence many pregnant applicants withhold this information during interviews or wear baggy clothing to conceal it. Their concerns are not unwarranted. Thousands of pregnant women are pushed out of their jobs every year, either by being put on unpaid leave or by being fired outright (cited in Bakst, 2012). Claims of job discrimination from pregnant women increased 23% between 2005 and 2011 (cited in Quart, 2012).

Segregation in the Workplace

In general, though, U.S. women have made remarkable progress in overcoming traditional obstacles

to employment. In 1950, a little over 30% of adult women were employed in the paid labor force; today, that figure is almost 60%, and it increases to 69.1% for married mothers, 70% for single mothers, and 79.7% for widowed, separated, and divorced mothers (ProQuest Statistical Abstract, 2013). Over half of all U.S. workers today are female. And a record 40% of all households with children younger than 18 include mothers who are either the sole or primary breadwinners for the family, up from just 11% in 1960 (Wang, Parker, & Taylor, 2013).

The increase in female labor force participation has been particularly dramatic in some traditionally male-dominated fields such as medicine and law. For instance, in 1983, 15% of lawyers and 16% of physicians in the United States were women; by 2011, those figures had doubled (U.S. Bureau of the Census, 2004; ProQuest Statistical Abstract, 2013).

Although such a trend is encouraging, sex segregation in the workplace is still the rule. Women constitute 95.9% of all secretaries, 91.1% of all registered nurses, 94.5% of all childcare workers, 97.5% of all dental hygienists, and 97.7% of all preschool and kindergarten teachers (ProQuest Statistical Abstract, 2013). Despite their increased presence in traditionally male occupations, women still tend to be underrepresented among dentists (22.2%), physicians (32.4%), engineers and architects (13.6%), lawyers (31.9%), police officers (12%), and firefighters (4.5%).

Most of the changes that have taken place in the sex distribution of different occupations have been the result of women entering male lines of work, not vice versa. Although women have entered traditionally male occupations at a steady clip since the 1980s, men have not noticeably increased their representation in female-dominated occupations. The number of male nurses, kindergarten teachers, and secretaries has increased only minimally, if at all (ProQuest Statistical Abstract, 2013). One study found that some men would rather suffer unemployment than accept "women's jobs," even high-paying ones, because of the potential damage to their sense of masculinity (Epstein, 1989).

This kind of "one-way" occupational shift may cause problems in the long run. Historically, when large numbers of women enter a particular occupation previously closed to them, the number of men in that occupation decreases. Given that greater value is usually awarded to male pursuits, such occupations become less prestigious as men leave them. In fact, the higher the proportion of female workers in an occupation, the less both male and female workers earn in that occupation (Padavic & Reskin, 2002).

Greater female entry into traditionally male lines of work doesn't necessarily mean sexual equality, either. For instance, sex segregation often occurs in jobs *within* a profession. In the field of medicine, female physicians are substantially overrepresented in specialties such as family practice, pediatrics, and obstetrics and gynecology and underrepresented in more prestigious and lucrative areas such as surgery and cardiology. Seventy-three percent of pediatric residents and 77% of obstetrics/gynecology residents today are women; but only 30% of surgical residents are women (Women Physicians Congress, 2008). Among lawyers, women are promoted at a lower rate than their male counterparts, and they remain underrepresented in private practice, in law firm partnerships, and in high positions such as judges on the federal courts, district courts, and circuit courts of appeals (Hull & Nelson, 2000).

In sum, although more women than ever work in the paid labor force, we continue to have some jobs that employ almost exclusively women and others that employ almost exclusively men. When people are allocated jobs on the basis of sex rather than ability to perform the work, chances for self-fulfillment are limited (Reskin & Hartmann, 1986). Society also loses, because neither men nor women are free to do the jobs for which they might best be suited. However, segregation is most harmful to individual women, because the occupations they predominantly hold tend to be less prestigious and to pay lower wages than those held predominantly by men.

The Wage Gap

The Lord spoke to Moses and said, "When a man makes a special vow to the Lord which requires your valuation of living persons, a male between twenty and sixty years old shall be valued at fifty silver shekels. If it is a female, she shall be valued at thirty shekels." (Leviticus 27:1–4)

You don't have to go back to biblical times to find evidence of the practice of setting women's pay at less than men's. Even though the 1963 Equal Pay Act guaranteed equal pay for equal work in the United States, and Title VII of the 1964 Civil Rights Act banned job discrimination on the basis of sex (as well as race, religion, and national origin), a gap in earnings persists. In 2011, the average earnings for all U.S. men working full time, year round was $48,202. All women working full time, year round earned about $37,118 per year (DeNavas-Walt, Proctor, & Smith, 2012). To put it another way, for every dollar a U.S. man earns, a woman earns only about 77 cents. Although women have been closing the wage gap over the past several decades, progress has been rather slow. At the current rate, they won't achieve full pay equity with men until the year 2057 (Institute for Women's Policy Research, 2013a).

Today's wage gap actually widens with age. Women between 25 and 34 working full time, year round earn about 91% of what their male counterparts do. But by the time they reach the years leading up to retirement (between the ages of 55 and 64), they earn only 73% of what men earn (Coontz, 2012). That means that over a 40-year career, the average working woman will earn $499,000 less than the average working man (Gault, 2013). And because women earn less when they're employed, their retirement pensions are also significantly smaller than men's (National Women's Law Center, 2006).

Moreover, the wage gap is especially pronounced for women of color. In 2012, the weekly earnings for African American women were 63% of men's earnings. Latinas earned 54% of men's pay. Asian American women were more successful, earning 80% of men's pay (Institute for Women's Policy Research, 2013b).

I should point out that the wage gap is a global phenomenon. To varying degrees, in every country around the world, men earn more than women. In Japan and Korea, women earn 30% to 40% less than men earn. In other countries, however, such as Belgium, Greece, Hungary, Italy, New Zealand, and Norway, the wage gap is actually narrower than it is in the United States, with women earning 90% or more of what men earn (Organisation for Economic Cooperation and Development, 2011).

Why is the U.S. wage gap so persistent? One reason, of course, is occupational segregation and the types of jobs women are most likely to have. For five of the "most female" jobs (that is, those that are around 95% female)—namely, preschool teacher, teacher's assistant, housekeeper, childcare worker, and dental assistant—the overall average weekly salary is $483. For five of the "most male" jobs (those around 95% male)—namely, airplane pilot, firefighter, aircraft engine mechanic, plumber, and steel worker—the overall average weekly salary is $1,027 (U.S. Bureau of Labor Statistics, 2013f). But segregation isn't the whole story. Even in the same occupations, men's earnings are higher than women's (Institute for Women's Policy Research, 2011).

Some economists and policymakers argue that the wage gap is essentially an institutional by-product that exists because men on the whole work more hours per year, are more likely to work a full-time schedule than women, and have more work experience and training (Dey & Hill, 2007). Now, you will recall from Chapter 10 that due to the current economic recession, large numbers of both men and women have been forced to work part time because their employers have cut back. But women are particularly susceptible to this trend. According to the U.S. Bureau of Labor Statistics (2013b), 11% of employed men work part time, compared with 27% of employed women. Not only do part-time workers earn less, but during hard times, they are usually the first ones pushed out of employment—not because they're women but because their jobs are the most expendable.

However, even after controlling for differences in experience, age, and education—factors that might justify discrepancies in salary—the wage gap between men and women remains (Weinberg, 2007). For instance, the average income of female workers in the United States is significantly lower than that of men with the same level of educational attainment. Women with bachelor's degrees earn, on average, about 65% of what men with bachelor's degrees earn. In fact, women with bachelor's degrees can expect to earn less than men with two-year associate's degrees (mean annual earnings of $45,044 compared with $46,524). Similarly, women with doctoral degrees (with mean annual earnings of $87,808) earn less than men with master's degrees (with mean annual earnings of $87,951; ProQuest Statistical Abstract, 2013).

One possible remedy for the wage gap is to increase women's access to occupations that have traditionally been closed to them. As I noted earlier, this is already happening, to a certain degree, although sex segregation is still the rule.

Another solution is *pay equity*. The principle behind this remedy is that the pay for particular jobs shouldn't be low simply because those jobs happen to be filled predominantly by women. Different jobs that are of equal value to society and require equal levels of training ought to have equal pay. In 2007, a bill was introduced in the U.S. Senate called the Fair Pay Act. It sought to end wage discrimination against those who work in female-dominated jobs by establishing equal pay guidelines for equivalent work. For example, within an individual company, employers could not pay less for jobs held predominately by women than for jobs held predominately by men if those jobs were similarly important to the employer (National Committee on Pay Equity, 2007). However, the bill was defeated. In 2009, President Obama signed into law a stripped-down version of the bill, which makes it easier for women to file equal-pay lawsuits.

THE GLOBAL DEVALUATION OF WOMEN

At first glance, women seem to be making tremendous advances worldwide—becoming better educated and more economically independent than ever before. For instance, in 1990, 79 girls were enrolled in secondary schools for every 100 boys around the world; by 2010, that figure had risen to 97 (Population Reference Bureau, 2011). And over the past several decades, women in most regions of the world have increased their representation in most sectors of the paid labor force.

Nevertheless, women remain physically and economically disadvantaged in most societies around the world. In sub–Saharan Africa, women make up close to 60% of all HIV-infected adults (UNAIDS, 2008). About 536,000 women around the world die each year in pregnancy and childbirth, but an astounding 99.5% of these deaths occur in poor, less developed countries (UNICEF, 2009). The chances of a woman in a developed country dying during childbirth are 1 in 3,600; for a woman in a less developed country, the chances are 1 in 90 (Population Reference Bureau, 2011). Women make up the vast majority of global factory workers in multinational corporations, often working in unsafe and unhealthy conditions at extremely low pay. And while women have made significant strides worldwide in access to education, they still lag far behind men in top political and decision making roles (Hausmann, Tyson, & Zahidi, 2008).

In many countries, women do not have the same legal, familial, and bodily protections that men enjoy:

- The Iranian constitution states that the value of a woman's life is half that of a man's. An Iranian woman cannot travel anywhere without her husband's permission (I. Watson, 2005).
- In Kyrgyzstan, it's estimated that more than half of all married women were abducted by their soon-to-be husbands in a centuries-old legal custom known as *ala kachuu* (which literally means "grab and run"). If the woman is kept in the man's home overnight,

her virginity becomes suspect, her name disgraced, and her future marriage chances destroyed. So most women (about 80%, according to estimates) eventually relent and marry their abductor, often at the urging of their own families (C. S. Smith, 2005).

- In Afghanistan, women are sometimes killed by their husbands for having sex outside the marriage or for not bearing a son (Bowley, 2012).
- In Syria, girls who bring dishonor to their families by having premarital sex are sometimes killed by relatives. Under Syrian law, these killings, called *ghasalat al arr* ("washing away the shame"), are not considered murder. If the killer is convicted of the lesser charge of "crime of honor" and sentenced to prison, he is typically released within months (Zoepf, 2007).
- In 2011, 8,600 Indian women—an average of 23 a day—were killed by their husbands for not providing adequate dowries (National Crime Records Bureau, 2012). Even though India officially banned dowry (gifts that a woman receives from her parents on marriage) in 1961, it is still an essential part of premarital negotiations and now encompasses the wealth that the bride's family pays the groom. Young brides, who by custom live with their new husbands' parents, are commonly subjected to severe abuse if the promised money is not paid. Sometimes dowry harassment ends in suicide or murder.

The public devaluation of women can sometimes hide a very different private reality. For instance, Japanese women have historically occupied a visibly subservient position in society and in families. Women in the workforce suffer discrimination in hiring, salary, and promotion despite the presence of equal-opportunity laws there. Only 40% of women currently work outside the home, even though many economists argue that their inclusion could help boost an economy that has been slumping for decades (French, 2003). They are expected to clean, cook, and tend to the needs of their husbands within the home.

Yet many Japanese wives dominate their husbands. Typically, they control the household finances, giving their husbands monthly allowances as they see fit. If a man wants to withdraw money from the family account, the savings bank will usually phone the wife to get her approval. Japanese men are even starting to take on some of the housework responsibilities, which would have been unthinkable a couple of decades ago.

Women are making significant strides in other parts of the world where they have traditionally suffered. In places like Uganda, Burundi, and Tunisia, women now account for around 30% of elected officials. For women in Rwanda, the figure is 56%—the highest in the world—up from just 17% in 2000 (Population Reference Bureau, 2011). Women in Iran, Afghanistan, Somalia, and Liberia are at the forefront of local and national reform movements (Foroohar, 2010). In Algeria, women make up 60% of university students, 70% of lawyers, and 60% of judges. They also contribute more to household income than men (Slackman, 2007).

To some extent, the improvement of women's lives in some parts of the world can be attributed to global forces for change, which sometimes spread democratic values and humanitarian principles (Giddens, 2005). For instance, following reports of beatings, burnings, and beheadings of female domestic workers at the hands of their bosses in Saudi Arabia, Indonesia, Sri Lanka, and elsewhere, the International Labor Organization adopted a treaty that protects women from such abuse. Observers estimate that such a pact could protect the 50 to 100 million domestic workers who heretofore had very few if any rights (Human Rights Watch, 2011).

In 1979, the United Nations General Assembly adopted a treaty known as the Convention on the Elimination of All Forms of Discrimination Against Women (Division for the Advancement of Women, 2009). By accepting the treaty, countries agreed to take measures to end discrimination against women in all forms by

- incorporating the principle of equality of men and women into their legal systems, abolishing all discriminatory laws, and adopting appropriate ones prohibiting discrimination against women
- establishing tribunals and other public institutions to ensure the effective protection of women against discrimination; and
- ensuring elimination of all acts of discrimination against women by persons, organizations, or enterprises

All but 8 of the 192 member countries of the United Nations have ratified this agreement, which legally binds them to put its provisions into practice (Crary, 2009). The only holdouts are Sudan, Somalia, Qatar, Iran, Nauru, Palau, Tonga . . . and the United States.

CONCLUSION

Inequality based on sex and gender goes beyond the degrading media and cultural images of women, the face-to-face interactions that reinforce the devaluation of women, and the stereotypical beliefs of individual people. It is woven into the institutional and cultural fabric of societies around the world. In the United States, it is as much a part of the social landscape as baseball, apple pie, and Fourth of July fireworks. Every woman has felt sexism at some level, whether as personal violence, annoying harassment, sexually suggestive leers and comments, fear of going out at night, job discrimination, legal obstacles, or subtle encouragement toward "appropriate" pursuits—whether they be sports, hobbies, or careers.

Men tend to benefit from living in a society where language, identity, intimacy, history, culture, and social institutions are built on gender distinctions, even if the men themselves do not support such inequality. Like most people whose interests are being served by the system, men are largely unaware of the small and large advantages the social structure provides them

(W. J. Goode, 1981). Thus, most men don't see sex and gender inequality as their problem—it's a "women's issue"—and they are less likely than women to see a need for large-scale social change.

So the first step toward gender equality is that men will have to come to understand their role in the process, even in the absence of blatant, personal sexism. All men are tacitly involved in the oppression of women each time they automatically giggle at sexist jokes, mistake female doctors for nurses, see women in purely physical terms, expect less from women on the job or in school, or expect more of them at home.

The next step will require a fundamental transformation of institutional patterns and cultural values. Such a solution sounds too massive to be possible. But today, we are seeing early steps in that direction: changing conceptions of family roles, women's increasing (though not yet equal) participation in the labor force, their growing (but not yet equal) political power, and greater awareness of sexual exploitation and violence worldwide. How far these changes will take us in the future remains to be seen.

CHAPTER HIGHLIGHTS

◆ Personal sexism is most apparent during the course of everyday interaction in the form of communication patterns and gestures. It can be particularly dangerous when expressed in the form of sexual harassment and sexual violence.

◆ Gender stratification is perpetuated by a dominant cultural ideology that devalues women on the basis of alleged biological differences between men and women. This ideology overlooks the equally important role of social forces in determining male and female behavior.

◆ Institutional sexism exists in the media, in the law, in the family, in the educational system, and in the economy. Women have entered the paid labor force in unprecedented numbers, but

they still tend to occupy jobs that are typically considered "female" and still earn significantly less than men.

◆ Not only are social institutions sexist in that women are systematically segregated, exploited, and excluded; they are also "gendered." Institutions themselves are structured along gender lines so that traits associated with success are usually stereotypically male characteristiscs: tough-mindedness, rationality, assertiveness, competitiveness, and so forth.

◆ Despite recent advances worldwide, women still tend to suffer physically, psychologically, economically, and politically in most societies.

KEY TERMS

institutional sexism: Subordination of women that is part of the everyday workings of economics, law, politics, and other social institutions

matriarchy: Female-dominated society that gives higher prestige and value to women than to men

objectification: Practice of treating people as objects

patriarchy: Male-dominated society in which cultural beliefs and values give higher prestige and value to men than to women

pay equity: Principle that women and men who perform jobs that are of equal value to society and that require equal training ought to be paid equally

sexism: System of beliefs that asserts the inferiority of one sex and justifies gender-based inequality

13

Demographic Dynamics

Population Trends

The Influence of Birth Cohorts

Demographic Dynamics

Population Trends in the United States

I admit it. I said those seven words I once vowed I'd never say. The ones that tag you as an over-the-hill relic. No, they weren't "Hey, have you guys heard of Twitter?" They were "I just don't understand you kids today!"

It all started about a decade ago when I was arguing with my two sons—one 16 at the time, the other 13—over what to watch on television. They wanted to watch the X Games; I wanted to watch a rerun of the sixth game of the 1975 World Series. I told them that my choice was a priceless piece of U.S. sports history, the best World Series game ever played. Besides, I still didn't quite understand the allure of the X Games. I knew it was an annual alternative sports festival based on recreational activities such as skateboarding, motocross, freestyle BMX, snowboarding, freestyle snowmobiling, and so on. But I didn't care to know the difference between a "noseslide" and a "backside disaster." To me, "grinding" is what you do with coffee beans in the morning and "getting clean air" means moving out of Los Angeles.

They told me that I was a dinosaur and that I had better wake up and smell the 21st century. The X Games, they claimed, were the future. And you know what? They turned out to be right. "Extreme" sports, as they have come to be called, have become part of a broader youth subculture with their own hard-edged language, fashion, and music. In fact, the word *extreme* has become a modifying adjective for any activity that pushes beyond what's commonly accepted: extreme camping, extreme bartending, extreme paintball, extreme pumpkin carving, extreme chess, extreme tanning, extreme couponing, and even extreme childbirth.

Extreme sports are self-consciously designed to be thrilling, dangerous, subversive, and rebellious. Their appeal resides not so much in grace, strategy, or face-to-face competition as in the chance of disaster striking. "The fact that they're called 'extreme' sports means, if you make a mistake, you die," said one admirer (quoted in Clemmitt, 2009, p. 301). And in the 2013 Winter X Games, a freestyle snowmobiler did indeed die after being knocked unconscious during a crash landing.

For the most part, extreme athletes bear little resemblance to athletes in more traditional sports. They tend to despise rules, regulations, and standard conceptions of the competitive spirit. Indeed, many extreme sports don't have objective measures of success—like finishing first in a race or scoring more points than an opponent—but are instead judged on their degree of risk and danger.

The allure has been powerful. One survey found that more teens and preteens prefer watching extreme sports on television to watching college basketball, college football, auto racing, hockey, tennis, or golf (G. Bennett, Henson, & Zhang, 2003). Indeed, the number of Americans who ride skateboards tripled between 1995 and 2005; during that same period, the number of baseball players dropped by 7%. There are now more skateboarders in this country than football players. Worldwide, there are more than 18.5 million snowboarders, ranging in age from 5 to 75 (Clemmitt, 2009). Tens of millions of people now regularly participate in other extreme sports such as wall climbing, mountain biking, and wakeboarding ("Extreme Facts," 2005). And once these sports become old hat, extreme athletes find new ways to push the limit, through activities like BASE jumping, waterfall kayaking, cliff face camping, or canyon swinglining.

Ironically, although extreme sports appear to be solidly antiestablishment, they have clearly become a marketing gold mine, generating tens of billions of dollars a year (Longman & Higgins, 2005). Corporate America has been scrambling to co-opt the language, image, and culture of extreme athletes in order to tap into this booming market. The champion snowboarder Shaun White earns tens of millions of dollars a year endorsing products ranging from Stride gum and Red Bull energy drinks to his own clothing line at Target. Extreme sports have also achieved a significant degree of societal acceptance. Events like freestyle skiing, snowboarding, mountain biking, and BMX cycling are now in the Olympics. And yet many older people still fail to understand the appeal of these sports.

What my sons didn't realize was that they had identified one of the most crucial dividing lines in society today. They and I may be members of the same family. We may share the same genes, ethnicity, social class, and political views. But we're also members of two extremely different, sometimes antagonistic, social groups that are distinguished by one simple and unchangeable fact: our ages.

In the past several chapters, I examined various interconnected sources of social stratification: class, race and ethnicity, and sex and gender. You have seen that the distance between the haves and the have-nots—both locally and globally—continues to grow wider as a result of their different levels of access to important cultural, economic, and political resources. But within the United States, as well as most other societies, imbalances between various age groups will also be a defining feature of social life in the decades to come. This chapter examines the relationship between broad population trends—which include not only a changing age structure but also population growth and immigration—and everyday life. How are these changes affecting the ability to provide people with the resources they need for a comfortable life? How are important social institutions functioning as a result of these population shifts?

THE INFLUENCE OF BIRTH COHORTS

If you're like most college students, you've no doubt asked yourself questions like these: Will I get a job after I graduate? Where will I live? Will I be able to afford a house? Will I have a spouse or lifetime partner? Will I ever be a parent? How will I save for my retirement? The answers to these questions are obviously influenced by your personal desires, traits, values, ambitions, and abilities. And as you've already read in this book so far, your social class, gender, race, religion, and ethnicity will shape the answers, too.

But they will also be influenced by your place in the population at a given point in time. *Birth cohorts* are sets of people who were born during the same time period and who face similar societal circumstances brought about by their position in the age structure of the population. Birth cohorts affect people's everyday lives in two fundamental ways (Riley, 1971):

- People born within a few years of one another tend to experience life course events or social rites of passage—such as puberty, marriage, childbearing, graduation, entrance into the workforce, and death—at roughly the same time. Sociologists call these experiences *cohort effects*. The size of your birth cohort, relative to other cohorts, can have a significant impact on your life experiences: It can determine things like the availability of affordable housing, high-paying jobs, and attractive potential mates and can also affect how satisfied you feel with your own life. One study found that large cohorts in developed countries tend to have higher rates of suicide than small cohorts because people face more economic disadvantage and have more difficulty integrating into their communities when there are large numbers of people in the same age range competing for limited resources (Stockard & O'Brien, 2002).
- Members of the same birth cohort also share a common history. A cohort's place in time tells us a lot about the opportunities and constraints placed on its members. Unexpected historical events (wars, epidemics, natural disasters, economic depressions, etc.), changing political conditions, and major cultural trends, called *period effects*, contribute to the unique shape and outlook of each birth cohort. Many historians, for instance, believe that a period of drought and famine caused the people of the Mayan civilization to abandon their great cities nearly a thousand years ago. Those who were adults when this period began enjoyed comfortable lives, reveled in the high culture of the Mayans, and had tremendous prospects for the future. But for their children, born just a generation later, starvation, death, and social dislocation were the basic facts of life (Clausen, 1986).

Cohort and period effects combine to give each birth cohort its distinctive properties, such as ethnic composition, average life expectancies, and age-specific birthrates. For instance, women who experienced the Great Depression of the 1930s during their peak childbearing years—when they were in their 20s and early 30s—had the lowest birthrate of any cohort during the 20th century. Therefore, women born between 1900 and 1910 tended as a group to

have smaller families to rely on in their old age, which for them occurred roughly between 1970 and 1980. These experiences contrasted sharply with those of women born a mere 10 years later, who were too young to have children during the Great Depression and entered adulthood during the prosperous years after World War II. They tended to have large families and therefore more sources of support in their old age (Soldo & Agree, 1988).

Cohort and period effects also influence your worldview and self-concept. Think how different your goals and ambitions would be had you experienced childhood during a time of economic uncertainty as opposed to a period of relative affluence, such as the late 1990s. Rights and privileges considered unattainable dreams by one cohort are likely to be taken for granted by a different one.

As we grow older, we develop and change in a society that itself is developing and changing. We start our lives in one historical period with a distinct set of social norms, and we end our lives in another. Early in the 20th century, for example, most people went to school for only six or seven years, which yielded an adequate education for the types of jobs their parents and older siblings held. Today, 87.6% of U.S. residents go to school for at least 12 years (ProQuest Statistical Abstract, 2013). As a result, older cohorts on the whole tend to score substantially lower on standardized intelligence tests than younger cohorts. Because of such test results, social scientists long assumed that intelligence declines markedly with age. But we now know that these differences are the result not of aging but of changing societal values regarding education (Clausen, 1986).

As you can see, birth cohorts are more than just a collection of individuals born around the same time; they are distinctive generations tied together by historical circumstances, population trends, and societal changes. However, we must also realize that when many individuals in the same cohort are affected by social events in similar ways, the changes in their collective lives can produce changes in society. Each succeeding cohort leaves its mark on the prevailing culture. In other words, cohorts are not only affected by social changes but contribute to them as well (Riley, Foner, & Waring, 1988).

Baby Boomers

The birth cohort that has received the most national attention is, without a doubt, the Baby

Boom generation, the 80 million or so people born between 1946 and 1964. They make up around 26% of the entire U.S. population (ProQuest Statistical Abstract, 2013).

The passing of this massive cohort through the life course has been described metaphorically as "a pig in a python." If you've ever seen one of those nature shows on TV where snakes devour and digest small animals, you know how apt the metaphor is. In 1980, the largest age group in the United States consisted of people between 15 and 24 years of age. In 1990, the largest group in the United States consisted of people between 25 and 34 years of age. In 2000, it was 35- to 44-year-olds. In 2011, it was people between 45 and 54 (ProQuest Statistical Abstract, 2013). So you see that as this cohort bulge works its way through the life course, it stretches the parameters of the relevant social institutions at each stage. Baby Boomers packed hospital nurseries as infants, school classrooms as children, and college campuses, employment lines, and the housing market as young adults (Light, 1988). In middle age, they are prime movers in the burgeoning markets for adventure travel, diet, nutrition, and wellness products as well as relaxed-fit fashion, high-tech gadgets, and financial services. Advertisers for companies like Kellogg's cereal, Skechers shoes, and 5-Hour Energy drinks have shifted their marketing focus from young people to those over 55 (B. Carter & Vega, 2011).

The trend will continue into the future. By the year 2030, there will be close to 73 million Baby Boomers of retirement age, about twice the number of retirees today (ProQuest Statistical Abstract, 2013). As they reach their golden years, programs concerned with later life—pension plans, Social Security, medical and personal care—will be seriously stretched. For instance, the number of older Americans covered by Medicare will increase by 30 million over the next two decades (Greenblatt, 2011). And sometime in the middle of the 21st century, there will likely be a surge in business for the funeral industry as this generation reaches the end of its collective life cycle (Schodolski, 1993).

Baby Boomers have left an especially influential mark on the institution of family. Their generation was the first to redefine families to include a variety of living arrangements, such as cohabitation, domestic partnerships, and never-married women with dependent children (Wattenberg, 1986). They were also the first to acknowledge the expectation of paid work as a central feature of women's lives. And they were the first to grow up with effective birth control, enabling delayed childbearing, voluntary childlessness, and low birthrates.

Consequently, as the Baby Boomers reach old age, they will have fewer children to turn to for the kind of help they gave their own grandparents and parents (Butler, 1989). Hence, they will be more likely than previous generations to turn to social service and health care organizations to care for them. Not surprisingly, most Baby Boomers are quite pessimistic about their ability to sustain their quality of life (Pew Research Center, 2010b).

Generation X

Although Baby Boomers have dominated the cultural spotlight for decades, U.S. society has also taken notice of the generation to follow them, known in the media as Generation X. Today, there are more than 61 million U.S. residents who were born between 1965 and 1979 (ProQuest Statistical Abstract, 2013). The birthrate during the 1970s, when most of these individuals were born, was about half what it was during the post–World War II years of the Baby Boom.

More Generation Xers—roughly 40% of them—experienced the divorce of their parents than any previous generation. As a result, they tend to be emotionally conflicted about marriage. They are less likely to get married than older generations and more likely to delay marriage and childbearing if they do (Carlson, 2009). In addition, they're more likely to be single—with or without children—than previous generations (Sayer, Casper, & Cohen, 2004).

Even more Generation Xers grew up as so-called latchkey children, the first generation of children to experience the effects of having two working parents. For many of these children, childhood was marked by dependence on secondary relationships—teachers, friends, babysitters, and day care workers.

The Millennium Generation

The 85 million or so individuals born between 1980 and the late 1990s make up the next noticeable cohort, known as the Millennium Generation. This cohort is comparable to the Baby Boom in size but differs in almost every other way. For one thing, unlike the Baby Boomers, Millennials are not evenly distributed across the nation. States that have large minority and immigrant populations (e.g., California, Florida, and Texas) account for a relatively high proportion of the Millennium Generation (Faust, Gann, & McKibben, 1999). Consequently, this cohort is more ethnically diverse than previous cohorts; one in three is not white (Mather, 2007). They are also more likely than preceding cohorts to grow up in a nontraditional family. One in four lives in a single-parent household; three in four have working mothers. In addition, compared with older cohorts, they are less religious, less likely to serve in the military, and on track to become the most educated cohort in American history.

The Millennium Generation is the most media connected of any cohort. They are the first generation to see computer technology as a birthright. According to a Kaiser Family Foundation report (Rideout, Roberts, & Foehr, 2005), children between the ages of 8 and 18 spend more than eight hours a day with some kind of communication or entertainment medium: watching TV, listening to MP3 players, streaming videos, sending e-mails, and communicating via cell phones. The average teenager sends or receives about 3,700 texts a month (cited in Dokoupil, 2012).

Although this preoccupation with technology may create a generation less interpersonally adept than generations of the past, the exposure to other cultures that the Internet provides will make these individuals significantly more worldly than any other generation in history. And as the Millennium Generation enters and exits college, it will come to the workforce with unprecedented technological savvy, forcing companies to think more creatively about how to meet its needs (Trunk, 2007). Indeed, some have argued that this cohort's seemingly constant participation in social networking, online gaming, and video sharing and its perpetual attachment to tablets and smartphones actually give its members the technological skills they'll need to succeed in the contemporary world. They have also become adept at maintaining and navigating intimate connections in an "always on," full-time technological community (Ito et al., 2008).

On some issues, members of the Millennium Generation seem to be more socially conservative and less risky than prior generations. For one thing, today's high school seniors smoke less, use marijuana less, and drink alcohol less than their 1980 counterparts (Parker-Pope, 2012a). In addition, the proportion of high school students who have ever had sexual intercourse decreased from 54.1% in 1991 to 47.4% in 2011 (Centers for Disease Control and Prevention, 2013). Indeed, rates of pregnancy,

abortion, unprotected sex, and births for girls between 15 and 19 have all declined since 1990 (Centers for Disease Control and Prevention, 2013; ProQuest Statistical Abstract, 2013).

At the same time, though, members of the Millennium Generation are more likely than older cohorts to self-identify as liberals (Pew Research Center, 2010b). They also seem even less eager to get married in their early 20s than either the Generation Xers or the Baby Boomers. The median age at first marriage in the early 1970s—when Baby Boomers were young—was 21 for women and 23 for men; by 2013, it had increased to 27 for women and 29 for men (cited in Coontz, 2013). In addition, compared with older cohorts, they are more inclined to be tolerant of single women having children, people living together without being married, mothers of young children working outside the home, people of different races marrying one another, and gay couples legally marrying and raising children.

As the Millennium Generation ages and begins to control important social institutions, their attitudes and behaviors will shape reality for other cohorts in U.S. society.

DEMOGRAPHIC DYNAMICS

Many aspects of our personal lives are influenced by our birth cohort, but our lives are also affected by societywide and worldwide population trends. Sociologists who study fluctuations in population characteristics are called *demographers*. Demographers examine several important and interrelated population processes to explain current social problems or to predict future ones: birth or fertility rates, death or mortality rates, and patterns of migration. These three processes influence a population's growth, overall age structure, and geographic distribution.

Population Growth

The most fundamental population characteristic is, of course, size. Changes in population size are mostly a function of birth and death rates. As long as people are dying and being born at similar rates, the size of the population remains stable (barring large changes caused by migration). But when birthrates increase and death rates decrease, the population grows.

It took hundreds of thousands of years, from the beginning of humanity to the early 19th century, for Earth's human population to reach 1 billion. However, it took only an additional hundred years for it to reach 2 billion. Then, 3 billion was reached 30 years later; 4 billion, 16 years later; and 5 billion, a little over 10 years after that. Today's population is 7.1 billion and will likely exceed 10 billion by 2100 (Haub & Gribble, 2011; United Nations, 2011).

People disagree about the consequences of such growth. In the past, large numbers of people were seen as a precious resource. The Bible urged humanity to be fruitful and multiply. One 18th-century British scholar, referring to the strategic importance of a large population, called a high birthrate "the never-failing nursery of Fleets and Armies" (quoted in Mann, 1993, p. 49).

Although few individuals today sing the praises of massive population growth, some argue that it isn't particularly troublesome. A larger population creates greater division of labor and a larger market to support highly specialized services. More people are available to contribute to the production of needed goods and services.

Others, however, aren't so optimistic. When a particular population is excessively large, people are forced to compete for limited food, living space, and jobs. According to some contemporary demographers, population growth can compound, magnify, or even create a wide variety of social problems, such as pollution, environmental degradation, housing shortages, high inflation, energy shortages, illiteracy, and the loss of individual freedom (J. Weeks, 1995).

Global Imbalances in Population Growth

On a global scale, population growth could widen the gap between rich and poor nations, perpetuate social and economic inequality within nations, give rise to racial and ethnic separatism, and increase the already high levels of world hunger and unemployment (Ehrlich & Ehrlich, 1993). Environmental threats are growing, too. Humanity's use of once-plentiful natural resources—fossil fuel, rich soil, and certain plant and animal species—is now 50% higher than Earth's biologically productive capacity. By 2030, we'll need more than two planets to support the consumption of all humans (World Wildlife Fund, 2012).

The problem, however, is not just that the overall population is growing rapidly but also that different countries are experiencing vastly different rates of growth. Populations in poor, developing countries tend to expand rapidly, whereas those in wealthy, developed countries have either stabilized or are declining. The annual growth rate of the world's population is approximately 1.2% (Population Reference Bureau, 2012). But that figure masks the dramatic regional differences that will exist for several decades to come:

- In Africa, the rate of natural population increase (that is, without taking migration into consideration) is about 2.4% each year; Europe, in contrast, is experiencing a growth rate of 0%. Sub–Saharan Africa alone has seen its population triple in the past 50 years (cited in Rosenthal, 2012). If current trends continue, by the middle of the 21st century, the population of Germany will be 13% smaller, Bulgaria's 21% smaller, and Ukraine's 24% smaller than it is today. In contrast, Malawi's population will be 312% bigger; Zambia's, 325% bigger; and Niger's, 332% bigger (Population Reference Bureau, 2012).

- In 1950, half of the 10 most populous nations were in the industrialized world. In 2011, two industrialized countries were in the top 10: Japan and the United States. By 2050, demographers predict that the United States will be the only developed country among the world's 10 most populous nations. The rest will be developing countries in Asia, Africa, and South America (Crossette, 2001; Population Reference Bureau, 2012).

- In 1950, over 28% of the world's population lived in North America and Europe. Today, it's 15.5%, and by 2050, about 12.5% will live in these regions. Much of the rest of the world's population will reside in the developing countries of Africa, Asia, and Latin America (Population Reference Bureau, 2012; United Nations Population Division, 2005).

These imbalances will influence how people view one another; affect global and domestic policies; and determine the availability of food, energy, and adequate living space (Kennedy, 1993). When the most highly industrialized and economically productive countries begin to experience shrinking populations, their role as major global producers and consumers of goods is thrown into doubt. The result can be economic and political turmoil as other countries jockey for global advantage.

Why would populations in poor, developing countries grow at such a high rate when so many people are already struggling to survive? When societies begin to industrialize, living conditions improve. New technology often means better food supplies and increased knowledge about disease. Societies learn how to keep their water supplies clean and how to dispose of garbage and sewage. So people begin to live longer. In 1990, 33% of all deaths worldwide occurred to people over 70; in 2010, that figure increased to 43%, indicating that infectious and communicable diseases are claiming fewer young victims (cited in Tavernise, 2012).

But for a considerable time after the death rate begins to fall, the birthrate remains high, resulting in a dramatic increase in the size of the population. In sub–Saharan Africa, for instance, women will bear an average of 5.1 children in their lifetimes. By comparison, U.S. women have, on average, 1.9 children. In Canada, the figure is 1.7, and in the countries of Southern Europe, it's a minuscule 1.4 (Population Reference Bureau, 2012). In the mid 2000s, some low-birthrate countries in the more developed world were beginning to show an increase in the number of babies being born. But the current global recession has slowed or reversed this trend in the majority of these countries (Haub, 2012b).

One of the reasons birthrates are so high in less developed countries is the lack of access to effective contraception. Only 44% of women in these regions use some form of modern contraception, compared with 63% in the more developed world (Population Reference Bureau, 2012). In sub–Saharan Africa, the figure is 20%. In contrast, 73% of U.S. women and 78% of Northern European women use modern contraception. In addition, established laws, customs, and religious norms often continue to exert strong influences on people's reproductive behavior. In developing nations, children are likely to be perceived as productive assets and "social security" for old age (Mann, 1993).

Politics, Culture, and Population Growth

You may have the impression that population growth is a "natural" process working relentlessly and inevitably on unsuspecting populations. Yet human intervention—government intervention, more specifically—has at times purposefully altered the size or even the configuration of a population for political or economic reasons.

Take China, for example. Because of its massive population of more than 1.35 billion and its limited resources, Chinese leaders have been struggling for decades to limit family size. One of every five humans alive today is Chinese, but China has only 7% of Earth's farmland, much of it of poor quality. To address the problem, the government enacted a strict family planning policy in the early 1970s that limited most families to one child. Couples had to wait until their mid 20s to marry. Provinces and cities were assigned yearly birth quotas. Neighborhood committees determined which married couples could have a baby and which would be subjected to forced sterilizations (Ignatius, 1988). They also charted the menstrual cycles and pelvic-exam results of every woman of childbearing age in the area (Jian, 2013). Women who lacked approval to be pregnant could be subjected to forced abortions (Kahn, 2007). According to data from the Chinese Health Ministry, since the policy was enacted, Chinese doctors have performed 336 million abortions and 196 million sterilizations (Rabinovitch, 2013).

A 2010 report by the Chinese Human Rights Defenders found that the government still uses a variety of coercive family planning tactics in poor rural areas, such as financial penalties for households that violate the restrictions, monetary gifts for citizens who divulge the reproductive secrets of their neighbors, and forced sterilizations of women who have already had one child (cited in Jacobs, 2010). Wealthy couples tend not to be subjected to such coercion. They can purchase the ability to have additional children by paying a fine—called a "social compensation fee"—or by traveling abroad to give birth (Jian, 2013).

The effectiveness of China's family planning policy has amazed population experts. The average number of births per woman has decreased from more than 7 in the 1960s to 1.5 today (Population Reference Bureau, 2012). In contrast, the average number of births per woman in India, a country with similar population problems, is 2.5. The Chinese government estimates that without the policy, the country's population of 1.35 billion would be 30% larger (Rabinovitch, 2013).

But the success of this policy has created some serious social problems. So few babies are being born now—and so many more elderly people are living longer—that the overall age of the population is growing steadily. Chinese officials fear that the country will likely encounter what is sometimes called the "four-two-one problem"—a generation of only children who will have to find the resources to care for two aging parents and four elderly grandparents ("One Child Left Behind," 2009). Today, there are six

Chinese working adults for every one retired person; by 2040, there will be just two (French, 2007). It's estimated that by that same year, China will have an older population than the United States but with only about one fourth the average per capita income (Kahn, 2004). Retirement funds and pension plans are scarce. Only 40% of elderly men and 13% of elderly women receive any kind of support from a pension. And the social networks that once supported aging Chinese are no longer there. Migration to urban areas and the work pressures of an increasingly industrialized economy have fractured family ties (Population Reference Bureau, 2010a). The problem has become so bad that the Chinese government had to enact a law that requires children to take care of their elderly parents (FlorCruz, 2013).

Like those in China, officials in many other countries are now starting to worry that their populations aren't growing enough. In contemporary Russia, for instance, many couples postpone childbearing or decide not to have children altogether because of severe economic instability and uncertainty about the future. Russia now has one of the world's lowest birthrates. At the same time, because of skyrocketing rates of poverty, stress, and alcoholism, Russians are dying much earlier than the rest of the developed world. As a result, over the past decade and a half, the Russian population has shrunk by about 700,000 people a year ("Vladimir Putin on Raising Russia's Birth Rate," 2006). Population experts project that it will decrease by an additional 11% between now and 2050 (Population Reference Bureau, 2012). Fearing that such a dramatic population decline will lead to economic catastrophe, Russian politicians have promoted a variety of policies to reverse the trend, such as a nationwide ban on abortions, financial incentives for couples to have children, increased funds for prenatal care and maternity leave, and a tax on childlessness ("Fearing Demographic Abyss," 2006; Karush, 2001). In one central Russian region, the governor decreed September 12 to be a "Day of Conception," in which couples are given the day off from work to ... well ... procreate. Those who have a baby nine months later receive money, cars, and other prizes ("Baby, and a Car," 2011).

Cultural tradition also continues to play a powerful role in people's decisions about having children. Some patriarchal cultures express a deep preference for male children because only they can perpetuate the family line. As one Chinese mother put it, "If you

have only girls, you don't feel right inside. You feel your status is lower than everyone else" (quoted in Jacobs, 2009, p. 8).

Parents in such cultures may take extreme measures to have sons rather than daughters. In rural China—where the one-child policy coupled with a tradition of favoring boys over girls has led many parents to fear they will be left to take care of themselves in old age—the abduction and sale of baby boys has become a thriving business (Jacobs, 2009). Elsewhere, female babies are aborted, killed at birth, abandoned, neglected, or given up for foreign adoption (Kristof, 1993). Although it is illegal, couples often seek to determine the sex of their fetus through sonograms, and if it's a girl, they have an abortion. In South Korea, for instance, 1 out of 12 female fetuses—or 30,000 girls a year—is aborted, even though disclosure of the sex of a fetus and abortion are against the law (WuDunn, 1997). In India, as many as 12 million female fetuses have been aborted over the past three decades as families have tried to secure male heirs (Yardley, 2011).

Such practices have led to a conspicuous shortage of females in many developing countries. Under normal circumstances in every society, there are between 103 and 107 boys born for every 100 girls; but higher male infant mortality works to even the distribution of boys to girls. In India, however, there are 109 males for every 100 females, the lowest sex ratio in that country since it achieved independence in 1947 (Jha, 2011). In some areas of China, the ratio is 120 males for every 100 females. There are 32 million more Chinese males under 20 than females; in 2005 alone, there were 1.1 million more boys born than girls (Zhu, Lu, & Hesketh, 2009). Demographers have identified similar shortages of females in South Korea, Pakistan, Bangladesh, Nepal, and Papua New Guinea, and some estimate that about 163 million females are "missing" from Asia's population (Hvistendahl, 2011).

Age Structure

In addition to population growth, demographers also study the *age structure* of societies—the balance of old and young people. Age structure, like the size of a population, is determined principally by birthrates and life expectancy.

The proportion of old people in the world has been growing steadily for decades. Currently, 8% of the global population is over 65 (Population Reference Bureau, 2012). By 2050, that figure is projected to be 17% (Scommegna, 2012). During the same period, the proportion of the "oldest old" (those over 80) will increase more than fivefold (United Nations Population Division, 2003).

But as with population growth in general, the global growth of the elderly population is not spread evenly across countries. In developing countries where recent population growth is exceedingly rapid and where life expectancy remains relatively low—as in most countries of Southeast Asia, Latin America, the Indian subcontinent, the Middle East, and especially Africa—the age structure tends to be dominated by young people. Forty-three percent of the population in sub–Saharan Africa is under the age of 15 (Population Reference Bureau, 2012). The median age of the population in the world's three youngest countries—Uganda, Mali, and Niger—is about 16 (United Nations, 2011). In contrast, developed countries that are experiencing low birthrates coupled with increasing life expectancy have a very different age structure. More old people are living, and fewer people are being born. Only 16% of Europe's population is under 15 (Population Reference Bureau, 2012). The median age of the population in the world's three oldest countries (Italy, Japan, and Germany) is about 44 (United Nations, 2011). In Japan, it's estimated that over the next 25 years, the proportion of elderly people in the population will increase from one in four to one in three (Harney, 2012).

The global implications of these different age structures cannot be understated. In Germany, Austria, France, and other European countries, a decreasing number of young people are paying into a pension system that must support a growing number of older people (R. Bernstein, 2003). Governments have reacted to the aging of their populations by reducing social services, including the pensions that millions of retirees have been counting on. A growing proportion of older people can strain economies in other ways. For instance, the World Health Organization (2012) projects that by the middle of the 21st century, the number of people with age-related dementia worldwide will more than triple to 115 million. The cost of caring for these people will approach $2 trillion.

In contrast, when young people outnumber the elderly in a particular country, they are likely to overwhelm labor markets and educational systems (K. Davis, 1976). The result is a steady decline in living standards. When combined with a skewed sex ratio—due to a shortage of young females and an overabundance of young males—the likelihood of instability and sometimes violent political unrest increases (Hvistendahl, 2011). In the spring of 2011, we witnessed massive angry demonstrations in many parts of the Middle East that continue today in places like Syria and Egypt. Not surprisingly, over 60% of the populations of Syria, Saudi Arabia, Iraq, Yemen, Jordan, Oman, Egypt, and Libya are under 30 years of age (U.S. Bureau of the Census, 2011a). Increasing rates of unemployment leave more and more young people angry and dissatisfied. Some authors even go so far as to predict that if these young men cannot find spouses or jobs, they will pose such a threat to the internal stability of these countries that their governments may decide they have to go to war with other countries simply to occupy the surplus male population (Hudson & den Boer, 2004).

The obvious consequence of today's trends is that developing nations will have the burden of trying to accommodate populations dominated by young people, whereas developed nations will have the burden of trying to support millions of people over the age of 65.

Geographic Distribution

Many people seek to escape these kinds of problems through **migration**, or moving to another place where prospects for a comfortable life are brighter. Through the centuries, migration has played a crucial role in history as people have contended for territory and the resources that go with it. Today, global media expose people more quickly and more consistently than ever to appealing lifestyles elsewhere. Large-scale migration includes both within-country movement and cross-border movement.

Migration Within a Country

Migration trends within a country can have a considerable effect on social life. In the United States, such internal migration usually consists of people moving from colder to warmer climates or from large cities to outer suburbs (Lalasz, 2006). But in less developed countries these days, in-country migration is more likely to reflect **urbanization**, the process by which people leave rural areas and begin to concentrate in large cities. For instance, in 1950, fewer than a billion people worldwide lived in cities. By 2027, that figure is projected to increase to 2.5 billion. Indeed, by 2050 70% of the world's population will be urban dwellers (Organisation for Economic Cooperation and Development, 2010). In Asia and Africa, four times more people live in cities today than in 1950 (Population Reference Bureau, 2008). It's estimated that in India alone, 700 million people will move from villages to cities by 2050 (cited in Giridharadas, 2007).

This transformation has changed assumptions about what urban living means worldwide. In the past, cities were meccas of commerce and culture and tended to have higher standards of living and better health conditions than rural areas. Even today, legislators in some countries believe that urbanization will spur economic growth and provide people with access to better hospitals, schools, and other services. For instance, in 2013, China announced a massive 12-year plan to relocate 250 million rural residents to newly constructed cities (I. Johnson, 2013).

But when cities grow rapidly, as many are in the developing world, their economies and infrastructures have a hard time keeping up. In sub–Saharan Africa, only about 43% of city dwellers have access to adequate sanitation facilities, compared with 99% in more developed countries (Population Reference Bureau, 2010b). Moreover, cities typically have much higher rates of poverty, crime, violence, and sexually transmitted diseases than rural areas.

Migration From One Country to Another

Population movement from one country to another is equally significant. It's estimated that about 200 million people worldwide live outside their countries of birth (cited in DeParle, 2007). International migration is encouraged by disparities in opportunities. Poverty, political instability, war, famine, environmental deterioration, high unemployment, and the lure of high wages in richer countries continue to drive the world's poorest people to give up their life savings and risk death to find a better life in more prosperous nations. According to the United Nations, each year hundreds of thousands of undocumented immigrants from poor countries in Africa, Central Asia, and the Middle East try to enter the wealthy nations of Western Europe (cited in Cowell, 2002).

You might think that when people migrate from underdeveloped, overcrowded countries to more developed, technologically advanced countries, everyone would benefit. After all, migration lowers population pressures and unemployment at home while offsetting the problems of negative population growth and an aging workforce in developed destination countries. Indeed, the only way Japan and Western Europe will be able to sustain a stable population in the future is through immigration.

From a sociological point of view, however, international migration often creates conflict. The immigrants themselves often experience tension between the values of their new homes and the values of their countries of origin. Take, for instance, cultural mores regarding virginity and premarital sex. As the Middle Eastern immigrant population in Europe grows, young Muslim women are caught between the relative sexual freedoms of European society and the deep, and often very restrictive, traditions of their parents and grandparents. Although there are no reliable statistics, French cosmetic surgeons report increasing numbers of young Muslim women seeking a surgical procedure called hymenoplasty—the restoration of the hymen, the vaginal membrane that breaks during the first act of intercourse—to give the appearance of virginity (Sciolino & Mekhennet, 2008).

People seeking opportunities abroad can no longer move to uncharted areas but rather must push into territories where other people already live. Instead of seeing immigrants for their contribution to the overall economy, the people already in residence see immigrants as an immediate and personal threat. The immigrants require jobs, housing, education, and medical attention, all of which are in limited supply. They also bring with them foreign habits, traditions, and norms.

Immigration creates a variety of cultural fears: fear that a nation can't control its own borders, fear that an ethnically homogeneous population will be altered through intermarriage, fear of the influx of a "strange" way of life, and fear that newcomers will encroach on property, clog the educational system, and suck up social benefits owned and largely paid for by "natives" (Kennedy, 1993). Many people also express concern that immigrants are responsible for outbreaks of diseases such as HIV/AIDS, tuberculosis, measles, and cholera, which strain health care systems and thus create even more resentment. Above all, they fear that immigrants and their offspring may one day become a statistical majority, rendering the "natives" powerless in their own country.

Even though laws in most countries ban discrimination against immigrants, antiforeigner resentment and prejudice are global phenomena. For instance, legislators in Denmark, France, and Italy continue to look for ways to tighten their borders so they can limit the free flow of immigrants, chiefly from North Africa. In Great Britain, the antipathy is usually directed toward immigrants from India and Pakistan. In Australia, politicians talk of being swamped by South and East Asians. And in the United States, immigrants from Latin America bear the brunt of the public's anti-immigrant animosity. In Japan, the resentment is directed toward almost anyone who isn't Japanese. Despite a severe labor shortage that could cripple its economy, Japan has done little to loosen its tight restrictions on immigration. In fact, the government actively encourages foreign workers and foreign graduates of its universities to return home as quickly as possible (Tabuchi, 2011).

Antiforeigner sentiment tends to be more pronounced in places with a large proportion of foreign populations, where economies are less prosperous, and where there is greater support for extreme right-wing political parties (Semyonov & Raijman, 2006). It's important to note, though, that such hostility is not inevitable. Peaceable contact with immigrants at work, at school, or in the community can reduce feelings of threat and the willingness to expel legal immigrants from the country (McLaren, 2003). In any case, the trend toward greater immigration is unlikely to slow down as long as communication and transportation technologies continue to shrink the globe and economic disparities between countries continue to exist.

POPULATION TRENDS IN THE UNITED STATES

In the United States, two important demographic trends will exert a profound effect on the population in the future: the growing proportion of non-white, non–English-speaking immigrants and their children and the shifting age structure of the population, marked by a growing proportion of elderly and a shrinking proportion of young people. These two trends together will strain the social fabric in years to come, raising questions about the fair distribution of social resources.

Immigration and the Changing Face of the United States

Because the U.S. population is currently growing at a manageable rate, residents may have trouble understanding the impact of population explosions in other countries on their everyday lives here. But as populations burst the seams of national boundaries elsewhere, many of those seeking better opportunities end up in the United States. Newly arrived immigrants believe that chances to get ahead, protection of women's rights, treatment of the poor, and availability of schools are all better here than in their countries of origin (Rieff, 2005). Some arrive legally by plane, boat, or train. Others arrive illegally by foot or are smuggled in the backs of trucks or the holds of cargo ships.

In the mid 1980s, the U.S. Bureau of the Census predicted that by the year 2050, the United States would have a population of 300 million (Pear, 1992). But that number was surpassed in 2007. Subsequently, the Census Bureau has revised its estimate to 399 million by 2050 (ProQuest Statistical Abstract, 2013).

Part of the reason this projection had to be adjusted was that immigration increased more than had been anticipated. In 2011, over 40 million people immigrated to the United States, about 11 million of whom were undocumented (Pew Hispanic Center, 2013). The share of the U.S. population that is foreign born rose from 5% in 1967 to 13% in 2011. And if you count the U.S.-born children and grandchildren of immigrants, immigration accounts for about half of U.S. population growth (P. Martin & Midgley, 2010).

Of course, this isn't the first time a surge of immigration has radically increased the U.S. population. In the first decade of the 20th century, nearly 9 million immigrants entered the country. By 1915, foreign-born residents constituted 15% of the population (U.S. Bureau of the Census, 2006). But what makes contemporary immigration different is that fewer of today's newcomers are of European descent.

Consequently, the racial and ethnic composition of the United States has changed dramatically over the past century. In 1900, one out of every eight U.S. residents was of a race other than white; in 2010, the ratio was one in three; and by 2050, it is projected to be one in two (P. Martin & Midgley, 2010). The majority of births in the United States are now to Latina, black, and Asian mothers. At the same time, the number of white people who die each year now exceeds the number of white babies born each year (cited in Roberts, 2013). Trends like these will continue to alter the look of the American population into the foreseeable future.

Until quite recently, the non–European immigrant population was not spread evenly across the country. Immigrants tended to settle in large urban areas that serve as ports of entry, such as New York, Los Angeles, Houston, and Miami. In the mid 1980s, for example, two thirds of Mexican immigrants lived in California and 20% more lived in Texas and Illinois (G. Thompson, 2009). Of the 20 metropolitan areas with the largest proportion of Asian immigrants in the early 2000s, eight were in California and six were cities in the eastern corridor that runs from Boston to Washington, DC (Zhao, 2002).

However, new immigrants can now be found all across the United States. Just like everyone else, they're motivated to go where the jobs are. In the past decade, the growth of the immigrant population has been largest in counties where immigrants comprised less than 5% of the population in 2000. In fact, more immigrants now settle in suburbs and small towns than in large urban centers (cited in Tavernise & Gebeloff, 2010). Consequently, the need for people to teach English as a second language has grown most rapidly in school districts in these regions. Between 1993 and 2002, the number of students in Idaho, Nebraska, Tennessee, and Georgia who speak little if any English tripled. In North Carolina, the number of such students increased sixfold (Zhao, 2002). Students who do not know English represent the fastest-growing group of students in the nation (G. Thompson, 2009). Questions of how best to integrate immigrants and their children are now being debated in every corner of the country.

U.S. residents have always had a love–hate relationship with immigrants. In good times, immigrants have been welcome contributors to the economy. Early in the 20th century, their labor helped build roads and the rail system. Immigrants have filled unwanted jobs, opened businesses, and improved the lives of many U.S. residents by working cheaply as housekeepers, dishwashers, and gardeners.

When times are bad, however, or when the political winds shift, many U.S. residents are inclined to shut the door and blame immigrants for many of the country's economic and social woes. During these periods, people often describe the influx of immigrants as a "flood," subtly equating their arrival with disaster. As in Europe, immigrants to the United States often find they are targets of a variety of social anxieties, from economic tension to outright hostility (Sontag, 1992).

The "Graying" of the United States

At the same time that the United States grapples with the changing ethnic and racial configuration of its population, it also must address its shifting age structure. Perhaps the most important and most problematic demographic trend in the United States today involves the increasing average age of the population. In 1910, 38% of the U.S. population was under 18; today, that figure is 24% (Mather, Pollard, & Jacobsen, 2011). Two hundred years ago, the median age for U.S. residents was 16; in 1980, it was 30; today, it is 36.2. And it's expected to be close to 41 by the middle of this century (ProQuest Statistical Abstract, 2013).

Two developments in the past few decades have conspired to alter the U.S. age structure. The first has been a decrease in the number of children being born. In 1960, there were approximately 24 births per 1,000 people in the population. By 2011, the rate had dropped to 13 per 1,000 (Population Reference Bureau, 2012). More U.S. women than ever are choosing not to have children at all (Dye, 2008). Like many countries in the developed world, the U.S. fertility rate is barely at the level necessary to replace the current population in the next generation. Most of the conditions that have helped lower fertility—improved educational and employment opportunities for women and more effective contraception, for example—are not likely to reverse in the future.

The other development has been a rapid increase in the number of people surviving to old age. The number of Americans over the age of 65 has nearly doubled in the last four decades (Greenblatt, 2011). Technological advances in medicine and nutrition have extended the lives of many U.S. residents, whose historical counterparts would not have lived nearly as long. Life expectancy has risen from 67.1 for males and 74.7 for females born in 1970 to 76.2 for males and 81.1 for females born in 2010 (ProQuest Statistical Abstract, 2013). By 2050, old people will constitute a greater proportion of the U.S. population than children. The number of people over 85, an age group for which health care costs are exceptionally high, will grow fastest of all, increasing from 5.7 million today to almost 9 million by 2030 and soaring to around 18 million by 2050 (ProQuest Statistical Abstract, 2013). Some demographers project that by 2050, there will be 10 times the number of centenarians (people living to 100) that we have today (cited in Dominus, 2004).

Why should we be concerned about the "graying" of the U.S. population? The answer is that a society with an aging population will inevitably experience increased demands for pensions, health care, and other social services for the elderly. Although older people in the United States tend to be healthier than their counterparts in the past, a significant proportion suffer from health problems and chronic disease and will eventually need some kind of long-term care (National Institute on Aging, 2006). The ability and willingness of society, and in particular the working population, to bear the additional burden of caring for the growing number of elderly people is an open question.

Political debate rages today over how—or even whether—the Social Security system should be transformed to accommodate the growing number of people who will turn 65 in the coming years. One survey found that 18% of Americans feel that the Social Security system is in crisis, 53% believe it has major problems, and 24% feel it has minor problems. About 60% of people fear that by the time they retire, there will not be enough money in the system to pay the benefits they're entitled to (Pew Research Center, 2005). Unless elderly Americans are better able to support themselves financially in the future than they are today, the government will have to play an even larger role in providing health care and other services. To do that, it will have to devote more tax dollars to the needs of older citizens, a prospect that seems unlikely given the current congressional atmosphere that advocates reduced rather than increased government spending.

The graying of the United States is challenging businesses and service providers to gear their products and amenities toward older clientele. For instance, some hospitals now provide emergency rooms specifically designed for the elderly. They include more soothing décor, limited medical machinery, and volunteers who circulate among the patients offering reading glasses, hearing aids, and pleasant conversation (Hartocollis, 2012a). Employers may have to restructure the workplace as well. Already, fewer young workers are available to replace retiring workers. Some employers will be forced to pay higher wages or provide additional benefits to attract new workers or will be forced to focus more attention on employee productivity, perhaps turning to machines to replace workers.

On the positive side, however, employers must find innovative ways to keep older workers interested in the job. Business owners are beginning to realize that older workers are more stable and trustworthy employees than younger workers. A recent study found that 54% of employed Millennials would rather be working somewhere else, compared to 21% of older Baby Boomers (that is, those born between 1946 and 1955; cited in Moeller, 2012). Indeed, the turnover rate for workers under 30 is six times higher than the rate for workers over 50 (The Silver Lining at Borders, 2011). So employers are developing new strategies to recruit older employees. Home Depot, for example, offers its older workers "snowbird specials"—winter jobs in warm-climate regions like Florida and summer jobs in cooler states like Maine. Employers may also have to keep older workers interested in continuing to work by offering substantial bonuses or by creating prestigious and well-paid part-time positions.

CONCLUSION

In discussing current and future demographic trends, I can't help but think about my own children. Their Millennium Generation cohort is the first to reach the teen years during the 21st century. I wonder what kind of impact being born in the late 1980s and growing up in the 1990s and early 2000s will have on their lives. Will the world's population reach the predicted catastrophic proportions, or will we figure out a way to control population growth and enable all people to live quality lives? Will the growing ethnic diversity of U.S. society continue to create tension and conflict, or will Americans eventually learn how to be a truly multicultural nation? What will be the single, most definitive "punctuating" event for my sons' cohort: a war, an assassination, a severe economic depression, a terrorist attack, a natural disaster, a political scandal, or some environmental catastrophe? Or will it be world peace, an end to hunger and homelessness, or a cure for cancer?

I also wonder how well social institutions will serve my children's generation. Will jobs be waiting for them when they're ready to settle down and go to work? What will be their share of the national debt? How will they perceive family life? Will marriage be an outdated mode of intimacy by the time they reach middle age? What will be a desirable family size?

As a parent, of course, I'm more than a little curious about how these questions will be answered. But as a sociologist, I realize that they will emerge only from the experiences and interactions of my kids, and others their age, as they progress through their lives. Herein lies the unique and fundamental message of the sociological perspective.

As powerful and relentless as the demographic and generational forces described in this chapter are in determining my children's life chances, the responsibility for shaping and changing this society in the 21st century ultimately rests in the hands of their generation. This topic—the ability of individuals to change and reconstruct their society—is the theme of the next and final chapter.

CHAPTER HIGHLIGHTS

◆ Often overlooked in our quest to identify the structural factors that shape our everyday experiences are the effects of our birth cohort. Birth cohorts are more than just a collection of individuals born within a few years of each other; they are distinctive generations tied together by historical events, national and global population trends, and large-scale societal changes.

◆ Earth's population is growing at an unprecedented rate. But different countries experience different rates of growth. Poor, developing countries are expanding rapidly, whereas the populations in wealthy, developed countries have either stabilized or, in some cases, declined.

◆ When the population of a country grows rapidly, the age structure is increasingly dominated by young people. In slow-growth countries with low birthrates and high life expectancy, the population is much older, on average.

◆ As conditions in developing countries grow worse, pressures to migrate increase, creating a variety of cultural, political, and economic fears in countries experiencing high levels of immigration.

◆ The changing age structure of the U.S. population—more older people and fewer younger people—suggests that a number of adjustments will have to be made in both employment policies and social programs.

KEY TERMS

age structure: Population's balance of old and young people

birth cohort: Set of people who were born during the same era and who face similar societal circumstances brought about by their shared position in the overall age structure of the population

cohort effect: Phenomenon in which members of a birth cohort tend to experience a particular life course event or rite of passage—puberty, marriage, childbearing, graduation, entry into the workforce, death—at roughly the same time

demographer: Sociologist who studies trends in population characteristics

migration: Movement of populations from one geographic area to another

period effect: Phenomenon in which a historical event or major social trend contributes to the unique shape and outlook of a birth cohort

urbanization: Process by which people leave rural areas and begin to concentrate in large cities

14

Architects of Change

Reconstructing Society

Social Change

Social Movements

The Sociological Imagination Revisited

Jonathan Simms, a 17-year-old student from a working-class family in Belfast, Northern Ireland, was a gifted soccer player who some felt had a chance of playing professionally. In September 2001, however, things began to change. He seemed to lose interest in soccer, and his playing suffered. Around the house, he became clumsy and began falling down, dropping things, and slurring his words. His parents suspected that he was drinking or taking drugs.

Within weeks, Jonathan became so weak that he had to be rushed to the hospital. He was diagnosed with a condition called variant Creutzfeldt-Jakob disease, popularly known as mad cow disease. This malady is a debilitating condition that results from eating infected beef. It can incubate in the body for years, even decades, before manifesting itself by attacking the brain (Belkin, 2003). By the middle of 2002, Jonathan could no longer walk or talk. His parents had to bathe him. Soon he became totally unresponsive, lying in bed in a vegetative state.

Doctors told Jonathan's parents that there was no chance he would live more than a year. But his father, Don, refused to accept the prognosis. And so he set out on a single-minded mission: to save his son's life. Don quit his job and spent days on the Internet trying to find doctors, researchers, anybody who could commute his son's death sentence.

Don Simms eventually found a researcher, Steven Dealler, who had been experimenting with a powerful and sometimes lethal new drug called pentosan polysulfate (PPS). PPS had shown some effectiveness in treating animals suffering from a similar disease called scrapie but had never been tested on humans. The problem with PPS is that it must be injected directly into the brain to achieve its intended effect. Most doctors were convinced that injecting this drug directly into a human's brain would be fatal.

So Don embarked on another quest: to find someone who would be willing to use this technique on his son. He found Dr. Nikolai Rainov, a neurosurgeon who was an expert on injecting cancer drugs directly into the brain. Dr. Rainov agreed to treat Jonathan, but the board of neurosurgery at Rainov's hospital refused to approve the treatment plan, stating that it was simply too dangerous (Belkin, 2003). Britain's Committee on Safety of Medicines entered the fray, saying that there was no rational basis for prescribing the drug ("Family of VCJD Victim Claim Untried Treatment Is a Success," 2003).

Don didn't give up. He found a hospital in Germany that would allow the PPS treatment. He chartered a medical transport plane—at his own expense—and prepared his son for the trip. But days before the family was set to leave, the German Department of Health blocked them. Germany had no cases of mad cow disease and wanted to keep it that way.

Again, Don refused to quit. He hired a lawyer and took the case to court in Great Britain. Numerous legal battles ensued. But in December 2002, 15 months after the initial diagnosis, a High Court judge ruled that the family could proceed with the treatment.

Jonathan began PPS treatments in February 2003. After several months, his doctors noticed that his heart rhythms were improving, that he had regained his ability to swallow, and that he was more responsive to light and pain. There were none of the adverse side effects that critics had predicted. By all accounts, the disease had been brought under control. In 2008, his condition was upgraded from "critical" to "non-life threatening." However, in 2011, Jonathan Simms finally died. Nevertheless, he lived for a decade with the disease—that's about a decade longer than anyone except his father thought possible at the time of his diagnosis. To date, he is the world's longest known survivor of mad cow disease (Yurkiewicz, 2012).

The message of the Jonathan Simms case is sociologically compelling: An individual was able to overcome the institutional obstacles of a massive international medical establishment to find an answer to a seemingly insoluble problem. As we have seen throughout this book, institutions must operate in a highly structured, standardized, and impersonal way, at a level above the interests and personalities of the individual people they are created to serve. Imagine the chaos that would ensue if the system were set up so that any parent with a terminally ill child could compel researchers, physicians, and hospitals to concoct unique and risky treatments. The entire health care system would quickly collapse. That hasn't stopped some patient advocacy groups from lobbying for laws that would allow the "compassionate use" of not-yet-approved experimental drugs for seriously ill patients who have run out of other options (Harmon, 2009). The Food and Drug Administration (FDA) now permits the use of some experimental drugs, but only in extreme emergency cases and with many safeguards and restrictions.

But from an institutional perspective, new drugs must be tested meticulously—and sometimes slowly—to determine their effectiveness and to identify all potentially dangerous side effects before they are made available to the public. A sharp line must be drawn between the need to satisfy the principles of sound scientific method and the desire to help people who are suffering (D. J. Rothman & Edgar, 1992). Insurance companies usually won't pay for drugs that have not completed rigorous scientific testing (Harmon, 2009). Indeed, in 2005, the FDA slowed down its drug approval process in response to several reports of unsafe drugs on the market (G. Harris, 2005). But Jonathan's story shows that individuals can overcome bureaucratic slowness and actually change a part of the social structure. As a result of Don Simms's actions, the standard medical approach to treating people infected with mad cow disease changed.

In the past, only the most dedicated individuals, such as Don Simms, were able to become highly involved in medical decisions. Today, however, such involvement is almost routine. At the first appearance of a symptom—even before a doctor mentions a diagnosis or prescribes a drug—people can immediately go online and consult one of the thousands of medical websites or blogs that offer information (some of it more trustworthy than others) on everything from common colds to exotic diseases. And when they do visit their doctors, patients typically arrive with information they've downloaded from the Internet.

By working together, individuals with the same illnesses or medical concerns have also been able to act as their own best advocates. For instance, in the early 1990s, AIDS deaths were mounting while the slow progress of the government drug-approval process kept drugs out of the hands of the people who needed them. But AIDS activists demanded that the FDA loosen rules for clinical trials and speed up the approval process (L. K. Altman, 2011). They were successful and thus altered the way AIDS drugs are developed and regulated. Effective treatments—called antiretroviral therapies (ARVs)—are now being produced more quickly and are making an impact (McNeil, 2011). For many people who are HIV positive, AIDS is now merely a chronic illness, not the inevitable death sentence it once was (D. Brown, 2011).

AIDS activists have also successfully pressured pharmaceutical companies to allow developing countries in sub–Saharan Africa and elsewhere to import cheaper, generic ARVs (Swarns, 2001). As a result, access to ARVs has expanded dramatically over the last few years, increasing by 63% between 2009 and 2011. In 2011, 8 million people in the developing world received treatment, the first time the number of people being treated for HIV exceeded the number of those who were eligible but who didn't have access to the treatment (about 6.8 million). In some sub–Saharan African countries with high rates of HIV infection—Botswana, Swaziland, Zambia, Namibia, and South Africa—over 80% of people in need now have access to ARVs (Avert, 2013). Activists working together magnified the influence that none of them could have had acting individually. The reach of their achievements goes beyond sick individuals to global institutions and concerns.

This theme—the power of individuals acting collectively to change the structural elements of their society—guides this final chapter of the book. I have spent the previous 13 chapters discussing how our society and everything in it is socially constructed and how these social constructions, in turn, shape the lives of individuals. You may feel a little helpless when considering how much control culture, bureaucracies, institutions, and systems of social stratification have over our lives. It's only fitting, then, to end this book on a more encouraging note, with a discussion of social change and the ways individuals can reconstruct their society.

SOCIAL CHANGE

Change is the preeminent characteristic of modern human societies, whether it occurs in personal relationships, cultural norms and values, systems of stratification, or institutions. Everywhere you look—your school, your job, your home, your government, and every aspect of your very way of life—institutional and cultural change is the rule, not the exception.

As a result of substantive changes affecting many social institutions simultaneously, the United States and other technologically advanced societies have become what sociologists call *postindustrial societies*. Economies that once centered on farms and agriculture or factories and the production of material goods now revolve around information and service industries, including communication, mass media, research and development, tourism, insurance, banking and finance, and technology. The everyday lives of ordinary people in these societies are qualitatively different from the lives of those in agricultural or industrial societies.

Change is clear when we look at specific institutions. Consider how the nature of education has changed in the past half century. If you had taken this sociology course 50 years ago, your instructor would have needed only a few tools: a good collection of books on the subject, a manual typewriter, some pencils, a ditto machine, a stack of carbon paper, a slide projector, and a love of the discipline. Good instructors today still need a love of the discipline (I hope!), but it's becoming difficult to teach interestingly, effectively, and efficiently without taking advantage of state-of-the-art technology: high-speed, in-class Internet access; databases, videos, and course materials available online; social networking sites for quick responses to course-related topics; and computerized test banks. Instructors can now use software programs that instantaneously grade essay exams (Markoff, 2013) or allow them to monitor whether students are keeping up with their online reading assignments (Streitfeld, 2013). Indeed, the growing popularity of massive open online courses (MOOCs) could very well reshape the entire college experience in years to come.

Indeed, technological advances have made similar inroads into almost every occupation—as well as almost every social institution. Family life in the United States has also changed considerably over the past 60 years. Divorce rates were low in the 1950s, skyrocketed in the 1960s and 1970s, stabilized in the

1980s and 1990s, and have dropped a bit in the 2000s. Women have entered the workforce in unprecedented numbers. People are waiting longer to marry, and once they do, they are having fewer children. Cultural concerns about gender equality have altered the way men and women relate to one another inside and outside the home. Social and sexual rules that once seemed permanent and natural have disintegrated: Same-sex couples can legally marry in some states. Unmarried couples can live openly together, unmarried women can have and keep their babies without community condemnation, and remaining single and remaining childless are acceptable lifestyle options. In short, today's family bears little resemblance to the cultural ideal of the 1950s.

These changes in family life have, in turn, affected other institutions. Because so many families are headed by dual-earner couples these days, children spend less time with their parents than they did in the past, forcing families to depend on others to look after their children: paid caregivers, friends, neighbors, and/or teachers. More parents than ever rely on professional day care centers to watch over their preschool-age children. Many of these centers require that children be toilet trained before they enroll, compelling parents to exert premature pressure on their children to comply. As a result, many pediatricians report an increase in children with toilet training problems, such as lack of daytime and nighttime urine control (Erica Goode, 1999).

Schools are also being called on to address many of the problems families used to deal with at home. They now routinely provide students with training in moral values, technological and financial "literacy," adequate nutrition, and practical instruction to help them avoid drug and alcohol abuse, teen pregnancy, and sexually transmitted diseases.

Not surprisingly, the very nature of childhood is also changing. Contemporary social critics argue that childhood has all but disappeared in the modern world. In the United States, children are exposed to events, devices, images, and ideas that would have been inconceivable to their Baby Boom grandparents or Generation X parents when they were young. Moreover, the increasingly competitive nature of childhood is making some parents feel obligated to give their young children every conceivable edge to help them succeed.

More seriously, children these days seem to have more trouble getting along in society than they once did. Harassment, bullying, verbal abuse and disrespect of teachers, and gang activity have become common elements of many children's school experiences. In 2011, there were 1.2 million nonfatal victimizations of 12- to 18-year-olds at school consisting of 649,000 thefts and 597,000 violent incidents. About 7% of teachers nationwide have been threatened with injury or physically attacked by a student. The majority of public schools now control access to school grounds, require faculty and staff to wear photo IDs, limit students' access to social networks, forbid student cell phone use at school, or use surveillance cameras on campus (National Center for Education Statistics, 2013). According to the National Center for Education Statistics (2012a), 24.5% of public high school students are suspended each year and another 3.2% are expelled. And it's not just teenage students. A nationwide study found that about 7 out of every 1,000 three- and four-year-old preschoolers are expelled each year for misbehavior, a rate more than three times as high as for K–12 students (Gilliam, 2005).

In 1990, about 66,000 juveniles in the United States were arrested for the sale, manufacture, or possession of illegal drugs; in 2009, that figure increased to more than 130,000 (ProQuest Statistical Abstract, 2013). The National Longitudinal Study of Adolescent Health found that one in four young people between the ages of 12 and 17 has used a gun or a knife or has been in a situation where someone was injured by a weapon in the past year ("Study Finds Increase in Weapons Use," 2000). No wonder that since the late 1980s, 44 states have adopted new laws enabling courts to try more children as adults. Between 1990 and 2008, the number of juveniles sent to adult jails and prisons increased by over 300% (Minton & Sabol, 2009). In fact, 85% of youthful offenders are held in adult facilities rather than juvenile detention centers (Minton, 2013).

The state of childhood is even more precarious in other parts of the world:

- UNICEF (2010) estimates that between 500 million and 1.5 billion children worldwide experience violence annually. And every year as many as 275 million children witness domestic violence.
- About 830,000 children around the globe die each year from preventable accidents, such as drowning, burns, car crashes, poisoning, and falls (cited in McNeil, 2008).
- The United Nations estimates that about 1.1 million children worldwide are deprived of their liberty and

detained in prisons, military facilities, immigration detention centers, welfare centers, or educational facilities (Hamilton, Anderson, Barnes, & Dorling, 2011).

- More than 158 million children under 14 are engaged in child labor, many in hazardous conditions involving mines, agricultural chemicals and pesticides, and heavy machinery (UNICEF, 2011). Some are as young as five or six. Often they're not even paid for their labor (Wines, 2006).

Clearly, social change doesn't always make children's lives as carefree as we would wish.

The Speed of Social Change

In the distant past, societies tended to change slowly, almost imperceptibly, during the course of one's lifetime. Family and community traditions typically spanned many generations. Although the traditional societies that exist today still change relatively slowly, change in postindustrial societies is particularly fast paced. Even while writing this book, I've had to revise several examples at the last minute because things have changed so abruptly. The pre-Facebook, pre-Twitter, pre-Instagram early 2000s already seem like a nostalgic, bygone era.

Because we live in a world that seems to be in a constant state of flux, we're often tempted to believe that social change is an exclusively contemporary issue. Keep in mind, however, that sociologists and other scholars have long expressed deep concern over the effects that social change has on people. The 19th-century sociologist Émile Durkheim (1897/1951) argued that rapid social change creates a vacuum in norms, which he called *anomie*, where the old cultural rules no longer apply. When things change quickly—through sudden economic shifts, wars, natural disasters, population explosions, or rapid transitions from a traditional to a modern society—people become disoriented and experience anomie as they search for new guidelines to govern their lives.

Widespread anomie affects the larger society as well. When change disrupts social norms, it unleashes our naturally greedy impulses. Without norms to constrain our unlimited aspirations and with too few resources to satisfy our unrestrained desires, we are in a sense doomed to frustrating lives of striving for unattainable goals (Durkheim, 1897/1951). The result, Durkheim felt, is higher rates of suicide and criminal activity as well as weakened ties to family, neighborhood, and friends.

But change isn't always bad. Sometimes speedy change is necessary to effectively address shifting social conditions. For instance, over the span of a few years in the early 2000s, school districts around the country drastically modified their curricula in response to the sudden ascendancy of the Internet in students' everyday lives, forever changing the face of U.S. education. At least 70% of public school teachers now use computers in their classes at least some of the time (National Center for Education Statistics, 2010).

The velocity of change today has affected the way sociologists go about their work, too. When U.S. society was understood to be relatively stable, sociological study was fairly straightforward. Most social researchers in the 1950s believed that one could start a 5- or 10-year study of some social institution, say the family or higher education, and assume that the institution would still be much the same when the study ended (Wolfe, 1991). Today, such assumptions about the staying power of institutions are dubious at best.

There is no such thing as a permanent social institution. Thus, sociologists, like everyone else in contemporary society, have had to adjust their thinking and their methods to accommodate the rapid pace of social change.

Causes of Social Change

The difficulty of pinning down any aspect of society when change is so rapid has led sociologists to study change itself. Following in the footsteps of Durkheim, they ask, what causes all these technological, cultural, and institutional changes? On occasion, massive change—in the private lives of individuals as well as in entire social institutions—can result from a single dramatic event, such as the attacks of September 11, 2001, Hurricane Katrina in 2005, the global economic meltdown of 2008, Superstorm Sandy in 2012, or the federal government shutdown in 2013. We can be thankful that such momentous events are relatively rare. Sociologists who focus on change tell us that institutional transformations are more likely to be caused over time by a variety of social forces, including environmental and population pressures, cultural innovation, and technological and cultural diffusion.

Environmental and Population Pressures

As you saw in Chapter 13, the shifting size and shape of the population—globally and locally—is enough by itself to create change in societies. As populations grow, more and more people move either into urban areas, where jobs are easier to find, or into previously uninhabited areas, where natural resources are plentiful.

Environmental sociologists note the complex interplay among humans, social structure, and natural resources as previously undeveloped territories are settled. For instance, one social scientist has argued that many civilizations throughout history—such as the Easter Islanders, the Mayans, and the Norse colony in Greenland— collapsed because deforestation led to soil erosion, which led to food shortages and ultimately political and social collapse (Diamond, 2005).

Even when new areas are developed for food production, environmental damage often occurs. Of course, improved food supplies have had obvious benefits for societies around the world. Fewer and fewer people today die from famine and malnutrition than ever before. But the positive effects of a growing global food supply have been tempered by the serious environmental harm that new production techniques have caused. For instance, pesticide use has increased 17-fold over the past several decades, threatening the safety of water supplies. Some insects have developed resistance, which leads to increased pesticide use. New crop varieties often require more irrigation than old varieties, which has been accompanied by increased erosion and water runoff. As demand for meat products increases, cattle ranches expand, destroying natural habitats, displacing native animal species, and polluting water sources. Modern factory farming practices helped spread mad cow disease throughout Great Britain (Cowley, 2003), affecting people like Jonathan Simms.

More broadly, the clearing of forests and the burning of fossil fuels, such as coal, oil, and natural gas, have been implicated as the chief cause of *global climate change*—a steady rise in Earth's average temperature as a result of increasing amounts of carbon dioxide in the atmosphere. We are already seeing the consequences of climate change: Polar ice caps and glaciers are melting; sea levels are rising; plants and animals are being forced out of their habitats; certain diseases, like malaria, are spreading to higher altitudes; and the number of severe storms, heat waves, and droughts is increasing. Many scientists believe that the long-term effects of global climate change may lead to unprecedented worldwide catastrophe.

Cultural and Technological Innovation

But population and environmental pressures have the potential to create more positive social change in the form of cultural and technological innovation. For example, natural disasters, such as earthquakes, hurricanes, and tornadoes, often inspire improvements in emergency response technology, home safety products, and architectural design that improve everyone's lives. Likewise, concerns about pollution and global climate change have fostered innovative changes in people's behavior (e.g., recycling and conserving energy); the creation of environmentally safe, "green" products and services (low-watt light bulbs, low-flow showerheads, and biodegradable detergent); and the development of energy-efficient hybrid vehicles and nonpolluting energy sources, such as solar power and wind power. The result is felt not only on an individual level but also on a societal level, as eco-efficient and environmentally sustainable businesses grow around these innovations and attract investors. The Apollo Alliance (2011), a coalition of business, labor, environmental, and community groups, estimates that a $500 billion investment over 10 years could produce 5 million jobs in renewable energy, hybrid cars, and infrastructure replacement. Most universities, companies, and even city governments routinely employ full-time "sustainability officers" to look for cost-saving ways to minimize the wasting of electricity and natural gas, improve energy efficiency, and reduce harmful greenhouse gasses (Greenblatt, 2009).

Sometimes, these scientific discoveries and technological inventions spur further innovations within a society. Improvements in motor vehicle safety, such as air bags, safety belts, child safety seats, and motorcycle helmets, have contributed to large reductions in motor vehicle deaths and fundamentally changed the way we drive. Water fluoridation is credited for a 40% to 60% reduction in tooth loss in adults. Safer and healthier foods have all but eliminated nutritional deficiency diseases such as rickets, goiter, and pellagra in the United States (Centers for Disease Control and Prevention, 1999).

Often, revolutionary innovations seem insignificant at first. Imagine what life would be like without the invention of corrective eyeglasses, which dramatically extended the activities of near- and farsighted people and fostered the belief that physical limitations could be overcome with a little ingenuity. (For one thing, instead of reading these wonderful words, you'd be reading strings of random letters and symbols since I wouldn't be able to see what I was typing.) The invention of indoor plumbing, the internal combustion engine, television, telephones, the microchip, nuclear fusion, and effective birth control have been instrumental in determining the course of human history. Sometimes the smallest innovation has the largest impact: According to one author, without the machine-made precision screw—the most durable way of attaching one object to another—entire fields of science would have languished; routine maritime commerce would have been impossible; and there would have been no machine tools and hence no industrial products and no industrial revolution (Rybczynski, 1999).

But social institutions can sometimes be slow to adjust to scientific and technological innovations. Consider, for instance, the medical treatment of infertility. Artificial insemination, in vitro fertilization, surrogate motherhood, and other medical advances have increased the number of previously infertile people who can now bear and raise children. And more and more same-sex couples are utilizing infertility treatments to have children. According to one of the nation's largest sperm banks, about one third of its clients are lesbian couples (Holson, 2011). Yet these technological developments were changing the face of parenthood well before society began to recognize and address the ethical, moral, and legal issues they raised. For instance, close to half a million embryos created through in vitro fertilization are kept frozen at fertility clinics around the country. Many of them belong to couples that no longer need them because they are finished having children. But it's unclear exactly what should be done with the embryos. Some couples are opposed to destroying them for moral or religious reasons. Most couples don't want to donate them to other couples because of genetic links to their own children. (In fact, state and federal regulations make donation to other couples difficult because they require donors to come back to the clinics to be tested for infectious diseases.) Still others would like to donate them for research, but that option is not always available (Grady, 2008).

The very definition of family and parenthood can also become complicated when technology plays a role in childbearing. Surrogacy—an arrangement in which a woman agrees to become pregnant and give birth to a child others will raise—divides motherhood into three distinct roles, which may be occupied by three separate people: the *genetic* mother (the one who supplies the egg from which the fetus develops), the *gestational* mother (the one who becomes pregnant and gives birth), and the *social* mother (the one who raises the child). Add to the mix the *genetic* father and the *social* father, and you can see how difficult it can sometimes be to establish legal parenthood. There is little uniformity among states about whether to recognize and enforce surrogacy agreements. Some states grant preference to surrogacy contracts; others assume the woman giving birth to the child is the mother and will reverse that determination only when the commissioning couple files a prebirth order to legally adopt the child after he or she is born (Shapo, 2006).

Moreover, the technological innovations that are meant to improve our lives can also change people's behavior in unanticipated, and sometimes dangerous, ways. Consider these examples:

- Smokestacks were originally developed to reduce *local* ground-level air pollution. But they spread pollution at high altitudes, thereby contributing to acid rain and harming the air quality of other cities, states, and even countries (Likens, Wright, Galloway, & Butler, 1979).
- Antibiotics were a revolutionary advance in the treatment of infectious diseases. But doctors soon began prescribing them for minor illnesses just to be safe. As a result of the overuse of antibiotics, some infectious and highly dangerous organisms have become resistant to the drugs. Some public health experts estimate that perhaps as many as 100,000 deaths a year in the United States occur as a result of antibiotic-resistant infections (cited in Interlandi, 2010).
- The distractions caused by technological devices used in cars—smartphones, onboard navigation systems, entertainment centers—may be responsible for as many as 1.5 million crashes each year. The National Highway Safety Administration estimates that 18% of fatal and injurious car accidents involve a driver distracted by a mobile device. The risk of a driver getting into an accident or near accident is 23 times greater when she or he is texting while driving than when she or he is not doing so (cited in Federal Communication Commission, 2013).
- Not only do hybrid cars reduce air pollution and reliance on fossil fuels, but they also reduce noise

pollution. However, pedestrians and bicyclists sometimes have difficulty hearing these cars coming their way, thereby increasing the risk of being struck or run over. At intersections, parking lots, and other places where cars travel slowly, pedestrians and bicyclists get hit by hybrids at up to twice the normal rate. To address the problem, manufacturers now market fake car noise so unwary pedestrians and cyclists can hear them coming (Mihm, 2009).

Diffusion of Technologies and Cultural Practices

Another cause of social change is *cultural diffusion*: the process by which beliefs, technology, customs, and other cultural items are spread from one group or society to another. You may not realize it, but most of the taken-for-granted aspects of our daily lives originally came from somewhere else. For instance, pajamas, clocks, toilets, glass, coins, newspapers, and soap were initially imported into Western cultures from elsewhere (Linton, 1937).

Diffusion often occurs because one society considers the culture or technology of another society to be useful. However, the diffusion process is not always friendly, as you may recall from the discussion of colonization in Chapter 10. When one society's territory is taken over by another society, the indigenous people may be required to adapt to the customs and beliefs of the invaders. When Europeans conquered the New World, Native American peoples were forced to abandon their traditional ways of life and become more "civilized." Hundreds of thousands of Native Americans died in the process, not only from violent conflict but also from malnutrition and new diseases inadvertently brought by their conquerors. Whether diffusion is invited or imposed, the effect is the same: a chain reaction of social changes that affect both individuals and the larger social structure.

SOCIAL MOVEMENTS

One danger of talking about the sources of social change or its cultural, environmental, and institutional consequences is that we then tend to see change as a purely macrolevel structural phenomenon, something that happens to us rather than something we create. But social change is not some huge, invisible hand that descends from the heavens to arbitrarily alter our routine way of life. It is, in the end, a phenomenon driven by human action.

Collective action by large numbers of people has always been a major agent of social change, whether it takes the form of mothers marching on Washington, DC, to demand gun control legislation; people holding a pray-in outside the Capitol building to encourage lawmakers to pass a budget "that is more reflective of the moral values of our nation" ("Religious Groups Gather," 2005); or a sit-in by students in the Harvard University president's house to demand higher wages for the school's blue-collar workers. When people organize and extend their activities beyond the immediate confines of the group, they may become the core of a *social movement* (Zurcher & Snow, 1981).

Underlying all social movements is a concern with social change: the desire to enact it, stop it before it begins, or reverse it. That desire may be expressed in a variety of ways, from peaceful activities such as signing petitions, participating in civil demonstrations, donating money, and campaigning during elections to violent activities such as rioting and overthrowing a government.

Types of Social Movements

Depending on the nature of their goals, social movements can be categorized as reform movements, countermovements, or revolutionary movements. A *reform movement* attempts to change limited aspects of a society but does not seek to alter or replace major social institutions. Take the U.S. civil rights movement of the 1960s. It did not call for an overhaul of the U.S. economic system (capitalism) or political system (two-party democracy). Instead, it advocated a more limited change: opening up existing institutions to full and equal participation by members of minority groups (DeFronzo, 1991). Similarly, the anti–Vietnam War movement questioned government policy (and in the process brought down two presidents—Lyndon Johnson and Richard Nixon), but it didn't seek to change the form of government itself (Fendrich, 2003). Other recent examples of reform movements include the women's movement, the nuclear freeze movement, the labor union movement, the school prayer movement, and the environmental movement. The recent Tea Party movement is a reform movement that espouses the values of individual liberty and limited government. Their message resonated with enough voters in 2010 that several Tea Party candidates won election to Congress (though they were less successful in 2012). However, although adherents express a desire to dismantle the federal government for what they perceive to be out-of-control spending, debt, and deficits, the politicians they helped elect still must enact any change within the confines of the present system of government.

Because reform movements seek to alter some aspect of existing social arrangements, they are usually opposed by some people and groups. *Countermovements* are designed to prevent or reverse the changes sought or accomplished by an earlier movement. A countermovement is most likely to emerge when the reform movement against which it is reacting becomes large and effective in pursuing its goals and therefore comes to be seen as a threat to personal and social interests (Chafetz & Dworkin, 1987; Mottl, 1980).

For instance, the emergence in the 1980s and 1990s of a conservative social countermovement often called the "religious right" or the "Christian right" was provoked by a growing perception among its members of enormous social upheaval in U.S. society: the breakdown of traditional roles and values and a concerted challenge to existing institutions such as education, religion, and the family. Although members of the religious right blamed these changes on the civil rights, antiwar, student, and women's movements of the 1960s and 1970s (Klatch, 1991), they perceived the women's movement as particularly dangerous. Indeed, the leaders of the religious right were the first, in modern times, to articulate the notion that the push for women's equality was responsible for the unhappiness of many individual women and the weakening of the American family (Faludi, 1991). Access to legal abortion, the high divorce rate, and the increased number of children who grow up with working mothers are often offered as proof that the moral bases of family life are eroding (Klatch, 1991).

Over the past few decades, the religious right has had some success in shifting the political and social mood of the country. It first gained legitimacy in 1980, when presidential candidate Ronald Reagan and several Senate candidates who were supported by the group won the election. It reasserted its influence in 1994 with the takeover of Congress by conservative Republicans. And it gained even more power and visibility with the election and reelection of George W. Bush in the early 2000s, who promoted

many religious-right themes. Today, it remains a formidable and influential wing of the Republican Party.

In the late 2000s and early 2010s, the religious right turned its focus to opposing the increasing visibility of homosexuality in U.S. society. Through organizations such as the Eagle Forum, the Christian Coalition, the Family Research Council, the Traditional Values Coalition, Concerned Women for America, Focus on the Family, the Alliance for Marriage, and many smaller groups around the United States, it has achieved some notable triumphs at the state and local levels. It has succeeded in influencing public school curricula as well as promoting anti–gay-rights legislation and defense of marriage acts at the city and state levels. Hours after the U.S. Supreme Court rolled back the federal Defense of Marriage Act in 2013, various religious organization began mounting a counteroffensive to try to reinstate it.

Over the years, the religious right has been especially effective in limiting access to abortion. Even though the majority of U.S. citizens still favor the legal right to abortion (Pew Research Center, 2013), virtually every state in the nation over the past two decades has enacted new restrictions, such as mandatory waiting periods, gestational limits, state-mandated counseling, spousal consent, and parental notification (Alan Guttmacher Institute, 2013). In recent years, legislatures in states such as Kansas, Oklahoma, and Indiana have been successful in passing restrictive laws that make it even more difficult or uncomfortable for women to get abortions, such as requiring doctors to show the woman a picture of the fetus or regulating the amount and type of equipment, drugs, and resources available in clinics. Few medical schools or residency programs in obstetrics and gynecology provide training in abortion techniques, although pressure from medical student advocacy groups has led a few programs to reinstate abortion instruction into the curriculum (Bazelon, 2010).

Given such an environment, it's not surprising that abortion services have become less and less available. About 87% of all U.S. counties (and 97% of rural counties) have no abortion provider. These counties are home to 35% of all American women. Nationwide, the number of abortion providers decreased by about 40% between 1982 and 2008 (Alan Guttmacher Institute, 2011; Henshaw & Finer, 2003; Kaiser Family Foundation, 2008). In addition, rates of legal abortion have declined steadily over the past two decades. In 1990, there were about 27 abortions per 1,000 women between the ages of 15 and 44; today, that figure is 19.4 per 1,000 (ProQuest Statistical Abstract, 2013).

The women's movement, the gay-rights movement, and the religious right all remain quite active today, creating numerous colorful conflicts in the national political arena. However, it is important to remember that all of these movements are pursuing their interests within the existing social system—as do all reform movements and countermovements. In contrast, *revolutionary movements* attempt to overthrow the entire system itself, whether it is the government or the existing social structure, in order to replace it with another (Skocpol, 1979). The American Revolution of 1776, the French Revolution of 1789, the Russian Revolution of 1917, the Iranian Revolution of 1979, and the Afghan Revolution of 1996 are examples of movements that toppled existing governments and created a new social order.

Revolutionary change in basic social institutions can be brought about through nonviolent means, such as peaceful labor strikes, democratic elections, and civil disobedience. However, most successful revolutions have involved some level of violence on the part of both movement participants and groups opposing the revolution (DeFronzo, 1991).

Elements of Social Movements

Whichever type they are, social movements occur when dissatisfied people see their condition as resulting from society's inability to meet their needs. Movements typically develop when certain segments of the population conclude that society's resources—access to political power, higher education, living wages, legal justice, medical care, a clean and healthy environment, and so on—are distributed unequally and unfairly (Roger Brown, 1986). People come to believe that they have a moral right to the satisfaction of their unmet expectations and that this satisfaction cannot or will not occur without some effort on their part. This perception is often based on the experience of past failures in working within the system.

As individuals and groups who share this sense of frustration and unfairness interact, the existing system begins to lose its perceived legitimacy (Piven & Cloward, 1977). Individuals who ordinarily might have considered themselves helpless come to believe that as a social movement they have the capacity to change things and significantly alter their lives and the lives of others. For instance, in 2006, a website called MomsRising.org was launched, bringing mothers together to talk about ways to change public policy. In "house parties" all across the country, small groups of mothers meet regularly to discuss ways to lobby legislators on issues like family leave, pay equity, health insurance, childcare, and after-school activities (St. George, 2007). They now have over a million members nationwide and a blogging/social media readership of over 3 million and have been influential in changing paid family-leave policies in several states (MomsRising.org, 2013).

Ideology

Any successful social movement must have an *ideology*, a coherent system of beliefs, values, and ideas that justifies its existence (R. W. Turner & Killian, 1987; Zurcher & Snow, 1981). An ideology fulfills several functions. First, it helps frame the issue in moral terms. Once people perceive the moral goodness of their position, they become willing to risk arrest, personal financial costs, or more for the good of the cause. Second, the ideology defines the group's interests and helps to identify people as either supporters or detractors, creating identifiable "good guys" and "villains." Finally, an ideology provides participants with a collective sense of what the specific goals of the movement are or should be.

Consider the antiabortion (or pro-life) movement. Its ideology rests on several assumptions about the nature of childhood and motherhood (Luker, 1984). For instance, it assumes that each conception is an act of God and so abortion violates God's will. The ideology also states that life begins at conception, the fetus is an individual who has a constitutional right to life, and every human life should be valued (Michener, DeLamater, & Schwartz, 1986). This ideology reinforces the view among adherents that abortion is immoral, evil, and self-indulgent.

The power of an ideology to mobilize support for a social movement often depends on the broader cultural and historical context in which the movement exists. For instance, it would have seemed in the 2003 buildup to the invasion of Iraq that antiwar activists would be able to make a strong case against going to war by using an ideology based on a portrayal of the United States as a hostile aggressor. After all, the country we were set to invade, Iraq, posed no direct threat to the United States, hadn't undertaken a large-scale military mobilization, wasn't involved in planning or carrying out the 9/11 attacks that precipitated our military action, and wasn't harboring those who were involved. Internationally, the sympathetic response that we received from other countries immediately after 9/11 was short lived, replaced by a growing perception that the United States was a global bully whose policies ignore the interests of people in other countries. The vast majority of nations around the world—foes and allies alike—strongly opposed the invasion.

But the post–9/11 cultural context in this country was a mixture of anger, fear, lingering shock, and heightened patriotism, which made an ideology of military restraint intolerable to many Americans. Enduring memories of earlier antiwar protestors' hostility toward soldiers returning from Vietnam during the late 1960s and early 1970s complicated the task. Reluctant to disrespect the individual soldiers in Iraq who were willing to put their lives at risk, antiwar activists had to walk a thin line between opposing U.S. aggression and expressing support for the young men and women who were being asked to carry out that aggression on the front lines. Against such a backdrop, the ideology of the 2003 antiwar movement—which advocated a diplomatic, reflective, and measured approach—sounded unpatriotic, weak, and inadequate, not to mention disloyal to the thousands who died in the 9/11 attacks. Not surprisingly, the movement failed to prevent the onset of war.

Although an ideology might be what attracts people to a movement, it must be spread through social networks of friends, family, coworkers, and other contacts (Zurcher & Snow, 1981). For some people, in fact, the ideology of the movement is secondary to other social considerations. Potential participants are unlikely to join without being introduced to the movement by someone they know (Gladwell, 2010). The ideological leaders of a social movement might want to believe that participants are there because of "the cause," but chances are the participants have a friend or acquaintance who persuaded them to be there (Gerlach & Hine, 1970; Stark & Bainbridge, 1980).

Sometimes the activities required to promote or sustain a particular movement run counter to the ideological goals of the movement itself. The leaders of successful political revolutions, for example, soon realize that to run the country they now control, they must create highly structured bureaucracies not

unlike the ones they have overthrown. Two years after helping to topple a dictatorial regime that had ruled for 30 years, leaders of the Egyptian pro-democracy movement issued an ultimatum calling for the resignation of the new democratically elected president, Mohammed Morsi, who was eventually forced out by the Egyptian military.

Furthermore, an ill-defined, unarticulated ideology—or one that is too broadly defined—may in the end muffle any headway the movement is able to make in the first place. For instance, the Occupy Wall Street movement generated significant attention in 2011. Its "We are the 99%" slogan became a popular call for economic justice nationwide. President Obama came out in support of it during the 2012 election campaign; so did House Minority Leader Nancy Pelosi. But the movement has not sustained the same level of interest or effectiveness since. Although its general goal was to reduce economic inequality, it advocated a slew of specific objectives that included a reduction of corporate influence in politics, a more balanced distribution of income, job creation, bank reform, relief for indebted students, housing reform, and so on. In addition, it expanded its interests to include protection of workers in Bangladesh and solidarity for protestors in Turkey, Brazil, and Greece. Some critics, as well as members of the movement itself, argued that its ideological purview has been spread too thin to effectively influence policy.

Participants in reform movements and countermovements may also have to engage in behaviors that conflict with the ideological beliefs of the movement. The religious right movement's pro-family, pro-motherhood positions are clearly designed to turn back the feminist agenda. However, early in the movement, it became clear that to be successful, it would have to enlist high-profile women to campaign against feminist policies. Women on the religious right frequently had to leave their families, travel the country to make speeches, and display independent strength—characteristics that were anything but the models of traditional womanhood they were publicly promoting.

Ironically, social movements sometimes require the involvement of individuals from outside the group whose interests the movement represents. For example, many of the people who fought successfully for Blacks' right to vote in Alabama and Mississippi during the civil rights movement of the 1950s and 1960s were middle-class white college students from the North. Similarly, it wasn't until mainstream religious organizations, labor groups, and college students got involved that the living wage movement—an effort to require cities and counties to pay their low-wage workers an amount above the federal minimum wage—became successful. As of 2008, 140 cities had passed living wage laws (Living Wage Resource Center, 2006). The Chicago City Council, for instance, passed an ordinance requiring large retail stores, such as Wal-Mart and Home Depot, to pay a minimum wage that was almost twice as high as the federal minimum wage (Eckholm, 2006). In 2007, Maryland became the first state to require a living wage for all state employees.

The ideology of a social movement gains additional credibility when voiced by those whose interests seem contrary to its goals. In the mid 2000s, opposition to the war in Iraq gained some traction not because people took a second look at the original antiwar ideology or because street protests and rallies suddenly gained their attention. Instead, it grew because many U.S. soldiers who fought there and saw the conditions firsthand started speaking out in opposition, often under the threat of disciplinary action (Houppert, 2005). Combatants knew the reality of war in ways that civilian protestors never could (Utne, 2006). Some even spoke out while on the front lines, posting daily blogs that criticized the condition of military equipment and resources, our lack of understanding of Iraqi insurgents, and ultimately our very involvement in the war (Finer, 2005). Membership in organizations with names like Operation Truth, Gold Star Families for Peace, and Iraq and Afghanistan Veterans of America grew during the early years of the war (N. Banerjee, 2005).

Furthermore, people who are already disadvantaged by particular social conditions may not be as effective as others in promoting their causes because they lack the money, time, skills, and connections that successful movements require. For instance, the people who would stand to benefit the most from environmental improvement—individuals in poor, polluted communities—have historically been uninvolved in the environmental movement. Residents tend to see environmentalists as middle- and upper-middle-class outsiders whose own neighborhoods are relatively unpolluted and who don't appreciate the community's concerns (Bullard, 1993). Nobody wants garbage dumps, landfills, incinerators, or polluting factories in their backyards. But if these are the only ventures that will provide steady employment

for residents, poor communities are left with little choice but to support them. Consequently, they often fear that outside environmentalists will take away their jobs and economic livelihoods. Recently, however, many members of poor communities have joined the environmental movement, motivated not by a "Save the earth" ideology but by a more immediately relevant one that emphasizes the unfairness and discrimination to which they are exposed. As one successful local activist put it, "People here aren't going to install solar panels on their roofs or drive a Prius, but they can demand institutional change and decent business practices" (quoted in Breslau, 2007, p. 69). In some developing nations, poor communities have mobilized resistance to commercial tree plantations, oil drilling, mining, or dam construction when these developments are perceived to constitute a threat to people's livelihoods (Martinez-Alier, 2003).

Resource Mobilization

At any given point, numerous problems in a society need to be fixed, and people's grievances remain more or less constant from year to year. Yet relatively few major social movements exist at any one time. If widespread dissatisfaction and frustration were all that was needed to sustain a social movement, "the masses would always be in revolt" (Trotsky, 1930/1959). What else is needed for a social movement to get started, gain support, and achieve its goals?

According to *resource mobilization theory*, the key ingredient is effective organization. No social movement can exist unless it has an organized system for acquiring needed resources: money, labor, participants, legal aid, access to the media, and so on (J. D. McCarthy & Zald, 1977). How far a movement goes in attaining its goals depends on its ability to expand its ranks, build large-scale public support, and transform those who join into committed participants (Zurcher & Snow, 1981).

Most large, long-term social movements involve a national and even international coalition of groups. Such widespread organization makes the movement more powerful by making recruiting and fundraising more efficient. Movements that historically have lasted the longest—the women's movement, the anti-abortion movement, the civil rights movement, the environmental movement—are those supported by large organizational bureaucracies. The National

Organization for Women, the Christian Coalition, the National Association for the Advancement of Colored People (NAACP), the Sierra Club, and the like have full-time lobbyists or political action committees in Washington that connect them to the national political system. Few movements can succeed without such connections, because achieving social change often requires changing laws or convincing courts to interpret laws in particular ways.

Highly organized social movements use an established network of communication (J. D. McCarthy & Zald, 1977). Movements need an effective system both for getting information to all participants and for recruiting and fundraising (Tarrow, 1994). The ability to quickly mobilize large numbers of people for, say, a flash mob or a march to the nation's capital depends on the ability to tell them what is going to happen and when and where it will happen. Modern social movements must use websites, Facebook, Twitter, direct mailing strategies, and networked phone and computer systems to be successful.

In 2009, a crowd of more than 10,000 youth in Moldova gathered to protest the country's communist leadership. Protestors ransacked government buildings and clashed with the police. To older observers and government officials, the sea of young people seemed to materialize out of nowhere. What they didn't realize was that protest organizers had mobilized participants through Twitter (E. Barry, 2009). Similar technological mobilization occurred during the so-called Arab Spring in 2011 when antigovernment protestors in Egypt, Tunisia, Yemen, Morocco, Libya, Syria, Bahrain, Saudi Arabia, Jordan, and elsewhere used Twitter, Facebook, and YouTube to mobilize collective actions and export images of their plight around the world. Cell phones replaced traditional reporters as the world's "eyes and ears" on the protests (Preston & Stelter, 2011). Media outlets referred to the movement variously as the Facebook Revolution, the Twitter Revolution, and the Keystroke Revolution. Today, it would be inconceivable for a movement's organizers to mobilize support *without* Facebook or Twitter.

The mass media play an equally important part in the success of a social movement by helping to validate and enlarge the scope of its cause. In other words, the media play a key role in constructing a particular social reality useful to the movement. The media spotlight sends the message that the movement's concerns are valid and that the movement is an important force in society. A small group of people disrupting a town hall meeting on health care reform is, for all intents and purposes, a nonevent without media coverage. Media recognition is often a necessary condition before those who are the targets of influence respond to the movement's claims and demands (Gamson & Wolfsfeld, 1993).

In sum, movements that succeed in enacting substantial social change are not necessarily those with the most compelling ideological positions or the greatest emotional appeal (Ferree, 1992). Instead, they are the ones with the necessary high-level organization and communication networks to mobilize supporters and the necessary media access and technological savvy to neutralize the opposition and transform the public into sympathizers.

Bureaucratization

It makes sense that the most successful social movements are those that are the best organized. However, high-level organization can backfire if it leads to rigidity and turf wars, common to any bureaucracy. When organizations within a movement differ in their philosophies and tactics, tremendous infighting and bickering may break out among organizations ostensibly working toward the same goal.

For instance, the U.S. civil rights movement during the 1950s and 1960s included many diverse, seemingly incompatible organizations. The NAACP was large, racially integrated, legalistic, and bureaucratic in form; the Student Non-violent Coordinating Committee (SNCC) was younger and more militant in its tactics and after a while excluded Whites from participation; the Southern Christian Leadership Conference (SCLC) was highly structured, had a religious ideology, and was dominated by male clergy; the Black Muslims and the Black Panthers advocated violent methods to achieve civil rights. The ideologies and methods of these diverse civil rights groups often conflicted, which arguably slowed down the extension of civil rights to African Americans.

No matter their shape, size, or motive, social movements require sustained activity over a long period (R. W. Turner & Killian, 1987). Thus, unlike riots, which are of limited duration, social movements may become permanent fixtures in the political and social environment. Ironically, a social movement whose goal is the large-scale alteration of some aspect of society can, in time, become so large and bureaucratic itself that it becomes part of the establishment it seeks to change. For instance, Sinn Féin was a movement founded in 1905 to end British rule in Ireland. Among its offshoots over the years was the Irish Republican Army, which carried out a bombing and terror campaign in Northern Ireland and England for decades. In recent years, most of the violence has been stopped, and the people of Ireland have won some autonomy. Sinn Féin is now the third-largest political party in Ireland, with its own news organization, a highly structured network of local branches, and representatives in both the Irish Parliament and the European Parliament.

In addition, people who devote their lives to a movement come to depend on it for their own livelihood. Hence, social movements organized for the purpose of enacting social change actually provide structure and order in the lives of their members, acting as sources of opportunities, careers, and rewards (Hewitt, 1988).

Political Opportunity Structure

Social movements also depend on conditions outside their reach. One such condition is the structure of existing political institutions. Political systems are more or less vulnerable and more or less receptive to challenge at different times (McAdam, McCarthy, & Zald, 1988). These ebbs and flows of political opportunities produce cycles of protest and movement activity. When political systems are firm, unyielding, and stable, people have to deal individually with their problems or air their grievances through existing channels. But when a system opens up and people realize it is vulnerable—that they can actually make a difference—movements are likely to develop.

Sometimes these opportunities are unintentional and exist quite independently of the actions of movement members. For instance, in the 1970s, two antinuclear movements arose in (what was then West) Germany and France. The movements had similar ideologies and used similar mobilization techniques. However, the German movement flourished and remains highly influential in national politics today. The French movement was weak and quickly died off. Why were the outcomes of these two movements so different? In Germany, the government procedure for reviewing nuclear power facilities provided opportunities for those opposed to nuclear power to legally intervene. The procedure in place in France

was closed and unresponsive to public sentiment (Nelkin & Pollak, 1981). Similarly, the emergence in the 1970s of the contemporary environmental movement in the United States was possible because government agencies were already sympathetic to environmental concerns (Gale, 1986).

The idea that unintentional political opportunities can encourage social movements for change was dramatically supported during the 1989 pro-democracy movement in the former Soviet Union and Eastern Europe. In the mid 1980s, the Soviet government under Mikhail Gorbachev embarked on a massive program of economic and structural reforms (*perestroika*) as well as a relaxation of constraints on freedom of expression (*glasnost*). The ensuing liberties encouraged open criticism of the political order and created new opportunities for political action (Tarrow, 1994). Protest movements took advantage of these opportunities, leading to the sometimes violent struggles for independence on the part of small, ethnically homogeneous republics that we saw during the 1990s and continue to see today in a few remaining areas. In other words, only when the political structure became less repressive could these monumental changes take place.

Political instability can sometimes spawn less dramatic reform movements. The changing fortunes of a government can create uncertainty among supporters and encourage challengers to try to take advantage of the situation. Consider once more the civil rights movement in the United States in the 1950s and 1960s. During the 1950s, as the first calls for racial equality were being heard, many conservative Southern Democrats defected to the Republican Party, where their segregationist leanings met with more sympathy. The ensuing decline of Southern white support for the Democratic Party, coupled with the movement of African Americans to large cities in the North, where they were more likely to vote, forced the Democrats to seek black support in the presidential election of 1960. The black vote is widely credited with John Kennedy's narrow victory that year (McAdam, 1982). Hence, the Kennedy administration (and later the Johnson administration) felt compelled to campaign for civil rights (Tarrow, 1994). Increased political power, in turn, enhanced the bargaining position of civil rights forces, culminating in two landmark pieces of legislation: the Civil Rights Act of 1964 and the Voting Rights Act of 1965.

At other times, existing political regimes intentionally create or actively support structural opportunities for change. For example, the U.S. anti–drunk-driving movement is strong and influential today because it enjoys substantial support from federal, state, and local governments; state and federal highway agencies; and state and local police departments (J. D. McCarthy & Wolfson, 1992). When in the 1980s the movement advocated a national drinking age of 21, many state legislatures balked, fearing a backlash from powerful alcohol producers, distributors, and retailers. However, the federal government enacted legislation threatening to withhold significant amounts of federal highway funds from states that didn't establish a drinking age of 21—a strong incentive for states to pass such a law.

Political opportunities provide the institutional framework within which social movements operate. Movements form when ordinary citizens respond to changes in the opportunity structure that lower the costs of involvement and reveal where the authorities are vulnerable. Unlike money and power, these conditions are external to the movement. If political opportunities exist, then even groups with fairly mild grievances or few resources can develop a successful movement (see also J. C. Jenkins & Perrow, 1977). In contrast, groups with deep grievances and ample resources—but few political opportunities—may never get their movements off the ground (Tarrow, 1994).

THE SOCIOLOGICAL IMAGINATION REVISITED

In the summer of 1981 with my brand new bachelor's degree in hand, I had the good fortune to visit Florence, Italy. While there, I made a point of visiting the Galleria dell'Accademia, the museum where one of my favorite works of art, Michelangelo's statue of David, resides. To my eye, it is truly a masterpiece of sculpture, nearly flawless in its detail. I stood there admiring this amazing work of art for close to two hours. As I left, I noticed several sculptures that had escaped my attention when I first entered the museum. I soon discovered that they, too, were created by Michelangelo. What made them particularly interesting was that they were all unfinished. Some were obviously near completion, but others looked to me like shapeless blocks of granite. As I looked closer, I could see the actual chisel marks the great sculptor

had made. I imagined the plan Michelangelo had in his head as he worked. I envisioned him toiling to bring form to the heavy stone.

These imperfect slabs of rock showed evidence of human creation in a way that the perfect, finished statue of David never could. At that moment, I saw Michelangelo as a real guy who fashioned beauty from shapelessness. I began to admire the genius of the creator and not just the creation. I went back to look at David again with a newfound appreciation.

Society isn't nearly as perfect as Michelangelo's David, yet we can still fall into the trap of seeing social structure as a product that exists on its own and not as something that people have collectively chiseled. We sometimes forget that many of the realities of our lives that we take for granted were the result, at some point in history, of the handiwork of individuals. One generation's radical changes become another's common features of everyday life. The fact that you can't be forced to work 70 or 80 hours a week, can't be exposed to dangerous working conditions without your knowledge, and are entitled to a certain number of paid holidays a year are a result of the actions of real people in early labor union movements.

Because we take many of our freedoms, rights, and desires for granted, we may not only overlook the struggles of those who came before us but also downplay the extent to which inequities and injustices existed in the past. For instance, many young women today have never even considered that they are only a generation or two removed from a time when they might have been prohibited from attending the college or pursuing the career of their choice, when they might have been expected to abandon their own dreams and ambitions to provide the support their husbands needed to succeed, or when they might have had to take sole responsibility for household chores and their children's daily care while their husbands focused on work and the outside world. The majority of young women polled in a survey a few years ago indicated that they didn't know that abortion was once illegal (Zernike, 2003). Like most beneficiaries of past movements, young women today simply take their freedoms and opportunities for granted, sometimes even expressing contempt for the feminists responsible for winning the rights they so casually enjoy (Stacey, 1991). A British columnist put it this way:

When I talk to girls they go, "I'm not a feminist . . . "
And I say: "What? You don't want to vote? Do

you want to be owned by your husband? Do you want your money from your job to go into his bank account? If you were raped, do you still want that to be a crime? Congratulations: you are a feminist." (quoted in Lyall, 2012, p. 40)

So the irony of social movements, then, is that the more profound and far reaching their accomplishments, the more likely we are to eventually forget the original inequities that fostered them and the efforts of the individuals who produced them.

Fundamentally, societies remain stable because enough individuals define existing conditions as satisfactory, and societies change because enough individuals define situations that were once tolerable as problems that must be acknowledged and solved. Some influential acts of individuals may at first blush appear rather insignificant. Early in 1960, four black students at North Carolina Agricultural and Technical State University, in Greensboro, engaged in a series of discussions in their dormitory room about the state of the civil rights movement. They came to the conclusion that things weren't progressing quickly enough in the still-segregated South and that it was time for action. So they decided to go to the lunch counter at the local Woolworth's store and order coffee and doughnuts. Now that might not sound like much. But in the early-1960s South, public eating facilities that weren't reserved for Blacks were forbidden by law to serve Blacks. And Greensboro at the time was the sort of place where any act of racial rebelliousness was routinely met with violence (Gladwell, 2010).

After purchasing some school supplies in another part of the store, the four students sat down at the lunch counter and placed their orders. As anticipated, the reply was, "I'm sorry, we don't serve you here" (McCain, 1991, p. 115). They remained seated for 45 minutes, citing the fact that they had been served in another part of the store without any difficulty. They were subjected to the verbal taunts, racial slurs, and even violence of angry Whites in the store.

Their actions attracted the attention of area religious leaders, community activists, and students from other local colleges, both black and white. Despite the abuses they knew awaited them, these four young men returned to Woolworth's a few days later, only this time with more demonstrators. At one point, they and their fellow protestors occupied 63 of the

65 seats available at the lunch counter. This was the first social movement covered by television, too, so word of their actions spread quickly. They received endorsements from religious organizations like the North Carolina Council of Churches. Within weeks, young African Americans and sympathetic Whites had engaged in similar acts in nine states and 54 cities in the South as well as several areas in the North, where stores were picketed. After several months of protests, Woolworth's integrated its lunch counters.

Some historians argue that many of the political movements for change that burst onto the scene in the 1960s—including the women's movement, the antiwar movement, and the student free speech movement—could trace their philosophical and tactical roots to this small act by four students (Cluster, 1979). Admittedly, the participants in all of these movements might have developed the sit-in as a tactic on their own, even if in 1960 the four students *had* been served coffee and doughnuts at Woolworth's. The point is, though, that the collective movement that arose from the actions of these seemingly insignificant individuals in 1960 had an enormous impact on the massive changes that occurred in the United States over the next 50 years and probably beyond

We recreate society not only through acts of defiance and organized social movements but also through our daily interactions. The driving theme throughout this book has been that society and its constituent elements are simultaneously human creations and phenomena that exist independently of us, influencing and controlling our private experiences at every turn.

Organizations and institutions exist and thrive because they implicitly or explicitly discourage individuals from challenging the rules and patterns of behavior that characterize them. Imagine what would happen to the system of higher education if you and others like you challenged the authority of your school. You could establish a new order in which students would dictate the content of courses, take control of the classroom, abolish grading or any other evaluative mechanism used for assessing student performance, do away with tuition, and so on. But because you have an education and a career to gain from the institutional structure as it stands, you're not very likely to do something to jeopardize it.

Are we then to believe that we are all leaves in the wind, buffeted here and there by the powerful and permanent forces of a structure that dwarfs us? To some extent, the answer is yes. I subscribe to the sociological imagination and strongly believe that to fully understand our lives, we must acknowledge that processes larger than ourselves determine some of our private experiences. Along the way, though, we sometimes lose sight of our important role as shapers of society. Although society presents itself as largely unchangeable, U.S. culture is based at least in part on the "can do" attitude. I recall, as a child in 1969, sitting in a darkened living room with my parents on a warm July evening. The only light in the room came from the gray-blue glow of our little black-and-white television. I watched with great amazement the fuzzy, almost imperceptible image of astronaut Neil Armstrong taking the first tentative steps on the moon and stating, "That's one small step for man, one giant leap for mankind." I didn't realize at the time how far beyond the space program the power of that statement stretched. But since then, I have come to realize that people do indeed leave footprints on the world in which they live.

CONCLUSION AND FAREWELL

Sociology is not one of those disciplines that draw from a long-standing body of scientific facts and laws. We do have some useful explanations for why certain important social phenomena happen, and we can make reasonable projections about future developments. But sociology is not inherently a discipline of answers. It's a discipline of questions, one that provides a unique and useful method for identifying the puzzles of your life and your society.

This discipline scrutinizes, analyzes, and dissects institutional order and its effects on our thinking.

It exposes the vulnerable underbelly of both objective and official reality and, by doing so, prods us into taking a closer look at ourselves and our private worlds—not an easy thing to do. Sociology makes life an unsafe place. I don't mean that it makes people violent or dangerous; I mean that it makes perceptions of social stability unstable or at least fair game for analysis. It's not easy to admit that our reality may be a figment of our collective minds and just one of many possible realities. We live under a belief system that tells us that our unchallenged assumptions are simply the way things are.

Sociology is thus a "liberating" perspective (Liazos, 1985). It forces us to look at the social processes that influence our thoughts, perceptions, and actions and helps us see how social change occurs and the impact we can have on others. In doing so, sociology also points out the very limits of liberation. We become aware of the chains that restrict our "movements." But sociology also gives us the tools to break those chains. The sociological imagination gives us a glimpse of the world both as it is and as it could be. To be a sociologically astute observer of the world as it is, you must be able to strip away fallacies and illusions and see the interconnected system underneath. Only then can you take full advantage of your role as a cocreator of society.

I leave you with one final thought: If you now look at your life and the lives of those around you differently, if you now question things heretofore unquestionable, if you now see where you fit in the bigger societal picture, if you now see orderly patterns in areas you previously thought were chaotic, or chaos in areas you previously thought were orderly, then you are well on your way to understanding the meaning—and the promise—of sociology.

CHAPTER HIGHLIGHTS

◆ Whether at the personal, cultural, or institutional level, change is the preeminent feature of modern societies.

◆ Social change is not some massive, impersonal force that arbitrarily disrupts our routine way of life; it is a human creation.

◆ Social change has a variety of causes: adaptation to environmental pressures, internal population changes, technological discoveries and innovations, and the importation of cultural practices from other countries.

◆ Social movements are long-term collective actions that address an issue of concern to large numbers of people.

◆ Societies remain stable because enough people define existing conditions as satisfactory and they change because enough people define the once accepted conditions as problems that must be solved.

KEY TERMS

anomie: Condition in which rapid change has disrupted society's ability to adequately regulate and control its members and the old rules that governed people's lives no longer seem to apply

countermovement: Collective action designed to prevent or reverse changes sought or accomplished by an earlier social movement

cultural diffusion: Process by which beliefs, technology, customs, and other elements of culture spread from one group or society to another

global climate change: Steady rise in Earth's average temperature as a result of increasing amounts of carbon dioxide in the atmosphere

ideology: Coherent system of beliefs, values, and ideas

postindustrial society: Society in which knowledge, the control of information, and service industries are more important elements of the economy than agriculture or manufacturing and production

reform movement: Collective action that seeks to change limited aspects of a society but does not seek to alter or replace major social institutions

revolutionary movement: Collective action that attempts to overthrow an entire social system and replace it with another

social movement: Continuous, large-scale, organized collective action motivated by the desire to enact, stop, or reverse change in some area of society

References

Abramsky, S. (2012, May 14). The other America 2012. *The Nation*.

Acitelli, L. (1988). When spouses talk to each other about their relationship. *Journal of Social and Personal Relationships, 5*, 185–199.

Acker, J. (1992). From sex roles to gendered institutions. *Contemporary Sociology, 21*, 565–569.

ActionAid. (2009). *Hate crimes: The rise of "corrective" rape in South Africa*. www.actionaid.org/assets/pdf/CorrectiveRapeRep_final.pdf. Accessed June 3, 2009.

Aday, D. P. (1990). *Social control at the margins*. Belmont, CA: Wadsworth.

Adler, P. (1985). *Wheeling and dealing*. New York, NY: Columbia University Press.

AFL-CIO. (2013). *Executive pay watch*. www.aflcio.org/Corporate-Watch/CEO-Pay-and-You. Accessed June 2, 2013.

Ainlay, S. C., Becker, G., & Coleman, L. M. (1986). *The dilemma of difference*. New York, NY: Plenum Press.

Alan Guttmacher Institute. (2011). *Facts on induced abortion in the United States*. www.guttmacher.org/pubs/fb_induced_abortion.html. Accessed June 30, 2011.

Alan Guttmacher Institute. (2013). *State policies in brief: An overview of abortion laws*. www.guttmacher.org/statecenter/spibs/spib_OAL.pdf. Accessed July 1, 2013.

Alexander, M. (2012, March 11). Go to trial: Crash the justice system. *The New York Times*.

Allport, G. (1954). *The nature of prejudice*. Reading, MA: Addison-Wesley.

Altman, D. (2003, April 26). Does a dollar a day keep poverty away? *The New York Times*.

Altman, L. K. (2011, May 31). 30 years in, we are still learning from AIDS. *The New York Times*.

Amato, P. R. (2000). The consequences of divorce for adults and children. *Journal of Marriage and the Family, 62*, 126–288.

Amato, P. R., & Sobolewski, J. M. (2001). The effects of divorce and marital discord on adult children's psychological well-being. *American Sociological Review, 66*, 900–921.

American Association of University Women. (2013). *Crossing the line: Sexual harassment at school*. www.aauw.org/files/2013/02/crossing-the-line-sexual-harassment-at-school-executive-summary.pdf. Accessed June 19, 2013.

American Lung Association. (2008). *State of tobacco control: 2008*. www.stateoftobaccocontrol.org/2008/ALA_SOTC_08.pdf. Accessed January 14, 2009.

American Psychiatric Association. (2013). *Diagnostic and statistical manual of mental disorders* (5th ed.). Washington, DC: Author.

American Society of Plastic Surgeons. (2011). *2010 plastic surgery procedural statistics*. www.plastic surgery.org/News-and-Resources/Statistics.html. Accessed May 31, 2011.

American Sociological Association. (2002). Statement of the American Sociological Association on the importance of collecting data and doing social scientific research on race. www.asanet.org/governance/racestmt.htm. Accessed June 18, 2003.

American Sociological Association. (2005, July). *Race, ethnicity, and the health of Americans* (ASA Series on How Race and Ethnicity Matter). Washington, DC: Author.

Ammerman, N. T. (1987). *Bible believers: Fundamentalists in the modern world*. New Brunswick, NJ: Rutgers University Press.

Amnesty International. (2004). *Rape as a tool of war: A fact sheet*. www.amnestyusa.org/women/pdf/rapeinwartime.pdf. Accessed September 4, 2009.

Amnesty International. (2013). *The death penalty and deterrence*. www.amnestyusa.org/our-work/issues/death-penalty/us-death-penalty-facts/the-death-penalty-and-deterrence. Accessed January 23, 2013.

Andreescu, T., Gallian, J. A., Kane, J. M., & Mertz, J. E. (2008). Cross-cultural analysis of students with exceptional talent in mathematical problem solving. *Notices of the American Mathematical Society, 55,* 1248–1260.

Andrews, E. L. (2007, January 8). Bush tax cuts offer most for very rich, study finds. *The New York Times.*

Andriote, J. M. (2005, March). *HIV/AIDS and African Americans: A "state of emergency"* (PRB Report). Washington, DC: Population Reference Bureau. www.prb.org. Accessed March 16, 2005.

Angier, N. (1997a, May 13). New debate over surgery on genitals. *The New York Times.*

Angier, N. (1997b, March 14). Sexual identity not pliable after all, report says. *The New York Times.*

Angier, N., & Chang, K. (2005, January 24). Gray matter and the sexes: Still a scientific gray area. *The New York Times.*

Ansell, A. E. (2000). The new face of race: The metamorphosis of racism in the post-civil rights era United States. In P. Kivisto & G. Rundblad (Eds.), *Multiculturalism in the United States.* Thousand Oaks, CA: Pine Forge Press.

Antill, J. K., Goodnow, J. J., Russell, G., & Cotton, S. (1996). The influence of parents and family context on children's involvement in household tasks. *Sex Roles, 34,* 215–236.

Apollo Alliance. (2011). *Mission.* http://apolloalliance.org/about/mission/. Accessed June 29, 2011.

Appiah, K. A. (2007, March 18). A slow emancipation. *The New York Times Magazine.*

Archer, D. (1985). Social deviance. In G. Lindzey & E. Aronson (Eds.), *Handbook of social psychology* (3rd ed., Vol. 2). New York, NY: Random House.

Arendell, T. (1995). *Fathers and divorce.* Thousand Oaks, CA: Sage.

Astbury, J. (1996). *Crazy for you: The making of women's madness.* Melbourne, Victoria, Australia: Oxford University Press.

Austen, I. (2012, November 23). Crackdown in Quebec: "Le Gap." *New York Times.*

Avert. (2013). *Universal access to HIV/AIDS treatment.* www.avert.org/universal-access.htm#contentTable2. Accessed July 2, 2013.

Babbie, E. (1986). *Observing ourselves: Essays in social research.* Belmont, CA: Wadsworth.

Babbie, E. (1992). *The practice of social research.* Belmont, CA: Wadsworth.

Babbie, E. (2007). *The practice of social research* (11th ed.). Belmont, CA: Wadsworth.

Baby, and a car! Russians hold Conception Day. (2011, September 11). MSNBC Online. www.msnbc.msn.com/id/20730526/ns/world_news-europe/t/baby-car-russians-hold-conception-day/#.Tm418k_b8xk. Accessed September 12, 2011.

Baca Zinn, M., & Eitzen, D. S. (1996). *Diversity in families* (4th ed.). New York, NY: HarperCollins.

Bagdikian, B. H. (1991). Missing from the news. In J. H. Skolnick & E. Currie (Eds.), *Crisis in American institutions.* New York, NY: HarperCollins.

Bailey, B. L. (1988). *From front porch to back seat: Courtship in 20th century America.* Baltimore, MD: Johns Hopkins University Press.

Bailey, C. A. (1993). Equality with difference: On androcentrism and menstruation. *Teaching Sociology, 21,* 121–129.

Bailey, J. (2007, March 18). Airlines learn to fly on a wing and an apology. *The New York Times.*

Bailey, W. C. (1990). Murder, capital punishment, and television: Execution publicity and homicide rates. *American Sociological Review, 55,* 628–633.

Bainbridge, W. L. (2005, February 5). Longer school year would benefit students. *Columbus Dispatch.*

Baird, J. (2013, July 6). In Australia, misogyny lives on. *The New York Times.*

Bajaj, V., & Fessenden, F. (2007, November 4). What's behind the race gap? *The New York Times.*

Baker, P., & Herszenhorn, D. M. (2010, April 23). Obama chastises Wall St. in call to stiffen rules. *The New York Times.*

Bakst, D. (2012, January 31). Pregnant and pushed out of a job. *New York Times.*

Ballard, C. (1987). A humanist sociology approach to teaching social research. *Teaching Sociology, 15,* 7–14.

Bandura, A., & Walters, R. H. (1963). *Social learning and personality development.* New York, NY: Holt, Rinehart & Winston.

Banerjee, N. (2005, January 23). Aided by elders and Web, Iraq veterans turn critics. *The New York Times.*

Banks, J., Marmot, M., Oldfield, Z., & Smith, J. P. (2006). Disease and disadvantage in the United States and in England. *Journal of the American Medical Association, 295,* 2037–2045.

Barber, B. (1992, March). Jihad vs. McWorld. *Atlantic Monthly,* pp. 53–65.

The Barna Group. (2007). *Barna's annual tracking study shows Americans stay spiritually active, but biblical views wane.* www.barna.org/barna-update/article/18-congregations/103-barnas-annual-tracking-study-shows-americans-stay-spirituallyactive-but-biblical-views-wane. Accessed September 4, 2009.

Baron-Cohen, S. (2003). *The essential difference: Men, women, and the extreme male brain.* London, UK: Allen Lane.

Barrionuevo, A. (2007, June 16). Globalization in every loaf. *The New York Times.*

Barro, R. J., & McCleary, R. M. (2003). Religion and economic growth across countries. *American Sociological Review, 68,* 760–781.

Barron, J. (2012, January 24). Connecticut police officers accused of mistreating Latinos. *The New York Times.*

Barry, E. (2009, April 8). Protests in Moldova explode, with a call to arms on Twitter. *The New York Times*.

Barstow, D. (2003, December 22). U.S. rarely seeks charges for deaths in workplace. *The New York Times*.

Baruchin, A. (2011, August 30). Stigma is toughest foe in an epilepsy fight. *The New York Times*.

Bazelon, E. (2008, July 20). The next kind of integration. *The New York Times Magazine*.

Bazelon, E. (2010, July 18). The new abortion providers. *The New York Times Magazine*.

Bearak, B. (2010, September 6). Dead join the living in a family celebration. *The New York Times*.

Becker, H. S. (1963). *Outsiders: Studies in the sociology of deviance*. New York, NY: Free Press.

Becker, H. S., & Geer, B. (1958). The fate of idealism in medical school. *American Sociological Review, 23*, 50–56.

Begley, S. (2011, January 31). Why almost everything you hear about medicine is wrong. *Newsweek*.

Beinart, P. (2012, August 27). The violence we don't see. *Newsweek*.

Belkin, L. (2003, May 11). Why is Jonathan Simms still alive? *The New York Times Magazine*.

Bell, S. T., Kuriloff, P. J., & Lottes, I. (1994). Understanding attributions of blame in stranger rape and date rape situations: An examination of gender, race, identification, and students' social perceptions of rape victims. *Journal of Applied Social Psychology, 24*, 1719–1734.

Bellah, R., Madsen, R., Sullivan, W. M., Swidler, A., & Tipton, S. M. (1985). *Habits of the heart*. New York, NY: Harper & Row.

Belluck, P. (2001, January 20). A nation's voices: Concern and solace, resentment and redemption. *The New York Times*.

Belluck, P. (2002, January 15). Doctors' new practices offer deluxe service for deluxe fee. *The New York Times*.

Belluck, P. (2004, November 14). To avoid divorce, move to Massachusetts. *The New York Times*.

Benedict, H. (2009). *The lonely soldier: The private war of women serving in Iraq*. Boston, MA: Beacon Press.

Bennett, G., Henson, R. K., & Zhang, J. (2003). Generation Y's perceptions of the action sports industry segment. *Journal of Sports Management, 17*, 95–115.

Bennett, J. (2008, February 25). Say "cheese" and now say "airbrush." *Newsweek*.

Bennett, J. (2010, July 28). The beauty advantage. *Newsweek*.

Benokraitis, N. V., & Feagin, J. R. (1993). Sex discrimination: Subtle and covert. In J. Henslin (Ed.), *Down-to-earth sociology* (7th ed.). New York, NY: Free Press.

Ben-Yehuda, N. (1990). *The politics and morality of deviance*. Albany: State University of New York Press.

Berenson, A. (2005, May 31). Despite vow, drug makers still withhold data. *The New York Times*.

Berenson, A. (2008, December 8). Weak patchwork of oversight lets bad hospitals stay open. *The New York Times*.

Berg, B. (1992). The guilt that drives working mothers crazy. In J. Henslin (Ed.), *Marriage and family in a changing society*. New York, NY: Free Press.

Berger, D. L., & Williams, J. E. (1991). Sex stereotypes in the United States revisited: 1972–1988. *Sex Roles, 24*, 413–423.

Berger, J. (2004, October 24). Pressure to live by an outmoded tradition is still felt among Indian immigrants. *The New York Times*.

Berger, P. L. (1963). *Invitation to sociology*. Garden City, NY: Anchor Books.

Berger, P. L., & Kellner, H. (1964). Marriage and the construction of reality: An exercise in the microsociology of knowledge. *Diogenes, 46*, 1–23.

Berger, P. L., & Luckmann, T. (1966). *The social construction of reality*. Garden City, NY: Anchor Books.

Bernard, J. (1972). *The future of marriage*. New York, NY: Bantam Books.

Bernard, J. (1981). The good provider role: Its rise and fall. *American Psychologist, 36*, 1–12.

Bernard, T. S. (2010, July 19). Need a mortgage? Don't get pregnant. *The New York Times*.

Berndt, T. J., & Heller, K. A. (1986). Gender stereotypes and social inferences. *Journal of Social and Personality Psychology, 50*, 889–898.

Bernstein, J., & Ellison, J. (2011, June 5). Hotel confidential. *Newsweek*.

Bernstein, N. (2012, November 22). Chefs, butlers, and marble baths: Not your average hospital room. *The New York Times*.

Bernstein, R. (2003, June 29). Aging Europe finds its pension is running out. *The New York Times*.

Bertelsmann Stiftung. (2011). *Social justice in the OECD—How do the member states compare*. www.sqi-network.org/pdf/SGI-11_Social_Justice_OECD.pdf. Accessed June 3, 2013.

Berthelsen, C. (1999, July 28). Suit says advanced-placement classes show bias. *The New York Times*.

Bhattacharya, J., DeLeire, T., Haider, S., & Currie, J. (2003). Heat or eat? Cold-weather shocks and nutrition in poor American families. *American Journal of Public Health, 93*, 1149–1154.

Bianchi, S. M., Robinson, J. P., & Milkie, M. A. (2006). *Changing rhythms of American family life*. New York, NY: Russell Sage.

Bibbins-Domingo, K. (2009). Racial differences in incident heart failure among young adults. *The New England Journal of Medicine, 360*, 1179–1190.

Billings, A. C., Angelini, J. R., & Eastman, S. T. (2005). Diverging discourses: Gender differences in televised golf announcing. *Mass Communication and Society, 8*, 155–171.

Birenbaum, A., & Sagarin, E. (1976). *Norms and human behavior*. New York, NY: Praeger.

Bisgaier, J., & Rhodes, K. V. (2011). Auditing access to specialty care for children with public insurance. *The New England Journal of Medicine, 364*, 2324–2333.

Black, M. C., Basile, K. C., Breiding, M. J., Smith, S. G., Walters, M. L., Merrick, M. T., Chen, J., & Stevens, M. R. (2011). *The national intimate partner and sexual violence survey*. National Center for Injury Prevention and Control, Centers for Disease Control and Prevention. www.cdc.gov/violenceprevention/pdf/nisvs_report2010-a.pdf. Accessed January 16, 2013.

Blackhealthcare.com. (2003). *Sickle-cell anemia: Description*. www.blackhealthcare.com/BHC/SickleCell/Description.asp. Accessed June 17, 2003.

Blackmon, D. A. (2009). *Slavery by another name: The re-enslavement of black Americans from the Civil War to World War II*. New York, NY: Anchor.

Blakeslee, S. (2012, April 3). Mind games: Sometimes a white coat isn't just a white coat. *The New York Times*.

Blanton, K. (2007, March 16). A "smoking gun" on race, subprime loans. *The Boston Globe*.

Blau, P. M., & Meyer, M. W. (1987). The concept of bureaucracy. In R. T. Schaeffer & R. P. Lamm (Eds.), *Introducing sociology*. New York, NY: McGraw-Hill.

Blauner, R. (1992). The ambiguities of racial change. In M. L. Anderson & P. H. Collins (Eds.), *Race, class and gender: An anthology*. Belmont, CA: Wadsworth.

Bleyer, A., & Welch, G. (2012). Effect of three decades of screening mammography on breast cancer incidence. *New England Journal of Medicine, 367*, 1998–2005.

Block, F., Korteweg, A. C., & Woodward, K. (2013). The compassion gap in American poverty policy. In D. Newman & J. O'Brien (Eds.), *Sociology: Exploring the architecture of everyday life (Readings)*. Thousand Oaks, CA: Sage.

Blow, C. M. (2008, August 9). Racism and the race. *The New York Times*.

Blow, C. M. (2009, February 21). A nation of cowards? *The New York Times*.

Blow, C. M. (2010, June 12). Friends, neighbors, and Facebook. *The New York Times*.

Blow, C. M. (2013, April 27). The morose middle class. *New York Times*.

Blumstein, P., & Schwartz, P. (1983). *American couples*. New York, NY: Morrow.

Bocian, D. G., Ernst, K. S., & Li, W. (2006). *Unfair lending: The effect of race and ethnicity on the price of subprime mortgages*. Durham, NC: Center for Responsible Lending. www.responsiblelending.org. Accessed October 10, 2007.

Bollen, J., Gonçalves, B., Ruan, G., & Mao, H. (2012). Happiness is assertive in online social networks. *Artificial Life, 17*, 237–251.

Bonilla-Silva, E. (2003). *Racism without racists: Color-blind racism and the persistence of racial inequality in the United States*. Lanham, MD: Rowman & Littlefield.

Bonilla-Silva, E. (2008). "New racism," color-blind racism, and the future of whiteness in America. In S. J. Ferguson (Ed.), *Mapping the social landscape*. New York, NY: McGraw-Hill.

Booth, A., Johnson, D. R., Branaman, A., & Sica, A. (1995). Belief and behavior: Does religion matter in today's marriage? *Journal of Marriage and the Family, 57*, 661–671.

Bowley, G. (2012, January 30). Afghan kin are accused of killing woman for not bearing a son. *New York Times*.

Bradsher, K. (1993, July 22). Mark Twain would understand the water crisis that's corrupting Iowans. *The New York Times*.

Bragg, R. (1998, January 4). Proposal to ban sofas from porches creates culture clash. *The Indianapolis Star*.

Bramlett, M. D., & Mosher, W. D. (2002). *Cohabitation, marriage, divorce, and remarriage in the United States*. Hyattsville, MD: National Center for Health Statistics. www.cdc.gov/nchs/data/series/sr_23/sr23_022.pdf. Accessed August 11, 2006.

Braun, D. (1997). *The rich get richer: The rise of income inequality in the United States and the world*. Chicago, IL: Nelson-Hall.

Breaking the rules of engagement. (2002, July/August). *American Demographics*, p. 35.

Breslau, K. (2007, December 25). Majora Carter. *Newsweek*.

Bricker, J., Kennickell, A. B., Moore, K. B., & Sabelhaus, J. (2012). Changes in U.S. family finances from 2007 to 2010: Evidence from the survey of consumer finances. *Federal Reserve Bulletin, 98*, 1–80. www.federalreserve.gov/Pubs/Bulletin/2012/articles/scf/scf.htm. Accessed May 31, 2013.

Brizendine, L. (2006). *The female brain*. New York, NY: Broadway.

Brody, J. E. (2011, December 13). The twice-victimized of sexual assault. *The New York Times*.

Bronner, E. (1998a, January 10). Inventing the notion of race. *The New York Times*.

Bronner, E. (1998b, April 1). U of California reports big drop in black admission. *The New York Times*.

Bronner, E. (2012, July 3). Poor land in jail as companies add huge fees for probation. *The New York Times*.

Bronner, E. (2013, March 16). Right to lawyer can be empty promise for poor. *The New York Times*.

Brookings Institution. (2006). *From poverty, opportunity: Putting the market to work for lower income families*. www.brookings.edu/metro/pubs/20060718_PovOp.pdf. Accessed July 18, 2006.

Brooks, M. (2011). *How has Internet dating changed society? An insider's look*. Internet Dating Executive

Alliance. January. www.onlineperonalswatch.com. Accessed January 15, 2013.

Broverman, I., Vogel, S., Broverman, D., Clarkson, F., & Rosenkrantz, P. (1972). Sex role stereotypes: A current appraisal. *Journal of Social Issues, 28,* 59–78.

Brown, D. (2011, July 13). Two studies show that drugs used to treat AIDS can be used to prevent HIV infection too. *The Washington Post.*

Brown, P. (1998). Biology and the social construction of the "race" concept. In J. Ferrante & P. Brown (Eds.), *The social construction of race and ethnicity in the United States.* New York, NY: Longman.

Brown, P. L. (2011, March 6). Bill to ban Chinese delicacy has some fuming. *The New York Times.*

Brown, Robbie. (2009, January 22). Nashville won't make English official language. *The New York Times.*

Brown, Roger. (1986). *Social psychology.* New York, NY: Free Press.

Brownmiller, S. (1975). *Against our will: Men, women, and rape.* New York, NY: Simon & Schuster.

Bruni, F. (2012, January 15). Running from millions. *The New York Times.*

Buckley, C. (2010, December 9). To test housing program, some are denied aid. *The New York Times.*

Bullard, R. D. (1993). Anatomy of environmental racism and the environmental justice movement. In R. D. Bullard (Ed.), *Confronting environmental racism.* Boston, MA: South End Press.

Bullard, R. D. (2001). Decision making. In L. Westra & B. E. Lawson (Eds.), *Faces of environmental racism: Confronting issues of global justice.* Lanham, MD: Rowman & Littlefield.

Bullington, B. (1993). All about Eve: The many faces of United States drug policy. In F. Pearce & M. Woodiwiss (Eds.), *Global crime connections.* Toronto, Ontario, Canada: University of Toronto Press.

Bunk busters unravel the art of spin. (2007). *National Public Radio.* www.npr.org/templates/story/story.php?storyId=10416827. Accessed September 5, 2009.

Bureau of Transportation Statistics. (2012). *Number of U.S. aircraft, vehicles, vessels, and other conveyances.* www.rita.dot.gov/bts/sites/rita.dot.gov.bts/publications/national_transportation_statistics/html/table_01_11.html. Accessed December 31, 2012.

Burke, T. W., & Owen, S. S. (2006, January/February). Same-sex domestic violence: Is anyone listening? *Gay & Lesbian Review, 8*(1), 6–7.

Burning through oil, or conserving it. (2008, April 20). *The New York Times.*

Bush, M. (2009). *International benchmarking—time.* Education Commission of the States. www.ecs.org/clearinghouse/80/66/8066.pdf. Accessed June 12, 2011.

Butler, R. (1989). A generation at risk: When the baby boomers reach Golden Pond. In W. Feigelman (Ed.),

Sociology full circle. New York, NY: Holt, Rinehart & Winston.

Butterfield, F. (2000, April 26). Racial disparities seen as pervasive in juvenile justice. *The New York Times.*

Cameron, P. (2003). Domestic violence among homosexual partners. *Psychological Reports, 93,* 410–416.

Campbell, A. (1987). Self-definition by rejection: The case of gang girls. *Social Problems, 34,* 451–466.

Campbell, A., Converse, P. E., & Rodgers, W. L. (1976). *The quality of American life.* New York, NY: Russell Sage.

Campbell, M. E., & Troyer, L. (2007). The implications of racial misclassification by observers. *American Sociological Review, 72,* 750–765.

Caplan, B. (2011). *Selfish reasons to have more kids: Why being a great parent is less work and more fun than you think.* New York, NY: Basic Books.

Caplan, P. J. (1995). *They say you're crazy: How the world's most powerful psychiatrists decide who's normal.* Reading, MA: Addison-Wesley.

Carey, B. (2007, January 14). Can Johnny come out and (be taught) to play? *The New York Times.*

Carey, B. (2012, January 19). New autism rule will trim many, a study suggests. *The New York Times.*

Carlson, E. (2009). 20th-century U.S. generations. *Population Bulletin, 64,* 1–17.

Carmichael, M. (2008, December 1). Katrina kids: Sickest ever. *Newsweek.*

Carnevale, A. P., & Rose, S. J. (2003). *Socioeconomic status, race/ethnicity, and selective college admissions.* Washington, DC: Century Foundation. www.tcf.org/Publications/Education/carnevale_rose.pdf. Accessed September 4, 2009.

Carothers, B. (2013, April 21). The tangle of the sexes. *The New York Times.*

Carson, E. A., & Sabol, W. J. (2012). *Prisoners in 2011.* U.S. Bureau of Justice Statistics. NCJ239808. bjs.ojp.usdoj.gov/content/pub/pdf/p11.pdf. Accessed January 21, 2013.

Carter, B., & Vega, T. (2011, May 14). In shift, ads try to entice over-55 set. *The New York Times.*

Carter, H., & Glick, P. C. (1976). *Marriage and divorce: A social and economic study.* Cambridge, MA: Harvard University Press.

Cast, A. D. (2004). Role taking and interaction. *Social Psychology Quarterly, 67,* 296–309.

Catalano, S. (2012). *Intimate partner violence, 1993–2010.* U.S. Bureau of Justice Statistics, NCJ239203. bjs.ojp.usdoj.gov/content/pub/pdf/ipv9310.pdf. Accessed January 16, 2013.

Center for Public Integrity. (2008). *Iraq: The war card.* www.publicintegrity.org/projects/entry/276. Accessed May 3, 2009.

Center for Responsive Politics. (2013). *Millionaire freshmen make Congress even wealthier.* www.opensecrets.org/

news/2013/01/new-congress-new-and-more-wealth. html. Accessed May 31, 2013.

Centers for Disease Control and Prevention. (1999). Ten great public health achievements in the United States, 1900–1999. *Mortality and Morbidity Weekly Report, 48,* 241–243.

Centers for Disease Control and Prevention. (2006). *Smoking and tobacco use.* www.cdc.gov/tobacco/ data_statistics/Factsheets/index.htm. Accessed June 18, 2007.

Centers for Disease Control and Prevention. (2009). *Intimate partner violence fact sheet.* www.cdc.gov/ violenceprevention/pdf/IPV_factsheet-a.pdf. Accessed July 2, 2010.

Centers for Disease Control and Prevention. (2010). Vital signs: Nonsmokers' exposure to secondhand smoke—United States, 1999–2008. *Morbidity and Mortality Weekly Reports, 59,* 1141–1146.

Centers for Disease Control and Prevention. (2011a). *Highlights in minority health & health disparities.* www.cdc.gov/omhd/Highlights/Highlight. htm#DISPARITIES0. Accessed June 17, 2011.

Centers for Disease Control and Prevention. (2011b). *Occupational cancer.* www.cdc.gov/niosh/topics/ cancer. Accessed June 8, 2011.

Centers for Disease Control and Prevention. (2011c). *Tobacco-related mortality.* www.cdc.gov/tobacco/ data_statistics/fact_sheets/health_effects/tobacco_ related_mortality/index.htm. Accessed June 8, 2011.

Centers for Disease Control and Prevention. (2012a). Comprehensive smoke-free laws—50 largest cities, 2000 to 2012. *Morbidity and Mortality Weekly Report, 61,* 914–917.

Centers for Disease Control and Prevention. (2013). *Trends in the prevalence of sexual behaviors and HIV testing, National YRBS: 1991–2011.* www.cdc. gov/healthyyouth/yrbs/pdf/us_sexual_trend_yrbs.pdf. Accessed June 26, 2013.

Chafetz, J. S. (1978). *A primer on the construction and testing of theories in sociology.* Itasca, IL: Peacock.

Chafetz, J. S., & Dworkin, A. G. (1987). In the face of threat: Organized anti-feminism in comparative perspective. *Gender & Society, 1,* 33–60.

Chambliss, W. (1964). A sociological analysis of the law of vagrancy. *Social Problems, 12,* 66–77.

Charles, M. (2011, Spring). What gender is science? *Contexts.* http://contexts.org/articles/spring2011/ what-gender-is-science/. Accessed June 21, 2011.

Charon, J. (1992). *Ten questions: A sociological perspective.* Belmont, CA: Wadsworth.

Charon, J. (1998). *Symbolic interactionism.* Upper Saddle River, NJ: Prentice Hall.

Chase-Dunn, C., & Rubinson, R. (1977). Toward a structural perspective on the world system. *Politics and Society, 7,* 453–476.

Chaudhry, L. (2006, April 7). Acting your race. *In These Times.*

Chen, E., Matthews, K. A., & Boyce, W. T. (2002). Socioeconomic differences in children's health: How and why do these relationships change with age? *Psychological Bulletin, 128,* 295–329.

Cherlin, A. J. (1992). *Marriage, divorce, remarriage.* Cambridge, MA: Harvard University Press.

Cherlin, A. J., Furstenberg, F. F., Jr., Chase-Lansdale, P. L., Kiernan, K. E., Robins, P. K., Morrison, D. R., & Teitler, J. O. (1991). Longitudinal studies of effects of divorce on children in Great Britain and the United States. *Science, 252,* 1386–1389.

Cherney, I. D., & London, K. (2006). Gender-linked differences in the toys, television shows, computer games, and outdoor activities of 5- to 13-year-old children. *Sex Roles, 54,* 717–726.

Child Welfare Information Gateway. (2010). *Child abuse and neglect fatalities: Statistics and interventions.* www.childwelfare.gov/pubs/factsheets/fatalities.pdf. Accessed June 6, 2011.

China changes death penalty law. (2006, October 31). *The New York Times.*

Ching, C. L., & Burke, S. (1999). An assessment of college students' attitudes and empathy toward rape. *College Student Journal, 33,* 573–584.

Chotiner, I. (2010, May 31). Globish for beginners. *The New Yorker.*

Chua, A. (2011). *Battle hymn of the Tiger Mother.* New York, NY: Penguin.

Ciancanelli, P., & Berch, B. (1987). Gender and the GNP. In B. B. Hess & M. M. Ferree (Eds.), *Analyzing gender: A handbook of social science research.* Newbury Park, CA: Sage.

Clark, C. (1997). *Misery and company: Sympathy in everyday life.* Chicago, IL: University of Chicago Press.

Clausen, J. A. (1986). *The life course: A sociological perspective.* Englewood Cliffs, NJ: Prentice Hall.

Clear Channel Communications. (2012). *Clear Channel corporate.* www.clearchannel.com/Corporate/. Accessed December 28, 2012.

Clemmitt, M. (2009). Extreme sports. *CQ Researcher, 19,* 297–320.

Cluster, D. (1979). *They should have served that cup of coffee.* Boston, MA: South End Press.

CNN.com. (2009). *Most blacks say MLK's vision fulfilled, poll finds.* http://edition.cnn.com/2009/ POLITICS/01/19/king.poll/. Accessed August 13, 2009.

Cohen, A. K. (1955). *Delinquent boys: The culture of the gang.* New York, NY: Free Press.

Cohen, A. K. (1966). *Deviance and control.* Englewood Cliffs, NJ: Prentice Hall.

Cohen, F. G. (1986). *Treaties on trial: The continuing controversy over Northwest Indian fishing rights.* Seattle: University of Washington Press.

Cohen, J., & Agiesta, J. (2008, June 22). 3 in 10 Americans admit to race bias. *The Washington Post.*

Cohen, N. (2006, August 6). So English is taking over the globe. So what? *The New York Times.*

The College Board. (1998). *SAT and gender differences* (Research Summary RS-04). http://professionals.collegeboard.com/profdownload/pdf/rs04_3960.pdf. Accessed August 13, 2009.

Collegiate Employment Research Institute. (2012). *Recruiting trends: 2012–2013.* www.ceri.msu.edu/wp-content/uploads/2012/11/FRecruiting-Trends-201202013.pdf. Accessed December 21, 2012.

Collins, G. (2011, April 7). Medicine on the move. *The New York Times.*

Collins, R. (1971). Functional and conflict theories of educational stratification. *American Sociological Review, 36,* 1002–1019.

Collins, R. (1981). On the microfoundations of macrosociology. *American Journal of Sociology, 86,* 984–1014.

Common Sense Media. (2011). *Zero to eight: Children's media use in America.* www.commonsensemedia.org/sites/default/files/research/zerotoeightfina12011.pdf. Accessed 1/8/2013.

Congeni, J. (2009). Management of the adolescent concussion victim. *Adolescent Medicine: State of the Art Reviews, 20,* 41–56.

Congressional Budget Office. (2011). *Trends in the distribution of household income between 1997 and 2007.* www.cbo.gov/sites/default/files/cbofiles/attachments/10–25-HouseholdIncome.pdf. Accessed June 2, 2013.

Congressional Budget Office. (2013). *The distribution of major tax expenditures in the individual income tax system.* www.cbo.gov/sites/default/files/cbofiles/attachments/43768_DistributionTaxExpenditures.pdf. Accessed May 31, 2013.

Conrad, P. (1975). The discovery of hyperkinesis: Notes on the medicalization of deviant behavior. *Social Problems, 23,* 12–21.

Conrad, P. (2005). The shifting engines of medicalization. *Journal of Health and Social Behavior, 46,* 3–14.

Conrad, P., & Leiter, V. (2004). Medicalization, markets, and consumers. *Journal of Health and Social Behavior, 45,* 158–176.

Conrad, P., & Schneider, J. W. (1992). *Deviance and medicalization: From badness to sickness.* Philadelphia, PA: Temple University Press.

A continuing abomination. (2008, November 1). *The Economist.*

Cookson, P., & Persell, C. (1985). *Preparing for power.* New York, NY: Basic Books.

Cooley, C. H. (1902). *Human nature and social order.* New York, NY: Scribner.

Coontz, S. (1992). *The way we never were.* New York, NY: Basic Books.

Coontz, S. (2005). *Marriage, a history: From obedience to intimacy, or how love conquered marriage.* New York, NY: Viking.

Coontz, S. (2012, September 30). The myth of male decline. *The New York Times.*

Coontz, S. (2013, June 23). The disestablishment of marriage. *The New York Times.*

Cose, E. (2009, February 2). Revisiting "The rage of the privileged class." *Newsweek.*

Cose, E. (2011, May 23 & 30). Meet the new optimists. *Newsweek.*

Coser, R. L. (1960). Laughter among colleagues: A study of the social functions among staff of a mental hospital. *Psychiatry, 23,* 81–95.

Cosgrove, L., Bursztaja, H., & Krimsky, S. (2009). Developing unbiased diagnostic and treatment guidelines in psychiatry. *New England Journal of Medicine, 360,* 2035–2036.

Coulson, M. A., & Riddell, C. (1980). *Approaching sociology.* London, UK: Routledge & Kegan Paul.

Cowan, R. (1991). More work for mother: The postwar years. In L. Kramer (Ed.), *The sociology of gender.* New York, NY: St. Martin's Press.

Cowell, A. (2002, April 28). Migrants feel chill in a testy Europe. *The New York Times.*

Cowell, A. (2007, March 8). Commons moves again to erode nobles' power in Britain. *The New York Times.*

Cowley, G. (1997, May 9). Gender limbo. *Newsweek.*

Cowley, G. (2003, May 5). How progress makes us sick. *Newsweek.*

Coyle, M. (2003). *Race and class penalties in crack cocaine sentencing* (Sentencing Project Report No. 5077). www.sentencingproject.org/doc/publications/5077.pdf. Accessed September 4, 2009.

Crandall, M., Nathens, A. B., Kernic, M. A., Holt, V. L., & Rivara, F. P. (2004). Predicting future injury among women in abusive relationships. *Journal of Trauma: Injury, Infection, and Critical Care, 56,* 906–912.

Crary, D. (2003, June 1). Internet can speed up divorces. *The Indianapolis Star.*

Crary, D. (2007, June 3). TB case raises ethical questions. *The Indianapolis Star.*

Crary, D. (2009, March 8). Women's rights pact worries right, left. *The Indianapolis Star.*

Crawford, S. P. (2011, December 4). The new digital divide. *The New York Times.*

The Criminal Justice Project. (2012). *Death Row U.S.A.* Quarterly report of the NAACP Legal Defense and Educational Fund. www.deathpenaltyinfo.org/documents/DRUSAFa112012.pdf. Accessed January 23, 2013.

Cross, J., & Guyer, M. (1980). *Social traps.* Ann Arbor: University of Michigan Press.

Crossette, B. (2001, February 28). Against a trend, U.S. population will bloom, UN says. *The New York Times.*

Croteau, D., & Hoynes, W. (2000). *Media/society: Industries, images, and audiences.* Thousand Oaks, CA: Pine Forge Press.

Crystal, D. (2003). *English as a global language.* Cambridge, UK: Cambridge University Press.

Cumulus Media. (2012). *Local radio.* www.cumulus.com/local-radio-2. Accessed December 28, 2012.

Curra, J. (2000). *The relativity of deviance.* Thousand Oaks, CA: Sage.

Currier, C. (2012). *The 24 states that have sweeping self-defense laws just like Florida's.* ProPublica. www.propublica.org/article/the-23-states-that-have-sweeping-self-defense-laws-just-like-floridas. Accessed January 21, 2013.

Cushing, R., & Bishop, B. (2005, July 20). The rural war. *The New York Times.*

Cushman, J. H. (1993, November 19). U.S. to weigh Blacks' complaints about pollution. *The New York Times.*

Dahrendorf, R. (1959). *Class and class conflict in industrial society.* Stanford, CA: Stanford University Press.

Daily Mail. (2012). South Korean girls' obsession with double eyelid surgery as they strive to look like "pretty western celebrities." www.dailymail.co.uk/femail/article-2222481/South-Korean-girls-obsession-double-eyelid-surgery-strive-look-like-pretty-western-celebrities.html?printingPage=true. Accessed January 11, 2013.

Daley, S. (1996, May 9). A new charter wins adoption in South Africa. *The New York Times.*

Daley, S. (2000, April 9). More and more, Europeans find fault with U.S. *The New York Times.*

Dao, J. (2010a, February 12). Single mother is spared court-martial. *The New York Times.*

Dao, J. (2010b, July 8). V.A. is easing rules to cover stress disorder. *The New York Times.*

Dao, J. (2011, May 14). Unfounded suspicions wreak havoc on lives of two Muslim soldiers. *The New York Times.*

Dao, J. (2013, June 24). When victims of military sex assaults are men. *The New York Times.*

Dargis, M. (2011, May 25). 3 men and a monkey-baby. *The New York Times.*

Davey, M. (2011, September 7). Families feel sharp edge of state budget cuts. *The New York Times.*

Davidson, A. (2011, November 27). When did the rules change? *The New York Times Magazine.*

Davidson, A. (2013, January 13). A tax on annoying behavior? *The New York Times Magazine.*

Davis, D. B. (2006). *Inhuman bondage: The rise and fall of slavery in the New World.* New York, NY: Oxford University Press.

Davis, F. J. (1991). *Who is black?* University Park: Pennsylvania State University Press.

Davis, K. (1937). The sociology of prostitution. *American Sociological Review, 2,* 744–755.

Davis, K. (1976). The world's population crisis. In R. K. Merton & R. Nisbett (Eds.), *Contemporary social problems.* New York, NY: Harcourt Brace Jovanovich.

Davis, K., & Moore, W. (1945). Some principles of stratification. *American Sociological Review, 10,* 242–247.

Dawes, R. M., & Messick, D. M. (2000). Social dilemmas. *International Journal of Psychology, 35,* 111–116.

Death Penalty Information Center. (2013a). *Death penalty representation.* www.deathpenaltyinfo.org/death-penalty-representation. Accessed January 23, 2013.

Death Penalty Information Center. (2013b). *Murder rates nationally and by state.* www.deathpenaltyinfo.org/murder-rates-nationally-and-state. Accessed January 23, 2013.

Deaux, K., & Kite, M. E. (1987). Thinking about gender. In B. B. Hess & M. M. Ferree (Eds.), *Analyzing gender: A handbook of social science research.* Newbury Park, CA: Sage.

Decker, G. (2011, July 4). More Hispanics are identifying themselves as Indians. *The New York Times.*

Declaration of sentiments and resolutions, Seneca Falls Convention, 1848. (2001). In P. S. Rothenberg (Ed.), *Race, class, and gender in the United States.* New York, NY: Worth.

DeFronzo, J. (1991). *Revolutions and revolutionary movements.* Boulder, CO: Westview Press.

de la Baume, M. (2011, May 12). Enforcing veil ban, the French have stopped 46 violators. *The New York Times.*

de la Baume, M. (2013, May 24). Bid in France to add courses in English raises fear for language. *New York Times.*

DeNavas-Walt, C., Proctor, B. D., & Lee, C. H. (2006). *Income, poverty, and health insurance: Coverage in the United States: 2005* (U.S. Census Bureau, Current Population Reports, P60–231). Washington, DC: Government Printing Office.

DeNavas-Walt, C., Proctor, B. D., & Smith, J. C. (2012). *Income, poverty, and health insurance coverage in the United States: 2011.* (U.S. Census Bureau, Current Population Reports, P60–243). www.census.gov/prod/2012pubs/p60–243.pdf. Accessed May 31, 2013.

Denzin, N. (1977). *Childhood socialization: Studies in the development of language, social behavior, and identity.* San Francisco, CA: Jossey-Bass.

Denzin, N. (1989). *The research act: A theoretical introduction to sociological methods.* Englewood Cliffs, NJ: Prentice Hall.

DeParle, J. (2007, April 22). A good provider is one who leaves. *The New York Times Magazine.*

DeParle, J. (2012, April 8). Welfare limits left poor adrift as recession hit. *The New York Times.*

DeParle, J., Gebeloff, R., & Tavernise, S. (2011, November 18). Meet the near poor: Older, married, suburban, & struggling. *The New York Times*.

DeParle, J., & Tavernise, S. (2011, September 15). Poor are still getting poorer, but downturn's punch varies. *The New York Times*.

Derber, C. (1979). *The pursuit of attention*. New York, NY: Oxford University Press.

Deutsch, K. W. (1966). *Nationalism and social communication*. Cambridge, MA: MIT Press.

Dey, J. G., & Hill, C. (2007). *Behind the pay gap*. Washington, DC: American Association of University Women Educational Foundation. www.aauw.org. Accessed April 1, 2007.

Diamond, J. (2005). *How societies choose to succeed or fail*. New York, NY: Viking.

Diekman, A. B., & Murnen, S. K. (2004). Learning to be little women and little men: The inequitable gender equality of nonsexist children's literature. *Sex Roles, 50*, 373–385.

Diekmann, A., & Engelhardt, H. (1999). The social inheritance of divorce: Effects of parent's family type in postwar Germany. *American Sociological Review, 64*, 78–93.

Diller, L. H. (1998). *Running on Ritalin*. New York, NY: Bantam Books.

Dillon, S. (2008, September 1). Hard times hitting students and schools in double blow. *The New York Times*.

Dillon, S. (2010, March 10). Many nations passing US in education, experts say. *The New York Times*.

Dillon, S. (2011, July 6). Saving money means less time for school. *The New York Times*.

DiMaggio, P. J., & Powell, W. W. (1983). The iron cage revisited: Institutional isomorphism and collective rationality in organizational fields. *American Sociological Review, 48*, 147–160.

DiMaggio, P. J., & Powell, W. W. (1991). Introduction. In W. W. Powell & P. J. DiMaggio (Eds.), *The new institutionalism in organizational analysis*. Chicago, IL: University of Chicago Press.

Dion, K., Berscheid, E., & Walster, E. (1972). What is beautiful is good. *Journal of Personality and Social Psychology, 24*, 285–290.

Division for the Advancement of Women. (2009). *Convention on the elimination of all forms of discrimination against women: Overview of the convention*. www.un.org/womenwatch/daw/cedaw/. Accessed June 4, 2009.

Dixon, T. L., & Linz, D. (2000). Race and the misrepresentation of victimization on local television news. *Communication Research, 27*, 547–573.

Dobash, R. E., & Dobash, R. P. (1979). *Violence against wives: A case against the patriarchy*. New York, NY: Free Press.

Do fines ever make corporations change? (2010, September 13). *Newsweek*.

Dokoupil, T. (2009, March 2). Men will be men. *Newsweek*.

Dokoupil, T. (2012, July 16). Is the onslaught making us crazy? *Newsweek*.

Domhoff, G. W. (1983). *Who rules America now? A view from the eighties*. Englewood Cliffs, NJ: Prentice Hall.

Domhoff, G. W. (1998). *Who rules America? Power and politics in the year 2000*. Mountain View, CA: Mayfield.

Domino's. (2012). *Domino's 101: Basic facts*. www.dominosbiz.com/Biz-Public-EN/Site+Content/Secondary/About+Dominos/Fun+Facts/. Accessed December 31, 2012.

Dominus, S. (2004, February 22). Life in the age of old, old age. *The New York Times Magazine*.

Dosomething.org. (2007). *11 facts about environmental racism*. www.dosomething.org/tipsandtools/11-facts-about-environmental-racism. Accessed June 19, 2011.

Doucleff, M. (2012). *HIV infections rise among young black men in U.S.* National Public Radio. www.npr.org/blogs/health/2012/11/27/166012216/hiv-infections-rise-among-young-black-men?sc=17&f=1001. Accessed November 28, 2012.

Drug Policy Alliance. (2013). *Cocaine and crack facts*. www.drugpolicy.org/drug-facts/cocaine-and-crack-facts. Accessed January 23, 2013.

Dugger, C. W. (1996, February 29). Immigrant cultures raising issues of child punishment. *The New York Times*.

Dugger, C. W. (1999, April 25). India's poorest are becoming its loudest. *The New York Times*.

Dugger, C. W. (2004, December 28). Supermarket giants crush Central American farmers. *The New York Times*.

Duncan, G. J. (2007). School readiness and later achievement. *Developmental Psychology, 43*, 1428–1446.

Duncan, G. J., & Chase-Lansdale, P. L. (2001). For better and for worse: Welfare reform and the well-being of children and families. In G. J. Duncan & P. L. Chase-Lansdale (Eds.), *For better and for worse*. New York, NY: Russell Sage.

Durkheim, É. (1947). *The division of labor in society* (G. Simpson, Trans.). Glencoe, IL: Free Press. (Original work published 1893)

Durkheim, É. (1951). *Suicide*. New York, NY: Free Press. (Original work published 1897)

Durkheim, É. (1954). *The elementary forms of religious life* (J. Swain, Trans.). New York, NY: Free Press. (Original work published 1915)

Durkheim, É. (1958). *Rules of sociological method* (G. E. G. Catlin, Ed.; A. Solovay & J. H. Mueller, Trans.). Glencoe, IL: Free Press. (Original work published 1895)

Dye, J. L. (2008). *Fertility of American women: 2006* (U.S. Census Bureau, Current Population Reports, P20–558). www.census.gov/prod/2008pubs/p20–558.pdf. Accessed September 4, 2009.

Eagly, A. H., & Karau, S. J. (2002). Role congruity theory of prejudice toward female leaders. *Psychology Review, 109,* 573–598.

Eappen, S. (2013). Relationship between occurrence of surgical complications and hospital finances. *Journal of the American Medical Association, 309,* 1599–1606.

Ebaugh, H. R. F. (1988). *Becoming an ex.* Chicago, IL: University of Chicago Press.

Eckholm, E. (2006, July 27). Chicago orders "big box" stores to raise wages. *The New York Times.*

Eckholm, E. (2010, September 29). Saying no to "I do," economy in mind. *The New York Times.*

Eckholm, E. (2011, December 27). Battling anew over the place of religion in public schools. *The New York Times.*

Eckholm, E. (2013, February 28). In gay marriage case, a corporate call for change. *The New York Times.*

Economic Policy Institute. (2012). Long-term unemployment, by demographic group, education, and occupation, 2000–2011. *The state of working America.* www.stateofworkingamerica.org/chart/swa-jobs-table-5–7-long-term-unemployment. Accessed December 21, 2012.

Edidin, P. (2005, March 6). How to shake hands or share a meal with an Iraqi. *The New York Times.*

Edney, J. J. (1979, August). Free riders en route to disaster. *Psychology Today,* pp. 80–102.

The Education Trust. (2002). *The funding gap: Low-income and minority students receive fewer dollars.* www.edtrust.org. Accessed January 16, 2003.

Edwards, L. (2013, March 17). The gender gap in pain. *The New York Times.*

Egan, T. (2007, January 7). Little Asia on the hill. *The New York Times.*

Ehrenreich, B. (1990). Is the middle class doomed? In B. Ehrenreich (Ed.), *The worst years of our lives.* New York, NY: Harper & Row.

Ehrenreich, B., & English, D. (1979). *For her own good: 150 years of the experts' advice to women.* Garden City, NY: Anchor Books.

Ehrlich, P. R., & Ehrlich, A. H. (1993). World population crisis. In K. Finsterbusch & J. S. Schwartz (Eds.), *Sources: Notable selections in sociology.* Guilford, CT: Dushkin.

Eitzen, D. S., & Baca Zinn, M. (1991). *In conflict and order: Understanding society.* Boston, MA: Allyn & Bacon.

Elder, G. H., & Liker, J. K. (1982). Hard times in women's lives: Historical influences across 40 years. *American Journal of Sociology, 88,* 241–269.

Elias, P. (2006, February 18). Execution reignites medical debate. *The Indianapolis Star.*

Eligon, J. (2013, January 16). An oil town where men are many, and women are hounded. *The New York Times.*

Eliot, L. (2010). *Pink brain, blue brain: How small differences grow into troublesome gaps and what we can do about it.* New York, NY: Mariner Books.

Elliott, D., & Simmons, T. (2011). *Marital events of Americans: 2009.* (U.S. Bureau of the Census, American Community Survey Report ACS-13). www.census.gov/prod/2011pubs/acs-13.pdf. Accessed September 4, 2011.

Emanuel, E. J. (2011, October 30). How much does health cost? *The New York Times.*

England, P., & Thomas, R. J. (2007). The decline of the date and the rise of the college hook-up. In A. S. Skolnick & J. H. Skolnick (Eds.), *Family in transition.* Boston, MA: Allyn & Bacon.

Enloe, C. (1993). *The morning after: Sexual politics at the end of the cold war.* Berkeley: University of California Press.

Epstein, C. F. (1989). Workplace boundaries: Conceptions and creations. *Social Research, 56,* 571–590.

Erdely, S. R. (2012, February 4). One town's war on gay teens. *Reader Supported News.* readersupportednews.org/news-section2/328–121/9792-one-towns-war-on-gay-teens. Accessed February 5, 2012.

Erikson, K. (1966). *Wayward Puritans.* New York, NY: Wiley.

Erlanger, S. (2000, April 2). Across a new Europe, a people deemed unfit for tolerance. *The New York Times.*

Erlanger, S. (2008, November 12). After U.S. breakthrough, Europe looks in mirror. *The New York Times.*

Erlanger, S. (2009, June 30). Study says Blacks and Arabs face bias from Paris police. *The New York Times.*

Erlanger, S. (2010, August 19). France intensifies effort to expel Roma, raising questions. *The New York Times.*

Evans, L., & Davies, K. (2000). No sissy boys here: A content analysis of the representation of masculinity in elementary school reading textbooks. *Sex Roles, 42,* 255–270.

Evans, T., & Nichols, M. (2009, March 22). Waiting for help in Indy. *The Indianapolis Star.*

Evered, R. (1983). The language of organizations: The case of the Navy. In L. R. Pondy, P. J. Frost, G. Morgan, & T. C. Dandridge (Eds.), *Organizational symbolism.* Greenwich, CT: JAI Press.

Extreme facts. (2005, June 4). *The Indianapolis Star.*

Faleiro, S. (2013, January 2). The unspeakable truth about rape in India. *The New York Times.*

Faludi, S. (1991). *Backlash: The undeclared war against women.* New York, NY: Crown.

Family of VCJD victim claim untried treatment is a success. (2003). *Vegsource Newsletter.* www.vegsource.com/talk/madcow/messages/422.html. Accessed June 30, 2003.

Farb, P. (1983). *Word play: What happens when people talk*. New York, NY: Bantam Books.

Farley, J. (1982). *Majority-minority relations*. Englewood Cliffs, NJ: Prentice Hall.

Farmer, R. (2002, Spring). Same sex couples face post–September 11 discrimination. *National NOW Times*.

Farrar, L. (2010). Chinese companies "rent" white foreigners. *CNN Online*. www.cnn.com/2010/BUSINESS/06/29/china.rent.white.people/index.html. Accessed June 1, 2011.

Faust, K., Gann, M., & McKibben, J. (1999). The boomlet goes to college. *American Demographics, 21*, 4–5.

Fausto-Sterling, A. (1985). *Myths of gender: Biological theories about women and men*. New York, NY: Basic Books.

Fausto-Sterling, A. (2000). *Sexing the body: Gender politics and the construction of sexuality*. New York, NY: Basic Books.

Feagin, J. R. (1975). *Subordinating the poor*. Englewood Cliffs, NJ: Prentice Hall.

Feagin, J. R., & McKinney, K. D. (2003). *The many costs of racism*. New York, NY: Rowman & Littlefield.

Fearing demographic abyss, Putin promises mums more money. (2006, May 10). *Agence France Presse—English*.

Fears, D., & Deane, C. (2001, July 5). Biracial couples report tolerance. *The Washington Post*.

Federal Bureau of Investigation. (2012). *FBI releases 2011 hate crime statistics*. www.fbi.gov/news/pressrel/press-releases/fbi-releases-2011-hate-crime-statistics. Accessed June 19, 2013.

Federal Communication Commission. (2013). *The dangers of texting while driving*. www.fcc.gov/guides/texting-while-driving. Accessed June 30, 2013.

Fee, D. (2013). Covenant marriage: Reflexivity and retrenchment in the politics of intimacy. In D. Newman & J. O'Brien (Eds.), *Sociology: Exploring the architecture of everyday life (Readings)*. Thousand Oaks, CA: Sage.

Feldman, M., & Weinberg, L. (2012). The Obama victory and near hysteria of the American far right. *Truthout*. truthout.org/opinion/item/12844-the-obama-victory-and-the-american-far-right?tmpl=components&print=1. Accessed November 21, 2012.

Feldmann, L., Marlantes, L., & Bowers, F. (2003, March 14). The impact of Bush linking 9/11 and Iraq. *Christian Science Monitor*.

Felmlee, D., Sprecher, S., & Bassin, E. (1990). The dissolution of intimate relationships: A hazard model. *Social Psychology Quarterly, 53*, 13–30.

Fendrich, J. M. (2003). The forgotten movement: The Vietnam antiwar movement. *Sociological Inquiry, 73*, 338–358.

Ferguson, N. (2004, April 4). Eurabia? *The New York Times Magazine*.

Ferree, M. M. (1992). The political context of rationality. In A. D. Morris & C. M. Mueller (Eds.), *Frontiers in social movement theory*. New Haven, CT: Yale University Press.

Festinger, L., Riecken, H., & Schacter, S. (1956). *When prophecy fails*. New York, NY: Harper & Row.

Feuer, A. (2004, May 15). Vatican discourages marriage with Muslims for Catholic women. *The New York Times*.

Fiese, B. H., & Skillman, G. (2000). Gender differences in family stories: Moderating influence of parent gender role and child gender. *Sex Roles, 43*(5/6), 267–283.

Figert, A. (1996). *Women and the ownership of PMS*. New York, NY: Aldine de Gruyter.

Fincham, F., & Bradbury, T. N. (1987). The impact of attributions in marriage: A longitudinal analysis. *Journal of Personality and Social Psychology, 53*, 510–517.

Fine, C. (2010). *Delusions of gender: How our minds, society, and neurosexism create difference*. New York: Norton.

Finer, J. (2005, August 12). The new Ernie Pyles: Sgtlizzie and 67shdocs. *The Washington Post*.

First, A. (2011). 14 most outdated pieces of baby advice. *Parenting*. Shine.yahoo.com/channel/parenting/14-most-outdated-pieces-of-baby-advice-2554194. Accessed September 27, 2011.

Fish, S. (2000). The nifty nine arguments against affirmative action in higher education. *Journal of Blacks in Higher Education, 27*, 79–81.

FlorCruz, M. (2013, January 2). Chinese law requires children to visit elderly parents. *International Business Times*. www.ibtimes.com/chinese-law-requires-children-visit-elderly-parents-987796#. Accessed June 27, 2013.

Folbre, N., & Yoon, J. (2006, January 5). *The value of unpaid child care in the U.S. in 2003*. Paper presented at the meeting of the Allied Social Science Association, Boston, MA. (Cited with permission of author)

Forbes Magazine. (2013). The world's most powerful celebrities. www.forbes.com/celebrities/list/#p_1_s_a3_Allcategories_. Accessed May 31, 2013.

Forman, T. A., Williams, D., & Jackson, J. (1997). Race, place, and discrimination. *Perspectives on Social Problems, 9*, 231–261.

Foroohar, R. (2010, April 26). The Burqa revolution. *Newsweek*.

Fowler, J. H., & Christakis, N. A. (2008). Dynamic spread of happiness in a large social network: Longitudinal analysis over 20 years in the Framingham Heart Study. *British Medical Journal, 338*, 23–31.

Fox, J. A. (2012). *Intimate partner violence: Down but far from out*. Boston College. boston.com/community/blogs/crime_punishment/2012/ 11/intimate_partner_violence_down.html. Accessed January 16, 2013.

Frank, A. G. (1969). *Capitalism and under-development in Latin America*. New York, NY: Monthly Review Press.

Frankenberg, E. (2006). *The segregation of American teachers*. Cambridge, MA: Civil Rights Project at Harvard University.

Franklin, D. (2006, August 15). Patient power: Making sure your doctor really hears you. *The New York Times*.

Free Press. (2012). *Who owns the media?* www.freepress.net/ownership/chart. Accessed December 29, 2012.

Freiberg, P. (1991). Self-esteem gender gap widens in adolescence. *APA Monitor, 22*, 29.

French, H. W. (1999a, November 15). "Japanese only" policy takes body blow in court. *The New York Times*.

French, H. W. (1999b, October 12). Japan's troubling trend: Rising teen-age crime. *The New York Times*.

French, H. W. (2000, May 3). Japan unsettles returnees, who yearn to leave again. *The New York Times*.

French, H. W. (2002, September 23). Educators try to tame Japan's blackboard jungles. *The New York Times*.

French, H. W. (2003, July 25). Japan's neglected resource: Female workers. *The New York Times*.

French, H. W. (2007, March 22). China scrambles for stability as its workers age. *The New York Times*.

Frese, B., Moya, M., & Megias, J. L. (2004). Social perception of rape: How rape myth acceptance modulates the influence of situational factors. *Journal of Interpersonal Violence, 19*, 143–161.

Freund, P. E. S., & McGuire, M. B. (1991). *Health, illness, and the social body: A cultural sociology*. Englewood Cliffs, NJ: Prentice Hall.

Friedman, T. L. (2005, April 3). It's a flat world after all. *The New York Times Magazine*.

Fry, R. (2013). *A rising share of young adults live in their parents' home*. Pew Research Social and Demographic Trneds. www.pewsocialtrends.org/2013/08/01/a-rising-share-of-young-adults-life-in-their-parents-home. Accessed August 15, 2013.

Fryer, R. G. (2006, Winter). "Acting white": The social price paid by the best and brightest minority students. *Education Next*, pp. 53–59.

Furstenberg, F. F., & Harris, K. M. (1992). The disappearing American father? Divorce and the waning significance of biological parenthood. In S. J. South & S. E. Tolnay (Eds.), *The changing American family: Sociological and demographic perspectives*. Boulder, CO: Westview Press.

Fustos, K. (2010a, June). *Marriage and partnership turnover for American families*. Population Reference Bureau. http://www.prb.org/Articles/2010/usmarriagepolicyseminar.aspx. Accessed August 28, 2011.

Fustos, K. (2010b). *Marriage benefits men's health*. Population Reference Bureau. www.prb.org/Articles/2010/usmarriagemenshealth.aspx? p=1. Accessed June 5, 2011.

Fuwa, M. (2004). Macro-level gender inequality and the division of household labor in 22 countries. *American Sociological Review, 69*, 751–767.

Gale, R. P. (1986). Social movements and the state: The environmental movement, countermovement and governmental agencies. *Sociological Perspectives, 29*, 202–240.

Galinsky, E., Bond, J. T., Kim, S. S., Backon, L., Brownfield, E., & Sakai, K. (2006). *Overwork in America: When the way we work becomes too much*. New York, NY: Families and Work Institute. www.familiesandwork.org/summary/overwork2005.pdf. Accessed July 19, 2006.

Galles, G. M. (1989, June 8). What colleges really teach. *The New York Times*.

Galliher, J. M., & Galliher, J. F. (2002). A "commonsense" theory of deterrence and the "ideology" of science: The New York State death penalty debate. *Journal of Criminal Law and Criminology, 92*, 307–333.

Gamson, W. A., & Wolfsfeld, G. (1993). Movements and media as interactive systems. *Annals of the American Academy of Political and Social Science, 528*, 114–125.

Gans, H. (1971, July/August). The uses of poverty: The poor pay for all. *Social Policy*, pp. 20–24.

Gans, H. (1996). Positive functions of the undeserving poor: Uses of the underclass in America. In J. Levin & A. Arluke (Eds.), *Snapshots and portraits of society*. Thousand Oaks, CA: Pine Forge Press.

Gans, H. (2005). Race as class. *Contexts, 4*, 17–21.

Garcia-Moreno, C., Jansen, H., Ellsberg, M., Heise, L., & Watts, C. H. (2006). Prevalence of intimate partner violence: Findings from the WHO multi-country study on women's health and domestic violence. *Lancet, 368*, 1260–1269.

Garfinkel, J. (2003, February 24). Boutique medical practices face legal, legislative foes. *Cincinnati Business Courier*. www.bizjournals.com/cincinnati/stories/2003/02/24/focus2.html. Accessed July 12, 2004.

Garner, B. A. (2010, February 28). Webinar: What makes for a successful mash-up neologism. *The New York Times Magazine*.

Gates, H. L. (2007, November 18). Forty acres and a gap in wealth. *The New York Times*.

Gaubatz, K. T. (1995). *Crime in the public mind*. Ann Arbor: University of Michigan Press.

Gault, B. (2013). *The wage gap and occupational segregation*. Institute for Women's Policy Research. www.iwpr.org/initiatives/the-wage-gap-and-occupational-segregation. Accessed June 24, 2013.

Geena Davis Institute on Gender in Media. (2012). *Research facts*. www.seejane.org/research. Accessed January 9, 2013.

Gelles, R. J., & Straus, M. A. (1988). *Intimate violence*. Newbury Park, CA: Sage.

Gentleman, A. (2007, June 3). Indian shepherds stoop to conquer caste system. *The New York Times.*

Gergen, K. J. (1991). *The saturated self.* New York, NY: Basic Books.

Gerlach, P., & Hine, V. H. (1970). *People, power, change: Movements of social transformation.* Indianapolis, IN: Bobbs-Merrill.

Gershon, I. (2010). *The breakup 2.0: Disconnecting over new media.* Ithaca, NY: Cornell University Press.

Getahun, D., Jacobsen, S. J., Fassett, M. J., Chen, W., Demissie, K., & Rhoads, G. G. (2013). Recent trends in childhood Attention-Deficit/Hyperactivity Disorder. *JAMA Pediatrics, January 21,* E1–E7.

Getlin, J., & Wilkinson, T. (2003, April 3). "Embedded" reporters are mixed blessing for the military. *The Seattle Times.*

Gettleman, J. (2010, October 4). 4-day frenzy of rape in Congo reveals U.N. troops' weakness. *The New York Times.*

Gettleman, J. (2011, December 28). For Somali women, pain of being a spoil of war. *The New York Times.*

Giddens, A. (1984). *The construction of society: Outline of the theory of structuration.* Berkeley: University of California Press.

Giddens, A. (2005). The global revolution in family and personal life. In A. S. Skolnick & J. H. Skolnick (Eds.), *Family in transition.* Boston, MA: Allyn & Bacon.

Gillen, B. (1981). Physical attractiveness: A determinant of two types of goodness. *Personality and Social Psychology Bulletin, 7,* 277–281.

Gilliam, W. S. (2005). *Prekindergarteners left behind: Expulsion rates in state prekindergarten systems.* New York, NY: Foundation for Child Development. www.fcd-us.org/PDFs/NationalPreKExpulsionPaper03.02_new.pdf. Accessed May 17, 2005.

Gilligan, C. (1990). Teaching Shakespeare's sister: Notes from the underground of female adolescence. In C. Gilligan, N. P. Lyons, & T. J. Hanmer (Eds.), *Making connections.* Cambridge, MA: Harvard University Press.

Ginzel, L. E., Kramer, R. M., & Sutton, R. I. (2004). Organizational impression management as a reciprocal influence process: The neglected role of the organizational audience. In M. J. Hatch & M. Schultz (Eds.), *Organizational identity.* New York, NY: Oxford University Press.

Giridharadas, A. (2007, November 25). Rumbling across India: Stories of urban migration. *The New York Times.*

Giridharadas, A. (2010, August 8). Getting in (and out of) line. *The New York Times.*

Gitlin, T. (1979). Prime time ideology: The hegemonic process in television entertainment. *Social Problems, 26,* 251–266.

Gladwell, M. (2010, October 4). Small change. *The New Yorker.*

Glater, J. D. (2006, December 3). Straight "A" students? Good luck making partner. *The New York Times.*

Glaze, L. E., & Bonczar, T. P. (2010). *Probation and parole in the United States, 2009* (NCJ 231674). U.S. Bureau of Justice Statistics. http://bjs.ojp.usdoj.gov/content/pub/pdf/ppus09.pdf. Accessed March 31, 2011.

Glick, P., & Fiske, S. T. (1996). The ambivalent sexism inventory: Differentiating hostile and benevolent sexism. *Journal of Personality and Social Psychology, 70,* 491–512.

Glynn, S. J. (2012). *The new breadwinners: 2010.* Center for American Progress. www.american progress.org/wp-content/uploads/issues/2012/04/pdf/breadwinners.pdf. Accessed January 16, 2013.

Godofsky, J., Zukin, C., & Van Horn, C. (2011). *Unfulfilled expectations: Recent college graduates struggle in a troubled economy.* John J. Heldrich Center for Workforce Development. www.heldrich.rutgers.edu. Accessed May 19, 2011.

Godson, R., & Olson, W. J. (1995). International organized crime. *Society, 32,* 18–29.

Goffman, A. (2009). On the run: Wanted men in a Philadelphia ghetto. *American Sociological Review, 74,* 339–357.

Goffman, E. (1952). On cooling the mark out: Some aspects of adaptation to failure. *Psychiatry, 15,* 451–463.

Goffman, E. (1959). *The presentation of self in everyday life.* Garden City, NY: Doubleday.

Goffman, E. (1961). *Asylums.* Garden City, NY: Doubleday.

Goffman, E. (1963). *Stigma: Notes on the management of spoiled identity.* Englewood Cliffs, NJ: Prentice Hall.

Goffman, E. (1967). *Interaction ritual.* Chicago, IL: Aldine-Atherton.

Goldberg, S. (1999). The logic of patriarchy. *Gender Issues, 17,* 53–69.

Goleman, D. (1989, October 10). Sensing silent cues emerges as key skill. *The New York Times.*

Goleman, D. (1990, December 25). The group and the self: New focus on a cultural rift. *The New York Times.*

Goleman, D. (1993, May 4). Therapists find some patients are just hateful. *The New York Times.*

Golway, T. (2004, August 2–9). Redrafting America. *America.*

Gonnerman, J. (2004). *Life on the outside.* New York, NY: Farrar, Strauss, & Giroux.

Gonzalez, J. (2012, November 7). Latinos and other minorities boost President Obama's margin of victory in 2012 election. *New York Daily News.*

Goode, Erica. (1999, January 12). Pediatricians renew battle over toilet training. *The New York Times.*

Goode, Erica. (2011, May 21). States seeking new registries for criminals. *The New York Times.*

Goode, Erich. (1989). *Drugs in American society.* New York, NY: McGraw-Hill.

Goode, Erich. (1994). *Deviant behavior*. Englewood Cliffs, NJ: Prentice Hall.

Goode, W. J. (1971). World revolution and family patterns. *Journal of Marriage and the Family, 33,* 624–635.

Goode, W. J. (1981). Why men resist. In B. Thorne & M. Yalom (Eds.), *Rethinking the family: Some feminist questions*. New York, NY: Longman.

Goodman, J. C. (2005). *Aid to Katrina victims: A right/left consensus*. Dallas, TX: National Center for Policy Analysis. www.ncpa.org/pub/ba529. Accessed May 23, 2009.

Goodstein, L. (2003, September 11). Survey finds slight rise in Jews' intermarrying. *The New York Times*.

Goodstein, L. (2013, October 1). Poll shows major shift in identity of U.S. Jews. *The New York Times*.

Gorbis, E., & Kholodenko, Y. (2005, September 1). Plastic surgery addiction in patients with body dysmorphic disorder. *Psychiatric Times*.

Gordon, M. M. (1964). *Assimilation in American life*. New York, NY: Oxford University Press.

Gordon, R. G. (2005). *Ethnologue: Languages of the world* (15th ed.). Dallas, TX: SIL International.

Gould, S. J. (1981). *The mismeasure of man*. New York, NY: Norton.

Gould, S. J. (1997, June). Dolly's fashion and Louis's passion. *Natural History*.

Gove, W., Hughes, M., & Geerkin, M. R. (1980). Playing dumb: A form of impression management with undesirable effects. *Social Psychology Quarterly, 43,* 89–102.

Gove, W., Style, C. B., & Hughes, M. (1990). The effect of marriage on the well-being of adults. *Journal of Family Issues, 11,* 34–35.

Gracey, H. L. (1991). Learning the student role: Kindergarten as academic boot camp. In J. Henslin (Ed.), *Down-to-earth sociology*. New York, NY: Free Press.

Grady, D. (2008, December 4). Parents torn over extra frozen embryos from fertility procedures. *The New York Times*.

Grady, D. (2013, January 16). When pills fail, this, er, option provides a cure. *The New York Times*.

Graham, L. O. (1999). *Our kind of people: Inside America's black upper class*. New York, NY: HarperCollins.

Grall, T. S. (2011). *Custodial mothers and fathers and their child support: 2009* (U.S. Census Bureau, Current Population Reports, P60–240). www.census.gov/prod/2011pubs/p60–240.pdf. Accessed January 16, 2013.

Grant, A. (2013, July 21). Why men need women. *The New York Times*.

Greenblatt, A. (2009). Confronting warming. *CQ Researcher, 19,* 1–24.

Greenblatt, A. (2011). Aging population. *CQ Researcher, 21,* 577–600.

Greencastle Banner Graphic. (1992, March 7). [Letter to the editor].

Greenhouse, L. (2005, June 7). Justices say U.S. may prohibit the use of medical marijuana. *The New York Times*.

Greenhouse, L. (2007, June 29). Justices, 5–4, limit use of race for school integration plans. *The New York Times*.

Greenhouse, S. (2011, May 21). Sexual affronts a known hotel hazard. *The New York Times*.

Greywolfe359. (2011, March 9). The must see chart (This is what class war looks like) [Web log post]. www.dailykos.com/story/2011/03/09/ 954301/-The-Must-See-Chart-(This-is-What-Class-War-Looks-Like). Accessed June 14, 2011.

Griffin, S. (1986). *Rape: The power of consciousness*. New York, NY: Harper & Row.

Griffin, S. (1989). Rape: The all-American crime. In L. Richardson & V. Taylor (Eds.), *Feminist frontiers II*. New York, NY: Random House.

Griswold, W. (1994). *Cultures and societies in a changing world*. Thousand Oaks, CA: Pine Forge Press.

Groppe, M. (2010, July 19). More get welfare in hard times, right? Not here. *The Indianapolis Star*.

Gross, E., & Etzioni, A. (1985). *Organizations and society*. Englewood Cliffs, NJ: Prentice Hall.

Gross, E., & Stone, G. P. (1964). Embarrassment and the analysis of role requirements. *American Journal of Sociology, 70,* 1–15.

Gross, J. (2004, February 24). Older women team up to face future together. *The New York Times*.

Gross, J. (2006, July 16). Checklist for camp: Bug spray. Sunscreen. Pills. *The New York Times*.

Gusfield, J. R. (1963). *Symbolic crusade: Status politics and the American temperance movement*. Urbana: University of Illinois Press.

Hacker, A. (1992). *Two nations: Black and white, separate, hostile, unequal*. New York, NY: Scribner.

Hacker, A. (1994, October 31). White on white. *The New Republic*.

Hafferty, F. W. (1991). *Into the valley: Death and socialization of medical students*. New Haven, CT: Yale University Press.

Hagan, J. (2000). The poverty of a classless criminology: The American Society of Criminology 1991 presidential address. In R. D. Crutchfield, G. S. Bridges, J. G. Weis, & C. Kubrin (Eds.), *Crime readings*. Thousand Oaks, CA: Pine Forge Press.

Hagerty, B. B. (2011, May 23). Doomsday believers cope with an intact world. *NPR Online*. www.npr.org/2011/05/23/136560695/doomsday-believers-cope-with-an-intact-world. Accessed May 23, 2011.

Hall, W. (1986). Social class and survival on the *S.S. Titanic*. *Social Science and Medicine, 22,* 687–690.

Hallin, D. C. (1986). We keep America on top of the world. In T. Gitlin (Ed.), *Watching television*. New York, NY: Pantheon Books.

Hamilton, C., Anderson, K., Barnes, R., & Dorling, K. (2011). *Administrative detention of children: A global report*. UNICEF. www.unicef.org/protection/files/Administrative_detention_discussion_paper_April2011.pdf. Accessed June 29, 2011.

Hamilton, D. L. (1981). *Cognitive processes in stereotyping and intergroup behavior*. Hillsdale, NJ: Erlbaum.

Hamilton, J. A. (1996). Women and health policy: On the inclusion of women in clinical trials. In C. F. Sargent & C. B. Brettell (Eds.), *Gender and health: An international perspective*. Upper Saddle River, NJ: Prentice Hall.

Haney López, I. E. (1996). *White by law: The legal construction of race*. New York, NY: New York University Press.

Harden, B. (2000, April 6). Africa's gems: Warfare's best friend. *The New York Times*.

Hardin, G., & Baden, J. (1977). *Managing the commons*. New York, NY: Freeman.

Hareven, T. K. (1978). Transitions: The family and the life course in historical perspective. New York, NY: Academic Press.

Hareven, T. K. (1992). *American families in transition: Historical perspectives on change*. In A. S. Skolnick & J. H. Skolnick (Eds.), *Family in transition* (7th ed.). New York, NY: HarperCollins.

Harmon, A. (2009, May 17). Fighting for a last chance at life. *The New York Times*.

Harney, A. (2012, December 16). Without babies, can Japan survive? *The New York Times*.

Harrington, B., Van Deusen, F., & Ladge, J. (2010). *The new dad: Exploring fatherhood within a career context*. Boston College Center for Work & Family. http://www.bc.edu/content/dam/files/centers/cwf/pdf/BCCWF_Fatherhood_Study_The_New_Dad1.pdf. Accessed August 28, 2011.

Harris, G. (2003, December 7). If shoe won't fit, fix the foot? Popular surgery raises concern. *The New York Times*.

Harris, G. (2005, August 6). F.D.A. responds to criticism with new caution. *The New York Times*.

Harris, G. (2006, September 30). F.D.A. says Bayer failed to reveal drug risk study. *The New York Times*.

Harris, G. (2009, January 12). F.D.A. is lax on oversight during trials, inquiry finds. *The New York Times*.

Harris, G. (2011a, October 2). Calling the nurse "doctor," a title physicians oppose. *The New York Times*.

Harris, G. (2011b, December 31). F.D.A. finds short supply of attention deficit drugs. *The New York Times*.

Harris, G. (2011c, October 7). U.S. panel says no to prostate test for healthy men. *The New York Times*.

Harris, G. (2012, November 30). Giving new life to vultures to restore a human ritual of death. *The New York Times*.

Harris, M. C. (1996). Doctors implicated in Tutsi genocide. *Lancet, 347*, 684.

Harris-Perry, M. (2012, April 16). What it's like to be a problem. *The Nation*.

Hartocollis, A. (2012a, April 10). For elderly, E.R.'s of their own. *The New York Times*.

Hartocollis, A. (2012b, January 8). Young, obese, and drawn to surgery. *The New York Times*.

Hartzband, P., & Groopman, J. (2011). The new language of medicine. *New England Journal of Medicine, 365*, 1372–1373.

Hass, N. (1995, September 10). Margaret Kelly Michaels wants her innocence back. *The New York Times Magazine*.

Hatzenbuehler, M. L. (2011). The social environment and suicide attempts in lesbian, gay, and bisexual youth. *Pediatrics, 127*, 896–903.

Haub, C. (2012a). *Changing the way U.S. Hispanics are counted*. Population Reference Bureau. www.prb.org/Articles/2012/us-census-and-hispanics.aspx?p=1. Accessed November 9, 2012.

Haub, C. (2012b). *Fertility rates in low birth-rate countries, 1996–2011*. Population Reference Bureau. www.prb.org/Articles/2012/low-fertility-countries-tfr.aspx. Accessed April 4, 2012.

Haub, C. (2013). *Rising trend of births outside marriage*. Population Reference Bureau. www.prb.org/Articles/2013/nonmarital-births.aspx?p=1. Accessed May 20, 2013.

Haub, C., & Gribble, J. (2011). The world at 7 billion. *Population Bulletin, 66*, 1–12.

Hausmann, R., Tyson, L. D., & Zahidi, S. (2008). *The global gender gap report: 2008*. Geneva, Switzerland: World Economic Forum. www.weforum.org/pdf/gendergap/report2008.pdf. Accessed June 3, 2009.

Health Grades. (2011). *Health Grades Patient Safety in American Hospitals Study*. www.cpmhealthgrades.com/CPM/assets/File/HealthGradesPatientSafetyInAmericanHospitalsStudy2011.pdf. Accessed May 28, 2013.

Hebel, S. (2007, March 23). The graduation gap. *Chronicle of Higher Education*. http://chronicle.com/weekly/v53/i29/29a02001.htm. Accessed August 8, 2007.

Helmreich, W. B. (1992). The things they say behind your back: Stereotypes and the myths behind them. In H. E. Lena, W. B. Helmreich, & W. McCord (Eds.), *Contemporary issues in sociology*. New York, NY: McGraw-Hill.

Henderson, J. J., & Baldasty, G. J. (2003). Race, advertising, and prime-time television. *Howard Journal of Communication, 14*, 97–112.

Henley, N. (1977). *Body politics*. Englewood Cliffs, NJ: Prentice Hall.

Henning, P. J. (2012, September 17). Deferred prosecution agreements and cookie-cutter justice. *Dealbook/New York Times*. dealbook.nytimes.com/2012/09/17/deferred-prosecution-agreements-and-cookie-cutter-justice/. Accessed January 22, 2013.

Henriques, D. B. (1999, August 24). New take on perpetual calendar. *The New York Times*.

Henriques, D. B. (2009, June 30). Madoff, apologizing, is given 150 years. *The New York Times*.

Henshaw, S. K., & Finer, L. B. (2003). The accessibility of abortion services in the United States, 2001. *Perspectives on Sexual and Reproductive Health, 35,* 16–24.

Herbert, B. (2007, May 15). The right to paid sick days. *The New York Times*.

Herbert, B. (2009, February 21). The invisible war. *The New York Times*.

Herek, G. M. (2000a). The psychology of sexual prejudice. *Current Directions in Psychological Science, 9,* 19–22.

Herek, G. M. (2000b). Sexual prejudice and gender: Do heterosexuals' attitudes toward lesbians and gay men differ? *Journal of Social Issues, 56,* 251–266.

Hewitt, J. P. (1988). *Self and society: A symbolic interactionist social psychology*. Boston, MA: Allyn & Bacon.

Hewitt, J. P., & Hewitt, M. L. (1986). *Introducing sociology: A symbolic interactionist perspective*. Englewood Cliffs, NJ: Prentice Hall.

Hewitt, J. P., & Stokes, R. (1975). Disclaimers. *American Sociological Review, 40,* 1–11.

Hibbler, D. K., & Shinew, K. J. (2005). The social life of interracial couples. In R. H. Lauer & J. C. Lauer (Eds.), *Sociology: Windows on society*. Los Angeles, CA: Roxbury.

Higginbotham, E., & Weber, L. (1992). Moving up with kin and community: Upward social mobility for black and white women. *Gender & Society, 6,* 416–440.

Hill, C., & Silva, E. (2006). *Drawing the line: Sexual harassment on campus*. Washington, DC: American Association of University Women. www.aauw.org/research/upload/DTLFinal.pdf. Accessed September 5, 2009.

Hill, M. E. (2000). Color differences in the socioeconomic status of African American men: Results from a longitudinal study. *Social Forces, 78,* 1437–1460.

Hill, N. E. (1997). Does parenting differ based on social class? African American women's perceived socialization for achievement. *American Journal of Community Psychology, 25,* 67–97.

Hills, S. (1980). *Demystifying social deviance*. New York, NY: McGraw-Hill.

Hirschi, T. (1969). *Causes of delinquency*. Berkeley: University of California Press.

Hochschild, A. R. (1983). *The managed heart*. Berkeley: University of California Press.

Hochschild, A. R. (1997). *The time bind: When work becomes home and home becomes work*. New York, NY: Metropolitan Books.

Hoffman, J. (1997, January 16). Crime and punishment: Shame gains popularity. *The New York Times*.

Hoffman, J. (2005, January 25). Sorting out ambivalence over alcohol and pregnancy. *The New York Times*.

Hollander, J. A., Renfrow, D. G., & Howard, J. A. (2011). *Gendered situations, gendered selves*. Lanham, MD: Rowman & Littlefield.

Holson, L. M. (2011, July 5). Who's on the family tree? Now it's complicated. *The New York Times*.

Holtzworth-Munroe, A., & Jacobson, N. S. (1985). Causal attributions of married couples: When do they search for causes? What do they conclude when they do? *Journal of Personality and Social Psychology, 48,* 1398–1412.

Hooks, G., & Smith, C. L. (2004). The treadmill of destruction: National sacrifice areas and Native Americans. *American Sociological Review, 69,* 558–575.

Horon, I. L., & Cheng, D. (2001). Enhanced surveillance for pregnancy-associated mortality—Maryland, 1993–1998. *Journal of the American Medical Association, 285,* 1455–1459.

Horowitz, A. (2012, December 16). Walk like a fish. *New York Times*.

Horwitz, A. V. (2002). *Creating mental illness*. Chicago, IL: University of Chicago Press.

Hotez, P. J. (2012, August 19). Tropical diseases: The new plague of poverty. *The New York Times*.

Houppert, K. (2005, March 28). The new face of protest? *The Nation*.

House, J. (1981). Social structure and personality. In M. Rosenberg & R. H. Turner (Eds.), *Social psychology: Sociological perspectives*. New York: Basic Books.

Hout, M., & Lucas, S. R. (2001). Narrowing the income gap between rich and poor. In P. Rothenberg (Ed.), *Race, class, and gender in the United States*. New York, NY: Worth.

Huber, J., & Form, W. H. (1973). *Income and ideology*. New York, NY: Free Press.

Hudson, V. M., & den Boer, A. (2004). *Bare branches: The security implications of Asia's surplus male population*. Cambridge, MA: MIT Press.

Huff, R., Desilets, C, & Kane, J. (2010). *The 2010 National Public Survey on White Collar Crime*. National White Collar Crime Center. Crimesurvey.nw3c.org/docs/nw3c2010survey.pdf. Accessed January 22, 2013.

Hughes, D., & Chen, L. (1997). When and what parents tell children about race: An examination of race-related socialization among African American families. *Applied Developmental Science, 1,* 200–214.

Hull, K. E., & Nelson, R. L. (2000). Assimilation, choice, or constraint? Testing theories of gender differences in the careers of lawyers. *Social Forces, 79,* 229–264.

Human Rights Campaign. (2011a). *HRC statement on new data on domestic partner benefits*. www.hrc.org/15780.htm. Accessed September 4, 2011.

Human Rights Campaign. (2011b). *LGBT equality at the Fortune 500*. www.hrc.org/issues/fortune500.htm. Accessed June 3, 2011.

Human Rights Watch. (2009). *Time to tear down the wall of caste.* www.hrw.org/en/news/2009/10/09/time-tear-down-wall-caste. Accessed June 15, 2011.

Human Rights Watch. (2011). *ILO: New landmark treaty to protect domestic workers.* www.hrw.org/mews/2011/06/16/ilo-new-landmark-treaty-protect-domestic-workers. Accessed June 23, 2013.

Human Rights Watch. (2012). *India: UN members should act to end caste discrimination.* www.hrw.org/news/2012/05/14/india-un-members-should-act-end-caste-discrimination. Accessed June 4, 2013.

Hunsinger, D. (2009, March 15). New college grads scramble for jobs. *The Indianapolis Star.*

Hunt, J. (1985). Police accounts of normal force. *Urban Life, 13,* 315–341.

Hunter, T. W. (2011, August 2). Putting an antebellum myth to rest. *The New York Times.*

Hunter-Gault, C. (2012, May 28). Violated hopes. *The New Yorker.*

Hvistendahl, M. (2011). *Unnatural selection: Choosing boys over girls, and the consequences of a world full of men.* New York, NY: PublicAffairs.

Hyde, J. S. (1984). How large are gender differences in aggression? A developmental meta-analysis. *Developmental Psychology, 20,* 722–736.

Ignatius, A. (1988, July 14). China's birthrate is out of control again as one-child policy fails in rural areas. *The Wall Street Journal.*

IMS Health. (2012). Trends in attention deficit hyperactivity disorder ambulatory diagnosis and medical treatment in the United States, 2000–2010. www.imshealth.com/portal/site/ims. Accessed January 22, 2013.

Ingold, S. (2012). *At life's end, a final home on the (shooting) range.* National Public Radio. www.npr.org/2012/11/13/164957657/at-lifes-end-a-final-home-on-the-shooting-range?sc=17&f=1001. Accessed November 13, 2012.

Institute for Policy Research. (2002). Housework in double-income marriages still divides unevenly. *Institute for Policy Research News, 24,* 1–2. www.northwestern.edu/ipr/publications/newsletter/iprn0212/housework.html. Accessed September 5, 2009.

Institute for Women's Policy Research. (2011). *The gender wage gap by occupation* (IWPR #C350a). www.iwpr.org/publications/pubs/the-gender-wage-gap-by-occupation-updated-april-2011/at_download/file. Accessed June 21, 2011.

Institute for Women's Policy Research. (2013a). *At current pace of progress, wage gap for women expected to close in 2057.* IWPR#Q004 updated. www.iwpr.org/publications/pubs/at-current-pace-of-progress-wage-gap-for-women-expected-to-close-in-2057/at_download/file. Accessed June 18, 2013.

Institute for Women's Policy Research. (2013b). *The gender wage gap by occupation.* IWPR#C350a. www.iwpr.org/publications/pubs/the-gender-wage-gap-by-occupation-2/at_download/file. Accessed June 18, 2013.

Institute of Medicine. (2013). *U.S. health in international perspective: Shorter lives, poorer health.* Report Brief. www.iom.edu/~/Media/Files/Report%20files/2013/US-Health-International-Perspective/USHealth_Intl_PerspectiveRB.pdf. Accessed February 14, 2013.

Interlandi, J. (2010, December 13). Are we running out of antibiotics? *Newsweek.*

International Centre for Prison Studies. (2012). *Entire world—prison population rates per 100,000 of the national population.* www.prisonstudies.org/info/worldbrief/wpb_stats.php?area=all&category=wb_poprate. Accessed January 21, 2013.

International Society of Aesthetic Plastic Surgery. (2011). *ISAPS International survey on aesthetic/cosmetic procedures performed in 2010.* www.isaps.org/files/html-conten ts/ISAPS-Procedures-Study-Results-2011.pdf. Accessed January 11, 2013.

Ioannidis, J. P. A. (2005). Contradicted and initially stronger effects in highly cited clinical research. *Journal of the American Medical Association, 294,* 218–228.

Issenberg, S. (2007). *The sushi economy.* New York, NY: Gotham Books.

Is there a Santa Claus? (1897, September 21). *The New York Sun.*

Ito, M., Horst, H., Bittanti, M., Boyd, D., Herr-Stephenson, B., Lange, P. G., . . . Robinson, L. (2008). *Living and learning with new media: Summary of findings from the Digital Youth Project* (Reports on Digital Media and Learning). Chicago, IL: MacArthur Foundation. http://digitalyouth.ischool.berkeley.edu/files/report/digitalyouth-WhitePaper.pdf. Accessed June 7, 2009.

Jackson, D. (2011, February 15). Obama's citizenship questioned by GOP voters, polling firm says. *USA Today.* http://content.usatoday.com/communities/theoval/post/2011/02 /obamas-citizenship-questioned-by-gop- voters-polling-firm-says/1. Accessed May 24, 2011.

Jackson, S. (1995). The social context of rape: Sexual scripts and motivation. In P. Searles & R. J. Berger (Eds.), *Rape and society.* Boulder, CO: Westview Press.

Jacobs, A. (2009, April 5). Rural China's hunger for sons fuels traffic in abducted boys. *The New York Times.*

Jacobs, A. (2010, December 22). Abuses cited in enforcing China policy of one child. *The New York Times.*

Jacobs, A. (2011, April 15). For many bachelors in China, no property means no dates. *The New York Times.*

Jamail, D. (2007). *Another casualty: Coverage of the Iraq war.* New York, NY: Global Policy Forum. http://globalpolicy.org/component/content/article/168-general/36698.html. Accessed September 5, 2009.

Jamrisko, M., & Kolet, I. (2012). Cost of college degree in U.S. soars 12-fold: Chart of the day. *Bloomberg*

News. www.bloomberg.com/news/2012–08–15/cost-fo-college-degree-in-u-s-soars-12-fold-chart-of-the-day.html. Accessed January 16, 2013.

Jäntti, M. (2006). *American exceptionalism in a new light: A comparison of intergenerational earnings mobility in the Nordic countries, the United Kingdom, and the United States.* Discussion Paper #1938. Institute for the Study of Labor. ftp.iza.org/dp1938.pdf. Accessed June 2, 2013.

Jaschik, S. (2012, September 25). SAT scores drop again. *Inside Higher Education.* www.insidehighered.com/news/2012/09/25/sat-scores-are-down-and-racial-gaps-remain. Accessed June 17, 2013.

Jefferson, T. (1955). *Notes on the State of Virginia.* Chapel Hill: University of North Carolina Press. (Original work published 1781)

Jencks, C., & Phillips, M. (1998). *The black-white test score gap.* Washington, DC: Brookings Institute.

Jenkins, H. (1999, July). Professor Jenkins goes to Washington. *Harper's Magazine.*

Jenkins, J. C., & Perrow, C. (1977). Insurgency of the powerless: Farm worker movements (1946–1972). *American Sociological Review, 42,* 249–268.

Jennings, D. (2010, March 16). With cancer, let's face it: Words are inadequate. *The New York Times.*

Jha, M. (2011). Trends in selective abortions of girls in India: Analysis of nationally representative birth histories from 1990–2005 and census data from 1991–2011. *The Lancet, 377,* 1921–1928.

Jian, M. (2013, May 22). China's brutal one-child policy. *New York Times.*

Johnson, I. (2013, June 16). China embarking on vast program of urbanization. *The New York Times.*

Johnson, J. (2013, May 23). Paul Tudor Jones: In macro trading, babies are a "killer" to a woman's focus. *The Washington Post.*

Johnson, R. (1987). *Hard time: Understanding and reforming the prison.* Pacific Grove, CA: Brooks/Cole.

Johnston, D. (2002, April 7). Affluent avoid scrutiny on taxes even as I.R.S. warns of cheating. *The New York Times.*

Jones, A. (2010). Your guide to dormcest: Avoiding the pitfalls, scoring the perks. *Her campus: A collegiate guide to life.* www.hercampus.com/love/your-guide-dormcest-avoiding-pitfalls-scoring-perks. Accessed June 6, 2011.

Jones, E. E., Farina, A., Hastorf, A. H., Markus, H., Miller, D. T., & Scott, R. A. (1984). *Social stigma: The psychology of marked relationships.* New York, NY: Freeman.

Jones, E. E., & Pittman, T. S. (1982). Toward a general theory of strategic self-presentation. In J. Suls (Ed.), *Psychological perspectives on the self* (Vol. 1). Hillsdale, NJ: Lawrence Erlbaum.

Jones, J. M. (1986). The concept of racism and its changing reality. In B. P. Bowser & R. G. Hunt (Eds.), *Impacts of racism on white Americans.* Beverly Hills, CA: Sage.

Jones, M. (2006, January 15). Shutting themselves in. *The New York Times Magazine.*

Jost, K. (2006a). Transgender issues. *CQ Researcher, 16,* 385–408.

Jost, K. (2006b). Understanding Islam. *CQ Researcher, 16,* 913–936.

Juergensmeyer, M. (1996, November). Religious nationalism: A global threat? *Current History.*

Kahlenberg, R. (2013, March 19). The untapped pool of low-income strivers. *Chronicle of Higher Education.*

Kahn, J. (2004, May 30). The most populous nation faces a population crisis. *The New York Times.*

Kahn, J. (2007, May 22). Harsh birth control steps fuel violence in China. *The New York Times.*

Kahn, J. (2012, May 11). Trouble, age 9. *The New York Times.*

Kahneman, D., Krueger, A. B., Schkade, D., Schwarz, N., & Stone, A. A. (2006). Would you be happier if you were richer? A focusing illusion. *Science, 312,* 1908–1910.

Kain, E. (1990). *The myth of family decline.* Lexington, MA: Lexington Books.

Kaiser Family Foundation. (2008). *Abortion in the U.S.: Utilization, financing, and access.* www.kff.org/womenshealth/upload/3269–02.pdf. Accessed September 5, 2009.

Kalb, C. (2010, October 4). Do no harm. *Newsweek.*

Kalmijn, M. (1994). Assortive mating by cultural and economic occupational status. *American Journal of Sociology, 100,* 422–452.

Kalmijn, M., & Flap, H. (2001). Assortive meeting and mating: Unintended consequences of organized settings for partner choices. *Social Forces, 79,* 1289–1312.

Kane, E. (2006). We put it down in front of him, and he just instinctively knew what to do: Biological determinism in parents' beliefs about the origin of gendered childhoods. Paper presented at Annual Meeting of American Sociological Association. Montreal.

Kang, C. (2013, February 27). Survey finds gap in Internet access between rich, poor students. *The Washington Post.*

Karp, D. A., & Yoels, W. C. (1976). The college classroom: Some observations on the meanings of student participation. *Sociology and Social Research, 60,* 421–439.

Karush, S. (2001, May 6). Russia's population drain could open a floodgate of consequences. *Los Angeles Times.*

Katbamna, M. (2009, October 27). Half a good man is better than none at all. *The Guardian.*

Katel, P. (2006). War on drugs. *CQ Researcher, 16,* 649–672.

Katel, P. (2008). Affirmative action. *CQ Researcher, 18,* 841–864.

Katz, J. (1975). Essences as moral identities: Verifiability and responsibility in imputations of deviance and charisma. *American Journal of Sociology, 80,* 1369–1390.

Kearl, M. C. (1980). Time, identity and the spiritual needs of the elderly. *Sociological Analysis, 41,* 172–180.

Kearl, M. C., & Gordon, C. (1992). *Social psychology.* Boston, MA: Allyn & Bacon.

Keith, V. M., & Herring, C. (1991). Skin tone and stratification in the black community. *American Journal of Sociology, 97,* 760–778.

Kennedy, P. (1993). *Preparing for the 21st century.* New York, NY: Random House.

Kent, M., & Lalasz, R. (2006, June). *In the news: Speaking English in the United States.* Washington, DC: Population Reference Bureau. www.prb.org. Accessed July 20, 2006.

Kerbo, H. R. (1991). *Social stratification and inequality.* New York, NY: McGraw-Hill.

Kershaw, S. (2005, January 26). Old law shielding a woman's virtue faces an updating. *The New York Times.*

Kershaw, S. (2008, October 30). Move over, my pretty, ugly is here. *The New York Times.*

Kershner, R. (1996). Adolescent attitudes about rape. *Adolescence, 31,* 29–33.

Kessler, S. J., & McKenna, W. (1978). *Gender: An ethnomethodological approach.* Chicago, IL: University of Chicago Press.

Kessler-Harris, A. (1982). *Out to work: A history of wage-earning women in the United States.* New York, NY: Oxford University Press.

Kilborn, P. T. (1999, September 16). Bias worsens for minorities buying homes. *The New York Times.*

Kimmel, M. S. (2004). *The gendered society.* New York, NY: Oxford University Press.

King, M. L., Jr. (1991). Letter from Birmingham City jail. In C. Carson, D. J. Garrow, G. Gill, V. Harding, & D. Clark Hine (Eds.), *The eyes on the prize civil rights reader.* New York, NY: Penguin Books.

Kirn, W. (2009, May 10). More than a numbers game. *The New York Times Magazine.*

Kirp, D. L. (2006, July 23). After The Bell Curve. *The New York Times Magazine.*

Kishor, S., & Johnson, K. (2004). *Profiling domestic violence: A multi-country study.* www.measuredhs.com/pubs/pdf/OD31/DV.pdf. Accessed June 1, 2005.

Klatch, R. (1991). Complexities of conservatism: How conservatives understand the world. In A. Wolfe (Ed.), *America at century's end.* Berkeley: University of California Press.

Kleck, R. (1968). Physical stigma and nonverbal cues emitted in face-to-face interaction. *Human Relations, 21,* 19–28.

Kleck, R., Ono, H., & Hastorf, A. (1966). The effects of physical deviance and face-to-face interaction. *Human Relations, 19,* 425–436.

Kleinfield, N. R. (2012, May 13). Why don't we have any white kids? *The New York Times.*

Klevens, R. M., Edwards, J. R., Richards, C. L., Horan, T. C., Gaynes, R. P., Pollock, D. A., & Cardo, D. M. (2007). Estimating health care-associated infections and deaths in U.S. hospitals, 2002. *Public Health Report, 122,* 160–166. www.cdc.gov/ncidod/dhqp/pdf/hicpac/infections_deaths.pdf. Accessed September 5, 2009.

Knight, D. (2006, May 21). Hiring frenzy. *The Indianapolis Star.*

Kobrin, F. E. (1976). The fall in household size and the rise of the primary individual in the United States. *Demography, 31,* 127–138.

Koch, K. (1999, October 22). Rethinking Ritalin. *CQ Researcher* [Special issue].

Kochhar, R., Fry, R., & Taylor, P. (2011). *Wealth gaps rise to record highs between Whites, Blacks, and Hispanics.* Pew Research Center Publications. http://pewresearch.org/pubs/2069/housing-bubble-subprime-mortgages-hispanics-blacks-household-wealth-disparity. Accessed September 8, 2011.

Kocieniewski, D. (2006, October 10). A history of sex with students, unchallenged over the years. *The New York Times.*

Koenig, S. (2011, August 26). Gossip. *This American Life.* www.thisamericanlife.org/radio-archives/episode/444/gossip. Accessed January 14, 2013.

Koeppel, B. (1999, November 8). Cancer Alley, Louisiana. *The Nation.*

Kohlberg, L. A. (1966). A cognitive-developmental analysis of children's sex-role concepts and attitudes. In E. Maccoby (Ed.), *The development of sex differences.* Stanford, CA: Stanford University Press.

Kohn, M. L. (1979). The effects of social class on parental values and practices. In D. Reiss & H. A. Hoffman (Eds.), *The American family: Dying or developing.* New York, NY: Plenum Press.

Kohut, A. (2012, January 27). Don't mind the gap. *The New York Times.*

Kokopeli, B., & Lakey, G. (1992). More power than we want: Masculine sexuality and violence. In M. L. Anderson & P. H. Collins (Eds.), *Race, class and gender: An anthology.* Belmont, CA: Wadsworth.

Kolata, G. (2011, February 6). Mysterious maladies. *The New York Times.*

Kosmin, B. A., & Keysar, A. (2009). *American religious identification survey (ARIS 2008).* Hartford, CT: Trinity College. www.livinginliminality.files.word

press.com/2009/03/aris_report_2008.pdf. Accessed May 6, 2009.

Kreider, R. M., & Ellis, R. (2011). *Number, timing, and duration of marriages and divorces: 2009* (U.S. Census Bureau, Current Population Reports, P70–125). www.census.gov/prod/2011pubs/p70–125.pdf. Accessed June 3, 2011.

Kress, M. (2005, April 20). Mormonism is booming in the U.S. and overseas. *The News-Sentinel.*

Kristof, N. D. (1993, July 21). Peasants of China discover new way to weed out girls. *The New York Times.*

Krueger, A. B. (2002, November 14). The apple falls close to the tree, even in the land of opportunity. *The New York Times.*

Krugman, P. (2008, February 18). Poverty is poison. *The New York Times.*

Krugman, P. (2012, January 8). America's unlevel field. *The New York Times.*

Kulick, D., & Machado-Borges, T. (2005). Leaky. In D. Kulick & A. Meneley (Eds.), *Fat: The anthropology of an obsession.* New York, NY: Tarcher/Penguin.

Kuperinsky, A. (2012, January 27). Trending. McDonald's Twitter fiasco. *The Star-Ledger.* www.nj.com/entertainment/index.ssf/2012/01/mcdonalds_twitter_jan_brewer_s.html. Accessed January 14, 2013.

Kurtz, L. R. (1995). *Gods in the global village.* Thousand Oaks, CA: Pine Forge Press.

Kurtzleben, D. (2010, August 3). Data show racial disparity in crack sentencing. *U.S. News & World Report.*

Lacey, M. (2006, December 14). Rwandan priest sentenced to 15 years for allowing deaths of Tutsi in church. *The New York Times.*

Lacey, M. (2011, September 25). In Arizona, complaints that an accent can hinder a teacher's career. *New York Times.*

LaCoste-Caputo, J. (2007, June 21). Academic ratings, teacher pay tied. *San Antonio Express-News.*

LaFraniere, S. (2011, April 24). For many Chinese, new wealth and a fresh face. *The New York Times.*

LaFraniere, S., & Levin, D. (2010, November 12). Assertive Chinese marooned in mental wards. *The New York Times.*

Lakshmi, R. (2005, February 27). India call centers suffer storm of 4-letter words. *The Washington Post.*

Lalasz, R. (2006). *Americans flocking to outer suburbs in record numbers.* Washington, DC: Population Reference Bureau. www.prb.org. Accessed May 9, 2006.

Lamont, M. (1992). *Money, morals and manners: The culture of the French and American upper middle class.* Chicago, IL: University of Chicago Press.

Lander, L. (1988). *Images of bleeding: Menstruation as ideology.* New York, NY: Orlando.

Landler, M. (2002, December 1). For Austrians, HoHoHo is no laughing matter. *The New York Times.*

Landrigan, C. P., Parry, G. J., Bones, C. B., Hackbarth, A. D., Goldmann, D. A., & Sharek, P. J. (2010). Temporal trends in rates of patient harm resulting from medical care. *New England Journal of Medicine, 363,* 2124–2134.

Lang, S. (1998). *Men as women, women as men: Changing gender in Native American cultures.* Austin: University of Texas Press.

Langan, P. A., & Levin, D. J. (2002). *Recidivism of prisoners released in 1994* (NCJ 193427). Washington, DC: Bureau of Justice Statistics. www.ojp.usdoj.gov/bjs/abstract/rpr94.htm. Accessed January 20, 2003.

Langman, L. (1988). Social stratification. In M. B. Sussman & S. K. Steinmetz (Eds.), *Handbook of marriage and the family.* New York, NY: Plenum Press.

Lanvers, U. (2004). Gender in discourse behaviour in parent-child dyads: A literature review. *Child: Care, Health, and Development, 30,* 481–493.

Lapchick, R. (2013). *The racial and gender report card.* www.bus.ucf.edu/sportbusiness/?page=1445. Accessed June 12, 2013.

Lareau, A. (2003). *Unequal childhoods: Class, race, and family life.* Berkeley: University of California Press.

Larew, J. (2003). Why are droves of unqualified, unprepared kids getting into our top colleges? Because their dads are alumni. In K. E. Rosenblum & T. C. Travis (Eds.), *The meaning of difference: American constructions of race, sex and gender, social class, and sexual orientation.* New York, NY: McGraw-Hill.

Larson, L. E., & Goltz, J. W. (1989). Religious participation and marital commitment. *Review of Religious Research, 30,* 387–400.

Lasch, C. (1977). *Haven in a heartless world.* New York, NY: Basic Books.

Lauer, R., & Handel, W. (1977). *Social psychology: The theory and application of symbolic interactionism.* Boston, MA: Houghton Mifflin.

Leape, L. L., & Bates, D. W. (1995). Systems analysis of adverse drug events. *Journal of the American Medical Association, 274,* 35–43.

LeBesco, K. (2004). *Revolting bodies? The struggle to redefine fat identity.* Amherst: University of Massachusetts Press.

Lee, S. M. (1993). Racial classifications in the U.S. Census: 1890–1990. *Ethnic and Racial Studies, 16,* 75–94.

Lee-St. John, J. (2007, February 12). A time limit on rape. *Time.*

Legewie, J., & DiPrete, T. A. (2012). School context and the gender gap in educational achievement. *American Sociological Review, 77,* 463–485.

Lehrer, J. (2012). The fragile teenage brain. *Grantland,* ESPN.com. www.grantland.com/story/_/id/7443714/jonah-lehrer-concussions-adolscents-future-football. Accessed, December 22, 2012.

Lemert, E. (1972). *Human deviance, social problems, and social control.* Englewood Cliffs, NJ: Prentice Hall.

Leonhardt, D. (2011, June 26). Even for cashiers, college pays off. *The New York Times.*

Leonhardt, D. (2013, July 22). In climbing income ladder, location matters. *The New York Times.*

Leonhardt, D., Parlapiano, A., & Waananen, L. (2012, August 14). A historical benchmark. *The New York Times.*

Leonnig, C. D. (2005, June 8). Tobacco escapes huge penalty. *The New York Times.*

Lerner, M. (1970). The desire for justice and reactions to victims. In J. Macauley & L. Berkowitz (Eds.), *Altruism and helping behavior.* New York, NY: Academic Press.

Levine, H. G. (1992). Temperance cultures: Concern about alcohol problems in Nordic and English-speaking cultures. In M. Lader, G. Edwards, & D. C. Drummond (Eds.), *The nature of alcohol and drug-related problems.* New York, NY: Oxford University Press.

Levinson, D. (1989). *Family violence in crosscultural perspective.* Newbury Park, CA: Sage.

Levitt, S. D., & Dubner, S. J. (2009). *Freakonomics: A rogue economist explores the hidden side of everything.* New York, NY: Harper Perennial.

Levy, A. (2006, May 29). Dirty old women. *The New York Magazine.* http://nymag.com/news/features/17064/index1.html. Accessed September 5, 2009.

Lewin, T. (1998, December 13). How boys lost out to girl power. *The New York Times.*

Lewin, T. (2000, April 11). Disabled student is suing over test-score labeling. *The New York Times.*

Lewin, T. (2001, October 21). Shelters have empty beds: Abused women stay home. *The New York Times.*

Lewin, T. (2006, July 9). At colleges, women are leaving men in the dust. *The New York Times.*

Lewin, T. (2007, January 26). Colleges regroup after voters ban race preferences. *The New York Times.*

Lewin, T. (2009a, February 5). A.P. program is growing, but black students lag. *The New York Times.*

Lewin, T. (2009b, December 10). College dropouts cite low money and high stress. *The New York Times.*

Lewin, T. (2012a, March 6). Black students punished more, data suggests. *The New York Times.*

Lewin, T. (2012b, March 17). Budget cuts threaten access to college placement tests. *The New York Times.*

Lewis, M. (1978). *The culture of inequality.* New York, NY: New American Library.

Lewis, M. M. (1948). *Language in society.* New York, NY: Social Science Research Council.

Lewis, P. H. (1998, August 15). Too late to say "extinct" in Ubykh, Eyak or Ona. *The New York Times.*

Lewis, R., & Yancey, G. (1997). Racial and nonracial factors that influence spouse choice in black/white marriages. *Journal of Black Studies, 28,* 60–78.

Liazos, A. (1985). *Sociology: A liberating perspective.* Boston, MA: Allyn & Bacon.

Liben, L. S., & Bigler, B. R. (2002). The developmental course of gender differentiation: Conceptualizing, measuring, and evaluating constructs and pathways. *Monographs of the Society for Research in Child Development, 67,* 1–112.

Lichtblau, E. (2003, March 18). U.S. lawsuit seeks tobacco profits. *The New York Times.*

Lichtblau, E. (2008, April 9). In justice shift, corporate deals replace trials. *The New York Times.*

Light, P. (1988). *Baby boomers.* New York, NY: Norton.

Likens, G. E., Wright, R. F., Galloway, J. N., & Butler, T. J. (1979). Acid rain. *Scientific American, 241,* 43–51.

Lindesmith, A. R., Strauss, A. L., & Denzin, N. K. (1991). *Social psychology.* Englewood Cliffs, NJ: Prentice Hall.

Link, B. G., Mirotznik, J., & Cullen, F. T. (1991). The effectiveness of stigma-coping orientations: Can negative consequences of mental illness labeling be avoided? *Journal of Health and Social Behavior, 32,* 302–320.

Link, B. G., & Phelan, J. C. (2001). Conceptualizing stigma. *Annual Review of Sociology, 27,* 363–385.

Lino, M. (2012). *Expenditures on children by families, 2011.* Center for Nutrition Policy and Promotion, U.S. Department of Agriculture. Miscellaneous Publication #1528–2011. www.cnpp.usda.gov/publications/CRC/crc2011.pdf. Accessed January 16, 2013.

Linton, R. (1937). One hundred percent American. *American Mercury, 40,* 427–429.

Lippmann, L. W. (1922). *Public opinion.* New York, NY: Harcourt Brace Jovanovich.

Lips, H. M. (1993). *Sex and gender: An introduction.* Mountain View, CA: Mayfield.

Liptak, A. (2004, March 17). Bans on interracial unions offer perspective on gay ones. *The New York Times.*

Little, A. G. (2007, September 2). Not in whose backyard? *The New York Times Magazine.*

Living Wage Resource Center. (2006). *Living wage wins.* www.livingwagecampaign.org/index.php?id=1959. Accessed June 10, 2009.

Lofland, L. H. (1973). *A world of strangers: Order and action in urban public space.* New York, NY: Basic Books.

Lohr, S. (2012, March 2). For impatient web users, an eye blink is just too long to wait. *The New York Times.*

Longman, J. (2006, June 4). Surge in racist mood raises concerns on eve of World Cup. *The New York Times.*

Longman, J. (2011, May 26). Badminton dress code for women criticized as sexist. *The New York Times.*

Longman, J., & Higgins, M. (2005, August 3). Rad dudes of the world, unite. *The New York Times.*

Longman, T. (2009). *Christianity and genocide in Rwanda.* Cambridge, UK: Cambridge University Press.

Lorber, J. (1989). Dismantling Noah's Ark. In B. J. Risman & P. Schwartz (Eds.), *Gender in intimate relationships: A microstructural approach.* Belmont, CA: Wadsworth.

Lorber, J. (2000). *Gender and the social construction of illness*. Walnut Creek, CA: AltaMira Press.

Lott, B. (1987). *Women's lives: Themes and variations in gender learning*. Pacific Grove, CA: Brooks/Cole.

Lovett, I. (2013a, May 7). Changing sex, and changing teams. *The New York Times*.

Lovett, I. (2013b, March 10). Neighborhoods seek to banish sex offenders by building parks. *The New York Times*.

Lowenstein, R. (2009, July 26). The new joblessness. *The New York Times Magazine*.

Lowrey, A. (2013, May 5). Movin' on up. *The New York Times Magazine*.

Lueders, B. (2006). *Cry rape: The true story of one woman's harrowing quest for justice*. Madison, WI: Terrace Books.

Luker, K. (1984). *Abortion and the politics of motherhood*. Berkeley: University of California Press.

Luo, M. (2007, July 22). God '08: Whose, and how much, will voters accept? *The New York Times*.

Luo, M. (2011, July 3). Mixing guns and mental illness. *The New York Times*.

Lutz, A. (2008). Who joins the military? A look at race, class, and immigration. *Journal of Political and Military Sociology, 36*, 167–188.

Lyall, S. (2000, July 8). Irish now face the other side of immigration. *The New York Times*.

Lyall, S. (2012, July 12). Caitlin Moran has her sights set on blowing up feminism. *The New York Times Magazine*.

MacDonald, J. (2006, March 25). Rising tide of applications lifts fortunes of Christian colleges. *The Washington Post*.

Macgillivray, I. K. (2000). Educational equity for gay, lesbian, bisexual, transgendered, and queer/questioning students: The demands of democracy and social justice for America's schools. *Education and Urban Society, 32*, 303–323.

Mann, C. C. (1993, February). How many is too many? *Atlantic Monthly*.

Manning, L. (2007). Nightmare at the day care: The Wee Care case. *Crime Magazine*. www.crimemagazine.com/nightmare-day-care-wee-care-case. Accessed June 7, 2011.

Manning, W. D., & Smock, P. J. (1999). New families and nonresident father-child visits. *Social Forces, 78*, 87–117.

Mannon, J. (1997). *Measuring up*. Boulder, CO: Westview Press.

Mansfield, H. (2006). *Manliness*. New Haven, CT: Yale University Press.

Marger, M. N. (1994). *Race and ethnic relations: American and global perspectives*. Belmont, CA: Wadsworth.

Marger, M. N. (2005). The mass media as a power institution. In S. J. Ferguson (Ed.), *Mapping the social landscape*. New York, NY: McGraw-Hill.

Markoff, J. (2013, April 4). Software subs for professors on essay test. *The New York Times*.

Marmot, M. (2004). *The status syndrome: How social standing affects our health and longevity*. New York, NY: Times Books.

Martin, C. L., & Ruble, D. (2004). Children's search for gender cues. *Current Directions in Psychological Science, 13*, 67–70.

Martin, P., & Midgley, E. (2010). *Immigration in America 2010* (Population Bulletin Update). www.prb.org/pdf10/immigration-update2010.pdf. Accessed July 6, 2010.

Martinez-Alier, J. (2003). *The environmentalism of the poor*. Cheltenham, UK: Edward Elgar.

Marx, K., & Engels, F. (1982). *The communist manifesto*. New York, NY: International. (Original work published 1848)

Mather, M. (2007). *The new generation gap*. Washington, DC: Population Reference Bureau. www.prb.org/Articles/2007/New Generation Gap.aspx. Accessed May 19, 2007.

Mather, M., & Adams, D. (2006). *The risk of negative child outcomes in low-income families*. Washington, DC: Population Reference Bureau. www.prb.org/pdf06/RiskNegOut_Families.pdf. Accessed July 27, 2006.

Mather, M., & Dupuis, G. (2012). *Rising share of U.S. children living in high-poverty neighborhoods*. Population Reference Bureau. www.prb.org/Articles/2012/us-high-poverty-neighborhoods.aspx?p=1. Accessed June 1, 2013.

Mather, M., & Jacobsen, L. A. (2010). *Hard times for Latino men in U.S.* Population Reference Bureau. www.prb.org/Articles/2010/latinomen.aspx. Accessed June 16, 2011.

Mather, M., Pollard, K., & Jacobsen, L. A. (2011). *First results from the 2010 Census*. Population Reference Bureau. www.prb.org/pdf11/reportson-america-2010-census.pdf. Accessed July 20, 2011.

Mathews, L. (1996, July 6). More than identity rides on a new racial category. *The New York Times*.

Matthews, J. (2012, December 12). Cash incentives for students. *The Washington Post*.

McAdam, D. (1982). *Political process and the development of black insurgency, 1930–1970*. Chicago, IL: University of Chicago Press.

McAdam, D., McCarthy, J. D., & Zald, M. N. (1988). Social movements. In N. J. Smelser (Ed.), *Handbook of sociology*. Newbury Park, CA: Sage.

McCain, F. (1991). Interview with Franklin McCain. In C. Carson, D. J. Garrow, G. Gill, V. Harding, & D. Clark Hine (Eds.), *The eyes on the prize civil rights reader*. New York, NY: Penguin Books.

McCall, G. J., & Simmons, J. L. (1978). *Identities and interactions*. New York, NY: Free Press.

McCarthy, J. D., & Wolfson, M. (1992). Consensus movements, conflict movements, and the cooptation of civic and state infrastructures. In A. D. Morris & C. M. Mueller (Eds.), *Frontiers in social movement theory*. New Haven, CT: Yale University Press.

McCarthy, J. D., & Zald, M. N. (1977). Resource mobilization and social movements: A partial theory. *American Journal of Sociology, 82*, 1212–1241.

McCarthy, T. (2001, May 14). He makes a village. *Time*.

McClain, P. D., Carter, N. M., Soto, V M. D., Lyle, M. L., Grynaviski, J. D., Nunnally, S. C., Scotto, T. J., Kendrick, J. A., Lackey, G. F., & Cotton, K. D. (2006). Racial distancing in a southern city: Latino immigrants' views of black Americans. *Journal of Politics, 68*, 571–584.

McCormick, J. S., Maric, A., Seto, M. C., & Barbaree, H. E. (1998). Relationship to victim predicts sentence length in sexual assault cases. *Journal of Interpersonal Violence, 13*, 413–420.

McEwan, J. (2005). Proving consent in sexual cases: Legislative change and cultural evolution. *International Journal of Evidence and Proof, 9*, 1–28.

McGee, C. (2010, August 23). The open road wasn't quite open to all. *The New York Times*.

McGeehan, P. (2012, February 8). For hotel staff, panic buttons and big raises. *New York Times*.

McIntosh, P. (2001). White privilege: Unpacking the invisible knapsack. In P. Rothenberg (Ed.), *Race, class, and gender in the United States*. New York, NY: Worth.

McKenry, P. C., & Price, S. J. (1995). Divorce: A comparative perspective. In B. B. Ingoldsby & S. Smith (Eds.), *Families in multicultural perspective*. New York, NY: Guilford Press.

McKinley, J. (2010, March 13). Conservatives on Texas panel carry the day on curricular change. *The New York Times*.

McKinley, J. (2011, February 17). "Non-English" tip policy raises eyebrows, then fades. *The New York Times*.

McLaren, L. M. (2003). Anti-immigrant prejudice in Europe: Contact, threat perception, and preferences for the exclusion of migrants. *Social Forces, 81*, 909–936.

McLean, R. (2005, January 12). Spaniards dare to question the way the day is ordered. *The New York Times*.

McLean, R. (2006, January 21). In the new year, a novel idea for Spanish government workers: A literal lunch hour. *The New York Times*.

McLoyd, V. C., Cauce, A. M., Takeuchi, D., & Wilson, L. (2000). Marital processes and parental socialization in families of color: A decade review of research. *Journal of Marriage and the Family, 62*, 1070–1094.

McNeil, D. G. (2008, December 10). Report sounds alarm on child accidents. *The New York Times*.

McNeil, D. G. (2011, May 23). AIDS: A price break for antiretroviral drugs in 70 of the world's poorest countries. *New York Times*.

McPhee, J. (1971). *Encounters with the archdruid*. New York, NY: Noonday.

Mead, G. H. (1934). *Mind, self and society*. Chicago, IL: University of Chicago Press.

Meier, B. (2004, June 15). Group is said to seek full drug-trial disclosure. *The New York Times*.

Mendoza, M. (2010, May 14). U.S. drug war is "on going tragedy." *The Indianapolis Star*.

Merton, R. (1948). The self-fulfilling prophecy. *Antioch Review, 8*, 193–210.

Merton, R. (1957). *Social theory and social structure*. New York, NY: Free Press.

Messick, D. M., & Brewer, M. B. (1983). Solving social dilemmas: A review. In L. Wheeler & P. Shaver (Eds.), *Review of personality and social psychology*. Beverly Hills, CA: Sage.

Messner, M. (2002). Boyhood, organized sports, and the construction of masculinities. In D. M. Newman & J. O'Brien (Eds.), *Sociology: Exploring the architecture of everyday life (Readings)*. Thousand Oaks, CA: Pine Forge Press.

Meyer, J. W., & Rowan, B. (1977). Institutionalized organizations: Formal structure as myth and ceremony. *American Journal of Sociology, 83*, 340–363.

Miall, C. E. (1989). The stigma of involuntary childlessness. In A. S. Skolnick & J. H. Skolnick (Eds.), *Family in transition*. Boston, MA: Little, Brown.

Michaels, K. (1993). Eight years in Kafkaland. *National Review, 45*, 36–38.

Michels, R. (1949). *Political parties*. Glencoe, IL: Free Press. (Original work published 1911)

Michener, H. A., DeLamater, J. D., & Schwartz, S. H. (1986). *Social psychology*. San Diego, CA: Harcourt Brace Jovanovich.

Mihm, S. (2009, December 13). Artificial car noise. *The New York Times Magazine*.

Milbank, D., & Deane, C. (2003, September 6). Hussein link to 9/11 lingers in many minds. *The Washington Post*.

Miller, E., & Almon, J. (2009). *Crisis in the kindergarten: Why children need to play in school*. College Park, MD: Alliance for Childhood.

Miller, L. (1997). Not just weapons of the weak: Gender harassment as a form of protest for army men. *Social Psychology Quarterly, 60*, 32–51.

Miller, L. (2008, May 5). An algorithm for Mr. Right. *Newsweek*.

Miller, L. (2011, July 25). How to raise a global kid. *Newsweek*.

Mills, C. W. (1940). Situated actions and vocabularies of motive. *American Sociological Review, 5*, 904–913.

Mills, C. W. (1956). *The power elite*. New York, NY: Oxford University Press.

Mills, C. W. (1959). *The sociological imagination.* New York, NY: Oxford University Press.

Mills, J. L. (1985, February). Body language speaks louder than words. *Horizons.*

Minton, T. D. (2012). *Jail inmates at midyear 2011: Statistical tables* (NCJ 237961). U.S. Bureau of Justice Statistics. bjs.ojp.usdoj.gov/content/pub/pdf/jim11st.pdf. Accessed January 21, 2013.

Minton, T. D. (2013). *Jail inmates at midyear 2012: Statistical tables.* NCJ241264. U.S. Bureau of Justice Statistics. www.bjs.gov/content/pub/pdf/jim12st.pdf. Accessed June 30, 2013.

Minton, T. D., & Sabol, W. J. (2009). *Jail inmates at midyear 2008: Statistical tables* (NCJ 225709). Washington, DC: Bureau of Justice Statistics. http://www.ojp.usdoj.gov/bjs/pub/pdf/jim08st.pdf. Accessed June 10, 2009.

Mishel, L., Bernstein, J., & Allegretto, S. (2007). *The state of working America: 2006/2007.* Washington, DC: Economic Policy Institute.

Mishel, L., Bernstein, J., & Shierholz, H. (2009). *The state of working America: 2008/2009.* Washington, DC: Economic Policy Institute.

Mishel, L., Bivens, J., Gould, E., & Shierholz, H. (2013). *The state of working America.* Economic Policy Institute. stateofworkingAmerica.org/subjects/overview/?reader. Accessed May 31, 2013.

Mnookin, S. (2011, January 10, 17). Autism and the affluent. *Newsweek.*

Mobius, M. M., & Rosenblat, T. S. (2006). Why beauty matters. *American Economic Review, 96,* 222–235.

Moeller, P. (2012, March 26). Top 10 reasons to hire older people. *US News & World Report.* money.usnews.com/money/blogs/the-best-life/2012/03/26/top-10-reasons-to-hire-older-people. Accessed June 28, 2013.

Moffatt, M. (1989). *Coming of age in New Jersey.* New Brunswick, NJ: Rutgers University Press.

Mokhiber, R. (1999, July/August). Crime wave! The top 100 corporate criminals of the 1990s. *Multinational Monitor,* pp. 1–9.

Mokhiber, R., & Weissman, R. (2004, December). The ten worst corporations of 2004. *Multinational Monitor,* pp. 8–21.

Molotch, H., & Lester, M. (1974). News as purposive behavior: On the strategic use of routine events, accidents, and scandals. *American Sociological Review, 39,* 101–112.

Molotch, H., & Lester, M. (1975). Accidental news: The great oil spill as local occurrence and national event. *American Journal of Sociology, 81,* 235–260.

MomsRising.org. (2013). *About MomsRising.* www.momsrising.org/page/moms/aboutmomsrising. Accessed July 10, 2013.

Monawad, J. (2011, November 21). Taking first-class coddling above and beyond. *The New York Times.*

Moore, R. B. (1992). Racist stereotyping in the English language. In M. L. Anderson & P. H. Collins (Eds.), *Race, class and gender: An anthology.* Belmont, CA: Wadsworth.

Morgan, G. (1986). *Images of organizations.* Newbury Park, CA: Sage.

Morgan, M. (1982). Television and adolescents' sex role stereotypes: A longitudinal study. *Journal of Personality and Social Psychology, 48,* 1173–1190.

Morgan, M. (1987). Television sex role attitudes and sex role behavior. *Journal of Early Adolescence, 7,* 269–282.

Morgan, R. (1996). *Sisterhood is global.* New York, NY: Feminist Press at the City University of New York.

Morrongiello, B. A., & Hogg, K. (2004). Mothers' reactions to children misbehaving in ways that can lead to injury: Implications for gender differences in children's risk taking and injuries. *Sex Roles, 50,* 103–118.

Mottl, T. L. (1980). The analysis of countermovements. *Social Problems, 27,* 620–635.

Mui, Y. Q. (2012, July 8). For black Americans, financial damage from subprime implosion is likely to last. *The Washington Post.*

Murdock, G. P. (1949). *Social structure.* New York, NY: Macmillan.

Murdock, G. P. (1957). World ethnography sample. *American Anthropologist, 59,* 664–687.

Murguia, E., & Telles, E. E. (1996). Phenotype and schooling among Mexican Americans. *Sociology of Education, 69,* 276–289.

Murphy, K. (2008, May 31). Job climate for the class of 2008 is a bit warmer than expected. *The New York Times.*

Mydans, S. (1995, February 12). A shooter as vigilante, and avenging angel. *The New York Times.*

Mydans, S. (2007, April 9). Across cultures, English is the word. *International Herald Tribune.*

Nanda, S. (1994). *Cultural anthropology.* Belmont, CA: Wadsworth.

Nasar, S., & Mitchell, K. B. (1999, May 23). Booming job market draws young black men into the fold. *The New York Times.*

National Academies. (2013). *Americans have worse health than people in other high-income countries; Health disadvantage is pervasive across age and socioeconomic groups.* www8.nationalacademies.org/onpinews/newsitem.aspx?RecordID=13497. Accessed January 10, 2013.

National Alliance to End Homelessness. (2013). *State of homelessness in America 2013.* www.endhomelessness.org/library/entry/the-state-of-homelessness-2013. Accessed June 2, 2013.

National Association to Advance Fat Acceptance. (2013). The Biggest Loser *promotes the bullying cycle.* www.naafaonline.com/dev2/. Accessed January 14, 2013.

National Center for Education Statistics. (2010). *Teachers' use of educational technology in U.S. public schools: 2009*. NCES 2010–040. nces.ed.gov/pubsearch/pubsinfo.asp?pubid=2010040. Accessed July 2, 2013.

National Center for Education Statistics. (2011). *Fast facts*. http://nces.ed.gov/fastfacts/display.asp?id=40. Accessed July 20, 2011.

National Center for Education Statistics. (2012a). *America's youth: Transitions to adulthood, Table 14*. nces.ed.gov/pubs2012/2012026/tables/table_14.asp. Accessed June 30, 2013.

National Center for Education Statistics. (2012b). *Trends in international mathematics and science study (TIMSS)*. nces.ed.gov/Timss/results11_science11.asp. Accessed May 28, 2013.

National Center for Education Statistics. (2013). *Indicators of school crime and safety: 2012*. nces.ed.gov/pubs2013/2013036.pdf. Accessed June 30, 2013.

National Center for Fair and Open Testing. (2011). *2010 college-bound seniors average SAT scores*. http://fairtest.org/2010-collegebound-seniors-average-sat-scores. Accessed April 13, 2011.

National Center for Fair and Open Testing. (2012). *ACT, SAT scores show failure of test-driven K-12 schools*. www.fairtest.org/act-sat-scores-show-failure-testdriven-K12-schools. Accessed June 21, 2013.

National Center for Law and Economic Justice. (2010). *Poverty in the United States: A snapshot*. www.nclej.org/poverty-in-the-us.php. Accessed June 14, 2011.

National Center on Time and Learning. (2013). *Mapping the field: A report on expanded time schools in America*. www.timeandlearning.org/mapping. Accessed May 28, 2013.

National Committee on Pay Equity. (2007). *Current legislation*. www.pay-equity.org/info-leg.html. Accessed July 11, 2007.

National Conference of State Legislatures. (2009). *State laws regarding marriage between first cousins*. www.ncsl.org/programs/cyf/cousins.htm. Accessed April 28, 2009.

National Crime Records Bureau. (2012). *Crime in India: 2011*. ncrb.nic.in/CD-CII-2011/Home.asp. Accessed June 20, 2013.

National Digestive Diseases Information Clearinghouse. (2011). *Hemochromatosis*. http://digestive.niddk.nih.gov/ddiseases/pubs/hemochromatosis. Accessed April 1, 2011.

National Employment Law Project. (2012). *The low-wage recovery and growing inequality*. nelp.3cdn.net/c54d93acdb96420855_03m612dq6.pdf. Accessed May 31, 2013.

National Fair Housing Alliance. (2012). *Fair housing in a changing nation: 2012*. Fair Housing Trends Report. www.nationalfairhousing.org. Accessed June 14, 2013.

National Institute of Mental Health. (2009). *Statistics*. www.nimh.nih.gov/health/topics/statistics/index.shtml. Accessed September 5, 2009.

National Institute of Mental Health. (2010). *Statistics*. www.nimh.nih.gov/statistics/index.shtml. Accessed June 9, 2011.

National Institute on Aging. (2006). *Dramatic changes in U.S. aging highlighted in new Census* (NIH report). www.nia.nih.gov/NewsAndEvents/PressReleases/PR2006030965PLusReport.htm. Accessed July 31, 2006.

National Institute on Alcohol Abuse and Alcoholism. (2007). *What colleges need to know now: An update on college drinking research* (NIH Publication 07–5010). www.collegedrinkingprevention.gov/1College_Bulletin-508_361C4E.pdf. Accessed September 5, 2009.

National Labor Committee for Worker and Human Rights. (2001). *Shah Haksdum Garments Factory, Dhaka, Bangladesh*. www.nlcnet.org/campaigns/shahmakhdum/0502/sm0201.shtml. Accessed June 16, 2003.

National Low Income Housing Coalition. (2012). *Out of reach 2012*. www.nlihc.org/oor/2012. Accessed June 2, 2013.

The National Marriage Project. (2010). *When marriage disappears: The new middle America*. www.virginia.edu/marriageproject/pdfs/Union_11_12_10.pdf. Accessed September 4, 2011.

National Urban League. (2009). *The state of black America 2009: Message to the President. Executive Summary*. www.nul.org/thestateofblackamerica.html. Accessed September 5, 2009.

National Women's Law Center. (2006). *The Paycheck Fairness Act: Helping to close the wage gap for women*. www.pay-equity.org/PDFs/PaycheckFairnessActApr06.pdf. Accessed September 5, 2009.

National Women's Law Center. (2013). *NWLC applauds final rule from HHS, banning gender rating and "pre-existing conditions."* www.nwlc.org/press-release/nwlc-applauds-final-rule-hhs-banning-gender-rating-and-pre-existing-conditions. Accessed June 21, 2013.

Nelkin, D., & Pollak, M. (1981). *The atom besieged*. Cambridge, MA: MIT Press.

Neubeck, K. (1986). *Social problems: A critical approach*. New York, NY: Random House.

Neuman, W. L. (1994). *Social research methods: Qualitative and quantitative approaches*. Boston, MA: Allyn & Bacon.

Newman, D. (2009). *Families: A sociological perspective*. New York: McGraw-Hill.

Newman, D. (2012). *Identities and inequalities: Exploring the intersections of race, class, gender, and sexuality* (2nd ed.). New York, NY: McGraw-Hill.

Newman, K. (2005). Family values against the odds. In A. S. Skolnick & J. H. Skolnick (Eds.), *Family in transition* (13th ed.). Boston, MA: Allyn & Bacon.

Niebuhr, G. (1998, April 12). Makeup of American religion is looking more like a mosaic, data say. *The New York Times.*

Noonan, D. (2008, November 10). No insurance? That's a killer. *Newsweek.*

Nugman, G. (2002). *World divorce rates.* Washington, DC: Heritage Foundation. www.divorcereform.org/gul.html. Accessed July 6, 2003.

O'Connell Davidson, J. (2002). The practice of social research. In D. M. Newman & J. O'Brien (Eds.), *Sociology: Exploring the architecture of everyday life (Readings).* Thousand Oaks, CA: Pine Forge Press.

Office of National Drug Control Policy. (2012). *The national drug control budget: FY2013 funding highlights.* The White House. www.whitehouse.gov/ondcp/the-national-drug-control-budget-fy-2013-funding-highlights. Accessed January 22, 2013.

Oldenburg, R., & Brissett, D. (1982). The third place. *Qualitative Sociology, 5,* 265–284.

Olsen, M. (1965). *The logic of collective action.* Cambridge, MA: Harvard University Press.

Omi, M., & Winant, H. (1992). Racial formations. In P. S. Rothenberg (Ed.), *Race, class and gender in the United States.* New York, NY: St. Martin's Press.

One child left behind. (2009, March/April). *UTNE Reader.*

Onishi, N. (2004, March 30). On U.S. fast food, more Okinawans grow super-sized. *The New York Times.*

Online Dating Statistics. (2012). *Statistic brain.* www.statisticbrain.com/online-dating-statistics/. Accessed January 15, 2013.

Oppel, R. A. (2011, September 26). Sentencing shift gives new clout to prosecutors. *The New York Times.*

Orenstein, P. (2008, February 10). Girls will be girls. *The New York Times Magazine.*

Orfield, G., & Lee, C. (2007). *Historical reversals, accelerating resegregation, and the need for new integration strategies.* The Civil Rights Project. www.civilrightsproject.ucla.edu/research/deseg/reversals_reseg_need.pdf. Accessed September 5, 2009.

Orfield, G., Siegel-Hawley, G., & Kucsera, J. (2011). *Divided we fail: Segregated and unequal schools in the Southland.* The Civil Rights Project. www.civilrightsproject.ucla.edu. Accessed June 17, 2011.

Organ Procurement and Transplant Network. (2013). *National data.* optn.transplant.hrsa.gov/latestData/step2.asp?. Accessed June 14, 2013.

Organisation for Economic Cooperation and Development. (2010). *Trends in urbanisation and urban policies in OECD countries: What lessons for China?* www.oecd.org/urban/roundtable/45159707.pdf. Accessed June 27, 2013.

Organisation for Economic Cooperation and Development. (2011). *Gender pay gaps for full-time workers and earnings differentials by educational attainment.* www.oecd.org/data oecd/29/63/38752746.pdf. Accessed June 22, 2011.

Organisation for Economic Cooperation and Development. (2012). *OECD (2009), doing better for children.* www.oecd.org/dataoecd/21/9/43590390.pdf. Accessed June 1, 2013.

O'Sullivan-See, K., & Wilson, W. J. (1988). Race and ethnicity. In N. Smelser (Ed.), *Handbook of sociology.* Newbury Park, CA: Sage.

Padavic, I., & Reskin, B. (2002). *Women and men at work* (2nd ed.). Thousand Oaks, CA: Sage.

Padawer, R. (2012, August 8). What's so bad about a boy who wants to wear a dress? *The New York Times Magazine.*

Palmer, B. (2012, November 15). Can we bring back the stockades? *Slate.* www.slate.com. Accessed July 3, 2013.

Pappas, A. (2013, May 22). Another lawmaker says Oklahoma disaster relief must be offset with spending cuts. *The Daily Caller.* dailycaller.com/2013/05/22/lawmaker-disaster-relief-must-be-offset-with-spending-cuts/. Accessed May 31, 2013.

Parenti, M. (1986). *Inventing reality.* New York, NY: St. Martin's Press.

Parenti, M. (1995). *Democracy for the few.* New York, NY: St. Martin's Press.

Parenti, M. (2006). Mass media: For the many, by the few. In P. S. Rothenberg (Ed.), *Beyond borders: Thinking critically about global issues.* New York, NY: Worth.

Parker-Pope, T. (2012a, February 5). The kids are more than all right. *The New York Times.*

Parker-Pope, T. (2012b, August 28). Overtreatment is taking a harmful toll. *The New York Times.*

Parsons, T. (1951). *The social system.* New York, NY: Free Press.

Parsons, T., & Bales, R. F. (1955). *Family, socialization and interaction process.* Glencoe, IL: Free Press.

Parsons, T., & Smelser, N. (1956). *Economy and society.* New York, NY: Free Press.

Pascoe, C. J. (2010). Dude, you're a fag? In S. Ferguson (Ed.), *Mapping the social landscape.* New York, NY: McGraw-Hill.

Paul, R. (2010, July 26). Perspectives. *Newsweek.*

Pear, R. (1992, December 4). New look at U.S. in 2050: Bigger, older and less white. *The New York Times.*

Pear, R. (2000, April 30). Studies find research on women lacking. *The New York Times.*

Pear, R. (2008, October 30). Women buying health policies pay a penalty. *The New York Times.*

Pear, R. (2010, June 22). Gay workers will get time to care for partner's sick child. *The New York Times.*

Pear, R. (2011, October 26). It's official: The rich get richer. *The New York Times.*

Pear, R. (2012, January 6). Report finds most errors at hospitals go unreported. *The New York Times.*

Pearce, D. (1979). Gatekeepers and homeseekers: Institutional patterns in racial steering. *Social Problems, 26,* 325–342.

Pearce, L. D., & Axinn, W. G. (1998). The impact of family religious life on the quality of mother child relations. *American Sociological Review, 63,* 810–828.

Peck, B. M., & Conner, S. (2011). Talking with me or talking at me? The impact of status characteristics on doctor–patient interaction. *Sociological Perspectives, 54,* 547–567.

Pérez-Peña, R. (2003, April 19). Study finds asthma in 25% of children in central Harlem. *The New York Times.*

Pérez-Peña, R. (2012, August 20). More Hispanics are in college, report finds. *The New York Times.*

Pérez-Peña, R. (2013, May 31). Limited success as colleges seek to attract poor. *The New York Times.*

Perlez, J. (1991, August 31). Madagascar, where the dead return, bringing joy. *The New York Times.*

Perlin, S. A., Sexton, K., & Wong, D. W. S. (1999). An examination of race and poverty for populations living near industrial sources of air pollution. *Journal of Exposure Analysis and Environmental Epidemiology, 9,* 29–48.

Perlman, D., & Fehr, B. (1987). The development of intimate relationships. In D. Perlman & S. Duck (Eds.), *Intimate relationships: Development, dynamics and deterioration.* Newbury Park, CA: Sage.

Pescosolido, B. A. (1986). Migration, medical care and the lay referral system: A network theory of role assimilation. *American Sociological Review, 51,* 523–540.

Peterson, R. D., & Bailey, W. C. (1991). Felony murder and capital punishment: An examination of the deterrence question. *Criminology, 29,* 367–395.

Peterson, S. B., & Lach, M. A. (1990). Gender stereotypes in children's books: Their prevalence and influence in cognitive and affective development. *Gender and Education, 2,* 185–197.

Pettit, B. (2012). *Invisible men: Mass incarceration and the myth of black progress.* New York: Russell Sage.

Pew Charitable Trusts. (2013). *How much protection does a college degree afford?* www.pewstates.org/uploadedFiles/PCS_Assets/2013/Pew_college_grads_recession_report.pdf. Accessed January 10, 2013.

Pew Forum on Religion and Public Life. (2004). *The American religious landscape and politics, 2004.* www.pewforum.org/publications/surveys/green.pdf. Accessed December 31, 2004.

Pew Forum on Religion and Public Life. (2010). *Religion among the millennials.* http://pewforum.org/Age/Religion-Among-the-Millennials.aspx. Accessed May 30, 2011.

Pew Forum on Religion and Public Life. (2012a). *"Nones" on the rise: Executive summary.* www.pewforum.org/Unaffiliated/nones-on-the-rise.aspx. Accessed January 8, 2013.

Pew Forum on Religion and Public Life. (2012b). *Overview of same-sex marriage in the United States.* www.pewforum.org/Gay-Marriage-and-Homosexuality/Overview-of-Same-Sex-Marriage-in-the-United-States.aspx. Accessed January 16, 2013.

Pew Forum on Religion and Public Life. (2013). *The world's Muslims: Religion, politics, and society.* www.pewforum.org/Muslim/the-worlds-muslims-religion-politics-society-exec.aspx. Accessed June 13, 2013.

Pew Hispanic Center. (2013). *A nation of immigrants.* www.pewhispanic.org/files/2013/01/statistical_portrait_final_jan_29.pdf. Accessed June 28, 2013.

Pew Research Center. (2005). *Social security polling: Cross-currents in opinion about private accounts.* http://people-press.org/commentary/pdf/106.pdf. Accessed September 5, 2009.

Pew Research Center. (2007). *Muslim Americans: Middle class and mostly mainstream.* http://pewresearch.org/assets/pdf/muslim-americans.pdf. Accessed September 5, 2009.

Pew Research Center. (2010a). *The decline of marriage and rise of new families.* http://pewsocial trends.org/files/2010/11/pew-social-trends-2010-families.pdf. Accessed June 2, 2011.

Pew Research Center. (2010b). *Millennials: A portrait of generation next.* http://pewsocialtrends.org/2010/12/20/files/2010/10/millennials-confident-connected-open-to-change.pdf. Accessed June 23, 2011.

Pew Research Center. (2011). *Pessimism about national economy rises, personal financial views hold steady.* http://people-press.org/2011/06/23/section-2-views-of-personal-finances/. Accessed June 27, 2011.

Pew Research Center. (2012a). *The rise of intermarriage.* www.pewsocialtrends.org/files/2012/02/SDT-Intermarriage-II.pdf. Accessed January 14, 2013.

Pew Research Center. (2012b). *Young, underemployed, and optimistic.* www.pewsocialtrends.org/2012/02/09/young-underemployed-and-optimistic/. Accessed June 26, 2013.

Pew Research Center. (2013). Roe v. Wade *at 40: Most oppose overturning abortion decision.* www.pewforum.org/uploadedFiles/Topics/Issues/Abortion/Roe-v-wade-full.pdf. Accessed January 22, 2013.

Pew Research Center for People and the Press. (2012). *Continued majority support for death penalty.* www.people-press.org/2012/01/06/continued-majority-support-for-death-penalty. Accessed January 21, 2013.

Pfohl, S. J. (1994). *Images of deviance and social control.* New York, NY: McGraw-Hill.

Phillips, K. (2002). *Wealth and democracy.* New York, NY: Broadway Books.

Piff, P. K., Stancato, D. M., Côté, S., Mendoza-Denton, R., & Keltner, D. (2012). Higher social class predicts increased unethical behavior. *Proceedings of the National Academy of Sciences, 109,* 4086–4091.

Piper, A. (1992). Passing for white, passing for black. *Transition, 58,* 4–32.

Piven, F. F., & Cloward, R. A. (1977). *Poor people's movements: Why they succeed, how they fail.* New York, NY: Vintage Books.

Pizza must go through: It's the law in San Francisco. (1996, July 14). *The New York Times.*

Planty, M., Langton, L., Krebs, C., Berzofsky, M., & Smiley-McDonald, H. (2013). *Female victims of sexual violence 1994–2010.* U.S. Bureau of Justice Statistics. NCJ240655. www.bjs.gov/content/pub/pdf/fvsv9410.pdf. Accessed June 18, 2013.

Polgreen, L. (2005, December 27). Ghana's uneasy embrace of slavery's diaspora. *The New York Times.*

Pollack, A. (2012, June 7). Tests of parents are used to map genes of a fetus. *New York Times.*

Pollan, M. (2007, January 28). Unhappy meals. *The New York Times Magazine.*

Pollan, M. (2013, May 19). Some of my best friends are bacteria. *The New York Times Magazine.*

Pope exalts women for roles as wife, mom. (2003, June 7). *The Indianapolis Star.*

Popenoe, D. (1993). American family decline, 1960–1990: A review and appraisal. *Journal of Marriage and the Family, 55,* 527–555.

Population Reference Bureau. (2008). *2008 world population data sheet.* www.prb.org/pdf08/08WPDS_Eng.pdf. Accessed May 27, 2009.

Population Reference Bureau. (2010a). China's rapidly aging population. *Today's Research on Aging, 20,* 1–5.

Population Reference Bureau. (2010b). *2010 world population data sheet.* www.prb.org/pdf10/10wpds_eng.pdf. Accessed June 14, 2011.

Population Reference Bureau. (2011). *The world's women and girls.* www.prb.org/pdf11/world-women-girls-2011-data-sheet.pdf. Accessed June 21, 2011.

Population Reference Bureau. (2012). *World population data sheet: 2012.* Accessed June 26, 2013.

Porter, E. (2006, October 17). Law on overseas brides is keeping couples apart. *The New York Times.*

Porter, E. (2012, June 13). Motherhood still a cause of pay inequity. *New York Times.*

Powell, B., Bolzendahl, C., Geist, C., & Steelman, L. C. (2010). *Counted out: Same-sex relations and Americans' definitions of family.* New York, NY: Russell Sage.

Powell, M. (2009, May 31). On diverse force, blacks still face special peril. *The New York Times.*

Powell, M. (2012, January 24). In police training, a dark film on U.S. Muslims. *New York Times.*

Prah, P. M. (2006). Domestic violence. *CQ Researcher, 16,* 1–24.

President's Council on Bioethics. (2003). *Beyond therapy: Biotechnology and the pursuit of happiness.* Washington, DC: Government Printing Office.

Preston, J., & Stelter, B. (2011, February 18). Cellphone cameras become the world's eyes and ears on protests across the Middle East. *The New York Times.*

Price paid in military lives equal to 9/11 toll. (2006, September 23). *Banner Graphic.*

Project for Excellence in Journalism. (2005). *Embedded reporters: What are Americans getting?* Washington, DC: Pew Research Center. www.journalism.org/sites/journalism.org/files/pejembedreport.pdf. Accessed September 5, 2009.

The Project on Student Debt. (2012). *Average student debt climbs to $26,600 for class of 2011.* The Institute for College Access & Success. http://ticas.org/files/pub//Release_SDR12_101812.pdf. Accessed December 21, 2012.

ProQuest Statistical Abstract. (2013). *Statistical abstract of the United States: 2013 Online edition.* si.conquestsystems.com/sa/index.html?id=5d40ca75–82e1=4194-b9dc-44cd63428eaa#. Accessed January 16, 2013.

Provine, R. R. (2000). *Laughter: A scientific investigation.* New York, NY: Penguin Books.

Provine, R. (2012). *Curious behavior.* Cambridge, MA: Belknap Press.

Pugliesi, K. (1987). Deviation in emotion and the labeling of mental illness. *Deviant Behavior, 8,* 79–102.

Putnam, R. D. (1995). Bowling alone: America's declining social capital. *Journal of Democracy, 6,* 65–78.

Qian, Z. (2012). *During the Great Recession, more young adults lived with their parents.* US2010 Project. www.s4.brown.edu/us2010/Data/Report/report08012012.pdf. Accessed December 21, 2012.

Quart, A. (2012, October 6). Why women hide their pregnancies. *The New York Times.*

Quenqua, D. (2012a, August 20). How well you sleep may hinge on race. *The New York Times.*

Quenqua, D. (2012b, November 19). Muscular body image lures boys into gym, and obsession. *The New York Times.*

Quinney, R. (1970). *The social reality of crime.* Boston, MA: Little, Brown.

Rabin, R. C. (2008, December 16). Living with in-laws linked to heart risks in Japanese women. *The New York Times.*

Rabin, R. C. (2011, May 18). Study finds fewer emergency rooms as need rises. *The New York Times.*

Rabinovitch, S. (2013, March 15). Data reveal scale of Chinese abortions. *Financial Times.*

Raftery, I. (2011, May 30). Changes in Oregon law put faith-healing parents on trial. *The New York Times.*

Raley, S., & Bianchi, S. (2006). Sons, daughters, and family processes: Does gender of children matter? *Annual Review of Sociology, 32,* 401–421.

Rampell, C. (2011, June 10). Companies spend on equipment, not workers. *The New York Times.*

Rampell, C. (2012, October 5). When job-creation engines stop at just one. *The New York Times.*

Rankin, S. R. (2003). *Campus climate for gay, lesbian, bisexual, and transgender people: A national perspective.* Washington, DC: National Gay and Lesbian Task Force. www.thetaskforce.org/downloads/reports/reports/CampusClimate.pdf. Accessed September 5, 2009.

Read, J. G., & Gorman, B. K. (2010). Gender and health inequality. *Annual Review of Sociology, 36,* 371–386.

Reardon, S. F. (2011). The widening academic achievement gap between the rich and the poor: New evidence and possible explanations. In R. Murname & G. Duncan (Eds.), *Whither opportunity? Rising inequality and the uncertain life chances of low-income children.* New York: Russell Sage.

Reardon, S. F. (2013, April 28). No rich child left behind. *New York Times.*

Reddy, G. (2005). *With respect to sex: Negotiating Hijra identity in South Asia.* Chicago, IL: University of Chicago Press.

Reiman, J., & Leighton, P. (2010). *The rich get richer and the poor get prison.* Boston, MA: Allyn & Bacon.

Reinharz, S. (1992). *Feminist methods in social research.* New York, NY: Oxford University Press.

Religious groups gather for "Justice Wednesday" pray in. (2005, April 26). *Worldwide Faith News.* www.wfn.org/2005/04/msg00274.html. Accessed July 24, 2005.

Rennison, C. M., & Welchans, S. (2000). *Intimate partner violence* (Special Report No. NCJ 178247). Washington, DC: United States Bureau of Justice Statistics.

Research findings affirm health of women hinges on reform of clinical research. (2003, August 14). *Women's Health Weekly.*

Reskin, B., & Hartmann, H. (1986). *Women's work, men's work: Sex segregation on the job.* Washington, DC: National Academy Press.

Restaurant Opportunities Center of New York. (2009). *The great service divide: Occupational segregation & inequality in the New York City restaurant industry.* www.rocunited.org/files/GREATSERVICEDIVIDE.pdf. Accessed June 17, 2011.

Reyes, L., & Rubie, P. (1994). *Hispanics in Hollywood: An encyclopedia of film and television.* New York, NY: Garland Press.

Rice, A. (2009, April 12). Mission from Africa. *The New York Times Magazine.*

Rich, M. (2010, December 20). Weighing costs, companies favor temporary help. *The New York Times.*

Rich, M. (2012, December 11). U.S. students still lag globally in math and science, tests show. *The New York Times.*

Richtel, M. (2011, December 15). As doctors use more devices, potential for distraction grows. *The New York Times.*

Richtel, M. (2012, April 23). New fashion wrinkle: Stylishly hiding the gun. *The New York Times.*

Rideout, V., Roberts, D. E., & Foehr, U. G. (2005). *Generation M: Media in the lives of 8–18 year olds.* www.kff.org/entmedia/upload/Generation-M-Media-in-the-Lives-of-8–18-Year-olds-Report.pdf. Accessed September 5, 2009.

Ridgeway, C. L., & Smith-Lovin, L. (1999). The gender system and interaction. *Annual Review of Sociology, 25,* 191–216.

Rieff, D. (2005, November 6). Migrant worry. *The New York Times Magazine.*

Rieff, D. (2006, July 2). America the untethered. *The New York Times Magazine.*

Riesman, D. (1950). *The lonely crowd.* New Haven, CT: Yale University Press.

Riley, M. W. (1971). Social gerontology and the age stratification of society. *Gerontologist, 11,* 79–87.

Riley, M. W., Foner, A., & Waring, J. (1988). Sociology of age. In N. J. Smelser (Ed.), *Handbook of sociology.* Newbury Park, CA: Sage.

Rimer, S., & Arenson, K. W. (2004, June 24). Top colleges take more blacks, but which ones? *The New York Times.*

Risen, J. (2012, November 2). Military has not solved problem of sexual assault, women say. *New York Times.*

Rittner, C. (2004). *Genocide in Rwanda: Complicity of the churches.* St. Paul, MN: Paragon House.

Roach, M. (2013). *Gulp: Adventures on the alimentary canal* (Kindle version). New York: Norton.

Robbins, A. (2004). *Pledged: The secret life of sororities.* New York, NY: Hyperion.

Robert Wood Johnson Foundation. (2005). *Characteristics of the uninsured: A view from the states.* www.rwjf.org/files/research/Full_SHADAC.pdf. Accessed September 5, 2009.

Roberts, S. (2006, February 12). So many men, so few women. *The New York Times.*

Roberts, S. (2008, August 17). A nation of none and all of the above. *The New York Times.*

Roberts, S. (2010, January 21). Census figures challenge views of race and ethnicity. *The New York Times.*

Roberts, S. (2013, June 13). For whites, more deaths than births, data show. *The New York Times.*

Robinson, B. A. (1999). *Facts about inter-faith marriages.* www.religioustolerance.org/ifm_fact.htm. Accessed July 6, 2003.

Robinson, R. V., & Bell, W. (1978). Equality, success and social justice in England and the United States. *American Sociological Review, 43,* 125–143.

Robinson, R. V., & Kelley, J. (1979). Class as conceived by Marx and Dahrendorf: Effects on income inequality and politics in the United States and Great Britain. *American Sociological Review, 44,* 38–58.

Rodriguez, C. E., & Cordero-Guzman, H. (2004). Placing race in context. In C. A. Gallagher (Ed.), *Rethinking the color line: Readings in race and ethnicity.* New York, NY: McGraw-Hill.

Rodriguez, M. N., & Emsellem, M. (2011). *65 million "need not apply."* The National Employment Law Project. www.nelp.org/page/-/65_Million_Need_Not_Apply.pdf?nocdn=1. Accessed March 31, 2011.

Roethlisberger, E. J., & Dickson, W. J. (1939). *Management and the worker.* Cambridge, MA: Harvard University Press.

Rohter, L. (2004, December 29). Learn English, says Chile, thinking upwardly global. *The New York Times.*

Roland, A. (1988). *In search of self in India and Japan.* Princeton, NJ: Princeton University Press.

Romano, A., & Samuels, A. (2012, April 16). Is Obama making it worse? *Newsweek.*

Romero, S. (1999, July 24). Cashing in on security woes. *The New York Times.*

Rosato, D. (2004, August). Flights of fancy: Part 2. Airlines' class warfare. *Money.*

Rosenfeld, M. J. (2005). A critique of exchange theory in mate selection. *American Journal of Sociology, 110,* 1284–1325.

Rosenthal, E. (2012, April 15). Nigeria tested by rapid rise in population. *The New York Times.*

Rosenthal, R., & Jacobson, L. (1968). *Pygmalion in the classroom.* New York, NY: Holt, Rinehart & Winston.

Rosner, S. (2013, May 5). New bills, similar faces. *New York Times.*

Ross, C. E., Mirowsky, J., & Goldstein, K. (1990). The impact of family on health: The decade in review. *Journal of Marriage and the Family, 52,* 1059–1078.

Rossi, A. (1968). Transition to parenthood. *Journal of Marriage and the Family, 30,* 26–39.

Rothenberg, P. S. (Ed.). (1992). *Race, class and gender in the United States.* New York, NY: St. Martin's Press.

Rothman, B. K. (1984). Women, health and medicine. In J. Freeman (Ed.), *Women: A feminist perspective.* Palo Alto, CA: Mayfield.

Rothman, B. K., & Caschetta, M. B. (1999). Treating health: Women and medicine. In S. J. Ferguson (Ed.), *Mapping the social landscape: Readings in sociology.* Mountain View, CA: Mayfield.

Rothman, D. J., & Edgar, H. (1992). Scientific rigor and medical realities: Placebo trials in cancer and AIDS research. In E. Fee & D. M. Fox (Eds.), *AIDS: The making of a chronic disease.* Berkeley: University of California Press.

Rothstein, R. (2001, December 12). An economic recovery will tell in the classroom. *The New York Times.*

Rubin, A. J. (2011, December 2). For Afghan women, justice runs into the static wall of custom. *The New York Times.*

Rubin, L. (1994). *Families on the fault line.* New York, NY: HarperCollins.

Rucker, P. (2009, April 8). Some link economy with spate of killings. *The New York Times.*

Rudman, L. A., & Glick, P. (1999). Feminized management and backlash toward agentic women: The hidden costs to women of a kinder, gentler image of middle managers. *Journal of Personality and Social Psychology, 77,* 1004–1010.

Rusbult, C. E., Zembrodt, I. M., & Iwaniszek, J. (1986). The impact of gender and sex-role orientation on responses to dissatisfaction in close relationships. *Sex Roles, 15,* 1–20.

Rwandan Stories. (2011). *With me, he behaved nicely.* www.rwandanstories.org/genocide/strangness_of_mind.html. Accessed May 19, 2011.

Rybczynski, W. (1999, April 18). One good turn. *The New York Times Magazine.*

Sack, K. (2011, September 15). Report finds improved performance by hospitals. *The New York Times.*

Sadker, M., & Sadker, D. (1999). Failing at fairness: Hidden lessons. In S. Ferguson (Ed.), *Mapping the social landscape.* Mountain View, CA: Mayfield.

Sadker, M., Sadker, D., Fox, L., & Salata, M. (2004). Gender equity in the classroom: The unfinished agenda. In M. S. Kimmel (Ed.), *The gendered society reader.* New York, NY: Oxford University Press.

Saenz, R. (2010). *Latinos in the United States: 2010.* Population Reference Bureau. www.prb.org/Publications/PopulationBulletins/2010/latinosupdate1.aspx. Accessed June 16, 2011.

Saez, E. (2012). *Striking it richer: The evolution of top incomes in the United States (updated with 2009 and 2010 estimates.* Working paper. University of California. elsa.berkeley.edu/~saez/saez-UStopincomes-2010.pdf. Accessed June 2, 2013.

Safer, D. J., Zito, J. M., & dosReis, S. (2003). Concomitant psychotropic medication for youths. *American Journal of Psychiatry, 160,* 438–449.

Saint Louis, C. (2010, July 4). What big eyes you have, dear, but are those contacts risky? *The New York Times.*

Saint Louis, C. (2011, May 15). Dessert, laid-back and legal. *The New York Times.*

Salganik, M. J., Dodds, P. S., & Watts, D. J. (2006). Experimental study of inequality and unpredictability in an artificial cultural market. *Science, 311,* 854–856.

Samuels, A. (2011, September 5). Reliving MLK's last hours. *Newsweek*.

Sanday, P. R. (1996). *A woman scorned: Acquaintance rape on trial*. New York, NY: Doubleday.

Sanders, B. (2011). Focus: Is poverty a death sentence? *Reader Supported News*. www.readersupportednews.org/opinion2/277–75/7429-focus-is-poverty-a-death-sentence. Accessed June 1, 2013.

Sanders, B., & Copps, M. (2012). FCC rule change would favor big media. *Politico*. www.politico.com/story/2012/12/fcc-rule-change-would-help-big-media-85262.html. Accessed December 30, 2012.

Sankaran, L. (2013, June 16). Caste is not past. *The New York Times*.

Sapir, E. (1929). The status of linguistics as a science. *Language, 5*, 207–214.

Sapir, E. (1949). *Selected writings* (D. G. Mandelbaum, Ed.). Berkeley: University of California Press.

Saul, L. (1972). Personal and social psychopathology and the primary prevention of violence. *American Journal of Psychiatry, 128*, 1578–1581.

Saulny, S. (2009a, November 8). Overweight Americans push back with vigor in the health care debate. *The New York Times*.

Saulny, S. (2009b, February 25). They stand when called upon, and when not. *The New York Times*.

Saulny, S. (2011, March 20). Black and white and married in the deep south: A shifting image. *The New York Times*.

Saunders, J. M. (1991). Relating social structural abstractions to sociological research. *Teaching Sociology, 19*, 270–271.

Savacool, J. (2009). *The world has curves: The global quest for the perfect body*. New York: Rodale.

Sayer, L., Casper, L., & Cohen, P. (2004, October). *Women, men, and work* (PRB Report). Washington, DC: Population Reference Bureau. www.prb.org. Accessed December 30, 2004.

Sayre, S. (2012, August 31). Hopes raised, Roma in France still face a date with the bulldozer. *The New York Times*.

Schemo, D. J. (2006, October 21). Turmoil at college for deaf reflects broader debate. *The New York Times*.

Schlesinger, A. (1992). *The disuniting of America*. New York, NY: Norton.

Schodolski, V. J. (1993, December 26). Funeral industry, pitching videos, 2-for-1 specials to baby boomers. *The Indianapolis Star*.

Schoenborn, C. A. (2004). Marital status and health: United States, 1999–2002. Centers for Disease Control and Prevention. *Vital and Health Statistics, 351*. http://www.cdc.gov/nchs/data/ad/ad351.pdf. Accessed September 5, 2009.

Schooler, C. (1996). Cultural and social structural explanations of cross-national psychological differences. *Annual Review of Sociology, 22*, 323–349.

Schreiber, N., Bellah, L. D., Martinez, Y., McLaurin, K. A., Strok, R., Garven, S., & Wood, J. M. (2006). Suggestive interviewing in the McMartin Preschool and Kelly Michaels day care abuse cases: A case study. *Social Influence, 1*, 16–47.

Schuman, H., & Krysan, M. (1999). A historical note on Whites' beliefs about racial inequality. *American Sociological Review, 64*, 847–855.

Schwartz, C. R., & Mare, R. D. (2005). Trends in educational assertive marriage from 1940 to 2003. *Demography, 42*, 621–646.

Schwartz, J., Revkin, A. C., & Wald, M. L. (2005, September 12). In reviving New Orleans, a challenge of many tiers. *The New York Times*.

Schwartz, N. D. (2013, July 2). Big companies paid a fraction of corporate tax rate. *The New York Times*.

Schwartzman, L. F. (2007). Does money whiten? Intergenerational changes in racial classification. *American Sociological Review, 72*, 940–963.

Schwarz, A. (2012, October 9). Attention disorder or not, pills to help in school. *The New York Times*.

Sciolino, E., & Mekhennet, S. (2008, June 11). Muslim world and virginity: 2 worlds collide. *The New York Times*.

Scommegna, P. (2012). *Dementia cases expected to triple by 2050 as world population ages*. Population Reference Bureau. www.prb.org/Articles/2012/global-dementia.aspx?p=1. Accessed June 27, 2013.

Scott, J., & Leonhardt, D. (2005, May 15). Class in America: Shadowy lines that still divide us. *The New York Times*.

Scott, L. D. (2003). The relation of racial identity and racial socialization to coping with discrimination among African American adolescents. *Journal of Black Studies, 33*, 520–538.

Scott, M., & Lyman, S. (1968). Accounts. *American Sociological Review, 33*, 46–62.

Scull, A., & Favreau, D. (1986). A chance to cut is a chance to cure: Sexual surgery for psychosis in three nineteenth-century societies. In S. Spitzer & A. T. Scull (Eds.), *Research in law, deviance and social control* (Vol. 8). Greenwich, CT: JAI Press.

Segal, D. (2009, March 12). Financial fraud rises as target for prosecutors. *The New York Times*.

Semyonov, M., & Raijman, R. (2006). The rise of anti-foreigner sentiment in European societies, 1988–2000. *American Sociological Review, 71*, 426–449.

Sengupta, S. (2004, October 26). Relentless attacks on women in West Sudan draw an outcry. *The New York Times*.

Sengupta, S. (2012, May 18). Reticent rich: Preferred style in Silicon Valley. *The New York Times*.

Sennett, R. (1984). *Families against the city: Middle-class homes in industrial Chicago*. Cambridge, MA: Harvard University Press.

Serrano, R. A. (2011, June 30). Federal panel OKs shorter sentences for crack offenders. *The Seattle Times*.

Sex offender's case denied in court. (2001, January 16). *Associated Press Online*. www.highbeam.com/doc/1P1–39751038.html. Accessed October 2, 2011.

Sexton, T. (2009). America's only winnable war: Invasion of the culture snatchers. *Yahoo voices*. Voices. yahoo.com/Americas-only-winnable-war-invasion-culture-2504076.html. Accessed December 31, 2012.

Sexual Harassment Support. (2009). *Sexual harassment in the workplace*. www.sexualharassmentsupport.org/SHworkplace.html. Accessed July 2, 2010.

Shah, A. (2009). Poverty facts and statistics. *Global Issues*. www.globalissues.org/article/26/poverty-facts-and-stats#src1. Accessed May 28, 2009.

Shah, A. (2013). Structural adjustments: A major cause of poverty. *Global Issues*. www.global issues.org/article/3/structural-adjustment- a-major-cause-of-poverty. Accessed June 3, 2013.

Shakin, M., Shakin, D., & Sternglanz, S. H. (1985). Infant clothing: Sex labeling for strangers. *Sex Roles, 12*, 955–964.

Shapiro, T. M. (2008). The hidden cost of being African American. In S. J. Ferguson (Ed.), *Mapping the social landscape*. New York, NY: McGraw-Hill.

Shapo, H. S. (2006). Assisted reproduction and the law: Disharmony on a divisive social issue. *Northwestern University Law Review, 100*, 465–479.

Shattuck, R. M., & Kreider, R. M. (2013). *Social and economic characteristics of currently unmarried women with a recent birth: 2011*. U.S. Bureau of the Census. American Community Survey Reports. ACS-21. www.census.gov/prod/2013pubs/acs-21.pdf. Accessed May 2, 2013.

Shear, M. D. (2010, April 16). Obama extends hospital visitation rights to same-sex partners of gays. *The Washington Post*.

Shenk, D. (2010, May/June). Are you a genius? *Brown Alumni Magazine*.

Shibutani, T. (1961). *Society and personality: An interactionist approach to social psychology*. Englewood Cliffs, NJ: Prentice Hall.

Shipler, D. K. (2004). *The working poor: Invisible in America*. New York, NY: Knopf.

Short, K. (2012). The research: Supplemental poverty measure, 2011. *Current Population Reports, P60–244*. www.census.gov/prod/2012pubs/p60–244.pdf. Accessed June 1, 2013.

Shorto, R. (2010, February 14). Founding father? *The New York Times Magazine*.

Shugart, H. A. (2003). She shoots, she scores: Mediated construction of contemporary female athletes in coverage of the 1999 U.S. Women's soccer team. *Western Journal of Communication, 67*, 1–31.

Shulevitz, J. (2012, September 9). Why fathers really matter. *New York Times Magazine*.

Shweder, R. A. (1997, March 9). It's called poor health for a reason. *The New York Times*.

Sidel, R. (1986). *Women and children last*. New York, NY: Penguin Books.

Sidel, R. (1990). *On her own: Growing up in the shadow of the American dream*. New York, NY: Penguin Books.

Siegel, R. B. (2004). A short history of sexual harassment. In C. A. MacKinnon & R. B. Siegel (Eds.), *Directions in sexual harassment law*. New Haven, CT: Yale University Press.

Signorielli, N. (1990). Children, television, and gender roles. *Journal of Adolescent Health Care, 11*, 50–58.

The silver lining at Borders. (2011, October 2). *HR Management*. www.hrmreport.com/article/The-silver-lining-at-Borders/. Accessed October 2, 2011.

Silverman, D. (1982). *Secondary analysis in social research: A guide to data sources and methods with examples*. Boston, MA: Allen & Unwin.

Simmel, G. (1950). *The sociology of Georg Simmel* (K. Wolff, Ed.). New York, NY: Free Press. (Original work published 1902)

Simon, S. (2009, April 13). Education board in Texas faces curbs. *The Wall Street Journal*.

Simons, M. (2001, April 30). An awful task: Assessing 4 roles in death of thousands in Rwanda. *The New York Times*.

Simons, M. (2011, June 25). Official gets life sentence for genocide in Rwanda. *The New York Times*.

Simpson, I. H. (1979). *From student to nurse: A longitudinal study of socialization*. Cambridge, UK: Cambridge University Press.

Sinclair Broadcast Group. (2012). *Company profile*. www.sbgi.net/about/profile.shtml. Accessed December 28, 2012.

Sindelar, R. (2004). *Recess: Is it needed in the 21st century?* Champaign, IL: Clearinghouse on Early Education and Parenting. http://ceep.crc.uiuc.edu/poptopics/recess.html. Accessed May 23, 2009.

Singer, N. (2009, August 5). Medical papers by ghostwriters pushed therapy. *The New York Times*.

Skocpol, T. (1979). *States and social revolutions: A comparative analysis of France, Russia and China*. New York, NY: Cambridge University Press.

Skolnick, A. S. (1991). *Embattled paradise*. New York, NY: Basic Books.

Slackman, M. (2006, August 6). The fine art of hiding what you mean to say. *The New York Times*.

Slackman, M. (2007, May 26). A quiet revolution in Algeria: Gains by women. *The New York Times*.

Slater, D. (2013, January/February). A million first dates. *The Atlantic*.

Smith, C. S. (2002, May 5). Risking limbs for height and success in China. *The New York Times*.

Smith, C. S. (2005, April 30). Abduction, often violent, a Kyrgyz wedding rite. *The New York Times*.

Smith, E. (2010, April 26). The Texas curriculum massacre. *Newsweek.*

Smith, S. L., Choueiti, M., Prescott, A., & Pieper, K. (2012). *Gender roles and occupations: A look at character attributes and job-related aspirations in film and television.* Geena Davis Institute on Gender in Media. www.seejane.org/downloads/KeyFindings_GenderROles.pdf. Accessed January 9, 2013.

Smith, W. (2002, April 5). Eroica trio offers beauty of more than one kind. *The Indianapolis Star.*

Snell, T. L. (2011). *Capital punishment, 2010—Statistical tables* (NCJ236510). bjs.ojp.usdoj.gov/content/pub/pdf/cp10st.pdf. Accessed January 21, 2013.

Sniderman, P. M., & Tetlock, P. E. (1986). Symbolic racism: Problems of motive attribution in political analysis. *Social Forces, 42,* 129–150.

Snipp, C. M. (1986). American Indians and natural resource development. *American Journal of Economics and Sociology, 45,* 457–474.

Soldo, B. J., & Agree, E. M. (1988). America's elderly. *Population Bulletin, 43,* 1–45.

Sontag, D. (1992, December 11). Across the U.S., immigrants find the land of resentment. *The New York Times.*

Sorkin, A. R. (2011, May 15). Rich and sort of rich. *The New York Times.*

South, S. J., & Lloyd, K. M. (1995). Spousal alternatives and marital dissolution. *American Sociological Review, 60,* 21–35.

South Africa: A biting critique of pets. (2012, December 27). *New York Times.*

Southern Poverty Law Center. (2013). *Hate map.* www.splcenter.org/get-informed/hate-map. Accessed June 12, 2013.

Springen, K. (2006, February 27). States: Time to stub out smoking. *Newsweek.*

Sroufe, L. A. (2012, January 29). Ritalin gone wrong. *The New York Times.*

Stacey, J. (1991). Backward toward the postmodern family. In A. Wolfe (Ed.), *America at century's end.* Berkeley: University of California Press.

Staggenborg, S. (1998). *Gender, family, and social movements.* Thousand Oaks, CA: Pine Forge Press.

Staples, R. (1992). African American families. In J. M. Henslin (Ed.), *Marriage and family in a changing society.* New York, NY: Free Press.

Starbucks. (2012). *Starbucks company profile.* globalassets.starbucks.com/assets/9a6616b98dc64271ac8c910fbee47884.pdf. Accessed December 31, 2012.

Stark, R., & Bainbridge, W. S. (1980). Networks of faith: Interpersonal bonds and recruitment in cults and sects. *American Journal of Sociology, 85,* 1376–1395.

Starr, P. (1982). *The social transformation of American medicine.* New York, NY: Basic Books.

Stein, R. (2007, May 27). Critical care without consent. *The Washington Post.*

Steinhauer, J. (2005, May 29). When the Joneses wear jeans. *The New York Times.*

Steinmetz, S. K., Clavan, R., & Stein, K. F. (1990). *Marriage and family realities: Historical and contemporary perspectives.* New York, NY: Harper & Row.

Steuerle, C. E. (2007). *Crumbs for children?* Washington, DC: Urban Institute. www.urban.org/publications/901068.html. Accessed June 24, 2007.

Stevenson, B., & Wolfers, J. (2003). *Bargaining in the shadow of the law: Divorce laws and family distress.* Stanford University Graduate School of Business, Research Paper #1828. gsbapps.stanford.edu/researchpapers/detai11.asp?Document_ID=2427. Accessed June 17, 2013.

Stevenson, B., & Wolfers, J. (2007). *Marriage and divorce: Changes and their driving forces* (Working Paper No. 12944). Cambridge, MA: National Bureau of Economic Research. http://bpp.wharton.upenn.edu/jwolfers/Papers/MarriageandDivorce(JEP).pdf. Accessed May 12, 2007.

Stewart, A. J., Copeland, A. P., Chester, A. L., Malley, J. E., & Barenbaum, N. B. (1997). *Separating together: How divorce transforms families.* New York, NY: Guilford Press.

St. George, D. (2007, May 13). Pushing the motherhood cause. *The Washington Post.*

Stille, A. (2002, June 29). Textbook publishers learn to avoid messing with Texas. *The New York Times.*

Stinnett, N., & DeFrain, J. (1985). *Secrets of strong families.* Boston, MA: Little, Brown.

Stockard, J., & O'Brien, R. M. (2002). Cohort effects on suicide rates: International variation. *American Sociological Review, 67,* 854–872.

Stokes, R., & Hewitt, J. P. (1976). Aligning actions. *American Sociological Review, 41,* 837–849.

Stolberg, S. G. (1998, April 5). Live and let die over transplants. *The New York Times.*

Stolberg, S. G. (2010, April 15). Obama widens medical rights for same-sex partners. *The New York Times.*

Stone, D., & Colarusso, L. (2011, November 21). Welfare for millionaires. *Newsweek.*

Stone, G. P. (1981). Appearance and the self: A slightly revised version. In G. P. Stone & H. A. Farberman (Eds.), *Social psychology through symbolic interaction.* New York, NY: Wiley.

Stonington, J., & McIntyre, A. (2011, November 10). The best and worst states for getting divorced. *Bloomberg News.* www.bloomberg.com/money-gallery/2011-11-10/best-and-worst-states-for-getting-divorced.html#slide1. Accessed January 16, 2013.

Straus, M. A. (1977). A sociological perspective on the prevention and treatment of wife beating. In M. Roy (Ed.), *Battered women.* New York, NY: Van Nostrand Reinhold.

Straus, M. A., & Gelles, R. J. (1990). How violent are American families? Estimates from the National Family Violence Resurvey and other studies. In M. A. Straus & R. J. Gelles (Eds.), *Physical violence in American families*. New Brunswick, NJ: Transaction.

Streitfeld, D. (2013, April 8). Teacher knows if you've done the e-reading. *The New York Times*.

Strube, M. J., & Barbour, L. S. (1983). The decision to leave an abusive relationship: Economic dependence and psychological commitment. *Journal of Marriage and the Family, 45*, 785–793.

Stryker, J. (1980). *Symbolic interactionism*. Menlo Park, CA: Benjamin/Cummings.

Stryker, J. (1997, July 13). The age of innocence isn't what it once was. *The New York Times*.

Study finds increase in weapons use. (2000, November 30). *The New York Times*.

Suarez, Z. (1998). The Cuban-American family. In C. H. Mindel, R. W. Habenstein, & R. Wright (Eds.), *Ethnic families in America: Patterns and variations*. Upper Saddle River, NJ: Prentice Hall.

Sudarkasa, N. (2001). Interpreting the African heritage in Afro-American family organization. In S. Ferguson (Ed.), *Shifting the center: Understanding contemporary families*. Mountain View, CA: Mayfield.

Sudnow, D. (1965). Normal crimes: Sociological features of the penal code in a public defender's office. *Social Problems, 12*, 255–264.

Sullivan, R. (2006, June 25). A slow-road movement. *The New York Times Magazine*.

Sullivan, T. A., Warren, E., & Westbrook, J. L. (2000). *The fragile middle class: Americans in debt*. New Haven, CT: Yale University Press.

Sussman, D. (2010, February 28). A question of what to ask. *The New York Times*.

Sutherland, E., & Cressey, D. (1955). *Criminology*. Philadelphia, PA: Lippincott.

Swanson, G. (1992). Doing things together: On some basic forms of agency and structuring in collective action and on some explanations for them. *Social Psychology Quarterly, 55*, 94–117.

Swarns, R. L. (2001, April 20). Drug makers drop South Africa suit over AIDS medicines. *The New York Times*.

Swarns, R. L. (2008a, September 2). Bipartisan calls for new federal poverty measure. *The New York Times*.

Swarns, R. L. (2008b, August 25). Blacks debate civil rights risk in Obama's rise. *The New York Times*.

Swartz, M. (2007, June 10). Shop stewards on Fantasy Island? *The New York Times Magazine*.

Sykes, G., & Matza, D. (1957). Techniques of neutralization: A theory of delinquency. *American Sociological Review, 22*, 664–670.

Tabuchi, H. (2011, January 3). Despite shortage, Japan keeps a high wall for foreign labor. *The New York Times*.

Takayama, H. (2003, January 13). The Okinawa way. *Newsweek*.

Talbot, M. (2000, February 27). A mighty fortress. *The New York Times Magazine*.

Tarrow, S. (1994). *Power in movement*. New York, NY: Cambridge University Press.

Tavernise, S. (2011a, August 16). Parents skip marriage for cohabitation, report finds. *The New York Times*.

Tavernise, S. (2011b, September 19). Poor young families soared in '10, data show. *The New York Times*.

Tavernise, S. (2012, December 14). Life expectancy rises around world, study finds. *The New York Times*.

Tavernise, S., & Gebeloff, R. (2010, December 15). Immigrants make paths to suburbia, not cities. *The New York Times*.

Tavris, C., & Offir, C. (1984). *The longest war: Sex differences in perspective*. New York, NY: Harcourt Brace Jovanovich.

Teachman, J. D. (1991). Contributions to children by divorced fathers. *Social Problems, 38*, 358–371.

Telles, E. E., & Murguia, E. (1990). Phenotypic discrimination and income differences among Mexican Americans. *Social Science Quarterly, 71*, 682–696.

This American Life. (2011b). *The psychopath test*. www.thisamericanlife.org/radio-archives/episode/436/the-psychopath-test. Accessed June 8, 2011.

Thoits, P. (1985). Self-labeling process in mental illness: The role of emotional deviance. *American Journal of Sociology, 91*, 221–249.

Thomas, K., & Schmidt, M. S. (2012, July 3). Drug firm guilty in criminal case. *The New York Times*.

Thompson, G. (2003, February 13). Behind roses' beauty, poor and ill workers. *The New York Times*.

Thompson, G. (2009, March 15). Where education and assimilation collide. *The New York Times*.

Thomson, D. S. (2000). The Sapir-Whorf hypothesis: Worlds shaped by words. In J. Spradley & D. W. McCurdy (Eds.), *Conformity and conflict*. Boston, MA: Allyn & Bacon.

Thomson-DeVeaux, A. (2013). *New survey illuminates differences among the world's Muslims*. Public Religion Research Institute. publicreligion.org/2013/05/new-survey-illuminates-differences-among-the-worlds-muslims/. Accessed June 17, 2013.

Thornton, M. (1997). Strategies of racial socialization among black parents: Mainstreaming, minority, and cultural messages. In R. Taylor, J. Jackson, & L. Chatters (Eds.), *Family life in black America*. Thousand Oaks, CA: Sage.

Thurn, S. (2012, April 27). U.S. firms add jobs, but mostly overseas. *Wall St. Journal*.

Tietz, J. (2006, April 20). The killing factory. *Rolling Stone*.

Timms, E., & McGonigle, S. (1992, April 5). Psychological warfare. *The Indianapolis Star*.

Tobin, J. J., Wu, D. Y. H., & Davidson, D. H. (1989). *Preschool in three cultures: Japan, China and the United States*. New Haven, CT: Yale University Press.

Tönnies, F. (1957). *Community and society* [Gemeinschaft und Gesellschaft] (C. P. Loomis, Ed.). East Lansing: Michigan State University Press. (Original work published 1887)

Towell, L. (2007, November 18). Patients without borders. *The New York Times Magazine*.

Transplant Living. (2013). *Costs*. www.transplantliving. org/before-the-transplant/financing-a-transplant/the-costs/. Accessed June 15, 2013.

Trautner, H. M., Ruble, D. N., Cyphers, L., Kirsten, B., Behrendt, R., & Hartmann, P. (2005). Rigidity and flexibility of gender stereotypes in childhood: Developmental or differential? *Infant and Child Development, 14,* 365–381.

Trepagnier, B. (2013). Silent racism: Passivity in well-meaning white people. In D. M. Newman & J, O'Brien (Eds.), *Sociology: Exploring the architecture of everyday life (Readings)*. Thousand Oaks, CA: Sage.

Triandis, H. C., McCusker, C., & Hui, C. H. (1990). Multimethod probes of individualism and collectivism. *Journal of Personality and Social Psychology, 59,* 1006–1020.

Trotsky, L. (1959). *The history of the Russian Revolution* (F. W. Dupee, Ed.). Garden City, NY: Doubleday. (Original work published 1930)

Trotter, R. T., & Chavira, J. A. (1997). *Curanderismo: Mexican American folk healing*. Athens: University of Georgia Press.

Truman, M., & Rand, J. (2010). *Criminal victimization, 2009* (NCJ 231327). U.S. Bureau of Justice Statistics. http://bjs.ojp.usdoj.gov/content/pub/pdf/cv09.pdf. Accessed June 20, 2011.

Trunk, P. (2007, July 16). What Gen Y really wants. *Time*.

Tsai, T. (2012). *China has too many bachelors*. Population Reference Bureau. www.prb.org/Articles/2012/china-census-excess-males.aspx?p=1. Accessed December 21, 2012.

Tsai, T., & Scommegna, P. (2012). *U.S. has world's highest incarceration rate*. Population Reference Bureau. www.prb.org/Articles/ 2012/us-incarceration. aspx?p=1. Accessed August 14, 2012.

Tumin, M. (1953). Some principles of stratification: A critical analysis. *American Sociological Review, 18,* 387–393.

Turkheimer, E., Haley, A., Waldron, M., D'Onofrio, B., & Gottesman, I. I. (2003). Socioeconomic status modifies heritability of IQ in young children. *Psychological Science, 14,* 623–628.

Turner, E. H., Matthews, A. M., Linardatos, E., Tell, R. A., & Rosenthal, R. (2008). Selective publication of antidepressant trials and its influence on apparent efficacy. *The New England Journal of Medicine, 358,* 252–260.

Turner, J. H. (1972). *Patterns of social organization*. New York, NY: McGraw-Hill.

Turner, R. W., & Killian, L. M. (1987). *Collective behavior*. Englewood Cliffs, NJ: Prentice Hall.

Twenge, J. M., Campbell, W. K., & Gentile, B. (2012). Increases in individualistic words and phrases in American books, 1960–2009. *PLoSONE, 7(7):* e40181. www.plosone.org/article/info%Adoi%2F10.1371%Fjournal.pone.0040181. Accessed May 28, 2013.

Tyre, P. (2006, January 30). The trouble with boys. *Newsweek*.

Ubiñas, L. A., & Gabrieli, C. (2011, August 23). Shortchanged by the bell. *The New York Times*.

Uchitelle, L. (2008, April 20). The wage that meant middle class. *The New York Times*.

Uchitelle, L. (2010, July 7). A new generation, an elusive American dream. *The New York Times*.

Uggen, C., & Blackstone, A. (2004). Sexual harassment as a gendered expression of power. *American Sociological Review, 69,* 64–92.

UNAIDS. (2008). *2008 report on the global AIDS epidemic*. http://data.unaids.org/pub/GlobalReport/2008/JC1511_GR08_ExecutiveSummary_en.pdf. Accessed September 5, 2009.

UNICEF. (2009). *The state of the world's children 2009*. www.unicef.org/sowc09/docs/SOWC09-FullReport-EN.pdf. Accessed September 5, 2009.

UNICEF. (2011). *Child protection from violence, exploitation, and abuse*. www.unicef.org/protection/index_childlabour.html. Accessed July 1, 2011.

UNICEF. (2013). *Female genital mutilation/cutting: A statistical overview and exploration of the dynamics of change*. http://www.unicef.org/media/files/FGCM_Lo_res.pdf. Accessed July 22, 2013.

United Nations. (2011). *World population prospects*. Department of Economic and Social Affairs. http://esa.un.org/unpd/wpp/index.htm. Accessed June 23, 2011.

United Nations Population Division. (2003). *World population prospects: The 2002 revision*. www.un.org/esa/population/publications/wpp2002/wpp2002-highlightsrev1.pdf. Accessed June 26, 2003.

United Nations Population Division. (2005). *World population prospects: The 2004 revision population database*. http://esa.un.org/unpp/index.asp?panel=2. Accessed July 15, 2005.

United States Bureau of Justice Statistics. (2001). *The sexual victimization of college women* [Press release]. www.ojp.usdoj.gov/bjs/pub/press/svcw.pr. Accessed September 5, 2009.

United States Bureau of Justice Statistics. (2010). *Criminal victimization, 2009*. NCJ231327. Bjs.ojp.usdoj.gov/content/pub/pdf/CV09.pdf. Accessed December 30, 2012. [ch3]

United States Bureau of Justice Statistics. (2011). *Homicide trends in the U.S.* http://bjs.ojp.usdoj.gov/content/homicide/relationship/cfm. Accessed May 24, 2011.

United States Bureau of Justice Statistics. (2012). *Sourcebook of criminal justice statistics online.* www.albany.edu/sourcebook/. Accessed January 21, 2013.

United States Bureau of Labor Statistics. (2010). *Median weekly earnings of full-time and salary workers by detailed occupation and sex—Table 39.* ftp://ftp.bls.gov/pub/special.requests/lf/aat39.txt. Accessed June 15, 2011.

United States Bureau of Labor Statistics. (2011). *The employment situation: May 2011.* (USDL-11–10809). www.bls.gov/news.release/pdf/empsit.pdf. Accessed June 16, 2011.

United States Bureau of Labor Statistics. (2012a). *Census of fatal occupational injuries (CFOI)—Current and revised data.* www.bls.gov/iif/oshcfoi1.htm. Accessed January 21, 2013.

United States Bureau of Labor Statistics. (2012b). *The employment situation—November 2012.* (USDL-12–2366). www.bls.gov/news.release/pdf/disabl.pdf. Accessed December 21, 2012.

United States Bureau of Labor Statistics. (2012c). *Extended mass layoffs in 2011.* www.bls.gov/mls/mlsreport1039.pdf. Accessed May 31, 2013.

United States Bureau of Labor Statistics. (2012d). *Workplace injury and illness summary.* USDL-12–2121. www.bls.gov/news.release/osh.nr0.htm. Accessed January 21, 2013.

United States Bureau of Labor Statistics. (2013a). *American Time Use Survey—2012 results.* USDL-13–1178. www.bls.gov/news.release/atus/nr0.htm. Accessed June 21, 2013.

United States Bureau of Labor Statistics. (2013b). *Employed persons by class of worker and part-time status. Table A-8.* www.bls.gov/news.release/empsit.t08.htm. Accessed May 31, 2013.

United States Bureau of Labor Statistics. (2013c). *Employment situation.* www.bls.gov/news.release/empsit.toc.htm. Accessed June 14, 2013.

United States Bureau of Labor Statistics. (2013d). *Expenditure table. Table 4.* www.bls.gov/cex/2011/standard/cusize.pdf. Accessed May 31, 2013.

United States Bureau of Labor Statistics. (2013e). *May 2012 national occupational and wage estimates: United States.* www.bls.gov/oes/current/oes_nat.htm#00–0000. Accessed May 31, 2013.

United States Bureau of Labor Statistics. (2013f). Median weekly earnings of full-time wage and salary workers by detailed occupation and sex. Table 39. www.bls.gov/cpsaat39.pdf. Accessed June 23, 2013.

United States Bureau of the Census. (2004). *Statistical abstract of the United States.* www.census.gov/prod/www/statistical-abstract-04.html. Accessed June 15, 2005.

United States Bureau of the Census. (2005). *Current population survey (CPS): Definitions and explanations.* www.census.gov/population/www/cps/cpsdef.html. Accessed September 21, 2005.

United States Bureau of the Census. (2006). *Special edition: 300 million.* www.census.gov/Press-Release/www/releases/archives/facts_for_features_special_editions/007276.htm. Accessed July 12, 2007.

United States Bureau of the Census. (2007). *Statistical abstract of the United States.* www.census.gov/prod/2006pub/07statab/pop.pdf. Accessed March 29, 2007.

United States Bureau of the Census. (2009). *Statistical abstract of the United States.* www.census.gov/compendia/statab/2009edition.html. Accessed March 27, 2009.

United States Bureau of the Census. (2011a). *International data base.* www.census.gov/ipc/www/idb. Accessed June 23, 2011.

United States Bureau of the Census. (2011b). *Statistical abstract of the United States.* www.census.gov/compendia/statab/2011 edition.html. Accessed July 4, 2011.

United States Commission on Human Rights. (1992). Indian tribes: A continuing quest for survival. In P. S. Rothenberg (Ed.), *Race, class and gender in the United States.* New York, NY: St. Martin's Press.

United States Conference of Mayors. (2012). *Hunger and homelessness survey: A status report on hunger and homelessness in America's cities.* www.usmayors.org/pressreleases/uploads/2012/1219-report-HH.pdf. Accessed June 2, 2013.

United States Department of Agriculture. (2001, June 17). *USDA estimates child rearing costs.* Washington, DC: Author.

United States Department of Defense. (2010). *Report on the impact of deployment of members of the armed forces on their dependent children.* www.militaryonesource.mil/12038/MOS/Reports/Report_to_Congress_on_Impact_of_Deployment_on_Military_Children.pdf. Accessed June 25, 2013.

United States Department of Defense. (2013). *Sexual assault prevention and responses—annual reports.* www.sapr.mil/public/docs/reports/FY12_DoD_SAPRO_Annual_Report_on_Sexual_Assault-VOLUME_ONE.pdf. Accessed June 19, 2013.

United States Department of Health and Human Services. (2006). *Sustaining state programs for tobacco control: Data highlights 2006.* www.cdc.gov/tobacco/data_statistics/state_data/data_highlights/2006/pdfs/dataHighlights06rev.pdf. Accessed September 5, 2009.

United States Department of Health and Human Services. (2012). *National healthcare disparities report 2011.* AHRQ Publication #12–0006. www.ahrq.gov/qual/qrdr11.htm. Accessed June 18, 2013.

United States Department of Justice. (2009). *UBS enters into deferred prosecution agreement.* www.usdoj.gov/opa/pr/2009/February/09-tax-136.html. Accessed May 21, 2009.

United States Department of Justice. (2013). *A national protocol for sexual assault medical forensic examinations—2nd edition.* NCJ241903. www.safeta.org/associations/8563/files/SAFE_PROTOCOL_2012–508.pdf. Accessed April 27, 2013.

United States Department of Labor. (2011). *Facts on Executive Order 11246—Affirmative action.* Office of Federal Contract Compliance Programs. www.dol.gov/OFCCP/regs/compliance/aa.htm. Accessed June 17, 2011.

United States Department of State. (2012). *Trafficking in persons report.* www.state.gov/documents/organization/192587.pdf. Accessed May 30, 2013.

United States Equal Employment Opportunity Commission. (2012). *Sexual harassment changes EEOC & FEPAs combined: FY1997-FY2011.* www.eeoc.gov/eeoc/statistics/enforcement/sexual_harassment.cfm. Accessed June 19, 2013.

United States Sentencing Commission. (2011). *2011 Annual Report.* www.ussc.gov/Data_and_Statistics/Annual_Reports_and_Sourcebooks/2011/ar11toc.htm. Accessed January 21, 2013.

Urbina, I. (2009, February 25). In push to end death penalty, some states cite cost-cutting. *The New York Times.*

Urbina, I. (2013, June 4). Blacks are singled out for marijuana arrests, federal data suggests. *The New York Times.*

USGovernmentSpending.com. (2013). *Government spending details.* www.usgovernmentspending.com/classic. Accessed June 3, 2013.

U.S. English. (2011). *Fact sheets: States with official English.* www.us-english.org/view/302. Accessed May 26, 2011.

U.S. PIRG Education Fund. (2012). *Transportation and the new generation.* www.pirg.org/sites/pirg/files/reports/Transportation%20%26%20the%20New%20Generation%20vUS_0.pdf. Accessed December 31, 2012.

Utne, L. (2006, March/April). Soldiers for peace. *Utne Reader.*

Van Ausdale, D., & Feagin, J. R. (2001). *The first R: How children learn race and racism.* Lanham, MD: Rowman & Littlefield.

van den Haag, E. (1975). *Punishing criminals: Concerning a very old and painful question.* New York, NY: Basic Books.

Vanek, J. (1980). Work, leisure and family roles: Farm households in the United States: 1920–1955. *Journal of Family History, 5,* 422–431.

van Nood, E. (2013). Duodenal infusion of donor feces for recurrent *Clostridium difficile. New England Journal of Medicine, 368,* 407–415.

Van Ryn, M., & Burke, J. (2000). The effect of patient race and socio-economic status on physicians' perceptions of patients. *Social Science and Medicine, 50,* 813–820.

Vaughan, D. (1986). *Uncoupling.* New York, NY: Vintage Books.

Vedantam, S. (2005, June 26). Patients' diversity is often discounted. *The Washington Post.*

Velázquez, N. (2002). In search of justice. In J. B. Schor & B. Taylor (Eds.). *Sustainable planet: Solutions for the twenty-first century.* Boston: Beacon Press.

Viets, E. (1992, November 29). Give a whistle, he'll love it. *St. Louis Post-Dispatch.*

Villarreal, A. (2010). Stratification by skin color in contemporary Mexico. *American Sociological Review, 75,* 652–678.

Virning, B. A. (2008). Associating insurance status with cancer stage at diagnosis. *The Lancet Oncology, 9,* 189–191.

Vladimir Putin on raising Russia's birth rate. (2006). *Population and Development Review, 32,* 385–389.

Voyandoff, P. (1990). Economic distress and family relations: A review of the eighties. *Journal of Marriage and Family, 52,* 1099–1115.

Wahl, O. (1999). *Telling is risky business.* New Brunswick, NJ: Rutgers University Press.

Waite, L. J., & Gallagher, M. (2000). *The case for marriage: Why married people are happier, healthier, and better off financially.* New York, NY: Doubleday.

Waldman, A. (2003, March 28). Broken taboos doom lovers in an Indian village. *The New York Times.*

Waldrop, J. (2013, March 13). State medical boards trying to limit who can be called "Doctor." *Clinical Advisor.*

Wal-Mart. (2012). *2012 Annual report.* walmartstores.com/sites/annual-report/2012/WalMart_AR.pdf. Accessed December 31, 2012.

Walton, J. (1990). *Sociology and critical inquiry.* Belmont, CA: Wadsworth.

Wang, W., & Morin, R. (2009). *Home for the holidays . . . and every other day.* Pew Research Center. http://pewsocialtrends.org/2009/11/24/home-for-the-holidays-and-every-other-day/. Accessed June 6, 2011.

Wang, W., Parker, K., & Taylor, P. (2013). *Breadwinner moms.* Pew Research Center. www.pewsocialtrends.org/2013/05/29/breadwinner-moms/. Accessed June 18, 2013.

Ward, L. M., & Friedman, K. (2006). Using TV as a guide: Associations between television viewing and adolescents' sexual attitudes and behavior. *Journal of Research on Adolescence, 16,* 133–156.

Warner, J. (2010, June 20). Dysregulation nation. *The New York Times.*

Warshaw, R. (1988). *I never called it rape.* New York, NY: Harper & Row.

Wartik, N. (2003, September 9). Muting the obsessions over perceived flaws. *The New York Times.*

Waters, M. C. (2008). Optional ethnicities: For Whites only? In D. Newman & J. O'Brien (Eds.), *Sociology: Exploring the architecture of everyday life (Readings).* Thousand Oaks, CA: Pine Forge Press.

Watson, I. (2005, June 13). As elections near, Iranian women stage protest. *National Public Radio.* www.npr.org/templates/story/story.php?story ID=4700486. Accessed June 13, 2005.

Wattenberg, E. (1986). The fate of baby boomers and their children. *Social Work, 31,* 20–28.

Watts, D. J. (2007, April 15). Is Justin Timberlake a product of cumulative advantage? *The New York Times Magazine.*

Watzlawick, P. (1976). *How real is real?* Garden City, NY: Doubleday.

Watzlawick, P. (1984). Self-fulfilling prophecies. In P. Watzlawick (Ed.), *The invented reality: How do we know what we believe we know? Contributions to constructivism.* New York, NY: Norton.

Weber, M. (1946). Bureaucracy. In H. H. Gerth & C. W. Mills (Eds.), *From Max Weber: Essays in sociology.* New York, NY: Oxford University Press.

Weber, M. (1947). *The theory of social and economic organization.* New York, NY: Free Press.

Weber, M. (1970). *From Max Weber: Essays in sociology* (H. H. Gerth & C. W. Mills, Eds.). New York, NY: Oxford University Press.

Weber, M. (1977). *The Protestant ethic and the spirit of capitalism.* New York, NY: Macmillan. (Original work published 1904)

Weber, M. (1978). *Economy and society* (G. Roth & C. Wittich, Trans.). Berkeley: University of California Press. (Original work published 1921)

Weeks, J. (1995). *Population: An introduction to concepts and issues* (Rev. 5th ed.). Belmont, CA: Wadsworth.

Weil, E. (2006, September 24). What if it's (sort of) a boy and (sort of) a girl? *The New York Times Magazine.*

Weinberg, D. H. (2007, July/August). Earnings by gender: Evidence from Census 2000. *Monthly Labor Review,* pp. 26–34.

Weiner, E. (2011, December 11). Americans: Undecided about God? *The New York Times.*

Weisberg, R. (2007). Pay-to-stay in California jails and the value of systematic self-embarrassment. *Michigan Law Review First Impressions, 106,* 55–59.

Weissman, J. (2012, April 23). 53% of recent college grads are jobless or underemployed–how? *The Atlantic.* www.theatlantic.com/business/archive/2012/04/53-of-recent-college-grads-are-jobless-or-underemployed-how/256237. Accessed December 21, 2012.

Weitzman, L., Eifler, D., Hodada, E., & Ross, C. (1972). Sex-role socialization in picture books for preschool children. *American Journal of Sociology, 77,* 1125–1150.

Welch, H. G., Schwartz, L., & Woloshin, S. (2007, January 2). What's making us sick is an epidemic of diagnoses. *The New York Times.*

Whalen, C. K., & Henker, B. (1977). The pitfalls of politicization: A response to Conrad's "The discovery of hyperkinesis: Notes on the medicalization of deviance." *Social Problems, 24,* 590–595.

What is coltan? (2002, January 21). *ABCNews.com.* http://abcnews.go.com/Nightline/story?id=128631&page=1. Accessed September 5, 2009.

Wheaton, S. (2013, May 8). For first time on record, black voting rate outpaced rate for whites. *The New York Times.*

Whorf, B. (1956). *Language, thought and reality.* Cambridge, MA: MIT Press.

Whoriskey, P. (2011, October 3). Cozy relationships and "peer benchmarking" send CEOs' pay soaring. *Washington Post.*

Whyte, M. K. (1990). *Dating, mating and marriage.* New York, NY: Aldine de Gruyter.

Wilcox, W. B. (2000). Conservative Protestant child discipline: The case of parental yelling. *Social Forces, 79,* 856–891.

Wildman, S. M., & Davis, A. D. (2002). Making systems of privilege visible. In P. S. Rothenberg (Ed.), *White privilege: Essential readings on the other side of racism.* New York, NY: Worth.

Wilford, J. N. (2007, September 19). Languages die, but not their last words. *The New York Times.*

Williams, J. C., Blair-Joy, M., & Berdahl, J. L. (2013). Cultural schemas, social class and the flexibility of stigma. *Journal of Social Issues, 69,* 209–234.

Williamson, R. C. (1984). A partial replication of the Kohn-Gecas-Nye thesis in a German sample. *Journal of Marriage and the Family, 46,* 971–979.

Wilson, C. (2012, April 7). Courtesy charter outlaws rude behavior. *Abacus News.*

Wilson, D. (2009a, August 30). Race, ethnicity, and care. *The New York Times.*

Wilson, D. (2009b, June 12). Senate approves tight regulation over cigarettes. *The New York Times.*

Wilson, D. (2010, November 14). Cigarette giants in a global fight on tighter rules. *The New York Times.*

Wilson, M., & Baker, A. (2010, October 8). Lured into a trap, then tortured for being gay. *The New York Times.*

Winerip, M. (2012, December 17). Same-sex marriage finds allies in conservatives of a certain age. *The New York Times.*

Wines, M. (2006, August 24). Africa adds to miserable ranks of child workers. *The New York Times.*

Winter, G. (2002, May 19). Workers say Coke sold old soda. *The New York Times.*

Witt, S. (2005). How television shapes children's gender roles. In R. H. Lauer & J. C. Lauer (Eds.), *Sociology: Windows on society.* Los Angeles, CA: Roxbury.

Wolfe, A. (1991). *America at century's end*. Berkeley: University of California Press.

Women Physicians Congress. (2008). *Statistics and history*. www.ama-assn.org/ama/pub/about-ama/our-people/member-groups-sections/women-physicians-congress/statistics-history.shtml. Accessed June 5, 2009.

Wood, N. (2005, February 6). Eight nations agree on plan to lift status of Gypsies. *The New York Times*.

World Bank. (2006). *Global monitoring report 2006*. http://web.worldbank.org. Accessed August 9, 2007.

World Bank. (2012). *Projects and lending*. www.worldbank.org. Accessed June 3, 2013.

World Health Organization. (2011). *WHO report on the global tobacco epidemic*. whqlibdoc.who.int/publications/2011/9789240687813_eng.pdf. Accessed January 22, 2013.

World Health Organization. (2012). *Dementia: A public health priority*. apps.who.int/iris/bitstream/10665/75263/1/9789241564458_eng.pdf. Accessed June 27, 2013.

World Health Organization. (2013). *Female genital mutilation*. Fact Sheet No. 241. www.who.int/mediacentre/factsheets/fs241/en/index.html. Accessed February 13, 2013.

World Hunger Education Service. (2012). *2012 world hunger and poverty facts and statistics*. www.worldhunger.org/articles/Learn/world hunger facts 2002.htm#Footnotes. Accessed June 3, 2013.

World Wildlife Fund. (e2012). *2012 Living planet report*. wwf.panda.org/about_our_earth/all_publications/living_planet_report/2012_lpr/. Accessed June 28, 2013.

Worsnop, R. (1996). Getting into college. *CQ Researcher, 6*, 169–192.

Wright, E. O. (1976). Class boundaries in advanced capitalist societies. *New Left Review, 98*, 3–41.

Wright, E. O., Costello, C., Hachen, D., & Sprague, J. (1982). The American class structure. *American Sociological Review, 47*, 709–726.

Wright, E. O., & Perrone, L. (1977). Marxist class categories and income inequality. *American Sociological Review, 42*, 32–55.

Wright, J. D., & Wright, S. R. (1976). Social class and parental values for children: A partial replication and extension of the Kohn thesis. *American Sociological Review, 41*, 527–537.

Wrong, D. (1988). *Power: Its forms, bases, and uses*. Chicago, IL: University of Chicago Press.

Wu, F. H. (2002). *Yellow: Race in America beyond black and white*. New York, NY: Basic Books.

WuDunn, S. (1996a, January 23). In Japan, even toddlers feel the pressure to excel. *The New York Times*.

WuDunn, S. (1996b, September 11). A taboo creates a land of Romeos and Juliets. *The New York Times*.

WuDunn, S. (1997, January 14). Korean women still feel demands to bear a son. *The New York Times*.

Wuthnow, R. (1994). *Sharing the journey*. New York, NY: Free Press.

Wynia, M. K., VanGeest, J. B., Cummins, D. S., & Wilson, I. B. (2003). Do physicians not offer useful services because of coverage restrictions? *Health Affairs, 22*, 190–198.

Xiao, H. (2000). Class, gender, and parental values in the 1990s. *Gender & Society, 14*, 785–803.

Yardley, J. (2011, May 25). As wealth and literacy rise in India, report says, so do sex-selective abortions. *The New York Times*.

Yi, C.-C., Chang, C.-E., & Chang, Y.-H. (2004). The intergenerational transmission of family values: A comparison between teenagers and parents in Taiwan. *Journal of Comparative Family Studies, 35*, 523–545.

Yong, W. (2010, December 7). Divorce soars in Iran as women say no, and work the system. *The New York Times*.

Yoshino, K. (2006). *Covering: The hidden assault on our civil rights*. New York, NY: Random House.

Young, J. Q., Ranji, S. R., Wachter, R. M., Lee, C. M., Niehaus, B., & Auerbach, A. D. (2011). "July effect": Impact of the academic year-end changeover on patient outcomes: A systematic review. *Annals of Internal Medicine, 155*, 309–315.

Younis, M. (2011). *Muslim Americans identify with God and country*. Abu Dhabi Gallup Center. www.gallup.com/poll/148799/Muslim-Americans-Identify-God-Country.aspx. Accessed September 8, 2011.

Yum! Brands. (2012). *About Yum! Brands*. www.yum.com/company/default.asp. Accessed December 31, 2012.

Yurkiewicz, I. (2012, June 12). Three bizarre tales of medical survivors, and what they can (and cannot) teach us about medicine. *Scientific American*.

Zernike, K. (2003, January 20). 30 years after *Roe v. Wade*, new trends but the old debate. *The New York Times*.

Zernike, K. (2004, December 19). Does Christmas need to be saved? *The New York Times*.

Zhao, Y. (2002, August 5). Wave of pupils lacking English strains schools. *The New York Times*.

Zhu, W. X., Lu, L., & Hesketh, T. (2009). China's excess males, sex selective abortion, and one child policy: Analysis of data from 2005 national intercensus survey. *British Medical Journal, 338*, 1211–1213.

Zimbardo, P. (2007). *The Lucifer effect: Understanding how good people turn evil*. New York, NY: Random House.

Zoepf, K. (2007, September 23). A dishonorable affair. *The New York Times Magazine*.

Zola, I. (1986). Medicine as an institution of social control. In P. Conrad & R. Kern (Eds.), *The sociology of health and illness*. New York, NY: St. Martin's Press.

Zoll, R. (2005, June 7). Poll reveals U.S. leads in religious devotion. *The Indianapolis Star*.

Zuckoff, M. (2000, June 8). Lawsuit accuses drug maker Eli Lilly of concealing Prozac data from trial. *The Boston Globe*.

Zuger, A. (1999, April 30). Take some strychnine and call me in the morning. *The New York Times*.

Zuger, A. (2005, October 30). For a retainer, lavish care by "boutique doctors." *The New York Times*.

Zurcher, L. A., & Snow, D. A. (1981). Collective behavior: Social movements. In M. Rosenberg & R. H. Turner (Eds.), *Social psychology: Sociological perspectives*. New York, NY: Basic Books.

Zwerdling, D. (2004). U.S. military whistle blowers face retribution. *National Public Radio*. www.npr.org/templates/story/story.php?storyId=1905858. Accessed June 19, 2007.

Photo Credits

Index

Abortion, 43, 103, 241–242

Absolute poverty: Inability to afford the minimal requirements for sustaining a reasonably healthy existence, 163

Abuse, child, 110

Account: Statement designed to explain unanticipated, embarrassing, or unacceptable behavior after the behavior has occurred, 89

Achieved status: Social position acquired through our own efforts or accomplishments or taken on voluntarily, 15

Acquisition
  of language, 67–68
  of self, 66–67

Adams, Bennie, 30

Adler, Patricia, 44

Affirmative action: Program designed to seek out members of minority groups for positions from which they had previously been excluded, thereby seeking to overcome institutional racism, 195–197

Affordable Health Care Act, 164

Afghanistan, 56, 206, 217

African Americans, 54, 71, 178, 179–180
  history of oppression of 182–183, 245
  affirmative action and, 196–197
  colorism and, 186–187
  drug use among, 128
  economic inequality and, 191–192, 215
  educational inequality and, 194–195
  ethnic socialization of, 72
  gains made by, 178
  health care inequality and, 193
  impression management by, 86
  institutional racism and, 196
  in the military, 70
  myth of innate racial inferiority of, 189–190
  political power of, 246, 248
  population trends and, 229
  poverty among, 165, 187
  prejudice and discrimination against, 186–187, 191

  racism in language and, 189–190
  stereotyping of, 116, 185
  views on racism, 188
  See also Race and ethnicity

Agency for Healthcare Research and Quality, 211

Agents of socialization: Various individuals, groups, and organizations that influence the socialization process, 66

Age structure: Population's balance of old and young people, 226–227
  in the United States, 230–231

AIDS activists, 235

Algeria, 217

Aligning action: Action taken to restore an identity that has been damaged, 89

Al-Qaeda, 34

Al-Shabab, 205

Amerco, 40

American Idol, 53–54

American Medical Association, 16

American Psychiatric Association, 33, 210

American Society of Plastic Surgeons, 85

Analysis of existing data: Type of unobtrusive research that relies on data gathered earlier by someone else for some other purpose, 41

Ancestor worship, 47, 48

Anomie: Condition in which rapid change has disrupted society's ability to adequately regulate and control its members and the old rules that governed people's lives no longer seem to apply, 237

Anticipatory socialization: Process through which people acquire the values and orientations found in statuses they will likely enter in the future, 66

Apollo Alliance, 238

Arab Spring of 2011, 7, 245

Ascribed status: Social position acquired at birth or taken on involuntarily later in life, 15

Asian Americans, 178, 180, 183–184
  prejudice and discrimination against, 187–188, 190
  population trends and, 229

Trustworthiness of social research, 42–44
Tucker, Sophie, 163
Tunisia, 217
Tutsi people, 11–12
Twain, Mark, 28
Twenge, Jean, 41
Twitter, 5, 14, 83, 88, 145, 219, 237, 245

Uganda, 217
Unemployment, 3, 4
   insurance, 171
   middle-class, 161–162
   sociological imagination and, 8–9
   working class, 162
Unhappiness, 3–4
United Nations General Assembly, 217
United Parcel Service, 172
United States, the
   class inequality in, 158–171
   cultural variation and health care in, 57
   graying of, 230–231
   immigration to, 229–230
   as individualist culture, 70
   Native Americans and, 181
   population trends in, 229–231
   poverty in, 163–165
   religious endogamy in, 96
   religious institutions in, 75
   sick role in, 57–58
Unobstrusive research: Research technique in which the
   researcher, without direct contact with the subjects,
   examines the evidence of social behavior that people
   create or leave behind, 41–42
Upper class: In a society stratified by social class, a group
   of people who have high income and prestige and
   who own vast amounts of property and other forms
   of wealth, such as owners of large corporations,
   top financiers, rich celebrities and politicians, and
   members of prestigious families, 160–161
   defined, 160
   enduring disparities in income and wealth and, 168
   impression management and, 86–87
   Marxian class model and, 157
   social class endogamy and, 97–98
   See also Class, social
Urbanization: Process by which people leave
   rural areas and begin to concentrate in
   large cities, 227–228
U.S. Bureau of Justice Statistics, 36
U.S. Bureau of Labor Statistics, 212
U.S. Bureau of the Census, 36, 98, 163, 166,
   167, 180, 229
U.S. Department of Agriculture, 163
U.S. Department of Defense, 102
U.S. Department of Education, 167, 194

U.S. Department of Health and Human Services,
   43–44, 166
U.S. Department of Justice, 207–208
U.S. Department of Veterans Affairs, 33
U.S. Equal Employment Opportunity Commission, 204
U.S. Food and Drug Administration, 234
U.S. Public Health Service, 210

Value: Standard of judgment by which people decide
   on desirable goals and outcomes, 20
   in sociological research, 43–44
Variable: Any characteristic, attitude, behavior, or
   event that can take on two or more values or
   attributes, 38–39
Variation, cultural, 56–60
   in intimacy and family, 100–101
Verbal and nonverbal expressions, 82
Via Campesina, 50
Victim blaming, 206–207
Violence
   ethnic, 11–12, 198
   family, 109–111
   against homosexuals and bisexuals, 204–205
   statistics, 36
   against women, 205–208
Voting Rights Act, 246

Wage gap, 215–216
Wal-Mart, 31, 50, 51, 172, 244
Washington, George, 190
Washington Post, 34
Wayward Puritans, 41–42
Wealth. See Upper class
Weber, Max, 140–141, 142, 148, 158
Weight stigma, 90, 91
Welfare, 170–171
Whites, 87, 179–181, 191
   drug use among, 128
   economic inequality and, 178, 182, 183,
      192, 196–197
   educational inequality and, 194–195, 243
   endogamy and, 96–97
   family life and, 99
   health care inequality and 192–194
   legal system and, 116, 123
   norms, 85–86
   politics and, 246, 248
   population trends and, 229–230
   poverty among, 164, 165
   privilege of having no color for, 187
   racism in language and, 189–190
   socialization of, 71–72
   stereotypes and, 185–187
   views on racism, 188
   See also Race and ethnicity

⑤SAGE research**methods**

The essential online tool for researchers from the world's leading methods publisher

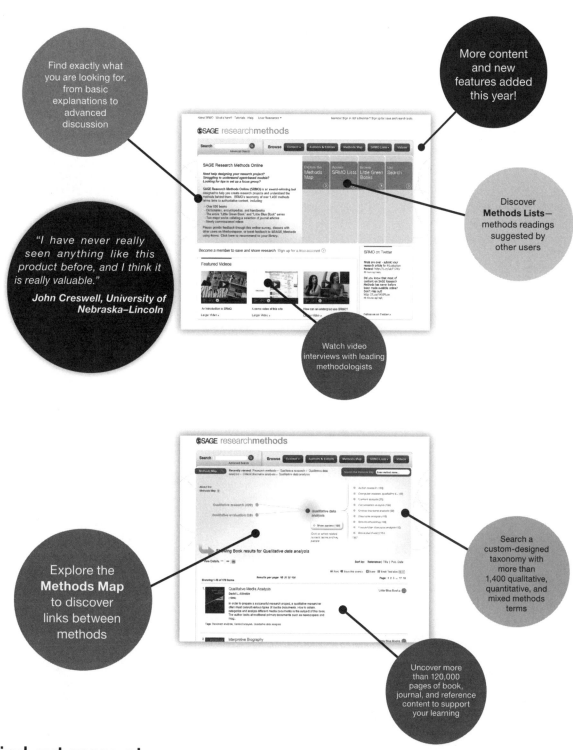

Find exactly what you are looking for, from basic explanations to advanced discussion

More content and new features added this year!

"I have never really seen anything like this product before, and I think it is really valuable."

John Creswell, University of Nebraska–Lincoln

Discover **Methods Lists**—methods readings suggested by other users

Watch video interviews with leading methodologists

Explore the **Methods Map** to discover links between methods

Search a custom-designed taxonomy with more than 1,400 qualitative, quantitative, and mixed methods terms

Uncover more than 120,000 pages of book, journal, and reference content to support your learning

Find out more at
www.sageresearchmethods.com